M000209399

Congratulations! With yc
People, Creating a Natic
Edition, Longman Publishers is pleased to offer you a
six-month subscription to *The History Place*, a unique Web
resource for history students. At *The History Place*, you'll find
a continually enriched learning resource that includes interactive maps, timelines, and other learning activities; a rich collection of source documents; the powerful TestFlight
testing tool for self-assessment; and more.

To explore this valuable teaching and learning resource:

1. Go to **www.awlonline.com/nash**
2. Click "*The History Place* Login" to enter *The History Place*.
3. Choose the Register Here Button
4. Enter your pre-assigned activation ID and password
   exactly as they appear below:

Activation ID   **HPPPST06005630**

Password   **think**

5. Complete the online form to establish your personal user
   ID and password.
6. Once your personal user ID and password are confirmed,
   go back to **www.ushistoryplace.com** to enter the site
   with your new user ID and password.

Your pre-assigned activation ID and password can be used
only once to establish your subscription, which is not
transferable and is limited to 6 months from the date of
activation. If you purchased a used textbook, this preas-
signed ID and password may already have been used.
However, you can purchase a subscription to *The History
Place* directly online by visiting *The HistoryPlace* at
www.ushistoryplace.com

THE AMERICAN PEOPLE

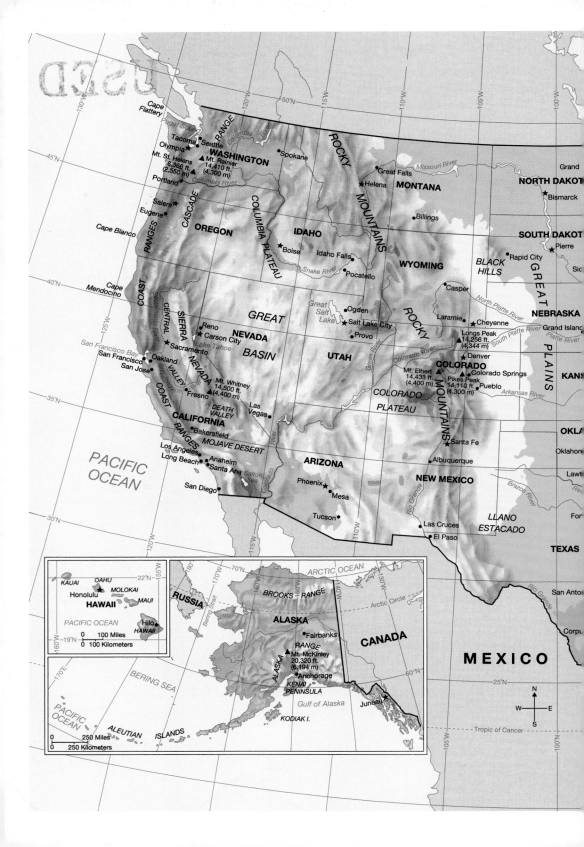

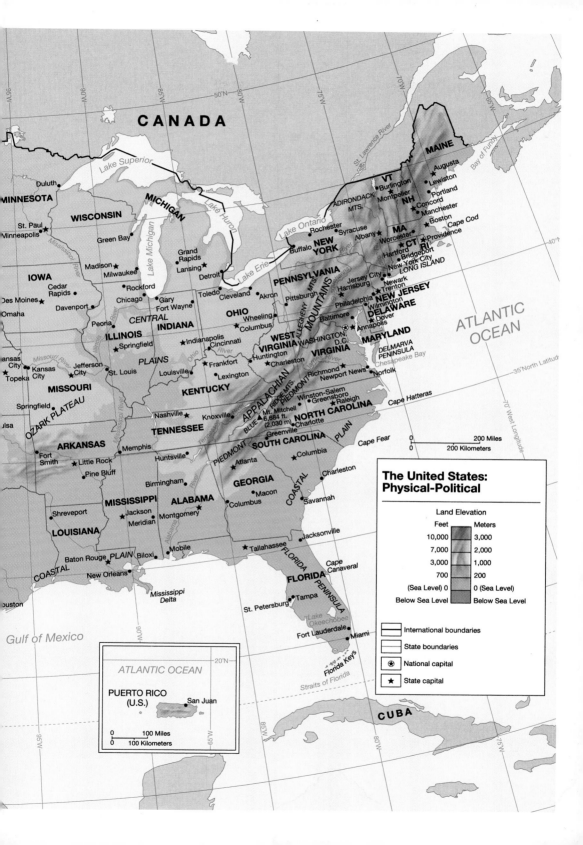

THE AMERICAN PEOPLE

Creating a Nation and a Society

Brief Third Edition

Volume II: From 1865

Gary B. Nash
University of California, Los Angeles
General Editor

Julie Roy Jeffrey
Goucher College
General Editor

John R. Howe
University of Minnesota

Peter J. Frederick
Wabash College

Allen F. Davis
Temple University

Allan M. Winkler
Miami University

An imprint of Addison Wesley Longman, Inc.

New York • Menlo Park, California • Reading, Massachusetts • Harlow, England
Don Mills, Ontario • Sydney • Mexico City • Madrid • Amsterdam

Editor-in-Chief: Priscilla McGeehon
Acquisitions Editor: Jay O'Callaghan
Development Manager: Betty Slack
Development Editor: Karen Helfrich
Executive Marketing Manager: Sue Westmoreland
Supplements Editor: Joy Hilgendorf
Full Service Production Manager: Valerie Zaborski
Project Coordination, Text Design, and Electronic Page Makeup: Elm Street Publishing
    Services, Inc.
Cover Design Manager: Nancy Danahy
Cover Designer: Kay Petronio
Cover Illustration: William Edward Lewis Bunn, "Festival at Hamburg" (study for the
    Hamburg, Iowa Post Office), 1941. Tempera on fiberboard. National Museum of
    American Art, Smithsonian Institution, Washington, DC, U.S.A. Art Resource, NY
Photo Researcher: Photosearch, Inc.
Senior Print Buyer: Hugh Crawford
Printer and Binder: R. R. Donnelley & Sons Company
Cover Printer: The Lehigh Press, Inc.

Please visit our website at http://www.awlonline.com/nash

ISBN 0-321-00564-3 (Single Volume Edition)
ISBN 0-321-00566-X (Volume I)
ISBN 0-321-00568-6 (Volume II)

12345678910—DOC—02010099

BRIEF CONTENTS

DETAILED CONTENTS

RECOVERING THE PAST

MAPS

PREFACE

The Yoruba people of West Africa have an old saying: "However far the stream flows, it never forgets its source." Why, we wonder, do such ancient societies as the Yoruba find history so important, while modern American students question its relevance? This book aims to end such skepticism about the usefulness of history.

As we begin the twenty-first century, in an ethnically and racially diverse society caught up in an interdependent global society, history is of central importance in preparing us to exercise our rights and responsibilities as free people. History cannot make good citizens, but without history we cannot understand the choices before us and think wisely about them. Lacking a collective memory of the past, we lapse into a kind of amnesia, unaware of the human condition and the long struggles of men and women everywhere to deal with the problems of their day and to create a better society. Unfurnished with historical knowledge, we deprive ourselves of knowing about the huge range of approaches people have taken to political, economic, and social life; to solving problems; and to conquering the obstacles in their way.

History has a deeper, even more fundamental importance: the cultivation of the private person whose self-knowledge and self-respect provide the foundation for a life of dignity and fulfillment. Historical memory is the key to self-identity; to seeing one's place in the long stream of time, in the story of humankind.

When we study our own history, we see a rich and extraordinarily complex human story. This country, whose written history began with a convergence of Native Americans, Europeans, and Africans, has always been a nation of diverse peoples—a magnificent mosaic of cultures, religions, and skin shades. This book explores how American society assumed its present shape and developed its present forms of government; how as a nation we have conducted our foreign affairs and managed our economy; how as individuals and in groups we have lived, worked, loved, married, raised families, voted, argued, protested, and struggled to fulfill our dreams and the noble ideals of the American experiment.

Several ways of making the past understandable distinguish this book from most textbooks written in the last 20 years. The coverage of public events like presidential elections, diplomatic treaties, and economic legislation is integrated with the private human stories that pervade them. Within a chronological framework, we have woven together our history as a nation, as a people, and as a society. When, for example, national political events are discussed, we analyze their impact on social and economic life at the state and local levels. Wars are described not only as they unfolded on the battlefield and in the salons of diplomats but also on the home front, where they are history's greatest motor of social change. The interaction of ordinary Americans with extraordinary events runs as a theme throughout this book.

Above all, we have tried to show the "humanness" of our history as it is revealed in people's everyday lives. The authors have often used the words of ordinary Americans to capture the authentic human voices of those who participated in and responded to epic events such as war, slavery, industrialization, and reform movements.

GOALS AND THEMES OF THE BOOK

Our primary goal is to provide students with a rich, balanced, and thought-pro-
voking treatment of the American past. By this we mean a history that treats the
lives and experiences of Americans of all national origins and cultural backgrounds, at all levels of society, and in all regions of the country. It also means a history that seeks connections between the many factors—political, economic,
technological, social, religious, intellectual, and biological—that have molded and
remolded American society over four centuries. And, finally, it means a history that
encourages students to think about how we have all inherited a complex past
filled with both notable achievements and thorny problems. The only history befit-
ting a democratic nation is one that inspires students to initiate a frank and searching dialogue with their past.

   To speak of a dialogue about the past presumes that history is interpretive.
Students should understand that historians are continually reinterpreting the past.
New interpretations may result from the discovery of new evidence, but more
often they emerge because historians reevaluate old evidence in the light of new
ideas that spring from the times in which they write and from their personal views
of the world.

   Through this book, we also hope to promote class discussions, which can be
organized around six questions that we see as basic to the American historical
experience:

1. How has this nation been peopled, from the first inhabitants to the many
   groups that arrived in slavery or servitude during the colonial period to the
   voluntary immigrants of today? How have these waves of newcomers contributed to the American cultural mosaic? To what extent have different
   immigrant groups preserved elements of their ethnic, racial, and religious
   heritages?
2. To what extent have Americans developed a stable, democratic political
   system flexible enough to address the wholesale changes occurring in the
   last two centuries and to what degree has this political system been consistent with the principles of our nation's founding?
3. How have economic and technological changes affected daily life, work,
   family organization, leisure, sexual behavior, the division of wealth, and
   community relations in the United States?
4. Has American religion served more to promote or retard social reform in
   our history? Whatever their varied sources, how have the recurring reform
   movements in our history dealt with economic, political, and social problems in attempting to square the ideals of American life with the reality?
5. What has been the role of our nation in the world? To what extent has the
   United States served as a model for other peoples, as an interventionist
   savior of other nations around the globe, and as an interfering expansionist
   in the affairs of other nations?
6. How have American beliefs and values changed over time, and how have
   they varied between different groups—women and men; Americans of many
   colors and cultures; people of different regions, religions, sexual orientations,
   ages, and classes?

In writing a history that revolves around these themes, we have tried to convey two dynamics that operate in all societies. First, we observe people continuously adjusting to new developments, such as industrialization and urbanization, over which they seemingly have little control; yet we realize that people are not paralyzed by history but are the fundamental creators of it. They retain the ability, individually and collectively, to shape the world in which they live and thus in considerable degree to control their own lives. Second, we emphasize the connections that always exist among social, political, economic, and cultural events.

STRUCTURE OF THE BOOK

The chapters of this book are grouped into six parts that relate to major periods in American history. The titles for each part suggest the large themes uniting the chapters.

Individual chapters have a clear structure, beginning with a personal story recalling the experience of an ordinary or lesser-known American. Chapter 1, for example, is introduced with the tragic account of Opechancanough, a Powhatan tribesman whose entire life of nearly 90 years was consumed by a struggle against the land, hunger, and alien values brought by Spanish and English newcomers. This brief anecdote serves several purposes. First, it introduces the overarching themes and major concepts of the chapter, in this case the meeting of three societies—Native American, European, and African—each with different cultural values, lifestyles, and aspirations. Second, the personal story suggests that ordinary as well as extraordinary people shaped our history. At the end of the personal story, a *brief overview* links the biographical sketch to the text by elaborating the major themes of the chapter.

We aim to facilitate the learning process for students in other ways as well. Every chapter ends with pedagogical features to reinforce and expand the presentation. A *conclusion* briefly summarizes the chapter's main concepts and developments and serves as a bridge to the following chapter. A list of *recommended readings* provides supplementary sources for further study; novels contemporary to the period are often included. Finally, a *time line* reviews the major events covered in the chapter. Each map, figure, and table has been chosen to relate clearly to the narrative. *Captions* are specially written to help students understand and interpret these visual materials.

THE BRIEF THIRD EDITION

This Brief Third Edition is condensed from the very successful full Fourth Edition of *The American People,* with its balance of political, social, and economic history. While we have eliminated detail and extra examples, and compressed the text, we have retained the interpretive connections and the "humanness" of history, the focus on history as it is revealed through the lives of ordinary Americans, and the interplay of social and political factors.

New Format and Features

The Brief Third Edition offers a new format and a more compact size than the previous brief edition. The new four-color design enhances the value of the maps and graphs and gives the book a vibrant appearance. We believe these changes make the book extremely accessible, easy to read, and convenient for students to carry to and from class.

An important new addition is the inclusion of one of the most popular features of *The American People,* the two-page sections entitled *Recovering the Past.* Twelve RTPs, as the authors affectionately call them, introduce students to the fascinating variety of evidence—ranging from novels, political cartoons, and diaries to houses, clothing, and popular music—that historians have learned to employ in reconstructing the past. Each RTP gives basic information about the source and its use by historians and then raises questions for students to consider as they study the example reproduced for their inspection. The RTPs included in this edition are Novels (Chapter 16), Political Cartoons (Chapter 20), Documentary Photographs (Chapter 21), Movies (Chapter 24), Clothing (Chapter 26), and Popular Music (Chapter 29).

Major Changes

Throughout the Brief Third Edition there are new materials on the role of religion, the environment, and the West. The structure and organization of the text—parts, chapters, sections, and subsections—reflect the full Fourth Edition where the authors significantly reorganized chapters focusing on the period following World War II and the contemporary period (Chapters 26–30). Chapter-by-chapter changes include the following:

- **Chapter 21:** new material on religion, progressive social justice, and Protestant social gospel movements
- **Chapter 23:** expanded discussion of religion during the 1920s
- **Chapter 24:** new material on The New Deal and the West
- **Chapter 25:** added material on the impact of war industry on the West
- **Chapter 26:** covers postwar growth and social change from 1945 to 1970; added material on African-American families and communities
- **Chapter 27:** covers foreign policy and the Cold War through the 1960s
- **Chapter 28:** covers domestic politics from 1945 to 1980
- **Chapter 29:** provides post-World War II background to reform movements and covers reform movements to 1980
- **Chapter 30:** carries the story from 1980 to the present, including discussion of the 1996 election; covers the economy, the political shift to the right, the end to social reform, and the end of the Cold War

In this Brief Third Edition we have tried to present American history in its rich complexity but in a form that students will find comprehensible and interesting. Additionally, we have tried to provide the support materials necessary to make teaching and learning enjoyable and rewarding. The reader will be the judge of our success. The authors and Addison Wesley Longman welcome your comments.

ACKNOWLEDGMENTS

The authors wish to thank the following reviewers who gave generously of their time and expertise and whose thoughtful and constructive work have contributed greatly to this edition:

Linda J. Borish, Western Michigan University
Thomas A. Britten, Briar Cliff College
Steven J. Bucklin, University of South Dakota
Stacy A. Cordery, Monmouth College
Stephen A. Harmon, Pittsburg State University
Jeff Livingston, California State University, Chico
Elizabeth Neumeyer, Kellogg Community College
A.J. Scopino, Jr., Central Connecticut State University
Michael Welsh, University of Northern Colorado

Over the years, as previous editions of this text were being developed, many of our colleagues read and criticized the various drafts of the manuscript. For their thoughtful evaluations and constructive suggestions, the authors wish to express their gratitude to the following reviewers:

Richard H. Abbott, Eastern Michigan University; John Alexander, University of Cincinnati; Kenneth G. Alfers, Mountain View College; Terry Alford, Northern Virginia Community College; Gregg Andrews, Southwest Texas State University; Robert Asher, University of Connecticut at Storrs; Harry Baker, University of Arkansas at Little Rock; Michael Batinski, Southern Illinois University; Gary Bell, Sam Houston State University; Virginia Bellows, Tulsa Junior College; Spencer Bennett, Siena Heights College; Jackie R. Booker, Western Connecticut State University; James Bradford, Texas A&M University; Neal Brooks, Essex Community College; Jeffrey P. Brown, New Mexico State University; Dickson D. Bruce, Jr., University of California at Irvine; David Brundage, University of California at Santa Cruz; Colin Calloway, Dartmouth University; D'Ann Campbell, Indiana University; Jane Censer, George Mason University; Vincent A. Clark, Johnson County Community College; Neil Clough, North Seattle Community College; Matthew Ware Coulter, Collin County Community College; David Culbert, Louisiana State University; Mark T. Dalhouse, Northeast Missouri State University; Bruce Dierenfield, Canisius College; John Dittmer, DePauw University; Gordon Dodds, Portland State University; Richard Donley, Eastern Washington University; Dennis B. Downey, Millersville University; Robert Downtain, Tarrant County Community College; Robert Farrar, Spokane Falls Community College; Bernard Friedman, Indiana University–Purdue University at Indianapolis; Bruce Glasrud, California State University at Hayward; Brian Gordon, St. Louis Community College; Richard Griswold del Castillo, San Diego State University; Carol Gruber, William Paterson College; Colonel William L. Harris, The Citadel Military College; Robert Haws, University of Mississippi; Jerrold Hirsch, Northeast Missouri State University; Frederick Hoxie, University of Illinois; John S. Hughes, University of Texas; Link Hullar, Kingwood College; Donald M. Jacobs, Northeastern University; Delores Janiewski, University of Idaho; David Johnson,

Portland State University; Richard Kern, University of Findlay; Robert J. Kolesar, John Carroll University; Monte Lewis, Cisco Junior College; William Link, University of North Carolina at Greensboro; Patricia M. Lisella, Iona College; Ronald Lora, University of Toledo; Paul K. Longmore, San Francisco State University; Rita Loos, Framingham State College; George M. Lubick, Northern Arizona University; Suzanne Marshall, Jacksonville State University; John C. Massman, St. Cloud State University; Vernon Mattson, University of Nevada at Las Vegas; Arthur McCoole, Cuyamaca College; John McCormick, Delaware County Community College; Sylvia McGrath, Stephen F. Austin University; James E. McMillan, Denison University; Otis L. Miller, Belleville Area College; Walter Miszczenko, Boise State University; Norma Mitchell, Troy State University; Gerald F. Moran, University of Michigan at Dearborn; William G. Morris, Midland College; Marian Morton, John Carroll University; Roger Nichols, University of Arizona; Paul Palmer, Texas A&I University; Albert Parker, Riverside City College; Judith Parsons, Sul Ross State University; Carla Pestana, Ohio State University; Neva Peters, Tarrant County Community College; James Prickett, Santa Monica Community College; Noel Pugash, University of New Mexico; Juan Gomez-Quiñones, University of California at Los Angeles; George Rable, Anderson College; Joseph P. Reidy, Howard University; Leonard Riforgiato, Pennsylvania State University; Randy Roberts, Purdue University; Mary Robertson, Armstrong State University; David Robson, John Carroll University; Judd Sage, Northern Virginia Community College; Sylvia Sebesta, San Antonio College; Phil Schaeffer, Olympic College; Herbert Shapiro, University of Cincinnati; David R. Shibley, Santa Monica Community College; Ellen Shockro, Pasadena City College; Nancy Shoemaker, University of Connecticut; Bradley Skelcher, Delaware State University; Kathryn Kish Sklar, State Univerity of New York at Binghamton; James Smith, Virginia State University; John Snetsinger, California Polytechnic State University at San Luis Obispo; Jo Snider, Southwest Texas State University; Stephen Strausberg, University of Arkansas; Katherine Scott Sturdevant, Pikes Peak Community College; Nan M. Sumner-Mack, Hawaii Community College; Cynthia Taylor, Santa Rosa Junior College; Thomas Tefft, Citrus College; John A. Trickel, Richland College; Donna Van Raaphorst, Cuyahoga Community College; Morris Vogel, Temple University; Michael Wade, Appalachian State University; Jackie Walker, James Madison University; Paul B. Weinstein, University of Akron-Wayne College; Joan Welker, Prince George's Community College; Kenneth H. Williams, Alcorn State University; Mitch Yamasaki, Chaminade University; and Charles Zappia, San Diego Mesa College.

GARY B. NASH

JULIE ROY JEFFREY

SUPPLEMENTS

For Qualified College Adopters

Teaching the American People. Julie Roy Jeffrey and Peter J. Frederick with Frances Jones-Sneed of Massachusetts College of Liberal Arts. This guide was written based on ideas generated in "active learning" workshops and is tied closely to the text. In addition to suggestions on how to generate lively class discussion and involve students in active learning, this supplement also offers a file of exam questions and lists of resources, including films, slides, photo collections, records, and audiocassettes.

Test Bank. This test bank, prepared by Diane Beers of Dickinson College, contains more than 3500 objective, conceptual, and essay questions. All questions are keyed to specific pages in the text.

Test Gen 3.0 Computerized Testing System. This flexible, easy-to-master computer test bank includes all the test items in the printed test bank. The software allows you to edit existing questions and add your own items. Tests can be printed in several different formats and can include figures such as graphs and tables. It comes with *QuizMaster,* a program that enables you to design Test Gen generated tests your students can take on a computer rather than in printed form. Available on CD-Rom for Windows and Macintosh, and on floppies.

The History Place Website (www.ushistoryplace.com). Available free to adopters of the text, this new website combines quality educational publishing with the immediacy and interactivity of the Internet. At *The History Place,* you'll find a continually updated source of maps, time lines, and other interactive learning activities, as well as a rich collection of primary documents, news, and online quizzes. A free subscription to *The History Place* is included with every new copy of the student text.

The American People, *Brief Third Edition Website* (www.awlonline.com/nash). This website, designed specifically for this book by Patrick McCarthy of the University of Georgia, is an invaluable tool for both students and instructors. It contains student resources such as self-testing, chapter outlines, web activities, and links to outside sources; instructor resources such as the instructor's manual and testing ideas; and our unique syllabus manager that gives instructors and students access to the up-to-date syllabus at any time from any computer.

American Impressions: A CD-ROM for U.S. History. This unique CD-ROM for the U.S. history course is organized in a topical and thematic framework which allows in-depth coverage with a media-centered focus. Hundreds of photos, maps, works of art, graphics, and historical film clips are organized into narrated vignettes and interactive activities to create a tool for both professors and students. Topics include "The Encounter Period," "Revolution to Republic," "A Century of Labor and Reform," and "The Struggle for Equality." A guide for instructors provides teaching tips and suggestions for using advanced media in the classroom. The CD-ROM is available in both Macintosh and Windows formats.

Visual Archives of American History, Second Edition. This two-sided video laserdisc explores history from the meeting of three cultures to the present. It is an encyclopedic chronology of U.S. history offering hundreds of photographs and illustrations, a variety of source and reference maps—several of which are animated—plus 50 minutes of video. For ease in planning lectures, a manual listing barcodes for scanning and frame numbers for all the material is available.

Video Lecture Launchers. Prepared by Mark Newman, University of Illinois at Chicago, these video lecture launchers (each two to five minutes in duration) cover key issues in American history from 1877 to the present. The launchers are accompanied by an instructor's manual.

"This Is America" Immigration Video. Produced by the American Museum of Immigration, this video tells the story of American immigrants, relating their personal stories and accomplishments. By showing how the richness of our culture is due to the contributions of millions of immigrant Americans, the videos make the point that America's strength lies in the ethnically and culturally diverse backgrounds of its citizens.

Discovering American History Through Maps and Views. Created by Gerald Danzer of the University of Illinois at Chicago, the recipient of the AHA's 1990 James Harvey Robinson Prize for his work in the development of map transparencies, this set of 140 four-color acetates is a unique instructional tool. It contains an introduction on teaching history through maps and a detailed commentary on each transparency. The collection includes cartographic and pictorial maps, views and photos, urban plans, building diagrams, and works of art.

Comprehensive American History Transparency Set. This vast collection of American history map transparencies includes more than 200 map transparencies ranging from the first Native Americans to the end of the Cold War, covering wars, social trends, elections, immigration, and demographics. Also included are a reproducible set of student map exercises, teaching tips, and correlation charts.

Text-Specific Map Transparencies. A set of 30 transparencies drawn from *The American People,* Fourth Edition, is available.

Longman American History Atlas Overhead Transparencies. These 69 acetates from our four-color historical atlas were especially designed for this volume.

A Guide to Teaching American History Through Film. Written by Randy Roberts of Purdue University, this guide provides instructors with a creative and practical tool for stimulating classroom discussion. The sections include "American Films: A Historian's Perspective," a list of films, practical suggestions, and bibliography. The film listing is presented in narrative form, developing connections between each film and the topics being discussed.

For Students

The History Place Website (www.ushistoryplace.com). Available free to adopters of the text, this new website combines quality educational publishing with the immediacy and interactivity of the Internet. At *The History Place,* you'll find a continually updated source of maps, time lines, and other interactive learning activities, as well as a rich collection of primary documents, news, and online quizzes. A free subscription to *The History Place* is included with every new copy of the student text.

The American People, *Brief Third Edition Website* (www.awlonline.com/nash). This website, designed specifically for this book by Patrick McCarthy of the University of Georgia, is an invaluable tool for both students and instructors. It contains student resources such as self-testing, chapter outlines, web activities, and links to outside sources; instructor resources such as the instructor's manual and testing ideas; and our unique syllabus manager that gives instructors and students access to the up-to-date syllabus at any time from any computer.

StudyWizard Computerized Tutorial. This interactive study guide by Ken Weatherbie of Del Mar College helps students learn major facts and concepts through drill and practice exercises and diagnostic feedback. StudyWizard provides correct answers, answer explanations, and the text page number on which the material is discussed. The easy-to-use CD-ROM for Windows and Macintosh is available to instructors through their sales representative. Also available on floppies.

Study Guides and Practice Tests. This two-volume study guide, created by Julie Roy Jeffrey and Peter J. Frederick, has been revised by Ken Weatherbie of Del Mar College. It includes chapter outlines, significant themes and highlights, a glossary, learning enrichment ideas, sample test questions, exercises for identification and interpretation, and geography exercises based on maps in the text.

Time Line to accompany The American People, *Brief Third Edition.* Created especially for this edition of the text, this five-page, fold-out, full-color, illustrated time line is designed to be hung on a wall and referred to throughout the semester. Arranged in an easy-to-read format around important political and diplomatic, social and economic, and cultural and technological events in United States history, it gives students a chronological context in which to place their knowledge.

Everything You Need to Know About Your History Course. Authored by Sandra Mathews-Lamb of Nebraska Wesleyan University and written for first-year university students, this guide provides invaluable tips on how to study, how to use a textbook, how to write a good paper, how to take notes, how to read a map, graph, or bar chart, and how to read primary and secondary sources.

Everything You Need To Know About The American People, *Brief Third Edition.* This guide to the text explains the text's organization, pedagogy, and special features.

Revised! Guide to the Internet for History, *Second Edition.* Written by Richard Rothaus of St. Cloud State University, this guide details all the World Wide Web has to offer and advises students on how to make the most of it.

Longman American History Atlas. This full-color historical atlas includes 69 maps, all designed especially for this course. This valuable reference tool is available shrinkwrapped with *The American People* at low cost.

Mapping America: A Guide to Historical Geography. Each volume of this workbook by Ken Weatherbie of Del Mar College contains 18 exercises corresponding to the map program in the text, each concluding with interpretive questions about the role of geography in American history. This free item is designed to be packaged with *The American People*.

Mapping American History: Student Activities. Written by Gerald Danzer of the University of Illinois at Chicago, this free map workbook for students features exercises designed to teach students to interpret and analyze cartographic materials as historical documents. This free item is designed to be packaged with *The American People*.

Retracing the Past, *Fourth Edition*. This two-volume reader is edited by Ronald Schultz of the University of Wyoming and Gary B. Nash of the University of California, Los Angeles. These secondary source readings cover economic, political, and social history with special emphasis on women, racial and ethnic groups, and working-class people.

America Through the Eyes of Its People: Primary Sources in American History, *Second Edition*. This one-volume collection of primary documents portrays the rich and varied tapestry of American life. It contains documents by women, Native Americans, African-Americans, Hispanics, and others who helped to shape the course of U.S. history along with student study questions and contextual headnotes. Available free when bundled with the text.

Sources of the African American Past. Edited by Roy Finkenbine of University of Detroit at Mercy, this collection of primary sources covers key themes in the African-American experience from the West African background to the present. Balanced between political and social history, it offers a vivid snapshot of the lives of African Americans in different historical periods and includes documents representing women and different regions of the United States. Available at a minimum cost when bundled with the text.

Women and the National Experience. Edited by Ellen Skinner of Pace University, this primary source reader contains both classic and unusual documents describing the history of women in the United States. The documents provide dramatic evidence that outspoken women attained a public voice and participated in the development of national events and policies long before they could vote. Chronologically organized and balanced between social and political history, this reader offers a striking picture of the lives of women across American history. Available at a minimum cost when bundled with the text.

Reading the American West. Edited by Mitchell Roth of Sam Houston State University, this primary source reader uses letters, diary excerpts, speeches, interviews, and newspaper articles to let students experience what historians really do and how history is written. Every document is accompanied by a contextual headnote and study questions. The book is divided into chapters with extensive introductions. Available at a minimum cost when bundled with the text.

A Short Guide to Writing About History. Written by Richard Marius of Harvard University, this short guide introduces students to the pleasures of historical research and discovery while teaching them how to write cogent history papers. Focusing on more than just the conventions of good writing, this supplement shows students first how to think about history and then how to organize their thoughts into coherent essays.

New! *Longman-Penguin Putnam Inc. Value Bundles.* A variety of classic texts are available at a significant discount when packaged with *The American People,* Brief Third Edition. Ask your local sales representative for details or visit our website at http://longman.awl.com/penguin.

Library of American Biography Series. Edited by Oscar Handlin of Harvard University, each of these interpretive biographies focuses on a figure whose actions and ideas significantly influenced the course of American history and national life. At the same time, each biography relates the life of its subject to the broader theme and developments of the times. Brief and inexpensive, they are ideal for any U. S. history course. New editions include *Abigail Adams: An American Woman,* Second Edition, by Charles W. Akers; *Andrew Carnegie and the Rise of Big Business,* Second Edition, by Harold C. Livesay; and *Eleanor Roosevelt: A Personal and Public Life,* Second Edition, by J. William T. Youngs.

Learning to Think Critically: Films and Myths About American History. Randy Roberts and Robert May of Purdue University use well-known films such as *Gone with the Wind* and *Casablanca* to explore some common myths about America and its past. This short handbook subjects some popular beliefs to historical scrutiny in order to help students develop a method of inquiry for approaching the subject of history in general.

ABOUT THE AUTHORS

Gary B. Nash received his Ph.D. from Princeton University. He is currently Director of the National Center for History in the Schools at the University of California, Los Angeles, where he teaches colonial and revolutionary American history. Among the books Nash has authored are *Quakers and Politics: Pennsylvania, 1681–1726* (1968); *Red, White, and Black: The Peoples of Early America* (1974, 1982, 1992, 1999); *The Urban Crucible: Social Change, Political Consciousness, and the Origins of the American Revolution* (1979); and *Forging Freedom: The Black Urban Experience in Philadelphia, 1720–1840* (1988). A former president of the Organization of American Historians, his scholarship is especially concerned with the role of common people in the making of history. He wrote Part I and served as a general editor of this book.

Julie Roy Jeffrey earned her Ph.D. in history from Rice University. Since then she has taught at Goucher College. Honored as an outstanding teacher, Jeffrey has been involved in faculty development activities and curriculum evaluation. Jeffrey's major publications include *Education for Children of the Poor* (1978); *Frontier Women: The Trans-Mississippi West, 1840–1880* (1979, 1997); *Converting the West: A Biography of Narcissa Whitman* (1991); and *The Great Silent Army of Abolitionism: Ordinary Women in the Antislavery Movement* (1998). She is the author of many articles on the lives and perceptions of nineteenth-century women. She wrote Parts III and IV in collaboration with Peter Frederick and acted as a general editor of this book.

John R. Howe received his Ph.D. from Yale University. At the University of Minnesota, his teaching interests include early American politics and relations between Native Americans and whites. His major publications include *The Changing Political Thought of John Adams* (1966) and *From the Revolution Through the Age of Jackson* (1973). His major research currently involves a manuscript entitled "The Transformation of Public Life in Revolutionary America." Howe wrote Part II of this book.

Peter J. Frederick received his Ph.D. in history from the University of California, Berkeley. Innovative student-centered teaching in American history has been the focus of his career at California State University, Hayward, and since 1970 at Wabash College (1992–1994 at Carleton College). Recognized nationally as a distinguished teacher and for his many articles and workshops for faculty on teaching and learning, Frederick has also written several articles on life-writing and a book, *Knights of the Golden Rule: The Intellectual as Christian Social Reformer in the 1890s*. He coordinated and edited all the "Recovering the Past" sections and coauthored Parts III and IV.

Allen F. Davis earned his Ph.D. from the University of Wisconsin. A former president of the American Studies Association, he is a professor of history at

Temple University and Director of the Center for Public History. He is the author of *Spearheads for Reform: The Social Settlements and the Progressive Movement* (1967) and *American Heroine: The Life and Legend of Jane Addams* (1973). He is coauthor of *Still Philadelphia* (1983), *Philadelphia Stories* (1987), and *One Hundred Years at Hull House* (1990). He is currently working on a book on masculine culture in America. Davis wrote Part V of this book.

Allan M. Winkler received his Ph.D. from Yale. He is presently teaching at Miami University. An award-winning historian, his books include *The Politics of Propaganda: The Office of War Information, 1942–1945* (1978); *Modern America: The United States from the Second World War to the Present* (1985); *Home Front U.S.A.: America During World War II* (1986); and *Life Under a Cloud: American Anxiety About the Atom* (1993). His research centers on the connections between public policy and popular mood in modern American history. Winkler wrote Part VI of this book.

THE AMERICAN PEOPLE

CHAPTER 16

The Union Reconstructed

In April 1864 Robert Allston died, leaving his daughter Elizabeth and his wife Adele to manage their many rice plantations. With Yankee troops moving through coastal South Carolina in the late winter of 1864–1865, Elizabeth's sorrow turned to "terror" as Union soldiers arrived and searched for liquor, firearms, and valuables. The women fled. Later, other troops encouraged the Allston slaves to take furniture, food, and other goods from the Big House. Before they left, the Union soldiers gave the keys to the crop barns to the semifree slaves.

After the war, Adele Allston swore allegiance to the United States and secured a written order for the former slaves to relinquish those keys. She and Elizabeth returned in the summer of 1865 to reclaim the plantations and reassert white authority. She was assured that although the blacks had guns, "no outrage has been committed against the whites except in the matter of property." But property was the issue. Possession of the keys to the barns, Elizabeth wrote, would be the "test case" of whether former masters or former slaves would control land, labor and its fruits, and even the subtle aspects of interpersonal relations.

Nervously, Adele and Elizabeth Allston confronted their ex-slaves at their old home. To their surprise, a pleasant reunion took place. A trusted black foreman handed over the keys to the barns. This harmonious scene was repeated elsewhere.

But at one plantation, the Allston women met defiant and armed ex-slaves. A former black driver, Uncle Jacob, was unsure whether to yield the keys to the barns full of rice and corn, put there by black labor. Mrs. Allston insisted. As Uncle Jacob hesitated, an angry young man shouted: "Ef yu gie up de key, blood'll flow." Uncle Jacob slowly slipped the keys back into his pocket.

The African-Americans sang freedom songs and brandished hoes, pitchforks, and guns to discourage anyone from going to town for help. Two blacks, however, slipped away to find some Union officers. The Allstons spent the night safely, if restlessly, in their house. Early the next morning, they were awakened by a knock at the unlocked front door. There stood Uncle Jacob. Silently, he gave back the keys.

<<<<<<

The story of the keys reveals most of the essential human ingredients of the Reconstruction era. Defeated southern whites were determined to resume control of both land and labor. The law and federal enforcement generally supported property owners. The Allston women were friendly to the blacks in a maternal way and insisted on restoring prewar deference. Adele and Elizabeth, in short, both feared and cared about their former slaves.

The African-American freedmen likewise revealed mixed feelings toward their former owners: anger, loyalty, love, resentment, and pride. They paid respect to the Allstons but not to their property and crops. They wanted not revenge, but economic independence and freedom.

Northerners played a most revealing role. Union soldiers, literally and symbolically, gave the keys of freedom to the blacks, but did not stay around long enough to guarantee that freedom. Although encouraging the freedmen to plunder the master's house and seize the crops, in the crucial encounter, northern officials had disappeared. Understanding the limits of northern help, Uncle Jacob handed the keys to land and liberty back to his former owner. The blacks knew that if they wanted to ensure their freedom, they had to do it themselves.

This chapter describes what happened to the conflicting goals and dreams of three groups as they groped toward new social, economic, and political relationships during the Reconstruction era. Amid devastation and class and race divisions, Civil War survivors sought to put their lives back together. Victorious but variously motivated northern officials, defeated but defiant southern planters, and impoverished but hopeful African-American black freedmen—they could not all fulfill their conflicting goals, yet each had to try. Reconstruction would be divisive, leaving a legacy of gains and losses.

THE BITTERSWEET AFTERMATH OF WAR

"There are sad changes in store for both races," the daughter of a Georgia planter wrote in the summer of 1865. To understand the bittersweet nature of Reconstruction, we must look at the state of the nation after the assassination of President Lincoln.

The United States in 1865

The "Union" faced constitutional crisis in April 1865. What was the status of the 11 former Confederate states? The North had denied the South's constitutional right to secede but needed four years of war and over 600,000 deaths to win the point. Lincoln's official position had been that the southern states had never left the Union and were only "out of their proper relation" with the United States. The president, therefore, as commander in chief, had the authority to decide how to set relations right again. Lincoln's congressional opponents retorted that the ex-Confederate states were now "conquered provinces" and that Congress should resolve the constitutional issues and direct reconstruction.

Differences between Congress and the White House over reconstruction mirrored a wider struggle between the two branches of the national government. During war, as has usually been the case, the executive branch assumed broad powers. Many believed, however, that Lincoln had far exceeded his constitutional authority. Now Congress reasserted its authority.

In April 1865, the Republican party ruled virtually unchecked. Republicans had made immense achievements in the eyes of the northern public: winning the war, preserving the Union, and freeing the slaves. They had enacted sweeping economic programs on behalf of free labor and free enterprise. But the party remained an uneasy grouping of former Whigs, Know-Nothings, Unionist Democrats, and antislavery idealists.

The Democrats were in shambles. Republicans depicted southern Democrats as rebels, murderers, and traitors, and they blasted northern Democrats as weak-willed, disloyal, and opposed to economic growth and progress. Nevertheless, in the elections of 1864 the Republicans, needing to show that the war was a bipartisan effort, nominated a Unionist Tennessee Democrat, Andrew Johnson, as Lincoln's vice president. Now the tactless Johnson headed the government.

The United States in the spring of 1865 presented stark contrasts. Northern cities and railroads hummed; southern cities and railroads lay in ruins. Southern financial institutions were bankrupt; northern banks flourished. Mechanizing northern farms were more productive than ever; southern farms and plantations, especially those along Sherman's march, resembled a "howling waste."

Despite widespread devastation in the South, southern attitudes towards the future were mixed. As a later southern writer, Wilbur Cash, explained, "If this war had smashed the Southern world, it had left the essential Southern mind and will . . . entirely unshaken." Many white southerners braced to resist Reconstruction and restore their old world, but the minority who had remained quietly loyal to the Union dreamed of reconciliation. And nearly four million former slaves were on their own, facing the challenges of freedom. After initial joy , freedmen quickly realized their continuing dependence on former owners. Everything—and nothing—had changed.

Hopes Among Freedmen

Throughout the South in the summer of 1865, optimism surged through the old slave quarters. The slavery chain, however, broke only link by link. After Union troops swept through an area, ex-Confederate soldiers would follow, or master and overseer would return, and freedmen learned not to rejoice too quickly or openly. Former slaves became cautious about what freedom meant.

Gradually, though, freedmen began to test the reality of freedom. Typically, their first step was to leave the plantation, if only for a few hours or days. "If I stay here I'll never know I am free," said a South Carolina woman who went to work as a cook in a nearby town. Some former slaves cut their ties entirely—returning to an earlier master, or going into towns and cities to find jobs, schools, churches, and association with other blacks, safe from whippings and retaliation.

Many freedmen left the plantation in search of a spouse, parent, or child sold away years before. Advertisements detailing these sorrowful searches filled African-American newspapers. For those who found a spouse or who had been living together in slave marriages, freedom meant getting married legally, sometimes in mass ceremonies common in the first months of emancipation. Legal marriage was important morally, but it also established the legitimacy of children and meant access to land titles and other economic opportunities. Marriage brought special burdens for black women who assumed the double role of housekeeper and breadwinner. Since many newly married blacks, however, were determined to create a traditional family life, their wives left plantation field labor altogether.

Freedmen also demonstrated their new status by choosing surnames. Names connoting independence, such as Washington, were common. Revealing freedmen's mixed feelings toward their former masters, some would adopt their master's name—while others would pick "any big name 'ceptin' their master's." Emancipation changed black manners around whites as well. Masks fell, and old expressions of humility disappeared. For African-Americans, these changes were necessary expressions of selfhood, proving that things were now different, while whites saw in such behaviors "insolence."

But the primary goal for most freedmen was getting land. "All I want is to git to own fo' or five acres ob land, dat I can build me a little house on and call my home," a Mississippi black said. Only through economic independence, the traditional American goal of controlling one's own labor and land, could former slaves prove to themselves that emancipation was real.

During the war, some Union generals had put liberated slaves in charge of confiscated and abandoned lands. In the Sea Islands of South Carolina and Georgia, blacks had been working 40-acre plots of land and harvesting their own crops for several years. Farther inland, most freedmen who received land were the former slaves of Cherokees and Creeks. Some blacks held title to these lands. Northern philanthropists had organized others to grow cotton for the Treasury Department to prove the superiority of free labor. In Mississippi, thousands of ex-slaves worked 40-acre tracts on leased lands formerly owned by Jefferson Davis. In this highly successful experiment, they made profits sufficient to repay the government for initial costs, then lost the land to Davis's brother.

Many freedmen expected a new economic order as fair payment for their years of involuntary work. "Gib us our own land," said one, "and we take care ourselves; but widout land, de ole massas can hire us or starve us, as dey please." Freedmen believed that "forty acres and a mule" had been promised. Once they obtained land, family unity, and education, they looked forward to civil rights and the vote.

The White South's Fearful Response

White southerners had equally mixed goals and expectations. Yeoman farmers and poor whites stood beside rich planters in bread lines, all hoping to regain land and livelihood. White southerners responded with feelings of outrage, loss, and injustice. Said one man, "my pa paid his own money for our niggers; and that's not all they've robbed us of. They have taken our horses and cattle and sheep and everything."

A dominant emotion was fear. The entire structure of southern society was shaken, and the semblance of racial peace and order that slavery had provided was shattered. Having lost control of all that was familiar and revered, whites feared everything—from losing their cheap labor to having blacks sit next to them on trains. But southern whites' worst fears were of rape and revenge. African-American "impudence," some thought, would lead to legal intermarriage, and then would come "Africanization" and the destruction of the purity of the white race. African-American Union soldiers seemed especially ominous. But demobilization came quickly, and violence by black soldiers against whites was extremely rare.

Believing their world turned upside down, the former planter aristocracy tried to set it right again. To reestablish white dominance, southern legislatures passed "black codes" in the first year after the war. Many of the codes granted freedmen the right to marry, sue and be sued, testify in court, and hold property. But these rights were qualified. Complicated passages explained under exactly what circumstances blacks could testify against whites, own property (mostly they could not), or exercise other rights of free people. Racial intermarriage, the bearing of arms, possessing alcoholic beverages, sitting on trains (except in baggage compartments), being on city streets at night, or congregating in large groups were all forbidden. Many of the qualified rights guaranteed by the black codes were only passed to induce the federal government to withdraw its remaining troops from the South. This was a crucial issue, for in many places marauding whites were terrorizing virtually defenseless freedmen.

Key provisions of the black codes regulated freedmen's economic status. "Vagrancy" laws provided that any blacks not "lawfully employed" (which usually meant by a white employer) could be arrested, jailed, fined, or hired out to a man who would assume responsibility for their debts and behavior. The codes regulated black laborers' work contracts with white landowners, including severe penalties for leaving before the yearly contract was fulfilled. A Kentucky newspaper was blunt: "The tune . . . will not be 'forty acres and a mule,' but . . . 'work nigger or starve.'"

NATIONAL RECONSTRUCTION

The black codes directly challenged the national government in 1865. How would it use its power—to uphold the codes and reimpose racial intimidation in the South, or to defend the freedmen? Would the federal government stress human liberty, or would it emphasize property rights, order, and self-interest? Although the primary drama of Reconstruction pitted white landowners against African-American freedmen over land and labor in the South, in the background of these local struggles lurked the debate over Reconstruction policy among politicians in Washington. This dual drama would extend well into the twentieth century.

The Presidential Plan

After initially demanding that the defeated Confederates be punished for "treason," President Johnson adopted a more lenient policy. On May 29, 1865, he issued two proclamations setting forth his reconstruction program. Like Lincoln's, it rested on the claim that the southern states had never left the Union.

Johnson's first proclamation continued Lincoln's policies by offering "amnesty and pardon, with restoration of all rights of property" to most former Confederates who would swear allegiance to the Constitution and the Union. Johnson revealed his Jacksonian hostility to "aristocratic" planters by exempting ex-Confederate government leaders and rebels with taxable property valued over $20,000. They could, however, apply for individual pardons, which Johnson granted to nearly all applicants.

In his second proclamation, Johnson accepted the reconstructed government of North Carolina and prescribed the steps by which other southern states could reestablish state governments. First, the president would appoint a provisional governor, who would call a state convention representing those "who are loyal to the United States," including persons who took the oath of allegiance or were otherwise pardoned. The convention must ratify the Thirteenth Amendment, which abolished slavery; void secession; repudiate Confederate debts; and elect new state officials and members of Congress.

Under Johnson's plan, all southern states completed Reconstruction and sent representatives to Congress, which convened in December 1865. Defiant southern voters elected dozens of former officers and legislators of the Confederacy, including a few not yet pardoned. Some state conventions hedged on ratifying the Thirteenth Amendment, and some asserted former owners' right to compensation for lost slave property. No state convention provided for black suffrage, and most did nothing to guarantee civil rights, schooling, or economic protection for the freedmen. Less than eight months after Appomattox, the southern states were back in the Union, ex-slaves were working for former masters, and the new president was firmly in charge. Reconstruction seemed to be over.

Congressional Reconstruction

Late in 1865, northern leaders painfully saw that almost none of their postwar goals—moral, political, or psychological—were being fulfilled and that the Republicans were likely to lose their political power. Would Democrats and the South gain by postwar elections what they had lost by civil war?

The answer was obvious. Congressional Republicans, led by Congressman Thaddeus Stevens of Pennsylvania and Senator Charles Sumner of Massachusetts, decided to set their own policies for Reconstruction. Although labeled "radicals," the vast majority of Republicans were moderates on the issues of the economic and political rights of freedmen.

Rejecting Johnson's position that the South had already been reconstructed, Congress exercised its constitutional authority to decide on its own membership. It refused to seat the new senators and representatives from the old Confederate states. It also established the Joint Committee on Reconstruction to investigate conditions in the South. Its report documented disorder, resistance, and the appalling situation of the freedmen.

Even before the final report came out in 1866, Congress passed a civil rights bill to protect the fragile rights of African-Americans and extended for two more years the Freedmen's Bureau, an agency providing emergency assistance at the end of the war. Johnson vetoed both bills and called his congressional opponents "traitors." His actions drove moderates into the radical camp, and Congress passed both bills over his veto—both, however, watered down by weakening the power of enforcement.

In such a climate, southern racial violence erupted. In a typical outbreak, in May 1866, white mobs in Memphis, encouraged by local police, rampaged for over 40 hours of terror, killing, beating, robbing, and raping virtually helpless black residents and burning houses, schools, and churches. Forty-eight people, all but two of them black, died. The local Union army commander took his time restoring order, arguing that his troops had "hated Negroes too." A congressional inquiry concluded that Memphis blacks had "no protection from the law whatever."

A month later, Congress sent to the states for ratification the Fourteenth Amendment, the single most significant act of the Reconstruction era. The first section of the amendment promised permanent constitutional protection of the civil rights of freedmen by defining them as citizens. States were prohibited from depriving "any person of life, liberty, or property, without due process of law," and all people were guaranteed the "equal protection of the laws." Section 2 granted

A white mob burned this freedmen's school during the Memphis riot of May 1866. (Library Company of Philadelphia)

black male suffrage in the South. Other sections of the amendment barred leaders of the Confederacy from national or state offices (except by act of Congress), repudiated the Confederate debt, and denied claims of compensation to former slave owners. Johnson urged the southern states to reject the Fourteenth Amendment, and ten immediately did so.

The Fourteenth Amendment was the central issue of the 1866 midterm election. Johnson barnstormed the country asking voters to throw out the radical Republicans and trading insults with hecklers. Democrats north and south appealed openly to racial prejudice in attacking the Fourteenth Amendment. Republicans responded in kind, branding Johnson a drunken traitor. Republicans freely "waved the bloody shirt," reminding voters of Democrats' treason and draft-dodging. Voters were moved more by self-interest and local issues than by such speeches, but the result was an overwhelming Republican victory. The mandate was clear: Presidential Reconstruction had not worked, and Congress must present an alternative.

Early in 1867, Congress passed three Reconstruction acts. The southern states were divided into five military districts, whose commanders had broad powers to maintain order and protect civil and property rights. Congress also defined a new process for readmitting a state. Qualified voters—including blacks but excluding unreconstructed rebels—would elect delegates to state constitutional conventions that would write new constitutions guaranteeing black suffrage. After the new voters of the states had ratified these constitutions, elections would be held to choose governors and state legislatures. When a state ratified the Fourteenth Amendment, its representatives to Congress would be accepted, completing its readmission to the Union.

The President Impeached

Congress also restricted presidential powers and established legislative dominance over the executive branch. The Tenure of Office Act, designed to prevent Johnson from firing the outspoken Secretary of War Edwin Stanton, limited the president's appointment powers. Other measures trimmed his power as commander in chief.

Johnson responded exactly as congressional Republicans had anticipated. He vetoed the Reconstruction acts, limited the activities of military commanders in the South, and removed cabinet officers and other officials sympathetic to Congress. The House Judiciary Committee charged the president with "usurpations of power" and of acting in the "interests of the great criminals" who had led the rebellion. But moderate House Republicans defeated the impeachment resolutions.

In August 1867, Johnson dismissed Stanton and asked for Senate consent. When the Senate refused, the president ordered Stanton to surrender his office, which he refused, barricading himself inside. Now the House quickly approved impeachment resolutions, charging the president with "high crimes and misdemeanors," mostly alleged violations of the Tenure of Office Act. The three-month trial in the Senate early in 1868 featured impassioned oratory. Evidence was skimpy, however, that Johnson had committed any crime justifying his removal. With seven moderate Republicans joining Democrats against conviction, the effort to find the president guilty fell exactly one vote short of the required two-thirds majority. Not until the 1970s—and again in 1998–99—would a president face removal from office through impeachment.

Moderate Republicans may have feared the consequences of removing Johnson, for the man in line for the presidency, Senator Benjamin Wade of Ohio, was a leading radical Republican. Wade had endorsed women's suffrage, rights for labor unions, and civil rights for African-Americans in both southern and northern states. As moderate Republicans gained strength in 1868 through their support of the presidential election winner, Ulysses S. Grant, radicalism lost much of its power within Republican ranks.

Congressional Moderation

Congress's political battle against President Johnson was not matched by an idealistic resolve on behalf of the freedmen. State and local elections of 1867 showed that voters preferred moderate Reconstruction policies. It is important to look not only at what Congress did during Reconstruction, but also at what it did not do.

With the exception of Jefferson Davis, Congress did not imprison Confederate leaders, and only one person, the commander of the infamous Andersonville prison camp, was executed. Congress did not insist on a long probation before southern states could be readmitted. It did not reorganize southern local governments. It did not mandate a national program of education for the four million ex-slaves. It did not confiscate and redistribute land to the freedmen, nor did it prevent Johnson from taking land away from freedmen who had gained titles during the war. It did not, except indirectly, provide economic help to black citizens.

Congress did, reluctantly, grant citizenship and suffrage to the freedmen. Northerners were no more prepared than southerners to make African-Americans equal citizens. Proposals to give black men the vote gained support in the North only after the presidential election of 1868, when General Grant, the supposedly invincible military hero, barely won the popular vote in several states. To ensure grateful black votes, Congressional Republicans, who had twice rejected a suffrage amendment, took another look at the idea. After a bitter fight, the Fifteenth Amendment, forbidding all states to deny the vote to anyone "on account of race, color, or previous condition of servitude," became part of the Constitution in 1870.

Congress, therefore, gave blacks the vote but not land, the opposite of the freedmen's priority. Almost alone, Thaddeus Stevens argued that "forty acres . . . and a hut would be more valuable . . . than the . . . right to vote." But Congress never seriously considered his plan to confiscate the land of the "chief rebels" and give a small portion of it, divided into 40-acre plots, to the freedmen. This would have violated deeply-held beliefs of the Republican party and the American people about the sacredness of private property. Moreover, northern business interests looking to develop southern industry and invest in southern land liked the prospect of a large pool of propertyless African-Americans workers.

Congress did pass the Southern Homestead Act of 1866, making public lands available to blacks and loyal whites in five southern states. But the land was poor and inaccessible, and most black laborers were bound by contracts that prevented them from moving onto claims before the deadline. Only about 4,000 black families even applied for the Homestead Act lands, and fewer than 20 percent of them saw their claims completed. White claimants did little better.

Women and the Reconstruction Amendments

One casualty of the Fourteenth and Fifteenth amendments was the goodwill of women who had worked for suffrage for two decades. They had hoped that male legislators would recognize their wartime service in support of the Union and were shocked when the Fourteenth Amendment for the first time inserted the word male into the Constitution in referring to a citizen's right to vote. Elizabeth Stanton and Susan B. Anthony, veteran suffragists and opponents of slavery, campaigned against the Fourteenth Amendment, breaking with abolitionist allies like Frederick Douglass, who had long supported woman suffrage yet declared that this was "the Negro's hour." When the Fifteenth Amendment was proposed, suffragists wondered why the word sex could not have been added to the "conditions" no longer a basis for denial of the vote. Largely abandoned by radical reconstructionists and abolitionist activists, they had few champions in Congress and their efforts were put off for half a century.

Disappointment over the suffrage issue helped split the women's movement in 1869. Anthony and Stanton continued their fight for a national amendment for woman suffrage and a long list of other rights, while other women concentrated on securing the vote state-by-state.

LIFE AFTER SLAVERY

Union army Major George Reynolds boasted late in 1865 that in the area of Mississippi under his command he had "kept the negroes at work, and in a good state of discipline." Clinton Fisk, a well-meaning white who helped found a black college in Tennessee, told freedmen in 1866 that they could be "as free and as happy" working again for their "old master . . . as any where else in the world." Such pronouncements reminded blacks of white preachers' exhortations during slavery to work hard and obey masters. Ironically, Fisk and Reynolds were agents of the Freedmen's Bureau, the agency intended to aid former slaves' transition to freedom.

The Freedmen's Bureau

Never in American history has one small agency—underfinanced, understaffed, and undersupported—been given a harder task than was the Bureau of Freedmen, Refugees and Abandoned Lands. Its fate epitomizes Reconstruction.

The Freedmen's Bureau performed many essential services. It issued emergency food rations, clothed and sheltered homeless victims of the war, and established medical and hospital facilities. It provided funds to relocate thousands of freedmen and white refugees. It helped blacks search for relatives and get legally married, and it served as a friend in local civil courts to ensure that freedmen got fair trials. Although not initially empowered to do so, the agency also became responsible for educating the ex-slaves in schools staffed by idealistic northerners.

The Bureau's largest task was to promote African-Americans' economic well-being. This included settling them on abandoned lands and getting them started with tools, seed, and draft animals, as well as arranging work contracts with white landowners. But in this area the Freedmen's Bureau served more to "reenslave" the freedmen than to set them on their way as independent farmers.

Although some agents were self-sacrificing young New Englanders eager to help ex-slaves adjust to freedom, others were Union army officers more concerned with social order than social transformation. Working in a postwar climate of resentment and violence, Freedmen's Bureau agents were constantly accused by local whites of being partisan Republicans, corrupt, and partial to blacks. But even the best-intentioned agents would have agreed with Bureau commissioner General O. O. Howard's belief in the traditional nineteenth-century American values of self-help, minimal government interference in the marketplace, the sanctity of private property, contractual obligations, and white superiority.

On a typical day, overworked agents would visit local courts and schools, supervise the signing of work contracts, and handle numerous complaints, most involving contract violations between whites and blacks or property and domestic disputes among blacks. One agent sent a man who had complained of a severe beating back to work: "Don't be sassy [and] don't be lazy when you've got work to do." Although helpful in finding work for freedmen, often agents defended white landowners by telling blacks to obey orders, trust employers, and accept disadvantageous contracts.

Despite numerous constraints, the agents accomplished much. In little more than two years, the Freedmen's Bureau issued 20 million rations (nearly one-third to poor whites), reunited families and resettled some 30,000 displaced war refugees, treated some 450,000 people for illness and injury, built 40 hospitals and hundreds of schools, provided books, tools, and furnishings—and even some land—to the freedmen, and occasionally protected their economic and civil rights. African-American historian W. E. B. Du Bois's epitaph for the bureau might stand for the whole of Reconstruction: "In a time of perfect calm, amid willing neighbors and streaming wealth," he wrote, it "would have been a herculean task" for the bureau to fulfill its many purposes. But in the midst of hunger, sorrow, spite, suspicion, hate, and cruelty, "the work of any instrument of social regeneration was . . . foredoomed to failure."

Economic Freedom by Degrees

The economic failures of the Freedmen's Bureau forced freedmen into a new dependency on former masters. Although the planter class did not lose its economic and social power in the postwar years, southern agriculture saw major changes.

First, a land-intensive system replaced the labor intensity of slavery. Land ownership was concentrated into fewer and even larger holdings than before the war. From South Carolina to Louisiana, the wealthiest tenth of the population owned about 60 percent of the real estate in the 1870s. Second, these large planters increasingly specialized in one crop, usually cotton, and were tied into the international market. This resulted in a steady drop in postwar food production (both grain and livestock). Third, one-crop farming created a new credit system whereby most farmers, black and white, rented seed, farm implements and animals, provisions, housing, and land from local merchants. These changes affected race relations and class tensions among whites.

This new system took a few years to develop after emancipation. At first, most freedmen signed contracts with white landowners and worked very much as during slavery. All members of the family had to work to receive their rations. The freedmen resented this new semiservitude, preferring small plots of land of their own to grow vegetables and grains. They wanted to be able to send their children to school and insisted on "no more outdoor work" for women.

Many blacks therefore broke contracts, ran away, engaged in work slowdowns or strikes, burned barns, and otherwise resisted. In the Sea Islands and rice-growing regions of coastal South Carolina and Georgia, where slaves had long held a degree of autonomy, resistance was especially strong. On the Heyward plantations, near those of the Allstons, the freedmen "refuse work at any price," a Freedman's Bureau agent reported, and the women "wish to stay in the house or the garden all the time." The Allstons' former slaves also refused to sign contracts, even when offered livestock and other favors, and in 1869, Adele Allston had to sell much of her vast landholdings.

Blacks' insistence on autonomy and land of their own was the major impetus for the change from the contract system to tenancy and sharecropping. Families would hitch mules to their old slave cabin and drag it to their plot, as far from the Big House as possible. Sharecroppers received seed, fertilizer, implements, food, and clothing. In return, the landlord (or a local merchant) told them what and how much to grow, and he took a share—usually half—of the harvest. The cropper's half usually went to pay for goods bought on credit (at high interest rates) from the landlord. Thus sharecroppers remained tied to the landlord.

Tenant farmers had only slightly more independence. Before a harvest, they promised to sell their crop to a local merchant in return for renting land, tools, and

Sharecroppers and tenant farmers, though more autonomous than contract laborers, remained dependent on the landlord for their survival. (Brown Brothers)

other necessities. From the merchant's store they also had to buy goods on credit (at higher prices than whites paid) against the harvest. At "settling up" time, income from sale of the crop was compared to accumulated debts. It was possible, especially after an unusually bountiful season, to come out ahead and eventually to own one's own land. But tenants rarely did; in debt at the end of each year, they had to pledge the next year's crop. World cotton prices remained low, and whereas big landowners still generated profits through their large scale of operation, sharecroppers rarely made much money. When they were able to pay their debts, landowners frequently altered loan agreements. Thus peonage replaced slavery, ensuring a continuing cheap labor supply to grow cotton and other staples in the South. Only a very few African-Americans became independent landowners— about 2 to 5 percent by 1880, and closer to 20 percent in some states by 1900.

These changes in southern agriculture affected yeoman and poor white farmers as well, and planters worried about a coalition between poor black and pro-Unionist white farmers. As a yeoman farmer in Georgia said in 1865, "We should tuk the land, as we did the niggers, and split it, and giv part to the niggers and part to me and t'other Union fellers." But confiscation and redistribution of land was no more likely for white farmers than for the freedmen. Whites, too, had to concentrate on growing staples, pledging their crops against high-interest credit and facing perpetual indebtedness. In the upcountry piedmont area of Georgia, for example, the number of whites working their own land dropped from nine in ten before the Civil War to seven in ten by 1880, while cotton production doubled.

Reliance on cotton meant fewer food crops and greater dependence on merchants for provisions. In 1884, Jephta Dickson of Jackson County, Georgia, purchased over $50 worth of flour, meal, meat, syrup, peas, and corn from a local store; 25 years earlier, he had been almost completely self-sufficient. Fencing laws seriously curtailed the livelihood of poor whites raising pigs and hogs, and restrictions on hunting and fishing reduced the ability of poor whites and blacks alike to supplement incomes and diets.

In the worn-out flatlands and barren mountainous regions of the South, poor whites' antebellum poverty, ill health, and isolation worsened after the war. Many poor white farmers were even less productive than black sharecroppers. Some became farmhands at $6 a month (with board). Others fled to low-paying jobs in cotton mills, where they would not have to compete against blacks.

The cultural life of poor southern whites reflected their lowly position and their pride. Their emotional religion centered on camp meeting revivals. Their ballads and folktales told of debt, chain gangs, and drinking prowess. Their quilt making and house construction reflected a marginal culture in which everything was saved and reused.

In part because their lives were so hard, poor whites clung to their belief in white superiority. Many poor whites joined the Ku Klux Klan and other southern white terror groups that emerged between 1866 and 1868. But however hard life was for poor whites, things were even worse for blacks. The freedmen's high hopes slowly soured. Recalled a former Texas slave, "We soon found out that freedom could make folks proud but it didn't make 'em rich."

Black Self-Help Institutions

Many African-American leaders realized that because white institutions could not fulfill the promises of emancipation, freedmen would have to do it themselves. Traditions of black community self-help survived in the churches and schools of the antebellum free Negro communities and in the "invisible" cultural institutions of the slave quarters. Emancipation brought a rapid increase in the growth of membership in African-American churches. The Negro Baptist Church grew from 150,000 members in 1850 to 500,000 in 1870, while the membership of the African Methodist Episcopal Church exploded.

African-American ministers continued to exert community leadership. Many led efforts to oppose discrimination, some by entering politics; over one-fifth of the black officeholders in South Carolina were ministers. Most preachers, however, focused on sin and salvation. An English visitor to the South in 1867 and 1868 noted the intensity of black "devoutness." As one black woman explained: "We make noise 'bout ebery ting else . . . I want ter go ter Heaben in de good ole way."

The freedmen's desire for education was as strong as for religion. Typically, a school official in Virginia said that the freedmen were "down right crazy to learn." The first teachers of these black children were the legendary "Yankee schoolmarms." Sent by groups such as the American Missionary Association, these high-minded young women sought to convert blacks to Congregationalism and white morality. In October 1865, Esther Douglass found "120 dirty, half naked, perfectly wild black children" in her schoolroom near Savannah, Georgia. Eight months later, she reported that they could read, sing hymns, and repeat Bible verses and had learned "about right conduct which they tried to practice."

Such glowing reports changed as white teachers grew frustrated with crowded facilities, limited resources, local opposition, and absenteeism caused by fieldwork.

Along with equal civil rights and land of their own, what the freedmen wanted most was education. Despite white opposition and limited facilities for black schools, one of the most positive outcomes of the Reconstruction era was education in freedmen's schools. (Valentine Museum, Richmond, Virginia)

In Georgia, for example, only 5 percent of black children went to school for part of any one year between 1865 and 1870, as opposed to 20 percent of white children. Blacks increasingly preferred their own teachers, who could better understand them. To train African-American preachers and teachers, northern philanthropists founded Howard, Atlanta, Fisk, Morehouse, and other black universities in the South between 1865 and 1867.

Black schools, like churches, became community centers. They published newspapers, provided training in trades and farming, and promoted political participation and land ownership. These efforts made black schools objects of local white hostility. As a Virginia freedman told a congressional committee, in his county, anyone starting a school would be killed and that blacks were "afraid to be caught with a book."

White opposition to black education and land ownership stimulated African-American nationalism and separatism. In the late 1860s, Benjamin "Pap" Singleton, a former Tennessee slave, urged blacks to abandon politics and migrate westward. He organized a land company in 1869, purchased public property in Kansas, and in the early 1870s took several groups from Tennessee and Kentucky to establish separate black towns in the prairie state. In following years, thousands of "exodusters" from the Lower South bought some 10,000 infertile acres in Kansas. But natural and human obstacles to self-sufficiency often proved insurmountable. By the 1880s, despairing of ever finding economic independence in the United States, Singleton and other nationalists advocated emigration to Canada and Liberia.

Other African-American leaders, notably Frederick Douglass, continued to press for full citizenship rights within the United States.

RECONSTRUCTION IN THE STATES

Douglass's confidence in the power of the ballot seemed warranted in the enthusiastic early months under the Reconstruction Acts of 1867. With President Johnson neutralized, Republican congressional leaders finally could prevail. Local Republicans, taking advantage of the inability or refusal of many southern whites to vote, overwhelmingly elected their delegates to state constitutional conventions in the fall of 1867. Guardedly optimistic and sensing the "sacred importance" of their work, black and white Republicans began creating new state governments.

Republican Rule

Southern state governments under Republican rule were not dominated by illiterate black majorities intent on "Africanizing" the South. Nor were these governments unusually corrupt or extravagant, nor use massive numbers of federal troops to enforce their will. By 1869, only 1,100 federal soldiers remained in Virginia, and most federal troops in Texas were guarding the frontier against Mexico and hostile Indians. Lacking strong military backing, the new state governments faced economic distress and increasingly violent harassment.

Diverse coalitions made up the new governments elected under congressional Reconstruction. These "black and tan" governments (as opponents called them) were actually predominantly white, except for the lower house of the South Carolina legislature. Some new leaders came from the old Whiggish elite of bankers, industrialists, and others interested more in economic growth and sectional reconciliation than in radical social reforms. A second group consisted of northern Republican capitalists who headed south to invest in land, railroads, and new industries. Others included Union veterans seeking a warmer climate, and missionaries and teachers inspired to work in Freedmen's Bureau schools. Such people were unfairly labeled "carpetbaggers."

Moderate African-Americans made up a third group in the Republican state governments. A large percentage of black officeholders were mulattoes, many of them well-educated preachers, teachers, and soldiers from the North. Others were self-educated tradesmen or representatives of the small landed class of southern blacks. In South Carolina, for example, of some 255 African-American state and federal officials elected between 1868 and 1876, two-thirds were literate and one-third owned real estate; only 15 percent owned no property at all. This class composition meant that black leaders often supported policies that largely ignored the economic needs of the black masses. Their goals fit squarely into the American republican tradition. African-American leaders reminded whites that they were also southerners, seeking only, as an 1865 petition put it, "that the same laws which govern white men shall govern black men [and that] we be dealt with as others are—in equity and justice."

The primary accomplishment of Republican rule in the South was to eliminate undemocratic features from prewar state constitutions. All states provided universal male suffrage and loosened requirements for holding office. Underrepresented counties got more legislative seats. Automatic imprisonment for debt was ended, and laws were enacted to relieve poverty and care for the handicapped. Many southern states received their first divorce laws and provisions granting property rights to married women. Lists of crimes punishable by death were shortened.

Republican governments financially and physically reconstructed the South by overhauling tax systems and approving generous railroad and other capital investment bonds. Harbors, roads, and bridges were rebuilt; hospitals and asylums were established. Most important, the Republican governments created the South's first public school systems. As in the North, these schools were largely segregated, but for the first time rich and poor, black and white alike had access to education. By the 1880s, black school attendance increased from 5 to over 40 percent, and white from 20 to over 60 percent. All this cost money, and so the Republicans also greatly increased tax rates and state debts.

These considerable accomplishments came in the face of opposition like that expressed at a convention of Louisiana planters, which labeled the Republican leaders the "lowest and most corrupt body of men ever assembled in the South." There was some corruption, mostly in land sales, railway bonds, and construction contracts. Such graft had become a way of life in postwar American politics, South and North. Given their lack of experience with politics, the black role was remarkable. As Du Bois put it, "There was one thing that the White South feared more than negro dishonesty, ignorance, and incompetence, and that was negro honesty, knowledge, and efficiency."

The Republican coalition did not survive. As the map indicates, Republican rule lasted for different periods in different states. It lasted the longest in the black belt states of the Deep South, where the black population was equal to or greater than the white. In Virginia, Republicans ruled hardly at all. Conservative Virginia Democrats professed agreement with Congress's Reconstruction guidelines while doing as they pleased and encouraging northern investors to rebuild shattered cities and develop industry. In South Carolina, African-American leaders' unwillingness to use their power to help black laborers contributed to their loss of political control to the Democrats. Class tensions and divisions among blacks in Louisiana helped to weaken that Republican regime as well.

Violence and "Redemption"

Democrats used violence to regain power. The Ku Klux Klan was only one of several secret organizations that forcibly drove black and white Republicans from office. The cases of North Carolina and Mississippi are representative.

After losing a close election in North Carolina in 1868, conservatives waged a concentrated terror campaign in several piedmont counties. If the Democrats could win these counties in 1870, they would most likely win statewide. In the year before the election, several prominent Republicans were killed, including a white state senator and a leading black Union League organizer, who was hanged in the

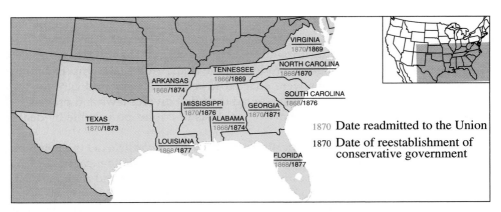

THE RETURN OF CONSERVATIVE DEMOCRATIC CONTROL IN SOUTHERN STATES DURING RECONSTRUCTION Note that the length of time Republican governments were in power to implement even moderate Reconstruction programs varied from state to state. In North Carolina and Georgia, for example, Republican rule was very brief while in Virginia it never took place at all. "Redemption," the return of conservative control, took longest in the three deep South states where electoral votes were hotly contested in the election of 1876.

courthouse square with a sign pinned to him: "Bewar, ye guilty, both white and black." Scores of citizens were fired, flogged, tortured, or driven in the middle of the night from burning homes and barns. The courts consistently refused to prosecute anyone for these crimes, which local papers blamed on "disgusting negroes and white Radicals." The conservative campaign worked. In the election of 1870, some 12,000 fewer Republicans voted in the two crucial counties than had voted two years earlier, and the Democrats swept back into power.

In Mississippi's state election in 1875, Democrats used similar tactics. Local Democratic clubs formed armed militias, marching defiantly through black areas, breaking up Republican meetings, and provoking riots to justify killing hundreds of blacks. Armed men posted during voter registration intimidated Republicans. At the election itself, voters were either "helped" by gun-toting whites to cast a Democratic ballot or chased away. Counties that had given Republican candidates majorities in the thousands managed a total of less than a dozen votes in 1875!

Democrats called their victory "redemption." As conservative Democrats resumed control of each state government, Reconstruction ended. Redemption succeeded with a combination of persistent white southern resistance, including violence and coercion, and a failure of northern persistence.

Congress and President Grant did not totally ignore southern violence. Three Force acts, passed in 1870 and 1871, gave the president strong powers to use federal supervisors to ensure that citizens were not prevented from voting by force or fraud. The third act, also known as the Ku Klux Klan Act, declared illegal secret organizations that used disguise and coercion to deprive others of equal protection of the laws. Congress created a joint committee to investigate Klan violence, and in 1872 its report filled 13 huge volumes with horrifying testimony. Grant, who had supported these measures, sent messages to Congress proclaiming the importance of the right to vote, issued proclamations condemning lawlessness, and dispatched additional troops to South Carolina. However, reform Republicans lost interest in defending blacks when they saw these voters supporting Grant, whom they opposed, and regular Republicans decided that they could do without black votes. Both groups were much more concerned with northern issues. In 1875, Grant's advisers told him that Republicans might lose important Ohio elections if he continued protecting African-Americans, so he rejected appeals by Mississippi blacks for troops to guarantee free elections. He and the nation "had tired of these annual autumnal outbreaks," the president said.

Mississippi Democrats' success in 1875, repeated a year later in South Carolina and Louisiana, indicated that congressional reports, presidential proclamations, and the Force acts did little to stop the reign of terror against black and white Republicans throughout the South. Despite hundreds of arrests, all-white juries refused to find whites guilty of crimes against blacks. The U.S. Supreme Court backed them, in two 1874 decisions throwing out cases against whites convicted of preventing blacks from voting and declaring key parts of the Force acts unconstitutional. Officially the Klan's power ended, but the attitudes (and tactics) of Klansmen would continue long into the next century.

Reconstruction, Northern Style

The American people, like their leaders, were tired of battles over the freedmen. The easiest course was to give citizenship and the vote to African-Americans, and move on. Americans of increasing ethnic diversity were primarily interested in starting families, finding work, and making money.

At both the individual and national levels, Reconstruction, northern style, meant the continuation of the enormous economic revolution of the nineteenth century. Although failing to effect a smooth transition from slavery to freedom for ex-slaves, Republican northerners did accelerate and solidify their program of economic growth and industrial and territorial expansion.

Thus as North Carolina Klansmen convened in dark forests in 1869, the Central Pacific and Union Pacific railroads met in Utah, linking the Atlantic and the Pacific. As southern cotton production revived, northern iron and steel manufacturing and western settlement of the mining, cattle, and agricultural frontiers also surged. As black farmers were "haggling" over work contracts with white landowners in Georgia, white workers were organizing the National Labor Union in Baltimore. As Elizabeth and Adele Allston demanded the keys to their barns in the summer of 1865, the Boston Labor Reform Association was demanding that "our . . . education, morals, dwellings, and the whole Social System" needed to be "reconstructed." If the South would not be reconstructed, labor relations might be.

The years between 1865 and 1875 featured not only the rise (and fall) of Republican governments in the South, but also a spectacular surge of working-class organization. Stimulated by the Civil War to improve working conditions in northern factories, trade unions, labor reform associations, and labor parties flourished, culminating in the founding of the National Labor Union in 1866. Before the depression of 1873, an estimated 300,000 to 500,000 American workers enrolled in some 1,500 trade unions, the largest such increase in the nineteenth century. This growth inevitably stirred class tensions. In 1876, hundreds of freedmen in the rice region along the Combahee River in South Carolina went on strike to protest a 40-cent-per-day wage cut, clashing with local sheriffs and white Democratic rifle clubs.

A year later, also fighting wage cuts, thousands of northern railroad workers went out in a nationwide wave of strikes, clashing with police and the National Guard.

As economic relations changed, so did the Republican party. Heralded by the moderate tone of the state elections of 1867 and Grant's election in 1868, the Republicans changed from a party of moral reform to one of material interest. In the continuing struggle in American politics between "virtue and commerce," self-interest was again winning. Abandoning the Freedmen's Bureau, Republican politicians had no difficulty handing out huge grants of money and land to the railroads. As blacks were told to help themselves, the Union Pacific was getting subsidies of between $16,000 and $48,000 for each mile of track it laid. As Susan B. Anthony and others tramped through the snows of Upstate New York with petitions for rights of suffrage and citizenship, Boss Tweed and other machine politicians defrauded New York taxpayers of millions of dollars. As Native Americans in the Great Plains struggled to preserve their sacred Black Hills from greedy gold prospectors protected by U.S. soldiers, corrupt government officials in the East "mined" public treasuries.

By 1869, the year financier Jay Gould almost cornered the gold market, the nation was increasingly defined by its sordid, materialistic "go-getters." Henry Adams, descendant of two presidents, was living in Washington, D.C., during this era. As he explained in his 1907 autobiography, *The Education of Henry Adams*, he had had high expectations in 1869 that Grant, like George Washington, would restore moral order and peace. But when Grant announced his cabinet, a group of army cronies and rich friends to whom he owed favors, Adams felt betrayed.

Honest himself, Grant showed poor judgment of others. The scandals of his administration touched his relatives, his cabinet, and his two vice-presidents. Outright graft, loose prosecution, and generally negligent administration flourished in a half dozen departments. The Whiskey Ring affair, for example, cost the public millions of dollars in tax revenues siphoned off to government officials. Gould's gold scam received the unwitting aid of Grant's Treasury Department and the knowing help of the president's brother-in-law.

Nor was Congress pure. Crédit Mobilier, a dummy corporation supposedly building the transcontinental railroads, received generous bonds and contracts in exchange for giving congressmen money, stock, and railroad lands. An Ohio congressmen described the House of Representatives in 1873 as an "auction room where more valuable considerations were disposed of under the speaker's hammer than any place on earth."

The election of 1872 showed the public uninterested in moral issues. "Liberal" Republicans, disgusted with Grant, formed a third party calling for lower tariffs and fewer grants to railroads, civil service reform, and the removal of federal troops from the South. Their candidate, Horace Greeley, editor of the New York *Tribune*, was also nominated by the Democrats, whom he had spent much of his career condemning. But despite his wretched record, Grant easily won a second term.

The End of Reconstruction

Soon after Grant's second inauguration, a financial panic, caused by railroad mismanagement and the collapse of some eastern banks, started a terrible depression that lasted throughout the mid-1870s. In these hard times, economic issues

Under a caption quoting a Democratic party newspaper, "This is a white man's government," this Thomas Nast cartoon from 1868 shows three white groups, stereotyped as apelike northern Irish workers, unrepentant ex-Confederates, and rich northern capitalists, joining hands to bring Republican Reconstruction to an end almost before it began. The immigrant's vote, the Kluxer's knife, and the capitalist's dollars would restore a "white man's government" on the back of the freedman, a Union soldier still clutching the Union flag and reaching in vain for the ballot box. No single image better captures the story of the end of Reconstruction. (*Harper's Weekly,* September 5, 1868)

dominated politics, further diverting attention from the freedmen. As Democrats took control of the House of Representatives in 1874 and looked toward winning the White House in 1876, politicians talked about new Grant scandals, unemployment and public works, the currency, and tariffs. No one said much about the freedmen. In 1875, a guilt-ridden Congress did pass Senator Charles Sumner's civil rights bill to put teeth into the Fourteenth Amendment. But the act was not enforced, and eight years later the Supreme Court declared it unconstitutional. Congressional Reconstruction, long dormant, had ended. The election of 1876 sealed the conclusion.

As their presidential candidate in 1876, the Republicans chose a former governor of Ohio, Rutherford B. Hayes, partly because of his reputation for honesty, partly because he had been a Union officer (a necessity for post-Civil War candidates), and partly because, as Henry Adams put it, he was "obnoxious to no one." The Democrats nominated Governor Samuel J. Tilden of New York, a famous civil service reformer who had broken the Tweed ring.

Tilden won a popular-vote majority and appeared to have enough electoral votes for victory—except for 20 disputed electoral votes, all but one in Louisiana, South Carolina, and Florida, where some federal troops remained and where Republicans still controlled the voting apparatus despite Democratic intimidation. To settle the dispute, Congress created a commission of eight Republicans and seven Democrats who voted along party lines to give Hayes all 20 votes and an electoral-college victory, 185 to 184.

Novels

We usually read novels, short stories, and other forms of fiction for pleasure, for the enjoyment of plot, style, symbolism, and character development. "Classic" novels such as *Moby Dick*, *Huckleberry Finn*, *The Great Gatsby*, *The Invisible Man*, and *Beloved*, for example, are not only written well, but also explore timeless questions of good and evil, of innocence and knowledge, or of noble dreams fulfilled and shattered. We enjoy novels because we often find ourselves identifying with one of the major characters. Through that person's problems, joys, relationships, and search for identity, we gain insights about our own.

We can also read novels as historical sources, for they reveal much about the attitudes, dreams, fears and ordinary everyday experiences of human beings in a particular historical period. In addition, they show how people responded to the major events of that era. The novelist, like the historian, is a product of time and place and has an interpretive point of view. Consider the two novels about Reconstruction quoted here. Neither is reputed for great literary merit, yet both reveal much about the various interpretations and impassioned attitudes of the post-Civil War era. *A Fool's Errand* was written by Albion Tourgée, a northerner; *The Clansman*, by Thomas Dixon, Jr., a southerner.

Tourgée was a young northern teacher and lawyer who fought with the Union army and moved to North Carolina after the war to begin a legal career. He became a judge and was an active Republican, supporting black suffrage and helping to shape the new state constitution. Because he boldly criticized the Ku Klux Klan, his life was threatened many times. When he left North Carolina in 1879, he published an autobiographical novel about his experiences as a judge challenging the Klan's campaign of violence and intimidation against the newly freed blacks.

The "fool's errand" in the novel is that of the northern veteran, Comfort Servosse, who like Tourgée seeks to fulfill human goals on behalf of both blacks and whites in post-Civil War North Carolina. His efforts are thwarted, however, by threats, intimidation, a campaign of violent "outrages" against republican leaders in the county, and a lack of support from Congress. Historians have verified the accuracy of the events in Tourgée's novel. While exposing the brutality of the Klan, Tourgée features loyal southern Unionists, respectable planters ashamed of Klan violence, and even guilt-ridden poor white Klansmen who try to protect or warn intended victims.

In the year of Tourgée's death, 1905, another North Carolinian published a novel with a very different analysis of Reconstruction and its fate. Thomas Dixon, Jr., was a lawyer, state legislator, Baptist minister, pro-Klan lecturer, and novelist. *The Clansman*, subtitled *A Historical Romance of the Ku Klux Klan*, reflects turn-of-the-century attitudes most white southerners still had about Republican rule during Reconstruction. According to Dixon, once the "Great Heart" Lincoln was gone, a power-crazed, vindictive radical Congress, led by scheming Austin Stoneman (Thaddeus Stevens), sought to impose corrupt carpetbagger and brutal black rule on a helpless South. Only through the inspired leadership of the Ku Klux Klan was the South saved from the horrors of rape and revenge.

Dixon dedicated *The Clansman* to his uncle, a Grand Titan of the Klan in North Carolina during the time when two crucial counties were being transformed from Republican to Democratic through intimidation and terror. No such violence shows up in Dixon's novel. When the novel was made the basis of D. W. Griffith's film classic, *Birth of a Nation*, in 1915, the novel's attitudes were firmly implanted on the twentieth-century American mind.

Both novels convey the events and issues of Reconstruction, especially attitudes toward the freedmen. Both create clearly defined heroes and villains. Both include exciting chase scenes, narrow escapes, daring rescues, and tragic deaths. Both include romantic subplots. Examining these brief excerpts is a poor substitute for reading the novels in their entirety, but notice the obvious differences of style and attitude in the depictions of Uncle Jerry and Old Aleck. How many differences can you find in these two short passages?

A Fool's Errand   Albion Tourgée (1879)

When the second Christmas came, Metta wrote again to her sister:

"The feeling is terribly bitter against Comfort on account of his course towards the colored people. There is quite a village of them on the lower end of the plantation. They have a church, a sabbath school, and are to have next year a school. You can not imagine how kind they have been to us, and how much they are attached to Comfort. . . . I got Comfort to go with me to one of their prayer-meetings a few nights ago. I had heard a great deal about them, but had never attended one before. It was strangely weird. There were, perhaps, fifty present, mostly middle-aged men and women. They were singing in soft, low monotone, interspersed with prolonged exclamatory notes, a sort of rude hymn, which I was surprised to know was one of their old songs in slave times. How the chorus came to be endured in those days I can not imagine. It was—

'Free! free! free, my Lord, free!
An' we walks de hebben-ly way!

"A few looked around as we came in and seated ourselves; and Uncle Jerry, the saint of the settlement, came forward on his staves, and said, in his soft voice,

"'Ev'nin', Kunnel! Sarvant, Missuss! Will you walk up, an' hev seats in front?'

"We told him we had just looked in, and might go in a short time; so we would stay in the back part of the audience.

"Uncle Jerry can not read nor write; but he is a man of strange intelligence and power. Unable to do work of any account, he is the faithful friend, monitor, and director of others. He has a house and piece of land, all paid for, a good horse and cow, and, with the aid of his wife and two boys, made a fine crop this season. He is one of the most promising colored men in the settlement: so Comfort says, at least. Everybody seems to have great respect for his character. I don't know how many people I have heard speak of his religion. Mr. Savage used to say he had rather hear him pray than any other man on earth. He was much prized by his master, even after he was disabled, on account of his faithfulness and character."

The Clansman   Thomas Dixon, Jr. (1905)

At noon Ben and Phil strolled to the polling-place to watch the progress of the first election under Negro rule. The Square was jammed with shouting, jostling, perspiring negroes, men, women, and children. The day was warm, and the African odour was supreme even in the open air . . . .

The negroes, under the drill of the League and the Freedman's Bureau, protected by the bayonet, were voting to enfranchise themselves, disfranchise their former masters, ratify a new constitution, and elect a legislature to do their will. Old Aleck was a candidate for the House, chief poll-holder, and seemed to be in charge of the movements of the voters outside the booth as well as inside. He appeared to be omnipresent, and his self-importance was a sight Phil had never dreamed. He could not keep his eyes off him . . . .

[Aleck] was a born African orator, undoubtedly descended from a long line of savage spell-binders, whose eloquence in the palaver houses of the jungle had made them native leaders. His thin spindle-shanks supported an oblong, protruding stomach, resembling an elderly monkey's, which seemed so heavy it swayed his back to carry it.

The animal vivacity of his small eyes and the flexibility of his eyebrows, which he worked up and down rapidly with every change of countenance, expressed his eager desires.

He was already mellow with liquor, and was dressed in an old army uniform and cap, with two horse-pistols buckled around his waist. On a strap hanging from his shoulder were strung a half-dozen tin canteens filled with whiskey.

Outraged Democrats threatened to stop the Senate from officially counting the electoral votes, thus preventing Hayes's inauguration. There was talk of a new civil war. But unlike the 1850s, a North-South compromise emerged. Northern investors wanted the government to subsidize a New Orleans-to-California railroad. Southerners wanted northern dollars but not northern political influence—no social agencies, no federal enforcement of the Fourteenth and Fifteenth amendments, and no military occupation, not even the symbolic presence left in 1876.

As the March 4 inauguration date approached, the forces of mutual self-interest concluded the "compromise of 1877." On March 2, Hayes was declared president-elect. After his inauguration, he ordered the last federal troops out of the South, appointed a former Confederate general to his cabinet, supported federal aid for economic and railroad development in the South, and promised to let southerners handle race relations themselves. On a goodwill trip to the South, he told blacks that "your rights and interests would be safer if this great mass of intelligent white men were let alone by the general government." The message was clear: Hayes would not enforce the Fourteenth and Fifteenth amendments, initiating a pattern of executive inaction not broken until the 1960s. But the immediate crisis was averted, officially ending Reconstruction.

✦✦✦✦✦✦

CONCLUSION

A Mixed Legacy

In the 12 years between Appomattox and Hayes's inauguration, victorious northern Republicans, defeated white southerners, and hopeful black freedmen each wanted more than the others would give. But each got something. The compromise of 1877 cemented reunion, providing new opportunities for economic development in both regions. The Republican party achieved its economic goals and generally held the White House, though not always Congress, until 1932. The ex-Confederate states came back into the Union, and southerners retained their grip on southern lands and black labor, though not without struggle and some changes.

And the freedmen? In 1880, Frederick Douglass wrote: "Our Reconstruction measures were radically defective . . . . To the freedmen was given the machinery of liberty, but there was denied to them the steam to put it in motion. . . . The old master class . . . retained the power to starve them to death, and wherever this power is held there is the power of slavery." The wonder, Douglass said, was "not that freedmen . . . have been standing still, but that they have been able to stand at all."

Freedmen had made strong gains in education and in economic and family survival. Despite sharecropping and tenancy, black laborers organized themselves to achieve a measure of autonomy and opportunity in their lives that could never be diminished. The three great Reconstruction amendments, despite flagrant violation over the next 100 years, held out the promise that equal citizenship and political participation would yet be realized.

TIMELINE

1865	1865–1866	1866	1867	1868
Civil War ends; Lincoln assassinated; Andrew Johnson becomes president; Johnson proposes general amnesty and reconstruction plan; Racial confusion, widespread hunger, and demobilization; Thirteenth Amendment ratified; Freedmen's Bureau established	Black codes; Repossession of land by whites and freedmen's contracts	Freedmen's Bureau renewed and Civil Rights Act passed over Johnson's veto; Southern Homestead Act; Ku Klux Klan formed; Tennessee readmitted to Union	Reconstruction acts passed over Johnson's veto; Impeachment controversy; Freedmen's Bureau ends	Fourteenth Amendment ratified; Impeachment proceedings against Johnson fail; Ulysses Grant elected president

1868–1870	1869	1870	1870s–1880s	1870–1871
Ten states readmitted under congressional plan	Georgia and Virginia reestablish Democratic party control	Fifteenth Amendment ratified	Black "exodusters" migrate to Kansas	Force acts; North Carolina and Georgia reestablish Democratic control

1872	1873	1874	1875	1876
General Amnesty Act; Grant reelected president	Crédit Mobilier scandal; Panic causes depression	Alabama and Arkansas reestablish Democratic control	Civil Rights Act; Mississippi reestablishes Democratic control	Hayes-Tilden election

1876–1877	1877	1880s		
South Carolina, Louisiana, and Florida reestablish Democratic control	Compromise of 1877; Rutherford B. Hayes assumes presidency and ends Reconstruction	Tenancy and sharecropping prevail in the South; Disfranchisement and segregation of southern blacks begins		

Recommended Reading

Overviews of Reconstruction

Laura Edwards, *Gendered Strife & Confusion: The Political Culture of Reconstruction* (1997); W. E. B. Du Bois, *Black Reconstruction* (1935); Eric Foner, *Reconstruction: America's Unfinished Revolution, 1863–1877* (1988); John Hope Franklin, *Reconstruction After the Civil War* (1961).

The Freedmen's Transition: Freedom by Degrees

James E. Bond, *No Easy Walk to Freedom: Reconstruction and the Ratification of the Fourteenth Amendment* (1997); Paul Cimbala, *Under the Guardianship of the Nation: The Freedmen's Bureau and the Reconstruction of Georgia, 1865–1870* (1997); Barbara J. Fields, *Slavery and Freedom on the Middle Ground* (1985); Eric Foner, *Nothing but Freedom: Emancipation and Its Legacy* (1983); Reginald F. Hildebrand, *The Times Were Strange and Stirring: Methodist Preachers and the Crisis of Emancipation* (1995); Jacqueline Jones, *Soldiers of Light and Love: Northern Teachers and Georgia Blacks, 1865–1873* (1980); Leon Litwack, *Been in the Storm So Long: The Aftermath of Slavery* (1980); William E. Montgomery, *Under Their Own Vine and Fig Tree: The African-American Church in the South, 1865–1900* (1993); Claude Oubré, *Forty Acres and a Mule: The Freedmen's Bureau and Black Land Ownership* (1978); Nell I. Painter, *Exodusters: Black Migration to Kansas After Reconstruction* (1977); Roger Ransom and Richard Sutch, *One Kind of Freedom: The Economic Consequences of Emancipation* (1977); Edward Royce, *The Origins of Southern Sharecropping* (1993); Julie Saville, *The Work of Reconstruction: From Slave to Wage Laborer in South Carolina, 1860–1870* (1994).

Reconstruction Politics: South and North

Richard H. Abbott, *The Republican Party and the South, 1855–1877* (1986); Michael Les Benedict, *A Compromise of Principle: Congressional Republicans and Reconstruction, 1863–1869* (1974); Dan T. Carter, *When the War Was Over: The Failure of Self-Reconstruction in the South* (1985); Richard N. Current, *Those Terrible Carpetbaggers* (1988); David Donald, *The Politics of Reconstruction* (1965); William Gillette, *Retreat from Reconstruction, 1869–1879* (1979); Thomas Holt, *Black over White: Negro Political Leadership in South Carolina During Reconstruction* (1977); William McFeeley, *Grant: A Biography* (1981); Edward A. Miller, *Gullah Statesman: Robert Smalls from Slavery to Congress, 1839–1915* (1995); George C. Rable, *But There Was No Peace: The Role of Violence in the Politics of Reconstruction* (1984); Brooks D. Simpson, *Let Us Have Peace: Ulysses S. Grant and the Politics of War and Reconstruction, 1861–1868* (1991); Hans L. Trefousse, *Thaddeus Stevens: Nineteenth-Century Egalitarian* (1997); Allen Trelease, *Andrew Johnson: A Biography* (1989); Richard Zuczek, *State of Rebellion: Reconstruction in South Carolina* 1996).

Race Relations and the Literature of Reconstruction

W. Fitzhugh Brundage, *Lynching in the New South: Georgia and Virginia, 1880–1930* (1993); Thomas Dixon, *The Clansman* (1905); W. E. B. Du Bois, *The Quest of the Silver Fleece* (1911); Howard Fast, *Freedom Road* (1944); Albion Tourgée, *A Fool's Errand* (1879); Joel Williamson, *The Crucible of Race* (1984) and *A Rage for Order: Black/White Relations in the American South Since Emancipation* (1986); C. Vann Woodward, *The Strange Career of Jim Crow*, 3d rev. ed. (1974).

CHAPTER 17

The Realities of Rural America

In 1873, Milton Leeper, his wife Hattie, and their baby Anna climbed into a wagon piled high with their possessions and set out to homestead in Boone County, Nebraska. Once on the claim, the Leepers dreamed confidently of their future. Wrote Hattie to her sister in Iowa, "I like our place the best of any around here." "When we get a fine house and 100 acres under cultivation," she added, "I wouldn't trade with any one." But Milton had broken in only 13 acres when disaster struck. Hordes of grasshoppers appeared, and the Leepers fled their claim and took refuge in the nearby town of Fremont.

There they stayed for two years. Milton worked first at a store, and then hired out to other farmers. Hattie sewed, kept a boarder, and cared for chickens and a milk cow. The family lived on the brink of poverty, but never gave up hope. "Times are hard and we have had bad luck," Hattie acknowledged, but "I am going to hold that claim . . . there will [be] one gal that won't be out of a home." In 1876, the Leepers triumphantly returned to their claim with $27 to help them start over.

The grasshoppers were gone, there was enough rain, and preaching was only half a mile away. The Leepers, like others, began to prosper. Two more daughters were born. The sod house was "homely" on the outside, but plastered and cozy within. Hattie thought that the homesteaders lived "just as civilized as they would in Chicago."

Their luck did not last. Hattie died in childbirth along with her infant son. Heartbroken, Milton buried his wife and child and left the claim. The last frontier had momentarily defeated him, although he would try farming in at least four other locations before his death in 1905.

The same year that the Leepers established their Boone County homestead, another family tried their luck in a Danish settlement about 200 miles west of Omaha. Rasmus and Ane Ebbesen and their 8-year-old son, Peter, had arrived in the United States from Denmark in 1868, lured by the promise of an "abundance" of free land "for all willing to cultivate it." By 1870, they had made it as far west as Council Bluffs, Iowa. There they stopped to earn the capital they needed to begin farming. Rasmus dug ditches for the railroad, Ane worked as a cleaning woman in a local boardinghouse, and young Peter brought water to thirsty laborers digging other ditches.

Like the Leepers, the Ebbesens eagerly took up their homestead and began to cultivate the soil. Peter later recalled that the problems that the family had anticipated never materialized. Even the rumors that the Sioux, "flying demons" in the settlers' eyes, were on the rampage proved false. The real obstacles facing the family were unexpected: rattlesnakes, prairie fires, grasshoppers—the latter just as devastating as they had been to the Leeper homestead. But unlike the Leepers, the Ebbesens stayed on the claim. Although the family "barely had enough" to eat, they survived the three years of grasshopper infestation.

In the following years, the Ebbesens thrived. Rasmus had almost all the original 80 acres under cultivation and purchased an additional 80 acres from the railroad. A succession of sod houses rose on the land and finally even a two-story frame house, paid for with money Peter earned teaching school. By 1873, Rasmus and Ane were over 50 and could look with pride at their "luxurient and promising crop." But once more natural disaster struck, a "violent hailstorm . . . which completely devastated the whole lot."

The Ebbesens were lucky, however. A banker offered to buy them out, for $1,000 under what the family calculated was the farm's "real worth." But it was enough for the purchase of a "modest" house in town. Later, there was even a "dwelling of two stories and nine rooms . . . with adjacent park."

⤚⤚⤚⤚⤚⤚

The stories of the Leepers and the Ebbesens, though different in their details and endings, hint at some of the problems confronting rural Americans in the last quarter of the nineteenth century. As a mature industrial economy transformed agriculture and shifted the balance of economic power permanently away from America's farmlands to the country's cities and factories, many farmers found it impossible to realize the traditional dream of rural independence and prosperity. Even bountiful harvests no longer guaranteed success. "We were told two years ago to go to work and raise a big crop; that was all we needed," said one farmer. "We went to work and plowed and planted; the rains fell, the sun shone, nature smiled, and we raised the big crop they told us to; and what came of it? Eight cent corn, ten cent oats, two cent beef and no price at all for butter and eggs—that's what came of it." Native Americans also discovered that changes threatened their values and dreams. As the Sioux leader Red Cloud told railroad surveyors in Wyoming, "We do not want you here. You are scaring away the buffalo."

This chapter explores the agricultural transformation of the late nineteenth century and highlights the ways in which rural Americans—red, white, and black—joined the industrial world and responded to new economic and social conditions. The rise of large-scale agriculture in the West, the exploitation of its natural resources, and the development of the Great Plains form a backdrop for the discussion of the impact of white settlement on western tribes and their reactions to white incursions. In an analysis of the South, the efforts of whites to create a "New South" form a contrast to the underlying realities of race and cotton. Although the chapter shows that discrimination and economic peonage scarred the lives of most black southerners during this period, it also describes the rise of new black protest tactics and ideologies. Finally, the chapter highlights the ways in which agricultural problems of the late nineteenth century, which would continue to characterize much of agricultural life in the twentieth century, led American farmers to become reformers and to form a new political party.

MODERNIZING AGRICULTURE

Between 1865 and 1900, the nation's farms more than doubled in number as Americans flocked west of the Mississippi. Farmers raised specialized crops with modern machinery and sped them to market over an expanding railroad system. And they became capitalists. Now, as one farmer observed, farmers had to "understand farming as a business; if they do not it will go hard with them."

This Currier and Ives print provides an idyllic view of rural life. Happy children greet hunters loaded down with game, while the woman of the family looks out from her cozy cabin at the cheerful sight. This image looked more to an idealized frontier past than to the reality of rural life after the Civil War. American agriculture was tied increasingly to national and international markets. Settlers on the Plains frontier lived in dugouts or shacks rather than in the cozy log cabin pictured here. (Museum of the City of New York, The Harry T. Peters Collection)

Rural Myth and Reality

The number of Americans still farming the land suggested the vigor of the country's rural tradition. As Thomas Jefferson had argued, many still maintained that the farmer was fundamental to the republic's virtue and health.

This vision persisted even as the United States industrialized. The popularity of cheap Currier and Ives prints romanticizing rural life testifies to this faith. But while Americans wanted to believe that no tension existed between technological progress and rural life, it did. In 1860, farmers represented almost 60 percent of the labor force; by 1900, less than 37 percent of employed Americans farmed. Meanwhile farmers' contribution to the nation's wealth declined from a third to a quarter.

The industrial and urban world increasingly affected farmers. Reliable, cheap transportation allowed them to specialize: wheat on the Great Plains, corn in the Midwest. Eastern farmers turned to vegetable, fruit, and dairy farming—or sold out. Cotton, tobacco, wheat, and rice dominated in the South, and grain, fruits, and vegetables in the Far West.

As farmers specialized for national and international markets, they became dependent on outside forces. Bankers provided capital to expand operations; middlemen stored and sometimes sold produce, and railroads carried it to market. A prosperous economy put money into laborers' pockets for food. After 1870, exports of wheat, flour, and animal products rose, with wheat becoming the country's chief cash crop. But later, as Russian, Argentine, and Canadian wheat also hit the world markets, American grain found competitors.

As a modern business, farming demanded particular attitudes and skills. "Watch and study the markets and the ways of marketmen [and] learn the art of 'selling well,'" one rural editor advised in 1887.

Like other post-Civil War businesses, farming stimulated technological innovation. "It is no longer necessary for the farmer to cut his wheat with sickle or cradle, nor to rake it and bind it by hand; to cut his cornstalks with a knife and shock the stalks by hand; to thresh his grain with a flail," an expert noted. Such tasks were now performed by animal-drawn mechanized harvesters and binders.

Machines made work easier and allowed far more land to be farmed. By 1900, more than twice the acreage was under cultivation as in 1860. But machinery was expensive, and many farmers borrowed to buy it. In the 1880s, mortgage indebtedness grew two and a half times faster than agricultural wealth.

New Farmers, New Farms

Thus American farmers learned to operate much like other nineteenth-century businessmen. Small family farms still typified American agriculture, but vast mechanized operations devoted to the cultivation of one crop appeared, especially west of the Mississippi. "Bonanza" wheat farms of thousands of acres, established in the late 1870s in the Dakotas, foreshadowed the trend to large-scale agriculture. Often owned by corporations, they required capital investment, machinery, hired workers, and efficient managers. Such farms dramatized agricultural changes that were occurring everywhere on a smaller scale.

Only gradually did farmers realize that technology might backfire. Productivity soared 40 percent between 1869 and 1899. But yields for some crops were so large that domestic markets could not absorb them. Prices steadily declined.

Falling prices did not hurt all farmers. Because the supply of money rose more slowly than productivity, all prices declined—by more than half between the 1865 and 1900 (see Chapter 19). Deflation meant that farmers received less for crops but also paid less for purchases.

But deflation may have encouraged overproduction. To make the same income, many farmers believed they had to produce larger crops, which drove prices even lower and raised the real value of debts. In 1888, it took 174 bushels of wheat to pay interest on a $2,000 mortgage at 8 percent; by 1895, it took 320 bushels. Falling prices hit hardest the newly settled farmers who had borrowed heavily.

Farming on the Western Plains, 1880s–1890s

Between 1870 and 1900, the acreage devoted to farming tripled west of the Mississippi. Prewar emigrants bound for the Far West had scorned the semiarid Plains. Such views changed after the Civil War. Railroads, town boosters, and speculators all needed settlers to make their investments in the Great Plains profitable, and lured them with extravagant claims. As one newspaper promised: "All that is needed is to plow, plant and attend to the crops properly; the rains are abundant." Abnormal rain in the 1880s bolstered such assertions.

Late-nineteenth-century industrial innovations helped settlers overcome natural obstacles to farming the Plains. In the 1870s, Joseph Glidden invented barbed wire as a cheap alternative to timber fencing. Twine binders speeded up grain harvesting and reduced the threat of losing crops to unpredictable weather. Mail-order steel windmills that pumped water from deep underground relieved water shortages by the 1890s.

In the first boom period of settlement from 1879 to the early 1890s, tens of thousands of eager families like the Leepers and Ebbesens began farming the Great Plains. Some claimed land under the Homestead Act, which granted 160 acres to any family head or adult who lived on the claim for five years or paid $1.25 an acre after six months of residence. Because homestead land was frequently less desirable, however, most settlers bought land from railroads or land companies.

Start-up costs were thus higher than the Homestead Act would suggest. Although western land was cheap compared with farmland in the East, a farmer was lucky to buy a good quarter section for under $500. Machinery would often cost $700. Although some thought it made economic sense to lease rather than buy land, many rented only because they lacked capital. In 1880, some 20 percent of the Plains farmers were tenants, and this percentage rose over time.

Like the Ebbesens, many new settlers were immigrants. The largest numbers came from Germany, the British Isles, and Canada, but Scandinavians, Czechs, and Poles also arrived. Unlike many immigrants to American cities, they came in family groups and intended to stay.

Life on the Plains frontier often proved difficult. Wrote one Kansas homesteader:

> I tell you Auntie no one can depend on farming for a living in this country. Henry is very industrious and this year had in over thirty acres of small grain, 8 acres of corn and about an acre of potatoes. We have sold our small grain . . . and it come to $100; now deduct $27.00 for cutting, $16.00 for threshing, $19.00 for hired help, say nothing of boarding our help, none of the trouble of drawing 25 miles to market and 25 cts on each head for ferriage over the river and where is your profit. I sometimes think this a God forsaken country, the [grass]hopper hurt our corn and we have 1/2 a crop and utterly destroyed our garden. If one wants trials, let them come to Kansas.

This letter highlights the uncertainties of frontier life: high costs, market fluctuations, pests and natural disasters, cash shortages. Many Plains pioneers took up homesteads with only a few dollars in their pockets, and survival often depended on how well families managed during the crucial first years.

Many settlers recoiled from a landscape without trees or human scale. As one New Englander observed, "It has been terrible on settlers, on the women especially, for there is no society and they get doleful and feel almost like committing suicide for want of society." Thousands of letters and diaries, however, provide a more positive picture of farming life. Church, parties, sings, and get-togethers brightened family life.

The Plains required many adjustments. Scarce water and violent weather called for resourcefulness. Without firewood, farmers burned corncobs and straw. The log cabin disappeared as settlers built houses of sod "bricks," frequently with glass windows, wooden shingles, and even plastered interiors. Walls 2 to 3 feet thick kept out summer heat and winter cold, winds, and prairie fires. The solidity of the sod house was a welcome contrast to the impersonal power and scale of nature.

The first boom on the Great Plains halted abruptly in the late 1880s and early 1890s. Falling prices cut profits; one wheat farmer reported in 1890 earnings of $41.48 and expenses of $56.00. Then the unusual rainfall that had lured farmers

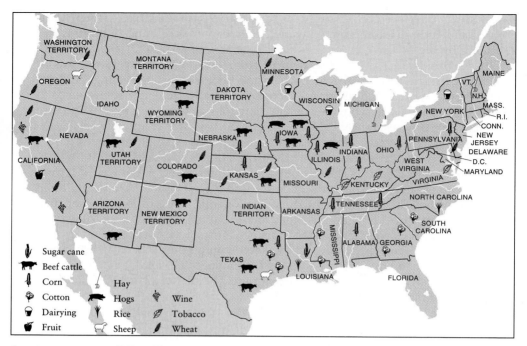

AGRICULTURE IN THE 1880s   This map reveals the patterns of regional agricultural specialization in the 1880s.

gave way to a devastating drought. The destitute survived on boiled weeds, a few potatoes, and a little bread and butter. Many lost their farms to creditors. Some stayed as tenants. Homesteaders like the Leepers gave up. By 1900, two-thirds of homestead farms had failed. In western Kansas, the population fell by half between 1888 and 1892, and eastward-bound wagons bore a sad epitaph: "In God We Trusted: In Kansas We Busted."

Agriculture damaged the Plains environment. The water table level dropped as the steel windmills pumped water from deep underground. When farmers removed sod to build their houses and plowed the prairies to plant their crops, they destroyed the earth's protective covering. Deep plowing, essential for dry farming techniques introduced after the drought of the 1880s, worsened the situation. The 1930s dust bowl was the eventual outcome of such agricultural interventions.

The Early Cattle Frontier, 1860–1890

Although cattle raising dated back to Spanish mission days, the commercial cattle frontier was an unexpected by-product of the Civil War when the North had cut Texas off from Confederate cattle markets. By war's end, millions of longhorns roamed the Texas range. The postwar burst of railroad construction made it possible to turn these cattle into dollars. If Texas ranchers drove their steers north to towns like Abilene, Kansas, they could be sent by rail to Chicago and Kansas City packinghouses. In the late 1860s and 1870s, cowboys herded thousands of longhorns north.

In 1886, Solomon Butcher photographed the Rawding family in Custer County, Nebraska. The family posed with all their prized possessions in front of their sod house. Although the younger Rawdings are barefoot, the women have dressed carefully for the picture. Despite their neat attire, women of farm families like this one worked both in and outside of the house. Although their husbands often had machinery to help them with their tasks, except for the sewing machine and cookstove, farm women did their work without the help of mechanization. (Solomon D. Butcher Collection, Nebraska State Historical Society)

Ranchers on the Great Plains, where grasses were ripe for grazing, bought some of the cattle and bred them with Hereford and Angus cows to create animals acclimatized to severe winters. In the late 1870s and early 1880s, huge ranches arose from eastern Colorado to the Dakotas. Such ventures, many owned by eastern or European investors, paid handsomely. Cattle on the public domain cost owners little but commanded good prices. Cowboys (a third of them Mexican and black) who herded the steers made meager wages of $25 to $40 a month, just enough for a fling at the trail's end.

By the mid-1880s, the first phase of the cattle frontier was ending as farmers moved onto the Plains, buying and fencing public lands once used for grazing. But the arrival of farmers was only one factor in the changing cattle frontier. Ranchers overstocked herds in the mid-1880s. Hungry cattle ate everything in sight, then weakened as grass became scarce. Memorable blizzards followed the very hot summer of 1886. By spring, 90 percent of the cattle were dead. Frantic owners dumped their remaining animals on the market, getting $8 or even less per head.

Ranchers who survived the disaster adopted new techniques. Experimenting with new breeds, they began to fence in their herds and feed them grain during the winter. Consumers wanted tender beef rather than tough cuts from free-range animals, and these new methods satisfied the market. Ranching, like farming, was becoming a modern business.

Just as plows and windmills disrupted Plains ecology, so, too, did the cattle. Ranchers killed off antelope, elk, wolves, and other wildlife. Cattle on overstocked ranges devoured perennial grasses. Less nutritious annual grasses appeared, which, in turn, sometimes disappeared. Lands once able to support large herds of cattle eventually became deserts of sagebrush, weeds, and dust.

Cornucopia on the Pacific

When gold was discovered in California, Americans rushed west to find it. But as one father told his son, "Plant your lands; these be your best gold fields." He was right; completion of a national railroad system made farming California's greatest asset. But California farming resembled neither the traditional picture of rural life nor the dreams of homesteaders.

Little of California's land was homesteaded or developed as family farms. When California entered the Union, speculators acquired much of the land held by Mexican ranchers. The prices speculators demanded put land out of the reach of many small farmers. By 1900, farms of 1,000 acres or more made up two-thirds of the state's farmland.

While small farmers and ranchers did exist, they found it hard to compete with large, mechanized operators using cheap migrant laborers, usually Mexican or Chinese. A San Joaquin Valley wheat farm was so vast that workers started plowing in the morning at one end of the 17-mile field, ate lunch at its halfway point, and camped at its end that night.

The value of much of California's agricultural land, especially the southern half of the Central Valley, depended on water. By the 1870s, water, land, and railroad companies, using the labor and expertise of Chinese workers, were building dams, headgates, and canals—at high costs that they passed on to buyers eager to acquire hitherto barren land and water rights. By 1890, over a quarter of California's farms were irrigated.

Although grain was initially California's most valuable crop, it faced stiff competition from farmers on the Plains and abroad. Some argued that land capable of raising luscious fruits "in a climate surpassing that of Italy, is too valuable for the cultivation of simple cereals." But high railroad rates and lack of refrigeration limited the volume of fresh fruit and vegetables sent to market. As railroad managers in the 1880s realized the potential profit that California's produce represented, they cut rates and introduced refrigerated cars. Before long, California fruit was sold as far away as London. Some travelers even began to grumble that the railroads treated produce better than people. Perhaps it was true. Successful agriculture in California depended on the railroad system, irrigation, and machinery.

Exploiting Natural Resources

The perspective that led Americans to treat farming as a business also appeared in their attitude toward the country's natural resources. Iron, copper, coal, lead, zinc, tin, and silver strikes lured thousands to Minnesota, Colorado, Montana, Idaho, and Nevada. Popular ideas of hardy forty-niners looking for nuggets bear little resemblance to late-nineteenth-century mining with its machinery, railroads, engineers, and large work forces. Mining was a big business with high costs and a dynamic that encouraged rapid and thorough exploitation of the earth's resources.

Devastation of the nation's forests went hand in hand with large-scale mining and the railroads that provided links to markets. Railroads and mines alike depended on wood—for ties, for shaft timber, and for ore reduction. The California State Board of Agriculture estimated in the late 1860s that one-third of the state's forests were already lost. Felling forests affected the flow of streams and destroyed the habitat supporting birds and animals. Like the farmers and cattle owners, the companies that stripped the earth of its forest cover were also contributing to soil erosion.

The idea that the public lands belonging to the federal government ought to be rapidly developed supported such exploitation of resources. Often, in return for royalties, the government leased parts of the public domain to companies planning to extract valuable minerals, not to own land permanently. Or companies bought land, not always legally. In 1878, Congress passed the Timber and Stone Act, which initially applied to Nevada, Oregon, Washington, and California. This legislation allowed the sale of 160-acre parcels of the public domain that were "unfit for cultivation" and "valuable chiefly for timber." Timber companies saw that they could hire men to register for claims and then turn them over to timber interests. By the end of the century, more than 3.5 million acres of the public domain had been sold under the law. Most of it was in corporate hands.

The rapacious exploitation of resources combined with accelerating industrialization made some Americans uneasy. Many believed that forests played a part in the rain cycle and that their destruction would adversely affect the climate. Others, like John Muir, lamented the destruction of the country's great natural beauty. In 1868, Muir came upon the Great Valley of California, "one smooth, continuous bed of honey-bloom." He soon realized, however, that aggressive agriculture and stock-raising would destroy this loveliness, and became a conservation champion. He helped create Yosemite National Park in 1890 and participated in a successful effort to get President Benjamin Harrison to classify parts of the public domain as forest reserves. In 1892, Muir established the Sierra Club. Conservation was more popular in the East, however, than in the West, where people were tempted with seemingly abundant natural resources and driven by the profit motive.

THE SECOND GREAT REMOVAL

Black Elk, an Oglala Sioux, listened to a story his father had heard from his father.

> A long time ago . . . there was once a Lakota [Sioux] holy man, called Drinks Water, who dreamed what was to be; and this was long before the coming of the Wasichus [white men]. He dreamed . . . that a strange race had woven a spider's web all around the Lakotas. And he said: "When this happens, you shall live in square gray houses, in a barren land, and beside those square gray houses you shall starve."

So great was the wise man's sorrow that he died soon after his strange dream. But Black Elk lived to see it come true.

As farmers settled the western frontier and became entangled in a national economy, they clashed with the Indians. In California, disease and violence killed 90 percent of the Native Americans in the 30 years following the gold rush. Elsewhere, the struggle among Native Americans, white settlers, the U.S. Army, officials, and reformers was prolonged and bitter. Some tribes moved onto government reservations with little protest. But most—including the Nez Percé in the Northwest, the Apache in the Southwest, and the Plains Indians—resisted stubbornly.

Background to Hostilities

The lives of most Plains Indians revolved around the buffalo. As migration to California and Oregon increased in the 1840s and 1850s, tribal life and animal migration patterns were disrupted.

During the Civil War, the eastern tribes that relocated in Oklahoma divided. Some, especially the slaveholders, sided with the Confederacy; others remained Unionist. But after the war all were "treated as traitors." The federal government callously nullified pledges and treaties, leaving Indians defenseless against incursions. As settlers pushed into Kansas, tribes there were shunted into Oklahoma.

The White Perspective

When the Civil War ended, red and white men on the Plains were already at war. In 1864, the Colorado militia massacred a band of friendly Cheyenne at Sand Creek. Cheyenne, Sioux, and Arapaho soon responded in kind. The Plains wars had begun.

Although not all whites condoned this butchery, the congressional commission authorized to make peace viewed Native Americans' future narrowly. The commissioners, including the commander of the army in the West, Civil War hero William T. Sherman, accepted as fact that the West belonged to an "industrious, thrifty, and enlightened population" of whites. Native Americans, the commission believed, must relocate to western South Dakota or Oklahoma to learn white ways. Annuities, food, and clothes would ease their transition to "civilized" life.

At two major conferences in 1867 and 1868, chiefs listened to these drastic proposals spelling the end of traditional native life. Some agreed; others, like a Kiowa chief insisted, "I don't want to settle. I love to roam over the prairies." In any case, the agreements were not binding because no chief had authority to speak for his tribe. For its part, the U.S. Senate dragged its feet in approving the treaties. Supplies promised to Indians who settled in the arid reserved areas failed to materialize, and wildlife proved too sparse to support them. These Indians soon drifted back to their former hunting grounds.

As Sherman warned, "All who cling to their old hunting ground are hostile and will remain so till killed off." When persuasion failed, the U.S. Army went to war. "The more we can kill this year," Sherman remarked, "the less will have to be killed the next war." In 1867, he ordered General Philip Sheridan to deal with the tribes. Sheridan introduced winter campaigning against Indians who divided into small groups during the winter.

Completion of the transcontinental railroad in 1869 added yet another pressure for "solving" the Indian question. Transcontinental railroads wanted rights-of-way through tribal lands and needed white settlers to make their operations profitable. Few of the settlers they carried thought Native Americans had any right to lands whites wanted.

In his 1872 annual report, the commissioner for Indian affairs, Francis Amasa Walker, addressed two fundamental questions: how to prevent Indians from blocking white migration to the Great Plains, and what to do with them over the long run. Walker suggested buying off the "savages" with promises of food and gifts, luring them onto reservations, and there imposing a "rigid reformatory discipline," necessary because Indians were "unused to manual labor." The grim reservations he proposed resembled prisons. Though Walker wished to save the Indians from destruction, he offered only one choice: "yield or perish."

The Tribal View

Native Americans defied such attacks on their ancient way of life. Black Elk remembered that in 1863, when he was only three, his father had his leg broken in a fierce battle with white men. "When I was older," he recalled,

> I learned what the fighting was about . . . . Up on the Madison Fork the Wasichus had found much of the yellow metal that they worship and that makes them crazy, and they wanted to have a road up through our country to the place where the yellow metal was; but my people did not want the road. It would scare the bison and make them go away, and also it would let the other Wasichus come in like a river. They told us that they wanted only to use a little land, as much as a wagon would take between the wheels; but our people knew better.

Black Elk's father and many others soon realized fighting was their only recourse. "There was no other way to keep our country."

Broken promises fueled Indian resistance. In 1875, the government allowed gold prospectors into the Black Hills, one of their sacred places and part of the Sioux reservation. Chiefs like Sitting Bull led the angry Sioux on the warpath. At the Battle of Little Big Horn in 1876, they vanquished the army's most famous Indian fighter, George Custer. But bravery and skill could not permanently withstand the well-supplied, well-armed, and determined U.S. Army.

The wholesale destruction of the buffalo was an important element in white victory. The animals were central to Indian life. Plains Indians could be wasteful of buffalo where the animals were abundant, but white miners and hunters wiped out the herds. Sportsmen shot the beasts from trains. Railroad crews ate the meat. Ranchers' cattle competed for grass. And demand for buffalo bones for fertilizer and hides for robes and shoes encouraged decimation.

The slaughter, which had claimed 13 million animals by 1883, was in retrospect disgraceful. The Indians considered white men demented. "They just killed and killed because they like to do that," said one, whereas when "we hunted the bison . . . [we] killed only what we needed." But the destruction pleased whites because it helped control the Indians.

The Dawes Act, 1887

Changing federal policy was aimed at ending Indian power and culture. In 1871, Congress stopped the practice, in effect since the 1790s, of treating the tribes as sovereign nations. Other measures supplemented this attempt to undermine tribal integrity and leaders. Federal authorities extended government jurisdiction to reservations and warned tribes not to gather for religious ceremonies.

The Dawes Severalty Act of 1887 pulled together the strands of federal Indian policy and set its course for the rest of the century. Believing that tribal bonds kept Indians in savagery, reformers intended to destroy them. Rather than allotting reservation lands to tribal groups, the act allowed the president to distribute these

INDIAN LANDS AND COMMUNITIES IN THE UNITED STATES   The map shows a rich variety of Indian groups, state reservations (primarily in the East), and federal reservations in the West.

lands to individuals. Holding out the lure of private property, the framers of the bill hoped to destroy communal norms and encourage Indians to settle as farmers. Those who accepted allotments would become citizens and presumably abandon their tribal identity.

The fact that speculators as well as reformers lobbied for the legislation revealed another motive. Even if each Indian family head claimed a typical share of 160 acres, millions of "surplus" acres would remain for sale to whites. Within 20 years of the Dawes Act, Native Americans lost 60 percent of their lands. The federal government held the profits from land sales "in trust" for the "civilizing" mission.

The Ghost Dance: An Indian Renewal Ritual

By the 1890s, their grim plight prepared many Native Americans for the message of Paiute prophet Wovoka. Although Wovoka did not urge Native Americans to attack whites, he predicted that natural disasters would eliminate the white race. Dancing Indians would not only avoid this destruction but gain new strength as their ancestors and wild game returned to life. Wovoka's prophecies spread rapidly. Believers expressed their hope through new rituals of ghost dancing, hypnosis, and meditation.

American settlers were uneasy. Indian agents tried to prevent ghost dances and filed hysterical reports. One agent determined that the Sioux medicine man Sitting Bull, a strenuous opponent of American expansion, was a leading trouble-maker and decided to arrest him. In the confusion, Indian police killed Sitting

Bull. Bands of Sioux fled the reservation with the army in swift pursuit. In late December 1890, the army caught up with them at Wounded Knee Creek. Although the Sioux had raised a flag of truce and started turning over weapons, a scuffle led to a bloody massacre. Using the most up-to-date machine guns and Hotchkiss cannons, the army killed over 200 men, women, and children.

In this way white Americans defeated the western tribes. Once proud, independent, and strong, Native Americans suffered dependency, poverty, and disorientation on reservations and in Indian schools and urban slums.

THE NEW SOUTH

Of all the nation's agricultural regions, the South was the poorest. In 1880, southerners' yearly earnings were half the national average. But despite poverty and backwardness, some late-nineteenth-century southerners dreamed of making the agricultural South the rival of the industrial North.

Postwar Southerners Face the Future

The vision of a modern, progressive, and self-sufficient South had roots in the troubled 1850s, when southern intellectuals argued that their region must throw off its dependence on the North and on cotton. Too few southerners had listened. Now, after war and Reconstruction, the cry for regional self-sufficiency grew sharper. Publicists of the "New South" movement argued that southern backwardness did not stem from the war, as so many southerners wished to believe, but from the conditions in southern life—especially its cotton-based economy. Defeat only made clearer the reality that power and wealth came not from cotton, but from factories, machines, and cities.

Pride and self-interest dictated a new course. As Atlanta newspaper publisher Henry Grady told a Boston audience in 1886, industrial advances would allow the South to match the North in a peaceful contest. In hundreds of speeches, editorials, pamphlets, articles, and books, spokesmen for the New South tried to persuade fellow southerners to abandon prewar ideals that glorified gentility and adopt the ethic of hard work. To lure northern bankers and capitalists, New South advocates held out attractive investment possibilities. Because the South was short of capital, northern assistance was critically important.

To attract manufacturers, several southern state governments offered tax exemptions and the cheap labor of leased convicts. Texas and Florida awarded the railroads land grants, and cities like Atlanta and Louisville mounted huge industrial exhibitions. Middle-class southerners increasingly accepted new entrepreneurial values. The most dramatic example of commitment to the New South vision may have come in 1886 when southern railroad companies, in a crash effort, relaid tracks and adjusted rolling stock to fit "standard" northern gauges.

During the late nineteenth century, northern money flowed south. In the 1880s, northerners increased investments in the cotton industry sevenfold and financed an expansion of southern railroads. Northern capital fuelled southern urban expansion. The percentage of southerners living in cities rose from 7 percent in 1860 to 15 percent in 1900 (as compared to national averages of 20 and 40 percent).

Birmingham, Alabama, symbolized the New South. In 1870 it was a cornfield. The next year, two northern real estate speculators arrived, attracted by rich iron deposits. Despite cholera and the depression of the 1870s, Birmingham rapidly became the center of the southern iron and steel industry. By 1890, a total of 38,414 people lived there. Coke ovens, blast furnaces, rolling mills, iron foundries, and machine shops belched smoke. Mills and factories poured out millions of dollars of finished goods, and eight railroad lines carried them away.

Other southern cities flourished, too. Memphis prospered from its lumber industry and the manufacturing of cottonseed products, and Richmond became the country's tobacco capital even as its flour mills and iron and steel foundries continued to produce wealth. Augusta, Georgia, led the emerging textile industry of Georgia, the Carolinas, and Alabama.

The Other Side of Progress

New South enthusiasts, a small group of merchants, industrialists, and planters, bragged about their iron and textile industries and paraded statistics to prove the success of modernization. But progress was slow, and older values persisted. Even New South spokesmen romanticized the recent past, impeding full acceptance of a new economic order. Despite modernization, southern schools lagged far behind the North's.

Although new industries and signs of progress abounded, two of the new industries depended on tobacco and cotton, crops long at the center of rural life. As they had before the war, commerce and government work drove urban growth. The South's economic achievements, though not insignificant, did not improve its position relative to the North.

Moreover, the South failed to reap many benefits from industrialization. The South remained an economic vassal of the North. Southern businessmen grew in number, but except for the American Tobacco Company, no great southern corporations arose. Instead, southerners worked for northern corporations, which absorbed southern businesses or dominated them financially. Profits and critical decision-making power flowed north. Southern manufacturers who did finish their products, hoping to compete in the marketplace, found that railroad rate discrimination robbed their goods of any competitive edge.

Individual workers in the new industries may have found factory life preferable to sharecropping, but their rewards were meager. The thousands of women and children in factories silently testified to their husbands' and fathers' inability to earn enough. As usual, women and children earned less than men. Justifying these policies, one Augusta factory president claimed that employing children was "a matter of charity with us; some of them would starve if they were not given employment . . . . The work we give children is very light." Actually, many children at his factory were doing adults' work for children's pay.

In general, workers earned less and toiled longer in the South than elsewhere. Per capita income was the same in 1900 as in 1860—and half the national average. In North Carolina in the 1890s, workers averaged 50 cents a day, with a 70-hour week. Black workers, who made up 6 percent of the southern manufacturing force in 1890 (but were excluded from textile mills), usually had the worst jobs and the lowest wages.

Cotton Still King

Although New South advocates envisioned the South's transformation from a rural to an industrial society, they always recognized the need for agricultural change. "It's time for an agricultural revolution," proclaimed Henry Grady, the New South's most vocal spokesman. Overdependence on "King Cotton" hobbled southern agriculture by making farmers the victims of faraway market forces and an oppressive credit system. Subdivide old cotton plantations into small diversified farms, Grady urged. Truck farming could produce "simply wonderful profits."

A new agricultural South with new class and economic arrangements did emerge, but not the one Grady envisioned. Despite the breakup of some plantations, large landowners were resourceful in keeping their property and dealing with postwar conditions, as Chapter 16 showed. As they adopted new agricultural arrangements, former slaves sank into peonage.

White farmers on small and medium-size holdings fared only slightly better than black tenants and sharecroppers. Immediately after the war, high cotton prices tempted them to raise as much cotton as they could. Then prices began a disastrous decline, from 11 cents a pound in 1875 to less than 5 cents in 1894. Yeoman farmers became entangled in debt. Each year, farmers bought supplies on credit from merchants so they could plant the next year's crop and support their families until harvest. In return, merchants demanded their exclusive business and acquired a lien (claim) on their crops. But when farmers sold their crops at declining prices, they usually discovered that they had not earned enough to settle with the merchant, who had charged dearly for store goods and whose annual interest rates might exceed 100 percent. Each year, thousands of farmers fell farther behind. By 1900, over half the South's white farmers and three-quarters of its black farmers were tenants. Tenancy increased all over rural America, but nowhere faster than in the Deep South.

These patterns had baneful results for individual southerners and for the South as a whole. Caught in a cycle of debt and poverty, few farmers could think of improving techniques or diversifying crops. Desperate to pay debts, they concentrated on cotton despite falling prices. Landowners pressured tenants to raise a market crop. Far from diversifying, farmers increasingly limited their crops. By 1880, the South was not growing enough food to feed its people adequately. Poor nutrition contributed to chronic bad health.

The Nadir of Black Life

Grady and other New South advocates expected that their region could deal with the race issue without the interference of any "outside power." He had few regrets over the end of slavery, which he thought had contributed to southern economic backwardness. Realizing that black labor would be crucial to the transformation he sought, he advocated racial cooperation. But racial cooperation did not mean equality. Grady assumed that blacks were inferior and therefore supported informal segregation.

By the time of Grady's death in 1889, a much harsher perspective on southern race relations was appearing. Congressional leaders' decision in 1890 to shelve a proposed act protecting black civil rights and the defeat of a bill giving federal assistance for educational institutions rendered black Americans vulnerable. The traditional sponsor of the freedmen rights, the Republican party, left blacks to fend for themselves. The courts also abandoned them. In 1878, the Supreme Court ruled unconstitutional a Louisiana statute banning discrimination in transportation. In 1882, the Court voided the Ku Klux Klan Act of 1871, finding that the civil rights protections of the Fourteenth Amendment applied to states, not to individuals. In 1883, provisions of the Civil Rights Act of 1875 that assured blacks of equal rights in public places were similarly voided.

Northern leaders did not oppose these actions; in fact, northerners increasingly promoted negative stereotypes. If blacks were inferior, they obviously could not be left to themselves or given the same rights and freedoms whites enjoyed. Instead, blacks needed the paternal protection of the superior white race. The *Atlanta Monthly* in 1890 expressed doubts that this "lowly variety of man" could ever be brought up to the intellectual and moral standards of whites. Other magazines opposed black suffrage as wasted on people too "ignorant, weak, lazy and incompetent" to make good use of it. *Forum* magazine suggested that "American Negroes" had "too much liberty." Only lynching and burning would deter "barbarous" rapists and other "sadly degenerated" Negroes corrupted since the Civil War by independence and too much education. Encouraged by northern public opinion, and with the blessing of Congress and the Supreme Court, southern whites sought to make blacks permanently second-class citizens.

In the political sphere, white southerners amended state constitutions to disfranchise black voters. By various legal devices—poll tax, literacy tests, "good character" and "understanding" clauses administered by white voter registrars, and all-white primary elections—blacks lost the right to vote. The most ingenious method was the "grandfather clause," which specified that only citizens whose grandfathers were registered to vote on January 1, 1867, could cast ballots. This virtually excluded blacks. Although the Supreme Court outlawed such blatantly discriminatory laws, other constitutional changes, beginning in Mississippi in 1890 and spreading to all 11 former Confederate states by 1910, effectively excluded the black vote.

In a second tactic in the 1890s, southern state and local laws legalized segregation in public facilities. Beginning with railroads and schools, "Jim Crow" laws soon covered libraries, hotels, hospitals, prisons, theaters, parks, cemeteries, toilets, sidewalks, drinking fountains—nearly every place where blacks and whites might mingle. The Supreme Court upheld these laws in 1896 in *Plessy* v. *Ferguson*, ruling that "separate but equal" facilities did not violate the Fourteenth Amendment's equal protection clause.

Political and social discrimination made it ever more possible to keep blacks permanently confined to agricultural and unskilled labor and dependent on whites. In 1900, nearly 84 percent of black workers nationwide either did some form of agricultural labor or had service jobs, mostly as domestic servants and in laundries.

IN SELF-DEFENSE

Southern Chiv. [Chivalrous Gentleman] "Ef I hadn't-er killed you, you would hev growd up to rule me."

In 1876, *Harper's Weekly* published this print entitled *Self-Defense*. The white man's comment, "Ef I hadn't-er killed you, you would hev growd up to rule me," is witness to the brutal treatment meted out to blacks in the late nineteenth-century South.

These had been the primary slave occupations. The remaining 16 percent worked in forests, sawmills, mines, and, with northward migration, in northern cities.

At the end of the Civil War, at least half of all skilled craftsmen in the South had been black, but by the 1890s the percentage dropped under 10 percent as whites systematically excluded blacks from the trades. Such factory work as blacks had been doing was also reduced, largely to separate poor blacks from whites and thus prevent unionization. Exclusion of blacks from industry prevented them from acquiring the skills and habits with which they could rise into the middle class, as would many European immigrants and their children by the mid-twentieth century.

Blacks did not accept their decline passively. In the mid-1880s, they enthusiastically joined the Knights of Labor (discussed in Chapter 18), making up at least a third of the membership in the South. But southern whites feared that the Knights' policies of racial and economic cooperation might lead to social equality. The Charleston *News and Courier* warned darkly about "mongrels and hybrids." As blacks continued to join, whites left the Knights. Their flight weakened the organization in the South until white violence finally killed it.

Lynchings and other violence against blacks increased. On February 21, 1891, the *New York Times* reported that in Texarkana, Arkansas, a mob caught a 32-year-old black man, Ed Coy, charged with raping a white woman, tied him to a stake, and burned him. As Coy pleaded his innocence to a large crowd, his alleged victim somewhat hesitatingly put the torch to his oil-soaked body. The *Times* report concluded that only by the "terrible death such as fire . . . can inflict" could other blacks "be deterred from the commission of like crimes." Ed Coy was one of more than 1,400 black men lynched or burned alive during the 1890s. About a third were charged with sex crimes. The rest were accused of a variety of "crimes" related to not knowing their place: marrying or insulting a white woman, testifying in court against whites, or having a "bad reputation."

Diverging Black Responses

White discrimination and exploitation nourished new protest tactics and ideologies among blacks. For years, Frederick Douglass had urged blacks to remain loyal Americans and count on the Republican party. In 1895 his dying words were allegedly "Agitate! Agitate! Agitate!"

Calls for black separatism within white America rang out. Insisting that blacks must join together to fight the rising tide of discrimination, T. Thomas Fortune in 1891 organized the Afro-American League. The League (the precursor of the NAACP) encouraged independent voting, opposed segregation and lynching, and urged the establishment of black institutions like banks to support black business-es. In the 1890s, black leaders lobbied to make the Oklahoma Territory, recently opened to white settlement, an all-black state. Blacks founded 25 towns there, as well as in other states and even Mexico. But these attempts, like earlier ones, were short-lived, crippled by limited funds and the hostility of white neighbors.

There were more radical black voices, too. Bishop Henry McNeal Turner, a former Union soldier and prominent black leader, despaired of ever securing equal rights for blacks in the United States. He described the Constitution as "a dirty rag, a cheat, a libel" and said that it ought to be "spit upon by every Negro in the land." In 1894, he organized the International Migration Society to return blacks to Africa, arguing that "this country owes us forty billions of dollars" to help. He sent two boatloads of emigrants to Liberia, but this effort worked no more successfully than those earlier in the century.

Douglass had long argued that no matter how important African roots might be, blacks had been in the Americas for generations and would have to win justice and equal rights here. W. E. B. Du Bois, the first black to receive a Ph.D. from Harvard, agreed. Yet in 1900, at the first Pan-African Conference in London, he argued that blacks must lead the struggle for liberation both in Africa and in the United States. It was at this conference that Du Bois first made his prophetic com-ment that "the problem of the Twentieth Century" would be "the problem of the color line."

Despite these militant voices, many blacks worked patiently but persistently within white society for equality and social justice. In 1887, J. C. Price formed the Citizens Equal Rights Association, which supported various petitions and direct-action campaigns to protest segregation. Other blacks boycotted segregated street-cars in southern cities. Most black Americans continued to follow the slow, moderate, self-help program of Booker T. Washington, the best-known black leader in America. Born a slave, Washington had risen through hard and faithful work to become the founder (in 1881) and principal of Tuskegee Institute in Alabama, which he personally and dramatically built into the nation's largest and best-known industrial training school. At Tuskegee, young blacks received a highly disciplined education in scientific agriculture and skilled trades. Washington believed that economic self-help and the familiar Puritan virtues of hard work, fru-gality, cleanliness, and moderation would help African-Americans succeed despite racism. He spent much time traveling through the North to secure philanthropic gifts for Tuskegee, becoming a favorite of the American entrepreneurial elite whose capitalist assumptions he shared.

In 1895, Washington delivered a speech at the Cotton States and International Exposition in Atlanta—his invitation had been a rare honor for a former slave—in which he proclaimed black loyalty to southern economic development while accepting the lowly status of southern blacks. "It is at the bottom of life we must begin, and not at the top," he declared. Although Washington worked behind the scenes for black civil rights, in Atlanta he publicly renounced black interest in the vote, civil rights, or social equality. Whites throughout the country enthusiastically acclaimed Washington's address, but many blacks called his "Atlanta Compromise" a serious setback.

Washington has often been charged with conceding too quickly that political rights should follow rather than precede economic well-being. In 1903, Du Bois confronted Washington directly in *The Souls of Black Folk*, arguing for the "manly assertion" of a program of equal civil rights, suffrage, and higher education in the ideals of liberal learning. A trip through Dougherty County, Georgia, showed Du Bois the "forlorn and forsaken" condition of southern blacks. Although "here and there a man has raised his head above these murky waters . . . a pall of debt hangs over the beautiful land." The lives of most blacks were still tied to the land of the South. To improve their lives, rural blacks would have to organize.

FARM PROTEST

During the post-Civil War period, many farmers, black and white, began organizing. Not all rural people were dissatisfied; farmers in the Midwest and near city markets adjusted to new economic conditions. But the new problems of southern and western farmers produced the first mass organization of farmers in American history.

The Grange in the 1860s and 1870s

The earliest effort to organize white farmers came in 1867 when Oliver Kelley founded the Order of the Patrons of Husbandry. Originally a social and cultural organization, it soon was protesting the powerlessness of the "immense helpless mob" of farmers, victims of "human vampires." The depression of the 1870s (discussed in Chapter 18) sharpened discontent. By 1875, an estimated 800,000 had joined Kelley's organization, now known as the National Grange.

The Grangers recognized some, but not all, of the complex changes that had created rural problems. Some of their "reforms" attempted to bypass middlemen by establishing buying and selling cooperatives. Although many cooperatives failed, they indicated that farmers realized the need to act collectively. Midwestern farmers also accused grain elevator operators of cheating them, and they pointed to the railroads, America's first big business, as the worst offenders. As Chapter 18 will show, cut-throat competition among railroad companies generally brought lower rates. But even though charges dropped nationwide, railroads often set high rates in rural areas, and their rebates to large shippers discriminated against small operators.

Farmers recognized that confronting the mighty railroads demanded cooperation with others, like western businessmen whose interests railroads also hurt, and it demanded political action. Between 1869 and 1874, businessmen and farmers successfully pressed Illinois, Iowa, Wisconsin, and Minnesota to pass so-called Granger laws (an inaccurate name, for the Grangers did not deserve complete credit for them) establishing maximum rates that railroads and grain elevators could charge. Other states set up railroad commissions to regulate railroad rates, or outlawed railroad pools, rebates, passes, and other practices that seemed to represent "unjust discrimination and distortion."

Railroad companies and grain elevators quickly challenged the new laws. In 1877, the Supreme Court upheld them in *Munn* v. *Illinois.* Even so, it soon became apparent that state commissions could not control long-haul rates. The tangle of questions that state regulation raised proved difficult to resolve locally. Although Granger laws failed to control the railroads, they did establish an important principle. The Supreme Court had made it clear that state legislatures could regulate businesses of a public nature like the railroads. Congress came under pressure to continue the struggle.

The Interstate Commerce Act, 1887

In 1887, Congress responded with the Interstate Commerce Act, requiring that railroad rates be "reasonable and just," that rate schedules be made public, and that rebates and similar practices be discontinued. The act also created the first federal regulatory agency, the Interstate Commerce Commission (ICC), empowered to investigate and prosecute lawbreakers. But the legislation limited its authority to commerce crossing state lines.

Like state railroad commissions, the ICC found it hard to define a reasonable rate, and thousands of cases overwhelmed its tiny staff. The ICC could only bring offenders into the federal courts and launch lengthy legal proceedings. Few railroads worried about defying it. When they appeared in court four or five years later, they often won their cases from judges suspicious of new federal authority. Between 1887 and 1906 the Supreme Court decided 15 of 16 such cases in the railroads' favor.

The Southern Farmers' Alliance in the 1880s and 1890s

The Grange declined in the late 1870s as the nation recovered from depression. But farm protest did not die. Depression struck farmers once again in the late 1880s and worsened in the early 1890s. Official statistics told the familiar, dismal story of falling grain prices on the plains and prairies. The national currency shortage, which usually reached critical proportions at harvest time, helped drive agricultural prices ever lower. Debt and shipping costs, however, climbed. It sometimes cost a farmer as much as one bushel of corn to send another bushel to market. Distraught farmers again tried organization, education, and cooperation.

The Southern Farmers' Alliance became one of the most important reform organizations of the 1880s. Its ambitious organizational drive sent lecturers across the South and onto the Plains. The farmer's plight was a "sin," an Alliance song had it, because he forgot that "he's the man that feeds them all."

The Alliance experimented with cooperatives to free farmers from the clutches of supply merchants, banks, and other credit agencies, but they often failed. It also supported legislative efforts to regulate powerful monopolies and corporations that, they believed, gouged farmers. Many Alliance members felt that increasing the money supply was critical to improving the position of farmers and supported a national banking system empowered to issue paper money.

Finally, the Alliance called for a variety of measures to improve the quality of rural life. Better rural public schools, state agricultural colleges, and improvements in the status of women were all on its agenda.

By 1890, rural discontent was sweeping the Plains states and the South, and more than a million farmers were Alliance members. In Kansas, hundreds of farmers packed their families into wagons and set off for Alliance meetings or parades through towns and villages.

The Alliance network included black farmers. The Colored Farmers' Alliance, organized in 1888, recognized that black and white farmers had common economic problems and must cooperate. But many southern cotton farmers, depending on black labor, had an different outlook from blacks. In 1891, cotton pickers on plantations near Memphis went on strike. White posses chased the strikers, lynching 15 and revealing the racial tensions simmering just below the surface.

The Ocala Platform, 1890

In December 1890, the National Alliance gathered in Ocala, Florida, to develop a platform. Most delegates felt that the federal government had failed to address the farmers' problems and attacked both parties as too subservient to the "will of corporation and money power."

In the context of late-nineteenth-century political life, almost all of the Alliance's program was radical. It called for the direct election of U.S. senators and supported lowering the tariff (a topic much debated in Congress) with the dangerous-sounding justification that prices must be reduced for the sake of the "poor of our land." Their money plank went far beyond what any national legislator would consider, boldly envisioning a new banking system controlled by the federal government. They demanded that the government take an active economic role by increasing the amount of money in circulation in the form of treasury notes and silver. More money would cause inflation and help debtors pay off loans.

The platform also called for subtreasuries (federal warehouses) in agricultural regions where farmers could store their produce at low interest rates until market prices favored selling. To tide farmers over, the federal government would lend farmers up to 80 percent of the current local price for their produce. Other demands included a graduated income tax and the regulation of transportation and communication networks—or, if regulation failed, their nationalization.

Even though a minority of farmers belonged to the Alliance, many Americans feared it. The New York *Sun* reported that the Alliance had caused a "panic" in the two major parties.

Although the Alliance was not formally in politics, it had supported sympathetic candidates in the fall elections of 1890. A surprising number of them had won. Alliance victories in the West hurt the Republican party enough to cause President Harrison to refer to "our election disaster."

Before long, many Alliance members were pressing for an independent political party. Alliance support did not necessarily bring action on issues of interest to farmers, or even respect. On the national level, no one had much interest in the Ocala platform. But among rural spokesmen, the first to realize the necessity of forming an independent third party was Georgia's Tom Watson, who also knew that success in the South would depend on unity between white and black farmers.

The People's Party, 1892

In February 1892, the People's, or Populist, party was established, with almost 100 black delegates taking part. Leonidas Polk, president of the Alliance, became the party's presidential candidate. "The time has arrived," he thundered, "for the great West, the great South, and the great Northwest, to link their hands and hearts together and march to the ballot box and take possession of the government, restore it to the principles of our fathers, and run it in the interest of the people." But by the time the party's convention met in Omaha, Polk had died. The party nominated James B. Weaver, a Union army veteran from Iowa, as its standard bearer and James G. Field, a former Confederate soldier, for vice president.

The platform preamble, written by Ignatius Donnelly, a Minnesota farmer, author, and politician, blazed with urgency:

> We meet in the midst of a nation brought to the verge of moral, political and material ruin. Corruption dominates the ballot box, the legislatures, the Congress, and touches even the ermine of the bench. The people are demoralized . . . . The fruits of the toil of millions are boldly stolen to build up colossal fortunes . . . we breed two great classes—paupers and millionaires.

The Omaha demands, drawn from the Ocala platform of 1890, were greatly expanded. They included more direct democracy (popular election of senators, direct primaries, initiative and referendum, and the secret ballot) and several planks intended to enlist support from urban labor. The People's party also endorsed a graduated income tax, the free and unlimited coinage of silver at a ratio of 16 to 1 (meaning that the U.S. Mint would have to buy silver for coinage at one-sixteenth the current official price of the equivalent amount of gold), and government ownership of railroads, telephone, and telegraph.

Populists attempted to widen political debate by promoting a new vision of government activism to resolve farmers' problems. But the obstacles they faced were monumental: weaning the South from the Democrats, encouraging southern whites to work with blacks, and persuading voters of both parties to abandon familiar political ties. Nor were all Alliance members eager to follow their leaders.

The new party nevertheless pressed ahead. Unlike the major-party candidates in 1892, Weaver campaigned actively. In the South, he faced egg- and rock-throwing Democrats. Although he won over a million popular votes (the first third-party candidate to do so), he carried only four western states with 22 electoral votes.

The Populists' support was substantial but regional. Miners and mine owners in Montana, Colorado, and New Mexico Territory favored their demand for silver coinage. Rural Americans in the South and West standing outside the mainstream of American life made up a majority of the party's following. While economic

TIMELINE

1860s	1865–1867	1867	1869	1869–1874
Cattle drives from Texas begin	Sioux Wars on the Great Plains	National Grange founded	Transcontinental railroad completed	Granger laws

1873	1874	1875	1876	1877
Financial panic triggers economic depression	Barbed wire patented	Black Hills gold rush incites Sioux War	Custer's last stand at Little Big Horn	*Munn v. Illinois;* Bonanza farms in the Great Plains

1878	1880s	1881	1883–1885	1884
Timber and Stone Act	"New South"	Tuskegee Institute founded	Depression	Southern Farmers' Alliance founded

1886	1887	1888	1890	1890s
Severe winter ends cattle boom; *Wabash v. Illinois*	Dawes Severalty Act; Interstate Commerce Act; Farm prices plummet	Colored Farmers' Alliance founded	Afro-American League founded; Sioux Ghost Dance movement; Massacre at Wounded Knee; Ocala platform; Yosemite National Park established	Black disenfranchisement in the South; Jim Crow laws passed in the South; Declining farm prices

1891	1892	1895	1896
Forest Reserve Act	Populist party formed; Sierra Club founded	Booker T. Washington's "Atlanta Compromise" address	*Plessy v. Ferguson*

grievances sharpened their political discontent, they were often no poorer or more debt-ridden than other farmers. However, they tended to lead more isolated lives, and they felt powerless.

The People's party failed to break the Democratic stranglehold on the South, defeated by Democratic racial demagogy, violence, and fraud. For example, in Richmond County, Georgia, Democrats won 80 percent in a total vote twice the size of the number of legal voters.

In the North, Weaver failed to appeal to workers, suspicious of the party's antiurban tone and its desire for higher agricultural prices (which meant higher food prices). Nor did Populism appeal to farmers east of the Mississippi. Their families enjoyed better farming weather, owed fewer debts, and were relatively prosperous. Their disinterest was significant, for the industrial northern states and the agriculturally prosperous Great Lake states formed an electoral majority by the 1890s. Farmers who were better integrated into their world tended to believe they could work through existing political parties. In 1892, when thousands of farmers and others were politically and economically discontented, they voted for the Democrats, not the Populists.

❖❖❖❖❖❖

CONCLUSION

Farming in the Industrial Age

The late nineteenth century brought turbulence to rural America. The "Indian problem," which had plagued Americans for 200 years, was tragically solved for a while, but not without resistance and bloodshed. Few whites found these events troubling. Most were caught up in the challenge of responding to a fast-changing world. Believing themselves to be the backbone of the nation, white farmers brought Indian lands into cultivation, modernized their farms, and raised bumper crops. But success and a comfortable competency eluded many of them. Some, like Milton Leeper, never gave up hope or farming. Many were caught in a cycle of poverty and debt. Others fled to the cities, where they joined the industrial work force described in the next chapter. Many turned to collective action and politics. Their actions demonstrate that they did not merely react to events but attempted to shape them.

Recommended Reading

General

Rodman W. Paul, with Martin Ridge, *The Far West and the Great Plains in Transition, 1859–1900* (1988); William G. Robbins, *Colony & Empire: The Capitalist Transformation of the American West* (1994); Patricia N. Limerick, *Legacy of Conquest: The Unbroken Past of the American West* (1987); Donald Worster, *Rivers of Empire: Water, Aridity, and the Growth of the American West* (1985) and *An Unsettled Country: Changing Landscapes of the American West* (1994); Donald J. Pisani, *Water, Land and Law in the West: The Limits of Public Policy, 1850–1920* (1996).

Regions and Groups

Fred C. Luebke, ed., *Ethnicity on the Great Plains* (1980); Carlos Schwantes, *The Pacific Northwest: An Interpretive History* (1989); Richard White, *Land Use, Environment, and Social Change: The Shaping of Island County, Washington* (1980); Sue Armitage and Elizabeth Jameson, eds., *The Women's West* (1987); Sarah Deutsch, *No Separate Refuge: Culture, Class, and Gender on an Anglo-Hispanic Frontier in the American Southwest, 1880–1940* (1987); David Montejano, *Anglos and Mexicans in the Making of Texas, 1831–1986* (1987).

Mining and Cattle Frontiers

Malcolm Rohrbough, *Aspen: The History of a Silver Mining Town, 1879–1893* (1986); Paula Petrik, *No Step Backward: Women and Family on the Rocky Mountain Mining Frontier, Helena, Montana* (1987); Blake Allmendinger, *The Cowboy: Representations of Labor in an American Work Culture* (1992); Peter Iverson, *When Indians Became Cowboys: Native Peoples and Cattle Ranching in the American West* (1994).

Native Americans

Ronald T. Takaki, *Iron Cages: Race and Culture in Nineteenth-Century America* (1979); Robert M. Utley, *The Indian Frontier of the American West* (1984); Richard White, *The Roots of Dependency* (1983); Catherine Price, *The Oglala People: 1841–1879: A Political History* (1996).

The New South

Orville Vernon Burton and Robert C. McMath, Jr., eds., *Toward a New South? Post-Civil War Southern Communities* (1982); Edward Royce, *The Origins of Southern Sharecropping* (1993); Lawrence H. Larsen, *The Rise of the Urban South* (1985); W. Fitzhugh Brundage, *Lynching in the New South; Georgia and Virginia, 1880–1930* (1993); William E. Montgomery, *Under Their Own Vine and Fig Tree: The African-American Church in the South, 1865–1900* (1993); Jacqueline Jones, *Labor of Love, Labor of Sorrow: Black Women, Work, and the Family from Slavery to the Present* (1985); Glenda Elizabeth Gilmore, *Gender and Jim Crow: Women and the Politics of White Supremacy in North Carolina, 1896–1920* (1996).

Populism

Bruce Palmer, *"Men over Money:" The Southern Populist Critique of American Capitalism* (1980); Steven Hahn, *The Roots of Southern Populism: Yeoman Farmers and the Transformation of the Georgia Upcountry, 1850–1890* (1983); Robert W. Larson, *Populism in the Mountain West* (1986); Jeffrey Ostler, *Prairie Populism: The Fate of Agrarian Radicalism in Kansas, Nebraska, and Iowa, 1880–1892* (1993).

Novels

Willa Cather, *My Antonia* (1918); O. E. Rölvaag, *Giants in the Earth* (1927).

CHAPTER 18

The Rise of Smokestack America

By 1883, Thomas O'Donnell, an Irish immigrant, had lived in the United States for over a decade. He was 30 years old, married with two young children, and in debt for the funeral of his third child who had died the year before. Money was scarce, for O'Donnell was a textile worker in Fall River, Massachusetts, and not well educated. "I went to work when I was young," he explained, "and have been working ever since." However, O'Donnell worked only sporadically at the mill, whose owners preferred to hire man-and-boy teams. Because O'Donnell's children were only one and three, he often saw others preferred for day work. Once, when he was passed over, he recalled, "I said to the boss . . . what am I to do; I have got two little boys at home . . . how am I to get something for them to eat; I can't get a turn when I come here . . . . I says, "Have I got to starve; ain't I to have any work?'"

O'Donnell and his family were barely getting by. He said that he had earned only $133 the previous year. Rent came to $72. The family spent $2 for a little coal, but depended on driftwood for heat. Clams were a major part of the family diet, but on some days, there was nothing to eat at all.

The children "got along very nicely all summer," but it was now November, and they were beginning to "feel quite sickly." It was hardly surprising. "One has one shoe on, a very poor one, and a slipper, that was picked up somewhere. The other has two odd shoes on, with the heel out." His wife was healthy, but not ready for winter. She had two dresses, one saved for church, and an "undershirt that she got given to her, and . . . an old wrapper, which is about a mile too big for her; somebody gave it to her."

O'Donnell was testifying to a Senate committee, which was gathering testimony in Boston in 1883 on the relations between labor and capital. The senators asked him why he did not go west. "It would not cost you over $1,500," said one. The gap between the worlds of the senator and the worker could not have been more dramatic. O'Donnell replied, "Well, I never saw over a $20 bill . . . if some one would give me $1,500 I will go." Asked by the senator if he had friends who could provide him with the funds, O'Donnell sadly replied no.

The senators, of course, were far better acquainted with the world of comfort and leisure than with the poverty of families like the O'Donnells. For them, the fruits of industrial progress were clear. As the United States became a world industrial leader in the years after the Civil War, its factories poured forth an abundance of ever-cheaper goods ranging from steel rails and farm reapers to mass-produced parlor sets. These were years of tremendous growth and broad economic and social change. Manufacturing replaced agriculture as the leading source of economic growth between 1860 and 1900. By 1890, a majority of the American work force held nonagricultural jobs; over a third lived in cities. A rural nation of farmers was becoming a nation of industrial workers and city dwellers.

✦✦✦✦✦✦

As O'Donnell's appearance before the senatorial committee illustrates, industrial and techno-logical advances profoundly changed American life. For O'Donnell and others like him, the benefits of this transformation were hard to see. Although no nationwide studies of poverty existed, estimates suggest that half the American population was too poor to take advantage of the new goods of the age. Eventually, the disparity between the reality of life for families like the O'Donnell's and American ideals would give rise to attempts to improve conditions for working-class Americans, but it is unlikely that O'Donnell ever profited from such efforts.

This chapter examines the new order that resulted from the maturing of the American industrial economy. Focusing on the years between 1865 and 1900, it describes the rise of heavy industry, the organization and character of the new industrial workplace, and the emer-gence of big business. It then examines the locus of industrial life, the fast-growing city, and its varied people, classes, and social inequities. The chapter's central theme grows out of O'Donnell's story: As the United States built up its railroads, cities, and factories, its production and profit orientation led to a maldistribution of wealth and power. Although many Americans were too exhausted by life's daily struggles to protest new inequalities, strikes and other forms of working-class resistance punctuated the period. The social problems that accompanied the country's industrial development would capture the attention of reformers and politicians for decades to come.

THE TEXTURE OF INDUSTRIAL PROGRESS

When America went to war in 1861, agriculture was its leading source of econom-ic growth. Forty years later, manufacturing had taken its place. During these years, the production of manufactured goods outpaced population growth. Per capita income increased by over 2 percent a year. But these aggregates disguise the fact that many people won no gains at all.

New regions grew in industrial importance. From New England to the Midwest lay the country's industrial heartland. New England remained a center of light industry, and the Midwest still processed natural resources. Now, however, the production of iron, steel, and transportation equipment joined older manufac-turing operations there. In the Far West, manufacturers concentrated on processing the region's natural resources, but heavy industry made strides as well. In the less industrialized South, the textile industry put down roots by the 1890s.

The Rise of Heavy Industry, 1880–1900

Although many factors contributed to the dramatic rise in industrial productivity, the changing nature of the industrial sector itself explains many of the gains. Pre-Civil War manufacturers had concentrated either on producing textiles, clothing, and leather goods or on processing agricultural and natural resources like grain, hogs, or lumber. Although these industries remained important, heavy industry grew rapidly after the war. Economic growth was driven by capital goods: farm machinery, factory equipment, and railroad track. All contributed to rising productivity and encouraged technological innovations that revolutionized production.

Technological innovations made possible the rise of heavy industries such as steel. Before the Civil War, skilled workers produced iron in a slow and expensive process. The iron was so soft that trains wore out the rails within a few years. The Bessemer converter changed soft iron into hard steel by forcing air through the molten iron, thus reducing the carbon. The converter also reduced the need for highly-paid skilled workers.

Dramatic changes in the steel industry resulted. Steel companies developed new forms of vertical organization providing access to raw materials and markets and brought all stages of steel manufacturing into one mill. Output soared and prices fell. When Andrew Carnegie introduced the Bessemer process in his plant in the mid-1870s, the price of steel dropped from $100 a ton to $50. By 1890, it cost only $12 a ton.

In turn, the production of a cheaper, stronger, more durable material than iron created new goods, new demands, and new markets, and it stimulated further technological changes. Bessemer furnaces, geared toward making steel rails, did not produce steel appropriate for building. Experimentation with the open-hearth process using high temperatures yielded steel usable by bridge builders, engineers, architects, and even designers of subways. Steel use increased dramatically, from naval vessels to screws.

New sources of power facilitated American industry's shift to mass production. In 1869, about half the industrial power came from water. The opening of new anthracite deposits, however, cut the cost of coal, and American industry rapidly converted to steam. By 1900, steam engines generated 80 percent of the nation's industrial energy supply. Then, thanks to inventions by Thomas Edison and George Westinghouse, electricity began to replace steam as a power source.

Completion of a national transportation and communications network was central to economic growth. Beginning in 1862, federal and state governments vigorously promoted railroad construction with land grants from the public domain. Eventually, railroads received lands one and a half times the size of Texas. Local governments gave everything from land for stations to tax breaks.

With such incentives, the first transcontinental railroad was finished in 1869. Four additional transcontinental lines and miles of feeder and branch roads were laid down in the 1870s and 1880s. By 1890, trains rumbled across 165,000 miles of tracks. Telegraph lines arose alongside them. Completion of the national system made possible mass production and mass marketing, and spurred the steel industry.

Financing Postwar Growth

Such changes demanded huge amounts of capital and posed big financial risks. Building the railroad system cost over $1 billion by 1859 (the prewar canal system's price tag was under $2 million); after the war, another $10 billion went to complete the national railroad network. Foreign investors contributed a third of it.

Americans began to put an increasing percentage of the national income into investment rather than consumption. Although savings and commercial banks continued to invest depositors' capital, investment banking houses like Morgan & Co. played a new and significant role. Because stocks were riskier than bonds, buyers were at first cautious. But when J. Pierpont Morgan, a respected investment banker, began to market stocks, they caught on. The market for industrial securities expanded rapidly in the 1880s and 1890s. Although some Americans feared the power of investment bankers and distrusted the financial market, both were integral to late-nineteenth-century economic expansion.

Railroads: Pioneers of Big Business

Big businesses became the characteristic form of economic organization. They could raise the capital to build huge factories, acquire the most efficient machinery, hire hundreds of workers, and use the most up-to-date methods. The result was more goods at lower prices.

Railroads were the pioneers of big business and a great modernizing force. After the Civil War, railroad companies expanded rapidly. The size of railroads, their huge costs, and the complexity of their operations required unprecedented amounts of capital and new management techniques. No single person could finance a railroad, supervise its vast operations, or resolve the questions such a large enterprise raised. How should the operations and employees be organized? What were long- and short-term needs? What were proper rates? What share of the profits did workers deserve?

Unlike small businesses, railroads faced high and constant costs and carried heavy loads of debt, encouraging aggressive business practices. When several lines competed, railroads often offered lower rates or secret rebates (cheaper fares in exchange for all of a company's business). Rate wars caused freight rates to drop steadily, but they could also plunge a railroad into bankruptcy. Instability plagued the industry.

In the 1870s, railroad leaders sought stability through eliminating ruinous competition. Railroad leaders established "pools," informal agreements that set uniform rates or divided up the traffic. Yet they never completely succeeded. Too often, companies broke agreements, especially during business downturns.

Railroad leaders often tried to control costs and counter late-nineteenth-century falling prices by slashing wages. Owners justified this by reasoning that they had taken all the risks. As a result, railroads faced powerful worker unrest.

The railroads' scale and complexity required new management techniques. In 1854, the Erie Railroad hired engineer and inventor Daniel McCallum to tell it how to make managers and employees more accountable. McCallum pointed out that only in small organizations could the manager watch all the details. But "any system that might be applicable to the business and extent of a short road would be found entirely inadequate to the wants of a long one." His system, emphasizing division of responsibilities and a regular flow of information, attracted widespread interest, and railroads pioneered rationalized administrative practices and management techniques. Facing similar economic conditions, big businesses emulated the railroads' competitiveness, their attempts to underprice one another, their eventual interest in mergers, and their tendency to cut wages.

Growth in Other Industries

By the last quarter of the century, the textile, metal, and machinery industries equaled the railroads in size. By 1900, more than 1,000 American factories had giant labor forces ranging between 500 and 1,000, and another 450 employed more than 1,000 workers.

Business expansion was accomplished in one of two ways (or a combination of both). Some owners like steel magnate Andrew Carnegie integrated vertically—adding operations either before or after the production process. Even though he had introduced the most up-to-date innovations in his steel mills, Carnegie realized he needed his own sources of pig iron, coal, and coke—"backward" integration to avoid dependence on suppliers. When Carnegie acquired steamships and railroads to transport his finished products, he was integrating "forward." Companies that integrated vertically frequently achieved economies of scale.

Other companies copied the railroads and integrated horizontally by combining similar businesses. They did not intend to control all stages of production, but rather, by monopolizing the market, hoped to eliminate competition and stabilize prices. While horizontal integration sometimes brought economies and greater profits, monopolistic control over prices did boost earnings.

John D. Rockefeller used horizontal integration to control the oil market. Rockefeller bought or drove out competitors of his Standard Oil of New Jersey. Although his company never achieved a complete monopoly, by 1898 it refined 84 percent of the nation's oil. In the oil business, Rockefeller said, "the day of individual competition . . . is past and gone." He was right. As giant businesses competed intensely, often cutting wages and prices, they absorbed smaller, weaker producers. Business ownership became increasingly concentrated. In 1870, some 808 American iron and steel firms competed. By 1900, fewer than 70 were left.

Like the railroads, many big businesses chose to incorporate. In 1860, most manufacturing firms were unincorporated. By 1900, corporations turned out two-thirds of the country's industrial goods. Corporations had many advantages. By selling stock, they could raise funds for large-scale operations. Limited liability protected investors, whereas the corporation's legal identity survived the death of original and subsequent shareholders.

The Erratic Economic Cycle

The transformation of the economy was neither smooth nor steady. Rockefeller described his years in the oil business as "hazardous."

Two depressions, from 1873 to 1879 and from 1893 to 1897, surpassed the severity of pre-Civil War downturns. Collapsing land values, unsound banking practices, and changes in the money supply had caused antebellum depressions. In the larger and more interdependent late-nineteenth-century economy, depressions were industrial, intense, and accompanied by widespread unemployment, a phenomenon new to American life.

The business cycle had a regular pattern. First, manufacturers flooded markets with goods. Falling prices and fierce competition encouraged overproduction. When the market was saturated, sales and profits declined and the economy spiraled downward. Owners laid off workers (who lived solely on their wages); and when workers economized on food, farm prices plummeted. Farmers, like wage workers, cut purchases. Business stagnated. Finally the railroads were hurt. Eventually the cycle bottomed out, but millions of workers had lost jobs, thousands of businesses had gone bankrupt, and many Americans had suffered hardship.

Pollution

The business cycle worried Americans more than widespread pollution. But by the late nineteenth century, industrial processes were polluting urban air, eastern and midwestern lakes and rivers, and creating acid soil.

The intellectual rationale of the times stressed growth, development, and the rapid exploitation of resources. As the last chapter pointed out, some steps were taken to protect the environment. Presidents Cleveland and Harrison both set aside forest reserves, and there was growing interest in creating national parks. But such limited actions did not begin to touch the problems created by the rise of heavy industry and rapid urban expansion.

URBAN EXPANSION IN THE INDUSTRIAL AGE

As postwar investors shifted from water to steam power, most favored urban locations that offered workers, specialized services, local markets, and railroad links to raw materials and distant markets. Industry, rather than commerce or finance, fueled urban expansion between 1870 and 1900.

Cities of all sizes grew. New York and Philadelphia doubled and tripled their populations. Smaller cities, especially in the industrial Midwest and the South, shared in the growth; Far Western cities increased explosively. In 1870, some 25 percent of Americans lived in cities; by 1900, fully 40 percent of them did.

A Growing Population

The American population grew at about 2 percent a year, but cities expanded far more rapidly. Why?

Not because of a high birthrate. Although more people were born than died in American cities, births contributed only modestly to the urban explosion. The general pattern of declining family size that had emerged before the Civil War continued. Urban families tended to have fewer children than rural ones, and urban children faced a host of health hazards. The death rate for infants was twice as high in cities as in the countryside. In the 1880s, half the children born in Chicago did not live to celebrate their fifth birthdays.

The real cause of rapid urban growth was the spectacular ability of the cities to attract newcomers. The nation's small town and farm population, as well as foreign immigrants, fed urban expansion. For rural Americans, the "push" came from agricultural modernization: Farm machines replaced human hands. By 1896, one man with machinery could harvest 18 times as much wheat as a farmer working with hand tools in 1830. Although urban jobs were often dirty, dangerous, and exhausting, so was farmwork, and by 1890 manufacturing workers were earning hundreds of dollars more a year than farm laborers. Part of the difference between rural and urban wages was eaten up by higher urban living costs, but not all of it.

Rural life was often drab compared to a "gilded metropolis." Shops, theaters, restaurants, department stores, and baseball games all amazed young people who had grown up in small towns and on farms. Said one, city life offered a "round of joy."

Southern blacks, often single and young, also fed the migratory stream into the cities. In the West and North, blacks formed only a tiny part of the population, but in southern cities they were more numerous. About 44 percent of late-nineteenth-century Atlanta's residents were black, and so were 38 percent of Nashville's. But all cities offered them few rewards as well as many dangers.

The New Immigration, 1880–1900

In the 40 years before the Civil War, five million immigrants poured into the United States; in 1860–1900, that volume almost tripled. Three-quarters of them stayed in the Northeast, and many of the rest settled in cities across the nation, where they soon outnumbered native-born whites.

Until 1880, three-quarters of the immigrants, so-called "old immigrants," hailed from the British Isles, Germany, and Scandinavia. Then the pattern slowly changed. By 1890, "old immigrants" composed only 60 percent of the total number of newcomers, and the "new immigrants" from southern and eastern Europe made up most of the rest. Italian Catholics and eastern European Jews were most numerous, followed by Slavs.

Better transportation facilitated the great tide of migration. Trains reached far into eastern and southern Europe. Steerage passengers on transatlantic vessels got slightly better treatment. But overpopulation, famine, and disease drove most to America. "We could have eaten each other had we stayed," said one Italian.

The modernization of European economies also stimulated immigration—some to European cities, many to Canada or South America, but the largest group to the United States. New agricultural techniques led landlords to consolidate their land, evicting longtime tenants. Artisans, their skills made obsolete by machinery, went abroad. Especially in Russia, government persecutions and the expansion of military drafts drove millions of Jews and other minorities to emigrate.

Opportunity in "golden" America lured thousands. State commissioners of immigration and American railroad and steamship companies wooed potential immigrants. Friends and relatives wrote optimistic letters promising help in finding work: American cities were great places for "blast frnises and Rolen milles," explained one unskilled worker. Often letters included passage money or pictures of friends in fashionable clothes.

Like rural and small-town Americans, Europeans came primarily to work. Most were young, single men with few skills. Jews, however, came most often in family groups, and women predominated among the Irish. When times were good and American industry needed many unskilled laborers, migration was heavy. In

These women and children, photographed as they landed at the Battery in New York City, were part of the new immigration from eastern Europe and Russia. (The Museum of the City of New York)

bad times, numbers fell off. Immigrants hoped to earn enough money in America to realize ambitions at home, and as many as a third eventually went back.

Although the greatest influx of Mexicans would come in the twentieth century, Mexican laborers also added to the stream of foreigners migrating to the late nineteenth-century United States. Like Europe, Mexico was modernizing. Overpopulation and new land policies uprooted many inhabitants, such as Gonzalo Plancarte. In the 1890s, he and his father supported themselves by raising cattle. When the owner of the hacienda decided to switch to producing goods for export, he ended the Plancartes' grazing privileges. After his father died, a desperately poor Gonzalo headed north. In 1895, completion of a 900-mile railroad from central Mexico to the Texas border helped migrants like him find work in the Southwest and West, often on railroads and in mines.

Overpopulation, turmoil, unemployment, and crop failures brought Asians, mostly from south China, to the "Land of the Golden Mountains." Although only 264,000 Chinese came to the United States between 1860 and 1900, they constituted a significant minority on the West Coast. Most were unskilled male contract laborers, away from wives and families for years. They held some of the worst jobs in the West. To serve them, contractors brought in virtually enslaved Chinese prostitutes.

THE INDUSTRIAL CITY, 1880–1900

The new physical and social arrangements of late-nineteenth-century industrial cities attracted comment. One Scottish visitor noted that urban "monotony" was

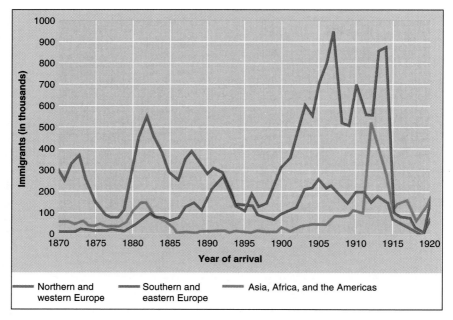

IMMIGRATION TO THE UNITED STATES, 1870–1920   This chart shows the changing pattern of immigration between 1870 and 1920. You can see the growing importance of immigration from southern and eastern Europe as well as a period of intensive immigration from China. Not only did newcomers make the United States more ethnically diverse, but more religiously diverse as well. The new European immigration contained large numbers of Jews and Roman Catholics. Source: U.S. Bureau of the Census.

"like a nightmare." Slums (nothing new) grew disturbingly large, but there were also grand mansions, handsome business and industrial buildings, impressive civic monuments, and acres of substantial middle-class homes.

By the last quarter of the nineteenth century, the jumbled arrangements of the antebellum "walking city," its size and shape defined by the necessity of walking to work, disappeared. Central business districts emerged, where many worked but few lived. Nearby were areas of light manufacturing and wholesale activity with housing for workers. Beyond lay middle-class residential areas. Then came the suburbs with their "pure air, peacefulness, quietude, and natural scenery." Scattered throughout were pockets of industrial activity surrounded by crowded working-class housing.

The new pattern, still characteristic of American cities today, reversed the early nineteenth-century urban form, in which the most desirable housing was in the heart of the city. The new living arrangements were also more segregated by race and class than those in the preindustrial walking city.

Transportation improvements enormously affected the development of American cities. The revolution had started modestly in the 1820s and 1830s, when slow horse-drawn "omnibuses" accommodated only 10 to 12 passengers; but their expensive fares obliged most people to live within walking distance of work. In the 1850s, many cities introduced faster and bigger horse railways, allowing the city to expand outward about four miles. The cost of a fare, however, limited ridership to the prosperous classes. Cable cars, trolleys, and subways after 1880 further extended city boundaries and enabled the middle class to escape grimy industrial districts.

Neighborhoods and Neighborhood Life

Working-class neighborhoods clustered near the center of most industrial cities. Here lived newcomers from rural America and crowds of foreigners.

Ethnic groups frequently chose to gather in neighborhoods near industries requiring their labor. Although such neighborhoods often had an ethnic flavor, they were not ethnic ghettos. Immigrants and native-born Americans often lived in the same neighborhoods, on the same streets, and even in the same houses.

Working-class neighborhoods were often what would be called slums today. Many workers lived in houses once occupied by middle- and upper-class residents, now subdivided to accommodate more people than originally intended. Others jammed into tenements, built to house as many families as possible. Outdoor privies, often shared by several families, were the rule. Water came from hydrants, and women had to carry it inside. Such indoor fixtures as existed frequently poured waste directly into unpaved alleys. Refuse piles stank in the summer and froze in the winter. Even when people kept their own living quarters clean, the outside environment was unhealthy. It was no surprise that urban death rates were so high. Only at the turn of the century did the public health movement make a difference.

Not every working-class family lived in abject circumstances. Skilled workers might rent comfortable quarters, and a few owned their homes. Unskilled and semiskilled workers were not so fortunate. But despite drab neighborhoods, working families created a community life. The expense of moving around the city encouraged a neighborhood and family focus. Long working hours meant that precious free time was apt to be spent close to home.

Working-class men and women were never mere victims. They found the energy, squeezed out the time, and even saved the money to set up religious or ethnic associations that made them feel at home, yet separated them from native-born Americans and other ethnic groups. Irish associational life, for example, focused around the parish church, its Irish priest, and its many religious services, clubs, and activities. Catholicism had fused with nationalism in Ireland, and in America it provided comfort and a shared sense of identity. In Irish nationalist organizations, in ward politics, and in Irish saloons, men met, socialized, drank, and talked politics. Jews gathered in their synagogues, Hebrew schools, and Hebrew- and Yiddish-speaking literary groups. Germans had their family saloons and their educational and singing societies.

Black Americans faced the worst living conditions in the city: in segregated black neighborhoods in the North, and in back alleys and small streets in the South. However, a rich religious and associational life tempered misery. Rapidly growing black churches retained the emotional exuberance of slave religion. Black members of mainline Protestant denominations establish separate branches, and the African Methodist Episcopal Church mushroomed. Some urban blacks, like the artist Henry Ossawa Tanner, rose into the middle class despite heavy odds.

Beyond working-class and black neighborhoods lay streets with the middle-class houses of clerks, shopkeepers, bookkeepers, salesmen, and small tradesmen.

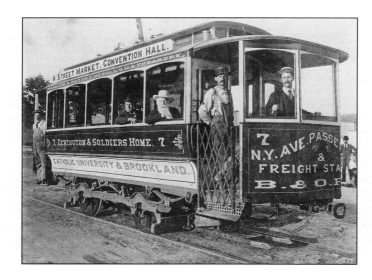

For the middle class, commuting to work from the suburbs became part of the daily routine. (Brown Brothers)

Separate spaces for cooking and laundry work kept unpleasant housekeeping tasks away from other living areas. Many houses boasted new gas lighting and bathrooms. Neighborhoods were cleaner than in the inner city because residents could pay for municipal services.

Streetcar Suburbs

On the fringes of the city lived the substantial middle class and the rich, who sped between downtown offices and home by public transportation. For example, Robert Work, a modestly successful merchant, moved his family to a $5,500 house in West Philadelphia in 1865 and commuted more than four miles to work. In 1880 his household contained two servants, two boarders, his wife, and their eldest son, who was still in school. The Works' house had running hot and cold water, indoor bathrooms, central heating, and other up-to-date conveniences. Upstairs, comfortable bedrooms provided a maximum of privacy for family members. The live-in servants, who did most of the housework, had attic bedrooms.

The Social Geography of the Cities

Industrial cities sorted people by class, occupation, and race. Physical distances between upper- and middle-class neighborhoods and working-class areas eliminated or distorted firsthand knowledge of other people and bred social disapproval. While middle-class newspapers criticized "crowds of idlers, who, day and night, infect Main Street," often the "idlers" were men unable to find work. A working-class woman's comments to temperance visitors that "when the rich stopped drinking, it would be time to speak to the poor about it," captures the critical view from the bottom of society.

THE LIFE OF THE MIDDLE CLASS

Middle-class Americans found much to value in the new age, including work and educational opportunities. Between 1865 and 1890, average middle-class income rose about 30 percent. Although living costs went up even faster, the difference was met by more family members holding jobs and taking in lodgers. By 1900, fully 36 percent of urban families owned their homes.

Industrial expansion raised living standards for the increasing numbers of Americans. They were able to purchase dozens of new products, many with still-familiar brand names like Del Monte, Nabisco, Lipton, and Aunt Jemima.

More leisure time and greater access to consumer goods signaled industrialism's power to transform the lives of middle-class Americans. Plentiful immigrant servant girls relieved urban middle-class wives of many housekeeping chores, and smaller families lightened the burdens of motherhood. New department stores began to appear in the central business districts in the 1870s, feeding women's desire for material possessions and revolutionizing retailing. Shopping for home furnishings and clothes became integral to many middle-class women's lives.

New Freedoms for Middle-Class Women

As many middle-class women acquired leisure time and enhanced purchasing power, they also won new freedoms. Several states granted women more property rights in marriage, adding to their growing sense of independence. Casting off confining crinolines, they now wore a shirtwaist blouse and ankle-length skirt that was more comfortable for working, school, and sports. The "new woman" was celebrated as *Life* magazine's attractively active, slightly rebellious "Gibson girl."

Using their new freedom, women joined organizations of all kinds—literary societies, charity groups, reform clubs. There they gained organizational experience, awareness of their talents, and contact with people and problems outside their traditional family roles. The depression of 1893 stimulated many women to investigate slum and factory conditions, and some began even earlier. Jane Addams, who told her college classmates in 1881 to lead lives "filled with good works and honest toil," went on to found Hull House, a famous social settlement.

Job opportunities for these educated middle-class women were generally limited to the social services and teaching. Still regarded as a suitable female occupation, teaching was a highly demanding but poorly paying field that grew as urban schools expanded under the pressure of a burgeoning population. By the 1890s, the willingness of middle-class women to work for low pay opened up new forms of employment in office work, nursing, and department stores. But moving up to high-status jobs proved difficult, even for middle-class women.

After the Civil War, educational opportunities for women expanded. New women's colleges offered programs similar to those at competitive men's colleges, while midwestern and western state schools dropped prohibitions against women. In 1890, some 13 percent of all college graduates were women; by 1900, nearly 20 percent were. Higher education prepared middle-class women for conventional female roles as well as for work and public service. A few courageous graduates overcame many barriers to enter the professions. By the early twentieth century,

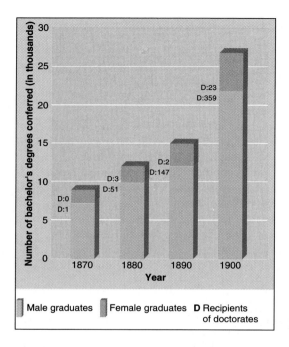

INCREASE IN HIGHER EDUCATION, 1870–1900 Note the rising pattern of college graduation, which suggests the professionalization of middle-class life. Source: U.S. Department of Commerce.

the number of women professionals (including teachers) was increasing at three times the rate for men.

One reason for the greater independence of American women was that they were having fewer babies. This was especially true of educated women. In 1900, nearly one married woman in five was childless. Decreasing family size and an increase in the divorce rate (one out of 12 marriages in 1905) fueled male fears about what Theodore Roosevelt called "race suicide"—the falling white birthrate.

Arguments against the new woman intensified as many men reaffirmed Victorian stereotypes of "woman's sphere." One male orator in 1896 inveighed against the new woman's public role because "a woman's brain involves emotions rather than intellect." Male campaigns against prostitution and for sex hygiene, as well as efforts to reinforce traditional sex roles, reflected deeper fears that female passions might weaken male vigor.

Male Mobility and the Success Ethic

The postwar economy opened up many new opportunities for middle-class men. As the lower ranks of the white-collar world became more specialized, the number of middle-class jobs increased.

These new careers required more education. Public high schools increased from 160 in 1870 to 6,000 in 1900. By 1900, most states and territories had compulsory school attendance laws. Enrollments in colleges and universities nearly doubled, from 53,000 in 1870 to 101,000 in 1900. Harvard introduced reforms ranging from higher faculty salaries to the elective system, and its growth reflected the rise of universities to a new stature in American life. Land-grant state colleges expanded, and philanthropists established research universities like Johns Hopkins.

These developments led to greater specialization and professionalism. By the 1890s, government licensing and the rise of professional schools helped to give the word *career* its modern meaning. No longer were tradesmen likely to read up on medicine in their spare time and become doctors. Organizations like the American Medical Association and the American Bar Association were regulating and professionalizing membership.

The need for lawyers, bankers, architects, and insurance agents to serve business and industry expanded opportunities. As the public sector grew, new careers in social services and government opened up as well, often filled by young professionals with graduate training in the social sciences. The professional disciplines of history, economics, sociology, psychology, and political science all date from the last 20 years of the nineteenth century.

The social ethic of the age stressed that economic rewards were available to anyone who fervently sought them. It was endlessly pointed out, for example, that John D. Rockefeller had raised turkeys as a boy. Horatio Alger's rags-to-riches novels were read by millions. A typical one told the story of a shoeshine-boyturned-office-boy who decided to "learn the business and grow up "spectable." Good fortune intervened when he rescued a girl who had tumbled into the harbor. His reward was a position as a clerk in her father's counting house. Virtuous habits were crucial for Alger's heroes, although success often depended as much on luck as on pluck.

Unlimited and equal opportunity for upward advancement in America has never been as easy as the "bootstraps" ethic maintains. But the persistence of the success myth owes something to the fact that many Americans, particularly those who began well, did rise rapidly. Native-born, middle-class whites tended to have the skills, resources, and connections that opened up the most desirable jobs. The typical big businessman was an Anglo-Saxon Protestant from a middle- or upper-class family whose father was most likely in business, banking, or commerce.

INDUSTRIAL WORK AND THE LABORING CLASS

David Lawlor, an Irish immigrant who came to the United States in 1872, might have agreed with the bootstrap ethic. As a child, he worked in textile mills and read Horatio Alger. Like Alger's heroes, he went to night school and rose in the business world, eventually becoming an advertising executive.

Lawlor's success was exceptional. Most working-class Americans labored long hours, in unpleasant or dangerous conditions, for meager wages. As industrialization transformed work, traditional opportunities for mobility and security eluded many working-class Americans.

The Impact of Ethnic Diversity

Late nineteenth-century immigrants formed 20 percent of the labor force and over 40 percent of laborers in the manufacturing and extractive industries. They tended to settle in cities and made up more than half the working-class population.

The fact that more than half the urban industrial class was foreign, unskilled, and often unable to speak English influenced industrial work, urban life, labor protest, and local politics. Immigrants often had little in common with native-born workers or even with one another.

Atop the working-class hierarchy, native-born Protestant whites held most well-paying skilled jobs. Their occupations bore the mark of late-nineteenth-century industrialism: machinists, iron puddlers and rollers, engineers, foremen, conductors, carpenters, plumbers, mechanics, and printers.

Skilled northern European immigrants filled most middle-rank positions. Often they had held similar jobs in their homelands. Jews, who had tailoring experience, became the backbone of the garment industry (where they faced little competition because American male workers considered it unmanly to work on women's clothes). But most "new immigrants" from southern and central Europe had no urban industrial experience. They got the unskilled, dirty jobs near the bottom of the occupational ladder: relining blast furnaces, carrying raw materials or finished products, or cleaning up. Often, they were day laborers on the docks, ditchdiggers, or construction workers. Hiring was often on a daily basis, often arranged through middlemen like the Italian *padrone.* Unskilled work seldom gave much job stability or paid much money.

At the bottom, blacks occupied the most marginal positions as janitors, servants, porters, and laborers. Racial discrimination generally kept them from industrial jobs, even though their occupational background differed little from that of rural white immigrants. There were always plenty of whites eager to work, so it was not necessary to hire blacks except occasionally as scabs during a strike.

The Changing Nature of Work

Big business and mechanization changed the size and shape of the work force and the nature of work. More and more Americans were wage earners rather than independent artisans. The number of manufacturing workers doubled between 1880 and 1900, with the fastest expansion in the unskilled and semiskilled ranks.

But skilled workers were still needed. New positions, as in steam fitting and structural ironwork, appeared as industries expanded and changed. Increasingly, though, older skills grew obsolete. And all skilled workers faced the possibility that technical advances would eliminate their favored status or that employers would eat away at their jobs by having unskilled helpers take over parts of them.

Work Settings and Experiences

A majority of American manufacturing workers now labored not in shops but in factories, and for them the unceasing rhythms of machinery increased steadily. For those Americans who still toiled in small shops and in basement, loft, or tenement sweatshops, pressures to produce were almost as relentless as in factories—volume, not hours, determined pay.

The organization of work kept workers apart. Those paid by the piece competed in speed, agility, and output. In large factories, workers were separated into small work groups often defined by ethnicity, and the entire work force rarely mingled.

All workers shared a very long working day—usually ten hours a day, six days a week—and often labored in unhealthy, dangerous, and comfortless work places. A few states passed laws to regulate work conditions, but enforcement was spotty, nor did owners concern themselves with health or safety. Women bent over sewing machines developed digestive illnesses and curved spines. In some mines, workers labored in temperatures above 120 degrees, handled dynamite, and died in cave-ins caused by inadequate timber supports. When new drilling machinery was introduced, the air was filled with tiny particles that caused lung disease. Accident rates in the United States far exceeded those of Europe's industrial nations. Nationwide, nearly one-quarter of the men reaching the age of 20 in 1880 would not live to see 44 (compared with 7 percent today). The law placed the burden of avoiding accidents on workers, who were expected to quit if they thought conditions unsafe.

Industrial jobs became increasingly specialized and monotonous. Even skilled workers did not produce a complete product, and the range of their skills narrowed.

Still, industrial work provided some personal benefits. New arrangements helped humanize the workplace. Workers who got their jobs through family and friends then worked with them. In most industries, the foreman controlled day-to-day activities. He chose workers from crowds at the gate, fired unsatisfactory ones, selected appropriate materials and equipment, and determined the order and pace of production. Himself a worker, he might sympathize with subordinates. Yet he could also be authoritarian and harsh, especially if his workers were unskilled or belonged to another ethnic group.

The Worker's Share in Industrial Progress

The huge fortunes accumulated by Andrew Carnegie and John D. Rockefeller during the late nineteenth century dramatized the pattern of wealth concentration that began in the early period of industrialization. In 1890, the top 1 percent of American families possessed over a quarter of the wealth, and the top 10 percent owned about 73 percent. But what of the workers who tended machines that created industrial wealth? Working-class Americans made up the largest segment of the labor force (more than 50 percent), so their experience reveals important facets of the American social and economic system and American values.

Statistics tell an important part of the story. Industry still needed skilled workers and paid them well. Average real wages rose more than 50 percent between 1860 and 1900. Skilled manufacturing workers, about a tenth of the nonagricultural working class in the late nineteenth century, saw their wages rise by about 74 percent. But wages for the unskilled increased by only 31 percent—a substantial differential that widened as the century drew to a close.

On the whole, the working class accrued solid benefits in the late nineteenth century, even if its share of total wealth did not increase. American workers had more material comforts than their European counterparts. But the general picture conceals realities of working-class economic life. A U.S. Bureau of Labor study in 1889 revealed great disparities of income: A young girl in a silk mill made $130 a year; a laborer earned $384 a year; a carpenter took home $686. The carpenter's family lived comfortably in a four-room house, usually breakfasting on meat or eggs, hotcakes, butter, cake, and coffee. The silk worker and the laborer generally ate bread and butter for two of their three daily meals.

For workers without steady employment, rising real wages were meaningless. Workers, especially unskilled ones, often found work only sporadically. When times were slow or conditions depressed, as they were in 1873–1879 and 1893–1897, employers, especially in small firms, laid off skilled and unskilled workers alike, and reduced wages. Even in a good year like 1890, one out of every five men outside of agriculture had been unemployed at least a month.

Unemployment insurance did not exist. One woman grimly recalled, "If the factory shuts down without warning, as it did last year for six weeks, we have a growing expense with nothing to counterbalance." Occasionally, kindhearted employers offered assistance in hard times, but it was rarely enough.

Although nineteenth-century ideology pictured men as breadwinners, many working-class married men could not earn enough to support their families alone. A working-class family's standard of living thus often depended on its number of workers. In the nineteenth century, married women did not usually take outside employment, although they contributed to family income by taking in sewing, laundry, and boarders. In 1890, only 3.3 percent of married women were to be found in the paid labor force.

The Family Economy

If married women did not work for pay outside their homes, their children did. The laborer whose annual earnings amounted to only $384 depended on his 13-year-old son, not his wife, to earn an extra $196, critical to the family's welfare. In 1880, one-fifth of the nation's children between the ages of 10 and 14 held jobs.

Child labor was closely linked to a father's income, which in turn depended on skill, ethnic background, and occupation. Immigrant families more frequently sent their young children out to work (and also had more children) than native-born families. Middle-class reformers who sentimentalized childhood disapproved of parents who put their children to work: "Father never attended school, and thinks his children will have sufficient schooling before they reach their tenth year, thinks no advantage will be gained from longer attendance at school, so children will be put to work as soon as able." Reformers believed that such fathers condemned their children to future poverty by taking them out of school. Actually, sending children to work was a means of coping with the immediate threat of poverty, of financing the education of one of the children, or even of ensuring that children stayed near their family.

Women at Work

Many more young people over the age of 14 were working for wages than was the case for children. Half of all Philadelphia's students had quit school by that age. Daughters as well as sons were expected to take jobs, although young women from immigrant families were more likely to work than young American women. By 1900, nearly 20 percent of American women were in the labor force.

An experienced female factory worker might be paid $5 or $6 a week, whereas an unskilled male laborer could make about $8. Discrimination, present from women's earliest days in the work force, persisted. Still, factory jobs were desirable because they often paid better than other kinds of work open to women.

Employment opportunities for women were narrow, and ethnic taboos and cultural traditions helped shape choices. About a quarter of working women secured factory jobs. Italian and Jewish women (whose cultural backgrounds virtually forbade their going into domestic service) clustered in the garment industry, and Poles and Slavs went into textiles, food processing, and meatpacking. In some industries, like textiles, women composed an important segment of the work force. But about 40 percent of them, especially those from Irish, Scandinavian, or black families, were maids, cooks, laundresses, and nurses.

Domestic service was arduous, nor could domestics count on much sympathy from their employers. "Do not think it necessary to give a hired girl as good a room as that used by members of the family," said one lady of the house. "She should sleep near the kitchen and not go up the front stairs or through the front hall to reach her room." A servant received room and board plus $2 to $5 a week. The fact that so many women took such work speaks clearly of their limited opportunities.

The dismal situation facing working women drove some, like Rose Haggerty, into prostitution. Burdened with a widowed and sickly mother and four young brothers and sisters, at 14 Rose started work at a New York paper bag factory. She earned $10 a month, of which $6 went for rent. Her fortunes improved when a friend helped her buy a sewing machine. Rose then sewed shirts at home, often working as much as 14 hours a day to support her family. Suddenly, the piecework rate for shirts was slashed in half. Rose contemplated suicide. But when a sailor offered her money for spending the night with him, she realized that she had an alternative. Prostitution meant food, rent, and heat for her family. "Let God Almighty judge who's to blame most," the 20-year-old Rose reflected, "I that was driven, or them that drove me to the pass I'm in."

Prostitution appears to have increased in the late nineteenth century, although there is no way of knowing the actual numbers of women involved. Probably most single women accepted the respectable jobs open to them. They tolerated discrimination and low wages because their families depended on their contributions. They also knew that when they married, they would probably leave the paid work force forever.

Marriage hardly ended women's work, however. Like colonial families, late-nineteenth-century working-class families operated as economic units. The unpaid domestic labor of working-class wives was critical to family survival. With husbands away for 10 to 11 hours a day, women bore the burden and loneliness of caring for children and doing all the domestic chores.

As managers of family resources, married women had important responsibilities. What American families had once produced for themselves now had to be bought. It was up to the working-class wife to scour secondhand shops for cheap clothes. Small domestic economies were vital.

Women also supplemented family income by taking in work. Jewish and Italian women frequently did piecework and sewing at home. In the Northeast and the Midwest, between 10 and 40 percent of all working-class families kept boarders. Immigrant families, in particular, often made ends meet by taking single young countrymen into their homes. The cost was the added burden of work (providing meals and clean laundry), the need to juggle work schedules, and the sacrifice of privacy. But the advantages of extra income far outweighed the disadvantages for many working-class families.

Black women's working lives reflected the obstacles African-Americans faced in late-nineteenth-century cities. Although few married white women worked outside the home, many black women did, both before and after marriage. In southern cities in 1880, about three-quarters of single black women and one-third of married ones worked outside the home. (For white women the rates were 24 and 7 percent, respectively.) Because industrial employers would not hire black women, most had to work as domestics or laundresses. The high percentage of married black women in the labor force reflected the marginal wages their husbands earned. But it may also be explained partly by the lesson learned during slavery that children could thrive without the constant attention of their mothers.

CAPITAL VERSUS LABOR

Class conflict permeated late-nineteenth-century industrial life. Although workers welcomed the progress the factory made possible, many rejected their employers' values, which emphasized individual gain at the expense of collective good. While owners reaped most of the profits, workers were becoming wage slaves. Fashioning their arguments from their republican legacy, workers claimed that the degradation of the country's citizen laborers threatened to undermine the republic itself.

On-the-Job Protests

Workers and employers struggled over who would control the workplace. Many workers staunchly resisted unsatisfactory working conditions and bosses' tendency to treat them "like any other piece of machinery, to be made to do the maximum amount of work with the minimum expenditure of fuel." Skilled workers had indispensable practical knowledge and were in a key position to direct on-the-job actions. Sometimes they tried to control critical work decisions or to humanize work. Cigar makers clung to their custom of having one worker read to others as they performed their tedious chores.

Workers also resisted owners' attempts to squeeze large profits from unlimited production. Too many goods meant an inhuman work pace and might result in overproduction, massive layoffs, and a reduction in piecework prices. So an experienced worker might whisper to a new hand, "See here, young fellow, you're working too fast. You'll spoil our job for us if you don't go slower."

Absenteeism, drunkenness at work, and general inefficiency—all widespread—contained elements of protest. In three industrial firms in the late nineteenth century, one-quarter of the workers stayed home at least one day a week. Some of these lost days were due to layoffs, but not all. The efforts of employers to impose stiff fines on absent workers suggested their frustration with uncooperative employees.

To a surprising extent, workers made the final protest by quitting their jobs altogether. Most employers responded by penalizing workers who left without giving sufficient notice—to little avail. A Massachusetts labor study in 1878 found that although two-thirds of them had been in the same occupation for more than ten years, only 15 percent of the workers surveyed were in the same job. A similar rate of turnover occurred in the industrial work force in the early twentieth century. Workers unmistakably and clearly voted with their feet.

Strike Activity After 1876

The most direct and strenuous attempts to change conditions in the workplace came in the form of thousands of strikes punctuating the late nineteenth century. In 1877, railroad workers staged the first and bloodiest nationwide industrial strike of the nineteenth century. The immediate cause of the disturbance was the railroad owners' decision to reduce wages. But the rapid spread of the strike all over the country, as well as the violence of the strikers, who destroyed railroad property and kept trains idle, indicated more fundamental discontent.

An erratic economy, high unemployment, and the lack of job security all fed the conflagration. Over 100 people died before federal troops ended the strike. The frenzied response of the propertied class, which saw the strike as the beginning of revolution and applauded military intervention, forecast the pattern of later conflicts. Time and time again, middle- and upper-class Americans would turn to state power to crush labor activism.

A wave of confrontations followed the strike of 1877. Between 1881 and 1905, there were 36,757 strikes involving over six million workers. These numbers indicate that far more than the "poorest part" of the workers were involved. Many investigations of this era found evidence of widespread working-class discontent. Such bitterness exploded into strikes, sabotage, and violence, most often linked to demands for higher wages and shorter hours.

Nineteenth-century strike activity underwent important changes as the consciousness of American workers expanded. In the period of early industrialization, discontented laborers rioted in their neighborhoods rather than at their workplaces. The Lowell protests of the 1830s (discussed in Chapter 10) were not typical. Between 1845 and the Civil War, however, strikes began to replace neighborhood riots. Although workers showed their anger against their employers by striking for higher wages, they had only a murky sense that the strike could also be a weapon to force employers to improve working conditions.

As industrialization transformed work and an increasing percentage of the labor force entered factories, collective actions at the workplace spread. Local and national unions played a more important role in organizing protest, conducting 60 percent of the strikes between 1881 and 1905. Coordination between strikers in different companies improved. Finally, wages among the most highly unionized workers became less of an issue. Workers sought more humane conditions. By the early 1890s, over one-fifth of strikes involved workplace rules.

Labor Organizing, 1865–1900

Civil War experience colored postwar labor organizing. As one working-class song pointed out, workers had borne the brunt of that struggle. "You gave your son to the war/ The rich man loaned his gold/ And the rich man's son is happy to-day,/

And yours is under the mold." Now workers who had fought to save the Union argued that wartime sacrifices justified efforts to gain justice and equality in the workplace.

Labor leaders quickly realized the need for national as well as local organizations to protect the laboring class against "despotic employers." In 1866, several craft unions and reform groups formed the National Labor Union (NLU). Claiming 300,000 members by the early 1870s, the organization supported a range of causes including temperance, women's rights, and the establishment of cooperatives to bring the "wealth of the land" into "the hands of those who produce it."

The call for an eight-hour day reveals some of the basic assumptions of the organized labor movement. Few workers saw employers as a hostile class or wanted to overturn the economic system. But they did believe bosses were often dangerous tyrants whose demands for their time threatened to turn citizens into slaves. The eight-hour day would curb the power of owners and allow workers the time to cultivate the qualities necessary for republican citizenship.

Many of the NLU's specific goals survived, although the organization did not. An unsuccessful attempt to create a political party and the depression of 1873 decimated the NLU. Survival and job searches took precedence over union causes.

The Knights of Labor and the AFL

As the depression wound down, a new mass organization, the Noble and Holy Order of the Knights of Labor, rose to prominence. Founded as a secret society in 1869, the order became public and national when Terence V. Powderly was elected Grand Master Workman in 1879. The Knights of Labor sought "to secure to the workers the full enjoyment of the wealth they create." Because the industrial system denied workers their fair share as producers, the Knights of Labor proposed a cooperative system of production paralleling the existing system. Cooperative efforts would give workers the economic independence necessary for citizenship, and an eight-hour day would provide them with the leisure for moral, intellectual, and political pursuits.

The Knights of Labor was open to all American "producers," defined as all contributing members of society—skilled and unskilled, black and white, men and women, even merchants and manufacturers. Only the idle and the corrupt (gamblers, saloonkeepers, speculators, bankers, lawyers) were excluded. Many shopkeepers joined, advertising themselves as "friend of the workingman."

This inclusive membership policy meant that the Knights potentially had the power of great numbers. The organization grew in spurts, attracting miners between 1874 and 1879, skilled urban tradesmen between 1879 and 1885, and unskilled workers thereafter.

Although Powderly frowned on strikes, the organization reaped the benefit of grass-roots strike activity. Local struggles proliferated after 1883. In 1884, unorganized workers of the Union Pacific Railroad walked off the job when management announced a wage cut. Within two days, the company caved in, and the men joined the Knights. The next year, a successful strike against the Missouri Pacific Railroad brought in another wave of members. Then, in 1886, the Haymarket Riot in Chicago caused such a growth in labor militancy that in that single year the membership of the Knights of Labor ballooned from 100,000 to 700,000.

The "riot" at Haymarket was, in fact, a peaceful protest meeting connected with a lockout at the McCormick Reaper Works. When the Chicago police arrived to disperse the crowd, a bomb exploded. Seven policemen died. Although no one knows who planted the bomb, eight anarchists were tried and convicted. Three were executed, one committed suicide, and the others served prison terms.

Labor agitation and turbulence spilled over into politics. In 1884 and 1885, the Knights lobbied for a national contract labor law that would demand work contracts and state laws outlawing convict labor. The organization also pressed successfully for the creation of a federal Department of Labor. As new members poured in, however, direct political action became increasingly attractive. Despite many local successes, no national labor party emerged. But in the 1890s, the Knights cooperated with the Populists' attempt to reshape American politics and society.

The Knights could not sustain momentum. Alerted by the Haymarket Riot, employers determined to break the organization. A strike against Jay Gould's southwestern railroad system in 1886 failed. Consumer and producer cooperatives fizzled; the policy of accepting both black and white workers led to strife and discord in the South. The two major parties co-opted labor politicians.

National leaders also failed. Powderly could never unify his diverse following, nor control militants opposing him. By 1890, membership had dropped to 100,000, although the Knights continued to play a role well into the 1890s.

In the 1890s, the American Federation of Labor (AFL), founded in 1886, became the nation's dominant union. The history of the Knights pointed up the problems of a national union that admitted all who worked for wages, but officially rejected strikes in favor of the ballot box and arbitration. The leader of the AFL, Samuel Gompers, had a different notion of effective worker organization. He was convinced that skilled workers should put their specific occupational interests first, so that they could control the supply of skilled labor and keep wages up.

Gompers organized the AFL as a federation of skilled trades—cigar makers, iron molders, ironworkers, carpenters, and others—each one autonomous, yet linked through an executive council to work together for prolabor national legislation and mutual support during boycott and strike actions. He repudiated dreams of a cooperative commonwealth or of ending the wage system, instead focusing on immediate "bread and butter" issues—higher wages, shorter hours, industrial safety, and the right to organize. Although Gompers rejected direct political action as a means of obtaining labor's goals, he believed in the value of the strike. A shrewd organizer, he knew from bitter experience the importance of dues high enough to sustain a strike fund through a long, tough fight.

Under Gompers's leadership, the AFL grew from 140,000 in 1886 to nearly one million by 1900. Although his notion of a labor organization was elitist, he steered his union through a series of crises, fending off challenges from socialists on his left and corporate opposition to strikes on his right. But there was no room in his organization for the unskilled or for blacks. The AFL did make a brief, half-hearted attempt to unionize women in 1892, but men resented women as co-workers and preferred them to stay in the home. The AFL agreed. In 1900, the

International Ladies' Garment Workers Union (ILGWU) was established. Although women were its backbone, men dominated the leadership.

Working-Class Setbacks

Despite the growth of working-class organizations, workers lost many battles. Some of the more spectacular clashes reveal why working-class activism often failed and why so many workers lived precariously.

In 1892, silver miners in Coeur d'Alene, Idaho, struck when their employers installed machine drills in the mines, reduced skilled workers to shovelmen, and cut wages. The owners, supported by state militiamen and the federal government, successfully broke the strike by using scabs, but not without fighting. Several hundred union men were eventually tried and found guilty of a wide variety of charges. Out of the defeat emerged the Western Federation of Miners (WFM), whose chief goal was an eight-hour law for miners.

The Coeur d'Alene struggle set the pattern for many subsequent strikes. Mine owners fought strikes by shutting off credit to union men, hiring strikebreakers and armed guards, and infiltrating unions with spies. Violence was frequent, usually ending with the arrival of state militia, arrests or intimidation, legal action, and blacklisting. Despite this, the WFM won as many strikes as it lost.

The Homestead and Pullman Strikes of 1892 and 1894

Labor's worst setback came in 1892 at the Homestead steel mills near Pittsburgh. Carnegie had purchased the Homestead plant and put Henry Clay Frick in charge. Together, they wanted to break the union that threatened to extend its organization of the steel industry. After three months of stalemated negotiations over a new wage contract, Frick issued an ultimatum. Workers must accept wage cuts or be replaced. Frick barricaded the entire plant and hired 300 armed Pinkerton guards. As they arrived on July 6, they and armed steelworkers fought a daylong gun battle. Several men on both sides were killed, and the Pinkertons retreated. Then, at Frick's request, the governor of Pennsylvania sent 8,000 troops to crush the strike and the union. Two and a half weeks later, a New York anarchist tried to assassinate Frick.

The Homestead strike dramatized the lengths to which both labor and capital would go. Eugene Debs, for many years an ardent organizer of railroad workers, wrote, "If the year 1892 taught the workingmen any lesson worthy of heed, it was that the capitalist class, like a devilfish, had grasped them with its tentacles and was dragging them down to fathomless depths of degradation."

Debs saw 1893 as the year in which organized labor would "escape the prehensile clutch of these monsters." Instead, 1893 brought a new depression and even worse setbacks for labor. Undaunted, Debs combined several of the separate railroad brotherhoods into a united American Railway Union (ARU). Within a year, over 150,000 railroadmen joined the ARU, and Debs won a strike against the Great Northern Railroad, which had attempted to slash wages.

In this 1892 engraving of the Homestead strikers surrendering, done for *Harper's Weekly*, the sympathy of the artist lies with the detectives in the foreground. The strikers appear as an unruly crowd in the distance, whereas the detectives' kindly faces are highlighted. (Library of Congress)

Debs faced his toughest crisis at the Pullman Palace Car Company in Chicago. The company maintained a model company town near Chicago—naturally, called Pullman—where management controlled all aspects of workers' lives.

Late in 1893, as the depression worsened, the Pullman Company cut wages by one-third and laid off many workers, without reducing rents or prices in its stores. Forced to pay in rent what they could not earn in wages, working families struggled through the winter. Those still at work suffered speedups, threats, and further wage cuts. Desperate Pullman workers joined the ARU in the spring of 1894 and struck.

In late June, after Pullman refused to submit the dispute to arbitration, Debs led the ARU into a sympathy strike in support of the striking Pullman workers. Remembering the ill-fated railroad strike of 1877, Debs advised his lieutenants to "use no violence" and "stop no trains." Rather, he sought to boycott trains handling Pullman cars throughout the West. As the boycott spread, the General Managers Association, which ran the 24 railroads centered in Chicago, came to Pullman's support. Hiring 2,500 strikebreakers, the GMA appealed to the state and federal governments for military and judicial support in stopping the strike.

Governor Richard Altgeld of Illinois, sympathizing with the workers and believing that local law enforcement was sufficient, opposed using federal troops. But U.S. Attorney General Richard Olney, a former railroad lawyer, on July 2 obtained a court injunction to end the strike as a "conspiracy in restraint of trade." Two days later, President Cleveland ordered federal troops to crush the strikers.

Violence escalated rapidly. Local and federal officials hired armed guards, and the railroads paid them to help the troops. Within two days, strikers and guards were fighting bitterly. As troops poured into Chicago, the violence worsened, leaving scores of workers dead.

Debs's resources were running out unless he could enlist wider labor support. "We must all stand together or go down in hopeless defeat," he warned other unions. When Gompers refused support, the strike collapsed. Debs and several other leaders were found guilty of contempt of court. Hitherto a lifelong Democrat, Debs became a staunch socialist. His arrest and the defeat of the Pullman strike killed the American Railway Union. In 1895, the Supreme Court upheld the legality of using an injunction to stop a strike, giving management a powerful weapon against unions. Most unions survived the difficult days of the 1890s, but the labor movement emerged as a distinct underdog in its conflicts with organized capital.

Although in smaller communities strikes against outside owners might receive local middle-class support, most labor conflicts encountered the widespread middle- and upper-class conviction that unions were un-American. Many people claimed to accept the idea of worker organizations, but would not concede that unions should participate in making economic or work decisions. Most employers violently resisted union demands as infringements of their right to manage their business. The sharp competition of the late nineteenth century, combined with a pattern of falling prices, stiffened employers' resistance to workers' demands. State and local governments and the courts frequently supported them.

The severe depressions of the 1870s and 1890s also undermined working-class activism. Workers could not focus on union issues when survival itself was in question. Many unions collapsed during hard times.

A far more serious problem was the reluctance of most workers to organize even in favorable times. In 1870, less than one-tenth of the industrial work force belonged to unions, about the same as on the eve of the Civil War. Thirty years later, despite the expansion of the work force, only 8.4 percent (mostly skilled workers) were union members.

Why were workers so slow to join unions? Certainly, diverse work settings and ethnic differences made it difficult for workers to recognize common bonds. Many unskilled workers sensed that labor "aristocrats" did not have their interests at heart. Moreover, many native-born American workers still clung to the tradition of individualism, or dreamed of entering the middle class.

An Irish woman highlighted another important point. "There should be a law . . . to give a job to every decent man that's out of work," she declared, "and another law to keep all them I-talians from comin' in and takin' the bread out of the mouths of honest people." Ethnic and religious diversity made it difficult to forge a common front. Many foreigners, planning to return to their homeland, had limited interest in changing conditions in the United States—and because their goal was to work, they took jobs as scabs. Much of the violence that accompanied working-class actions erupted when owners brought in strikebreakers. Some Americans blamed immigrants for both low wages and failed worker actions.

Tension within laboring ranks appeared most dramatically in the anti-Chinese campaign of the 1870s and 1880s as white workers in the West began to blame the Chinese for economic hardships. A meeting of San Francisco workers in 1877 in favor of the eight-hour day exploded into a rampage against the Chinese. In 1882

Congress passed the Chinese Exclusion Act with the support of the Knights of Labor, prohibiting the immigration of Chinese workers for a ten-year period. It was extended in 1892 and made permanent in 1902.

Many immigrants, especially skilled ones, supported unions and cooperated with native-born Americans. Often ethnic bonds tied members to one another and to the community. For example, in the 1860s and 1870s, as the Molders' Union in Troy, New York, battled with manufacturers, its Irish membership won sympathy and support from the Irish-dominated police force, the Roman Catholic Church, fraternal orders, and public officials.

The importance of workers' organizations lay not so much in their successful struggles and protests as in the implicit criticism they offered of American society. Using the language of republicanism, many workers lashed out at an economic order that robbed them of their dignity and humanity. As producers of wealth, they protested that so little of it was theirs. As members of the working class, they rejected the middle-class belief in individualism and social mobility.

The Balance Sheet

Except for skilled workers, most laboring people found it impossible to earn much of a share in the material bounty industrialization created. Newly arrived immigrants suffered especially. Long hours on the job, and walking to and from work left workers little free time. Family budgets included, at best, only small amounts for recreation.

Yet this harsh view of working-class life partly reflects our standards of what is acceptable today. Because so few working-class men or women recorded their thoughts, it is hard to know how they viewed their experiences. But culture and background influenced perspectives. The family tenement, one Polish immigrant said, "seemed quite advanced when compared with our home" in Poland. Jews found American poverty preferable to Russian pogroms.

Studies of several cities show that nineteenth-century workers achieved some occupational mobility. One worker in five in Los Angeles and Atlanta during the 1890s, for example, managed to climb into the middle class. Most immigrant workers were stuck in ill-paid, insecure jobs, but their children did better.

Mobility, like occupation, was related to background. Native-born whites, Jews, and Germans rose more swiftly and fell less often than Irish, Italians, or Poles. Cultural attitudes, family size, education, and group leadership all produced different ethnic mobility patterns. Jews, for example, valued education and sacrificed to keep children in school. With an education, they moved upward. Slavs, however, who valued a steady income over mobility and education, took their children out of school and sent them to work young. This not only helped the family, they thought, but also gave the child a head start toward reliable, stable employment. A southern Italian proverb, "Do not make your child better than you are," suggests valuing family success over individual success. Different attitudes led to different aspirations and career patterns.

Two groups found little mobility. African-Americans were largely excluded from the industrial occupational structure and restricted to unskilled jobs. Unlike immigrant industrial workers, they could not move to better jobs as new unskilled workers took the positions at the bottom. Hispanic residents in Los Angeles made minimal gains, and this was probably the pattern elsewhere.

Although occupational mobility was limited for immigrants, other rewards often compensated for the lack of workplace success. Home ownership—all but impossible in their homeland—loomed important for the Irish. Owning a home also meant extra income from boarders and some protection against uncertainties and old age. The Irish proved adept politicians and came to dominate big-city government in the late nineteenth century. They succeeded in the construction industry and dominated the hierarchy of the Catholic Church. Even Irish who did not share this upward mobility could benefit from ethnic connections and take pride in their group's achievements.

Likewise, social clubs and fraternal orders compensated in part for lack of advancement at work. Ethnic associations, parades, and holidays provided a sense of identity and security that offset the limitations of the job world.

A few rags-to-riches stories always encouraged the struggling masses. The family of John Kearney in Poughkeepsie, New York, for example, achieved modest success. After 20 years as a laborer, he started his own business as a junk dealer and even bought a simple house. His sons started off in better jobs than their father. One became a grocery store clerk, later a baker, a policeman, and, finally, at the age of 40, an inspector at the waterworks. Another was an iron molder, and the third son was a post office worker and eventually the superintendent of city streets. If this success paled next to that of industrial giants like Andrew Carnegie and John D. Rockefeller, it was still enough to keep the American dream alive.

✦✦✦✦✦

CONCLUSION

The Complexity of Industrial Capitalism

The rapid growth of the late nineteenth century made the United States one of the world's industrial giants. Many factors contributed to the "wonderful accomplishments" of the age. They ranged from sympathetic government policies to the rise of big business and the emergence of a cheap industrial work force. But it was also a turbulent period. Many Americans benefited only marginally from the new wealth. Some of them protested by joining unions, by walking out on strike, or by initiating on-the-job actions. Most lived their lives more quietly without Thomas O'Donnell's opportunity to tell their story. But middle-class Americans began to wonder about the O'Donnells of the country. It is to their concerns, worries, and aspirations that we now turn.

Recommended Reading

Industrialism and Economic Growth

Olivier Zunz, *Making America Corporate, 1870–1929* (1990); Louis Galambos and Barbara Barron Spence, *The Public Image of Big Business in America* (1975); James D. Norris, *Advertising and the Transformation of American Society, 1865–1920* (1990); Thomas P. Hughes, *American*

TIMELINE

1843–1884 "Old immigration"	1844 Telegraph invented	1850s Steam power widely used in manufacturing	1859 Value of U.S. industrial production exceeds value of agricultural production	1866 National Labor Union founded
1869 Transcontinental railroad completed; Knights of Labor organized	**1870** Standard Oil of Ohio formed	**1870s–1880s** Consolidation of continental railroad network	**1873** Bethlehem Steel begins using Bessemer process	**1873–1879** Depression
1876 Alexander G. Bell invents telephone; Thomas Edison establishes his "invention factory" at Menlo Park, New Jersey	**1877** Railroad workers hold first nationwide industrial strike	**1879** Thomas Edison invents incandescent light	**1882** Chinese Exclusion Act	**1885–1914** "New immigration"
1886 American Federation of Labor founded; Haymarket Riot in Chicago	**1887** Interstate Commerce Act	**1890** Sherman Anti-Trust Act	**1892** Standard Oil of New Jersey formed; Coeur d'Alene strike; Homestead steelworkers strike	**1893** Chicago World's Fair
1893–1897 Depression	**1894** Pullman railroad workers strike	**1900** International Ladies' Garment Workers Union founded; Corporations responsible for two-thirds of U.S. manufacturing		

Genius (1989); Thomas J. Misa, *A Nation of Steel* (1995); William G. Roy, *Socializing Capitalism: The Rise of the Large Industrial Corporation in America* (1997).

Urban Life

David Goldfield, *Cotton Fields and Skyscrapers: Southern City and Region* (1989); William Cronon, *Nature's Metropolis: Chicago and the Great West* (1991); Carl Smith, *Urban Disorder and the Shape of Belief: the Great Chicago Fire, the Haymarket Bomb, and the Model Town of Pullman* (1993); James Borchert, *Alley Life in Washington: Family, Community, Religion, and Folklife in the City, 1850–1970* (1980); David Nasaw, *Going Out: The Rise and Fall of Public Amusements* (1993); Priscilla Ferguson Clement, *Growing Pains: Children in the Industrial Age, 1850–1890* (1997); Kathie Friedman-Kasaba, *Memories of Migration: Gender, Ethnicity* (1996).

Work and Workers

Alan M. Kraut, *The Huddled Masses: The Immigrant in American Society, 1880–1921* (1982); Peter Jones and Melvin G. Holli, eds., *Ethnic Chicago* (1981); Kerby A. Miller, *Emigrants and Exiles: Ireland and the Irish Exodus to North America* (1985); Mark Wyman, *Round Trip to America: The Immigrants Return to Europe, 1880–1930* (1993); David M. Gordon, Richard Edwards, and Michael Reich, *Segmented Work, Divided Workers: The Historical Transformation of Labor in the United States* (1982); David Montgomery, *The Fall of the House of Labor: The Workplace, The State, and American Labor Activism, 1865–1925* (1987); James Whiteside, *Regulating Danger: The Struggle for Mine Safety in the Rocky Mountain Coal Industry* (1990); Theodore Hershberg, ed., *Philadelphia: Work, Space, Family, and Group Experience in the Nineteenth Century* (1981); Nell Irvin Painter, *Standing at Armageddon in the United States, 1877–1919* (1987); Leon Fink, *Workingmen's Democracy: The Knights of Labor and American Politics* (1983); Alice Kessler-Harris, *Out to Work: A History of Wage-earning Women in the United States* (1982); Ronald Takaki, *A Different Mirror: A History of Multicultural America* (1993).

Novels

Theodore Dreiser, *Sister Carrie* (1900); Stephen Crane, *Maggie: A Girl of the Streets* (1893); Abraham Cahan, *The Rise of David Levinsky* (1917); Thomas Bell, *Out of This Furnace* (1976 ed.).

CHAPTER 19

Politics and Reform

At the start of his bestseller *Looking Backward* (1888), Edward Bellamy likened the American society of his day to a huge stagecoach. Dragging the coach along sandy roads and over steep hills were the "masses of humanity." While they strained desperately "under the pitiless lashing of hunger," at the top sat the favored few—who, however, constantly feared that they might fall from their seats and have to pull the coach themselves.

Bellamy's famous coach allegory began a utopian novel in which the class divisions and pitiless competition of the nineteenth century were replaced by a classless, caring, cooperative new society. Economic anxieties and hardships were supplanted by satisfying labor and leisure.

The novel opens in 1887. The hero, a wealthy Bostonian, falls asleep worrying about the effect local labor struggles might have on his upcoming wedding. When he wakes up, it is the year 2000. Utopia has been achieved peacefully through the development of one gigantic trust, owned and operated by the national government. All citizens between the ages of 21 and 45 work in an industrial army with equalized pay and work difficulty. Retirement after 45 is devoted to hobbies, reading, culture, and the minimal leadership in a society without problems like crime or war.

Bellamy's book was popular with educated middle-class Americans who were attracted by his vision of a society in which humans were both morally good and materially well off—and in which core values of the 1880s survived intact, including individual incentive, private property, and rags-to-riches presidents. Like most middle-class Americans of his day, Bellamy disapproved of European socialism. Although some features of Bellamy's utopia were socialistic, he and his admirers called his system "nationalism." This appealed to a new generation of Americans who had put aside Civil War antagonisms to embrace the greatness of a growing, if now economically divided, nation. In the early 1890s, with Americans buying nearly 10,000 copies of *Looking Backward* every week, over 160 Nationalist clubs were formed to crusade for the adoption of Bellamy's ideas.

❖❖❖❖❖❖

The inequalities of wealth described in Bellamy's coach scene reflected a political life in which many participated, but only a few benefited. The wealthiest 10 percent, who rode high on the coach, dominated national politics while untutored bosses held sway in governing cities. Except for token expressions of support, national political leaders ignored the cries of factory workers, immigrants, farmers, African-Americans, Native Americans, and other victims of the vast transformation of American industrial, urban, and agrarian life in the late nineteenth century. But as the century closed, middle-class Americans like Bellamy, as well as labor, agrarian, and ethnic leaders themselves, proposed various reforms. Their concern was never more appropriate than during the depression of the mid-1890s, a real-life social upheaval that mirrored the worst features and fears of Bellamy's fictional coach.

In this chapter, we will examine American politics at the national and local level from the end of Reconstruction to the 1890s, a period that for the most part bolstered the rich and neglected the corrosive human problems of urban industrial life. Then we will look at the growing social and political involvement of educated middle-class reformers who, despite their distaste for mass politics, now acted to effect change both locally and nationally. We will conclude with an account of the pivotal importance of the 1890s, highlighted by the Populist revolt, the depression of 1893 to 1897, and the election of 1896. In an age of strong national identity and pride, the events of the 1890s shook many comfortable citizens out of their apathy and began the reshaping of American politics.

POLITICS IN THE GILDED AGE

Co-authoring a satirical book in 1873, Mark Twain coined the expression "Gilded Age" to describe Grant's corrupt presidency. The phrase has come to characterize social and political life in the last quarter of the nineteenth century. Although politics was marred by corruption and politicians avoided fundamental issues in favor of a politics of mass entertainment, voter participation in national elections between 1876 and 1896 hovered at an all-time high of 73 to 82 percent of all registered voters.

Behind the glitter, two gradual changes occurred that would greatly affect twentieth-century politics. First was the development of a professional bureaucracy. In congressional committees and executive branch offices, elite specialists and experts emerged as a counterfoil to the perceived dangers of majority rule represented by high voter participation. Second, after a period of close elections and party stalemate, new issues and concerns fostered a party realignment in the 1890s.

Politics, Parties, Patronage, and Presidents

American government in the 1870s and 1880s clearly supported the interests of riders atop Bellamy's coach. Few nineteenth-century Americans would have agreed that the national government should tackle problems of poverty, unemployment, and trusts. They mistrusted organized power and believed that all would benefit from an economic life free of government interference. Political leaders favored governmental passivity that would allow industrial expansion and wealth-creation.

"One might search the whole list of Congress, Judiciary, and Executive during the twenty-five years 1870–95," wrote Henry Adams, "and find little but damaged reputation." Few eras of American government were so corrupt, and Adams was especially sensitive to the low quality of politics compared to the exalted morality of his grandfather John Quincy Adams and great-grandfather John Adams.

During the weak Johnson and Grant presidencies, Congress emerged as the dominant branch of government. The moral quality of congressional leadership was typified by senators James G. Blaine (Maine) and Roscoe Conkling (New York). Despite lying about having been paid off by railroads, Blaine was probably

Although this 1892 painting by John Klir shows the outcome of a "Lost Bet" in the election that year, note the ethnic, racial, and class diversity of the street crowds, momentarily united in enjoyment of the humiliated loser pulling his victorious opponent (and a wagon full of American flags). Will a more diverse America hold together? (Library of Congress)

the most popular Republican politician of the era. Charming, intelligent, witty, and able, he served twice as secretary of state and was a serious contender for the presidency in every election from 1876 to 1892. His foe, Conkling, dispensed lucrative jobs at the New York customhouse and spent most of his career bickering over patronage. In more than two decades in Congress, he never drafted a bill.

In 1879, a disgusted student of legislative politics, Woodrow Wilson, wrote: "No leaders, no principles; no principles, no parties." The two big parties diverged not over principles, but patronage. A British observer, Lord Bryce, concluded that the two parties, like two bottles, bore different labels, yet "each was empty."

Republican votes came from northeastern Yankee industrial interests, New England migrants, and Scandinavian Lutherans across the Upper Midwest. Democrats depended on southern whites, northern workers, and urban immigrants. Affiliation reflected interest in important cultural, religious, and ethnic questions. Because the Republican party had proved its willingness in the past to mobilize the power of the state to reshape society, people who wished to regulate moral and economic life were attracted to it. Catholics and various immigrant groups preferred the Democratic party because it opposed government efforts to regulate morals. Said one Chicago Democrat, "A Republican is a man who wants you t' go t' church every Sunday. A Democrat says if a man wants t' have a glass of beer on Sunday he can have it."

For a few years, Civil War and Reconstruction issues generated party differences. But after 1876, on national issues at least, party labels did indeed mark "empty" bottles. Because the two parties were evenly matched, it made sense to avoid controversial stands. In three of the five presidential elections between 1876 and 1892, a mere 1 percent of the vote separated the two major candidates. In 1880, James Garfield won by only 7,018 votes; in 1884, Grover Cleveland squeaked by Blaine by a popular vote margin of 48.5 to 48.2 percent. In two elections (1876 and 1888), the electoral vote winner had fewer popular votes. Only twice, each time for only two years, did one party control the White House and both houses of Congress. Although all the presidents in the era except Cleveland were Republicans, the Democrats controlled the House of Representatives in eight of the ten sessions of Congress between 1875 and 1895.

Gilded Age presidents were undistinguished and played a minor role in natural life. None of them—Hayes (1877–1881), Garfield (1881), Chester A. Arthur (1881–1885), Cleveland (1885–1889 and 1893–1897), and Benjamin Harrison (1889–1893)—served two consecutive terms. The only Democrat in the group, Cleveland differed little from the Republicans. When Cleveland violated the expectation that presidents should not initiate ideas by devoting his entire annual message in 1887 to a call for a lower tariff, Congress did nothing. Voters turned him out of office a year later.

National Issues

Four issues were important at the national level in the Gilded Age: the tariff, currency, civil service, and government regulation of railroads (see Chapter 18). In confronting these issues, legislators tried to serve both their own self-interest and the national interest of an efficient, productive economy.

The tariff was one issue where party, as well as regional attitudes toward the use of government power, made some difference. Republicans wanted government to support business interests and stood for a high tariff to protect businessmen, wage earners, and farmers from foreign competition. Democrats demanded a low tariff because "the government is best which governs least." But politicians accommodated local interests when it came to tariffs. Democratic senator Daniel Vorhees of Indiana explained: "I am a protectionist for every interest which I am sent here by my constituents to protect."

Tariff revisions were bewilderingly complex as legislators catered to these many special interests. Most tariffs included a jumble of higher and lower rates. The federal government depended on tariffs and excise taxes (primarily on tobacco and liquor) for most of its revenue, so there was little chance that the tariff would be abolished or substantially lowered, and surpluses produced by the tariff during the Gilded Age helped the parties finance patronage jobs and government programs.

The money question was even more complicated. During the Civil War, the federal government had circulated paper money (greenbacks) that could not be exchanged for gold or silver (specie). In the late 1860s and 1870s, politicians debated whether the United States should return to a metallic standard, which would allow paper money to be exchanged for specie. "Hard-money" advocates supported either withdrawing all paper money from circulation or making it convertible to specie. They opposed increasing the volume of money, fearing inflation. "Soft money" Greenbackers argued that there was not enough currency in circulation for an expanding economy and urged increasing the supply of paper money in order to raise farm prices and cut interest rates.

Hard-money interests had more clout. In 1873, Congress demonetized silver. In 1875, it passed the Specie Resumption Act, gradually retiring greenbacks from circulation and putting the nation firmly on the gold standard. But as large supplies of silver were mined in the West, pressure resumed for increasing the money supply by coining silver. Soft-money advocates pushed for the unlimited coinage of silver in addition to gold. In an 1878 compromise, the Treasury was required to buy between $2 and $4 million of silver each month and coin it as silver dollars. Despite this increase in the money supply, the period was not inflationary. Prices fell, disappointing supporters of soft money. They pushed for more silver, continuing the controversy into the 1890s.

The issue of civil service reform was, Henry Adams said, a "subject almost as dangerous in political conversation in Washington as slavery itself in the old days before the war." The worst feature of the spoils system was that parties financed themselves by assessing holders of patronage jobs, often as much as 1 percent of their annual salaries. Reformers, mostly genteel native white Protestants, demanded competitive examinations to create an honest and professional civil service—but also one that would bar immigrants and their urban political machine bosses from the spoils of office.

Most Americans expected their presidents to reward the faithful with government jobs, but Garfield's assassination by a crazed office-seeker created a public backlash. "My God! Chet Arthur in the White House!" someone exclaimed, knowing that the new president was closely identified with Conkling's corrupt machine. Arthur surprised doubters by being a capable and dignified president, responsive to growing demands for civil service reform. Congress found itself forced into passing the Pendleton Act of 1883, mandating merit examinations for about one-tenth of federal offices. Gradually, more bureaucrats fell under its coverage, but parties became no more honest. As campaign contributions from government employees dried up, parties turned to corporate contributions.

The Lure of Local Politics

The fact that the major parties did not disagree substantially on issues like money and civil service does not mean that nineteenth-century Americans found politics dull. Far more eligible voters turned out in the late nineteenth century than at any time since. The 78.5 percent average turnout to vote for president in the 1880s contrasts sharply with the near 50 percent of eligible Americans who vote today.

American men were drawn to the polls in part by the hoopla, but also by local issues. Iowa farmers turned out to vote for state representatives who favored curbing the railroads. But emotional issues of race, religion, nationality, and alcohol often overrode economic self-interest. Voters expressed strong interest in temperance, anti-Catholicism, compulsory school attendance and Sunday laws, aid to parochial schools, racial issues, immigration restriction, and "bloody shirt" reminders of the Civil War.

The new urban immigrants played a large role in stimulating political participation. As traditional elites, usually native-born, left local government for more lucrative and higher-status business careers, city bosses stepped in. Their control rested on their ability to deliver the immigrant vote, which they secured by operating informal welfare systems. Bosses handed out jobs and money for rent, fuel, and bail, and they provided a personal touch in a strange environment.

Party leaders also won votes by making politics exciting. The parades, rallies, and oratory of nineteenth-century campaigns generated excitement even when substantive issues were not at stake. In the election of 1884, for example, emotions ran high over the moral lapses of the opposing candidates—Blaine's corruption and Cleveland's illegitimate child. Cleveland won in part because an unwise Republican clergyman called the Democrats the party of "rum, Romanism, and rebellion," ensuring Cleveland an outpouring of Catholic support in crucial New York.

Local and ethnocultural issues rather than national and economic questions explained party affiliation and mobilized voters. Spirited local contests occurred, particularly over prohibition. Many Americans considered drinking a serious social problem. Annual consumption of brewery beer had risen from 2.7 gallons per capita in 1850 to 17.9 in 1880. In one city, saloons outnumbered churches 31 to 1. Such statistics shocked those who believed that drinking would destroy character, corrupt politics, and cause poverty, crime, and unrestrained sexuality. Because they were often the targets of violent drunken men, women especially supported temperance. Rather than try to persuade individuals to give up drink, as the pre-Civil War temperance movement had done, many now sought to ban drinking by putting the question of prohibition on the ballot.

Emotional conflicts boiled in the 1880s at the state level over issues like education. Irish Catholics in New York sought political support for their parochial schools. In Iowa, Illinois, and Wisconsin, however, Republicans sponsored laws mandating that children attend "some public or private day school" where instruction was in English. These laws aimed to undermine parochial schools, which taught in the language of the immigrants. In Iowa, where a state prohibition law also passed, the Republican slogan was "A schoolhouse on every hill, and no saloon in the valley." Local Republicans bragged that "Iowa will go Democratic when hell goes Methodist," and indeed they won. But in Wisconsin, a law for compulsory school attendance was so strongly anti-Catholic that it backfired. Many voters, disillusioned with Republican moralism, shifted to the Democratic party.

MIDDLE-CLASS REFORM

Most middle-class Americans avoided reformist politics. But urban corruption and labor violence of the 1880s frightened many out of their aversion to politics.

Frances Willard and the Women's Christian Temperance Union (WCTU) is an example. As president of the WCTU from 1879 until 1898, Willard headed the largest women's organization in the country. Most WCTU members were churchgoing, white Protestant women who believed drunkenness caused poverty and family violence. But after 1886 the WCTU reversed its position, attributing drunkenness to poverty, unemployment, and bad labor conditions. Willard joined the Knights of Labor in 1887 and by the 1890s influenced the WCTU to extend its programs to alleviate the problems of workers, particularly women and children.

The Gospel of Wealth

Willard called herself a Christian socialist because she believed in applying the ethical principles of Jesus to economic life. For her and many other educated middle-class reformers, Christianity called for a cooperative social order that would reduce inequalities of wealth. But for most Gilded Age Americans, Christianity supported the competitive individualistic ethic. Philadelphia Baptist preacher Russell Conwell's famous sermon "Acres of Diamonds," delivered 6,000 times to an estimated 13 million listeners, praised riches as a sure sign of "godliness" and stressed the power of money to "do good."

Andrew Carnegie expressed the ethic most clearly. In an article, "The Gospel of Wealth" (1889), Carnegie celebrated competition for producing better goods at lower prices. The concentration of wealth in a few hands, he concluded, was "not only beneficial but essential to the future of the race." The fittest would bring order and efficiency out of the chaos of rapid industrialization. Carnegie's defense of the new economic order found as many supporters as Bellamy's *Looking Backward*. Partly this was because Carnegie insisted that the rich must spend some of their wealth to benefit their "poorer brethren." Carnegie built hundreds of libraries and later promoted world peace.

Carnegie's ideas reflected an ideology known as social Darwinism, based on the work of naturalist Charles Darwin, whose *Origin of Species* was published in 1859. Darwin had concluded that plant and animal species evolved through natural selection. Some managed to adapt to their environment and survived; others failed to adapt and perished. Herbert Spencer, an English social philosopher, applied this "survival of the fittest" notion to human society. Progress, Spencer said, resulted from relentless competition in which the weak were eliminated and the strong climbed to the top. Spencer warned against any interference in the economic world by tampering with the natural laws of selection.

Spencer's American followers, like Carnegie and Yale economist William Graham Sumner, insisted that poverty resulted from the struggle for existence. It was "absurd," Sumner wrote, to pass laws permitting society's "worst members" to survive.

The scientific vocabulary of social Darwinism injected scientific rationality into what often seemed a baffling economic order. Sumner and Spencer argued that underlying social laws, like those of the natural world, dictated economic affairs. Social Darwinists also believed in the superiority of the Anglo-Saxon race, which they maintained had reached the highest stage of evolution. Their theories were used to justify race supremacy and imperialism, as well as the monopolistic efforts of American businessmen.

Others questioned social Darwinism. Brooks Adams, Henry's brother, wrote that social philosophers like Spencer and Sumner were "hired by the comfortable classes to prove that everything was all right."

Reform Darwinism and Pragmatism

A number of intellectual reformers directly challenged the gloomy social Darwinian notion that nothing could be done to alleviate poverty and injustice.

With roots in antebellum abolitionism, women's rights, and other crusades for social justice, men like Wendell Phillips, Frederick Douglass, and Franklin Sanborn and women like Elizabeth Cady Stanton and Susan B. Anthony transferred their reform fervor to postbellum issues. Sanborn, for example, an Emersonian transcendentalist, founded the American Social Science Association in 1865 to "treat wisely the great social problems of the day." As the Massachusetts inspector of charities in the 1880s, he became known as the "leading social worker of his day."

Reformer Henry George, who was not a social scientist, nevertheless observed that wherever the highest degree of "material progress" had been realized, "we find the deepest poverty." George's book, *Progress and Poverty* (1879), was an early statement of the contradictions of American life. With Bellamy's *Looking Backward,* it was the most influential book of the age, selling two million copies by 1905. George admitted that economic growth had produced wonders, but pointed out the social costs and the loss of Christian values. His remedy was to break up landholding monopolists who profited from the increasing value of their land, which they rented to those who actually did the work. He proposed a "single tax" on the unearned increases in land value.

George's solution may seem simplistic, but his religious tone and optimistic faith in the capacity of humans to effect change appealed to many middle-class intellectuals. Some went further. Sociologist Lester Frank Ward and economist Richard T. Ely both found examples of cooperation in nature and demonstrated that competition and laissez-faire had proved both wasteful and inhumane. These reform Darwinists urged an economic order marked by cooperation and regulation.

Two pragmatists, John Dewey and William James, established a philosophical foundation for reform. James, a professor at Harvard, argued that while environment was important, so was human will. "What is the 'cash value' of a thought, idea, or belief?" James asked. What was its result? "The ultimate test for us of what a truth means," he suggested, was in the consequences of a particular idea in "the conduct it dictates."

James and young social scientists like Ward and Ely gathered statistics documenting social wrongs and rejected social determinism. They argued that the application of intelligence and human will could change the "survival of the fittest" into the "fitting of as many as possible to survive." Their position encouraged educators, economists, and reformers of every stripe, giving them an intellectual justification to struggle against misery and inequalities of wealth.

Settlements and Social Gospel

Jane Addams saw the gap between progress and poverty in the winter of 1893. She had long been aware that life in big cities for working-class families was bitter and hard. Born in rural Illinois, Addams founded Hull House in Chicago in 1889 "to aid in the solution of the social and industrial problems which are engendered by the modern conditions of life in a great city." Young Wellesley literature professor Vida Scudder and six other Smith graduates formed an organization of college women, also in 1889, to work in settlement houses.

Middle-class activists like Addams and Scudder worried about social conditions, particularly the degradation of life and labor in America's cities, factories, and farms. Most of them drew upon the ethical teachings of Jesus for inspiration

The young Jane Addams was one of the college-educated women who chose to remain unmarried and pursue a career as an "urban housekeeper" and social reformer, serving immigrant families in the Chicago neighborhood near her Hull House. (The University of Illinois at Chicago, The University Library, Jane Addams Memorial Collection)

in solving social problems. They preferred a society marked by cooperation rather than competition—where, as they liked to say, people were guided by the "golden rule rather than the rule of gold." Some preferred to put their goals in more secular terms; they spoke of radically transforming American society. Most, however, worked within existing institutions. As middle-class intellectuals and professionals, they tended to stress an educational approach to problems. But they were also practical, seeking tangible improvements by running for public office, crusading for legislation, mediating labor disputes, and living among the poor people they helped.

The settlement house movement typified 1890s middle-class reformers' blend of idealism and practicality. The primary purpose of settlement houses was to help immigrant families, especially women, adapt Old World rural styles of childrearing and housekeeping to American urban life. They launched day nurseries, kindergartens, and boarding rooms for working women; they offered classes in sewing, cooking, nutrition, health care, and English; and they tried to keep young people out of saloons by organizing sports clubs and coffeehouses.

A second purpose of the settlement house movement was to give college-educated women meaningful work at a time when they faced professional barriers and to allow them to preserve the strong feelings of sisterhood they had experienced at college. A third goal was to gather data exposing social misery in order to spur legislative action—developing city building codes for tenements, abolishing child labor, and improving factory safety. Hull House, Addams said, was intended in part "to investigate and improve the conditions in the industrial districts of Chicago."

The settlement house movement nourished the new discipline of sociology, first taught in divinity schools. Many organizations were founded to blend Christian belief and academic study in an attempt to change society. One was the American Institute of Christian Sociology, founded in 1893 by Josiah Strong, a Congregational minister, and economist Richard T. Ely.

A highly traditional Christianity was preached in the cities by Dwight Moody, who led hundreds of urban revivals in the 1870s. The revivals appealed to lower-class rural folk who were either drawn to the city by their hopes or pushed there by economic ruin. Supported by businessmen who felt that religion would make workers and immigrants more docile, revivalists battled sin through individual conversion. The revivals helped to nearly double Protestant church membership in the last two decades of the century. Although some urban workers drifted into socialism, most remained conventionally religious.

Unlike Moody, many Protestant ministers embraced the Social Gospel movement of the 1890s, which tied salvation to social betterment. Like the settlement house workers, these religious leaders sought to make Christianity relevant to urban problems. Congregational minister Washington Gladden advocated collective bargaining and corporate profit sharing. A young Baptist minister in the notorious Hell's Kitchen area of New York City, Walter Rauschenbusch, raised an even louder voice. Often called on to conduct funeral services for children killed by the airless, diseased tenements and sweatshops, Rauschenbusch scathingly attacked the selfishness of capitalism and church ignorance of socioeconomic issues. His progressive ideas for social justice and a welfare state were later published in two landmark books, *Christianity and the Social Crisis* (1907) and *Christianizing the Social Order* (1912).

Perhaps the most influential book promoting social Christianity was a best-selling novel *In His Steps,* published in 1897 by Charles Sheldon. The novel portrayed the dramatic changes made possible by a few community leaders who resolved to base all their actions on a single question: "What would Jesus do?" For a minister, this meant seeking to "bridge the chasm between the church and labor." For the idle rich, it meant settlement house work and reforming prostitutes. For landlords and factory owners, it meant improving the living and working conditions of tenants and laborers. Although streaked with naive sentimentality characteristic of much of the Social Gospel, Sheldon's novel prepared thousands of influential middle-class Americans for progressive civic leadership after 1900.

Reforming the City

No late-nineteenth-century institution needed reforming more than urban government. A Philadelphia committee pointed to years of "inefficiency, waste, badly paved and filthy streets, unwholesome and offensive water, and slovenly and costly management." New York and Chicago were even worse.

Rapid urban growth swamped city leaders with new demands for service. As city governments struggled, they raised taxes and incurred vast debts. All this, coupled with the influx of new immigrants, bred graft and "bossism."

The rise of the boss was directly connected to urban growth. Bosses awarded utility franchises and construction contracts to local businesses in return for kickbacks while new immigrant voters received jobs and welfare in return for their votes. Bosses tipped off friendly real estate men about projected city improvements and received favors from the owners of saloons, brothels, and gambling clubs in return for help with police protection, bail, and influence with judges. These institutions were vital to the urban economy and played an important role in easing the immigrants' way into American life. For many young women, prostitution meant economic survival. For men, the saloon was the center of social life and a source of cheap meals and job leads.

Bossism deeply offended middle-class urban reformers. "Goo-goos" (as bosses called advocates of "good government") opposed not only graft and vice, but also the perversion of democracy by the exploitation of ignorant immigrants. The immigrants, said one, "follow blindly leaders of their own race, are not moved by discussion, and exercise no judgment of their own"—and so were "not fit for the suffrage."

Urban reformers' programs were similar in most cities. They not only worked for the "Americanization" of immigrants in public schools (and opposed parochial schooling), but also formed voters' leagues to discuss the failings of municipal government. They delighted in spectacularly exposing electoral irregularities and large-scale graft. These discoveries led to strident calls for replacing the mayor, often an Irish Catholic, with an Anglo-Saxon Protestant reformer.

Politics colored every reform issue. Many Anglo-Saxon men favored prohibition partly to remove ethnic saloon owner influence from politics and supported woman suffrage partly to gain a middle-class political advantage against male immigrant voters. Most urban reformers disdained the "city proletariat mob." They proposed to replace the bosses with expert city managers, who would bring honest professionalism to city government. They hoped to make government cheaper and thereby lower taxes. One effect of their emphasis on cost efficiency was to cut services to the poor. Another was to disfranchise working-class and ethnic groups, whose political participation depended on the old ward-boss system.

Not all urban reformers were elitist. Samuel Jones, for example, both opposed bossism and passionately advocated political participation by urban immigrants. He himself had begun as a poor immigrant in the Pennsylvania oil fields but worked his way up to the ownership of several oil fields and a factory in Toledo, Ohio. In 1894 he decided to "apply the Golden Rule as a rule of conduct" in his factory, with an eight-hour day, a $2 minimum daily wage (50 to 75 cents higher than the local average for ten hours), cooperative insurance, and a Christmas dividend. He hired social outcasts, offered employees cheap lunches and recreational facilities, and established Golden Rule Hall where social visionaries could speak. In 1897 he was elected to the first of an unprecedented four terms as mayor. A maverick Republican who antagonized prominent citizens, Jones advocated municipal ownership of utilities, public works jobs and housing for the unemployed, more civic parks and playgrounds, and free vocational education and kindergartens (few of which were implemented). A pacifist, he took away policemen's weapons. In police court, he regularly dismissed most cases of petty theft and drunkenness on grounds that the accused were victims of social injustice, and he usually released prostitutes after fining every man in the room ten cents—and himself a dollar—for condoning prostitution. Crime in notoriously sinful Toledo fell. When "Golden Rule" Jones died in 1904, nearly 55,000 tearful people filed past his coffin.

The Struggle for Woman Suffrage

Women served, in Jane Addams's phrase, as "urban housekeepers" in the settlement house and good government movements, which reflected the tension many women felt between their public and private lives, between their obligations to self, family, and society. This tension was seldom expressed openly. A few women writers, however, began to vent the frustrations of middle-class domestic life. In her novel *The Awakening* (1899), Kate Chopin told the story of a young woman who, in discovering her own sexuality and life's possibilities beyond being a "mother-woman," defied conventional expectations of a woman's role. Her sexual affair and eventual suicide prompted a St. Louis newspaper to label the novel "poison."

Some middle-class women, Addams and Scudder, for example, avoided marriage, preferring the supportive relationships found in the female settlement house community. A few women boldly advocated free love or, less openly, formed lesbian relationships. Although most preferred traditional marriages and chose not to work outside the home, the generation of women that came of age in the 1890s married less—and later—than any other in American history.

One way women reconciled the conflicting pressures between their private and public lives, and deflected male criticism, was to see their work as maternal. Addams called Hull House the "great mother breast of our common humanity." Frances Willard told Susan B. Anthony in 1898 that "government is only housekeeping on the broadest scale," a job men had botched, requiring women's saving participation. One of the leading labor organizers was "Mother" Jones, and the fiery feminist anarchist Emma Goldman titled her monthly journal *Mother Earth.* By using nurturant language to describe their work, women furthered the very arguments used against them. Many, of course, remained economically dependent on men, and all women still lacked the essential rights of citizenship. How could they be municipal housekeepers if they could not even vote?

After the Seneca Falls Convention in 1848, women's civil and political rights advanced very slowly. Although several western states gave women the vote in municipal and school board elections, before 1890 only the territory of Wyoming (1869) granted full political equality. Colorado, Utah, and Idaho enfranchised women in the 1890s, but no other states granted suffrage until 1910. This slow pace resulted in part from an antisuffrage movement led by an odd combination of ministers, saloon interests, and men threatened in various ways by women's voting rights. "Equal suffrage," said a Texas senator, "is a repudiation of manhood."

In the 1890s, leading suffragists reappraised the situation. The two wings of the women's rights movement, split since 1869, combined in 1890 as the National American Woman Suffrage Association (NAWSA). Although Elizabeth Cady Stanton and Susan B. Anthony continued to head the association, both were in their seventies. Effective leadership passed to younger, more moderate women who, unlike Stanton and Anthony, concentrated on the single issue of the vote.

Changing leadership meant a shift in the arguments for the suffrage. Since 1848, suffragists had argued primarily from the principle of "our republican idea, individual citizenship." But the younger generation shifted to three expedient arguments. The first was that women needed the vote to pass self-protection laws to guard against rapists and unsafe industrial work. The second argument, Addams's notion of urban housekeeping, pointed out that political enfranchisement would further women's role in cleaning up the immoral cities and their corrupt politics.

The third expedient argument reflected urban middle-class reformers' prejudice against non-Protestant immigrants. Machine bosses saw to it that immigrant men got the vote. Suffragists argued that educated, native-born American women should get the vote to counteract the undesirable influence of male immigrants. In a speech in Iowa in 1894, Carrie Chapman Catt, who would succeed Anthony as president of NAWSA in 1900, argued that the "Government is menaced with great danger . . . in the votes possessed by the males in the slums of the cities," a danger that could be averted only by cutting off that vote and giving it instead to women. In the new century, under the leadership of women like Catt, suffrage would finally be secured.

THE PIVOTAL 1890s

Americans mistakenly think of the last decade of the nineteenth century as the "gay nineties," symbolized by mustached baseball players and sporty Gibson girls. The 1890s was indeed a decade of sports and leisure, urban electrification, and the enormous wealth of the few. But for many more Americans, it was also a decade of dark tenements, grinding work or desperate unemployment, and poverty. The early 1890s meant Populism and protesting farmers; Wounded Knee and the "second great removal" of Native Americans; lynchings, disfranchisement, and the "nadir of black life;" and the "new immigration," a changing workplace, and devastating labor defeats at Coeur d'Alene, Homestead, and Pullman.

The 1890s were years of contrasts and crises. Supreme Court Justice John Harlan saw a "deep feeling of unrest" everywhere among people worrying that the nation was in "real danger from . . . the slavery that would result from aggregations of capital in the hands of a few." Populist "Sockless" Jerry Simpson simply saw a struggle between "the robbers and the robbed."

Although Simpson was wrong about the absence of a middle ground, the gap was indeed huge between Kansas orator Mary E. Lease, who in 1890 said, "What you farmers need to do is to raise less corn, and more Hell," and the wealthy Indianapolis woman who told her husband, "I'm going to Europe and spend my money before these crazy people take it." The pivotal nature of the 1890s hinged on this feeling of polarizing unrest and upheaval as the nation underwent the traumas of change from a rural to an urban society. The new immigration from Europe and the northward, westward, and cityward internal migrations of blacks and farmers added to the "great danger" against which Catt warned. The depression of 1893 widened the rich-poor gap and accelerated demands for reform. The bureaucracy began to adapt to the needs of governing a complex specialized society, and Congress slowly abandoned laissez-faire to confront national problems.

Republican Legislation in the Early 1890s

Harrison's election in 1888 was accompanied by Republican control of both houses of Congress. The Republicans moved forward in the first six months of 1890 with legislation in five areas: pensions for Civil War veterans and their dependents, trusts, the tariff, the money question, and rights for blacks. A bill providing generous support of $160 million a year for Union veterans and their dependents sailed through Congress.

The Sherman Anti-Trust Act passed with only one nay vote. It declared illegal "every contract, combination . . . or conspiracy in restraint of trade or commerce." Although the Sherman Act was vague and not really intended to break up big corporations, it was an initial attempt to restrain large business combinations. But in *United States* v. *E. C. Knight* (1895), the Supreme Court ruled that the American Sugar Refining Company, which controlled more than 90 percent of the nation's sugar-refining capacity, was not in violation of the Sherman Act.

A tariff bill introduced in 1890 by Ohio Republican William McKinley stirred more controversy. McKinley's bill raised tariffs higher than ever. Despite heated opposition from agrarian interests, whose products were generally not protected, the bill passed the House and, after nearly 500 amendments, also the Senate.

Silver was trickier. Recognizing the appeal of free silver to agrarian debtors and the new Populist party, Republican leaders feared their party might be destroyed by the issue. Senator Sherman proposed a compromise that momentarily satisfied almost everyone. The Sherman Silver Purchase Act ordered the Treasury to buy 4.5 million ounces of silver monthly and to issue Treasury notes for it. Silverites were pleased by the proposed increase in the money supply. Opponents felt they had averted the worst—free coinage of silver. The gold standard still stood.

Republicans were also prepared to confront violations of the voting rights of southern blacks in 1890. Political considerations paralleled moral ones. Since 1877, the South had become a Democratic stronghold, where party victories could be traced to fraud and intimidation of black Republican voters. "To be a Republican . . . in the South," said one Georgian, "is to be a foolish martyr." Republican legislation, then, would honor old commitments to the freedmen and improve party fortunes in the South. An elections bill, proposed by Massachusetts Senator Henry Cabot Lodge, tried to ensure African-American voter registration and fair elections. A storm of Democratic disapproval arose. Ex-president Cleveland called it a "dark blow at the freedom of the ballot," and the Mobile *Daily Register* claimed that it "would deluge the South in blood." Senate Democrats delayed action with a filibuster.

To pass the McKinley Tariff, Republican leaders bargained away the elections bill, ending major-party efforts to protect African-American voting rights in the South until the 1960s. In a second setback for black southerners, the Senate defeated a bill to provide federal aid to schools in the South, mostly black, that did not receive a share of local and state funds. These two failed measures were the last gasp of the Republican party's commitment to Reconstruction ideals. "The plain truth is," said the New York *Herald*, "the North has got tired of the negro," foreshadowing a similar abandonment in the 1980s and 1990s.

The legislative efforts of the summer of 1890, impressive by nineteenth-century standards, fell far short of solving the nation's problems. Trusts grew more rapidly after the Sherman Act than before. Union veterans were pleased by their pensions, but southerners were incensed that Confederate veterans were left out. Others, seeing the pension measure as extravagant, labeled the 51st Congress the "billion-dollar Congress." Despite efforts to please farmers, many still viewed tariff protection as a benefit primarily for eastern manufacturers. Farm prices continued to slide, and gold and silver advocates were only momentarily silenced. African-American rights were put off to another time. Polarizing inequalities of wealth remained. Nor did Republican legislative activism lead the Republicans to a "permanent tenure of power," as party leaders had hoped. Voters abandoned the GOP in droves in the 1890 congressional elections, dropping the Republican contingent in the House from 168 to 88.

Two years later, Cleveland won a presidential rematch with Harrison. "The lessons of paternalism ought to be unlearned," he said in his inaugural address, "and the better lesson taught that while the people should . . . support their government, its functions do not include the support of the people."

The Depression of 1893

Cleveland's philosophy soon faced a difficult test. No sooner had he taken office than began one of the worst depressions ever to grip the American economy, lasting from 1893 to 1897. Its severity was heightened by the growth of a national economy and economic interdependence. The depression started in Europe and spread to the United States as overseas buyers cut back on purchases of American products. Shrinking markets abroad soon crippled American manufacturing. Foreign investors, worried about the stability of American currency, dumped some $300 million of their securities in the United States. As gold left the country to pay for these securities, the nation's money supply declined. At the same time, falling prices hurt farmers, many of whom discovered that it cost more to raise their crops and livestock than they could make in the market. Workers fared no better: Wages fell faster than the price of food and rent.

The collapse in 1893 was also caused by serious overextensions of the domestic economy, especially in railroad construction. Farmers, troubled by falling prices, planted more, hoping that the market would pick up. As the realization of overextension spread, confidence faltered, and then gave way to financial panic. When Wall Street crashed early in 1893, investors frantically sold their shares, companies plunged into bankruptcy, and disaster spread. People rushed to exchange paper notes for gold, reducing gold reserves and confidence in the economy even further. Banks called in loans, which by the end of the year led to 16,000 business bankruptcies and 500 bank failures.

The capital crunch and the diminished buying power of rural and small-town Americans (still half the population) forced massive factory closings. Within a year, an estimated three million Americans—20 percent of the work force—lost jobs. People fearfully watched tramps going from city to city, looking for work.

As in Bellamy's coach image, the misery of the many was not shared by the few, which only increased discontent. While unemployed men foraged in garbage dumps, the wealthy gave lavish parties sometimes costing $100,000. While poor families shivered in poorly heated tenements, the very rich built million-dollar summer resorts at Newport, Rhode Island, or grand mansions on New York's Fifth Avenue. While immigrants walked or rode streetcars, wealthy men luxuriated on huge pleasure yachts.

The depression of 1893 accentuated contrasts between rich and poor. While well-to-do children enjoyed the giant Ferris wheel and other midway attractions at the Chicago World's Columbian Exposition, slum children played in filthy streets nearby. (Library of Congress)

Nowhere were these inequalities more apparent than in Chicago during the World's Columbian Exposition, which opened on May 1, 1893, five days before a plummeting stock market began the depression. The Chicago World's Fair showed off, as President Cleveland said in an opening-day speech, the "stupendous results of American enterprise." When he pressed an ivory telegraph key, he started electric current that unfurled flags, spouted water through gigantic fountains, lit 10,000 electric lights, and powered huge steam engines. For six months, some 27 million visitors strolled around the White City, admiring its wide lagoons, its neoclassical buildings, and its exhibit halls filled with inventions. Built at a cost of $31 million, the fair celebrated the marvelous accomplishments of American enterprise and of a "City Beautiful" movement to make cities more livable.

But in immigrant wards less than a mile away, people drank contaminated water, crowded into packed tenements, and looked in vain for jobs. "If Christ came to Chicago," a British journalist, W. T. Stead, wrote in 1894, this would be "one of the last precincts into which we should care to take Him." Stead's book showed readers the "ugly sight" of corruption, poverty, and wasted lives in a city with 200 millionaires and 200,000 unemployed men.

Despite the magnitude of despair during the depression, national politicians and leaders were reluctant to respond. Only mass demonstrations forced city authorities to provide soup kitchens and places for the homeless to sleep. When an army of unemployed led by Jacob Coxey marched on Washington in the spring of 1894 to press for public work relief, its leaders were arrested for walking on the Capitol grass. Cleveland's reputation for callousness worsened later that summer when he sent federal troops to Chicago to crush the Pullman strike.

The president focused on tariff reform and repeal of the Silver Purchase Act, which he blamed for the depression. Although repeal was ultimately necessary to establish business confidence, in the short run Cleveland only worsened the financial crisis, highlighted the silver panacea, and hurt conservative Democrats. With workers, farmers, and wealthy silver miners alienated, in the midterm elections of

1894 voters abandoned the Democrats in droves. Populists and Republicans had high hopes for 1896.

The Crucial Election of 1896

The campaign of 1896, waged during the depression and featuring a climactic battle over the currency, was one of the most critical in American history. Although Cleveland was in disgrace for ignoring depression woes, few leaders in either major party thought the federal government was responsible for alleviating the suffering of the people. But the disadvantaged, unskilled, and unemployed everywhere wondered where relief might be found. Would either major party respond to the pressing human needs of the depression? Would the People's party set a new national agenda for politics? These questions were raised and largely resolved in the election of 1896.

As the election approached, Populist leaders emphasized the silver issue and debated whether to fuse with one of the major parties by agreeing on a joint ticket, which meant abandoning much of the Populist platform. Influenced by silver mine owners, many Populists became convinced that they must make a single-issue commitment to the free and unlimited coinage of silver at the ratio of 16 to 1.

In the throes of the depression in the mid-1890s, silver took on enormous importance as the symbol of the many grievances of downtrodden Americans. Popular literature captured the rural, moral dimensions of the silver movement. L. Frank Baum's *The Wonderful Wizard of Oz* (1900) was a free-silver allegory of rural values (Kansas, Auntie Em, the uneducated but wise scarecrow, and the good-hearted tin woodsman) and Populist policies (the wicked witch of the East and the magical silver shoes in harmony with the yellow brick road in "Oz"—ounces).

The Republicans nominated William McKinley. As a congressman and governor of Ohio, McKinley was happily identified with the high protective tariff that bore his name. Citing the familiar argument that prosperity depended on the gold standard and protection, Republicans blamed the depression on Cleveland's attempt to lower the tariff.

The excitement of the Democratic convention in July contrasted with the staid, smoothly organized Republican gathering. Cleveland had already been repudiated by his party, as state after state elected convention delegates pledged to silver. Gold Democrats, however, had enough power to wage a close battle for the platform plank on money. The Democrats' surprise nominee was an ardent young silverite, William Jennings Bryan, a 36-year-old congressman from Nebraska. Few saw him as presidential material, but Bryan arranged to give the closing argument for a silver plank himself. His dramatic speech swept the convention for silver and ensured his nomination. Concluding one of the most famous political speeches in American history, Bryan attacked the "goldbugs:"

> Having behind us the producing masses of this nation ... and toilers everywhere, we will answer their demand for a gold standard by saying to them: "You shall not press down upon the brow of labor this crown of thorns, you shall not crucify mankind upon a cross of gold."

Bryan stretched out his arms as if on a cross, and the convention exploded.

William Jennings Bryan, surprise
nominee at the 1896 Democratic
Convention, was a vigorous proponent
of the "cause of humanity." His
nomination threw the country into a
frenzy of fear and the Populist party
into a fatal decision over "fusion."
(Library of Congress)

Populist strategy lay in shambles when the Democrats named a silver candidate. Some party leaders favored fusion with the Democratic ticket (whose vice-presidential nominee was a goldbug), but antifusionists were outraged. Unwisely, the Populists nominated Bryan with Georgia Populist Tom Watson for vice president. Running on competing silverite slates damaged Bryan's chances.

During the campaign, McKinley stayed home in Canton, Ohio, where 750,000 admirers came to visit him, brought by low excursion rates offered by the railroads. The Republicans made an unprecedented effort to reach voters through a highly sophisticated mass-media campaign, heavily financed by major corporations. Party leaders hired thousands of speakers and distributed over 200 million pamphlets in 14 languages to a voting population of 15 million, all advertising McKinley as the "advance agent of prosperity."

McKinley appealed not only to the business classes but also to unemployed workers, to whom he promised a "full dinner pail." Free silver, he warned, would cause inflation and more economic disaster. Recovery depended not on money, but on tariff reform to stimulate industry and provide jobs.

Bryan took his case to the people. Three million people in 27 states heard him speak as he traveled over 18,000 miles, giving as many as 30 speeches a day. Bryan's message was simple: Prosperity required free coinage of silver. Government should attend to the needs of the producing classes rather than the vested interests. But his rhetoric favored rural toilers. "The great cities rest upon our broad and fertile prairies," he had said in the "Cross of Gold" speech. Urban workers were not inspired by this rhetoric, nor were immigrants by Bryan's prairie moralizing.

To influential easterners, the brash young Nebraskan represented a threat. Theodore Roosevelt wrote that "Bryan's election would be a great calamity." One newspaper editor said of Bryan that he was just like Nebraska's Platte River: "six inches deep and six miles wide at the mouth."

Voters turned out in record numbers. In key states like Illinois, Indiana, and Ohio, 95 percent of those eligible to vote went to the polls. McKinley won 271 electoral votes to Bryan's 176. Millionaire Mark Hanna jubilantly wired McKinley: "God's in his heaven, all's right with the world." Bryan had been defeated by the largest popular majority since Grant trounced Greeley in 1872.

Although Bryan won over six million votes (47 percent of the total), more than any previous Democratic winner, he failed to carry the Midwest or the urban middle classes and industrial masses, who had little confidence that the Democrats could stimulate economic growth or cope with industrialism. McKinley's promise of a "full dinner pail" was more convincing. Northern laborers feared that inflation would leave them even poorer—that prices and rents would rise faster than their wages. Catholic immigrants distrusted Populist Protestantism. In the Great Lakes states, prosperous farmers felt less discontent than farmers elsewhere. But chance also played a part in Bryan's defeat. Bad wheat harvests in India, Australia, and Argentina drove up world grain prices, and many of the complaints of American farmers evaporated.

The New Shape of American Politics

The landslide Republican victory broke the stalemate in post-Civil War American politics. Republicans dropped their identification with the politics of piety and strengthened their image as the party of prosperity and national greatness, which gave them a party dominance that lasted until the 1930s. The Democrats, under Bryan's leadership until 1912, put on the mantle of populist moralism, but were largely reduced to a sectional party, reflecting narrow southern views on money, race, and national power. The 1896 election demonstrated that the Northeast and Great Lakes states had acquired so many immigrants that they now controlled the nation's political destiny. The demoralized Populists disappeared. Within the next 20 years, however, many Populist issues were coopted by major-party politicians.

Another result of the election of 1896 was a change in political participation. Because the Republicans were so dominant outside of the South and Democrats so powerful in the South, few states had vigorous two-party political battles and less reason to mobilize large numbers of voters. With results so often a foregone conclusion, voters had little motivation to cast a ballot. Many black voters in the South, moreover, were disfranchised, and middle-class good government reformers discouraged the high turnouts achieved by urban party bosses. The tremendous rate of political participation that had characterized the nineteenth century since the Jackson era gradually declined. In the twentieth century, political involvement among poorer Americans lessened considerably, a phenomenon unique among western industrial countries.

McKinley had promised that Republican rule meant prosperity, and as soon as he took office the economy recovered. Discoveries of gold in the Yukon and the Alaskan Klondike increased the money supply, ending the silver mania until the next great depression in the early 1930s. Industrial production returned to full capacity. Touring the Midwest in 1898, McKinley spoke to cheering crowds about the hopeful economic picture.

McKinley's election marked not only the return of economic health, but also the emergence of the executive as the preeminent focus of the American political system. Just as McKinley's campaign set the pattern for the extravagant efforts to win office that have dominated modern times, his conduct as president foreshadowed the twentieth-century presidency. McKinley rejected traditional views of the president as the passive executor of laws, instead playing an active role in dealing with Congress and the press. His frequent trips away from Washington showed an increasing regard for public opinion. Some historians see McKinley as the first modern president for his emphasis on the role of the chief executive in contributing to industrial growth and national power. As we shall see in Chapter 20, he began the transformation of the presidency into a potent force, not only in domestic life, but in world affairs as well.

❦❦❦❦❦

Conclusion

Looking Forward

This chapter began with Edward Bellamy's imaginary look backward from the year 2000 at the grim economic realities and unresponsive politics of American life in the late nineteenth century. McKinley's triumph in 1896 indicated that in a decade marked by depression, Populist revolt, and cries for action to close the inequalities of wealth—represented by Bellamy's coach—the established order remained intact and politics remained as unresponsive as ever. Calls for change did not necessarily lead to change. But in the areas of personal action and the philosophical bases for social change, intellectual middle-class reformers like Edward Bellamy, Henry George, William James, Jane Addams, "Golden Rule" Jones, and many others were showing the way to progressive reforms in the new century. More Americans were able to look forward to the kind of cooperative, caring, and cleaner world envisioned in Bellamy's utopian novel.

As 1900 approached, people took a predictably intense interest in what the new century would be like. Henry Adams, still the pessimist, saw an ominous future, predicting the explosive and ultimately destructive energy of unrestrained industrial development, symbolized by the "dynamo" and other engines of American power. Such forces, he warned, would overwhelm the gentler, moral forces represented by art, woman, and religious symbols. But others were more optimistic, preferring to place their confidence in America's historic role as an exemplary nation, demonstrating to the world the moral superiority of its economic system, democratic institutions, and middle-class Protestant values. Surely the new century, most thought, would see not only the continued perfection of these values and institutions, but also the spread of American influence throughout the world. Such confidence resulted in foreign expansion by the American people even before the old century had ended. We turn to that in the next chapter.

TIMELINE

1873 Congress demonetizes silver	**1875** Specie Resumption Act	**1877** Rutherford B. Hayes becomes president	**1878** Bland-Allison Act	**1879** Henry George, *Progress and Poverty*
1880 James A. Garfield elected president	**1881** Garfield assassinated; Chester A. Arthur succeeds to presidency	**1883** Pendleton Civil Service Act	**1884** Grover Cleveland elected president; W. D. Howells, *The Rise of Silas Lapham*	**1887** College Settlement House Association founded
1888 Edward Bellamy, *Looking Backward;* Benjamin Harrison elected president	**1889** Jane Addams establishes Hull House; Andrew Carnegie promulgates "The Gospel of Wealth"	**1890** General Federation of Women's Clubs founded; Sherman Anti-Trust Act; Sherman Silver Purchase Act; McKinley Tariff; Elections bill defeated	**1890s** Wyoming, Colorado, Utah, and Idaho grant woman suffrage	**1892** Cleveland elected president for the second time; Populist party wins over a million votes; Homestead steel strike
1893 World's Columbian Exposition, Chicago	**1893–1897** Financial panic and depression	**1894** Pullman strike; Coxey's march on Washington	**1895** *United States* v. *E. C. Knight*	**1896** Charles Sheldon, *In His Steps;* Populist party fuses with Democrats; William McKinley elected president
1897 "Golden Rule" Jones elected mayor of Toledo, Ohio; Economic recovery begins				

Recommended Reading

Politics in the Gilded Age

John Allswang, *Bosses, Machines, and Urban Voters* (1977); Charles W. Calhoun, *The Gilded Age: Essays on the Origins of Modern America* (1996); Sean Dennis Cashman, *America and the Gilded Age: From the Death of Lincoln to the Rise of Theodore Roosevelt* (1984); Morton Keller, *Affairs of State: Public Life in Late Nineteenth-Century America* (1977); Paul Kleppner, *The Third*

Electoral System, 1853–1892: Parties, Voters, and Political Cultures (1979); H. Wayne Morgan, *From Hayes to McKinley: National Party Politics, 1877–1896* (1969); Nell I. Painter, *Standing at Armageddon in the United States, 1877–1919* (1987); William Riordon, *Plunkitt of Tammany Hall* (1963); R. Hal Williams, *Years of Decision: American Politics in the 1890s* (1978); Richard E. Welch, Jr., *The Presidencies of Grover Cleveland (1988)*.

Middle-Class Reform and Reformers

Jane Addams, *Twenty Years at Hull House* (1910); Ruth Bordin, *Frances Willard: A Biography* (1986) and *Women and Temperance: The Quest for Power and Liberty, 1873–1900* (1981); Mina Carson, *Settlement Folk: Social Thought and the American Settlement Movement, 1885–1930* (1990); Susan Curtis, *A Consuming Faith: The Social Gospel and Modern American Culture* (1991); Allen F. Davis, *American Heroine: The Life and Legend of Jane Addams* (1973) and *Spearheads for Reform: The Social Settlements and the Progressive Movement, 1890–1914* (1967); Richard Digby-Junger, *The Journalist as Reformer: Henry Demarest Lloyd and Wealth Against Commonwealth* (1996); Peter J. Frederick, *Knights of the Golden Rule: The Intellectual as Christian Reformer in the 1890s* (1976); Marnie Jones, *Holy Toledo: Religion and Politics in the Life of "Golden Rule" Jones* (1998); Aileen Kraditor, *The Ideas of the Woman's Suffrage Movement, 1890–1920* (1965); Daphne Pata, ed., *Looking Backward, 1988–1888: Essays on Edward Bellamy* (1988); Kathryn Kish Sklar, *Florence Kelley and the Nation's Work: The Rise of Women's Political Culture, 1830–1900* (1995); John L. Thomas, *Alternative America: Henry George, Edward Bellamy, Henry Demarest Lloyd and the Adversary Tradition* (1983); Marjorie Spruill Wheeler, ed., *One Woman, One Vote: Rediscovering the Woman Suffrage Movement* (1995).

Cultural Life, Thought, and Literature of the Late Nineteenth Century

Burton J. Bledstein, *The Culture of Professionalism: The Middle Class and the Development of Higher Education in America* (1976); Mark C. Carnes and Clyde Griffen, eds., *Meanings for Manhood: Constructions of Masculinity in Victorian America* (1990); John Cawelti, *Apostles of the Self-Made Man: Changing Concepts of Success in America* (1965); Paulette D. Kilmer, *The Fear of Sinking: The American Success Formula in the Gilded Age* (1996); Bruce Kuklick, *The Rise of American Philosophy: Cambridge, Massachusetts, 1860–1930* (1977); T. Jackson Lears, *No Place of Grace: Antimodernism and the Transformation of American Culture, 1880–1920* (1981); H. Wayne Morgan, *Unity and Culture: The United States, 1877–1890* (1971); Priscilla Murolo, *The Common Ground of Womanhood: Class, Gender, and Working Girls' Clubs, 1884–1928* (1997); Alan Trachtenberg, *The Incorporation of America: Culture and Society in the Gilded Age* (1982); Larzer Ziff, *The American 1890s: Life and Times of a Lost Generation* (1966).

Depression Politics, Populism, and the Election of 1896

Peter H. Argersinger, *The Limits of Agrarian Radicalism: Western Populism and American Politics* (1995); Gene Clanton, *Populism: The Humane Preference in America, 1890–1900* (1991); Robert F. Durden, *The Climax of Populism: The Election of 1896* (1965); Paul Glad, *McKinley, Bryan and the People* (1964); Lawrence Goodwyn, *Democratic Promise: The Populist Movement in America* (1976); Charles Hoffman, *The Depression of the Nineties: An Economic History* (1970).

Fiction

Kate Chopin, *The Awakening* (1899); Charles Sheldon, *In His Steps* (1897); Edward Bellamy, *Looking Backward* (1888); W. D. Howells, *The Rise of Silas Lapham* (1884).

CHAPTER 20

Becoming a World Power

In January 1899, the United States Senate was locked in a dramatic debate over whether to ratify the Treaty of Paris concluding the recent war with Spain over Cuban independence. At the same time, American soldiers uneasily faced Filipino rebels across a neutral zone around the outskirts of Manila, capital of the Philippines. Until recent weeks, the Americans and Filipinos had been allies, together defeating the Spanish to liberate the Philippines. The American fleet under Admiral George Dewey had destroyed the Spanish naval squadron in Manila Bay on May 1, 1898. Three weeks later, an American ship brought from exile the native Filipino insurrectionary leader Emilio Aguinaldo to lead rebel forces on land while U.S. gunboats patrolled the seas.

At first, the Filipinos looked on the Americans as liberators. Although the intentions of the United States were never clear, Aguinaldo believed that, as in Cuba, the Americans had no territorial ambitions. They would simply drive the Spanish out and then leave. In June, therefore, Aguinaldo declared the independence of the Philippines and began setting up a constitutional government. American officials pointedly ignored the independence ceremonies. When an armistice ended the war in August, American troops denied Filipino soldiers an opportunity to liberate their own capital city and shunted them off to the suburbs. The armistice agreement recognized American rights to the "harbor, city, and bay of Manila," while the proposed Treaty of Paris gave the United States the entire Philippine Island archipelago.

Consequently, tension mounted in the streets of Manila and along 14 miles of trenches separating American and Filipino soldiers. Taunts, obscenities, and racial epithets were shouted across the neutral zone. Barroom skirmishes and knifings filled the nights; American soldiers searched houses without warrants and looted stores. Their behavior was not unlike that of the English soldiers in Boston in the 1770s.

On the night of February 4, 1899, Privates William Grayson and David Miller of Company B, 1st Nebraska Volunteers, were on patrol in Santa Mesa, a Manila suburb surrounded on three sides by insurgent trenches. The Americans had orders to shoot any Filipino soldiers in the neutral area. As the two Americans cautiously worked their way to a bridge over the San Juan River, they heard a Filipino signal whistle, answered by another. Then a red lantern flashed from a nearby blockhouse. The two froze as four Filipinos emerged from the darkness on the road ahead. "Halt!" Grayson shouted. The native lieutenant in charge answered, "Halto!," either mockingly or because he had similar orders. Standing less than 15 feet apart, the two men repeated their commands. After a moment's hesitation, Grayson fired, killing his opponent with one bullet. As the other Filipinos jumped out at them, Grayson and Miller shot two more. Then they turned and ran back to their own lines shouting warnings of attack. A full-scale battle followed.

The next day, Commodore Dewey cabled Washington that the "insurgents have inaugurated general engagement" and promised a hasty suppression of the insurrection. The outbreak of hostilities ended the Senate debates. On February 6, the Senate ratified the Treaty of Paris, thus formally annexing the Philippines and sparking a war between the United States and Filipino nationalists.

In a guerrilla war similar to those fought later in the twentieth century in Asia and Central America, Filipino nationalists tried to undermine the American will by hit-and-run attacks. American soldiers, meanwhile, remained in heavily garrisoned cities and undertook search-and-destroy missions to root out rebels and pacify the countryside. The Filipino-American War lasted until July 1902, three years longer than the Spanish-American War that caused it and involving far more troops, casualties, and monetary and moral costs.

How did all this happen? What brought Private Grayson to "shoot my first nigger," as he put it, halfway around the world? For the first time in history, regular American soldiers found themselves fighting outside North America. The "champion of oppressed nations," as Aguinaldo said, had turned into an oppressor nation itself, imposing the American way of life and American institutions on faraway peoples against their will.

The war in the Philippines marked a critical transformation of America's role in the world. Within a few years at the turn of the century, the United States acquired an empire, however small by European standards, and established itself as a world power. In this chapter, we will review the historical dilemmas of America's role in the world, especially those of the expansionist nineteenth century. Then we will examine the motivations for intensified expansionism in the 1890s and how they were manifested in Cuba, the Philippines, and elsewhere. Finally, we will look at how the fundamental patterns of modern American foreign policy were established for Latin America, Asia, and Europe in the early twentieth century. Throughout, we will see that the tension between idealism and self-interest that has permeated America's domestic history has also guided its foreign policy.

STEPS TOWARD EMPIRE

The circumstances that brought Privates Grayson and Miller from Nebraska to the Philippines originated deep in American history. As early as the seventeenth-century Puritan migration, Americans worried about how to do good in a world that does wrong. John Winthrop sought to set up a "city on a hill" in the New World, a model community of righteous living for the rest of the world to imitate. "Let the eyes of the world be upon us," Winthrop had said. That wish, reaffirmed during the American Revolution, became a permanent goal of American policy toward the outside world.

America as a Model Society

Nineteenth-century Americans continued to believe in the nation's special mission. The Monroe Doctrine in 1823 warned Europe's monarchies to keep out of the republican New World. In succeeding decades, distinguished European visitors

Clustered in trenches against Filipino nationalists, American soldiers in the faraway Philippine Islands in 1899 were a harbinger of twentieth-century wars to come. (Library of Congress)

came to observe the "great social revolution." They found widespread democracy, representative and responsive political and legal institutions, a religious commitment to human perfectibility, unlimited energy, and an ability to apply unregulated economic activity and inventive genius to produce more things for more people.

In an evil world, Americans believed that they stood as a transforming force for good. But how could a nation committed to isolationism do the transforming? One way was to encourage other nations to observe and imitate the good example set by the United States. Often, however, other nations preferred their own society or were attracted to competing models of modernization, such as socialism. This implied the need for a more aggressive foreign policy.

Americans have rarely just focused on perfecting the good example at home, waiting for others to copy it. This requires patience and passivity, two traits not characteristic of Americans. Rather, throughout history, the American people have actively and sometimes forcefully imposed their ideas and institutions on others. The international crusades of the United States, well intentioned if not always well received, have usually been motivated by a mixture of idealism and self-interest. Hence, the effort to spread the American model to an imperfect world has been both a blessing and a burden—for others and for the American people.

Early Expansionism

Persistent expansionism marked the first century of American independence. Jefferson's purchase of Louisiana in 1803, the Jeffersonians' grasping for more territory in 1812, and the mid-century pursuit of "Manifest Destiny" spread the United States across North America. In the 1850s, Americans began to look beyond their own continent as Commodore Perry in 1853 "opened" Japan and southerners sought more cotton lands in the Caribbean. After the Civil War, Secretary of State William Seward spoke of an America that would hold a "commanding sway in the world," destined to exert commercial domination "on the Pacific ocean, and its islands and continents." He purchased Alaska from Russia in 1867 for $7.2 million and acquired a coaling station in the Midway Islands near Hawaii, where missionaries and merchants were already active. He advocated annexing Cuba and other West Indian islands, tried to negotiate a treaty for an American-built canal through Panama, and dreamed of "possession" of the entire North and Central American continent and ultimately "control of the world."

Expansion After Seward

In 1870, foreshadowing the Philippine debates 30 years later, supporters of President Grant tried to persuade the Senate to annex Santo Domingo on the island of Hispaniola. They cited the strategic importance of the Caribbean and argued forcefully for the economic value that Santo Domingo would bring. Opponents responded that expansionism violated American principles of self-determination and government by the consent of the governed. They claimed that the Caribbean peoples were unassimilable. Expansionism might also involve foreign entanglements, a large and expensive navy, bigger government, and higher taxes. So the Senate rejected the annexation treaty.

Although reluctant to add territory outright, Americans eagerly sought commercial dominance in Latin America and Asia. But American talk of building a canal across Nicaragua produced only Nicaraguan suspicions. In 1881, Secretary of State Blaine sought to convene a conference of American nations to promote hemispheric peace and trade. Latin Americans may have wondered what Blaine intended, for in 1881 he intervened in three separate border disputes in Central and South America, in each case at the cost of goodwill.

American expansion produced other incidents in the Pacific. In the mid-1870s, American sugar-growing interests in the Hawaiian Islands were strong enough to put whites in positions of influence over the monarchy. In 1875, they obtained a treaty admitting Hawaiian sugar duty-free to the United States, and in 1887 the United States also won exclusive rights to build a naval base at Pearl Harbor. Hawaiians resented the influence of American sugar interests, especially as they brought in Japanese to replace native people—many of whom died from white diseases—in the sugarcane fields. In 1891, the nationalistic queen Liliuokalani assumed the throne and pursued a policy of "Hawaii for the Hawaiians." So in 1893 white planters staged a coup with the help of U.S. gunboats and marines. An annexation treaty was presented to the Senate by the friendly Harrison administration. But then Grover Cleveland, who opposed imperial expansion, returned to the presidency for his second term and stopped the move. The white sugar growers waited patiently for a more desirable time for annexation, which came during the war in 1898.

Meanwhile the United States acquired a naval station in the Samoan Islands in 1878. American and German naval forces almost fought each other there in 1889—before a typhoon ended the crisis by wiping out both navies.

The United States sought to replace Great Britain as the most influential nation in Central America and northern South America. In 1895, a boundary dispute between Venezuela and British Guiana threatened to bring British intervention against the Venezuelans. President Cleveland, needing a popular political issue amid the depression, asked Secretary of State Richard Olney to send a message to Great Britain. Olney's note (stronger than Cleveland intended) called the United States "practically sovereign on this continent" and demanded international arbitration to settle the dispute. The British ignored the note, and war loomed. But then both sides realized that war would be an "absurdity." The dispute was settled by agreeing to an impartial American commission to settle the boundary.

Yet as of 1895, the United States had neither the means nor a consistent policy for enlarging its role in the world. The diplomatic service was small and unprofessional. The U.S. Army, with about 28,000 men, was smaller than Bulgaria's. The navy, dismantled after the Civil War and partly rebuilt under President Arthur, ranked no higher than tenth and included dangerously obsolete ships.

EXPANSIONISM IN THE 1890s

In 1893, historian Frederick Jackson Turner wrote that for three centuries "the dominant fact in American life has been expansion." The "extension of American influence to outlying islands and adjoining countries," he thought, indicated still more expansionism. Turner struck a responsive chord in a country that had always been restless and optimistic. With the western frontier closed, Americans would surely look for new frontiers, for mobility and markets as well as for morality and missionary activity. The motivations for the expansionist impulse of the late 1890s resembled those that had prompted Europeans to settle the New World in the first place: greed, glory, and God. We will examine expansionism as a reflection of profits, patriotism, piety, and politics.

Profits: Searching for Overseas Markets

Senator Albert Beveridge of Indiana bragged in 1898 that "American factories are making more than the American people can use; American soil is producing more than they can consume. Fate has written our policy for us; the trade of the world must and shall be ours." Americans like Beveridge revived older dreams of an American commercial empire in the Caribbean Sea and the Pacific Ocean. American businessmen saw huge profits beckoning in heavily populated Latin America and Asia, and wanted to get their share of these markets, as well as access to the sugar, coffee, fruits, oil, rubber, and minerals that were abundant in these lands.

Understanding that commercial expansion required a stronger navy and coaling stations and colonies, business interests began to shape diplomatic and military strategy. But not all businessmen in the 1890s liked commercial expansion or a vigorous foreign policy. Some preferred traditional trade with Canada and Europe rather than risky new ventures in Asia and Latin America. Some thought it more important to recover from the depression than annex islands.

But the drop in domestic consumption during the depression also encouraged businessmen to expand into new markets. The tremendous growth of American production in the post-Civil War years made expansionism more attractive than drowning in overproduction, cutting prices, or laying off workers, which would increase social unrest.

Despite the 1890s depression, products spewed from American factories at a staggering rate. The United States moved from fourth place in the world in manufacturing in 1870 to first place in 1900, doubling the number of factories and tripling the value of farm output. Manufactured goods grew nearly fivefold between 1895 and 1914. The total value of American exports tripled, from $434 million in 1866 to nearly $1.5 billion in 1900. By 1914, exports had risen to $2.5 billion, a 67 percent increase over 1900. The increased trade continued to go mainly to Europe rather than Asia. In 1900, for example, only 3 to 4 percent of U.S. exports went to China and Japan. Nevertheless, interest in Asian markets grew, especially as agricultural output continued to increase and prices stayed low.

Investments followed a similar pattern. American direct investments abroad increased from about $634 million to $2.6 billion between 1897 and 1914. Although investments were largest in Britain, Canada, and Mexico, most attention focused on actual and potential investment in Latin America and Asia. At the turn of the century came the formation and growth of America's biggest multinational corporations, including the United Fruit Company. Although slow to respond to investment and market opportunities abroad, these companies soon supported an aggressive foreign policy.

Patriotism: Asserting National Power

In 1898, a State Department memorandum stated that "we can no longer afford to disregard international rivalries now that we ourselves have become a competitor in the world-wide struggle for trade." The national state, then, should support commercial interests.

More Americans, however, saw expansion in terms of national glory and greatness. In the late 1890s, a group centered on Assistant Secretary of the Navy Theodore Roosevelt and Massachusetts Senator Henry Cabot Lodge emerged as highly influential leaders of a changing American foreign policy. These intensely nationalistic young men shifted official policy to what Lodge called the "large policy." Roosevelt agreed that economic interests should take second place to questions of what he called "national honor."

Naval strategist Alfred Thayer Mahan greatly influenced the new foreign policy elite. Mahan's books argued that in a world of Darwinian struggle for survival, national power depended on naval supremacy, control of sea lanes, and vigorous development of domestic resources and foreign markets. He advocated colonies in both the Caribbean and the Pacific, linked by a canal built and controlled by the United States. In a world of constant "strife," he said, it was imperative that Americans begin "to look outward."

Piety: The Missionary Impulse

As Mahan's and Roosevelt's statements suggest, a strong sense of duty and the missionary ideal of doing good for others also motivated expansionism—and sometimes rationalized the exploitation and oppression of weaker peoples. As a missionary put it in 1885, "The Christian nations are subduing the world in order to make mankind free." Josiah Strong, a Congregationalist minister, was another ardent advocate of American missionary expansionism. He argued that in the struggle for survival among nations, the United States had emerged as the center of Anglo-Saxonism and was "divinely commissioned" to spread political liberty, Protestant Christianity, and civilized values over the earth. "This powerful race," he wrote, "will move down upon Mexico, down upon Central and South America, out upon the islands of the sea, over upon Africa and beyond."

Missionaries carried similar Western values to non-Christian lands around the world, especially China. The number of American Protestant missionaries in China increased from 436 in 1874 to 5,462 in 1914, and the estimated number of Christian converts in China jumped from 5,000 in 1870 to nearly 100,000 in 1900 (much less than missionaries hoped). But this tiny fraction of the Chinese population included young reformist intellectuals who, absorbing Western ideas, in 1912 helped overthrow the Manchu dynasty. Economic relations between China and the United States increased at approximately the same rate as missionary activity.

Politics: Manipulating Public Opinion

Although less significant than the other factors, politics also played a role. For the first time in American history, public opinion on international issues helped shape presidential politics. The psychological tensions and economic hardships of the 1890s depression jarred national self-confidence. Foreign adventures provided an emotional release from domestic turmoil and promised to restore patriotic pride—and maybe even win votes.

This process was helped by the growth of a highly competitive popular press, which brought international issues before a mass readership. When New York City newspapers, notably William Randolph Hearst's *Journal* and Joseph Pulitzer's *World*, competed in stirring up public support for the Cuban rebels against Spain, politicians dared not ignore the outcry. Daily reports of Spanish atrocities in 1896 and 1897 kept public moral outrage constantly before President McKinley.

Politics, then, joined profits, patriotism, and piety in motivating the expansionism of the 1890s. These four impulses interacted to produce the Spanish-American War, the annexation of the Philippine Islands, and the foreign policy of President Theodore Roosevelt.

CUBA AND THE PHILIPPINES

Lying 90 miles off Florida, Cuba had been the object of intense American interest for a half century. Spain could not halt the continuing struggle of the Cuban people for relief from exploitive labor in the sugar plantations, even after slavery itself ended, and for a measure of autonomy. The most recent uprising, which lasted

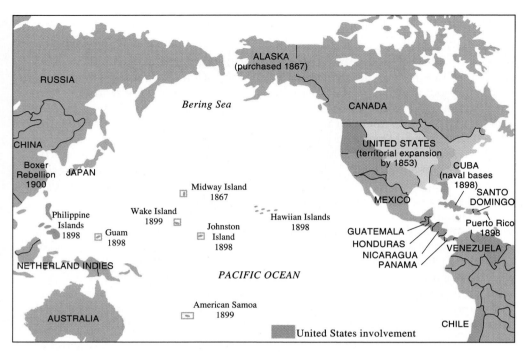

UNITED STATES TERRITORIAL EXPANSION TO 1900   Compare this map with the one on U.S. territorial expansion to 1860 on page 335 (represented in miniature in the U.S. portion of this map).

from 1868 to 1878, raised tensions between Spain and the United States, just as it whetted the Cuban appetite for complete independence.

The Road to War

When the Cuban revolt flared up anew in 1895, the Madrid government again failed to implement reforms. Instead, it sent General "Butcher" Weyler with 50,000 troops to quell the disturbance. When Weyler began herding rural Cubans into "reconcentration" camps, Americans were outraged. An outpouring of sympathy swept the nation, especially as sensationalists reports of horrible suffering and the deaths of thousands in the camps filled American newspapers.

The Cuban struggle appealed to a country convinced of its role as protector of the weak and defender of the right of self-determination. Motivated by genuine humanitarian concern and a sense of duty, many Americans held rallies to raise money and food for famine relief, to call for land reform, and sometimes to advocate armed intervention. But neither Cleveland nor McKinley wanted war.

Self-interest also played a role. For many years, Americans had noted the profitable resources and strategic location of the island. American companies had invested extensively in Cuban sugar plantations. Appeals for reform had much to do with ensuring a stable environment for further investments, as well as for protecting the sugar fields.

The election of 1896 only temporarily diverted attention from Cuba. A new government in Madrid made halfhearted concessions. Conditions worsened in the reconcentration camps, and the American press kept harping on the plight of the Cuban people. McKinley, eager not to upset recovery from the depression, skillfully resisted war pressures. But he could not control Spanish misrule or Cuban aspirations for freedom.

Events early in 1898 sparked the outbreak of hostilities. Rioting in Havana intensified both Spanish repression and American outrage. A letter from the Spanish minister to the United States, Depuy de Lôme, calling McKinley a "weak," hypocritical politician, was intercepted and made public. Americans fumed.

A second event was more serious. When the rioting broke out, the U.S. battleship *Maine* was sent to Havana harbor to protect American citizens. On February 15, a tremendous explosion blew up the *Maine,* killing 262 men. Newspapers trumpeted slogans like "Remember the *Maine!* To hell with Spain!"

Assistant Secretary of the Navy Theodore Roosevelt, who had been preparing for war for some time, said that he believed the *Maine* had been sunk "by an act of dirty treachery on the part of the Spaniards" and that he would "give anything if President McKinley would order the fleet to Havana tomorrow." When the president did not, Roosevelt privately declared that McKinley had "no more backbone than a chocolate éclair" and continued readying the navy for action. Although an official board of inquiry concluded that an external submarine mine caused the disaster, it is probable that a faulty boiler or some other internal problem set off the explosion. Even Roosevelt later conceded this possibility.

After the sinking of the *Maine,* Roosevelt took advantage of the Secretary of the Navy being absent from the office one day to cable Commodore George Dewey, commander of the United States' Pacific fleet at Hong Kong. Roosevelt ordered Dewey to fill his ships with coal and, "in the event" of a declaration of war with Spain, to sail to the Philippines and make sure "the Spanish squadron does not leave the Asiatic coast." "The Secretary is away and I am having immense fun running the Navy," Roosevelt wrote in his diary that night.

Roosevelt's act was consistent with policies he had been urging on his more cautious superior for more than a year. As early as 1895, the navy had contingency plans for attacking the Philippines. Influenced by Mahan and Lodge, Roosevelt wanted to enlarge the navy. He also believed that the United States should construct an interoceanic canal, acquire the Danish West Indies (the Virgin Islands), annex Hawaii, and oust Spain from Cuba. As Roosevelt told McKinley late in 1897, he was putting the navy in "the best possible shape" for the day "when war began."

The public outcry over the *Maine* drowned out McKinley's efforts to avoid war. The issues had become highly politicized. McKinley pressured the Madrid government to make the necessary concessions. But Spain refused to grant full independence to the Cubans.

On April 11, 1898, McKinley sent an ambiguous message to Congress that seemed to call for war. Two weeks later, Congress authorized using troops against Spain and recognized Cuban independence, actions amounting to a declaration of war. In a significant additional resolution, the Teller Amendment, Congress stated that the United States had no intention of annexing Cuba.

"A Splendid Little War"

As soon as war was declared, Roosevelt resigned from the Navy Department and prepared to lead a cavalry unit. African-American and white regiments headed to Tampa, Florida, to be shipped to Cuba. One black soldier, noting the stark differences in the southern reception of the segregated regiments, commented, "I am sorry that we were not treated with much courtesy while coming through the South." Blacks were especially sympathetic to the Cuban people's struggle. On arriving in Puerto Rico, a white soldier wrote that it was a "wonderful sight how the natives respect us." As the four-month war neared its end in August, Secretary of State John Hay wrote Roosevelt that "it has been a splendid little war; begun with the highest motives, carried on with magnificent intelligence and spirit."

It was also a short and relatively easy war. Naval battles were won almost without return fire. At both major naval engagements, Manila Bay and Santiago Bay, only two Americans died, one of them from heat prostration while stoking coal. Guam and Puerto Rico were taken virtually without a shot. Only 385 men died from Spanish bullets, but over 5,000 succumbed to tropical diseases.

The Spanish-American War seemed splendid in other ways, as letters from American soldiers suggest. One young man wrote that his comrades were all "in good spirits" because "every trooper has his canteen full of lemonade all the time." Another wrote his brother that he was having "a lot of fun chasing Spaniards." But the "power of joy in battle" that Theodore Roosevelt felt "when the wolf rises in the heart" was not a feeling all American soldiers shared. One soldier wrote that "words are inadequate to express the feeling of pain and sickness when one has the fever. For about a week every bone in my body ached and I did not care much whether I lived or not."

Roosevelt's celebrated charge up Kettle Hill near Santiago, his flank protected by African-American troops, made three-inch headlines and propelled him toward the New York governor's mansion. During the war, no one did as much as Roosevelt to advance not only his political career, but also expansionism.

The Philippines Debates and War

Roosevelt's ordering Dewey to Manila initiated a chain of events that led to the annexation of the Philippines. The most crucial battle of the Spanish-American War occurred on May 1, 1898, when Dewey destroyed the Spanish fleet in Manila Bay and cabled McKinley for additional troops. The president said later that when he received Dewey's cable, he was not even sure where "those darned islands were." Actually, McKinley had already approved Roosevelt's policies. He sent twice as many troops as Dewey had asked for and began shaping American public opinion to accept the "political, commercial [and] humanitarian" reasons for annexing the Philippines. The Treaty of Paris gave the United States the islands in exchange for a $20 million payment to Spain.

The treaty went to the Senate for ratification during the winter of 1898–1899. Senators hurled arguments across the floor of the Senate as American soldiers hurled oaths and taunts across the neutral zone at Aguinaldo's insurgents near

Manila. Private Grayson's encounter, as we have seen, led to the passage of the treaty in a close Senate vote—and began the Filipino-American War and the debates over what to do with the Philippines.

The entire nation joined the argument. At stake were two very different views of foreign policy and of America's vision of itself. After several months of quietly seeking advice and listening to public opinion, McKinley finally recommended annexation. Many Democrats supported the president out of fear of being labeled disloyal. At a time when openly racist thought flourished in the United States, fellow Republicans confirmed McKinley's arguments for annexation, adding even more insulting ones. Filipinos were described as childlike, dirty, and backward. "The country won't be pacified," a Kansas veteran of the Sioux wars told a reporter, "until the niggers are killed off like the Indians."

A small but vocal Anti-Imperialist League vigorously opposed war and annexation. Many felt displaced by the younger generation of expansionists. By attacking imperialism, the anti-imperialists struck out against the modernizing forces that they felt threatened their elite position. This cross-section of American dignitaries included ex-presidents Harrison and Cleveland, Samuel Gompers and Andrew Carnegie, William James, Jane Addams, and Mark Twain.

The major anti-imperialist arguments pointed out how imperialism in general and annexation in particular contradicted American ideals. First, the annexation of territory without immediate or planned steps toward statehood was unprecedented and unconstitutional. Second, to occupy and govern a foreign people without their consent violated the ideals of the Declaration of Independence. Third, social reforms needed at home demanded American energies and money before foreign expansionism.

Not all anti-imperialist arguments were so noble. A racist position alleged that Filipinos were unassimilable. A practical argument suggested that once in possession of the Philippines, the United States would have to defend them, possibly even acquiring more territories—in turn requiring higher taxes and bigger government, and perhaps demanding that American troops fight distant Asian wars.

The last argument became fact when Private Grayson's encounter started the Filipino-American War. Before it ended in 1902, some 126,500 American troops served in the Philippines, 4,234 died there, and 2,800 more were wounded. The cost was $400 million. Filipino casualties were much worse. In addition to 18,000 killed in combat, perhaps 200,000 Filipinos died of famine and disease as American soldiers burned villages and destroyed crops and livestock. General Jacob H. Smith told his troops that "the more you kill and burn, the better you will please me." Atrocities on both sides increased with the frustrations of a lengthening war, but American repressions were especially brutal.

As U.S. treatment of the Filipinos became more and more like Spanish treatment of the Cubans, the hypocrisy of American behavior became even more evident. This was especially true for black American soldiers who fought in the Philippines. They identified with the dark-skinned insurgents, whom they saw as tied to the land, burdened by debt, pressed by poverty, and were called "nigger" from morning to night. "I feel sorry for these people," a sergeant in the 24th Infantry wrote. "You have no idea the way these people are treated by the Americans here."

The war starkly exposed the hypocrisies of shouldering the white man's burden. On reading a report that 8,000 Filipinos had been killed in the first year of the war, Carnegie wrote a letter, dripping with sarcasm, congratulating McKinley for "civilizing the Filipinos . . . . About 8,000 of them have been completely civilized and sent to Heaven. I hope you like it."

The anti-imperialists failed either to prevent annexation or to interfere with the war effort. They were out of tune with the period of exuberant national pride, prosperity, and promise.

Expansionism Triumphant

By 1900, Americans had ample reason to be patriotic. But several questions arose over what to do with the new territories. Were they colonies? Would they be granted statehood or would they develop gradually from colonies to constitutional parts of the United States? Did Hawaiians, Puerto Ricans, Guamians, and Filipinos have the same rights as American citizens on the mainland? Were they protected by the U.S. Constitution?

Although slightly different governing systems were worked out for each new territory, the solution in each case was to define its status somewhere between a colony and a candidate for statehood. The indigenous people were usually allowed to elect their own legislature, but had presidentially-appointed governors and other judicial and administrative officials. The first full governor of the Philippines, McKinley appointee William Howard Taft, effectively moved the Filipinos toward self-government. Final independence did not come until 1946.

The question of constitutional rights was resolved by deciding that Hawaiians and Puerto Ricans, for example, would be treated differently from Texans and Oregonians. In the "insular cases" of 1901, the Supreme Court ruled that these people would achieve citizenship and constitutional rights only when Congress said they were ready.

In the election of 1900, Bryan was again the Democratic nominee and tried to make imperialism the "paramount issue" of the campaign. He failed, in part because the country strongly favored annexing the Philippines. In the closing weeks of the campaign, Bryan shied away from imperialism and focused on domestic issues.

That did Bryan no good either. Prosperity returned with the discovery of gold in Alaska, and cries for reform fell on deaf ears. The McKinley forces rightly claimed that four years of Republican rule had brought more money, jobs, thriving factories, and manufactured goods, as well as the tremendous growth in American prestige abroad. As Tom Watson put it, noting the end of the Populist revolt with the war fervor over Cuba, "The blare of the bugle drowned out the voice of the reformer."

He was more right than he knew. Within one year, expansionist Theodore Roosevelt went from assistant secretary of the navy to colonel of the Rough Riders to governor of New York. For some Republican politicos, who thought he was too vigorous, unorthodox, and independent, this quick rise as McKinley's potential rival came too fast. One way to eliminate Roosevelt politically, or at least slow him down, was to make him vice president, which they did in 1900. But six months into McKinley's second term, the president was killed by an anarchist, the third presidential assassination in less than 40 years. "Now look," exclaimed party boss Mark Hanna, who had opposed putting Roosevelt on the ticket, "that damned cowboy is President of the United States!"

THEODORE ROOSEVELT'S ENERGETIC DIPLOMACY

At a White House dinner party in 1905, a guest told a story about visiting the Roosevelt home when "Teedie" was a baby. "You were in your bassinet, making a good deal of fuss and noise," the guest reported, "and your father lifted you out and asked me to hold you." Secretary of State Elihu Root looked up and asked, "Was he hard to hold?" Whether true or not, the story reveals much about President Roosevelt's principles and policies on foreign affairs. As president from 1901 to 1909, and as the most dominating American personality for the 15 years between 1897 and 1912, Roosevelt made much fuss and noise about the activist role he thought the United States should play in the world. As he implemented his policies, he often seemed "hard to hold." Roosevelt's energetic foreign policy in Latin America, Asia, and Europe paved the way for the vital role of the United States as a world power.

Foreign Policy as Darwinian Struggle

Roosevelt advocated both individual physical fitness and collective national strength. An undersized boy, he had he pursued a rigorous body-building program, and as a young man on his North Dakota ranch he learned to value the "strenuous life." Reading Darwin taught him that life was a constant struggle for survival. As president, his ideal was a "nation of men, not weaklings." Although he believed in Anglo-Saxon superiority, he admired—and feared—Japanese military prowess. Powerful nations, like individuals, Roosevelt believed, had a duty to cultivate vigor, strength, courage, and moral commitment to civilized values. In practical terms, this meant developing natural resources, building large navies, and being ever prepared to fight.

Although famous for saying "speak softly and carry a big stick," Roosevelt often not only wielded a large stick but spoke loudly as well. In a speech in 1897, he used the word *war* 62 times, saying that "no triumph of peace is quite so great as the supreme triumphs of war." But despite his bluster, Roosevelt was usually restrained in exercising force. He won the Nobel Peace Prize in 1906 for helping end the Russo-Japanese War. The big stick and the loud talk were meant to preserve order and peace.

Roosevelt divided the world into civilized and uncivilized nations. The civilized ones had a responsibility to "police" the uncivilized, not only maintaining order but also spreading superior values and institutions. Taking on the "white man's burden," civilized nations sometimes had to wage war on the uncivilized— justly so, because the victors bestowed the blessings of culture and racial superiority on the vanquished. But a war between two civilized nations (for example, Germany and Great Britain) would be wasteful and foolish. Above all, Roosevelt believed in the balance of power. Strong, advanced nations like the United States had a duty to use their power to preserve order and peace. Americans could no

The "big stick" became a memorable image in American diplomacy as Teddy Roosevelt sought to make the United States a policeman not only of the Caribbean basin, but also of the whole world. "As our modern life goes on," Roosevelt said, "and the nations are drawn closer together for good and for evil, and this nation grows in comparison with friends and rivals, it is impossible to adhere to the policy of isolation." (*Puck*, 1901, Culver Pictures)

longer "avoid responsibilities." The 1900 census showed that the United States, with 75 million people, was much more populous than Great Britain, France, or Germany. It seemed time for Americans to exercise a greater role in world affairs.

Roosevelt developed a highly personal style of diplomacy. Bypassing the State Department, he preferred face-to-face contact and personal exchanges of letters with foreign diplomats and heads of state. A British emissary observed that Roosevelt had a "powerful personality" and a commanding knowledge of the world. Ministries from London to Tokyo respected both the president and the power of the United States.

When threats failed to accomplish his goals, Roosevelt used direct personal intervention. When he wanted Panama, Roosevelt bragged later, "I took the Canal Zone" rather than submitting a long "dignified State Paper" for congressional debate. And while Congress debated, he was fond of pointing out, the building of the canal began. Roosevelt's energetic executive activism in foreign policy set a pattern for nearly every twentieth-century president.

Taking the Panama Canal

Justifying the intervention of 2,600 American troops in Honduras and Nicaragua in 1906, Philander Knox, secretary of state from 1909 to 1913, said, "We are in the eyes of the world, and because of the Monroe Doctrine, held responsible for the order of

In 1904, a cartoonist showed the American eagle celebrating "his 128th birthday" with wings spanning the globe from Panama to the Philippines. In a prophetic anticipation of American overexpansion in the twentieth century, the eagle says, "Gee, but this is an awful stretch." (The Granger Collection, New York)

Central America, and its proximity to the Canal makes the preservation of peace in that neighborhood particularly necessary." The Panama Canal was not yet finished when Knox spoke, but it had already become a cornerstone of United States policy.

Three problems had to be surmounted in order to dig an interoceanic connection. First, an 1850 treaty bound the United States to build a canal jointly with Great Britain, a problem resolved in 1901 when the British canceled the treaty in exchange for an American guarantee that the canal would be open to all nations. A second problem was where to dig it. American engineers rejected a long route through Nicaragua in favor of a shorter, more rugged path across Panama, where a French firm had already begun work. This raised the third problem: Panama was a province of Colombia, which rejected the terms the United States offered. Roosevelt called the Colombians "Dagoes" who tried to "hold us up" like highway robbers.

Aware of Roosevelt's fury, encouraged by hints of American support, and eager for the economic benefits that a canal would bring, Panamanian nationalists in 1903 staged a revolution led by several rich families and a Frenchman, Philippe Bunau-Varilla of the French canal company. Colombian intervention was deterred by an American warship; local troops were separated from their officers, who were bought off. A bloodless revolution occurred on November 3; the next day, Panama declared its independence, and on November 6 the United States recognized it. Although Roosevelt did not directly encourage the revolution, it would not have occurred without American help.

On November 18, Hay and Bunau-Varilla signed a treaty establishing the American right to build and operate a canal through Panama and to exercise "titular sovereignty" over the ten-mile-wide Canal Zone. The Panamanian government protested, and a later government called it the "treaty that no Panamanian signed."

Roosevelt, in his later boast that he "took the canal," claimed that his diplomatic and engineering achievement, completed in 1914, would "rank . . . with the Louisiana Purchase and the acquisition of Texas."

Policeman of the Caribbean

As late as 1901, the Monroe Doctrine was still regarded, according to Roosevelt, as the "equivalent to an open door in South America." To the United States, this meant that although no nation had a right "to get territorial possessions," all nations had equal commercial rights in the Western Hemisphere south of the Rio Grande. But as American investments poured into Central America and the Caribbean, the policy changed to one of asserting U.S. dominance in the Caribbean basin.

This change was demonstrated in 1902 when Germany and Great Britain blockaded Venezuela's ports to force the government to pay defaulted debts. Roosevelt was especially worried that German influence would replace the British. He insisted that the European powers accept arbitration and threatened to "move Dewey's ships" to the Venezuelan coast. The crisis passed, largely for other reasons, but Roosevelt's threat of force made very clear the paramount presence and self-interest of the United States in the Caribbean.

The United States kept liberated Cuba under a military governor until 1902, when the Cubans elected a congress and president. The United States honored Cuban independence, as it had promised to do in the Teller Amendment. But through the Platt Amendment, which Cubans reluctantly added to their constitution in 1901, the United States obtained many economic rights in Cuba, a naval base at Guantanamo Bay, and the right to intervene if Cuban sovereignty were ever threatened.

American policy intended to make Cuba a model of how a newly independent nation could achieve orderly self-government with only minimal guidance. Cuban self-government, however, was shaky. When in 1906 a political crisis threatened to spiral into civil war, Roosevelt expressed his fury with "that infernal little Cuban republic." At Cuba's request, he sent warships to patrol the coastline and special commissioners and troops "to restore order and peace and public confidence." Along with economic development, which mostly benefitted American companies, American political and even military involvement in Cuban affairs would continue throughout the century.

The pattern was repeated throughout the Caribbean. The Dominican Republic, for example, suffered from unstable governments and great poverty. In 1904, as a revolt erupted, European creditors pressured the Dominican government for payment of $40 million in defaulted bonds. Sending its warships to discourage European intervention, the United States took over the collection of customs in the republic. Two years later, the United States intervened in Guatemala and Nicaragua, where American bankers controlled nearly 50 percent of all trade, the first of several twentieth-century interventions in those countries.

Roosevelt clarified his policy that civilized nations should "insist on the proper policing of the world" in his annual message to Congress in 1904. The goal of the United States, he said, was to have "stable, orderly and prosperous neighbors." A

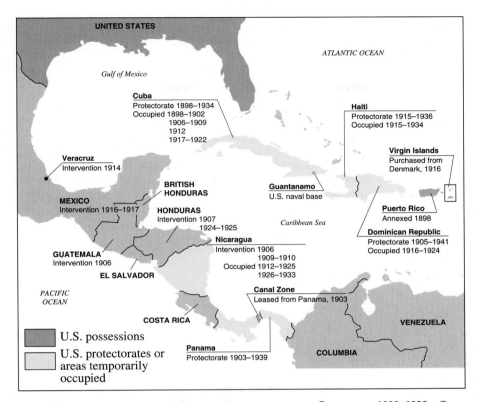

UNITED STATES INVOLVEMENT IN CENTRAL AMERICA AND THE CARIBBEAN, 1898–1939 Can you update the location of further interventions in Central America and the Caribbean since the 1950s?

country that paid its debts and kept order "need fear no interference from the United States." But "chronic wrong-doing" would require the United States to intervene as an "international police power." This policy became known as the Roosevelt Corollary to the Monroe Doctrine. Whereas Monroe's doctrine had warned European nations not to intervene in the Western Hemisphere, Roosevelt's corollary justified American intervention. Starting with a desire to protect property, loans, and investments, the United States wound up supporting the tyrannical regimes of elites who owned most of the land, suppressed the poor, blocked reforms, and acted as American surrogates.

After 1904, the Roosevelt Corollary was invoked in several Caribbean countries. Intervention usually required the landing of U.S. Marines to counter a threat to American property. Occupying the capital and major seaports, Marines, bankers, and customs officials usually remained for several years, until they were satisfied that stability had been reestablished. Roosevelt's successors, William Howard Taft and Woodrow Wilson, pursued the same interventionist policy. So would later presidents, most recently Ronald Reagan (Grenada and Nicaragua), George Bush (Panama), and Bill Clinton (Haiti).

Political Cartoons

One of the most enjoyable ways of recovering the values and attitudes of the past is through political cartoons. Ralph Waldo Emerson once said, "Caricatures are often the truest history of the times." A deft drawing can freeze ideas and events in time, conveying more effectively than columns of print the central issues—and especially the hypocrisies and misbehaviors of an era. Cartoonists are often at their best when they are critical, exaggerating a physical feature of a political figure or capturing public sentiment against the government.

The history of political cartoons in the United States goes back to Benjamin Franklin's "Join or Die" cartoon calling for colonial cooperation against the French in 1754. But political cartoons were rare until Andrew Jackson's presidency. Even after such cartoons as "King Andrew the First" in the 1830s, they did not gain notoriety until the advent of Thomas Nast's cartoons in *Harper's Weekly* in the 1870s. Nast drew scathing cartoons exposing the corruption of William "Boss" Tweed's Tammany Hall, depicting Tweed and his men as vultures and smiling deceivers. "Stop them damn pictures," Tweed ordered. "I don't care so much what the papers write about me. My constituents can't read. But, damn it, they can see pictures." Tweed sent some of his men to Nast with an offer of $100,000 to "study art" in Europe. The $5,000-a-year artist negotiated up to a half million dollars before refusing Tweed's offer. "I made up my mind not long ago to put some of those fellows behind bars," Nast said, "and I'm going to put them there." His cartoons helped to drive Tweed out of office.

The emergence of the United States as a world power at the same time as the rise of cheap newspapers, such as William Randolph Hearst's *Journal* and Joseph Pulitzer's *World*, provided a rich opportunity for cartoonists, whose clever images helped increase daily circulation to a million copies. When the Spanish-American War broke out, newspapers whipped up public sentiment by having artists draw fake pictures of fierce Spaniards stripping American women at sea and killing helpless Cubans. But by the time of the debates over Philippine annexation, many cartoonists took an anti-imperialist stance, pointing out American hypocrisy. Within a year, cartoonists shifted from depicting "The Spanish Brute Adds Mutilation to Murder" (1898) to "Liberty Halts American Butchery in the Philippines" (1899), both included here. Note the similarities in that both cartoons condemn the "butchery" of native peoples. But the villain has changed. Although Uncle Sam as a killer is not nearly as menacing as the figure of Spain as an ugly gorilla, both cartoons share a similarity of stance, blood-covered swords, and a trail of bodies behind. How would you account for the change? What attitudes and political positions are reflected in today's cartoons?

"The Spanish Brute Adds Mutilation to Murder," by Grant Hamilton, in Judge, July 9, 1898. (Culver Pictures)

"Liberty Halts American Butchery in the Philippines," from Life, 1899.

Opening the Door to China

Throughout the nineteenth century, American relations with China were restricted to a small but profitable trade. The British, in competition with France, Germany, and Russia, took advantage of the crumbling Manchu dynasty to force treaties on China creating "treaty ports" and granting exclusive trading privileges in various parts of the country. After 1898, Americans with dreams of exploiting the seemingly unlimited markets of China wanted to join the competition and enlarge their share. Those with moral interests, however, including many missionaries, reminded Americans of their revolutionary tradition against European imperialism. They made clear their opposition to crass U.S. commercial exploitation of a weak nation and supported the preservation of China's political integrity as the other imperial powers moved toward partitioning the country.

Although a few Americans admired China's ancient culture, the dominant American attitude viewed the Chinese as heathen, exotic, backward, and immoral. The Exclusion Act of 1882 and riots against Chinese workers in the 1870s and 1880s reflected this negative stereotype. The Chinese regarded the United States with a mixture of admiration, curiosity, resentment, suspicion, and disdain.

American annexations in the Pacific in 1898 and 1899 convinced Secretary of State Hay that the United States should announce a China policy. He did so in the Open Door notes of 1899–1900, which became the cornerstone of U.S. policy in Asia for half a century. The first note demanded an open door for American trade by declaring the principle of equal access to commercial rights in China by all nations. The second note, addressing Russian movement into Manchuria, called on all countries to respect the "territorial and administrative integrity" of China. This second principle announced a larger American role in Asia, offering China protection and preserving the East Asian balance of power.

An early test of this new role came during the Boxer Rebellion in 1900. The Boxers were a society of young traditionalist Chinese in revolt against both the Manchu dynasty and the growing Western presence in China. During the summer of 1900, Boxers killed some 242 missionaries and other foreigners and besieged the western quarter of Peking. Eventually an international military force of 19,000 troops, including some 3,000 Americans, marched on Peking to end the siege.

The relationship with China was plagued by the American exclusionist immigration policy. Despite barriers and riots, Chinese workers kept coming to the United States illegally. In 1905, Chinese nationalists at home boycotted American goods and called for a change in immigration policy. Roosevelt, contemptuous of the "backward" Chinese, bristled and sent troops to the Philippines as a threat. Halfheartedly, he also asked Congress for a modified immigration bill, but nothing came of it.

Despite exclusion and insults, the idea that the United States had a unique guardian relationship with China persisted into the twentieth century. Japan had ambitions in China, so this created a rivalry between Japan and the United States, testing the American commitment to the Open Door in China and the balance of power in Asia. Economic motives, however, proved to be less significant. Investments there developed very slowly, as did the dream of the "great China market" for American grains and textiles. The China trade always remained larger in imagination than in reality.

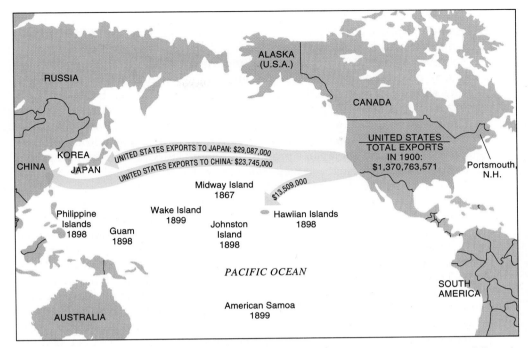

UNITED STATES INVOLVEMENT IN ASIA, 1898–1909 What major twentieth-century events have followed the acquisition of territories in the Pacific and the development of intensified trade with East Asian countries?

Japan and the Balance of Power

Population pressures, war, and a quest for economic opportunities caused Japanese immigration to the United States to increase dramatically around the turn of the century. Coming first as males working on western railroads and in West Coast canneries, mines, and logging camps, immigrants from Japan increased from 25,000 in the 1890s to 125,000 between 1901 and 1908. Like the earlier Chinese immigrants, they met nativist hostility. In 1906, the San Francisco school board segregated them into separate schools and asked Roosevelt to persuade Japan to stop the emigration. The insulted Japanese agreed to limit the migration of unskilled workers to the United States in a "gentleman's agreement" signed in 1907. In return, the segregation law was repealed, but not without costs in relations between the two nations.

Roosevelt worked hard to maintain the balance of power in East Asia. The Boxer Rebellion of 1900 left Russia with 50,000 troops in Manchuria, making it the strongest regional power. Roosevelt's admiration for the Japanese as a "fighting" people and valuable factor in the "civilization of the future" contrasted with his low respect for the Russians. As Japan moved into Korea and Russia into Manchuria, Roosevelt hoped that each would check the other.

Roosevelt welcomed news in 1904 that Japan had successfully mounted a surprise attack, beginning the Russo-Japanese War. But as Japanese victories continued, many Americans worried that Japan might play the game too well, shutting the United States out of Far Eastern markets. Roosevelt tilted toward Russia. When the Japanese expressed an interest in ending the war, the American president was pleased to exert his influence.

Roosevelt's goal was to achieve peace and leave a balanced situation. Nothing better symbolized the new American presence in the world than the 1905 negotiation and signing in Portsmouth, New Hampshire, of the peace treaty ending a war in Manchuria between Russia and Japan.

The Treaty of Portsmouth left Japan dominant in Manchuria. Roosevelt recognized this, as well as Japanese control of Korea. In return, in the Root-Takahira Agreement of 1908, he got Japan's promise to honor U.S. control in the Philippines and to make no further encroachments into China. This made the United States the major counterweight to Japan in East Asia.

These agreements barely papered over Japanese-American tensions. Some Japanese blamed Roosevelt that the Treaty of Portsmouth had not given them indemnities from Russia. American insensitivity on the immigration issue left bad feelings. In Manchuria, the U.S. consul general aggressively pushed an anti-Japanese program of financing capital investment projects in banking and railroads. This policy, known as "dollar diplomacy" under Roosevelt's successor, William Howard Taft, like the pursuit of markets, was larger in prospect than results. Nevertheless, the United States was in Japan's way, and rumors of war circulated.

It was clearly time for Roosevelt's "big stick." In 1907, he told Secretary of State Root that he was "more concerned over the Japanese situation than almost any other. Thank Heaven we have the navy in good shape." Although the naval buildup had begun over a decade earlier, under Roosevelt the U.S. Navy developed into a formidable force. In 1907, to make it clear that "the Pacific was as much our home waters as the Atlantic," Roosevelt sent his "Great White Fleet" on a goodwill world tour. The first stop was Yokohama. Although American sailors were greeted warmly, the act may have stimulated navalism in Japan, which came back to haunt the United States in 1941. But for the time being, the balance of power in Asia was preserved.

Preventing War in Europe

The United States had stretched the Monroe Doctrine to justify sending Marines and engineers to Latin America and the Navy and dollars to Asia. Treaties, agreements, and the protection of territories and interests entangled the United States with foreign nations from Panama and the Dominican Republic to the Philippines and Manchuria. Toward Europe, however, traditional neutrality continued.

Roosevelt believed that the most serious threats to world peace and civilized order lay in the relationships among Germany, Great Britain, and France. He established two fundamental policies toward Europe that would define the U.S. role throughout the century. The first was to make friendship with Great Britain the cornerstone of U.S. policy. Second, the crucial goal of a neutral power like the United States was to prevent a general war in Europe among strong nations. Toward this end, Roosevelt depended on his personal negotiating skills and began the practice of summit diplomacy.

The Venezuelan crisis of 1895 shocked the United States and Britain into an awareness of their mutual interests. Both nations appreciated the neutrality of the other in their respective colonial wars. Roosevelt supported British imperialism because he favored the dominance of the "English-speaking race" and believed that Britain was "fighting the battle of civilization." Furthermore, both nations worried about growing German power around the world. As German naval power increased, Britain had to bring its fleet closer to home. Friendly allies were needed to police parts of the world formerly patrolled by the British navy. The United Kingdom therefore concluded a mutual-protection treaty with Japan in 1902 and willingly let the Americans police Central America and the Caribbean Sea.

Language, cultural traditions, and strategic self-interest drew the two countries together. Roosevelt, moreover, was unashamedly pro-British. He knew, as he wrote to Lodge in 1901, that the United States had "not the least particle of danger to fear" from Britain and that German ambitions and militarism represented the major threat to peace in Europe. As Roosevelt left the presidency in 1909, one of his final acts was to proclaim the special American friendship with Great Britain.

German Kaiser Wilhelm II thought that Roosevelt was really pro-German. Roosevelt cultivated the Kaiser's illusion, and Wilhelm sought his support on several diplomatic issues between 1905 and 1909. In each case, Roosevelt flattered the Kaiser while politely rejecting his overtures. The relationship gave Roosevelt a unique advantage in trying to prevent war in Europe, most notably during the Moroccan crisis in 1905 and 1906. When Germany and France threatened to go to war over the control of Morocco, Roosevelt arranged the Algeciras Conference in Spain to head off conflict. The treaty signed in 1906 peacefully settled the Moroccan issue favorably for the French. Later, at the Hague conference on disarmament in 1907, the Kaiser sought an agreement to reduce British naval supremacy, a superiority Roosevelt thought "quite proper." The German emperor also tried to promote German-Chinese-American entente to balance the Anglo-Japanese Treaty in Asia. Roosevelt rebuffed all these efforts.

Touring Europe in 1910, the retired American president was warmly entertained by Wilhelm, who continued to misunderstand him. Roosevelt, meanwhile, kept urging his English friends to counter the German naval buildup in order to maintain peace in Europe. In 1911, Roosevelt wrote that there would be nothing worse than that "Germany should ever overthrow England and establish the supremacy in Europe she aims at." A German attempt "to try her hand in America," he thought, would surely follow. To avert it, Roosevelt's policy for Europe included cementing friendship with England and, while maintaining official neutrality, using diplomacy to prevent hostilities among European powers. The relationship between Great Britain and Germany continued to deteriorate, however, and by 1914, a new American president, Woodrow Wilson, would face the terrible reality that Roosevelt had skillfully sought to prevent. When World War I finally broke out, no American was more eager to fight on the British side against the Germans than the leader of the Rough Riders.

TIMELINE

1823	1857	1867	1870	1875
Monroe Doctrine	Trade opens with Japan	Alaska purchased from Russia	Failure to annex Santo Domingo (Hispaniola)	Sugar reciprocity treaty with Hawaii

1893	1895	1896	1897	1898
Hawaiian coup by American sugar growers	Cuban revolt against Spanish Venezuelan boundary dispute	Weyler's reconcentration policy in Cuba; McKinley-Bryan presidential campaign	Roosevelt's speech at Naval War College	**February** Sinking of the *Maine* **April** Spanish-American War; Teller Amendment **May** Dewey takes Manila Bay **July** Annexation of Hawaiian Islands **August** Americans liberate Manila; War ends **December** Treaty of Paris; Annexation of the Philippines

1903	1904	1904–1905	1904–1906	1905–1906
Panamanian revolt and independence; Hay-Bunau-Varilla Treaty	Roosevelt Corollary	Russo-Japanese War ended by treaty signed at Portsmouth, New Hampshire	United States intervenes in Nicaragua, Guatemala, and Cuba	Moroccan crisis

1914	1916
Opening of the Panama Canal; World War I begins	Partial home rule granted to the Philippines

❖❖❖❖❖

CONCLUSION

The Responsibilities of Power

The realities of power in the 1890s brought increasing international responsibilities. Roosevelt said in 1910 that because of "strength and geographical situation," the United States had itself become "more and more, the balance of power of the whole world." This ominous responsibility was also an opportunity to extend American economic, political, and moral influence around the globe.

1877 United States acquires naval base at Pearl Harbor	**1878** United States acquires naval station in Samoa	**1882** Chinese Exclusion Act	**1889** First Pan-American Conference	**1890** Alfred Mahan publishes *Influence of Sea Power upon History*
1899 Senate ratifies Treaty of Paris; Filipino-American War begins; American Samoa acquired	**1899–1900** Open Door notes	**1900** Boxer Rebellion in China; William McKinley reelected president	**1901** Supreme Court insular cases; McKinley assassinated; Theodore Roosevelt becomes president	**1902** Filipino-American War ends; U.S. military occupation of Cuba ends; Platt Amendment; Venezuela debt crisis
1906 Roosevelt receives Nobel Peace Prize	**1907** Gentleman's agreement with Japan	**1908** Root-Takahira Agreement	**1909** U.S. Navy ("Great White Fleet") sails around the world	**1911** United States intervenes in Nicaragua

As president in the first decade of the twentieth century, Roosevelt established aggressive American policies toward the rest of the world. The United States dominated and policed Central America and the Caribbean Sea to maintain order and protect its investments and other economic interests. In the Far East, Americans marched through Hay's Open Door with treaties, troops, navies, and dollars to protect the newly annexed Philippine Islands, to develop markets and investments, and to preserve the balance of power in Asia. In Europe, the United States sought to remain neutral and uninvolved in European affairs and at the same time to cement Anglo-American friendship and prevent "civilized" nations from going to war.

How well these policies worked would be seen later in the twentieth century. Whatever the particular judgment, the fundamental ambivalence of America's sense of itself as a model "city on a hill," an example to others, remained. As widening involvements around the world—the Filipino-American War, for example—painfully demonstrated, it was increasingly difficult for the United States to be both responsible and good, both powerful and loved. The American people thus learned to experience both the satisfactions and burdens, both the profits and costs, of the missionary role.

Recommended Reading

American Expansionism: Moving Toward Empire

Robert Beisner, *From the Old Diplomacy to the New, 1865–1900* (1975); Charles Campbell, *The Transformation of American Foreign Relations, 1865–1900* (1976); John Dobson, *Reticent Expansionism: The Foreign Policy of William McKinley* (1988); David Healy, *U.S. Expansion: Imperialist Urge in the 1890s* (1970); Walter LaFeber, *The Cambridge History of Foreign Relations: The Search for Opportunity, 1865–1913* (1993); H. Wayne Morgan, *America's Road to Empire: The War with Spain and Overseas Expansion* (1965); Milton Plesur, *America's Outward Thrust, 1865–1890* (1971); William Widenor, *Henry Cabot Lodge and the Search for an American Foreign Policy* (1980).

The Spanish-American War and the Philippines

Robert Beisner, *Twelve Against Empire: The Anti-Imperialists, 1898–1900* (1968); James E. Bradford, ed., *Crucible of Empire: The Spanish-American War and Its Aftermath* (1993); Willard Gatewood, Jr., *Black Americans and the White Man's Burden* (1975) and *"Smoked Yankees" and the Struggle for Empire: Letters from Negro Soldiers, 1898–1902* (1971); Stanley Karnow, *In Our Image: America's Empire in the Philippines* (1989); Gerald Linderman, *The Mirror of War: American Society and the Spanish-American War* (1974); Stuart Creighton Miller, *"Benevolent Assimilation:" The American Conquest of the Philippines, 1899–1903* (1982); John L. Offner, *An Unwanted War: The Diplomacy of the United States and Spain over Cuba, 1895–1898* (1992); Louis A. Perez, Jr., *The War of 1898: The United States and Cuba in History and Historiography* (1998); David Trask, *The War with Spain in 1898* (1981); Richard Welch, *Response to Imperialism: The United States and the Philippine-American War, 1899–1902* (1979);

Roosevelt's Energetic Foreign Policy and Relations with Asia and the Caribbean

Howard Beale, *Theodore Roosevelt and the Rise of America to World Power* (1956); Roger Daniels, *Asian Americans: Chinese and Japanese in the United States Since 1850* (1988); Walter La Feber, *Inevitable Revolutions: The United States in Central America* (1983); Frederick Marks III, *Velvet on Iron: The Diplomacy of Theodore Roosevelt* (1979); David McCollough, *The Path Between the Seas: The Creation of the Panama Canal, 1870–1914* (1977); Richard H. Collin, *Theodore Roosevelt's Caribbean: The Panama Canal, the Monroe Doctrine, and the Latin American Context* (1990); Ronald Takaki, *Strangers from a Different Shore: A History of Asian Americans* (1989); Marilyn B. Young, *The Rhetoric of Empire: American China Policy, 1895–1901* (1968).

CHAPTER 21

The Progressives Confront
Industrial Capitalism

Frances Kellor, a young woman who grew up in Ohio and Michigan, received her law degree in 1897 from Cornell University and became one of the small but growing group of professionally trained women. Deciding that she was more interested in solving the nation's social problems than in practicing law, she moved to Chicago, studied sociology, and trained herself as a social reformer. Kellor believed passionately that poverty and inequality could be eliminated in America. She also had the progressive faith that if Americans could only hear the truth about the millions of people living in urban slums, they would rise up and make changes. She was one of the experts who provided the evidence to document what was wrong in industrial America.

Like many progressives, Kellor believed that environment was more important than heredity in determining ability, prosperity, and happiness. Better schools and better housing, she thought, would produce better citizens. Even criminals, she argued, were simply victims of environment. Kellor demonstrated that poor health and deprived childhoods explained the only differences between criminals and college students. If it were impossible to define a criminal type, then it must be possible to reduce crime by improving the environment.

Kellor was an efficient professional. Like the majority of the professional women of her generation, she never married but devoted her life to social research and social reform. She lived for a time at Hull House in Chicago and at the College Settlement in New York, centers not only of social research and reform, but also of lively community. For many young people the settlement, with its sense of commitment and its exciting conversation around the dinner table, provided an alternative to the nuclear family or the single apartment.

While staying at the College Settlement, Kellor researched and wrote a muckraking study of employment agencies, published in 1904 as *Out of Work*. She revealed how employment agencies exploited immigrants, blacks, and other recent arrivals in the city. Kellor's book, like the writing of most progressives, sizzled with moral outrage. But Kellor went beyond moralism to suggest corrective legislation at the state and national levels. Kellor became one of the leaders of the movement to Americanize the immigrants pouring into the country in unprecedented numbers. Between 1899 and 1920, over eight million people came to the United States, most from southern and eastern Europe. Many feared that this flood of immigrants threatened the very basis of American democracy. Kellor and her co-workers represented the side of progressivism that sought state and federal laws to protect the new arrivals from exploitation and to establish agencies and facilities to educate and Americanize them. Another group of progressives, often allied with organized labor, tried to pass laws to restrict immigration. Kellor did not entirely escape her generation's ethnocentrism, but she did maintain that all immigrants could be made into useful citizens.

Convinced of the need for a national movement to push for reform legislation, Kellor helped to found the National Committee for Immigrants in America, which tried to promote a national policy "to make all these people Americans," and a federal bureau to organize the campaign. Eventually, she helped establish the Division of Immigrant Education within the Department of Education. A political movement led by Theodore Roosevelt excited her most. More than almost any other single person, Kellor had been responsible for alerting Roosevelt to the problems the immigrants faced in American cities. When Roosevelt formed the new Progressive party in 1912, she was one of the many social workers and social researchers who joined him. She campaigned for Roosevelt and directed the Progressive Service Organization, educating voters in all areas of social justice and welfare after the election. After Roosevelt's defeat and the collapse of the Progressive party, Kellor continued to work for Americanization. She spent the rest of her life promoting justice, order, and efficiency and looking for ways of resolving industrial and international disputes.

✦✦✦✦✦

Frances Kellor's life illustrates two important aspects of progressivism, the first nationwide reform movement of the modern era: first, a commitment to promote social justice, to assure equal opportunity, and to preserve democracy; and second, a search for order and efficiency in a world complicated by rapid industrialization, immigration, and spectacular urban growth. But no one person can represent all facets of so complex a movement. Borrowing from populism and influenced by a number of reformers from the 1890s, progressivism reached a climax in the years from 1900 to 1914. The progressive movement did not plot to overthrow the government; rather, it sought to reform the system in order to assure the survival of the American way of life.

This chapter traces the important aspects of progressivism. It examines the social justice movement, which sought to promote reform among the poor and to improve life for those who had fallen victim to an urban and industrial civilization. It surveys life among workers, a group the reformers sometimes helped but often misunderstood. Then it traces the reform movements in the cities and states, where countless officials and experts tried to reduce chaos and promote order and democracy. Finally, it examines progressivism at the national level during the administrations of Theodore Roosevelt and Woodrow Wilson, the first thoroughly modern presidents.

THE SOCIAL JUSTICE MOVEMENT

Historians write of a "progressive movement." Actually there were a number of movements, some of them contradictory, but all focusing on the problems created by a rapidly expanding urban and industrial world. Some reformers, often from the middle class, sought to humanize the modern city—improving housing and schools, and providing a better life for immigrants. Others focused on working conditions and the rights of labor. Still others sought to make politics responsive to popular interests, including women. Progressivism had roots in the 1890s, when many reformers were shocked by the devastation caused by the depression of 1893, and they were influenced by George's *Progress and Poverty* (1879), Bellamy's *Looking Backward* (1888), and the Social Gospel movement (see Chapter 19).

The Progressive World View

Intellectually, the progressives were influenced by Darwinism. Believing that the world was in flux, they rebelled against the fixed and the formal. Progressive philosopher John Dewey wrote that ideas could become instruments for change. William James, in his philosophy of pragmatism, denied that there were universal truths; ideas should be judged by their usefulness. Most progressives were convinced that social environment was much more important than heredity in forming character. Building better schools and houses would make better people and a more perfect society. Yet even the more advanced reformers thought in racial and ethnic categories, sure that some groups could be molded more easily than others. Progressivism did not usually mean progress for blacks.

In many ways, progressivism was the first modern reform movement. It sought to bring order and efficiency to a world that had been transformed by rapid growth and new technology. Yet elements of nostalgia infected the movement as reformers tried to preserve pre-industrial handicrafts and to promote small town and farm values in urban settings. Progressive leaders were almost always middle class, and they quite consciously tried to teach middle-class values to immigrants and working people. Often progressives seemed more interested in control than in reform; frequently, they displayed paternalism toward those they tried to help.

The progressives were part of a statistics-minded, realistic generation. They conducted surveys, gathered facts, wrote reports, and usually had faith that all this would lead to change. Their urge to document and to record came out in haunting photographs of young workers taken by Lewis Hine, in the stark and beautiful city paintings by John Sloan, and in the realist novels of Theodore Dreiser and William Dean Howells.

Optimistic about human nature, progressives believed that change was possible. They may seem naive or bigoted, but they wrestled with many social questions, some of them old but fraught with new urgency in an industrialized society. What is the proper relation of government to society? In a world of large corporations and huge cities, how much should the government regulate and control? How much responsibility does society have for its poor and needy? Progressives could not agree on the answers, but for the first time in American history they struggled with the questions.

The Muckrakers

Writers who exposed corruption and other social evils were labeled "muckrakers" by Theodore Roosevelt. Not all muckrakers were reformers—some just wrote for the money—but reformers learned from their techniques of exposé.

In part, the muckrakers were a product of the journalistic revolution of the 1890s. Nineteenth-century magazines had elite audiences. The new magazines had slick formats, more advertising, and wider sales. Competing for readers, editors eagerly published articles telling the public what was wrong in American society.

Lincoln Steffens, a young California journalist, wrote articles exposing the connections between respectable businessmen and corrupt politicians. When published as a book in 1904, *The Shame of the Cities* became a battle cry for people determined to clean up city government. Ida Tarbell, a teacher turned journalist, revealed the ruthlessness of John D. Rockefeller's Standard Oil Company. David Graham Phillips uncovered the alliance of politics and business in *The Treason of the Senate* (1906). Robert Hunter, a young settlement worker, shocked Americans in 1904 with his book *Poverty*. Upton Sinclair's novel *The Jungle* (1906) described the horrors of the Chicago meatpacking industry, and Frank Norris in *The Octopus* (1901) dramatized the railroads' stranglehold on farmers.

Working Women and Children

Nothing disturbed the social justice progressives more than the sight of children as young as eight or ten working long hours in dangerous and depressing factories. Florence Kelley was one of the most important leaders in the crusade against child labor. Kelley had grown up in an upper-class Philadelphia family and was a member of the first generation of college women. Refused admission to an American graduate school because of her sex, she went to the University of Zurich in Switzerland and became a socialist. After her marriage failed, Kelley moved into Hull House and poured her energies into the campaign against child labor. When no Chicago attorney would argue child labor cases against prominent corporations, she went to law school, passed the bar exam, and argued the cases herself.

Kelley and other child labor reformers quickly recognized the need for state laws. Marshaling their evidence about the tragic effects on growing children of long working hours in dark and damp factories, they pressured the Illinois legislature into passing an antichild labor law. A few years later, however, the state supreme court ruled it unconstitutional, showing reformers that national-level action was essential. Kelley led the charge.

The National Child Labor Committee was the brainchild of Edgar Gardner Murphy, a Social Gospel clergyman from Alabama. Headquartered in New York, it drew up a model state child labor law, encouraged state and city campaigns, and coordinated the movement around the country. Although two-thirds of the states passed some form of child labor law between 1905 and 1907, many had loopholes. The committee therefore supported a national bill introduced in Congress by Indiana Senator Albert Beveridge in 1906 "to prevent the employment of children in factories and mines." It went down to defeat, but reformers convinced Congress in 1912 to establish a children's bureau in the Department of Labor. Compulsory school attendance laws, however, did more to reduce the number of children who worked than federal and state laws, which proved difficult to pass and even more difficult to enforce.

The crusade against child labor was a typical social justice reform effort. Its origins lay in the moral indignation of middle-class reformers. But reform went beyond moral outrage as reformers gathered statistics, took photographs, and used their evidence to push for legislation, first on the local level, then in the states, and eventually in Washington.

Nothing tugged at the heartstrings of the reformers more than the sight of little children, sullen and stunted, working long hours in factory, farm, and mine. These children, breaker boys who spent all day sorting coal in western Pennsylvania, were carefully posed by documentary photographer Lewis Hine while he worked for the National Child Labor Committee in 1911. (Records of the Children's Bureau, The National Archives, Office of the Chief Signal Officer)

Like other progressive reform efforts, the battle against child labor was only partly successful. Too many businessmen profitably employed children. Too many politicians and judges were reluctant to regulate the work of children or adults. And some parents, desperately needing their childrens' earnings, opposed the reformers and broke the law.

Reformers worried over the young people who got into trouble with the law, often for pranks that in rural areas would have seemed harmless. By setting up juvenile courts, a progressive innovation, it was thought that young people could receive correction without being turned into hardened criminals by adult prisons. Yet juvenile courts frequently deprived young offenders of all rights of due process, as the Supreme Court finally recognized in 1967.

Closely connected with the anti-child labor movement was the effort to limit the hours of women's work. It seemed inconsistent to protect a girl until she was 16 and then give her the "right to work from 8 a.m. to 10 p.m., 13 hours a day, 78 hours a week for $6." Florence Kelley and the National Consumers League led the campaign. It was foolish and unpatriotic, they argued, to allow the "mothers of future generations" to work long hours in dangerous industries.

The most important court case on women's work came before the U.S. Supreme Court in 1908. Josephine Goldmark, Kelley's friend, wrote the brief for *Muller* v. *Oregon* that her brother-in-law, Louis Brandeis, used when he argued the case. The Court upheld the Oregon ten-hour law largely because Goldmark's sociological argument detailed the danger and disease that factory women faced. Brandeis opposed laissez-faire legal concepts, arguing that the government had a special interest in protecting citizens' health. Most states fell into line with the

Supreme Court decision and passed protective legislation for women, though many companies managed to circumvent the laws. But even the ten hours of work permitted by the law seemed too long for women who had to come home to child-care and housekeeping.

Contending that "women are fundamentally weaker than men in all that makes for endurance . . . ," reformers won some protection for women workers. But their arguments would later be used to reinforce gender segregation at work.

Besides seeking legislation to protect working women, the social justice progressives also campaigned for woman suffrage. Unlike some supporters who argued that middle-class women would offset the ignorant and corrupt votes of immigrant men, these social reformers supported votes for all women. Addams argued that urban women not only could vote intelligently, but also needed the vote to protect their families. The progressive insistence that all women needed the vote helped to push woman suffrage toward victory during World War I.

Much more controversial than either votes for women or protective legislation was the birth control movement. Even many advanced progressives could not imagine themselves teaching immigrant women how to prevent conception (which was also illegal under federal law).

Margaret Sanger, a nurse who had watched poor women suffer from too many births and even die from dangerous illegal abortions, was one of the founders of the modern American birth control movement. Middle-class Americans had limited family size in the nineteenth century through abstinence, withdrawal, abortion, and primitive birth control devices, but much ignorance remained, even among middle-class women. Sanger obtained the latest medical and scientific European studies and in 1914 explained in her magazine, *The Woman Rebel,* and in a pamphlet, *Family Limitation,* that women could separate sex from procreation. She was indicted for violation of the postal code and fled to Europe to avoid arrest.

Birth control long remained controversial, and in most states illegal. Yet Sanger helped to bring sexuality and contraception out into the open. When she returned to the United States in 1921, she founded the American Birth Control League, which became the Planned Parenthood Federation in 1942.

Home and School

Reformers believed that better housing and education could transform the lives of the poor and create a better world. Books such as Jacob Riis's *How the Other Half Lives* (1890) horrified them. With vivid language and haunting photographs, Riis had documented the misery of New York's slums.

In the first decade of the twentieth century, the progressives took a new approach to the housing problems. They collected statistics, conducted surveys, organized committees, and constructed exhibits to demonstrate the effect of urban overcrowding. Tenement house laws, passed in several cities, were often ineffectual. In 1910, reformers organized the National Housing Association, and some hoped for federal laws and even government-subsidized housing.

The housing reformers combined a moral sense of what needed to be done to create a more just society with practical ability to stir up the public and get laws passed. They also viewed the poor paternalistically. But often immigrants' family values differed from middle-class reformers'. They did not mind clutter and lack of privacy, and they hung religious objects rather than "good pictures" on the walls.

Many middle-class women reformers who tried to teach working-class families how to live in their tenements had never organized their own homes. Those who lived in settlement houses never worried about cooking or chores. Some, however, began to realize that domestic tasks kept women of all classes from taking their full place in society. Charlotte Perkins Gilman sketched an alternative to traditional notions of "the woman's sphere," suggesting that entrepreneurs build apartment houses in which women could combine motherhood with careers. Most Americans, however, of all political persuasions continued to view the home as sacred space where the mother ruled supreme and created domestic tranquillity for her husband and children.

Next to better housing, the progressives stressed better schools as a way to produce better citizens. Public school systems were often rigid and corrupt, and seemed to reinforce old habits. Barked a Chicago teacher: "Don't stop to think; tell me what you know."

Progressive education, like many other aspects of progressivism, opposed the rigid in favor of flexibility. John Dewey was the key philosopher of progressive education. He tried to create in the city a sense of the small rural community of his native Vermont. He experimented with new educational methods, including seats that could be arranged in small groups rather than bolted down in rows.

Dewey insisted that the schools be child-centered rather than subject-centered, that teachers teach children rather than history or mathematics. He did not mean that history and math should not be taught, but that those subjects should be related to the students' experience. Students should not just learn about democracy; the school itself should operate like a democracy.

Dewey also maintained, somewhat controversially, that the schools should become instruments for social reform. But like most progressives, Dewey was never clear whether he wanted the schools to help the students adjust to the existing world or to turn out graduates who would change the world. Although he wavered, the spirit of progressive education, like the spirit of progressivism in general, was optimistic. The schools could create more flexible, better-educated adults who would go out to improve society.

Crusades Against Saloons, Brothels, and Movie Houses

Given their faith in the reforming potential of healthy and educated citizens, it was logical that most social justice progressives opposed the sale of alcohol. Some came from Protestant homes where drinking was considered a sin, but most favored prohibition for pragmatic reasons: to reform the city and conserve human resources.

Americans did drink a lot, and the amount they consumed rose rapidly after 1900, peaking between 1911 and 1915. Only three states still had prohibition laws dating from the 1850s. The modern anti-liquor movement was spearheaded in the 1880s and 1890s by the Women's Christian Temperance Union and after 1900 by the Anti-Saloon League and a coalition of religious leaders and social reformers. Seven states passed temperance laws between 1906 and 1912.

Reformers were appalled by young children going into saloons to buy a pail of beer for the family and horrified by tales of abuse by alcoholic fathers. Most often, progressives focused on the saloon. "Why should the community have any more sympathy for the saloon . . . than . . . for a typhoid-breeding pool of filthy water?" an irate reformer asked.

Although they never quite understood the role alcohol played in the social life of many ethnic groups, Jane Addams and other settlement workers appreciated the saloon's importance as a social center. Addams started a coffeehouse at Hull House to lure people away from the saloon. The progressives never found a substitute for the saloon, but they did work for local and state prohibition laws. As in many other progressive efforts, they joined with diverse groups to push for change, and won. On December 22, 1917, Congress sent to the states for ratification a constitutional amendment prohibiting the sale, manufacturing, or importing of intoxicating liquor within the United States. The spirit of wartime sacrifice facilitated its rapid ratification.

Besides the saloon, progressives saw the urban dance hall and movie theater as threats to youthful morals. The motion picture, invented in 1889, developed as an important form of entertainment only during the first decade of the twentieth century, at first appealing mainly to a lower-class and largely ethnic audience.

Not until World War I, when D. W. Griffith produced long feature films, did the movies begin to attract a middle-class audience. The most popular of these early films was Griffith's *The Birth of a Nation* (1915), a blatantly racist and distorted epic of black debauchery during Reconstruction. Many early films were imported from France, Italy, and Germany; because they were silent, they could be subtitled in any language. But viewers did not need to know the language, or even be able to read, to enjoy the action. That was part of early films' attraction. Many depicted premarital sex, adultery, and violence, and, unlike later films, many attacked authority and had tragic endings. *The Candidate* (1907) showed an upper-class reform candidate who gets dirt thrown at him when he tries to clean up the town. In *Down with Women* (1907) well-dressed men denounced woman suffrage and the incompetence of the weaker sex, but throughout the film, only strong women were depicted.

Some of the films stressed slapstick humor or romance and adventure; others bordered on pornography. The reformers objected not only to the plots and content of the films, but also to the location of the theaters, near saloons and burlesque houses, and to their dark interiors. "In the dim auditorium which seems to float on the world of dreams . . . an American woman may spend her afternoon alone," one critic wrote. "She can let her fantasies slip through the darkened atmosphere. . . ." This disturbed reformers. But for young immigrant women, who made up the bulk of the audience at most urban movie theaters, the films provided rare exciting moments in their lives.

Saloons, dance halls, and movie theaters all seemed to progressives somehow connected with the worst evil of all, prostitution. Nineteenth-century anti-prostitution campaigns were nothing compared with the progressives' crusade to wipe out the "social evil." All major cities and many smaller ones appointed vice commissions, whose reports, often running to several thick volumes, were typical progressive documents, filled with elaborate statistical studies and moral outrage.

The progressive antivice crusade attracted many kinds of people, for often contradictory reasons. Racists and immigration restrictionists claimed that inferior people—blacks and recent immigrants—became prostitutes and pimps. Social hygiene progressives published vivid accounts of prostitution as part of their campaign to fight sexual ignorance. Some women reformers promoted a single moral standard for men and women. Others worried that prostitutes would spread venereal disease to unfaithful husbands, who would pass it on to wives and babies. Most progressives, however, stressed the environmental causes of vice. To them, prostitution, like child labor and poor housing, would be eliminated by education and reform.

Despite all their reports and publicity, the progressives failed to end prostitution and did virtually nothing to address its roots in poverty. "Do you suppose I am going back to earn five or six dollars a week in a factory," one prostitute asked an investigator, "when I can earn that amount any night and often much more?" Reformers wiped out a few red-light districts, closed some brothels, and managed to push a bill through Congress (the Mann Act of 1910) that prohibited the interstate transport of women for immoral purposes. Perhaps more important, in several states, they got the age of consent for women raised, and in 20 states they made the Wassermann test for syphilis mandatory for both men and women before a marriage license could be issued.

THE WORKER IN THE PROGRESSIVE ERA

Progressive reformers sympathized with industrial workers who struggled to earn a living for themselves and their families and sought legislation to protect working women and children. But often they had little understanding of what it was really like to sell one's strength by the hour. For example, they supported labor's right to organize at a time when labor had few friends, yet they often opposed the strike as a weapon against management. And neither organized labor nor the reformers, individually or in shaky partnership, had much power over industry.

Adjusting to Industrial Labor

Many workers, whether from eastern Europe or Michigan, found the factory bewildering. Unlike the farm or shop, it was ruled by the clock and the boss. Workers continued to resist the pace of factory work and subtly sabotaged employers' efforts to control them (see Chapters 10 and 18). They stayed home on holidays when they were supposed to work, took unauthorized breaks, and set their own productivity schedules. Often they were fired or quit. In New York needleworker shops in 1912 and 1913, the turnover rate was over 250 percent. Overall, one-third of the workers stayed at their jobs less than a year.

The industrial work force, still composed largely of immigrants, had a fluid character. Many migrants, especially those from southern and eastern Europe, expected to stay only for a short time. About 40 percent of those who came in the first decade of the twentieth century did return. In years of economic downturn, more Italians and Austro-Hungarians left the United States than entered. Many men came alone—70 percent in some years—and saved perhaps a third of their money by living in a boardinghouse.

Documentary Photographs

Photographs are a revealing way of recovering the past visually. But when looking at a photograph, especially an old one, it is easy to assume that it is an accurate representation of the past. Photographers, however, like novelists and historians, have a point of view. They take their pictures for a reason and often to prove a point. As one photographer remarked, "Photographs don't lie, but liars take photographs."

To document the need for reform in the cities, progressives collected statistics, made surveys, described settlement houses, and even wrote novels. But they discovered that the photograph was often more effective than words. Jacob Riis, the Danish-born author of *How the Other Half Lives* (1890), a devastating exposure of conditions in New York City tenement house slums, was also a pioneer in urban photography. Others had taken pictures of dank alleys and street urchins before, but Riis was the first to photograph slum conditions with the express purpose of promoting reform. At first he hired photographers, but then he bought a camera and taught himself how to use it. He even tried a new German flash powder to illuminate dark alleys and tenement rooms in order to record the horror of slum life.

Riis made many of his photographs into lantern slides and used them to illustrate his lectures on the need for housing reform. Although he was a creative and innovative photographer, his pictures were often far from objective. His equipment was awkward, his film slow. He had to set up and prepare carefully before snapping the shutter. His views of tenement ghetto streets and poor children now seem like clichés, but they were designed to make Americans angry, to arouse them to reform.

Another important progressive photographer was Lewis Hine; like Riis, he taught himself photography. Trained as a sociologist, Hine used his camera to illustrate his lectures at the Ethical Culture School in New York. In 1908, he was hired as a full-time investigator by the National Child Labor Committee. His haunting photographs of children in factories helped convince many Americans of the need to abolish child labor. Hine's children were appealing human beings. He showed them eating, running, working, and staring wistfully out factory windows. His photographs avoided the pathos that Riis was so fond of recording, but just as surely they documented the need for reform.

As you look at this, or any photographs, ask yourself: What is the photographer's purpose and point of view? Why was this particular angle chosen for the picture? And why center on these particular people or objects? What does the photographer reveal about his or her purpose? What does the photographer reveal unintentionally? How have fast film and new camera styles changed photography? On what subjects do reform-minded photographers train their cameras today?

Lewis Hine, *Carolina Cotton Mill*, 1908. (George Eastman House)

The nature of work continued to change in the early twentieth century as industrialists extended late-nineteenth-century efforts to make their factories and work forces more efficient, productive, and profitable. In some industries, new machines revolutionized work and eliminated highly paid skilled jobs. The moving assembly line, perfected by Henry Ford, transformed the nature of work and turned many laborers into unskilled machine-tenders.

The influence of the machine was uneven, having a greater impact in some industries than in others. Although some skilled weavers and glassblowers were transformed into unskilled operators, the machines themselves created the need for new skilled workers. In the auto industry, for example, the new elite workers were the mechanics and the tool and die men who kept the assembly line running. But the trend toward mechanization was unstoppable, and even the most skilled workers were eventually removed from making decisions about production.

The principles of scientific management were also important in altering industrial work. Here the key figure was Frederick Taylor, the son of a prominent Philadelphia family. Taylor had a nervous breakdown as a youth, and his physicians prescribed manual labor as a cure. Working in a Philadelphia steel plant and studying engineering at night, he became chief engineer in the 1880s. Later he used this experience to rethink the organization of industry.

Taylor was obsessed with efficiency. He emphasized centralized planning, systematic analysis, and detailed instructions. Most of all, he timed all kinds of workers with a stopwatch. Many owners enthusiastically adopted his concepts of scientific management, seeing an opportunity to increase their profits and their control of the workplace. Not surprisingly, many workers resented "Taylorism."

Union Organizing

Samuel Gompers, head of the American Federation of Labor, quickly saw that Taylorism would reduce workers to "mere machines." Under his guidance, the AFL prospered during the progressive era. By 1914, the AFL alone had over two million members. Gompers's "pure and simple unionism" was most successful among coal miners, railroad workers, and the building trades. As we saw in Chapter 18, Gompers ignored unskilled and immigrant workers and concentrated on raising the wages and improving the working conditions of the skilled craftsmen who were members of unions affiliated with the AFL.

For a time, Gompers's strategy seemed to work. Several industries negotiated with the AFL to avoid disruptive strikes. But cooperation was short-lived. Labor unions were defeated in a number of disastrous strikes, and the National Association of Manufacturers (NAM) launched an aggressive counterattack. The NAM and other employer associations provided strikebreakers, used industrial spies, and blacklisted union members to bar them from other jobs.

The Supreme Court came down squarely on management's side, ruling in the *Danbury Hatters* case in 1908 that trade unions were subject to the Sherman Anti-Trust Act. Thus union members could be held personally liable for money lost by a business during a strike. Courts at all levels often declared strikes illegal and were quick to issue restraining orders.

Although many social justice progressives sympathized with the working class, they spent most of their time promoting protective legislation. They found it difficult to comprehend what life was really like for people who had to work six days a week.

Working women and their problems aroused more sympathy among progressive reformers than the plight of working men. The number of women working outside the home increased steadily during the progressive era, from over 5 million in 1900 to nearly 8.5 million in 1920. But few belonged to unions, and the percentage had declined by 1910 before increasing a little after that date with aggressive organizing in the textile and clothing trades.

Although the AFL had hired Mary Kenney as an organizer in the 1890s and accepted a few women's unions into affiliation, Gompers and other labor leaders generally opposed organizing women workers (see Chapter 18). "The demand for female labor," one leader announced, "is an insidious assault upon the home."

Of necessity, women continued to work to support themselves and their families. Many well-born women reformers tried to help these working women. Tension and misunderstanding often cropped up between the reformers and the working women, but one organization in which there was genuine cooperation was the Women's Trade Union League. Founded in 1903, the league was organized by Kenney and other progressive reformers and drew leaders from the working class, such as Rose Schneiderman, a Jewish immigrant cap maker. The league established branches in most large eastern and midwestern cities and served for more than a decade as an important force in helping to organize women into unions. It forced the AFL to pay more attention to women, helped out in time of strikes, put up bail money for those arrested, and publicized the plight of working women.

Garment Workers and the Triangle Fire

Thousands of young women, most of them Jewish and Italian, were employed in the garment industry in New York City. Most were between the ages of 16 and 25. They worked a 56-hour, 6-day week that paid about $6. New York had over 600 shirtwaist (blouse) and dress factories employing more than 30,000 workers.

Like other industries, garment manufacturing had changed. Once conducted in thousands of dark and dingy tenement rooms, all operations were now centralized in large loft buildings in lower Manhattan. Though an improvement over the tenements, many were still overcrowded and had few safety features. Scientific management made life miserable for the workers. Most of the women rented their sewing machines and even paid for their electricity. They were penalized for mistakes or for talking loudly, and were usually supervised by a male contractor who badgered and sometimes sexually harassed them.

In 1909, some of the women went out on strike to protest the working conditions. The International Ladies' Garment Workers Union (ILGWU) and the Women's Trade Union League supported them. But strikers were beaten and sometimes arrested. On November 22, after an impassioned speech in Yiddish by a young shirtwaist worker who had been injured on the picket line, a mass meeting voted for a general strike.

This "uprising of the twenty thousand" startled the nation. Jews and Italians learned a little of each other's language so they could communicate on the picket line. A young state legislator, Fiorello La Guardia, later a congressman and mayor, was one of many public officials who joined clergy and social reformers in aiding the strikers.

The shirtwaist workers won, and in part, the success of the strike made the garment union one of the most powerful in the AFL. But some companies refused to go along, and work conditions remained oppressive and unsafe. That became dramatically obvious on Saturday, March 25, 1911, when a fire broke out on the eighth floor of the ten-story loft building housing the Triangle Shirtwaist Company. Within minutes, the top three floors of the factory were ablaze. Many exit doors were locked. The elevators broke down. With no fire escapes, 46 women jumped to their deaths and over 100 died in the flames.

A shocked state legislature appointed a commission to investigate working conditions in the state. One investigator for the commission was a young social worker, Frances Perkins, who in the 1930s would become secretary of labor. She took politicians on tour through the garment district to show them the miserable conditions under which young women worked. The result was state legislation limiting the work of women to 54 hours a week, prohibiting labor by children under the age of 14, and improving safety regulations in factories. One supporter of the bills was a young state senator named Franklin Delano Roosevelt.

The investigative commission was a favorite progressive tactic. When there was a problem, reformers often got a state legislature or the Federal government to appoint a commission, and if that did not work, they made their own studies, compiled statistics and consulted experts.

The federal Industrial Relations Commission, created in 1912 to study the causes of industrial unrest and violence, conducted one of the most important investigations, that of a dramatic labor-management conflict in Colorado called the Ludlow Massacre. When the mine workers, whom management forced to live in company towns, struck for an eight-hour day, better safety, and the removal of armed guards, the Rockefeller-dominated company refused to negotiate. The strike turned violent, and in the spring of 1914 strikebreakers and national guardsmen fired on the workers, killing eleven children and two women.

The Industrial Relations Commission forced John D. Rockefeller, Jr., to testify and implied that he was personally guilty of murder. Its report concluded that violent class conflict could be avoided only by limiting the use of armed guards and detectives, by restricting monopoly, by protecting workers' right to organize, and, most dramatically, by redistributing wealth through taxation. Not surprisingly, the report fell on deaf ears. Most progressives, like most Americans, denied its conclusion that class conflict was inevitable.

Radical Labor

Not everyone accepted the progressives' faith in investigations and protective labor legislation. Nor did everyone approve of Samuel Gompers's conservative tactics or his emphasis on getting better pay for skilled workers. About 200 radicals met in Chicago in 1905 to form a new union as an alternative to the AFL. They called it the Industrial Workers of the World (IWW). Like the Knights of Labor in the 1880s, the IWW welcomed all workers, regardless of skill, gender, or race.

Presiding at the Chicago meeting was "Big Bill" Haywood, a colorful radical worker. "This is the Continental Congress of the working class," he announced. "We are here to confederate the workers of this country into a working-class movement . . . for . . . the emancipation of the working class from the slave bondage of capitalism."

Eugene Debs attended the organizational meeting. He had become a socialist after the Pullman strike of 1894 and emerged by 1905 as one of the outstanding radical leaders in the country. Also attending was the legendary "Mother" Jones, who dressed like a society matron but attacked labor leaders "who sit on velvet chairs in conferences with labor's oppressors." Now in her sixties, she had been a dressmaker, a Populist, and a member of the Knights of Labor.

The IWW remained small and troubled by internal squabbling. Haywood dominated the movement, which played an important role in organizing the militant strike of textile workers in Lawrence, Massachusetts, in 1912 and the following year in Paterson, New Jersey, and Akron, Ohio. The IWW had its greatest success organizing lumbermen and migrant workers in the Northwest. Elsewhere, especially in times of high unemployment, the "Wobblies" helped the unskilled workers vent their anger against their employers.

Many American workers still did not feel, as European workers did, that they were fighting a perpetual class struggle. Some immigrant workers, intent on earning enough money to go home, had no time to join the conflict. Most of those who stayed dreamed the American dream—a better job or moving up into the middle class—and avoided labor militancy. They believed that even if they failed, their sons and daughters would profit from the American way. The AFL, not the IWW, became the dominant American labor movement.

REFORM IN THE CITIES AND STATES

The reform movements of the progressive era usually started at the local level, moved to the state, and finally reached the nation's capital. Progressivism in the cities and states had roots in the depression and discontent of the 1890s. The reform banners called for more democracy, more power for the people, and legislation regulating railroads and other businesses. Yet often the professional and business classes were the movement's leaders. They intended to bring order out of chaos and to modernize the city and the state during a time of rapid growth.

Municipal Reformers

American cities grew rapidly in the last part of the nineteenth and the first part of the twentieth centuries. New York, which had a population of 1.2 million in 1880, grew to 3.4 million by 1900 and 5.6 million in 1920. Chicago expanded even more dramatically. Los Angeles, a town of 11,000 in 1880, multiplied ten times by 1900 and then increased another five times, to more than a half million, by 1920.

The spectacular and continuing growth of the cities created a need for housing, transportation, and municipal services. But the kind of people who were filling the cities gave cause for worry. Fully 40 percent of New York's population and 36 percent of Chicago's were foreign-born in 1910; including immigrant children, the percentage approached 80 percent in some cities. "Beaten men from beaten races, representing the worst failures in the struggle for existence," was how the president of MIT described them.

Fear of the city and its new inhabitants motivated progressive municipal reform. Early twentieth-century reformers, mostly middle-class citizens, wanted to regulate the sprawling metropolis, restore democracy, cut corruption, and limit the power of bosses and their immigrant allies. When these reformers talked of restoring power to the people, they usually meant people like themselves.

Municipal reform movements varied from city to city. In Boston, reformers tried to strengthen the power of the mayor, break the hold of the city council, and eliminate council corruption. But in 1910 John Fitzgerald, grandfather of John F. Kennedy and a foe of reform, was elected mayor, defeating their reform candidate. Elsewhere reformers used different tactics, but they almost always conducted elaborate studies and campaigned to reduce corruption.

The most dramatic innovation was the replacement of both mayor and council with a nonpartisan commission of administrators. This innovation began quite accidentally when a hurricane devastated Galveston, Texas, in September 1900—one of the worst natural disasters in the nation's history, killing more than 6,000 people. The existing government was helpless to deal with the crisis, so the state legislature appointed five commissioners to run the city during the emergency.

The idea spread, proving most popular in small and mid-sized cities in the Midwest and the Pacific Northwest. Dayton, Ohio, went one step further. After a disastrous flood in 1913, the city hired a city manager to run the city and to report to the elected council. Government by experts was the perfect symbol of what most municipal reformers had in mind.

In most large cities, however, the commission and the expert manager did not replace the mayor. One of the most flamboyant and successful of the progressive mayors was Tom Johnson of Cleveland, a wealthy man converted to reform by Henry George's *Progress and Poverty*. Elected mayor of Cleveland in 1901, he cut transit fares and built parks and municipal bath houses throughout the city, and he broke the connection between the police and prostitution by promising madams and brothel owners that he would not bother them if they would not steal from customers or pay off the police. His most controversial move was to advocate city ownership of the street railroads and utilities. He was defeated in 1909, in part because he alienated many powerful business interests, but one of his lieutenants, Newton D. Baker, was elected mayor in 1911 and carried on many of his programs. Cleveland was one of many cities that began to regulate municipal utilities or to take them over from the private owners.

City Beautiful

In Cleveland, Tom Johnson and Newton Baker promoted the arts, music, and adult education, supervised construction of a civic center, and built a library and a museum. Such efforts were typical of progressivism.

Cities grew so rapidly that they often ceased to work. This 1909 photograph shows Dearborn Street looking south from Randolph in Chicago. Horse-drawn vehicles, streetcars, pedestrians, and even a few early autos clogged the intersection and created the urban inefficiency that angered municipal reformers. (Chicago Historical Society)

The architects of the "city beautiful movement" preferred the impressive and ceremonial architecture of Rome or the Renaissance for libraries, museums, railroad stations, and other public buildings. The huge Pennsylvania Station in New York (now replaced by Madison Square Garden) was modeled after imperial Rome's baths of Caracalla. The city beautiful leaders tried to make the city more attractive for the middle and upper classes. Unfortunately, the museums and libraries were closed on Sundays, the only day the working class could visit them.

The social justice progressives, especially those connected with the social settlements, were more concerned with neighborhood parks and playgrounds. Hull House established the first public playground in Chicago. Jacob Riis and Lillian Wald of the Henry Street Settlement campaigned in New York for small parks and the opening of schoolyards on weekends. Some progressives, remembering their own rural youth, tried to get urban children out of the city to summer camps. But they also tried to make the city more livable and beautiful.

Most progressives both feared and loved the city. Some saw the great urban areas filled with immigrants as a threat, but one of Tom Johnson's young assistants, Frederic C. Howe, wrote a book called *The City: The Hope of Democracy* (1905). Hope or threat, the progressives realized that the United States had become an urban nation and that the problems of the city had to be faced.

Reform in the States

The progressive movements in the states had many roots and took many forms. In some states, especially in the West, progressive attempts to regulate railroads and utilities were simply an extension of populism. In other states, progressivism bubbled up from urban reform efforts. Most states passed laws designed to extend democracy and give more authority to the people. Initiative and referendum laws allowed citizens to originate legislation and to overturn laws passed by the legislature, and recall laws gave the people a way to remove elected officials. Most of these "democratic" laws worked better in theory than in practice, but they did represent a genuine effort to remove special privilege from government.

Much progressive state legislation concerned order and efficiency, but many states passed social justice measures as well. Maryland enacted the first workers' compensation law in 1902, paying employees for days missed because of job-related injuries. Illinois approved a law aiding mothers with dependent children. Several states passed antichild labor bills, and Oregon's ten-hour law restricting women's labor became a model for other states.

States with the most successful reform movements elected strong governors, the most famous of whom was Wisconsin's Robert La Follette. Of small-town origin and an 1879 graduate of the University of Wisconsin, he began his career as a railroad lawyer and became a reformer only after the depression of 1893. Taking advantage of the general mood of discontent, he won the governorship in 1901. Ironically, La Follette owed his victory to his attack on the railroads. But La Follette was a shrewd politician. He used professors from the University of Wisconsin to prepare reports and do statistical studies. Then he worked with the legislature to pass a state primary law and an act regulating the railroads. "Go back to the first principles of democracy; go back to the people" was his battle cry. Journalists touted Wisconsin as the "laboratory of democracy." La Follette became a national figure and was elected to the Senate in 1906.

The progressive movement did improve government and make it more responsible to the people in states like Wisconsin. For example, the railroads were brought under the control of a railroad commission. But by 1910, the railroads no longer complained about the new taxes and restrictions. They had discovered that it was to their advantage to make their operations more efficient, and often they convinced the commission that they should raise rates or abandon unprofitable lines. Progressivism in the states, like progressivism everywhere, had mixed results. But the spirit of reform that swept the country was real, and progressive movements on the local level did eventually have an impact on Washington.

THEODORE ROOSEVELT AND THE SQUARE DEAL

An anarchist shot President McKinley in Buffalo on September 6, 1901. When McKinley died eight days later, Theodore Roosevelt, at 42, became history's youngest president. As the nation mourned its fallen leader, anarchists and other radicals were rounded up in many cities.

No one knew what to expect from Roosevelt. Some politicians thought he was too radical, but a few social justice progressives remembered his suggestion that the soldiers fire on strikers during the 1894 Pullman strike. Nonetheless, under his leadership, progressivism reshaped the national political agenda. Although early progressive reformers had attacked problems that they saw in their own communities, they gradually understood that some problems could not be solved at the state or local level. The emergence of a national industrial economy had spawned conditions that demanded national solutions.

Progressives at the national level turned their attention to the economic system—the railroads and other large corporations, the state of the natural environment, and the quality of American industrial products. And as they fashioned legislation to remedy economic flaws, they vastly expanded the national government's power.

A Strong and Controversial President

Roosevelt came to the presidency with considerable experience. He had run unsuccessfully for mayor of New York and served a term in the New York state assembly. He had spent four years as a United States civil service commissioner and two years as New York City's police commissioner. His exploits in the Spanish-American War brought him to the public's attention, but he had also been an effective assistant secretary of the navy and a reform governor of New York. While police commissioner and governor, he had been influenced by progressives like his friend Jacob Riis and New York City settlement workers. He seemed sympathetic to the problems of lower-class life.

But no one was sure how he would act as president. He came from an upper-class family, had associated with the important and the powerful all over the world, had written books, and was one of the most intellectual presidents since Thomas Jefferson. None of this assured that he would be a progressive in office.

Roosevelt loved being president. He called the office a "bully pulpit," and he enjoyed talking to the people and reporters. His appealing personality and sense of humor made him a good subject for the new mass-market press. The public quickly adopted him as their favorite. They called him "Teddy" and named a stuffed bear after him. Sometimes his exuberance got a little out of hand. On one occasion, he took a foreign diplomat on a nude swim in the Potomac River. You have to understand, someone remarked, that "the president is really only six years old."

Roosevelt, however, was more than an exuberant child; he was the strongest president since Lincoln. By revitalizing the executive branch, reorganizing the army command structure, and modernizing the consular service, he made many aspects of the federal government more efficient. He established the Bureau of Corporations, appointed commissions staffed with experts, and enlisted talented men to work for the government. "TR" called a White House conference on the care of dependent children, and in 1905 he even summoned college presidents and coaches to discuss ways to limit violence in football. He angered many social justice progressives by not going far enough. Once Florence Kelley slammed his office door. But he was the first president to listen to the pleas of the progressives and to invite them to the White House. Learning from experts like Frances Kellor, he became more concerned with social justice as time went on.

Dealing with the Trusts

One of Roosevelt's first actions as president was to attempt to control the large industrial corporations. He took office amid an unprecedented wave of business consolidation. Between 1897 and 1904, some 4,227 companies combined to form 257 large corporations. U.S. Steel, the first billion-dollar corporation, was formed in 1901 by joining Carnegie Steel with its eight main competitors. The new company controlled two-thirds of the market, and J. P. Morgan made $7 million on the deal.

The Sherman Anti-Trust Act of 1890 had been virtually useless in controlling the trusts, but a new outcry from muckrakers and progressives called for regulation. Some even demanded the return to the age of small business. Roosevelt opposed neither bigness nor the right of businessmen to make money. "We draw the line against misconduct, not against wealth," he said.

To the shock of much of the business community, he directed his attorney general to file suit to dissolve the Northern Securities Company, a giant railroad monopoly put together by Morgan and railroadman James J. Hill. "If we have done anything wrong," Morgan suggested, "send your man to my man and they can fix it up." A furious Roosevelt let Morgan and other businessmen know that the president of the United States was not just another tycoon. The government won its case and proceeded to prosecute some of the largest corporations, including Standard Oil of New Jersey and the American Tobacco Company.

Roosevelt's antitrust policy did not end the power of the giant corporations or even alter their methods of doing business. Nor did it force down the price of kerosene, cigars, or railroad tickets. But it breathed some life into the Sherman Anti-Trust Act and increased the role of the federal government as regulator. It also caused large firms such as U.S. Steel to diversify to avoid antitrust suits.

Roosevelt tried to strengthen the regulatory powers of the federal government in other ways. He steered the Elkins Act through Congress in 1903 and the Hepburn Act in 1906, which together increased the power of the Interstate Commerce Commission (ICC). The first act eliminated the use of rebates by railroads; the second broadened the power of the ICC and gave it the right to investigate and enforce rates. Opponents in Congress weakened both bills, and the legislation neither ended abuses nor satisfied farmers and small businessmen.

Roosevelt firmly believed in corporate capitalism, detested socialism, and was not comfortable around labor leaders. Yet he saw his role as mediator and regulator. His view of the power of the presidency was illustrated in 1902 during the anthracite coal strike. Led by the United Mine Workers, coal miners went on strike to protest low wages, long hours, and dangerous conditions. In 1901, a total of 513 coal miners had died in industrial accidents. The mine owners refused to talk to the miners, hiring strikebreakers and using private security forces to intimidate workers. In the fall of 1902, schools began closing for lack of coal, and it looked like many citizens would suffer through the winter. Over bosses' protests about talking to "outlaws," Roosevelt called owners and union leaders to the White House and

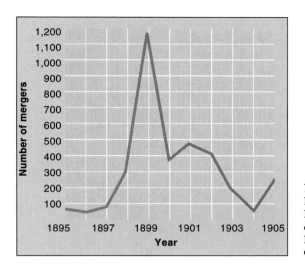

BUSINESS MERGERS, 1895–1905
Business mergers did decline during the Roosevelt years, but they did not cease entirely and they even rose again during his second term. Source: U.S. Bureau of the Census.

appointed a commission that included both union and community representatives. Within weeks, the miners were back at work with a 10 percent raise.

Meat Inspection and Pure Food and Drugs

Roosevelt's first major legislative reform began almost accidentally in 1904 when Upton Sinclair, a 26-year-old muckraking journalist, boarded at the University of Chicago Settlement House while doing research on the city's stockyards and writing *The Jungle*, which was published in 1906. The novel documented labor exploitation and tried to convert readers to socialism, but its description of contaminated meat turned stomachs and set off an outcry for better regulation of the meatpacking industry. Roosevelt, who read the book, reportedly could no longer enjoy his breakfast sausage. He ordered a study of the meatpacking industry and used the report to pressure Congress and the meatpackers to accept a reform bill.

In the end, the Meat Inspection Act of 1906 was a compromise. It enforced some federal inspection and mandated sanitary conditions in all companies selling meat in interstate commerce. The meatpackers defeated a provision that would have required the dating of all meat. Some large companies supported the compromise bill because it gave them an advantage against smaller firms. But the bill was a beginning. It illustrates how muckrakers, social justice progressives, and public outcry eventually led to reform legislation. It also shows how Roosevelt used the public mood and manipulated the political process to get a bill through Congress. He was always willing to settle for half a loaf rather than none at all. Ironically, the Meat Inspection Act restored public confidence in the meat industry and helped it increase profits.

Publicity surrounding *The Jungle* generated legislation to regulate food and drug sales. Many packaged and canned foods contained dangerous chemicals and impurities. Americans consumed an enormous quantity of patent medicines; one popular remedy was revealed to be 44 percent alcohol, and often medicines were laced with opium. Many people unwittingly became alcoholics or drug addicts. The Pure Food and Drug Act (1906) was not perfect, but it corrected some of the worst abuses, including eliminating cocaine from Coca-Cola.

Conservation Versus Preservation

Roosevelt, an outdoorsman and amateur naturalist, considered his conservation program his most important domestic achievement. Using his executive authority, he more than tripled the land set aside for national forests, bringing the total to more than 150 million acres.

Roosevelt understood, as few easterners did, the problems created by limited water in the western states. In 1902, with his enthusiastic support, Congress passed the Newlands Act, setting aside the proceeds from the sale of public land in sixteen western states to pay for the construction of irrigation projects in those states. Although it tended to help big farmers most, the Newlands Act federalized irrigation for the first time.

More important, Roosevelt raised public consciousness about saving natural resources. He appointed a National Conservation Commission charged with making an inventory of the natural resources in the entire country, chaired by Gifford Pinchot, probably the most important conservationist in the country. An advocate of selective logging, fire control, and limited grazing on public lands, Pinchot became a friend and adviser to Roosevelt.

Pinchot's conservation policies pleased many in the timber and cattle industries, and angered those who simply wanted to exploit the land. But his approach was denounced by the followers of John Muir, a passionate advocate of preserving wilderness. Muir had founded the Sierra Club in 1862 and had led a successful campaign to create Yosemite National Park in California. He looked eccentric, but thousands agreed when he argued that to preserve the wilderness was a spiritual and psychological necessity for overcivilized and overstimulated urbanites. Muir was one of the leaders in the turn-of-the-century "back-to-nature" movement, which also included the founding of the Boy Scouts (1910) and the Camp Fire Girls (1912).

The conflicting conservation philosophies of Pinchot and Muir were most dramatically demonstrated by the controversy over Hetch-Hetchy, a remote valley deep within Yosemite National Park. It was a pristine wilderness area, and Muir and his followers wanted to keep it that way. But in 1901, the mayor of San Francisco decided the valley would make a perfect place for a dam and reservoir to supply his growing city with water. Muir argued that wilderness soon would be scarcer than water, though more important for the nation's moral strength. Pinchot and other conservationists argued that it was silly to sacrifice the welfare of the great majority to the aesthetic enjoyment of a tiny group. In the end, Roosevelt and Congress sided with the conservationists, and the valley became (and remains) a lake. The debate between conservationists and preservationists still goes on.

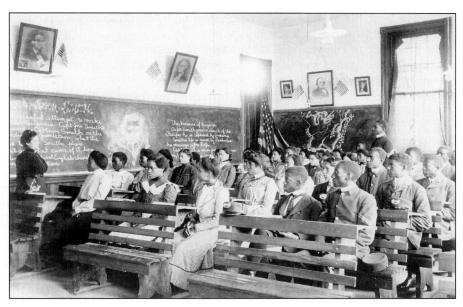

Tuskegee Institute followed Booker T. Washington's philosophy of black advancement through accommodation to the white status quo. Here students study white American history, but most of their time was spent on more practical subjects. This photo was taken in 1902 by Francis Benjamin Johnson, a pioneer woman photographer. (Library of Congress)

Progressivism for Whites Only

Like most whites of his generation, Roosevelt believed that blacks, Indians, and Asians were inferior, and he feared that massive migrations from southern and eastern Europe threatened Anglo-Saxon dominance. But Roosevelt was a politician, so he made gestures of goodwill to most groups. He even invited Booker T. Washington to the White House in 1901, despite vicious southern protests, and appointed several qualified blacks to minor federal posts. But he could also be insensitive to African-Americans, as in his handling of the Brownsville, Texas, riot of 1906. Members of a black army unit stationed there rioted, angered by discrimination against them. No one is sure exactly what happened, but one white man was killed and several were wounded. After the midterm elections of 1906, Roosevelt ordered all 167 members of three companies dishonorably discharged—an unjust punishment for an unproven crime. Sixty-six years later, the secretary of the army granted honorable discharges to the men, most of whom were dead by then.

The progressive era coincided with the years of greatest segregation in the South, but even the most advanced progressives seldom included blacks in their reform schemes. Hull House, like most settlements, was segregated, although Addams more than most progressives struggled to overcome the racist attitudes of her day. She helped found a settlement that served a black neighborhood in Chicago, and she spoke out repeatedly against lynching. Addams also supported the founding of the National Association for the Advancement of Colored People

(NAACP) in 1909, the most important organization of the progressive era aimed at promoting equality and justice for blacks.

The founding of the NAACP is the story of cooperation between a group of white social justice progressives and courageous black leaders. Even in the age of segregation and lynching, blacks in all parts of the country—through churches, clubs, and schools—sought to promote a better life for themselves.

The most important black leader who argued for equality and opportunity for his people was W. E. B. Du Bois. As discussed in Chapter 17, Du Bois differed dramatically with Booker T. Washington on the proper position of blacks in American life. Whereas Washington advocated vocational education, Du Bois argued that "talented tenth" of the black population should get the best education possible. Against Washington's talk of compromise and accommodation to the dominant white society, Du Bois increasingly urged aggressive action for equality.

Denouncing Washington in 1905, Du Bois called a meeting of young and militant blacks across from Niagara Falls in Canada. "We believe in taking what we can get but we don't believe in being satisfied with it and in permitting anybody for a moment to imagine we're satisfied," said the Niagara movement's angry manifesto. Du Bois's small band was soon augmented by white liberals concerned with violence against blacks, including Jane Addams and Oswald Garrison Villard, grandson of abolitionist William Lloyd Garrison. In 1910 it merged with the NAACP, and Du Bois became editor of its journal, *The Crisis*. He toned down his rhetoric but tried to promote equality for all blacks. The NAACP was a typical progressive organization, seeking to work within the American system to promote reform. But Roosevelt and many other progressives thought it dangerously radical.

William Howard Taft

After two terms as president, Roosevelt decided to step down and go big-game hunting in Africa. But he soon regretted leaving the White House. He was only 50 years old and at the peak of his popularity and power.

William Howard Taft, Roosevelt's choice for the Republican nomination in 1908 and winner over Bryan for the election, was a distinguished lawyer, federal judge, and public servant—the first civil governor of the Philippines and Roosevelt's secretary of war. In some ways, he was more progressive than Roosevelt. His administration instituted more suits against monopolies in one term than Roosevelt had in two. He supported the eight-hour workday and legislation to make mining safer. He supported the Mann-Elkins Act in 1910, which strengthened the ICC. Taft and Congress also authorized the first tax on corporate profits, and he encouraged the process that eventually led to the passage of the federal income tax, which was authorized under the Sixteenth Amendment, ratified in 1913.

But Taft's presidency quickly ran into difficulties. His biggest problem was his style. He weighed over 300 pounds, wrote ponderously, and spoke uninspiringly. He also lacked Roosevelt's political skills and angered many of the progressives in the Republican party, especially the midwestern insurgents led by La Follette.

Even Roosevelt was infuriated when his successor reversed many of his conservation policies and fired Chief Forester Gifford Pinchot, who had attacked Secretary of the Interior Richard A. Ballinger for giving away rich coal lands in Alaska to mining interests. Roosevelt broke with Taft, letting it be known that he was willing to run again for president. This set up one of the most exciting and significant elections in American history.

The Election of 1912

Woodrow Wilson won the Democratic presidential nomination in 1912. The son and grandson of Presbyterian ministers, he grew up in a comfortable and intellectual southern household. He graduated from Princeton in 1879, got a Ph.D., and published *Congressional Government* (1885), which established his reputation as a shrewd political analyst. He taught history and became a Princeton professor. Less flamboyant than Roosevelt, he was a persuasive speaker. In 1902 he was elected president of Princeton University, and during the next few years established a national reputation as an educational leader. He eagerly accepted the Democratic machine's offer to run for governor of New Jersey in 1910, but then showed courage by quickly alienating some of the conservatives who had helped elect him. Building a reform coalition, he put through a direct primary law and other progressive reforms. By 1912, Wilson had acquired the reputation of a progressive.

Roosevelt, who had been speaking out on a variety of issues since 1910, competed with Taft for the Republican nomination. As the incumbent president and party leader, Taft won it—but Roosevelt startled the nation by walking out of the convention and forming a new political party, the Progressive party. It appealed to progressives who had become frustrated with the conservative leadership in both major parties. Its platform contained provisions that reformers had been advocating for years: an eight-hour day; a six-day week; abolition of child labor under age 16; federal accident, old age, and unemployment insurance; and—unlike the Democrats—woman suffrage.

Most supporters of the Progressives in 1912 hoped to organize a new political movement that would replace the Republican party, just as the Republicans had replaced the Whigs after 1856. Progressive leaders, led by Kellor, had plans to apply the principles of social research by educating voters between elections.

The Progressive convention in Chicago seemed like a religious revival or a social work conference. Delegates sang "Onward Christian Soldiers" and "The Battle Hymn of the Republic," and when Jane Addams seconded Roosevelt's nomination, a large group of women marched around the auditorium with a "Votes for Women" banner. The Progressive cause "is based on the eternal principles of righteousness," Roosevelt cried.

But behind the unified facade lurked many disagreements. Roosevelt had become more progressive on many issues since leaving the presidency. He even attacked the financiers "to whom the acquisition of untold millions is the supreme goal of life, and who are too often utterly indifferent as to how these millions are obtained." But he was less committed to social reform than some delegates. A number of social justice progressives fought hard to include a plank in the platform supporting equality for blacks and for seating a black delegation, but Roosevelt hoped to carry several southern states. In the end no blacks were seated and the platform made no mention of black equality.

The 1912 campaign became a contest primarily between Roosevelt and Wilson, who vigorously debated the proper relationship of government to society in a modern industrial age. Advancing what he called the New Nationalism, Roosevelt argued that in a modern industrial society large corporations were "inevitable and necessary." What was needed was a strong president and increased power in the hands of the federal government to regulate business and industry for the benefit of the people. He argued for using Hamiltonian means to assure Jeffersonian ends, for using strong central government to guarantee the rights of the people."

Wilson responded with a program and a slogan of his own, the New Freedom. Drawing on the writings of Louis Brandeis, he emphasized the Jeffersonian tradition of limited government with open competition. He spoke of the "curse of bigness" and argued against too much federal power. "What I fear is a government of experts," Wilson declared, implying that Roosevelt's New Nationalism would mean regulated monopoly and even collectivism.

This was one of the few elections in American history in which important ideas were actually discussed. It also marked a watershed for political thought for liberals who rejected Jefferson's distrust of a strong central government. It is easy to exaggerate the differences between Roosevelt and Wilson. Both urged reform within the American system, defended corporate capitalism, and opposed socialism and radical labor organizations. Both wanted more democracy and stronger but conservative labor unions. Both were very different in style and substance from the fourth candidate, Eugene Debs, who ran on the Socialist party ticket in 1912.

Debs, at the time, was the most important socialist leader in the country. Socialism has always been a minority movement in the United States, but it stood at its pinnacle in the first decade of the twentieth century. Thirty-three cities had socialist mayors, and two socialists sat in Congress. The most important socialist periodical increased its circulation from about 30,000 in 1900 to nearly 300,000 in 1906. Its following was quite diverse. In the cities, some who called themselves socialists merely favored municipal ownership of street railways. Some reformers, such as Florence Kelley, joined out of frustration with the slow pace of reform. Many recent immigrants brought to the party a European sense of class and loyalty to socialism.

A tremendously appealing figure and a great orator, Debs had run for president in 1900, 1904, and 1908, but in 1912, he reached much wider audiences in more parts of the country. His message differed radically from that of Wilson or Roosevelt. Unlike the progressives, socialists argued for fundamental change in the American system. The Socialist party is "organized and financed by the workers themselves," Debs announced, "as a means of wresting control of government and industry from the capitalists and making the working class the ruling class of the nation and the world." Debs polled almost 900,000 votes in 1912 (6 percent of the popular vote), the best showing ever for a socialist in the United States. Wilson received 6.3 million votes, Roosevelt a little more than 4 million, and Taft 3.5 million. Wilson garnered 435 electoral votes, Roosevelt 88, and Taft only 8.

WOODROW WILSON AND THE NEW FREEDOM

Wilson was elected largely because Roosevelt and the Progressive party split the Republican vote. But once elected, Wilson became a vigorous and aggressive chief executive who set out to translate his ideas about progressive government into legislation. He was the first southerner elected president since Zachary Taylor in 1848 and only the second Democrat since the Civil War. Wilson, like Roosevelt, had to work with his party, and that restricted how progressive he could be. He was also constrained by his background and inclinations. Still, like Roosevelt, Wilson became more progressive during his presidency.

Tariff and Banking Reform

Wilson had a more difficult time than Roosevelt relating to small groups, but he was an excellent public speaker who dominated through the force of his intellect. He probably had an exaggerated belief in his ability to persuade and tended to trust his own intuition too much. His accomplishment in pushing a legislative program through Congress during his first two years in office was matched only by Franklin Roosevelt during the first months of the New Deal and by Lyndon Johnson in 1965. But his early success bred overconfidence, portending trouble.

Within a month of his inauguration, Wilson went before a joint session of Congress to outline his legislative program. He recommended reducing the tariff, freeing the banking system from Wall Street control, and restoring industrial competition. By appearing in person before Congress, he broke a precedent of written presidential messages established by Thomas Jefferson.

First on Wilson's agenda was tariff reform. The Underwood Tariff, passed in 1913, was not a free-trade bill, but it did reduce the schedule for the first time in many years. Attached to the Underwood bill was a provision for a small and slightly graduated income tax, recently allowed by passage of the Sixteenth Amendment. It imposed a modest rate of 1 percent on income over $4,000 (thus exempting a large portion of the population), with a surtax rising to 6 percent on high incomes. The income tax was enacted to replace the money lost from lowering the tariff. Wilson seemed to have no interest in using it to redistribute wealth.

A financial panic in 1907 had revealed the need for a central bank, and much of the private banking system was dominated by J. P. Morgan, but few people could agree on what should be done. Progressive Democrats argued for a banking system and currency controlled by the federal government. But talk of banking reform raised the specter among conservative Democrats and the business community of socialism, populism, and the monetary ideas of William Jennings Bryan.

The Federal Reserve System, created by compromise legislation in 1913, was the first reorganization of the banking system since the Civil War. The law gave the federal government some control over the banking system. It also created a flexible currency, based on Federal Reserve notes, that could be expanded or contracted as need required. The Federal Reserve System was not without its flaws, as later developments would show, and it did not end the power of the large eastern banks; but it was an improvement, and it appealed to the part of the progressive movement that sought order and efficiency.

Wilson was not very progressive in some of his early actions. He failed to support a plan for long-term rural credit financed by the federal government. He opposed a woman suffrage amendment and refused to back an antichild labor bill. And he ordered the segregation of blacks in several federal departments. "I sincerely believe it to be in their [the blacks'] best interest, "he said in rejecting the NAACP's protests.

Moving Closer to a New Nationalism

Wilson and Roosevelt had vigorously debated how to control the great corporations. Wilson's solution was the Clayton Act, which prohibited various unfair trading practices, outlawed the interlocking directorate, and forbade corporations to purchase stock in other corporations if this tended to reduce competition. But the law was vague and hard to enforce, and the courts interpreted it to mean that labor unions remained subject to court injunctions during strikes.

More important was the creation of the Federal Trade Commission (FTC). Powerful enough to move directly against corporations accused of restricting competition, the FTC was the idea of Louis Brandeis. Wilson accepted it even though it seemed to move him more toward the philosophy of New Nationalism.

The FTC and the Clayton Act did not end monopoly. The success of Wilson's reform agenda appeared minimal in 1914, but the outbreak of war in Europe and the need to win the election of 1916 would force him into becoming more progressive.

Neither Wilson nor Roosevelt satisfied advanced progressives. Most of the efforts of the two progressive presidents were spent trying to regulate economic power rather than promote social justice. Yet their most important legacy was their attempts to strengthen the office of president and the executive branch of the federal government. The nineteenth-century American presidents after Lincoln had been relatively weak, and much of the federal power had resided with Congress. The progressive presidents reasserted presidential authority, modernized the executive branch, and began the creation of the federal bureaucracy, which has had a major impact on the lives of Americans in the twentieth century.

Both Wilson and Roosevelt used the presidency as what TR called a bully pulpit. Roosevelt strengthened the Interstate Commerce Commission and Wilson created the Federal Trade Commission, forerunners of many other federal regulatory bodies. By personally delivering his annual message before Congress, Wilson symbolized the new power of the presidency.

More than the increased power of the executive branch changed the nature of politics. The new bureaus, committees, and commissions brought to Washington a new kind of expert, trained in the universities, at the state and local level, and in the voluntary organizations. Julia Lathrop, a co-worker of Jane Addams at Hull House, was typical. Appointed by President Taft in 1912 to become chief of the newly created Children's Bureau, she was the first woman ever named to such a position. She used her post not only to work for better child labor laws, but also to train a new generation of women experts who would take their positions in state,

TIMELINE

1901	1902	1903	1904	1905
McKinley assassinated; Theodore Roosevelt becomes president; Robert La Follette elected governor of Wisconsin; Tom Johnson elected mayor of Cleveland; Model tenement house bill passed in New York; U.S. Steel formed	Anthracite coal strike	Women's Trade Union League founded; Elkins Act	Roosevelt reelected; Lincoln Steffens, *The Shame of the Cities*	Frederic C. Howe, *The City: The Hope of Democracy;* Industrial Workers of the World formed

1906	1907	1908	1909	1910
Upton Sinclair, *The Jungle;* Hepburn Act; Meat Inspection Act; Pure Food and Drug Act	Financial panic	*Muller v. Oregon;* Danbury Hatters case; William Howard Taft elected president	Herbert Croly, *The Promise of American Life;* NAACP founded	Ballinger-Pinchot controversy; Mann Act

1911	1912	1913	1914
Frederick Taylor, *The Principles of Scientific Management;* Triangle Shirtwaist Company fire	Progressive party founded by Theodore Roosevelt; Woodrow Wilson elected president; Children's Bureau established; Industrial Relations Commission founded	Sixteenth Amendment (income tax) ratified; Underwood Tariff; Federal Reserve System established; Seventeenth Amendment (direct election of senators) passed	Clayton Act; Federal Trade Commission Act; AFL has over two million members; Ludlow Massacre in Colorado

federal, and private agencies in the 1920s and 1930s. Other experts emerged in Washington during the progressive era to influence policy in subtle and important ways. The expert, the commission, the statistical survey, and the increased power of the executive branch were all legacies of the progressive era.

✦✦✦✦✦✦

CONCLUSION

The Limits of Progressivism

The progressive era was a time when many Americans set out to promote reform because they saw poverty, despair, and disorder in the country transformed by immigration, urbanism, and industrialism. The progressives, unlike the socialists, however, saw nothing fundamentally wrong with the American system. Progressivism was largely a middle-class movement that sought to help the poor, the immigrants, and the working class. Yet the poor were rarely consulted about policy, and many groups, especially African-Americans, were almost entirely left out of reform plans. Progressives had an optimistic view of human nature and an exaggerated faith in statistics, commissions, and committees. They talked of the need for more democracy, but they often succeeded in promoting bureaucracy and a government run by experts. They believed there was a need to regulate business, promote efficiency, and spread social justice, but these were often contradictory goals. In the end, their regulatory laws tended to aid business and to strengthen corporate capitalism, while social justice and equal opportunity remained difficult to achieve. By contrast, most of the industrialized nations of western Europe, especially Germany, Austria, France, and Great Britain, passed legislation during this period providing for old-age pensions and health and unemployment insurance.

Progressivism was a broad, diverse, and sometimes contradictory movement that had its roots in the 1890s and reached a climax in the early twentieth century. It began with many local movements and voluntary efforts to deal with the problems created by urban industrialism and moved to the state and finally the national level. Women played important roles in organizing reform, and many became experts at gathering statistics and writing reports. Eventually they began to fill positions in the new agencies in the state capitals and in Washington. Neither Theodore Roosevelt nor Woodrow Wilson was an advanced progressive, but during both their administrations, progressivism achieved some success. Both presidents strengthened the power of the presidency, and both promoted the idea that the federal government had the responsibility to regulate and control and to promote social justice. Progressivism would be altered by World War I, but it survived, with its strengths and weaknesses, to affect American society through most of the twentieth century.

Recommended Reading

General Accounts

Arthur S. Link and Richard L. McCormick, *Progressivism* (1983); Robert Wiebe, *The Search for Order, 1877–1920* (1967); Richard Hofstadter, *The Age of Reform* (1955); Alan Dawley, *Struggle for Justice: Social Responsibility and the Liberal State* (1991); Steven J. Diner, *A Very Different Age: Americans of the Progressive Era* (1998).

The Progressive Impulse

Paul Boyer, *Urban Masses and Moral Order in America, 1820–1920* (1978); Peter Conn, *The Divided Mind: Ideology and Imagination in America, 1890–1927* (1983); Morton White, *Social Thought in America* (1949); Robert B. Westbrook, *John Dewey and American Democracy* (1991); George Cotkin, *Reluctant Modernism: American Thought and Culture, 1880–1900* (1992).

A Diversity of Progressive Movements

Allen F. Davis, *Spearheads for Reform: The Social Settlements and the Progressive Movement* (1967); Walter I. Trattner, *Crusade for Children* (1970); Ruth Rosen, *The Lost Sisterhood: Prostitutes in America, 1900–1918* (1982); Mark T. Connelly, *The Response to Prostitution in the Progressive Era* (1980); Linda Gordon, *Woman's Body, Woman's Right: A Social History of Birth Control* (1976); Lary May, *Screening Out the Past: The Birth of Mass Culture and the Motion Picture Industry* (1980); James H. Timberlake, *Prohibition and the Progressive Movement* (1963); David P. Thelen, *The New Citizenship* (1972); Dewey Grantham, *Southern Progressivism* (1983); Aileen S. Kraditor, *The Ideas of the Woman Suffrage Movement, 1890–1920* (1965); August Meier, *Negro Thought in America, 1880–1915* (1963); David L. Lewis, *W.E.B. Du Bois, Biography of a Race, 1868–1919* (1993); Samuel P. Hays, *Conservation and the Gospel of Efficiency* (1959); David Brody, *Workers in Industrial America* (1980); Alice Kessler-Harris, *Out to Work: A History of Wage Earning Women in the United States* (1983); Rivka Shpak Lissak, *Pluralism and Progressivism* (1989); Robyn Muncy, *Creating a Female Dominion in American Reform, 1890–1935* (1991); David Nasaw, *Going Out: The Rise and Fall of Public Amusements* (1993); Kathy Peiss, *Cheap Amusements: Working Women and Leisure in Turn of the Century New York* (1986).

National Politics

John Morton Blum, *The Progressive Presidents* (1980); John Milton Cooper, Jr., *The Warrior and the Priest* (1983); Nick Salvatore, *Eugene V. Debs* (1982); David P. Thelen, *Robert LaFollette and the Insurgent Spirit* (1976); William A. Link, *The Paradox of Southern Progressivism, 1880–1930* (1992); Morton Keller, *Regulating a New Society: Public Policy and Social Change in America, 1900–1930* (1994).

Fiction

Fiction from the period includes Theodore Dreiser, *Sister Carrie* (1900), a classic of social realism; Upton Sinclair, *The Jungle* (1906), a novel about the meatpacking industry and the failure of the American dream; David Graham Phillips, *Susan Lenox* (1917), an epic of slum life and political corruption; and Charlotte Perkins Gilman, *Herland* (1915), the story of a female utopia.

CHAPTER 22

The Great War

In April 7, 1917, the day after the United States declared war on Germany, 22-year-old Edmund P. Arpin, Jr., from Grand Rapids, Wisconsin, enlisted in the Army. The war seemed to provide a solution for his aimless drifting. It was not patriotism but his craving for adventure that led him to join the Army. A month later, he was at Fort Sheridan, Illinois, along with hundreds of other eager young men, preparing to become an Army officer. He felt pride, purpose, and especially comradeship, but the war was far away.

Arpin finally arrived with his unit in Liverpool on December 23, 1917, aboard the *Leviathan,* a German luxury liner that the United States had seized and turned into a troop transport. American troops were not greeted as saviors. English hostility simmered partly because of the previous unit's drunken brawls. Despite the efforts of the United States government to protect soldiers from the sins of Europe, drinking seems to have been a preoccupation of Arpin's outfit. He also learned something about French wine and women, but he spent most of the endless waiting time learning to play contract bridge.

Arpin saw some of the horror of war when he went to the front with a French regiment, but his own unit did not go into combat until October 1918, when the war was almost over. He took part in the bloody Meuse-Argonne offensive, which helped end the war. But he discovered that war was not the heroic struggle of carefully planned campaigns that newspapers and books described. War was filled with misfired weapons, mix-ups, and erroneous attacks. Wounded in the leg in an assault on an unnamed hill and awarded a Distinguished Service Cross for his bravery, Arpin later learned that the order to attack had been recalled, but word had not reached him in time.

When the armistice came, Arpin was in a field hospital. He was disappointed that the war had ended so soon, but he was well enough to go to Paris to take part in the victory celebration and to explore famous restaurants and nightclubs. In many ways, the highlight of his war experiences was not a battle or his medal, but his postwar adventure. With a friend, he went AWOL and explored Germany, making it back without being arrested.

Edmund Arpin was one of 4,791,172 Americans who served in the Army, Navy, or Marines, one of the two million who went overseas, and one of the 230,074 who were wounded. Some of his friends were among the 48,909 who were killed. Mustered out in March 1919, he felt confused. Being a civilian was not nearly as exciting as being in the Army and visiting exotic places.

In time, Arpin settled down. He became a successful businessman, married, and reared a family. A member of the American Legion, he periodically went to conventions and reminisced with men from his division about their escapades in France. Although the war changed their lives in many ways, most would never again feel the same sense of common purpose and adventure. "I don't suppose any of us felt, before or since, so necessary to God and man," one veteran recalled.

For Edmund P. Arpin, Jr., the Great War was the most important event of a lifetime. Just as war changed his life, so, too, did it alter the lives of most Americans. Trends begun during the progressive era accelerated. The power and influence of the federal government increased. Not only did the war promote woman suffrage, prohibition, and public housing, but it also helped create an administrative bureaucracy that blurred the lines between public and private, between government and business—a trend that continued through the twentieth century.

In this chapter, we examine the complicated circumstances that led the United States into war and share the wartime experiences of American men and women overseas and at home. We will study not only military actions, but also the war's impact on domestic policies and on the lives of ordinary Americans, including the migration of African-Americans into northern cities. The war left a legacy of prejudice and hate and raised a basic question: Could the tenets of American democracy, such as freedom of speech, survive participation in a major war? The chapter concludes with a look at the idealistic efforts to promote peace at the end of the war, and the disillusion that followed. The Great War thrust the United States into world leadership, but many Americans were reluctant to accept that role.

THE EARLY WAR YEARS

Few Americans expected the Great War that erupted in Europe in the summer of 1914 to affect their lives or alter their comfortable world. When a Serbian terrorist shot Archduke Franz Ferdinand of Austria-Hungary in Sarajevo, a place almost no Americans had heard of, things soon spiraled into the most destructive war the world had ever known.

The Causes of War

Despite Theodore Roosevelt's successful peacekeeping attempts (see Chapter 20), intense European rivalries turned minor incidents in Africa, Asia, and the Balkans into threats to world peace. Nationalism was fanned by mass newspapers. Anglo-Germany tensions led to a race to build bigger battleships.

As European nations armed, they drew up treaties pitting Austria-Hungary and Germany (the Central Powers) against Britain, France, and Russia (the Allied Powers). Despite peace conferences and international agreements, many promoted by the United States, the European balance of power rested precariously on layers of treaties that barely obscured years of jealousy and distrust.

The incident in Sarajevo destroyed that balance. The leaders of Austria-Hungary wanted to punish Serbia for killing Franz Ferdinand, the heir to the throne. Russia mobilized to aid Serbia. Germany, supporting Austria-Hungary, declared war on Russia and its ally, France. When Germany invaded Belgium to attack France, Britain declared war. The slaughter began.

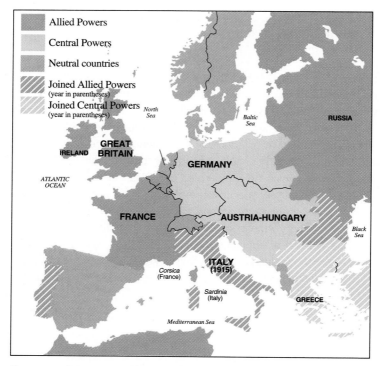

EUROPEAN ALIGNMENTS, 1914 The Great War had an impact on all of Europe, even on the few countries that managed to remain neutral. Russia left the war in 1917, the same year that the United States joined the fight.

Despite much evidence to the contrary, many intelligent people on both sides of the Atlantic believed that education, science, social reform, and negotiation had replaced war as a way of solving international disputes. But as reports of the first bloody battles began to reach the United States, most Americans felt that madness had replaced reason.

The American sense that the nation would never succumb to the barbarism of war, combined with the knowledge that they were insulated by the Atlantic, brought relief after the first shock wore off. Wilson's official proclamation of neutrality on August 4, 1914, reinforced the belief that the United States had no major stake in the outcome and would stay uninvolved. The president urged Americans to "be neutral in fact as well as in name . . . impartial in thought as well as in action." But it was difficult to stay uninvolved, at least emotionally.

American Reactions

Many social reformers despaired at the news from Europe. War abroad seemed to deflect energy from reform at home. Jane Addams, one of many women recognizing this, helped to organize the Woman's Peace party. Drawing on traditional ideas, she argued that women had a special responsibility to work for peace.

Although many people worked to promote an international plan to end the war through mediation, others could hardly wait to leap into the adventure. Hundreds of young American men, mostly college students or recent graduates, joined ambulance units. Among the most famous were Ernest Hemingway, John Dos Passos, and e. e. cummings (as he spelled his name), who later turned their wartime adventures into literary masterpieces. Others volunteered for the French Foreign Legion or the Lafayette Escadrille, volunteer American pilots attached to the French army. Many were inspired by their elders, like Theodore Roosevelt, who talked of war as something like a football game.

Many Americans saw war in such terms because the only conflict they remembered was the "splendid little war" of 1898. Older Americans recalled the Civil War, whose horrors had faded, leaving only the memory of heroic triumphs. But Oliver Wendell Holmes, the Supreme Court justice who had been wounded in the Civil War, remarked, "War, when you are at it, is horrible and dull. It is only when time has passed that you see that its message was divine."

Early reports from the battlefields should have indicated that the message was anything but divine. This would be a modern war in which men died by the thousands, cut down by an improved and efficient technology of killing.

The New Military Technology

The Germans' plan called for a rapid strike through Belgium to attack Paris and the French army from the rear. However, the French stopped the Germans in September 1914, and the fighting bogged down. Soldiers on both sides dug miles of trenches and strung out barbed wire. Thousands died in battles that gained only a few yards or nothing at all. Rapid-firing rifles, improved explosives, incendiary shells, smokeless bullets, and tracer bullets all added to the destruction. Most devastating of all was the improved artillery that could hit targets miles behind the lines. Machine guns neutralized frontal assaults. Explained one writer: "Three men and a machine gun can stop a battalion of heroes." But generals on both sides continued to order their men to charge to almost certain death.

The war was the last major conflict in which cavalry was used and the first to employ a new generation of military technologies. By 1918, airplanes were creating terror with their bombs. Tanks made a tentative appearance in 1916, but not until the last days of the war did this new offensive weapon began to neutralize the machine gun. Poison gas, first used in 1914, added fear—but soon both sides developed the gas mask.

Difficulties of Neutrality

Despite Wilson's efforts to promote neutrality, most Americans favored the Allied cause. About eight million people of German and Austro-Hungarian descent lived in the United States, and some supported the Central Powers. The anti-British feelings of some Irish Americans led them to side not so much with Germany as against England. A number of American scholars, physicians, and intellectuals fondly remembered studying in Germany and admired its culture and progressive social planning. For most Americans, however, the ties of language and culture tipped the balance toward the Allies. After all, did not the English-speaking people of the world have special bonds and responsibilities? Memories of Lafayette's role in the American Revolution and France's gift of the Statue of Liberty made many Americans pro-French.

Other reasons made real neutrality nearly impossible. The fact that trade with the Allies was much more important than with the Central Powers favored the Allies. Wilson's advisers openly supported the French and British. Most newspaper owners and editors had close ethnic, cultural, and sometimes economic ties to the British and the French. The newspapers were quick to picture the Germans as barbaric Huns and to accept and embellish atrocity stories, some of them planted by British propaganda experts. Gradually for Wilson, and probably for most Americans, the perception that England and France were fighting to preserve civilization from evil Prussians replaced the idea that all Europeans were decadent. But as for going to war to save civilization, let France and England do that.

Wilson sympathized with the Allies for practical and idealistic reasons. He wanted to keep the United States out of the war, but he did not object to using force to promote diplomatic ends. "When men take up arms to set other men free, there is something sacred and holy in the warfare," he had written. Wilson believed that by keeping the United States out of the war, he might control the peace. The war, he hoped, would show the futility of imperialism and would usher in a world of free trade in both products and ideas, a world in which the United States had a special role to play.

Remaining neutral while maintaining trade with the belligerents became increasingly difficult. The need to trade and the desire to control the peace finally led the United States into the Great War.

World Trade and Neutrality Rights

The United States was part of an international economic community in 1914 in a way that it had not been during the nineteenth century. The outbreak of war in the summer of 1914 caused immediate economic panic in the United States. On July 31, 1914, the Wilson administration closed the stock exchange. It also discouraged loans by American banks to belligerent nations. Most difficult was the matter of neutral trade. Wilson insisted on Americans' right to trade with both sides and with other neutrals, but Great Britain instituted an illegal naval blockade, mined the North Sea, and began seizing American ships. The first crisis that Wilson faced was whether to accept the illicit British blockade. To do so would be to surrender one of the rights he supported most ardently, free trade.

Wilson eventually accepted British control of the sea. His conviction that the destinies of the United States and Great Britain were intertwined outweighed his idealistic belief in free trade and caused him to react more harshly to German than to British violations of international law. Consequently, American trade with the Central Powers declined between 1914 and 1916 from $169 million to just over $1 million, whereas with the Allies it increased during the same period from $825 million to over $3 billion. At the same time, the United States government eased restrictions on private loans to belligerents. With dollars as well as sentiments, the United States gradually ceased to be neutral.

Germany retaliated against British control of the seas with submarine warfare. International law obligated a belligerent warship to warn a passenger or merchant ship before attacking, but a U-boat rising to the surface to do that would have been blown out of the water by an armed merchant ship.

On February 4, 1915, Germany announced a submarine blockade of the British Isles. Until Britain gave up its campaign to starve the German population, the Germans would sink even neutral ships. Wilson warned Germany that it would be held to "strict accountability" for illegal destruction of American ships or lives.

In March 1915, a German U-boat sank a British liner, killing 103 people, including one American. Wilson's advisers could not agree on an appropriate response. Robert Lansing, a legal counsel at the State Department, urged the president to issue a strong protest, charging a breach of international law. William Jennings Bryan, the secretary of state, argued that an American traveling on a British ship was guilty of "contributory negligence" and urged Wilson to ban Americans from belligerent ships in the war zone. Before Wilson could decide what to do, on May 7, 1915, a U-boat torpedoed the British luxury liner *Lusitania* off the Irish coast. The unarmed liner, which was carrying war supplies, sank in 18 minutes with a loss of nearly 1,200 lives, including 128 Americans. Suddenly Americans realized that modern war killed civilians as easily as it killed soldiers.

Despite earlier warnings by the Germans in American newspapers that it was dangerous to travel in war zones, the same newspapers denounced the act as "mass murder." Some called for war. Wilson and most Americans had no intention of fighting, but the president rejected Bryan's advice that Americans be prohibited from traveling on ships from the countries at war. Instead, he demanded reparation for the loss of American lives and a German pledge to cease attacking ocean liners without warning. Bryan resigned as secretary of state, charging that the United States was not being truly neutral. The president replaced him with Robert Lansing, who was more eager to oppose Germany, even at the risk of war.

The tense situation eased late in 1915. After a German U-boat sank the British steamer *Arabic*, which claimed two American lives, the German ambassador promised that Germany would not attack ocean liners without warning. But the *Lusitania* crisis caused an outpouring of books and articles urging the nation to prepare for war. However, a group of progressive reformers formed the American Union Against Militarism, fearing that preparedness advocates planned to destroy liberal social reform at home and promote imperialism abroad.

Wilson sympathized with the preparedness groups to the extent of asking Congress on November 4, 1915, for an enlarged and reorganized Army. The bill met great opposition, especially from southern and western congressmen, but the Army Reorganization Bill that Wilson signed in June 1916 increased the regular Army to just over 200,000 and integrated the National Guard into the defense structure. Few Americans expected those young men to go to war. But soon Wilson used the Army and the Marines in Mexico and Central America.

Intervening in Mexico and Central America

Wilson envisioned a world purged of imperialism, a world of free trade, and a world where American ideas and American products would find their way. Combining the zeal of a Christian missionary with the conviction of a college professor, he spoke of "releasing the intelligence of America for the service of mankind." Along with Secretary of State Bryan, Wilson denounced the "big stick" and "dollar diplomacy" of the Roosevelt and Taft years. Yet Wilson's administration used force more systematically than those of his predecessors. The rhetoric was different, yet like Roosevelt, Wilson tried to maintain stability in the countries to the south in order to promote American economic and strategic interests.

At first, Wilson's foreign policy seemed to reverse the most callous aspects of dollar diplomacy in Central America. Bryan signed a treaty with Colombia in 1913 paying $5 million for the loss of Panama and virtually apologizing for Roosevelt's treatment of Colombia. But the Senate refused to ratify the treaty.

The change in spirit proved illusory. After a disastrous civil war in the Dominican Republic, the United States offered in 1915 to take over the country's finances and police force. When Dominican leaders rejected a treaty making their country virtually an American protectorate, Wilson ordered in the Marines. They took control of the government in May 1916. Although Americans built roads, schools, and hospitals, people resented their presence. Americans also intervened in Haiti, with similar results. In Nicaragua, Wilson kept the Marines sent by Taft in 1912 to prop up a pro-American regime and acquired the right to intervene at any time to preserve order and protect American property. Except briefly in the mid-1920s, the Marines remained until 1933.

Wilson's policy of intervention ran into greatest difficulty in Mexico, a country that had been ruled by dictator Porfirio Díaz, who had long welcomed American investors. By 1910, more than 40,000 American citizens lived in Mexico, and more than $1 billion of American money was invested there. In 1911, however, Francisco Madero, a reformer who wanted to destroy the privileges of the upper classes, overthrew Díaz. Two years later, Madero was deposed and murdered by Victoriano Huerta, the head of the army.

To the shock of many diplomats and businessmen, Wilson refused to recognize the Huerta government. Everyone admitted that Huerta was a ruthless dictator, but diplomatic recognition, the exchange of ambassadors, and the regulation of trade and communication had never meant approval. But Wilson set out to remove what he called a "government of butchers."

At first, Wilson applied diplomatic pressure. Then, using a minor incident as an excuse, he asked Congress for power to involve American troops if necessary. Few Mexicans liked Huerta, but they liked North American interference even less, and rallied around the dictator. As it had in 1847, the United States landed troops at Veracruz. Mexican mobs destroyed American property wherever they could find it. Wilson's action outraged many in Europe, Latin America, and the United States.

Wilson's intervention drove Huerta from power, but a civil war between the forces of Venustiano Carranza and those under General Francisco "Pancho" Villa ensued. The United States sent arms to Carranza, who was considered less radical than Villa, and Carranza's soldiers defeated Villa's. When Villa led what was left of his army in a raid on Columbus, New Mexico, in March 1916, Wilson sent an expedition under Brigadier General John Pershing to track down Villa and his men. An American Army charged 300 miles into Mexico unable to catch the elusive villain. Mexicans feared that Pershing's army was planning to occupy northern Mexico. Carranza shot off a bitter note to Wilson, but Wilson refused to withdraw. Tensions rose. An American patrol attacked a Mexican garrison. At length Wilson agreed to recall the troops and to recognize the Carranza government. But this was in January 1917, and had it not been for the growing crisis in Europe, war would likely have resulted.

Wilson, who wanted the best for the people of Mexico and Central America and thought he knew exactly what they needed, had intervened too often and too blatantly to protect strategic and economic U.S. interests. His policy alienated one-time friends of the United States and would contribute to future difficulties in both Latin America and Europe.

THE UNITED STATES ENTERS THE WAR

A significant minority of Americans opposed going to war in 1917, and that decision would remain controversial when it was reexamined in the 1930s. But once involved, the government and the American people made the war into a patriotic crusade that influenced all aspects of American life.

The Election of 1916

American political campaigns do not stop even for international crisis. In 1915 and 1916, Wilson had to think of reelection as well as of preparedness, submarines, and Mexico. His chances seemed poor. If supporters of the Progressives in 1912 returned to the Republican fold, Wilson would probably lose. Because the Progressive party had done very badly in the 1914 congressional elections, Roosevelt seemed ready to seek the Republican nomination.

Wilson knew that he had to win over voters who had favored Roosevelt in 1912. In January 1916, he nominated Louis D. Brandeis to the Supreme Court. Becoming the first Jewish justice, Brandeis was confirmed over strong opposition. His appointment pleased the social justice progressives because he had always championed reform causes. They made it clear to Wilson that the real test for them was whether or not he supported the anti-child labor and workers' compensation bills pending in Congress.

Within a few months, Wilson reversed his earlier New Freedom doctrines and aligned the federal government on the side of reform. In August 1916, he pushed through Congress the Workmen's Compensation Bill, which gave some protection to federal employees, and the Keatings-Owen Child Labor Bill, which barred from interstate commerce goods produced by children under the age of 14 and in some cases under the age of 16. This bill, later declared unconstitutional, was a far-reaching proposal that for the first time used federal control over interstate commerce to dictate the conditions under which products could be manufactured. To attract farm support, Wilson backed the Federal Farm Loan Act to extend long-term credit to farmers. Urged on by organized labor as well as by many progressives, he supported the Adamson Act, establishing an eight-hour day for all interstate railway workers.

The flurry of legislation early in 1916 provided a climax to the progressive movement. The strategy seemed to work, for progressives of all kinds enthusiastically endorsed the president.

The election of 1916, however, turned as much on foreign affairs as on domestic policy. Ignoring Roosevelt, Republicans nominated staid Charles Evans Hughes, a former governor of New York and future Supreme Court chief justice. Their platform called for "straight and honest neutrality" and "adequate preparedness." Hughes attacked Wilson for not promoting American rights in Mexico more vigorously and for giving in to what he called labor's unreasonable demands. Wilson implied that electing Hughes would guarantee war with both Mexico and Germany and that his opponents were somehow not "100 percent Americans." As the campaign progressed, the peace issue became more important, and the cry "He kept us out of war" echoed through every Democratic rally. It was a slogan that would soon seem strangely ironic.

The election was extremely close. Wilson went to bed on election night thinking he had lost, and the result was not clear until he took California by less than 4,000 votes. Wilson won by carrying the West as well as the South.

Deciding for War

Wilson's victory in 1916 seemed to be a mandate for staying out of the European war. But the campaign rhetoric made the president nervous. He had tried to emphasize Americanism, not neutrality.

People who supported Wilson as a peace candidate applauded in January 1917 when he went before the Senate to clarify the American position on a negotiated settlement of the war. The German government had earlier indicated that it might be willing to go to the conference table. Wilson outlined a plan for a negotiated settlement, without indemnities or annexations. The agreement Wilson outlined could have worked only if Germany and the Allies were willing to settle for a draw.

Early in 1917, however, German leaders thought they could win. On January 31, 1917, Berlin announced that any ship, belligerent or neutral, sailing toward Britain or France would be sunk on sight. A few days later, the United States broke diplomatic relations with Germany. An intercepted telegram from the German foreign secretary, Arthur Zimmermann, to the German minister in Mexico increased anti-German feeling. If war broke out, the German minister was to offer Mexico the territory it had lost in Texas, New Mexico, and Arizona. In return, Mexico would join Germany in a war against the United States. When this telegram was released to the press on March 1, 1917, many Americans demanded war against Germany. Wilson still hesitated.

As the country waited on the brink of war, news of revolution in Russia reached Washington. That event would prove as important as the war itself. The March 1917 revolution in Russia was a spontaneous uprising of workers, housewives, and soldiers against the tsarist government's inept conduct of the war. The army had suffered staggering losses. Civilian conditions were desperate. Food was scarce, and the railroads and industry had nearly collapsed. At first, Wilson and other Americans were enthusiastic about the new republic led by Alexander Kerensky, who promised to continue the struggle against Germany. But within months, the revolution took a more extreme turn. Vladimir Ilyich Ulyanov, known as Lenin, returned from exile in Switzerland and led the radical Bolsheviks to victory over the Kerensky regime in November 1917.

Lenin, a brilliant revolutionary tactician, was a follower of Karl Marx (1818–1883). Marx was a German radical philosopher who had described the alienation of the working class under capitalism and predicted a growing split between the proletariat (unpropertied workers) and the capitalists. Lenin extended Marx's ideas and argued that capitalist nations eventually would be forced to go to war over raw materials and markets. Believing that capitalism and imperialism went hand in hand, Lenin argued that the only way to end imperialism was to end capitalism. Communism, Lenin predicted, would eventually dominate the globe. The Russian Revolution threatened Wilson's vision of the world and to his plan to bring the United States into the war "to make the world safe for democracy."

More disturbing than the first news of revolution in Russia, however, was the situation in the North Atlantic, where U-boats sank five American ships between March 12 and March 21, 1917. On April 2, Wilson urged Congress to declare war. "It is a fearful thing," he concluded, "to lead this great, peaceful people into war, into the most terrible and disastrous of all wars." The war resolution swept the Senate 82 to 6 and the House of Representatives 373 to 50.

Once war was declared, most Americans forgot their doubts. Young men rushed to enlist; women volunteered to become nurses or to serve in other ways.

A Patriotic Crusade

But not all Americans applauded. Some pacifists and socialists opposed the war, and a black newspaper, *The Messenger,* decried the conflict. "To whom does war bring prosperity?" Senator George Norris of Nebraska asked on the Senate floor.

> Not to the soldier, . . . not to the broken hearted widow, . . . not to the mother who weeps at the death of her brave boy . . . . War brings no prosperity to the great mass of common patriotic citizens. We are going into war upon the command of gold . . . . I feel that we are about to put the dollar sign on the American flag.

For most Americans in the spring of 1917, the war seemed remote. A few days after war was declared, a Senate committee listened to a member of the War Department staff list the vast quantities of materials needed to supply an American army in France. One of the senators, jolted awake, exclaimed, "Good Lord! You're not going to send soldiers over there, are you?"

To convince senators and citizens alike that the war was real and that American participation was just, Wilson appointed a Committee on Public Information, headed by journalist George Creel. His committee launched a gigantic campaign to persuade the American public that the United States had gone to war to promote democracy and prevent the "Huns" from overrunning the world.

The patriotic crusade soon became stridently anti-German and anti-immigrant. Most school districts forbade teaching German. Sauerkraut was renamed "liberty cabbage." Many families Americanized German surnames. Several cities banned music by German composers. South Dakota prohibited speaking German on the telephone, and in Iowa a state official announced, "If their language is disloyal, they should be imprisoned. If their acts are disloyal, they should be shot." The most notorious incident occurred in East St. Louis, Illinois, which had a large German population. In April 1918, a mob seized Robert Prager, a young German

GEE !!
I WISH I WERE
A MAN

I'd JOIN
The NAVY

BE A MAN AND DO IT
UNITED STATES NAVY
RECRUITING STATION
34 East 23rd Street, New York

Recruiting posters helped to create a sense of purpose and patriotism, and often used pictures of attractive women to make their point. To be a soldier was to be a real man; to avoid service was to be something less than a man. (The Granger Collection, New York)

American, stripped off his clothes, dressed him in an American flag, marched him through the streets, and lynched him. Brought to trial, the ringleaders were acquitted on the grounds that the lynching was a "patriotic murder."

The Wilson administration did not condone domestic violence and murder, but the heated patriotism fanned by the war led to irrational hatreds and fears. Suspect were not only German Americans, but also radicals, pacifists, and anyone with doubts about the American war efforts or the government's policies. In New York, the black editors of *The Messenger* were given 2 1/2-year jail sentences for the paper's article "Pro-Germanism Among Negroes." The Los Angeles police ignored complaints that Mexicans were being harassed because they believed that all Mexicans were pro-German. Senator La Follette, who had voted against declaring war, was burned in effigy and censured by the University of Wisconsin. At a number of universities, professors were dismissed, sometimes for questioning the morality or necessity of America's participation in the war.

On June 15, 1917, Congress, at Wilson's behest, passed the Espionage Act, providing imprisonment of up to 20 years or a fine of up to $10,000, or both, for people who aided the enemy or who "willfully cause . . . insubordination, disloyalty, mutiny or refusal of duty in the military . . . forces of the United States . . . ." The act also authorized the postmaster general to bar from the mails any matter he thought advocated treason or forcible resistance to United States laws. The act was used to stamp out dissent, even to discipline anyone who questioned the administration's policies.

Congress later added the Trading with the Enemy Act and a Sedition Act. The latter prohibited disloyal, profane, scurrilous, or abusive remarks about the form of government, flag, or uniform of the United States. It even prohibited citizens from opposing the purchase of war bonds. In the most famous case tried under the act, Eugene Debs was sentenced to ten years in prison for opposing the war. In 1919, the Supreme Court upheld the conviction, even though Debs had not explicitly urged violating the draft laws. While still in prison, Debs polled close to one million votes in the presidential election of 1920. Ultimately, the government prosecuted 2,168 people under the Espionage and Sedition acts and convicted about half of them. These figures do not include the thousands informally persecuted.

A group of amateur loyalty enforcers, the American Protective League, cooperated with the Justice Department. League members often reported nonconformists; people were arrested for criticizing the Red Cross or a government agency. One woman was sentenced to prison for writing, "I am for the people and the government is for the profiteers." Ricardo Flores Magon, a leading Mexican-American labor organizer and radical in the Southwest, got 20 years in prison for criticizing Wilson's Mexican policy and violating the Neutrality Acts. The attorney general of the United States, speaking of critics, said, "May God have mercy on them for they need expect none from an outraged people and an avenging government."

The Civil Liberties Bureau, an outgrowth of the American Union Against Militarism, protested the blatant abridgment of freedom of speech during the war, but the protests fell on deaf ears at the Justice Department and in the White House. Rights and freedoms have been reduced or suspended during all wars, but the massive disregard for basic rights was greater during World War I than during the Civil War—ironically, because Wilson had often written and spoken of the need to preserve freedom of speech and civil liberties. During the war, however, he tolerated the vigilante tactics of his own Justice Department. Wilson was so convinced his cause was just that he ignored the rights of those who opposed him.

Raising an Army

The debate over a volunteer army versus the draft had been going on for several years before the United States entered the war. People who favored some form of universal military service argued that college graduates, farmers, and young men from eastern slums could learn from one another as they trained together. Critics pointed out that people making such claims were usually the college graduates, who assumed they would command the boys from the slums. The draft, they argued, was simply the tool of an imperialist power bent on ending dissent. Memories were revived of massive draft riots during the Civil War.

Wilson and his secretary of war, Newton Baker, both initially opposed the draft, but in the end concluded that it was the most efficient way to organize military manpower. Ironically, Theodore Roosevelt tipped Wilson in favor of the draft. With failing health and blind in one eye, the old Rough Rider wanted to recruit a volunteer division and lead it personally against the Germans.

The thought of Roosevelt, whom Wilson considered his enemy, blustering about Europe so frightened Wilson that he supported the Selective Service Act in part, at least, to forestall such volunteer outfits as Roosevelt planned. Yet the House finally insisted that the minimum age for draftees should be 21, not 18. On June 5, 1917, some 9.5 million men between the ages of 21 and 31 registered, with little protest. In August 1918, Congress extended the act to men 18 to 45. In all, over 24 million men registered and over 2.8 million were inducted—over 75 percent of soldiers who served in the war.

The draft worked well, but it was not quite the perfect system that Wilson claimed. Most Americans took seriously their obligation of "service" during time of war. But because local draft boards had so much control, favoritism and political influence allowed some to stay at home. Draft protests erupted in a few places, the largest in Oklahoma, where a group of tenant farmers planned a march on Washington to take over the government and end the "rich man's war." A local posse arrested about 900 protesters and took them off to jail.

Some men escaped the draft. Some were deferred because of war-related jobs, and others resisted by claiming exemption for reasons of conscience. The Selective Service Act did exempt men who belonged to pacifist religious groups, but religious motivation was often difficult to define, and nonreligious conscientious objection was even more complicated. Thousands of conscientious objectors were inducted. Some served in noncombat positions; others went to prison.

THE MILITARY EXPERIENCE

For years afterward, men and women who lived through the war remembered rather sentimentally what it had meant to them. For some, it was a tragedy in which they saw the horrors of the battlefield firsthand. For others, it was liberating—the most exciting period in their lives.

The American Doughboy

The typical soldier stood 5 feet 7 1/2 inches tall, weighed 141 1/2 pounds, and was about 22 years old. He took a physical exam, an intelligence test, and a psychological test, and he probably watched a movie called *Fit to Fight,* warning about venereal disease. The majority of American soldiers had not attended high school. The median amount of education for native whites was 6.9 years and for immigrants 4.7 years, but only 2.6 years for southern blacks. As many as 31 percent of the recruits were declared illiterate, but the tests were so primitive that they probably tested social class more than anything else. Fully 29 percent of the recruits were rejected as physically unfit for service, shocking health experts.

Most World War I soldiers were ill-educated, unsophisticated young men from farms, small towns, and urban neighborhoods. Coming from all classes and ethnic groups, most were transformed into soldiers. In the beginning, they didn't look the part, because uniforms and equipment were in short supply. Many men had to wear their civilian clothes for months, and they often wore out their shoes before they were issued army boots.

The military experience changed the lives and often the attitudes of many young men. Women also contributed to the war effort as telephone operators and clerk-typists in the Navy and the Marines, as nurses, or with organizations like the Red Cross. Yet the military experience was predominantly male. Even going to training camp was new and often frightening. A leave in Paris or London, or even in New York or New Orleans, was an adventure to remember for a lifetime. Many soldiers saw their first movie or their first truck in the army. Men learned to shave with the new safety razor and to wear the new wristwatch. The war also popularized the cigarette, which, unlike a pipe or cigar, could be smoked during a short break.

The Black Soldier

Blacks had served in all American wars, and many fought valiantly in the Civil War and the Spanish-American War. Yet black soldiers had most often performed menial work in segregated units. Black leaders hoped it would be different this time. W. E. B. Du Bois urged blacks to support the war, predicting that the war experience would cause the "walls of prejudice" to crumble gradually before the "onslaught of common sense." But the walls did not crumble.

The Selective Service Act made no mention of race, and African-Americans in most cases registered without protest. Many whites, especially in the South, at first feared having too many blacks trained in the use of arms. In some areas, draft boards exempted single white men, but drafted black fathers. Still, most southern whites found it difficult to imagine a black man in the uniform of the U.S. Army.

White attitudes toward African-Americans sometimes led to conflict. In August 1917, violence erupted in Houston, Texas, involving soldiers from the regular Army's all-black 24th Infantry Division. Harassed by the Jim Crow laws, which had been tightened for their benefit, a group of soldiers went on a rampage, killing 17 white civilians. Over 100 soldiers were court-martialed; 13 were condemned to death and hanged three days later before appeals could be filed.

This violence, coming only a month after a race riot in East St. Louis, Illinois, brought on in part by the migration of southern blacks to the area, caused great concern about the handling of African-American soldiers. Secretary of War Baker made it clear that the army had no intention of upsetting the segregated status quo.

Some African-Americans were trained as junior officers and were assigned to the all-black 92nd Division, where the high-ranking officers were white. But blacks were officially considered unfit to fight. Most of the black soldiers, including about 80 percent of those sent to France, worked as stevedores and common laborers under white noncommissioned officers. Other black soldiers acted as servants, drivers, and porters for the white officers. It was a demeaning and ironic policy for a government that advertised itself as standing for justice, honor, and democracy.

Over There

The conflict that Wilson called the war "to make the world safe for democracy" had become a contest of stalemate and slaughter. To this ghastly war, Americans

World War I, especially on the Western front, was a war of position and defense. Troops on both sides lived in elaborate trenches that turned into a sea of mud when it rained. The men tried to protect themselves with barbed wire and gas masks against new and terrifying technology. But there was little defense against the machine gun that mowed down the troops as they charged from their trenches. Here American soldiers from the New York National Guard, part of the 42nd Division, dig in behind their sandbag-lined trenches in the woods near the Marne River in June, 1918. (U.S. Signal Corps., National Archives)

made important contributions; without their help, the Allies might have lost. But the American contribution was most significant only in the war's final months.

When the United States went to war in the spring of 1917, the fighting had dragged on for nearly three years. In one battle in 1916, a total of 60,000 British soldiers were killed or wounded in a single day, yet the battle lines did not move an inch. By the spring of 1917, the British and French armies were down to their last reserves. Italy's army had nearly collapsed. In the East, Russia plunged into a bitter internal struggle, and soon Lenin would make a separate peace, freeing German divisions in the East to join in one final assault in the West. The Allies desperately needed fresh American troops, but those troops had to be trained, equipped, and transported to the front.

Token American regiments arrived in France in the summer of 1917 under the command of "Black Jack" Pershing, who had led the Mexican expedition in 1916. When they paraded in Paris on July 4, 1917, the crowd showered them with flowers. But the American commanders worried that many of their soldiers were so inexperienced they did not know how to march, let alone fight. The first Americans saw action near Verdun in October 1917. By March 1918, over 300,000 American soldiers had reached France, and by November 1918, that number had risen to more than two million.

One reason that the United States forces were slow to see actual combat was Pershing's insistence that they be kept separate from French and British divisions. An exception was made for four regiments of black soldiers who were assigned to the French army. Despite the American warning to the French not to "spoil the Negroes" by allowing them to mix with the French civilian population, these soldiers fought so well that the French later awarded three of the regiments the Croix de Guerre, their highest unit citation.

In the spring of 1918, with Russia out of the war and the British blockade becoming more and more effective, the Germans launched an all-out offensive to win the war before full American military and industrial power became a factor. By late May, the Germans pushed within 50 miles of Paris. American troops helped stem the German advance at Château-Thierry, Belleau Wood, and Cantigny, names that proud survivors would later endow with almost sacred significance. Americans also took part in the Allied offensive in the summer of 1918.

In September, over a half million American troops fought near St. Mihiel, the first battle where large numbers of Americans went into action. One enlisted man "saw a sight which I shall never forget. It was zero hour and in one instant the entire front as far as the eye could reach in either direction was a sheet of flame, while the heavy artillery made the earth quake." The Americans suffered over 7,000 casualties, but they captured more than 16,000 German soldiers. The victory, even if it came against exhausted and retreating German troops, seemed to vindicate Pershing's insistence on a separate American army. The British and French commanders were critical of what they considered the disorganized, inexperienced, and ill-equipped American forces. They especially denounced the quality of the American high-ranking officers.

In the fall of 1918, the combined British, French, and American armies drove the Germans back. Faced with low morale among the German soldiers and finally the mutiny of the German fleet and Austria-Hungary's surrender, Kaiser Wilhelm II abdicated, and the Armistice was signed on November 11. More than a million American soldiers took part in the final Allied offensive. Many were inexperienced, and some "90-day wonders" had never handled a rifle before arriving in France. Edmund Arpin got his wound by mistake. There were many other mistakes, some disastrous. The most famous blunder was the "lost battalion," which advanced beyond its support and was cut off and surrounded. It suffered 70 percent casualties.

The performance of the all-black 92nd Division was also controversial. The 92nd had been deliberately dispersed around the United States and had never trained as a unit. Its higher officers were white, and they repeatedly asked to be transferred. Many of its men were partly trained and poorly equipped, and they were continually being called away to work as common laborers. At the last minute during the Meuse-Argonne offensive, the 92nd was assigned to a particularly difficult position on the line, without maps or wire-cutters. Battalion commanders lost contact with their men, and several times the troops ran in the face of enemy fire. The division was withdrawn in disgrace. For years politicians and military leaders used this incident to claim that black soldiers would never make good fighting men, ignoring the difficulties under which the 92nd fought and the valor shown by black troops assigned to the French army.

The war produced a few American heroes. Joseph Oklahombie, a Choctaw, overran several German machine gun nests and captured more than 100 German soldiers. Sergeant Alvin York, a former conscientious objector from Tennessee, single-handedly killed or captured 160 Germans using only his rifle and pistol. But his heroics were not typical. Artillery, machine guns, and, near the end, tanks, trucks, and airplanes won the war.

With few exceptions, the Americans fought hard and well. Although the French and British criticized the Americans' inexperience and disarray, they admired their exuberance, "pep," and ability to move large numbers of men and equipment efficiently. Sometimes the Americans simply overwhelmed the enemy with their numbers. They suffered over 120,000 casualties in the Meuse-Argonne campaign alone. One officer estimated that he lost ten soldiers for every German his men killed in the final offensive.

The United States entered the war late, but still lost more than 48,000 service personnel and had many more wounded. Disease claimed 15 of every 1,000 soldiers each year (compared with 65 per 1,000 in the Civil War). But the British lost 900,000 men, the French 1.4 million, and the Russians 1.7 million. The United States contributed huge amounts of men and supplies in the last months of the war, and that finally tipped the balance. But it had entered late and sacrificed little compared with France and England. That would influence the peace settlement.

DOMESTIC IMPACT OF THE WAR

For at least 30 years before the United States entered the Great War, a debate raged over the proper role of the federal government in regulating industry and protecting people who could not protect themselves. Even within the Wilson administration, advisers disagreed on the proper role of the federal government. But the war and the problems it raised increased the power of the federal government and forged a more modern nation.

Financing the War

The war, by one calculation, cost the United States over $33 billion, and interest and veterans' benefits brought the total to nearly $112 billion. Early on, when an economist suggested that the war might cost the United States $10 billion, everyone had laughed. Yet many in the Wilson administration knew the war was going to be expensive, and they set out to raise the money by borrowing and by increasing taxes.

Secretary of the Treasury William McAdoo shouldered the task of financing the war. Studying the policies that Treasury Secretary Salmon Chase had followed during the Civil War, he decided that Chase should have appealed to popular emotions. His campaign to sell liberty bonds to ordinary American citizens at a very low interest rate stirred patriotism. "Lick a Stamp and Lick the Kaiser," one poster urged. Celebrities promoted the bonds, Boy Scouts sold them, and McAdoo implied that people who did not buy them were traitors.

The public responded enthusiastically, but they discovered after the war that their bonds had dropped to about 80 percent of face value. Because the interest on the bonds was tax-exempt, well-to-do citizens profited more from buying the bonds than did ordinary people. But the wealthy were not as pleased with McAdoo's other plan to finance the war by raising taxes. The War Revenue Act of 1917 boosted the tax rate sharply, taxed excess profits, and increased estate taxes. The next year the tax rate on the largest incomes soared to 77 percent. The wealthy protested, but a number of progressives were just as unhappy, for they wanted to confiscate all income over $100,000 a year. Despite taxes and liberty bonds, however, World War I, like the Civil War, was financed in large part by inflation. Food prices, for example, nearly doubled between 1917 and 1919.

Increasing Federal Power

At first, Wilson tried to work through state agencies to mobilize resources. The need for more central control soon led Wilson to create a series of emergency federal agencies. The first crisis was food. Poor grain crops for two years and an increasing demand for American food in Europe caused shortages. Wilson appointed Herbert Hoover, a young engineer who had won great prestige organizing relief for Belgium, to direct the Food Administration. Hoover set out to meet the crisis not so much through government regulation as through an appeal to the patriotism of farmers and consumers alike. He instituted "wheatless" and "meatless" days and urged housewives to cooperate. Women emerged during the war as the most important group of consumers. The government urged them to save, just as later it would urge them to buy.

The Wilson administration used the authority of the federal government to organize resources for the war effort. The War Industries Board, led by Bernard Baruch, a shrewd Wall Street broker, used government power to control scarce materials and, on occasion, to set prices and priorities. The government itself went into the shipbuilding business and ran the railroads. When a severe winter and a lack of coordination brought the rail system near collapse in December 1917, Wilson put all the nation's railroads under the control of the United Railway Administration. The government spent more than $500 million to improve the rails and equipment, and in 1918 the railroads did run more efficiently than they had under private control. Some businessmen complained of "war socialism" and regulation. But most agreed with Baruch that a close relationship with government could improve product quality, promote efficiency, and increase profits.

War Workers

The Wilson administration sought to protect and extend the rights of organized labor during the war, while mobilizing workers to keep the factories running. The National War Labor Board insisted on adequate wages and reduced hours, and it tried to prevent exploitation of working women and children. If a munitions

Women proved during the war that they could do "men's work." These shipyard workers even dressed like men, but the war did not change the American ideal that woman's place was in the home. Notice that in this photograph the two black women in the center of the picture seem to have the same status as the white workers. This would have been unusual during World War I. (National Archives)

plant refused to accept the board's decision, the government seized it. When workers threatened to strike, the board often ruled that they either had to work or be drafted.

The Wilson administration favored the conservative labor movement of Samuel Gompers and his AFL, and the Justice Department put the radical Industrial Workers of the World "out of business." After September 1917, federal agents conducted massive raids on IWW offices and arrested most of the leaders. Yet the government tolerated ruthless vigilante groups. In Bisbee, Arizona, the sheriff and 2,000 deputies rounded up 1,200 striking workers and sent them by boxcar to New Mexico. They spent two days in the desert without food or water before help came.

Gompers took advantage of the crisis to strengthen the AFL's position. He lent his approval to administration policies by making it clear that he opposed the IWW, socialists, and communists. As the AFL won a voice in home front policy, its membership increased from 2.7 million in 1916 to over 4 million in 1917. Organized labor's wartime gains, however, would prove only temporary.

The war opened up industrial opportunities for black men. With four million men in the armed forces and the flow of immigrants ended by the war, factories for the first time hired African-Americans in large numbers. Northern labor agents and the railroads actively recruited southern blacks, but the news of jobs in northern cities spread by word of mouth as well. By 1920, more than 300,000 blacks had joined the "great migration" north. This massive movement, which continued into the 1920s, had a permanent impact on the South as well as on the northern cities. As African-Americans trekked north, thousands of Mexicans crossed into the United States. Immigration officials relaxed regulations because of the need for labor in the farms and factories of the Southwest.

The war also created new employment opportunities for women. Posters and patriotic speeches urged women to do their duty for the war effort. One poster showed a woman at her typewriter, the shadow of a soldier in the background, with the message: "STENOGRAPHERS, WASHINGTON NEEDS YOU."

Women responded to these appeals out of both patriotism and a need to increase their earnings and to make up for inflation, which cut real wages. Women went into every kind of industry. They labored in brickyards and factories, as railroad conductors, and in munitions plants. The Woman's Land Army mobilized female labor for the farms. They demonstrated that women could do any kind of job. "It was not until our men were called overseas," one woman banking executive reported, "that we made any real onslaught on the realm of finance, and became tellers, managers of departments, and junior and senior officers." Black women left domestic service for textile mills and even stockyards. But racial discrimination, even in the North, kept them from moving very far up the ladder.

Even though women demonstrated that they could do "male" jobs, their wartime progress proved temporary. Only about 5 percent of the women employed during the war, mostly unmarried, were new to the work force. For most, it meant a shift of occupations or a move up to a better-paying position. Moreover, the war accelerated trends already under way. It increased the need for telephone operators, sales personnel, secretaries, and other white-collar workers, and in these occupations women soon became a majority. Telephone operator became an almost exclusively female job by 1917.

In the end, the war did provide limited opportunities for some women, but it did not change the dominant perception that a woman's place was in the home. After the war was over, the men returned, and women's gains almost disappeared. There were 8 million women in the work force in 1910 and only 8.5 million in 1920.

The Climax of Progressivism

Many progressives, especially the social justice progressives, opposed the United States's entry into the war until a few months before Congress declared war. But after April 1917, many began to see the "social possibilities of war." They deplored the war's death and destruction, the abridgment of freedom of speech, and the ultrapatriotism, but praised the social planning that war stimulated. They approved the Wilson administration's support of collective bargaining, the eight-hour day, and protection for women and children in industry. They welcomed government-owned housing projects, woman suffrage, and prohibition. Many endorsed the government takeover of the railroads and control of business. For many social justice progressives who had fought hard, long, and frustrating battles to humanize the industrial city, it was refreshing that suddenly people in high places were listening and approving.

One of the best examples of the progressives' influence on wartime activities was the Commission on Training Camp Activities, set up early in the war to mobilize, entertain, and protect American servicemen at home and abroad. It organized community singing and baseball, established post exchanges and theaters, and even provided university extension lectures. The overriding assumption was that the military experience would produce citizens ready to vote for social reform.

The Commission on Training Camp Activities also incorporated the progressive crusades against alcohol and prostitution. Laws banned liquor sales to men in uniform and prostitution and alcohol around military bases. "Fit to fight" was the motto. It was a typical progressive effort, combining moral indignation with scientific prophylaxis. The commissioners prided themselves on eliminating all redlight districts near the training camps. When the boys go to France, the secretary of war remarked, "I want them to have invisible armour to take with them."

France tested that "invisible armour." Despite hundreds of letters from American mothers, the government decided that it could not stop soldiers from drinking wine, but it did forbid them to buy or accept as gifts anything but light wine and beer. If Arpin's outfit is typical, troops ignored the rules. Sex was even more difficult to regulate. The British and the French armies tried to control venereal disease by licensing and inspecting prostitutes. French premier Georges Clemenceau accused the Americans of spreading disease throughout the French population and offered to provide the Americans with licensed prostitutes. When Clemenceau's letter reached Baker, the secretary of war said, "For God's sake, . . . don't show this to the President or he'll stop the war." The offer was never accepted.

Suffrage for Women

In the fall of 1918, Wilson asked the Senate's support of woman suffrage as "vital to the winning of the war." Wilson had earlier opposed the vote for women. His positive statement at this late date was not necessary, but his voice was a welcome addition to a rising chorus of support for an amendment to the Constitution that would permit the female half of the population to vote. Many still argued that voting would make women less feminine and less fit as wives and mothers. The National Association Opposed to Woman Suffrage declared that woman suffrage, socialism, and feminism were "three branches of the same Social Revolution."

Carrie Chapman Catt, an efficient administrator and tireless organizer, devised the strategy that finally secured the vote for women. In 1915, she became president of the National American Woman Suffrage Association (NAWSA), coordinating the state campaigns from the office in Washington and directing a growing army of dedicated workers. The careful planning began to produce results, but a group of more militant reformers, impatient with the slow progress, broke off from NAWSA to form the National Woman's Party (NWP) in 1916. This group was led by Alice Paul, who had participated in suffrage battles in England. Paul and her group picketed the White House, chained themselves to the fence, and blocked the streets. They carried banners that asked, "MR. PRESIDENT, HOW LONG MUST WOMEN WAIT FOR LIBERTY?" In the summer of 1917, the government arrested more than 200 women and charged them with "obstructing the sidewalk." It was just the kind of publicity the militant group sought, and it made the most of it. Wilson, fearing more embarrassment, began to cooperate with moderate reformers.

Careful organizing by the NAWSA and the NWP's more militant tactics both contributed to the final success of the woman suffrage crusade. The war did not cause the passage of the Nineteenth Amendment, but it did accelerate it. In 1917, 14 state legislatures petitioned Congress as did 26 in 1919, urging enactment. Early in 1919, the House of Representatives passed the amendment 304 to 90, and the Senate approved 56 to 25. Fourteen months later, the required 36 states had ratified, and women at last had the vote. But this would not prove the triumph of feminism, nor the signal for the beginning of a new reform movement that the women leaders expected.

PLANNING FOR PEACE

Wilson turned U.S. participation in the war into a crusade to make the world safe for democracy—and more. On January 8, 1918, partly to counter Bolshevik charges that the war was merely an imperialist struggle, he announced his plan. Called the Fourteen Points, it argued for "open covenants of peace openly arrived at," freedom of the seas, equality of trade, and the self-determination of all peoples. But his most important point, the fourteenth, called for a "league of nations" to preserve peace.

The Paris Peace Conference

Late in 1918, Wilson announced that he would head the American delegation to Paris, revealing his belief that he alone could bring peace to the world. Wilson and his entourage of college professors, technical experts, and advisers sailed for France on December 4, 1918. Secretary of State Lansing, Wilson's confidante Edward House, and a number of other advisers were there. Conspicuously missing was Henry Cabot Lodge, the most powerful man in the Senate, or any other Republican senator—a serious blunder, for the Republican-controlled Senate would have to approve the treaty. It is difficult to explain Wilson's lack of political insight, except to say that he hated Lodge and compromise with equal intensity and had supreme confidence in his ability to persuade.

Wilson's self-confidence grew during a triumphant tour through Europe before the conference. Enthusiastically received by ordinary people, he had greater difficulty convincing the political leaders at the peace conference.

Though Wilson was more naive and idealistic than his European counterparts, he won many concessions at the peace table, sometimes by threatening to go home. The Allied leaders were determined to punish Germany and enlarge their empires. Wilson, however, believed that he could create a new kind of international relations based on his Fourteen Points. He achieved limited endorsement of self-determination, his dream that each national group could have its own country and that people should decide in what country they wanted to live.

The peacemakers carved Austria, Hungary, and Yugoslavia out of what had been the Austro-Hungarian Empire. They hoped that the new countries of Poland, Czechoslovakia, Finland, Estonia, Latvia, and Lithuania would help contain bolshevism in eastern Europe. France was to occupy Germany's industrial Saar region for 15 years, until a plebiscite determined whether its people wanted to be part of

Germany or France. Italy gained the port of Trieste. Dividing up the map of Europe was difficult at best, but perhaps the biggest mistake that Wilson and other major leaders made was to give the small nations little power at the negotiating table and to exclude Soviet Russia entirely.

Wilson had to make major concessions. He was forced to agree that Germany should pay reparations (later set at $56 billion), lose much of its oil- and coal-rich territory, and admit war guilt. He accepted a mandate system that allowed France and Britain to take over portions of the Middle East and gave Germany's Pacific colonies to Japan. He acquiesced when the Allies turned Germany's African colonies into "mandate possessions" because they did not want to allow colonized blacks self-determination.

This was not a "peace without victory," and German feelings of betrayal would later have grave repercussions. Wilson did not achieve freedom of the seas or the abolition of trade barriers, but he did get the League of Nations, which he hoped would prevent future wars. The key to collective security was Article 10 of the League covenant, which pledged all members "to respect and preserve against external aggression the territorial integrity" of all other members.

Women for Peace

While the statesmen met at Versailles to make peace and divide up Europe, a group of prominent and successful women (some from the Central Powers) convened in Zurich, Switzerland. The American delegation was led by Jane Addams and included Montana Congresswoman Jeannette Rankin, who had voted against war in 1917. They formed the Women's International League for Peace and Freedom with Addams as president, and denounced the one-sided peace terms of the Versailles treaty that called for disarmament of only one side and pinned the Central Powers with gigantic economic penalties.

Hate and intolerance were legacies of the war. Clemenceau especially wanted to humiliate Germany. The peace conference was also haunted by the Bolshevik success in Russia. This threat seemed so great that the Allies sent American and Japanese troops to Russia in 1919 to defeat bolshevism and create a moderate republic. But by 1920 the mission failed. The troops withdrew, but the Russians never forgot.

Wilson's Failed Dream

Probably most Americans supported the concept of the League of Nations in the summer of 1919, yet the Senate refused to accept American membership. The League of Nations treaty, one commentator has suggested, was killed by its friends and not by its enemies.

First there was Lodge, who had earlier endorsed some kind of international peacekeeping organization. He objected to Article 10, claiming that it would force Americans to fight the wars of foreigners. Chairman of the Senate Foreign Relations Committee, Lodge, like Wilson, was a lawyer and a scholar as well as a politician. He disliked all Democrats, especially Wilson, whose missionary zeal infuriated him.

TIMELINE

1914	1915	1916	1917	1918
Archduke Franz Ferdinand assassinated; World War I begins; United States declares neutrality; American troops invade Mexico and occupy Veracruz	Germany announces submarine blockade of Great Britain; *Lusitania* sunk; *Arabic* pledge; Marines land in Haiti	Army Reorganization Bill; Expedition into Mexico; Wilson reelected; Workmen's Compensation Bill; Keatings-Owen Child Labor Bill; Federal Farm Loan Act; National Women's Party founded	Germany resumes unrestricted submarine warfare; United States breaks relations with Germany; Zimmermann telegram; Russian Revolution; United States declares war on Germany; War Revenue Act; Espionage Act; Committee on Public Information established; Trading with the Enemy Act; Selective Service Act; War Industries Board formed	Sedition Act; Flu epidemic sweeps nation; Wilson's Fourteen Points; American troops intervene in Russian Revolution

1919	1920
Paris peace conference; Eighteenth Amendment prohibits alcoholic beverages; Senate rejects Treaty of Versailles	Nineteenth Amendment grants woman suffrage

Then there was Wilson, whose only hope of passage of the treaty in the Senate was a compromise to bring moderate senators to his side. But Wilson refused to compromise or to modify Article 10. Angry at his opponents, who were exploiting the disagreement for political advantage, he stumped the country to convince the American people of the rightness of his plan. They did not need to be convinced. They greeted Wilson much the way the people of France had. Traveling by train, he gave 37 speeches in 29 cities in the space of three weeks. When he described the graves of American soldiers in France and announced that American boys would never again die in a foreign war, the people responded with applause.

After one dramatic speech in Pueblo, Colorado, Wilson collapsed. His health had been failing for some months, and the strain of the trip was too much. He was rushed back to Washington, where a few days later he suffered a massive stroke. For the final year and a half of his term, the president was incapable of running the government and could not lead a fight for the League.

The Senate finally killed the League treaty in March of 1920. Had the United States joined the League of Nations, it probably would have made little difference in the international events of the 1920s and 1930s, nor would American participation have prevented World War II. The United States did not resign from the world of diplomacy or trade, nor by that single act become isolated. But the rejection of the League treaty was symbolic of the refusal of many Americans to admit that the world and America's place in it had changed dramatically since 1914.

✦✦✦✦✦✦

CONCLUSION

The Divided Legacy of the Great War

For Edmund Arpin and many of his friends who left small towns and urban neighborhoods to join the military forces, the war was a great adventure. For the next two decades, at American Legion conventions and Armistice Day parades, they continued to celebrate their days of glory. For others who served, the war's results were more tragic. Many died. Some came home injured, disabled by poison gas, or unable to cope with the complex world that had opened up to them.

In a larger sense, the war was both a triumph and a tragedy for the American people. The war created opportunities for blacks who migrated to the North, for women who found more rewarding jobs, and for farmers who suddenly discovered a demand for their products. But much of the promise and the hope proved temporary.

The war provided a certain climax to the progressive movement. The passage of the woman suffrage amendment and the use of federal power in a variety of ways to promote justice and order pleased reformers, who had been working toward these ends for many decades. But the results were often disappointing. Once the war ended, much federal legislation was dismantled or reduced in effectiveness and votes for women had little initial impact on social legislation.

The Great War marked the coming of age of the United States as a world power, but the country seemed reluctant to accept the new responsibility. The war stimulated patriotism and pride in the country, but it also increased intolerance. With this mixed legacy from the war, the country entered the new era of the 1920s.

Recommended Reading

General Accounts

Frank Freidel, *Over There: The Story of America's First Great Overseas Crusade* (1964); Ellis W. Hawley, *The Great War and the Search for Modern Order* (1979); Barbara W. Tuchman, *The Guns of August* (1962); Martin Gilbert, *The First World War: A Complete Account* (1994).

Diplomacy and Peace

P. Edward Haley, *Revolution and Intervention* (1970); C. C. Clemenden, *The United States and Pancho Villa* (1961); Robert H. Ferrell, *Woodrow Wilson and World War I* (1985); N. Gordon Levin, Jr., *Woodrow Wilson and World Politics* (1968); C. Roland Marchand, *The American Peace Movement and Social Reform* (1973); Thomas J. Knock, *To End All Wars: Woodrow Wilson and the Quest for a New World Order* (1992).

The Battlefield Experience and Beyond

Edward M. Coffman, *The War to End All Wars: The American Military Experience in World War I* (1968); Arthur D. Barbeau and Florette Henri, *The Unknown Soldiers: Black American Troops in World War I* (1974); Paul Fussell, *The Great War and Modern Memory* (1975); Michael C. C. Adams, *The Great Adventure: Male Desire and the Coming of World War I* (1990).

The War at Home

David M. Kennedy, *Over Here: The First World War and American Society* (1980); Maurine W. Greenwald, *Women, War, and Work* (1980); Donald Johnson, *The Challenge to American Freedoms: World War I and the Rise of the American Civil Liberties Union* (1963); Florette Henri, *Black Migration: Movement Northward, 1900–1920* (1975); James P. Grossman, *Land of Hope: Chicago, Black Southerners, and the Great Migration* (1989); Ronald Schaffer, *America in the Great War: The Rise of the War Welfare State* (1991).

Fiction

Erich Maria Remarque highlights the horror of the war in his classic *All Quiet on the Western Front* (1929); John Dos Passos describes the war as a bitter experience in *Three Soldiers* (1921); and Ernest Hemingway portrays its futility in *A Farewell to Arms* (1929). In *Regeneration* (1991), Pat Barker recreates the nightmare of the western front through British eyes.

CHAPTER 23

Affluence and Anxiety

John and Lizzie Parker were black sharecroppers living in a "stubborn, ageless hut squatted on a little hill" in central Alabama. They had two daughters, one age six, the other already married. The whole family worked hard in the cotton fields with little to show for it. One day in 1917, Lizzie declared, "I'm through. I've picked my last sack of cotton. I've cleared my last field."

Like many southern African-Americans, the Parkers sought a better life in the North. World War I cut off the flow of immigrant workers from Europe. Some companies sent trains into the South to recruit African-Americans. John Parker signed up with a mining company in West Virginia. The company offered free transportation for his family. "You will be allowed to get your food at the company store and there are houses awaiting for you," the agent promised.

But it turned out that the houses in the company town in West Virginia were little better than those they left in Alabama. After deducting for rent and for supplies from the company store, almost no money was left at the end of the week. John hated the dirty and dangerous work in the mine and realized that he would never get ahead by staying there. He ran away, leaving his family in West Virginia.

John drifted to Detroit, where he got a job with the American Car and Foundry Company. It was 1918, and the pay was good, more than he had ever made before. After a few weeks, he rented an apartment and sent for his family. For the first time, Lizzie had a gas stove and an indoor toilet, and Sally, now seven, started school. It seemed as if their dream had come true.

Detroit was not quite the dream, however. It was crowded with all kinds of migrants, attracted by the wartime jobs at the Ford Motor Company and other factories. The new arrivals increased racial tensions already present in the city. Sally was beaten up by a gang of white youths at school. Even in their neighborhood, which had been solidly Jewish before their arrival, the shopkeeper and the old residents made it clear that they did not like blacks moving in. The Ku Klux Klan, which gained many new members in Detroit, also made life uncomfortable for the blacks who had moved north to seek jobs and opportunity. Suddenly the war ended, and almost immediately John lost his job. Then the landlord raised the rent, and the Parkers had to leave their apartment for housing in a section just outside the city near Eight Mile Road. The surrounding suburbs had paved streets, wide lawns, and elegant houses, but this black ghetto's dirt streets and shacks reminded the Parkers of the company town in West Virginia. Lizzie had to get along without her bathroom. There was no indoor plumbing and no electricity, only a pump in the yard and an outhouse.

The recession winter of 1921–1922 was particularly difficult. The auto industry and the other companies laid off most of their workers. John found only part-time employment, while Lizzie worked as a servant for white families. Because no bus route connected the black community to surrounding suburbs, she often had to trek miles through the snow. Their shack was freezing cold, and it was cramped because their married daughter and her husband had joined them in Detroit.

Lizzie did not give up her dream. With strength, determination, and a sense of humor, she kept the family together. In 1924, Sally entered high school. By the end of the decade, Sally had graduated from high school, and the Parkers finally had electricity and indoor plumbing, though the streets were still unpaved. Those unpaved streets symbolized their unfulfilled dream. The Parkers, like most African-Americans who moved north in the decade after World War I, had improved their lot, but they still lived outside Detroit—and, in many ways, outside America.

Like most Americans in the 1920s, the Parkers pursued the American dream of success. For them, a comfortable house, a steady job, a new bathroom, and an education for their younger daughter constituted that dream. For others during the decade, the symbol of success was a new automobile, a new suburban house, or perhaps making a killing on the stock market. The 1920s, the decade between the end of World War I and the stock market crash, has often been referred to as the "jazz age," a time when the American people had one long party complete with flappers, speakeasies, illegal bathtub gin, and young people doing the Charleston long into the night. This frivolous interpretation has some basis in fact, but most Americans did not share in the party, for they were too busy struggling to make a living.

In this chapter we will explore some of the conflicting trends of an exciting decade. First, we will examine the intolerance that influenced almost all the events and social movements of the time. We will also look at technological developments, especially the automobile, which changed life for almost everyone during the 1920s and created the illusion of prosperity for all. We will then focus on groups—women, blacks, industrial workers, and farmers—whose hopes were raised but not always fulfilled. We will close by considering how business, politics, and foreign policy intertwined in the era of Harding, Coolidge, and Hoover.

POSTWAR PROBLEMS

Enthusiasm for social progress evaporated in 1919. The year after the war ended was marked by strikes and violence and by fear that Bolsheviks, blacks, foreigners, and others were destroying the American way of life. Some of the anxiety grew out of wartime patriotism, and some reflected the postwar economic and political turmoil that forced Americans to deal with new and immensely troubling situations.

Red Scare

Radicals and dissidents have often been feared as threats to the American way of life. In the early twentieth century, anarchists seemed the worst danger, but the

Russian Revolution of 1917 suddenly made *Bolshevik* the most dangerous radical, somehow mixed with that other villain, the German. In the spring of 1919, with the Bolsheviks advocating worldwide revolution, many Americans feared that the Communists planned to take over the United States.

Immediately after the war, there were perhaps 25,000 to 40,000 American Communists, at first split into two groups, but they never threatened the United States. Some were idealists such as John Reed, the son of a wealthy businessman, who had been converted to socialism in New York's Greenwich Village. Appalled by the carnage of the capitalistic war, Reed went to Russia as a journalist in 1917. His eyewitness account of the Bolshevik takeover, *Ten Days That Shook the World*, optimistically predicted a worldwide revolution. Seeing little hope for that revolution in postwar America, he returned to Moscow, where he died in 1920, disillusioned by the new regime's authoritarianism.

Working-Class Protest

Though small in number, the Communists seemed to be a menace by 1919. American workers had suffered from wartime inflation, which had almost doubled prices between 1914 and 1919 while most wages remained the same. In 1919, more than four million workers staged 4,000 strikes. Few wanted to overthrow the government; they demanded higher wages, shorter hours, and sometimes more control over the workplace.

On January 21, 1919, some 35,000 shipyard workers struck in Seattle. Within a few days, a general strike paralyzed the city. The mayor called for federal troops. Within five days, using strong-arm tactics, he put down the strike and was hailed as a "red-blooded patriot."

Yet other strikes continued. In September 1919, all 343,000 employees of U.S. Steel walked out in an attempt to win an eight-hour day and an "American living wage." Within days, the strike spread to Bethlehem Steel. Owners blamed the steel strikes on Bolsheviks. They imported strikebreakers, provoked riots, broke up union meetings, and used police and soldiers to end the strike. Eighteen strikers were killed. Because most people believed the Communists had inspired the strike, the issue of long hours and poor pay got lost, and eventually the union surrendered.

The Boston police also walked out. Like most other workers, they were struggling to survive on prewar salaries in inflationary times. Again there was talk of Communist influence. College students and army veterans volunteered to replace the police and prevent looting. The government quickly broke the strike and fired the policemen. When Gompers urged Governor Calvin Coolidge to ask the Boston authorities to reinstate them, Coolidge's answer made him famous: "There is no right to strike against the public safety by anybody, anywhere, anytime."

From the beginning, corporate owners blamed the strikes on Bolsheviks and the "bomb-throwing radical" became almost a cliché. On April 28, 1919, a bomb was discovered in a small package delivered to the home of the mayor of Seattle. The next day, the maid of a former senator opened a package and had her hands blown off. Other bombings occurred in June; one shattered the front of Attorney General A. Mitchell Palmer's home. The bombings seem to have been the work of misguided radicals who thought they might spark a revolution. But their effect was to convince many that revolution was a real and immediate threat.

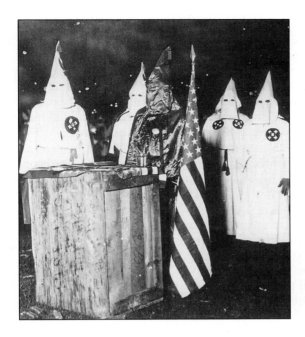

The Klan, with its elaborate rituals and its white uniforms, exploited the fear of blacks, Jews, liberals, and Catholics while preaching "traditional" American values. (Library of Congress)

No one was more convinced than Palmer. In the summer of 1919 he decided to destroy the Red network. He organized a special antiradical division within the Justice Department and put young J. Edgar Hoover in charge of coordinating information on domestic radical activities. Obsessed by the "Red Menace," Palmer instituted a series of raids to round up radical foreign workers. In December, 249 aliens, including the famous anarchist Emma Goldman, were deported, although very few were Communists and even fewer had any desire to overthrow the government of the United States.

The Palmer raids, probably the most massive violation of civil liberties in America up to then, found few dangerous radicals but did increase fear and intolerance. An Indiana jury quickly acquitted a man who had killed an alien for yelling "To hell with the United States." Palmer briefly became a national hero, though in the end only about 600 aliens were deported, out of more than 5,000 arrested. The worst of the "Red Scare" was over by the end of 1920, but antiradicalism and hyperpatriotism colored almost every aspect of life during the 1920s.

The Red Scare promoted many patriotic organizations and societies determined to purge communists. These organizations made little distinction between Communists, Socialists, progressives, and liberals, and they saw Bolsheviks everywhere. The best-known of the superpatriot organizations was the American Legion, but all provided a sense of purpose and belonging by attacking radicals and preaching patriotism.

Ku Klux Klan

Among the superpatriotic organizations claiming to protect the American way of life, the Ku Klux Klan was the most extreme. The Klan was revived in Georgia by

William J. Simmons, a lay preacher, salesman, and member of many fraternal organizations. He adopted the name and white-sheet garb of the old antiblack Reconstruction organization that was glorified in 1915 in the immensely popular but racist film *Birth of a Nation*. Simmons appointed himself head ("Imperial Wizard") of the new Klan. The new Klan was thoroughly Protestant and antiforeign, anti-Semitic, and anti-Catholic. It opposed the teaching of evolution; glorified old-time religion; supported immigration restriction; denounced short skirts, petting, and "demon rum;" and upheld patriotism and the purity of women. The Klan grew slowly until after the war, but added over 100,000 new members in 1920 alone. Not only aggressive recruiting, but also postwar fear and confusion, explained its explosive growth.

The Klan flourished in the small-town and rural South, where it aimed to keep returning black soldiers in their "proper place," but soon it spread throughout the country. The Klan was especially strong in the working-class neighborhoods of Chicago, Detroit, Indianapolis, and Atlanta, where African-Americans and other ethnic minorities were settling. At the peak of its power, it had several million members, many of them middle-class. Especially in Indiana, Oregon, Oklahoma, Louisiana, and Texas, it influenced politics. The Klan declined after 1924, but widespread fear of everything "un-American" remained.

The Sacco-Vanzetti Case

One result of the Red Scare was the conviction and sentencing of two Italian anarchists, Nicola Sacco and Bartolomeo Vanzetti. Arrested in 1920 for allegedly murdering a guard during a robbery in Massachusetts, the two were sentenced to die in 1921 on what many liberals considered flimsy evidence. To many, it seemed that the two Italians were punished for their anarchism and foreign appearance.

Even now, it is not clear whether Sacco and Vanzetti were guilty, but the case took on symbolic significance as many intellectuals in Europe and America rallied to their defense. Appeal after appeal failed, but finally the governor of Massachusetts appointed a commission to reexamine the evidence. The commission reaffirmed the verdict, and the two were electrocuted on August 23, 1927. But their cause did not die. On the fiftieth anniversary of their deaths in 1977, the governor of Massachusetts exonerated them.

Religious Intolerance

The KKK and well-publicized cases like Sacco-Vanzetti touched relatively few people, but intolerance affected millions of lives. Henry Ford published anti-Semitic diatribes. Barred from fashionable resorts, Jews built their own hotels in the Catskills in New York State and elsewhere. Many colleges, private academies, and medical schools had Jewish quotas, and many suburbs explicitly limited residents to "Christians." Catholics, too, were prohibited from many organizations, and few even tried to enroll in the elite colleges. Prejudice and intolerance had always existed but during the 1920s much of that intolerance was made more fixed and formal.

A PROSPERING ECONOMY

The decade after World War I was also a time of industrial expansion and wide prosperity. After recovering from a postwar depression in 1921 and 1922, the economy took off. Fueled by new technology, more efficient management, and innovative advertising, industrial production almost doubled during the decade. The gross national product rose by an astonishing 40 percent. A construction boom created new suburbs around American cities, and new skyscrapers transformed the cities themselves. However, the benefits of this prosperity were not distributed evenly.

The Rising Standard of Living

Signs of the new prosperity abounded. Millions of homes and apartments were built and equipped with the latest conveniences. Plastics and cellophane altered the habits of millions, and new products, such as cigarette lighters, dry ice, and Pyrex glass, created demands unheard of a decade before.

Perhaps the most tangible sign of the new prosperity was the modern American bathroom. In the early 1920s the enameled tub, toilet, and washbasin became standard. The bathroom, with unlimited hot water, privacy, and clean white fixtures, symbolized American affluence.

Americans now had more leisure time. Persistent efforts by labor unions had gradually reduced the 60-hour workweek of the late nineteenth century to a 45-hour week. Paid vacations, unknown in the nineteenth century, became prevalent. The American diet also improved. The consumption of cornmeal and potatoes declined, but the sale of fresh vegetables increased by 45 percent. Health improved and life expectancy lengthened. But not all Americans enjoyed better health and more leisure. A white male born in 1900 had a life expectancy of 48 years and a white female of 51 years. By 1930, these figures had increased to 59 and 63 years. For a black male born in 1900, however, the life expectancy was only 33 years, and for the black female, 35 years. These figures increased to 48 and 47 by 1930, but the discrepancy remained.

Yet almost all Americans benefited to some extent from the new prosperity. Some took advantage of expanding educational opportunities. In 1900, only one in ten young people of high school age was in school. By 1930, that number had increased to six in ten, and much of the improvement came in the 1920s. College enrollment also grew, but it was by no means common for young people.

The Rise of the Modern Corporation

The structure and practice of American business were transformed in the 1920s. After the economic downturn of 1920 to 1922, business boomed until the crash of 1929. Mergers increased during the decade at a rate greater than at any time since the end of the 1890s. What emerged was not monopolies but oligopolies (industry domination spread among a few large firms). By 1930, the 200 largest corporations—which were becoming more diversified—controlled almost half the corporate wealth.

Perhaps the most important business trend of the decade was the emergence of a new kind of manager. The prototype was Alfred P. Sloan, Jr., an engineer who reorganized General Motors. He divided the company into components, freeing top managers to concentrate on planning, controlling inventory, and integrating operations. Marketing and advertising became as important as production. The new manager, often a business school graduate, had a large staff, but owned no part of the company.

Continuing the trends started by Frederick Taylor (see Chapter 21), the new managers tried to keep employees working efficiently, but now they introduced pensions, recreation facilities, cafeterias, and even paid vacations and profit-sharing plans. This "welfare capitalism" was designed to reduce worker discontent and discourage labor unions. The key to the new corporate structure was planning— often a continuation of the business-government cooperation that had developed during World War I. It failed to prevent economic collapse in 1929, but the modern corporation survived the depression to exert a growing influence on American life in the 1930s and after.

Electrification

The 1920s also marked the climax of the "second industrial revolution," a trend in American industry away from a primary concentration on manufacturing goods intended for other producers. By the 1920s, as older industries stabilized or declined, new manufacturing companies focused on goods for consumers, such as silk stockings, washing machines, and cars, and they introduced synthetic fabrics, chemicals, and petroleum products.

Powering the second industrial revolution was electricity, which rapidly replaced steam power after 1900. This change, largely in place by 1920, worked as profound a change as had the substitution of steam for water power after the Civil War. By 1929, electrical generators provided 80 percent of the power used in industry. Less than one of every ten American homes had electricity in 1907; by 1929, more than two-thirds did, and workers were turning out twice as many goods as a similarly sized work force had ten years before.

Electricity brought dozens of gadgets and labor-saving devices into the home. But the new machines did not reduce the time the average housewife spent doing housework. In many ways, the success of the electric revolution increased the contrast in American life. Urban "Great White Ways" symbolized progress, but they also made slums and rural hamlets seem even darker. For poor women, the traditional female tasks of carrying water, pushing, pulling, and lifting continued.

Automobile Culture

Automobile manufacturing, like electrification, grew spectacularly in the 1920s. The automobile was a major factor in the postwar boom. It stimulated and transformed the petroleum, steel, and rubber industries; it forced the construction and upgrading of streets and highways at the cost of millions of dollars for labor and concrete. From the beginning the United States loved autos. There were nearly a million in 1912, and in the 1920s autos came within the reach of the middle class. In

1929, Americans purchased 4.5 million cars, and by the end of that year nearly 27 million were registered.

The auto created new suburbs and allowed families to live miles from work. Filling stations, diners, and tourist courts (forerunners of motels) became familiar on the American scene. But there was an environmental downside as oil and gasoline contaminated streams, piles of old tires and rusting hulks of discarded cars began to line the highways, and emissions from thousands and then millions of internal combustion engines fouled the air.

The auto transformed American life in other ways. Small crossroads stores and many small churches disappeared as rural families drove into town. Trucks and tractors changed farming. Buses began to eliminate the one-room school. Autos freed young people from parental chaperoning, too, and though the car was hardly the "house of prostitution on wheels" that one judge called it, it did change courting habits.

Over the decade, the automobile became a sign of status. Advertising made it the symbol of the good life, sex, freedom, and speed. The auto transformed advertising and altered the way products were purchased. By 1926, three-fourths of the cars sold were bought on some kind of deferred-payment plan, and "buy now, pay later" was soon used to sell other consumer products. The auto industry, like most American businesses, consolidated. In 1908, more than 250 companies were making automobiles in the United States. By 1929, only 44 remained. But one name became synonymous with the automobile itself—Henry Ford.

Ford had a reputation as a progressive industrial leader and champion of ordinary people. As with all men and women who become symbols, the truth is less dramatic. For example, his famous assembly line was invented by a team of engineers. Introduced in 1913, it cut production time for a car from 14 hours to an hour and a half. Here was the perfect application of Taylor's system. The product of the carefully planned system was the Model T, the prototype of the inexpensive family car.

In 1914, Ford startled the country by increasing the minimum pay of the Ford assembly-line worker to $5 a day (almost twice the national average pay for factory workers). Ford was not a humanitarian. He wanted a dependable work force and knew that skilled workers were less likely to quit if well paid. Ford was one of the first to appreciate that workers were also consumers who might buy Model Ts. But despite the high wages work on the assembly line was numbing, and when the line closed down, workers were released without compensation.

Henry Ford was not an easy man for whom to work. One newspaper in 1928 called him "the Mussolini of Detroit." He ruthlessly pressured dealers and used them to bail him out of difficult financial situations by forcing them to buy more cars. He used spies on the assembly lines and fired workers and executives at the least provocation.

The Model T, which cost $600 in 1912, was reduced gradually in price until it sold for only $290 in 1924. The "Tin Lizzie" was light and easily repaired. Some owners claimed a pair of pliers and some baling wire would keep it running. Except for adding a self-starter, offering a closed model, and making a few minor face-lifts, Ford kept the Model T in 1927 as he had introduced it in 1909. By that time, its popularity had declined as many people traded up to sleeker, more colorful, and, they thought, more prestigious autos put out by Ford's competitors. Ford's new Model A, introduced in 1927, never had the appeal of the Model T.

The Exploding Metropolis

The automobile both pushed urban areas out into the countryside and brought industry to the suburbs. The great expansion of suburban population came in the 1920s. Shaker Heights, outside Cleveland, was typical. Two businessmen planned and built the new suburb on the site of a former Shaker community. No blacks were allowed. Landscape design lent a parklike atmosphere. Between 1919 and 1929 the population grew from 1,700 to over 15,000, and the price of lots multiplied by ten. Other suburbs grew just as rapidly—none more than Beverly Hills, California, whose population soared by 2,485 percent. The biggest land boom of all occurred in Florida, where Miami mushroomed from 30,000 in 1920 to 75,000 in 1925. A plot in West Palm Beach sold for $800,000 in 1923 and two years later was worth $4 million.

The 1920 census indicated that for the first time more than half the American population lived in "urban areas" of more than 2,500. The census designation of an urban area was a little misleading because a town of 5,000 could still be mainly rural. A more significant concept was the metropolitan area of at least 100,000 people. There were only 52 of these areas in 1900. By 1930, there were 115.

The automobile transformed every city, but the growth was most spectacular in two cities that the car virtually created. Detroit grew from 300,000 in 1900 to 1,837,000 in 1930. Los Angeles, held together by a network of roads, expanded from 114,000 in 1900 to 1,778,000 in 1930.

Cities expanded horizontally in the 1920s, sprawling into the countryside, but city centers grew vertically. A building boom that peaked near the end of the decade created new skylines for most urban centers. The most famous skyscraper of all, the 102-story Empire State Building in New York, was finished in 1931 but was not completely occupied until after World War II.

A Communications Revolution

Changing communications altered the way Americans lived as well as the way they conducted business. The telephone was first demonstrated in 1876, and by 1899 more than a million phones were in operation. During the 1920s, the number of homes with phones increased from 9 to 13 million. Still, by the end of the decade, more than half of American homes lacked them.

Even more than the telephone, the radio symbolized the changes of the 1920s. The first station began commercial broadcasting in the summer of 1920, and that fall election returns were broadcast for the first time. The next year a Newark station transmitted the World Series, beginning a process that would transform American sports. In 1922, a radio station in New York broadcast the first commercial.

Much early broadcasting consisted of classical music, but soon came news analysis and coverage of important events. Serials made radio a national medium, with millions tuning in to the same program. The record industry grew just as rapidly. By the end of the decade, people everywhere were humming the same popular songs. Actors and announcers became celebrities.

Even more dramatic was the phenomenon of the movies. Forty million viewers a week went to the movies in 1922, and by 1929 that total exceeded 100 million. To countless Americans, the stars were more famous and important than most government officials. Motion pictures before the war had attracted mostly the working class, but now they seemed to appeal to everyone. Many parents feared that they would dictate ideas about sex and life. One young college woman admitted that movies taught her how to smoke, and in some movies "there were some lovely scenes which just got me all hot 'n' bothered."

Sports heroes like Babe Ruth and Jack Dempsey were as famous as the movie stars. The great spectator sports of the decade owed much to the increase of leisure time and to the automobile, the radio, and the mass-circulation newspaper. Thousands drove to college towns to watch football; millions listened for scores or read about the results the next day. The popularity of sports, like the movies and radio, was a product of technology.

The year 1927 seemed to mark the beginning of the new age of mechanization and progress. Henry Ford produced his fifteen millionth car and introduced the Model A. Radio-telephone service linked San Francisco and Manila. The first radio network was organized (CBS), and the first sound movie was released (*The Jazz Singer*). The Holland Tunnel, the first underwater vehicular roadway, connected New York and New Jersey, and Charles Lindbergh flew his single-engine plane from New York to Paris and captured the world's imagination. Lindbergh always said "we," meaning his airplane as well. When Americans cheered Lindbergh, they were reaffirming their belief in the American dream and their faith in individual initiative as well as in technology.

HOPES RAISED, PROMISES DEFERRED

The 1920s was a time when all kinds of hopes seemed realizable. "Don't envy successful salesmen—be one!" one ad screamed. Buy a car. Build a house. Start a career. Invest. Make a fortune.

Some Americans, of course, merely wished to retain traditional values in a society that seemed to question them. Others wanted a steady job and a little respect. Still others hungered for the new appliances. Many discovered that even the most modest hopes lay tantalizingly out of reach.

Clash of Values

During the 1920s, radio, movies, advertising, and mass-circulation magazines promoted a national, secular culture. But this new culture of consumption, pleasure, upward mobility, and sex clashed with traditional values: hard work, thrift, church, family, home. This was not simply an urban-rural conflict, for many people clinging to old ways had moved into the cities. Still, many Americans feared that familiar ways of life were threatened by new values, scientific breakthroughs, bolshevism, relativism, Freudianism, and biblical criticism. A trial over the teaching of evolutionary ideas in a high school in the little town of Dayton, Tennessee, symbolized (even as it exaggerated) the clash of traditional versus modern, city versus country.

The scientific community and most educated people had long accepted Darwinian evolution. But many evangelical Protestants saw the Bible as literal truth and the dramatic changes of the 1920s as a major spiritual crisis. The theory of evolution epitomized the challenge to traditional faith, and in some states its teaching was outlawed. John Scopes, a young biology teacher, broke the law, and Tennessee put him on trial. The famous lawyer Clarence Darrow defended Scopes, while the World Christian Fundamentalist Association hired former presidential candidate and Secretary of State William Jennings Bryan to assist the prosecution. Bryan was old and tired (he died only a few days after the trial), but he was deeply religious and still eloquent. In cross-examination, Darrow reduced Bryan's statements to intellectual rubble. Nevertheless, the jury declared Scopes guilty.

The national press covered the trial and upheld science and academic freedom. The journalist H. L. Mencken had a field day poking fun at Bryan and the fundamentalists. "Heave an egg out a Pullman window," Mencken wrote, "and you will hit a Fundamentalist almost anywhere in the United States today . . . . They are everywhere where learning is too heavy a burden for mortal minds to carry."

Religious Fundamentalism

Some, including Mencken, thought that the Scopes trial ended "the fundamentalist menace." Yet fundamentalism continued to survive in an urbanizing, modernizing, and sophisticated world. All fundamentalists believed in the literal interpretation and infallibility of the Bible. They rejected secularism, liberal theology, pluralism, the Social Gospel, and any sense that earthly reform could lead to perfection. They had an unshakable belief in what they believed was the truth.

Throughout the 1920s and the 1930s, attendance at Christian colleges and the circulation of fundamentalist publications increased dramatically. Evangelical preachers reached large audiences, sometimes using flamboyant performances. Aimee Semple McPherson, a glamorous faith healer, became famous for chasing the devil out of her auditorium with a pitchfork.

Radio extended the reach of the fundamentalist preachers even more dramatically. McPherson was the first woman to hold a radio license, and she had the second most popular radio show in Los Angeles in the late 1920s. For many, the period between the wars was an age of secular humanism, technological marvels, and modernism in all fields, but for many others, it was a time when fundamentalist religion and old-fashioned values prospered.

Immigration and Migration

Immigrants and anyone else "un-American" seemed to threaten old ways. The fear and intolerance of the war years and the period right after the war resulted in major restrictive legislation.

John Steuart Curry was one of the 1920s regionalist painters who found inspiration in the American heartland. In *Baptism in Kansas,* he depicts a religious ritual that underscores the persistence of faith and the importance of religion in creating a sense of community. (The Whitney Museum of American Art, New York)

The first strongly restrictive immigration law passed in 1917 over Wilson's veto. It required a literacy test for the first time and barred radicals. This did not stop the more than one million immigrants who poured into the country in 1920 and 1921.

In 1921 and again in 1924, Congress imposed quotas on European immigration. The tighter 1924 quota was 2 percent of those from each country who were in the United States in 1890—before the great flood of newcomers had begun arriving from southern and eastern Europe. All immigrants from Asia were banned. In 1927 a ceiling of 150,000 European immigrants a year was set; more than 60 percent could come from Great Britain and Germany, but fewer than 4 percent from Italy.

Ethnicity increasingly became a factor in political alignments. Republican-sponsored immigration laws drove Jews, Italians, and Poles to the Democrats. By 1924, the Democratic party was so evenly divided between northern urban Catholics and southern rural Protestants that its convention voted—by a very small margin—to condemn the Klan.

The immigration acts of 1921, 1924, and 1927 cut off the streams of cheap labor that had provided muscle for industrialization since the early nineteenth century. At the same time, by exempting Western Hemisphere immigrants, the new laws opened the country to Mexicans eager to work in the fields and farms of California and the Southwest. Mexicans soon became the country's largest first-generation immigrant group. Mexican farm workers often lived in primitive camps, where conditions were unsanitary and health care nonexistent. "When they have finished harvesting my crops I will kick them out on the country road," one employer announced.

Mexicans also migrated to industrial cities, recruited by northern companies that paid for their transportation. During the 1920s, El Paso became more than half Mexican. The Mexican population in California reached 368,000 in 1929, and Los Angeles was about 20 percent Mexican. Like African-Americans, the Mexicans found opportunity by migrating, but they did not escape prejudice or hardship.

African-Americans migrated north in great numbers from 1915 to 1920. The black population of Chicago increased from 44,000 in 1910 to 234,000 by 1930. Reduced European immigration and continuing industrial growth caused many northern companies to recruit southern blacks. Trains in small southern depots sometimes picked up hundreds of blacks in a single day. "I don't care where so long as I go where a man is a man," wrote one. It was the young and mostly unskilled who tended to move.

African-Americans unquestionably improved their lives by moving north. But for most, like the Parkers, dreams were only partly fulfilled. Most crowded into segregated housing and faced hatred. "Black men stay South," the *Chicago Tribune* advised, and offered to pay the transportation for any who would return.

Often the young black men moved first, and only later brought their wives and children, putting great pressure on many black families. Some young men, like John Parker, restrained their anger, but others, like Richard Wright's fictional Bigger Thomas portrayed movingly in *Native Son* (1940), struck out violently against white society. The concentration of African-Americans in northern industrial cities created black ghettos and increased the racial tension that sometimes flared into violence.

One of the worst race riots took place in Chicago in 1919. The riot began on a hot July day when a black youth drowned in a white swimming area—hit by stones, blacks said, but the police refused to arrest any white men. When African-Americans attacked the police, a four-day riot was on. Several dozen were killed, and hundreds were wounded. The tension between the races did not die when the riot was over. Nor were other cities exempt.

The wave of violence and racism angered and disillusioned W. E. B. Du Bois, who had urged African-Americans to support the American cause during the war. In an angry editorial for *The Crisis,* he called on blacks to

> fight a sterner, longer, more unbending battle against the forces of hell in our own land. We return. We return from fighting. We return fighting. Make way for Democracy; we saved it in France, and by the Great Jehovah, we will save it in the United States of America, or know the reason why.

Marcus Garvey: Black Messiah

Du Bois was not the only postwar militant black leader. Marcus Garvey, a flamboyant Jamaican who arrived in New York at the age of 29, fed black pride.

Marcus Garvey, (second from the right), shown dressed in his favorite uniform, became a hero for many black Americans. (Archive Photos)

Although he never abandoned Booker T. Washington's self-help philosophy, Garvey thoroughly transformed it. Washington focused on economic betterment; Garvey saw self-help as political empowerment by which African peoples would reclaim their homelands.

In Jamaica, Garvey had founded the Universal Negro Improvement Association. By 1919, he had established 30 branches in the United States and the Caribbean. He also set up a newspaper, the Black Cross Nurses, and chains of stores and restaurants. His biggest project was the Black Star Line, a steamship company, to be owned and operated by African-Americans. Advocating blacks' return to Africa, he declared himself the "provisional president of Africa."

He won converts, mostly among lower-middle-class blacks, through the force of his oratory and powerful personality, but especially through his message of black pride. "Up you mighty race, you can accomplish what you will," Garvey thundered. Thousands of blacks cheered his Universal African Legions, marching in blue and red uniforms and waving a red-black-green flag. Thousands invested in the Black Star Line—which soon collapsed, in part because white entrepreneurs sold Garvey inferior ships. Garvey was arrested for using the mails to defraud shareholders and sentenced to five years in prison. Coolidge commuted the sentence. Ordered deported, Garvey left America in 1927. Despite his failures, he convinced thousands of black Americans, especially the poor and discouraged, that they could unite and feel pride in their heritage.

The Harlem Renaissance and the Lost Generation

A group of black writers, artists, and intellectuals who settled in Harlem after the war led a movement related in some ways to Garvey's black nationalism crusade and in the end more important. They studied anthropology, art, history, and music, and in their novels, poetry, dance, and music explored the ambivalent role of blacks in America. Like Garvey, they expressed black pride and sought African and folk roots. Unlike Garvey, they wanted to be both black and American and had no desire to go back to Africa.

Alain Locke, the first black Rhodes scholar, was the father of the renaissance. His *The New Negro* (1925) announced the movement to the outside world and outlined black contributions to American culture and civilization. Langston Hughes, a poet and novelist, wrote bitter but laughing poems, using black vernacular to describe the pathos and pride of African-Americans. In *Weary Blues*, he adapted the rhythms of jazz and the blues.

Jazz was an important force in Harlem in the 1920s, and prosperous whites came to listen to Louis Armstrong, Duke Ellington, and other black musicians. Many brought up in Victorian white America were intrigued by what they saw as Harlem's primitive emotions and erotic atmosphere, as well as its music and illegal sex, drugs, and liquor. Jamaican Claude McKay wrote about the underside of life in Harlem in *Home to Harlem* (1925), one of the most popular "new Negro" novels. McKay portrayed two black men—one, Jake, who finds a life of simple and erotic pleasure in Harlem's cabarets, the other an intellectual unable to make such an easy choice and conscious that "My damned white education has robbed me of . . . primitive vitality."

Many Harlem writers agonized about how to be both black and intellectual. They worried about white patrons who pressured them to conform to the white elite's idea of black authenticity, but they knew that patronage was their only hope to be recognized. Jean Toomer, more self-consciously avant-garde than most other black writers, wrote haunting poems about the difficulty of black identity, and in a novel, *Cane* (1923), he sketched maladjusted, almost grotesquely alienated characters.

Many African-American writers felt alienated from American society. They tried living in Paris or Greenwich Village, but most felt drawn to Harlem, which in the 1920s was rapidly becoming the center of New York's black population. Over 117,000 whites left during the decade, while over 87,000 blacks moved in. Countee Cullen remarked, "In spite of myself I find that I am activated by a strong sense of race consciousness." So was Zora Neale Hurston, who came to New York to study at Barnard College, earned an advanced degree in anthropology from Columbia University, and used her interest in folklore to write stories of robust and passionate rural blacks. Much of the work of the Harlem writers was read by very small numbers, but another generation of young black intellectuals in the 1960s would rediscover it.

Many white intellectuals, writers, and artists also felt estranged from what they saw as the narrow materialism of American life. Some, like F. Scott Fitzgerald, Ernest Hemingway, e. e. cummings, and T. S. Eliot, moved to Europe—where they wrote novels, plays, and poems about America. Like so many American intellectuals in all periods, they had a love-hate relationship with their country.

For many writers, disillusionment began with the war. Hemingway eagerly volunteered to go to Europe as an ambulance driver. But when he was wounded on the Italian front, he reevaluated the meaning of all the slaughter. His novel *The Sun Also Rises* (1926) is the story of the purposeless European wanderings of a group of Americans, and also the story of Jake Barnes, made impotent by a war injury. His "unreasonable wound" symbolized the futility of postwar life.

Fitzgerald, who loved the cafés and parties in Paris, became a celebrity during the 1920s. He epitomized some of the despair of his generation, which had "grown up to find all Gods dead, all wars fought, all faiths in man shaken." His best novel, *The Great Gatsby* (1925), was a critique of the American success myth. But wealth won't buy happiness, and Gatsby's life ends tragically, as in many other of the decade's novels.

It was not necessary to live in France to criticize American society. Sherwood Anderson created a fictional midwestern town in *Winesburg, Ohio* (1919), describing the dull, narrow, warped lives that seemed to provide a metaphor for American culture. Sinclair Lewis, another midwesterner, wrote scathing parodies of middle-class, small-town life in *Main Street* (1920) and *Babbitt* (1922). The "hero" of the latter novel is a salesman from the town of Zenith. He is a "regular guy" who distrusts "red professors," foreign-born people, and anyone from New York. But no one had more fun laughing at the American middle class than Baltimore's H. L. Mencken, whose magazine *The American Mercury* overflowed with his assaults on "the booboisie." Harding's speeches reminded him of "a string of wet sponges, . . . of stale bean soup, of college yells, of dogs barking idiotically through endless nights."

Ironically, while intellectuals despaired over American society and complained that art could not survive in a business-dominated civilization, literature flourished. The 1920s were one of the most creative decades in American literature.

Women Struggle for Equality

An indelible image of the 1920s is the flapper—a young woman with a short skirt, bobbed hair, and a boyish figure doing the Charleston, smoking, drinking, and being very casual about sex. Fitzgerald's heroines in novels like *This Side of Paradise* (1920) and *The Great Gatsby* (1925) provided such role models for young people, and movie stars such as Clara Bow and Gloria Swanson, aggressively seductive on the screen, supplied even more vivid examples of provocative behavior.

Without question, women acquired more sexual freedom in the 1920s. "None of the Victorian mothers had any idea how casually their daughters were accustomed to being kissed," Fitzgerald wrote. However, it is difficult, if not impossible, to know how accustomed those daughters (and their mothers) were to kissing and enjoying other sexual activity. Contraceptives became more readily available, and Margaret Sanger (who had been indicted for sending birth control information through the mail in 1914) organized the first American birth control conference in 1921. Birth control devices and literature, however, were still often illegal.

Family size declined during the decade (from 3.6 children in 1900 to 2.5 in 1930), and young people were apparently more inclined to marry for love than for security. More women expected sexual satisfaction in marriage (nearly 60 percent in one poll) and felt that divorce was the best solution for an unhappy marriage. Nearly 85 percent in another poll approved of sexual intercourse as an expression of love and affection, rather than simply for procreation. But these polls tended to be biased toward urban middle-class attitudes. Despite more freedom for women, the double standard persisted.

Middle-class women lives' were shaped by innovations like electricity, running water, and labor-saving devices. But as standards of cleanliness rose, they spent more time on housework while being bombarded with advertising urging them to make themselves better housekeepers yet still be beautiful. The young adopted new styles quickly, and they also learned to swim, play tennis, and ride bicycles.

More women worked outside the home—22 percent in 1933, compared to 17 percent in 1890. But their share of manufacturing jobs fell from 19 to 16 percent between 1900 and 1930. The greatest expansion of jobs was in white-collar occupations that were being feminized—secretary, bookkeeper, clerk, telephone operator. Although more married women had jobs (an increase of 25 percent during the decade), most held low-paying jobs, and most single women assumed that marriage would end their employment.

For some working women—secretaries and teachers, for example—marriage indeed often led to dismissal. Yet an office was a good place to meet eligible men, and a secretary learned endurance, self-effacement, and obedience—traits that many thought would make her a good wife. Considering these attitudes, it is not surprising that the male-female pay disparity widened. By 1930, women earned only 57 percent of what men were paid.

The image of the flapper in the 1920s promised more freedom and equality for women than they actually achieved. The flapper was young, white, slender, and upper-class, and most women did not fit those categories. Although the proportion of women lawyers and bankers increased slightly, the rate of growth declined. The number of women doctors and scientists dropped.

The promise of prewar feminists and suffrage advocates remained unfulfilled. Often, they could not serve on juries. In some states, without their husband's consent women could not hold office, own a business, or sign a contract. Women were usually held responsible for an illegitimate birth, and divorce laws almost always favored men. Many women leaders were disappointed in the small turnout of women voters in the presidential election of 1920.

Alice Paul, who had led the militant National Woman's Party in 1916, chained herself to the White House fence once again to promote an equal rights amendment to the Constitution. The amendment got support in several states, but many women opposed it, fearing that it would cancel the special legislation to protect women in industry. Feminists disagreed in the 1920s on the proper way to promote equality and rights for women, but the political and social climate was not conducive to feminism.

Rural America in the 1920s

Most farmers did not share in the decade's prosperity. During the war, farmers had responded to worldwide demand and rising commodity prices by investing in land and equipment. Then prices and farm income tumbled. Because the value of land fell, they often lost both mortgage and land and still owed the bank.

The changing nature of farming was part of the problem. Chemical fertilizers and new hybrid seeds increased yields. Farming became more mechanized and efficient. Production swelled just as worldwide demand for American farm products tumbled.

Not all farmers suffered. During the 1920s, the farming class separated into those who were getting by barely or not at all and those who earned large profits. Large, mechanized operations produced most of the cash crops. In 1900, fully 40 percent of the labor force worked on farms; by 1930, only 21 percent did.

Few farmers could afford the products of the new technology. Although many middle-class urban families were more prosperous than ever before, only one farm family in ten had electricity in the 1920s. The lot of the farm wife had not changed for centuries.

As they had done in the nineteenth century, farmers tried to act collectively. After the failure of the People's Party in 1896, they turned to influencing legislation. Most of their effort went into the McNary-Haugen Farm Relief Bill, which provided for government support for key agricultural products. The government would buy crops at a "fair exchange value" and then market the excess on the world market at a lower price. The bill passed Congress twice, in 1927 and 1928, and twice was vetoed by President Coolidge. But farm organizations across the country learned how to cooperate and influence Congress, with important future ramifications.

The Workers' Share of Prosperity

Hundreds of thousands of workers improved their standard of living in the 1920s, yet inequality grew. Between 1923 and 1929, real wages increased 21 percent, but corporate dividends went up by nearly two-thirds. The richest 5 percent of the population increased their share of the wealth from a quarter to a third, and the wealthiest 1 percent controlled a whopping 19 percent of all income. Workers did not profit from the increased production they helped generate. That boded ill.

Even among workers there was great disparity. For example, those employed on auto assembly lines saw their wages go up and their hours down. Yet the majority of American working-class families could not move much beyond subsistence. One study suggested that a family needed $2,000 to $2,400 in 1924 to maintain an "American standard of living." That year, 16 million families earned under $2,000.

Although some workers prospered in the 1920s, organized labor did not. Union membership dropped from about 5 million in 1921 to under 3.5 million in 1929. Although a majority of American workers had never supported them, unions now faced competition from employers who lured workers with profit-sharing plans. The National Manufacturing Association and individual businesses carried on a vigorous campaign to restore the open shop. The increasingly conservative AFL had little interest in organizing the large industries.

The more aggressive unions like the United Mine Workers, led by the bombastic John L. Lewis, also encountered difficulties. The union's attempt to organize

West Virginia mines had led to violent clashes with imported guards. But internal strife weakened the union, and Lewis had to accept wage reductions in 1927.

Organized labor, like so many other groups, struggled desperately to share in the 1920s prosperity. It won some victories and made some progress. But affluence was beyond the reach of many. Eventually, the inequality would lead to disaster.

THE BUSINESS OF POLITICS

"Among the nations of the earth today America stands for one idea: *Business*," a popular writer announced in 1921. Bruce Barton, the head of the largest advertising firm in the country, published one of the most popular nonfiction books of the decade. In *The Man Nobody Knows* (1925), he depicted Christ as "the founder of modern business." He took 12 men from the bottom of society and forged them into a successful organization.

Business, especially big business, prospered in the 1920s, and the image of businessmen rose higher. The government reduced regulation, lowered taxes, and helped aid business expansion at home and abroad. Business and politics, always intertwined, became especially close. Wealthy financiers played important roles in formulating policy. Even more significant, a new kind of businessman was elected president in 1928. Herbert Hoover, international engineer and efficiency expert, was the very symbol of world-transforming modern techniques and practices.

Harding and Coolidge

The Republicans, almost assured of victory in 1920 because of bitter reaction against Woodrow Wilson, might have preferred nominating their old standard-bearer, Theodore Roosevelt, but he had died the year before. Warren G. Harding, a former Ohio newspaper editor, captured the nomination after meeting late at night with some of the party's most powerful men in a Chicago hotel room. What was promised in this legendary "smoke-filled room," no one ever discovered. To balance the ticket, the Republicans chose for vice-president Calvin Coolidge of police strike fame. Meanwhile, after 44 roll calls, the Democrats nominated Governor James Cox of Ohio and for vice-president picked Franklin D. Roosevelt, the assistant secretary of the Navy who so far had done little to distinguish himself.

Harding won in a landslide. His 60.4 percent of the vote was the widest margin yet recorded in a presidential election. More significant, fewer than 50 percent of the eligible voters went to the polls. Newly enfranchised women, especially in working-class neighborhoods, avoided the voting booths. So did large numbers of men. Many people did not care who was president.

In contrast to the reform-minded presidents Roosevelt and Wilson, Harding reflected the conservatism of the 1920s. A visitor to the White House found Harding and his cohorts discussing the problems of the day, with "the air heavy with tobacco smoke, trays with bottles containing every imaginable brand of whiskey." A few blocks away, Harry Daugherty, Harding's attorney general and longtime associate, did a brisk business in selling favors, taking bribes, and organizing illegal schemes.

Warren G. Harding (left) and Calvin Coolidge were immensely popular in the 1920s, but later historians have criticized them and rated them among the worst of American presidents. (Corbis/UPI)

Harding was not personally corrupt, and the nation's leading businessmen approved of his high-tariff, low-tax policies. Nor did Harding spend all his time drinking with his pals. He called a conference on disarmament and another on unemployment, and he pardoned Eugene Debs. Harding once remarked that he could never be considered a great president, but he thought perhaps he might be "one of the best loved." When he died suddenly in August 1923, the American people genuinely mourned.

Only after Coolidge became president did the full extent of the Harding scandals come out. A Senate committee discovered that Secretary of the Interior Albert Fall had illegally leased government-owned oil reserves in the Teapot Dome section of Wyoming to businessmen for over $300,000 in bribes. Illegal activities were turned up in the Veterans Administration and elsewhere. Harding's attorney general resigned in disgrace, the secretary of the Navy barely avoided prison, two of Harding's advisers committed suicide, and Fall went to jail.

Coolidge was dour, taciturn—and honest. Born in a little town in Vermont, he was sworn in as president by his father, a justice of the peace, whom he was visiting when news of Harding's death came. To many, Coolidge represented old-fashioned values, simple religious faith, and personal integrity. But Coolidge was no yokel. He felt ill at ease posing for photographers holding a pitchfork, and much more comfortable around corporate executives.

Coolidge ran for reelection in 1924 with the financier Charles Dawes as his running mate. There was little question that he would win. The Democrats were so equally divided between northern urban Catholics and southern rural Protestants that it took 103 ballots to nominate John W. Davis, an affable corporate lawyer.

Dissidents, mostly representing the farmers and laborers dissatisfied with both nominees, formed a new Progressive party. They adopted the name, but little else, from Theodore Roosevelt's party of 1912. Nominating Robert La Follette for president, their platform called for government ownership of railroads and ratification of a child labor amendment. La Follette attacked the "control of government and industry by private monopoly." He received nearly 5 million votes, only 3.5 million short of Davis's total. But Coolidge and prosperity won easily.

Like Harding, Coolidge was popular. Symbolizing his administration was the wealthy secretary of the treasury, Andrew Mellon. In 1922, Congress, with Mellon's endorsement, repealed the wartime excess profits tax. Although it raised some taxes slightly, it exempted most families from any tax by giving everyone a $2,500 exemption, plus $400 for each dependent. In 1926, the rate was lowered to 5 percent and the maximum surtax to 40 percent. Only families with incomes above $3,500 paid anything. In 1928, Congress slashed taxes further, removed most excise taxes, and lowered the corporate tax rate. The 200 largest corporations increased their assets during the decade from $43 to $81 billion.

"The chief business of the American people is business," Coolidge said. His idea of the proper role of the federal government was to have as little as possible to do with the functioning of business and the lives of the people. "No other president in my time slept so much," a White House usher remembered. But most Americans approved.

Herbert Hoover

One bright light in the lackluster Harding and Coolidge administrations was Secretary of Commerce Herbert Hoover. He had made a fortune as a mining engineer before 1914 and earned the reputation of a great humanitarian during the war. Many Progressives supported him as a presidential candidate in 1920.

Hoover was a dynamo. He expanded his department to regulate the airlines, radio, and other new industries. Through the Bureau of Standards, Hoover standardized the size of almost everything manufactured in the United States. He supported zoning codes, the eight-hour day in major industries, better nutrition for children, and conservation. He pushed through the Pollution Act of 1924, the first attempt to control coastal oil pollution.

While secretary of commerce, Hoover used the authority of the federal government to regulate, stimulate, and promote, but he believed first of all in American free enterprise and local volunteer action. In 1921, he convinced Harding of the need to do something about unemployment during the postwar recession. The president's conference on unemployment, convened in September 1921, marked the first time the national government had admitted any responsibility to the unemployed. The conference (the first of many that Hoover was to organize) unleashed a flood of publicity and expert advice. Most of all, the conference urged state and local governments and businesses to cooperate voluntarily to solve the problem. The primary responsibility of the federal government, Hoover believed, was to educate and promote. Hoover got the reputation as an efficient and progressive administrator, and he became one of the most popular figures in government service.

Foreign Policy in the 1920s

The 1920s are often called a time of isolation. But the United States remained involved—indeed, increased its involvement—in international affairs. Although the United States never joined the League of Nations, and a few staunch isolationists blocked membership in the World Court, the United States cooperated with many

League agencies. And it took the lead in trying to reduce naval armaments and to solve the problems of international finance caused in part by the war.

The seven-fold expansion of American corporate investments overseas turned the United States from a debtor to a creditor nation. Yet the United States took up its role of international power reluctantly and with a number of contradictory and disastrous results.

"We seek no part in directing the destiny of the world," Harding announced in his inaugural address, but he discovered that international problems would not go away. One that required immediate attention was the naval arms race, for which purpose the United States convened the Washington Conference on Naval Disarmament, the first international disarmament conference, in November 1921.

Secretary of State Charles Evans Hughes startled the conference by proposing a ten-year "holiday" on warship construction and offering to sink or scrap 845,000 tons of American ships, including 30 battleships. He urged Britain and Japan to do the same. The delegates cheered Hughes's speech, and they sank more ships than all their admirals had managed to do in a century. The conference ultimately fixed the tonnage of capital ships at a ratio of the United States and Great Britain, 5; Japan, 3; and France and Italy, 1.67. Japan agreed only reluctantly, after the United States promised not to fortify its Pacific islands.

The Washington Conference has often been criticized in the light of Pearl Harbor, but in 1921 it was appropriately hailed as the first time in history that the major nations of the world had agreed to disarm. The conference neither caused nor averted World War II. But it was a creative beginning to reducing tensions and to meeting the challenges of the modern arms race.

American foreign policy in the 1920s tried to reduce the risk of international conflict, resist revolution, and make the world safe for trade and investment. Nobody in the Republican administrations even suggested that the United States remain isolated from Latin America. American diplomats argued for an open door to trade in China, but in Latin America the United States had always assumed a special and distinct role. Throughout the decade, American investment increased in the Western Hemisphere. The United States bought nearly 60 percent of Latin America's exports and sold the region nearly 50 percent of its imports.

By the end of the decade, the United States controlled the financial affairs of ten Latin American nations. The Dominican Republic remained a virtual protectorate of the United States until 1941. Only briefly were the Marines out of Nicaragua, in 1925 and 1926. First the Marines, and later the Nicaraguan troops they trained, had a difficult time containing a guerrilla band led by charismatic Augusto Sandino. The Sandinistas, supported by the great majority of peasants, came out of the hills to attack the politicians and their American supporters. "Today we are hated and despised," an American coffee planter announced in 1931. In 1934, Sandino was murdered by General Anastasio Somoza, a ruthless leader supported by the United States. For more than 40 years, Somoza and his two sons would rule Nicaragua.

Mexico frightened American businessmen in the mid-1920s by beginning to nationalize foreign holdings in oil and mineral rights. Fearing that further military activity would "injure American interests," businessmen and bankers urged Coolidge to negotiate. Coolidge did, and his ambassador's conciliatory attitude led to agreements protecting American investments.

The United States' policy of promoting peace and trade was not always consistent, especially toward Europe. The United States was owed more than $10 billion in war loans, three-fourths of it by Britain and France. Both countries, mired in economic problems, suggested that the United States forgive the debts, arguing that they had paid for the war in lives and property destroyed. But the United States, although adjusting the interest and the payment schedule, refused. "They hired the money, didn't they?" Coolidge supposedly asked.

International debt was not the same as money borrowed at the neighborhood bank. The only way European nations could repay the United States was by exports, but Congress established protective barriers. In 1930, the Hawley-Smoot Tariff raised rates even further, despite the protests of many economists and 35 countries. American policy of high tariffs (a counterproductive policy for a creditor nation) caused retaliation and restrictions on American trade, which American corporations were trying to increase.

Europeans' inability to export to the United States and repay their loans was intertwined with the reparation agreement made with Germany. The postwar German economy was beset by inflation and its industrial plant throttled by the peace treaty. By 1921, Germany was defaulting on reparations payments. Hoping to maintain international stability, the United States introduced the Dawes Plan, under which the German debt would be spread over a longer period while American bankers and the American government lent Germany hundreds of millions of dollars. This enabled Germany to pay reparations to Britain and France so that they could continue debt repayments to the United States.

Although the United States had displaced Great Britain as the dominant force in international finance, it was a reluctant and inconsistent world leader. The United States stayed out of the League and hesitated to join multinational agreements. But the Kellogg-Briand pact seemed irresistible. French foreign minister Aristide Briand suggested a Franco-American pact, in large part commemorating long years of friendship between the two countries, but Secretary of State Frank B. Kellogg in 1928 expanded the idea to a multinational treaty outlawing war. Fourteen nations initially signed the treaty and 62 eventually did, but the only power behind it was moral force.

The Survival of Progressivism

The decade of the 1920s saw a reaction against reform, but progressivism did not simply die. Progressives interested in efficiency and order were perhaps happier during the 1920s than those who tried to promote social justice, but the fights against poverty and for better housing persisted, as did campaigns to protect children. The reformers did not disappear. They worked to promote a child labor constitutional amendment after the 1919 law was declared unconstitutional in 1922.

The greatest success of the social justice movement was the 1921 Sheppard-Towner Maternity Act, one of the first pieces of federal social welfare legislation and the product of long progressive agitation. The bill, controversial from the beginning, called for a million dollars a year to assist states in providing medical aid, consultation centers, and visiting nurses to teach expectant mothers how to care for themselves and their babies. The American Medical Association attacked it as socialistic; those who had opposed woman suffrage argued that it was put forward by extreme feminists and Communists.

But the bill passed Congress and was signed by President Harding in 1921. The appropriation for the bill was only for six years, and the opposition, still trembling at a feminist-Socialist-Communist plot, got it repealed in 1929. Yet the Sheppard-Towner Act, promoted and fought for by a group of progressive women, indicated that concern for social justice was not dead in the age of Harding and Coolidge.

Temperance Triumphant

By 1918, over three-fourths of Americans lived in dry states or counties, but the war allowed antisaloon advocates to link prohibition and patriotism. At first, beer manufacturers supported limited prohibition, but in the end, patriotic fervor prohibited the sale of all alcoholic beverages. "We have German enemies across the water," one prohibitionist disclosed. "We have German enemies in this country too. And the worst of all our German enemies, the most treacherous, the most menacing are Pabst, Schlitz, Blatz and Miller."

The Volstead Act, passed in 1919, banned the brewing and selling of beverages containing more than 0.5 percent alcohol. The Eighteenth Amendment was ratified in June 1919, but the country had been effectively dry since 1917. A social worker predicted that the Eighteenth Amendment would reduce poverty, nearly wipe out prostitution and crime, improve labor, and "substantially increase our national resources by setting free vast suppressed human potentialities."

The prohibition experiment probably did reduce the total consumption of alcohol in the country, especially in rural areas and urban working-class neighborhoods. Fewer arrests for drunkenness were made, and deaths from alcoholism declined. But prohibition showed the difficulty of using law to promote moral reform. Most people who wanted to drink during the "noble experiment" found a way. Speakeasies replaced saloons, and people consumed many strange and dangerous homemade concoctions. Bartenders invented the cocktail to disguise the poor quality of liquor, and middle- and upper-class women began to drink in public.

Prohibition also created great bootlegging rings, in many cities tied to organized crime. Chicago's Al Capone was the most famous underworld figure whose power and wealth were based on the sale of illegal alcohol. His organization alone supposedly grossed over $60 million in 1927. Many prohibition supporters slowly came to favor repeal, some because it reduced the power of the states, others because it stimulated too much illegal activity and it did not seem worth the costs.

The Election of 1928

On August 2, 1927, President Coolidge announced, "I do not choose to run for President in 1928." Although he and the president were not especially close, Hoover immediately became the logical Republican candidate, and he easily got the nomination. Few doubted that the prospering country would elect him.

The Democrats nominated Alfred Smith, the colorful, "wet," and Catholic governor of New York who contrasted sharply with Hoover. Anti-Catholicism disgraced the campaign. But two candidates differed little. Both were self-made men, and both were progressives. Social justice reformers campaigned for each candidate. Both sought women voters, favored organized labor, defended capitalism, and were advised by millionaires and corporate executives.

Hoover won in a landslide, receiving 444 electoral votes to Smith's 76. But the campaign revitalized the Democratic party. Smith polled nearly twice as many votes as Davis had in 1924, and for the first time Democrats carried the 12 largest cities.

Stock Market Crash

Hoover had only six months to apply his progressive, efficient methods to running the country. In the fall of 1929, the seemingly endless prosperity suddenly fizzled.

In 1928 and 1929, rampant speculation made the stock market boom. Money could be made everywhere—in real estate, business ventures, and especially the stock market. "Everybody ought to be Rich," Al Smith's campaign manager proclaimed in an article in the *Ladies' Home Journal* early in 1929. But only a small percentage of the American people invested in the stock market. A large number got into the game in the late 1920s because it seemed a safe and sure way to make money. The *New York Times* index of 25 industrial stocks reached 100 in 1924, moved up to 181 in 1925, dropped a bit in 1926, and rose again to 245 by the end of 1927.

Then the orgy started. During 1928, the market zoomed to 331. Many investors and speculators began to buy on margin (borrowing to invest). Money went into the market that would ordinarily have gone into houses, cars, and other goods. Yet even at the peak, probably only about 1.5 million Americans owned stock.

In early September 1929, the *New York Times* index peaked at 452 and then began to drift downward. On October 23, the market lost 31 points. The next day ("Black Thursday"), it first seemed that everyone was trying to sell, but at the end of the day, the panic appeared over. It was not. By mid-November, the market had plummeted to 224, about half what it had been two months before—a loss on paper of over $26 billion. Still, a month later, some businessmen got back into the market, thinking that it had reached its low point. But it continued to go down. Tens of thousands of investors lost everything. Those who had bought on margin had to keep coming up with money to pay off their loans as the value of their holdings fell. There was panic and despair, but the legendary stories of executives jumping out of windows were grossly exaggerated.

←←←←←

CONCLUSION

A New Era of Prosperity and Problems

The stock market crash ended the decade of prosperity. The crash did not cause the depression, but the stock market debacle revealed the weakness of the economy. The fruits of economic expansion had been unevenly distributed. Not enough people could afford to buy the autos, refrigerators, and other products pouring from American factories. Prosperity had been built on a shaky foundation. When that foundation crumbled in 1929, the nation slid into a major depression.

TIMELINE

1900–1930	1917	1918	1919	1920
Electricity powers the "second industrial revolution"	Race riot in East Saint Louis, Illinois	World War I ends	Treaty of Versailles; Strikes in Seattle, Boston, and elsewhere; Red Scare and Palmer raids; Race riots in Chicago and other cities; Marcus Garvey's Universal Negro Improvement Association spreads	Warren Harding elected president; Women vote in national elections; First commercial radio broadcast; Sacco and Vanzetti arrested; Sinclair Lewis, *Main Street*

1921	1921–1922	1922	1923	1924
Immigration Quota Law; Disarmament Conference; First birth control conference; Sheppard-Towner Maternity Act	Postwar depression	Fordney-McCumber Tariff; Sinclair Lewis, *Babbitt*	Harding dies; Calvin Coolidge becomes president; Teapot Dome scandal	Coolidge reelected president; Peak of Ku Klux Klan activity; Immigration Quota Law

1925	1926	1927	1928	1929
Scopes trial in Dayton, Tennessee; F. Scott Fitzgerald, *The Great Gatsby*; Bruce Barton, *The Man Nobody Knows*; Alain Locke, *The New Negro*; Claude McKay, *Home to Harlem*; Five million enameled bathroom fixtures produced	Ernest Hemingway, *The Sun Also Rises*	National Origins Act; McNary-Haugen Farm Relief Bill; Sacco and Vanzetti executed; Lindbergh flies solo, New York to Paris; First talking movie, *The Jazz Singer*; Henry Ford produces 15 millionth car	Herbert Hoover elected president; Kellogg-Briand Treaty; Stock market soars	27 million registered cars in country; 10 million households own radios; 100 million people attend movies; Stock market crash

Looking back from the vantage point of the 1930s or later, the 1920s seemed a golden era—an age of flappers, bootleg gin, constant parties, literary masterpieces, sports heroes, and easy wealth. The truth is much more complicated. More than most decades, the 1920s was a time of paradox and contradictions.

The 1920s was a time of prosperity, yet a great many people, including farmers, blacks, and other ordinary Americans did not prosper. It was a time of modernization, but only about 10 percent of rural families had electricity. It was a time when women achieved more sexual freedom, but the feminist movement declined. It was a time of prohibition, but many Americans increased their consumption of alcohol. It was a time of reaction against reform, yet progressivism survived. It was a time when intellectuals felt disillusioned with America, yet it was one of the most creative and innovative periods for American writers. It was a time of flamboyant heroes, yet the American people elected the lackluster Harding and Coolidge as their presidents. It was a time of progress, when almost every year saw a new technological breakthrough, but it was also a decade of hate and intolerance. The complex and contradictory legacy of the 1920s continues to fascinate and to influence our time.

Recommended Reading

General References

William E. Leuchtenburg, *The Perils of Prosperity, 1914–1932* (1970); Lynn Dumenil, *The Modern Temper: America in the 1920s* (1995).

Politics, Economics, and Foreign Policy

John Kenneth Galbraith, *The Great Crash, 1929* (1954); Andrew Sinclair, *The Available Man* (1965); Donald R. McCoy, *Calvin Coolidge* (1967); Oscar Handlin, *Al Smith and His America* (1958); Joan Hoff Wilson, *Herbert Hoover: The Forgotten Progressive* (1975) and *American Business and Foreign Policy, 1920–1933* (1971); Warren I. Cohen, *Empire Without Tears* (1987).

Society and Culture

Robert K. Murray, *Red Scare* (1955); Frederick Hoffman, *The Twenties: American Writing in the Postwar Decade* (1955); Houston A. Baker, Jr., *Modernism and the Harlem Renaissance* (1987); Arnold Rampersand, *The Life of Langston Hughes*, 2 vols. (1986-88); Gary Wills, *Under God: Religion and American Politics* (1990); George M. Marsden, *Fundamentalism and American Culture* (1980); David M. Chalmers, *Hooded Americanism: The History of the Ku Klux Klan* (1965); John Higham, *Strangers in the Land: Patterns of American Nativism, 1860–1925* (1955); Paula Fass, *The Damned and Beautiful: American Youth in the 1920s* (1977); Robert Sklar, *Movie Made America* (1975); James J. Flink, *The Car Culture* (1976); Roland Marchand, *Advertising the American Dream* (1985); William H. Chafe, *The American Woman: Her Changing Social and Economic Roles, 1920–1970* (1972); Ruth Schwartz, *More Work for Mother* (1983); Margaret Marsh, *Suburban Lives* (1990); Lizabeth Cohen, *Making a New Deal: Industrial Workers in Chicago, 1919–1939* (1990); George J. Sanchez, *Becoming Mexican American* (1993); David E. Nye, *Electrifying America: Social Meaning of a New Technology* (1991); Tom Lewis, *Empire of the Air: The Men Who Made Radio* (1991); Ellen Chesler, *Woman of Valor: Margaret Sanger and the Birth Control Movement* (1992); George Chauncey, *Gay New York: Gender, Urban Culture and the Meaning of the Gay Male World* (1994).

Fiction

Ernest Hemingway's novel *The Sun Also Rises* (1926) is a classic tale of disillusionment and despair in the 1920s; F. Scott Fitzgerald gives a picture of the life of the rich in *The Great Gatsby* (1925); and Claude McKay's novel *Home to Harlem* (1928) is one of the best to come out of the Harlem Renaissance.

CHAPTER 24

The Great Depression and the New Deal

Diana Morgan grew up in a small North Carolina town, the daughter of a prosperous cotton merchant. She lived the life of a "southern belle," oblivious to national problems. But the Great Depression changed that. She came home from college one Christmas to discover that the telephone had been disconnected. Her world suddenly fell apart. Her father's business had failed, her family didn't have a cook or a cleaning woman anymore, and their house was being sold for back taxes. Sometimes the little things were the hardest. Out-of-town friends would come, and there would be no ice because her family did not own an electric refrigerator and could not afford ice. "There were those frantic arrangements of running out to the drugstore to get Coca-Cola with crushed ice, and there'd be this embarrassing delay, and I can remember how hot my face was."

Like many Americans, Diana Morgan and her family blamed themselves for what happened during the Great Depression. Americans had been taught to believe that if they worked hard, saved their money, and lived upright and moral lives, they could succeed. Success was an individual matter for Americans. When so many failed during the Depression, they blamed themselves, not society or larger forces. Shame and guilt affected people at all levels. The businessman who lost his business, the farmer who watched his farm being sold at auction, the worker who was suddenly unemployed and felt his manhood stripped away because he could not provide for his family were all devastated by the Depression.

Diana Morgan had never intended to get a job; she expected to get married and let her husband support her. But the failure of her father's business forced her to join the growing number of women who worked outside the home in the 1930s. She finally found a position with the Civil Works Administration, a New Deal agency, where at first she had to ask humiliating questions of people applying for assistance to make sure they were destitute. "Do you own a car?" "Does anyone in the family work?" Diana was appalled at the conditions she saw when she traveled around the county to corroborate their stories: dilapidated houses, a dirty, "almost paralyzed-looking mother," a drunken father, malnourished children. She felt helpless. One day, a woman who had formerly cooked for her family came in to apply for help. Each was embarrassed to see the other in changed circumstances.

Diana had to defend the New Deal programs to many of her friends, who accused her of being sentimental and told her that the poor, especially poor blacks, did not know any better. "If you give them coal, they'd put it in the bathtub," was a charge she often heard. But she knew "they didn't have bathtubs to put coal in. So how did anybody know that's what they'd do with coal if they had it?"

Diana Morgan's experience working for a New Deal agency influenced her life and her attitudes; it made her more of a social activist. Her Depression experience gave her a greater appreciation for the struggles of the country's poor and unlucky. Although she prospered in the years after the Depression, the sense of guilt and the fear that the telephone might again be cut off never left her.

↞↞↞↞↞

The Great Depression changed the lives of all Americans and haunted that generation. An exaggerated need for security, the fear of failure, a nagging sense of guilt, and a real sense that it might happen again divided the Depression generation from everyone born after 1940. Like Diana Morgan, most Americans never forgot those bleak years.

This chapter explores the causes and consequences of the Great Depression. We will look at Herbert Hoover's efforts to combat it and then turn to Franklin Roosevelt, the dominant personality of the 1930s. We will examine the New Deal and Roosevelt's program of relief, recovery, and reform. But we will not ignore the other side of the 1930s, for the decade did not just mean unemployment and New Deal agencies. It also brought great strides in technology, and innovations in radio, movies, and the automobile affected the lives of most Americans.

THE GREAT DEPRESSION

There had been recessions and depressions in American history, notably in the 1830s, 1870s, and 1890s, but nothing compared to the devastating economic collapse of the 1930s. The Great Depression was all the more shocking because it came after a decade of unprecedented prosperity, when most experts assumed that the United States was immune to a business-cycle downturn. The Great Depression affected all areas of American life; perhaps most important, it destroyed American confidence in the future.

The Depression Begins

Few people anticipated the stock market crash in the fall of 1929. But even after the collapse of the stock market, few expected the entire economy to go into a tailspin. General Electric stock, selling for $396 in 1929, fell to $34 in 1932. By 1932, the median income had plunged to half what it had been in 1929. Construction spending fell to one-sixth of the 1929 level. By 1932, at least one of every four American breadwinners was out of work, and industrial production ground almost to a halt.

Why this ever-deepening downturn? After all, only about 2 percent of the population owned stock. The answer is complex, but the prosperity of the 1920s, it appears in retrospect, was superficial. Farmers and coal and textile workers had suffered all through the 1920s from low prices, and the farmers were the first group in the 1930s to plunge into depression. But other economic sectors also lurched out of balance. Two percent of the population received about 28 percent of the national income, but the lower 60 percent got only 24 percent. Businesses increased profits while holding down wages and the prices of raw materials. This pattern depressed consumer purchasing power. Workers, like farmers, did not have the money to buy the goods they helped to produce. There was a relative decline in purchasing power in the late 1920s, unemployment was high in some industries, and the housing and automobile industries were already slackening before the crash.

Well-to-do Americans were speculating a significant portion of their money in the stock market. Their illusion of permanent prosperity helped fire the boom of the 1920s, just as their pessimism and lack of confidence helped exaggerate the depression in 1931 and 1932.

But there were other factors. The stock market crash revealed serious structural weaknesses in the financial and banking systems. The Federal Reserve Board, fearing inflation, tightened credit—the opposite of what it should have done. High American tariffs during the 1920s had reduced trade, and when American investment in Europe slackened in 1928 and 1929, European economies declined. As the European financial situation worsened, the American economy spiraled downward.

The federal government might have prevented the Wall Street crash and the Depression by more careful regulation of business and the stock market. Central planning might have assured a more equitable distribution of income. But that kind of policy would have taken more foresight than most people had in the 1920s. It certainly would have required different people in power, and it is unlikely that the Democrats, had they been in control, would have altered fundamental policies.

Hoover and the Great Depression

Initial business and government reactions to the stock market crash were optimistic. "All the evidence indicates that the worst effects of the crash upon unemployment will have been passed during the next sixty days," Herbert Hoover reported, tailoring his upbeat first statements to prevent further panic.

The Agricultural Marketing Act of 1929 set up a $500 million revolving fund to help farmers organize cooperative marketing associations and to establish minimum prices. But as agricultural prices plummeted and banks foreclosed on farm mortgages, the available funds proved inadequate. The Farm Board was helpless to aid the farmer who could not meet mortgage payments because the price of grain had fallen so rapidly, nor the Arkansas woman who stood weeping as her possessions were sold one by one.

Hoover acted aggressively. More than any president before him, he used the power of the federal government and the office of the president to deal with a crisis that seemed much like earlier cyclic recessions. Hoover called conferences of businessmen and labor leaders. He encouraged mayors and governors to speed up public works projects. He created agencies and boards, such as the National Credit Corporation and the Emergency Committee for Employment, to obtain voluntary action to solve the problem. Hoover even supported the tax cut that Congress enacted in December 1929, but it did little to stimulate spending. Hoover also went on the radio to assure the American people that the fundamental structure of the economy was sound.

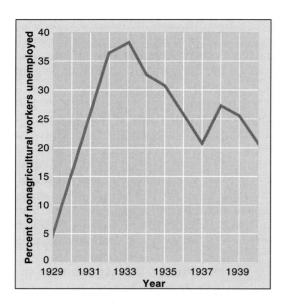

UNEMPLOYMENT RATE, 1929–1940
Although the unemployment rate declined
during the New Deal years, the number still
unemployed remained tragically high until
World War II brought full employment.
Source: U.S. Bureau of the Census.

The Collapsing Economy

Voluntarism and psychological campaigns could not stop the Depression. The
stock market, after appearing to bottom out in the winter of 1930 and 1931, continued its decline, responding in part to the European economic collapse that
threatened international finance and trade. Of course, not everyone lost money.
Joseph Kennedy, film magnate, entrepreneur, and father of a future president, was
among those who made millions by selling short as the market went down.

More than a collapsing market afflicted the economy. Over 1,300 banks failed
in 1930. Despite Hoover's pleas, many factories cut production, and some simply
closed. More than 4 million Americans were out of work in 1930, and that number
increased to at least 12 million by 1932. Foreclosures and evictions created thousands of personal tragedies. While the middle class watched in horror as life savings and dreams disappeared, the rich worried increasingly as the price of
government bonds (the symbol of safety and security) dropped. They began to
hoard gold and fear revolution.

There was never any real danger of revolution. Some farmers organized to
dump their milk to protest low prices, and when a neighbor's farm was sold, they
gathered to hold a penny auction, bidding only a few cents for equipment and
returning it to their dispossessed neighbor. But everywhere people despaired as the
Depression deepened in 1931 and 1932. For unemployed blacks and many tenant
farmers, the Depression had little immediate effect because their lives were already
so depressed. The 98 percent of Americans who did not own stock hardly noticed
the crash; for them, the Depression meant a lost job or a foreclosure. For Diana
Morgan, it was the discovery that the telephone had been cut off; for some farmers,
it was burning corn rather than coal because the price of corn had fallen so low that
it was not worth marketing. For some in the cities, the Depression meant not

having enough money to feed the children. In Chicago, children fought with men and women over the garbage dumped by the city trucks.

Not everyone went hungry, stood in breadlines, or lost jobs, but almost everyone was affected, and many tended to blame themselves. A businessman who lost his job and had to stand in a relief line remembered years later how he would bend his head low so nobody would recognize him.

The Depression probably disrupted women's lives less than men's. When men lost their jobs, their identity and sense of purpose as the family breadwinner generally collapsed. Some helped out with family chores, usually with bitterness. For women, however, even when money was short, there were still chores, and they were still in command of their households. Yet many women had to do extra work: taking in laundry, finding room for a boarder, and making clothes they formerly would have bought. They also bore the psychological burden of unemployed husbands, hungry children, and unpaid bills. Many families moved in with relatives. The marriage rate, the divorce rate, and the birthrate all dropped during the decade, creating tensions that statistics cannot capture.

Hoover kept urging more voluntary action. "We are going through a period," he announced in February 1931, "when character and courage are on trial." He insisted on maintaining the gold standard and a balanced budget, but so did almost everyone else. New York Governor Franklin Roosevelt accused him of spending too much. Hoover increasingly blamed the Depression on international economic problems, and he was not entirely wrong. But Americans began to blame Hoover. The president became isolated and bitter. The shanties that grew near all the large cities were called "Hoovervilles." Unable to admit mistakes and take a new tack, he could not communicate personal empathy for the poor and the unemployed.

Hoover did try innovative schemes. More public works projects were built during his administration than in the previous 30 years. In the summer of 1931, he organized a pool of private money to rescue banks and businesses that were near failure. When that private effort failed, he turned reluctantly to Congress, which in 1932 authorized the Reconstruction Finance Corporation. The RFC was capitalized at $500 million and soon increased to $3 billion. It lent to banks, insurance companies, farm mortgage companies, and railroads. Some critics charged that it was simply a trickle-down measure while the unemployed were ignored. Hoover, however, understood the immense costs to individuals and communities when a bank or mortgage company failed. The RFC helped shore up shaky financial institutions and remained the major government finance agency until World War II. But it became much more effective under Roosevelt because it lent directly to industry.

Hoover also asked Congress for a Home Financing Corporation to make mortgages more readily available. The Federal Home Loan Bank Act of 1932 became the basis for the Federal Housing Administration of the New Deal years. He also pushed the passage of the Glass-Steagall Banking Act of 1932, which expanded credit in order to make more loans available to businesses and individuals.

But Hoover rejected calls for the federal government to restrict production in hopes of raising farm prices—that, he believed, was too much federal intervention. He firmly believed in loans, not direct subsidies, and he thought it was the responsibility of state and local governments, as well as private charity, to provide direct relief to the unemployed and the needy.

The worst result of the Depression was hopelessness and despair. Those emotions are captured in this painting of an unemployment office by Isaac Soyer. (Employment Agency, 1937/Collection Whitney Museum of American Art, New York)

The Bonus Army

Many World War I veterans lost their jobs during the Great Depression, and beginning in 1930 they lobbied for payment of their veterans' bonuses that were due in 1945. In May 1932, about 17,000 veterans marched on Washington. Some took up residence in a shantytown, called Bonus City, outside town.

In mid-June the Senate defeated the bonus bill, and most of the disappointed vets accepted a free railroad ticket home. Several thousand remained, however, along with some wives and children, in the unsanitary shacks during the steaming summer heat. Among them were a few Communists and other radicals. Hoover, who exaggerated the subversive elements among those still camped out in Bonus City, refused to talk to the leaders, and finally called out the U.S. Army.

General Douglas MacArthur, the Army chief of staff, ordered troops to disperse the veterans, "a mob," he said, " . . . animated by the essence of revolution." With tanks, guns, and tear gas, troops routed men who 15 years before had worn the same uniform. Two Bonus marchers died. Far from attacking revolutionaries in the streets of Washington, the Army was routing bewildered, confused, unemployed men whose American dream had collapsed.

The Bonus army fiasco, breadlines, and Hoovervilles became the symbols of Hoover's presidency. He deserved better because he tried to use the power of the federal government to solve growing and increasingly complex economic problems. But his personality and background limited him. He could not understand why veterans marched on Washington to ask for a handout when they should be back home working hard, practicing self-reliance, and cooperating. He believed that the greatest problem besetting Americans was a lack of confidence. He could not communicate with these people or inspire their confidence. Willing to give federal support to business, he could not accept giving federal aid to the unemployed. He feared an unbalanced budget and a large federal bureaucracy that would interfere with the "American way." Ironically, his actions and inactions soon led to a massive increase in federal power and in federal bureaucracy.

ROOSEVELT AND THE FIRST NEW DEAL

The first New Deal, from 1933 to early 1935, focused mainly on recovery and relief for the poor and unemployed. Some of its programs were borrowed from the Hoover administration, or went back to the progressive period. Others were inspired by the nation's experiences in mobilizing for World War I. No single ideological position united all the programs, for Roosevelt was a pragmatist who was willing to try different programs. More than Hoover, however, he believed in economic planning and in government spending to help the poor.

Roosevelt's caution and conservatism shaped the first New Deal. He did not promote socialism. The basic assumption of the New Deal was that a just society could be created by superimposing a welfare state on the capitalist system, leaving the profit motive in place. Roosevelt believed he could achieve this through cooperation with the business community. Later he would move toward reform, but at first his concern was simply relief and recovery.

The Election of 1932

In the summer of 1932 the Republicans renominated Hoover for a second term, but the Depression and Hoover's unpopularity opened the way for the Democrats. Franklin D. Roosevelt won the nomination. Distantly related to Theodore Roosevelt, he had served as assistant secretary of the Navy during World War I and was the Democratic vice presidential candidate in 1920. Crippled by polio not long after, he had recovered enough to serve as governor of New York for two terms, though he was not especially well known by the general public in 1932.

As governor, Roosevelt had promoted cheaper electric power, conservation, and old-age pensions, and he became the first governor to support state aid for the unemployed. But it was difficult to tell during the campaign exactly what he stood for. Ambiguity was probably the best strategy in 1932, but Roosevelt had no master plan to save the country. Yet he won overwhelmingly, carrying more than 57 percent of the popular vote.

Campaigning, Roosevelt had promised a "new deal for the American people." But the New Deal had to wait for four months because the Constitution provided for presidents to be inaugurated on March 4. (This was changed to January 20 by the Twentieth Amendment, ratified in 1933.) During the long interregnum, the state of the nation deteriorated badly. The banking system veered near collapse and hardship increased. Despite his bitter defeat, Hoover tried to cooperate with the president-elect and a hostile Congress. But he could accomplish little. Everyone waited for the new president to take office.

In his inaugural address, Roosevelt announced confidently, "The only thing we have to fear is fear itself." This, of course, was not true: The country faced the worst crisis since the Civil War. But Roosevelt's confidence and ability to communicate with ordinary Americans were obvious early in his presidency. He had clever speech writers, a sense of pace and rhythm in his speeches, and an ability, in his "fireside chats," to convince listeners that he was speaking directly to them. When he said "my friends," millions believed that he meant it.

The Cabinet and the "Brain Trust"

During the interregnum, Roosevelt surrounded himself with intelligent and innovative advisers. His cabinet consisted of a mixture of people from different backgrounds who often did not agree with one another. Harold Ickes, the secretary of the interior, was a Republican lawyer from Chicago and onetime supporter of Theodore Roosevelt. Another Republican, Henry Wallace of Iowa, a plant geneticist and agricultural statistician, became the secretary of agriculture. Frances Perkins, the first woman ever appointed to a cabinet post, became the secretary of labor. A disciple of Jane Addams and Florence Kelley, she had been a settlement resident, the secretary of the New York Consumers League, and an adviser to Al Smith.

Besides the formal cabinet, Roosevelt had an informal "Brain Trust," including Adolph Berle, Jr., a young expert on corporation law, and Rexford Tugwell, a Columbia University authority on agricultural economics and a committed national planner. Roosevelt also listened to Raymond Moley, another Columbia professor who later became one of the president's severest critics, and to Harry Hopkins, a nervous, energetic man who loved to bet on horse races and was passionately concerned for the poor and unemployed.

Eleanor Roosevelt made a controversial first lady. She wrote a newspaper column, made radio broadcasts, traveled widely, and was constantly giving speeches and listening to the concerns of women, minorities, and ordinary Americans. Attacked by critics who thought she had too much power, she took courageous stands for social justice and civil rights, pushing the president toward social reform.

Roosevelt was an adept politician. He was not well-read, especially on economic matters, but he could learn from his advisers and yet not be dominated by them. He took ideas, plans, and suggestions from conflicting sources and combined them. An improviser who once likened himself to a quarterback who called one play and if it did not work called a different one, Roosevelt was an optimist by nature. And he believed in action.

ONE HUNDRED DAYS

Congress was ready to pass almost any legislation that Roosevelt put before it. In three months, a bewildering number of bills were rushed through. Some were not well thought out, and some contradicted other bills. But many of these laws would have far-reaching implications for the relationship of government to society. Roosevelt was an opportunist, but unlike Hoover, he was willing to use direct government action against depression and unemployment. None of the bills passed during the first 100 days cured the Depression, but taken together, the "Hundred Days" were one of the most innovative periods in American political history.

The Banking Crisis

The most immediate problem Roosevelt faced was the banking crisis. Many banks had closed, and citizens were hoarding money and gold. Roosevelt immediately declared a four-day bank holiday. Three days later, an emergency session of Congress approved his action and within hours gave the president broad powers over financial transactions, prohibited the hoarding of gold, and allowed for the reopening of sound banks, sometimes with RFC loans.

Over the next few years, Congress gave the federal government more regulatory power over the stock market and over the process by which corporations issued stock. The Banking Act of 1933 strengthened the Federal Reserve System, established the Federal Deposit Insurance Corporation (FDIC), and insured individual deposits up to $5,000. Although the American Bankers Association opposed the plan, banks were soon attracting depositors by advertising that they were protected by government insurance.

The Democratic platform in 1932 called for reduced government spending and an end to prohibition. Roosevelt moved quickly on both. The Economy Act, which passed easily, called for a 15 percent reduction in government salaries and a reorganization of federal agencies to save money. The bill also cut veterans' pensions, over their protests. However, the Economy Act's small savings were dwarfed by other bills passed the same week, which called for increased spending. The Beer-Wine Revenue Act legalized 3.2 beer and light wines and levied a tax on both. The Twenty-first Amendment, ratified on December 5, 1933, repealed the Eighteenth Amendment and officially ended prohibition. The veterans and the antiliquor forces, two of the strongest lobbying groups in the nation, were overwhelmed by a Congress that seemed ready to give the president free rein.

Congress granted Roosevelt broad power to devalue the dollar and induce inflation. Some members revived the old Populist solution of free and unlimited silver coinage, while others called for issuing billions of dollars in paper currency. Bankers and businessmen feared inflation, but farmers and debtors favored some inflation to put more dollars in their pockets. Roosevelt rejected the more extreme inflationary plans of many congressmen from agricultural states, but he did take the country off the gold standard. No longer would paper currency be redeemable in gold. The action terrified some conservative businessmen, and even Roosevelt's director of the budget announced solemnly that it "meant the end of Western Civilization."

Devaluation neither ended Western civilization nor produced instant recovery. Roosevelt and his advisers fixed the price at $35 an ounce in January 1934 (against the old price of $20.63), inflating the dollar by about 40 percent. Soon the country settled down to a slightly inflated currency and a dollar based on both gold and silver. Some experts still believed that gold represented fiscal responsibility, even morality, while others still cried for more inflation.

Relief Measures

Roosevelt believed in economy in government and in a balanced budget, but he also wanted to help the unemployed and the homeless. One survey estimated in 1933 that 1.5 million Americans were homeless. A man with a wife and six children who was being evicted wrote, "I have 10 days to get another house, no job, no means of paying rent, can you advise me as to which would be the most humane way to dispose of myself and family, as this is about the only thing that I see left to do."

Roosevelt's answer was the Federal Emergency Relief Administration (FERA), which Congress authorized with an appropriation of $500 million in direct grants to cities and states. A few months later, Roosevelt created a Civil Works Administration (CWA) to put more than four million people to work on various state, municipal, and federal projects. Hopkins, who ran both agencies, believed it was much better to pay people to work than to give them charity. So did most people in need. An accountant working on a road project said, "I'd rather stay out here in that ditch the rest of my life than take one cent of direct relief."

The CWA was not always effective, but in just over a year it built or restored a half-million miles of roads and constructed 40,000 schools and 1,000 airports. It hired 50,000 teachers to keep rural schools open and others to teach adult education courses in the cities. The CWA helped millions of people get through the bitterly cold winter of 1933–1934. It also put over a billion dollars of purchasing power into the economy. Roosevelt, who later would be accused of deficit spending, feared that the program was costing too much and might create a permanent class of relief recipients. In the spring of 1934, he ordered the CWA closed down.

The Public Works Administration (PWA), directed by Harold Ickes, lasted longer. Between 1933 and 1939, the PWA built hospitals, courthouses, and school buildings. Its projects included the port of Brownsville, Texas, two aircraft carriers, and low-cost slum housing.

One purpose of the PWA was economic pump priming—to stimulate the economy through government outlays. Afraid of scandals, Ickes spent money slowly and carefully. Thus during the first years PWA projects, worthwhile as most of them were, provided little economic stimulus.

Agricultural Adjustment Act

By 1933, most farmers were desperate, caught between mounting surpluses and falling prices. Some in the Midwest talked of revolution. Many observers saw only despair in farmers who had worked hard but were still losing their farms.

Congress passed a number of bills in 1933 and 1934 to deal with the agricultural crisis, including foreclosures and evictions. But the New Deal's principal solution was the Agricultural Adjustment Act (AAA), which sought to control the overproduction of basic commodities so that farmers might regain their pre-World War I purchasing power. To guarantee these "parity prices" (the average prices in the years 1909 to 1914), the production of major agricultural staples—wheat, cotton, corn, hogs, rice, tobacco, and milk—would be controlled by paying the farmers to reduce their acreage under cultivation. The AAA levied a tax at the processing stage to pay for the program.

For many people, the Depression meant homeless despair. Here an Oklahoma family who has lost their farm walk with all their possessions along the highway. This compelling photograph was taken by Dorothea Lange, one of several accomplished photographers who documented the impact of the Depression for the Farm Security Administration. (Corbis-Bettmann)

The act caused great disagreement among farm leaders and economists, but the controversy was nothing compared with the public outcry in the summer of 1933, when, to boost prices, the AAA ordered ten million acres of cotton plowed up and six million young pigs slaughtered. It seemed immoral to kill pigs and plow up cotton when millions of people were hungry and ill-clothed.

The Agricultural Adjustment Act did raise the prices of some agricultural products. But it helped the larger farmers more than the small operators, and it was often disastrous for the tenant farmers and sharecroppers, made expendable by crop reduction. When they reduced their acreage, landowners often discharged tenant families. Many were simply cast out on the road with nowhere to go. Large farmers cultivated their fewer acres more intensely, so that the total crop was little reduced. In the end, the prolonged drought that hit the Southwest in 1934 did more than the AAA to limit production and raise agricultural prices. But the long-range significance of the AAA, which was later declared unconstitutional, was to entrench the idea that the government should subsidize farmers for limiting production.

Industrial Recovery

The legislation during the first days of the Roosevelt administration contained something for almost every group. The National Industrial Recovery Act (NIRA) was designed to help business, raise prices, control production, and put people back to work. The act established the National Recovery Administration (NRA) with the power to set fair competition codes in all industries. For a time, everyone forgot about antitrust laws and talked of cooperation.

To run the NRA, Roosevelt appointed Hugh Johnson, who used his wartime administrative experiences (he had run the draft) and the enthusiasm of bond drives to rally the country around the NRA and, implicitly, around the New Deal. There were parades and rallies, a postage stamp, and "We Do Our Part" posters for cooperating industries. But the results were somewhat less than the promise.

Section 7a of the NIRA, included at labor unions' insistence, guaranteed labor's right to organize and to bargain collectively and established the National Labor Board to see that unions' rights were respected. But the board, usually dominated by businessmen, often interpreted the labor provisions of the contracts loosely. In addition, small businessmen complained that the NIRA was unfair to their interests. Any attempt to set prices led to controversy.

Many consumers suspected that the codes and contracts were raising prices, while others feared the return of monopoly. Johnson's campaign backfired because anyone with a complaint about the New Deal seemed to take it out on the NIRA's blue eagle symbol. When the Supreme Court declared the NIRA unconstitutional in 1935, few complained. Still, the NIRA was an ambitious attempt to bring some order into a confused business situation, and its labor provisions were picked up later by the National Labor Relations Act.

Civilian Conservation Corps

One of the most popular and successful New Deal programs, the Civilian Conservation Corps (CCC), combined work relief with the preservation of natural resources. It put young unemployed men between the ages of 18 and 25—2.5 million of them—to work on reforestation, road and park construction, flood control, and other projects. The men lived in work camps and earned $30 a month, $25 of which had to be sent home to their families. A few separate camps were organized for unemployed young women. Overall, the CCC was one of the most successful and least controversial of all the New Deal programs.

Tennessee Valley Authority

FDR, like TR, believed in conservation. He promoted flood-control projects and added millions of acres to the country's national forests, wildlife refuges, and fish and game sanctuaries. But the most important New Deal conservation project, the Tennessee Valley Authority (TVA), owed more to Republican George Norris, a progressive senator from Nebraska, than to Roosevelt.

During World War I, the federal government had built a hydroelectric plant and two munitions factories at Muscle Shoals, on the Tennessee River in Alabama. The government tried unsuccessfully to sell these facilities to private industry, but all through the 1920s Norris campaigned to have the federal government operate them for the benefit of the valley's residents. Twice Republican presidents vetoed bills providing for federal operation, but Roosevelt endorsed Norris's idea and expanded it into a regional development plan.

Congress authorized the TVA as an independent public corporation to sell electricity and fertilizer and to promote flood control and land reclamation. The TVA built nine major dams and many minor ones between 1933 and 1944, affecting parts of Virginia, North Carolina, Georgia, Alabama, Mississippi, Tennessee, and Kentucky. Some private utility companies claimed that the TVA unfairly competed with private industry, but it was an imaginative experiment in regional planning. For residents of the valley, it meant cheaper electricity and changed lifestyles. The largest federal construction project ever launched, it also created jobs for many thousands who helped build the dams. But government officials and businessmen who feared that the experiment would lead to socialism always curbed the regional planning possibilities of the TVA.

Critics of the New Deal

The furious legislative activity during the first 100 days of the New Deal helped alleviate the country's pessimism and despair. The stock market rose slightly, and industrial production was up 11 percent at the end of 1933. Still, the country remained locked in depression, and nearly 12 million Americans lacked jobs.

Roosevelt captured the imagination of ordinary Americans everywhere, but conservatives were not so happy. Many businessmen, after being impressed with Roosevelt's early economy measures and approving programs such as the NIRA, began to fear that the president was leading the country toward socialism.

The conservative revolt against Roosevelt surfaced in the summer of 1934 as the congressional elections approached. A group of disgruntled politicians and businessmen formed the Liberty League. Led by Alfred E. Smith and John W. Davis, the league supported conservative or at least anti-New Deal candidates for Congress, but it had little influence. In the election of 1934, the Democrats increased their majority from 310 to 319 in the House and from 60 to 69 in the Senate (only the second time in the twentieth century that the party in power had increased its control of Congress in the mid-term election). A few people were learning to hate "that man in the White House," but most Americans approved of what he was doing.

Much more disturbing to Roosevelt and his advisers in 1934 and 1935 than people who thought the New Deal too radical were those on the left who maintained that the government had not done enough to help the poor. The Communist party increased its membership from 7,500 in 1930 to 75,000 in 1938. Communists organized protest marches and tried to reach out to the oppressed and unemployed. While a majority who joined the party came from the working class, communism had a special appeal to writers, intellectuals, and some college students during a decade when the American dream had turned into a nightmare.

More Americans, however, were influenced by other movements promising easy solutions. In Minnesota, Governor Floyd Olson accused capitalism of causing the Depression and thundered, "I hope the present system of government goes right to hell." In California, Upton Sinclair, the muckraking socialist and author of *The Jungle,* ran for governor on the EPIC platform ("End Poverty in California"). He promised to pay everyone over 60 years of age a pension of $50 a month, financed by higher income and inheritance taxes. He won the primary but lost the election, and his movement collapsed.

California also produced Dr. Francis E. Townsend, who claimed a national following of over five million. His supporters backed a scheme that promised $200 a month to all unemployed citizens over age 60 on the condition that they spend it in the same month they received it. Economists laughed, but followers organized thousands of Townsend Pension Clubs across the country.

More threatening to Roosevelt and the New Deal were the protest movements led by Father Charles E. Coughlin and Senator Huey P. Long. Father Coughlin, a Roman Catholic priest from a Detroit suburb, attracted an audience of 30 to 45 million to his national radio show. At first he supported Roosevelt's policies, but later he savagely attacked the New Deal as excessively pro-business. Mixing religious commentary with visions of a society without bankers and big businessmen, he roused his audience with blatantly anti-Semitic tirades. Anti-Semitism reached a peak in the 1930s, as Jews bore the brunt of nativist fury.

Huey Long, like Coughlin, had a charisma that won support from the millions still trying to survive in a country where the continuing depression made day-to-day existence a struggle. Elected governor of Louisiana in 1928, Long called his program "Share the Wealth." He taxed the oil refineries and built hospitals, schools, and thousands of miles of new highways. By 1934, he was the virtual dictator of his state, personally controlling the police and the courts. Long talked about a guaranteed $2,000 to $3,000 income for all American families (18.3 million families earned less than $1,000 per year in 1936) and promised pensions for the elderly and college educations for the young, all to be paid for by soaking the rich. Had not an assassin killed Long in September 1935, he might have mounted a third-party challenge to Roosevelt.

THE SECOND NEW DEAL

Responding in part to lower-middle-class discontent but also to head off utopian schemes, Roosevelt moved his programs in 1935 toward the goals of social reform and social justice. At the same time, he ceased trying to cooperate with the business community. "In spite of our efforts and in spite of our talk, we have not weeded out the overprivileged and we have not effectively lifted up the underprivileged," Roosevelt announced in his annual message to Congress in January 1935.

Work Relief and Social Security

The Works Progress Administration (WPA), authorized by Congress in April 1935, was the first massive attempt to deal with unemployment and its demoralizing effect on millions of Americans. The WPA employed about three million people a year (at wages below what private industry paid) on projects ranging from bridges to libraries. It built nearly 6,000 schools, more than 2,500 hospitals, and 13,000 playgrounds. Nearly 85 percent of its funds went directly to workers. A minor but important part of its funding supported writers, artists, actors, and musicians.

Only one member of a family could get a WPA job—always a man unless a woman headed the household. But eventually more than 13 percent of the people who worked for the WPA were women, usually making over old clothes. "For unskilled men we have the shovel. For unskilled women we have only the needle," one official explained.

The WPA was controversial from the beginning. Its initials, said wags, stood for "We Putter Around." Yet the WPA not only did useful work but also gave millions of unemployed Americans a sense that they were working and supporting their families.

The National Youth Administration (NYA) supplemented the work of the WPA and assisted young men and women between the ages of 16 and 25 (including a young law student at Duke University named Richard Nixon). Lyndon Johnson began his political career as director of the Texas NYA.

By far the most enduring reform was passage of the Social Security Act of 1935. Since the progressive period, reformers had argued for national health and unemployment insurance and old-age pensions. By the 1930s, the United States was the only major industrial country without them. Secretary of Labor Perkins argued most strongly for social insurance, but Roosevelt also wanted to head off popular schemes like the Townsend Plan.

The Social Security Act of 1935 was a compromise. To appease the medical profession, Congress quickly dropped a plan for federal health insurance. The act's central provision was old-age and survivor insurance, paid for by a tax of 1 percent on both employers and employees. The act also established a cooperative federal-state system of unemployment compensation, gave federal grants to the states for the disabled and the blind, and provided aid to dependent children—the provision that years later expanded to become the largest federal welfare program.

Conservatives denounced Social Security for regimenting people and destroying self-reliance. But in no other country was social insurance paid for in part by a regressive tax on the workers' wages. "With those taxes in there, no damn politician can ever scrap my Social Security program," Roosevelt later explained, insisting that by paying the taxes wage earners won a moral claim on their benefits. But farm laborers and domestic servants were not covered. The system discriminated against married women wage earners and failed to protect against sickness. Still, it was one of the most important New Deal measures, and it marked the beginning of the welfare state that would expand greatly after World War II.

Aiding the Farmers

The Social Security Act and the Works Progress Administration were only two signs of Roosevelt's greater concern for social reform. The flurry of legislation in 1935 and early 1936, often called the "second New Deal," also included an effort to help American farmers. The Resettlement Administration (RA), motivated in part by a Jeffersonian ideal of yeoman farmers working their own land, tried to relocate tenant farmers to land purchased by the government. But it failed to accomplish much, a victim of underfunding and of scare talk about Soviet-style collective farms.

Much more important in improving the lives of farm families was the Rural Electrification Administration (REA), which was authorized in 1935 to lend money to cooperatives to generate and distribute electricity in isolated rural areas not served by private utilities. Only 10 percent of the nation's farms had electricity in 1936. When the REA's lines were finally attached, they dramatically changed the lives of millions of farm families who had only been able to dream about the radios, washing machines, and farm equipment advertised in magazines.

A farmer and his sons race to find shelter from a dust storm in Cimarron County,
Oklahoma, in 1936. A combination of factors, including overplanting which
destroyed the natural sod of the Great Plains, resulted in the devastating dust storms
of the 1930s. Without sod to protect the soil from the wind, thousands of acres of the
Great Plains just blew away. (Library of Congress)

The Dust Bowl: An Ecological Disaster

Those who tried to farm on the Great Plains fell victim to years of drought and
dust storms, as record heat waves and below-average rainfall in the 1930s turned
the Oklahoma panhandle and western Kansas into a giant dust bowl. Thousands
died of "dust pneumonia." By the end of the decade 10,000 farm homes were
abandoned, 9 million acres of farmland were reduced to wasteland, and 3.5 million
people had joined a massive migration to find a better life. Many tenant farmers
and hired hands were evicted, their plight immortalized by John Steinbeck in his
novel *The Grapes of Wrath* (1939).

The dust bowl was a natural disaster, aided and exaggerated by human actions
and inactions. The semiarid plains west of the 98th meridian were not suitable for
intensive agriculture, and 60 years of improper land use had exposed the thin soil
to the elements. When the winds came, much of the land simply blew away. In the
end it was a matter of too little government planning and regulation and too many
farmers using new technology to exploit nature.

Whatever the administration tried to do was too little and too late. Even worse,
according to some authorities, government measures applied after the disaster of
1930 encouraged farmers to return to raising wheat and other inappropriate crops,
leading to more dust bowl crises in the 1950s and 1970s.

The New Deal and the West

The New Deal probably aided the West more than any other region. The CCC, the AAA, drought relief measures, and various federal agencies helped the region out of proportion to the people who lived there. Most important were the large-scale water projects, such as Boulder Dam (later renamed Hoover Dam) on the Colorado River and (the largest of all) Grand Coulee Dam on the Columbia River, which produced massive amounts of hydroelectric power, poured millions of dollars into the economy, and provided enormous amounts of water for cities and irrigation.

Despite all the federal aid to the region, many Westerners bitterly criticized the regulation and the bureaucracy that went with the grants. The cattlemen in Wyoming, Colorado, and Montana desperately needed the help of the federal government, but even as they accepted the aid they denounced the New Deal.

Controlling Corporate Power and Taxing the Wealthy

In the summer of 1935, Roosevelt also moved to control the large corporations, and he even toyed with radical plans to tax the well-to-do heavily and redistribute wealth in the United States. The Public Utility Holding Company Act, passed in 1935, attempted to restrict the power of the giant utility companies, the 12 largest of which controlled more than half the country's power. It gave each company five years to demonstrate that its services were efficient or face being dissolved. This was one of the most radical attempts to control corporate power in American history.

In the same year Roosevelt urged higher taxes on the rich and a heavy inheritance tax. When Congress dropped the inheritance tax provision, however, Roosevelt did not fight for it. Even the weakened bill angered many in the business community who thought that FDR had sold out to Huey Long's "Share the Wealth" scheme.

The New Deal for Labor

Like many progressive reformers, Roosevelt was more interested in helping working people by social legislation than by strengthening unions. Yet he saw labor as an important balance to the power of industry, and he listened to his advisers, especially to Frances Perkins and to Senator Robert Wagner of New York, who persistently brought up the needs of organized labor.

After a series of strikes, Roosevelt supported the Wagner Act (officially the National Labor Relations Act), which outlawed blacklisting and a number of other practices and reasserted labor's right to organize and to bargain collectively. The act also established a Labor Relations Board with the power to certify a properly elected bargaining unit. The act did not require workers to join unions, but it made the federal government a regulator, or at least a neutral force, in management-labor relations. That alone made the National Labor Relations Act one of the most important New Deal reform measures.

The Roosevelt administration's friendly attitude helped increase union membership from under 3 million in 1933 to 4.5 million by 1935. Many groups, however,

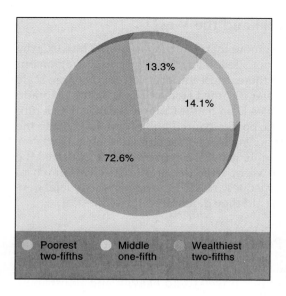

DISTRIBUTION OF INCOME, 1935–1936
Roosevelt and the New Deal never sought consistently to redistribute wealth in America, and a great disparity in income and assets remained. Source: U.S. Bureau of the Census.

were left out, including farm laborers, unskilled workers, and women. Only about 3 percent of working women belonged to unions, and they earned only about 60 percent of wages paid to men for equivalent work. Still, many resented the women being employed at all. One writer had a perfect solution for unemployment: "Simply fire the women, who shouldn't be working anyway, and hire the men."

The AFL had never organized unskilled workers, but a new group of committed and militant labor leaders emerged in the 1930s to take up that task: John L. Lewis of the United Mine Workers, David Dubinsky of the International Ladies' Garment Workers, and Sidney Hillman of the Amalgamated Clothing Workers. The latter two were socialists who believed in economic planning and had worked closely with social justice progressives. These new progressive labor leaders formed the Committee of Industrial Organization (CIO) within the AFL and set out to organize workers in the steel, auto, and rubber industries. Rather than separating workers by skill or craft as the AFL preferred, they organized industrywide unions. They also used aggressive new tactics, such as declaring a spontaneous strike when management made unwanted demands. This "brass knuckle unionism" worked especially well in the auto and rubber industries.

In 1936, the workers at three rubber plants in Akron, Ohio, went on unauthorized strikes. Instead of picketing, they took over the buildings. The "sit-down strike" became a new protest technique, disorderly but largely nonviolent (as would be civil rights demonstrations in the 1960s). After several such strikes, General Motors finally accepted the United Auto Workers (UAW) as their employees' bargaining agent. The GM strike was the most important event in a critical period of labor upheaval. Labor's voice now began to be heard in the decision-making process in major industries where labor had long been denied any role, raising the status of organized labor in the eyes of many Americans.

Violence spread along with the sit-down strikes. Chrysler capitulated, but Ford fought back with armed guards, and it took a bloody struggle before the UAW was accepted as the bargaining agent. Militantly anti-union U.S. Steel agreed to a 40-hour week and an eight-hour day, but other steel companies refused to go along. In the "Memorial Day Massacre" in 1937, police fired into a crowd of workers and their families peacefully picketing the Republic Steel plant in Chicago. All ten who died were shot in the back.

The CIO's aggressive tactics gained many members, to the horror of AFL leaders. They expelled the CIO leaders, only to see them form a separate Congress of Industrial Organization (the initials stayed the same). Accepting unskilled workers, African-Americans, and others who had never belonged to a union before, the CIO won increased pay, better working conditions, and the right to bargain collectively in most basic industries, and infused the labor movement with a new spirit.

America's Minorities in the 1930s

A half-million African-Americans joined unions through the CIO, and New Deal agencies aided many blacks. Yet familiar patterns of poverty, discrimination, and violence persisted. Lynchings in the South increased in the New Deal years.

Throughout the decade the nation was gripped by the "Scottsboro Boys" case in Alabama, which began in 1931 when two young white women accused nine black youths of rape. Convicted and condemned to death by an all-white jury, the blacks were given a new trial in 1933 by order of the Supreme Court on the grounds that they had not received proper legal counsel. Liberal and radical northerners (including the Communist party) mobilized in defense of the youths' civil rights, while many southerners saw the honor of white women at stake. Evidence supporting the alleged rapes was never presented, and eventually one of the women recanted. Yet in new trials, five of the young men were convicted and given long prison terms. Charges against the other four were dropped in 1937. Four of the remaining five were paroled in 1944, and the fifth escaped to Michigan.

The migration of blacks to northern cities, which had accelerated during World War I, continued during the 1930s. The collapse of cotton prices forced black farmers and farm laborers to flee north for survival. But since most were poorly educated, they soon became trapped in northern ghettos, where they got only the most menial jobs. The black unemployment rate was triple that of whites, and blacks often received less per person in welfare payments.

Black leaders attacked the Roosevelt administration for supporting or allowing segregation in government-sponsored facilities. Roosevelt, dependent on the vote of the solid South and fearing to antagonize powerful southern congressmen, refused to support the two major civil rights bills of the era, an antilynching bill and a bill to abolish the poll tax. Yet Ickes and Hopkins worked to ensure that blacks were given opportunities in New Deal agencies. By 1941, black federal employees totaled 150,000, more than three times the number during the Hoover administration. Most worked in the lower ranks, but some were lawyers, architects, office managers, and engineers.

Partly responsible for the presence of more black employees was the "black cabinet," a group of more than 50 young blacks working in various New Deal agencies and led by Mary McLeod Bethune, the daughter of a sharecropper and organizer of the National Council of Negro Women. She had a large impact on

New Deal policy—speaking out forcefully, picketing and protesting, and intervening shrewdly to obtain civil rights and more jobs for African-Americans.

Although FDR appointed some blacks to government positions, he was never particularly committed to civil rights. That was not true of Eleanor Roosevelt, who was educated in part by Bethune. In 1939, when the Daughters of the American Revolution denied black concert singer Marian Anderson their stage, Mrs. Roosevelt protested by resigning her DAR membership and arranged for Anderson to sing from the steps of the Lincoln Memorial before an audience of 75,000.

Hundreds of thousands of Mexicans, brought to the United States for work in the 1920s, lost their jobs in the Depression. Drifting to the Southwest or settling in urban *barrios*, they met signs like "No Niggers, Mexicans, or Dogs Allowed." Some New Deal agencies helped destitute Mexicans, but as aliens and migrants, most could not qualify for relief. The preferred solution was to ship them back to Mexico, often after illegal roundups. One estimate placed the number sent back in 1932 at 200,000, which included some American citizens. But some who remained adopted militant tactics to obtain fair treatment.

By the 1930s, Native American hunger, disease, and despair had been compounded by years of exploitation. Native Americans had lost over 60 percent of the 138 million acres allocated to them under the Dawes Act in 1887 (see Chapter 17), and many who remained on the reservations were not even citizens. In 1924, Congress granted citizenship to all Indians born in the United States, but that did not end their suffering.

FDR brought a new spirit to Indian policy by appointing John Collier as commissioner of Indian affairs. Collier was primarily responsible for passage of the Indian Reorganization Act of 1934, which sought to restore tribes' political independence, to end the Dawes Act's allotment policy, and to promote the "study of Indian civilization." Not all Indians agreed with the new policies. Some Americans charged that the act was inspired by Communism or would increase government bureaucracy, while missionaries claimed that the government was promoting paganism.

The paradox of United States policy toward the Indians can be illustrated by Collier's attempt to solve the Navajo problem. Genuinely sympathetic to Native Americans, he also believed in soil conservation, science, and progress. The Navajo lands, like most of the West, were overgrazed, and soil erosion threatened to fill the new lake behind Hoover Dam with silt. By supporting a policy of reducing the herds of sheep and goats on Indian land and by promoting soil conservation, Collier contributed to the change in the Navajo lifestyle and to the end of their self-sufficiency, something his other policies supported.

Women and the New Deal

Women made some gains during the 1930s, and more women occupied high government positions than in any previous administration. Some of these women had collaborated as social workers and now joined government bureaus to continue the fight for social justice. But they were usually in offices where they did not threaten male prerogatives.

Despite the number of women working for the government, feminism declined in the 1930s. The older feminists died or retired, and younger women did not replace them. Despite some dramatic exceptions, the image of woman's proper role in the 1930s continued to be housewife and mother.

THE LAST YEARS OF THE NEW DEAL

The New Deal was not a consistent or well-organized effort to end the Depression and restructure society. A pragmatic politician, Roosevelt was unconcerned about consistency. The first New Deal in 1933 and 1934 had concentrated on relief and recovery; the legislation of 1935 and 1936 stressed social reform. In many ways, the election of 1936 marked the high point of Roosevelt's power and influence. After 1937, in part because of the growing threat of war but also because of increasing opposition in Congress, the pace of social legislation slowed. Yet several measures passed in 1937 and 1938 had such far-reaching significance that some historians refer to a third New Deal.

The Election of 1936

The Republicans in 1936 nominated a moderate, Governor Alfred Landon of Kansas. Although he attacked the New Deal, charging it with waste and too much bureaucracy, Landon promised to do the same thing more efficiently. The *Literary Digest* magazine predicted his victory on the basis of its "scientific" telephone poll.

Roosevelt, helped by signs of economic recovery and supported by a coalition of the Democratic South, organized labor, farmers, and urban voters, won easily. A majority of African-Americans for the first time deserted the GOP—"the party of Lincoln"—out of appreciation for New Deal relief programs. No viable candidate to the left of the New Deal materialized. Winning by over ten million votes and carrying every state except Maine and Vermont, Roosevelt now had a mandate to continue his New Deal reforms. "To some generations much is given," Roosevelt announced in his acceptance speech; "of other generations much is expected. This generation has a rendezvous with destiny."

The Battle of the Supreme Court

"I see one-third of a nation ill-housed, ill-clad, ill-nourished," Roosevelt declared in his second inaugural address, and he vowed to alter it. But the president's first action in 1937 was a plan to reform the federal judiciary and the Supreme Court, whose "nine old men" had struck down various important New Deal measures.

To create a more sympathetic Court, FDR asked for power to appoint an extra justice for each justice over 70 years of age, of whom there were six. He also called for modernizing the court system at all levels, but that plan got lost in the public outcry over "court-packing."

Roosevelt's plan foundered. Republicans accused him of subverting the Constitution. Many congressmen from his own party refused to support him. Led by Vice President John Nance Garner of Texas, a number of southern Democrats broke with the president and formed a coalition with conservative Republicans that lasted for more than 30 years. Finally Roosevelt admitted defeat. He had perhaps misunderstood his mandate, and he certainly underestimated the respect, even reverence, that most Americans felt for the Supreme Court. Even amid economic catastrophe, Americans proved themselves fundamentally conservative toward their institutions.

Ironically, though he lost the battle of the Supreme Court, Roosevelt won the war. By the spring of 1937, the Court began to reverse its position and in a 5–4 decision upheld the National Labor Relations Act. When a conservative justice retired, Roosevelt made his first Supreme Court appointment, thus ensuring at least a shaky liberal majority on the Court. But Roosevelt triumphed at great cost. His attempt to reorganize the Court slowed the momentum of his legislative program. The most unpopular action he took as president, it made him vulnerable to criticism from New Deal opponents, and even some of his supporters were dismayed by what they regarded as an attack on the separation of powers.

In late 1936 and early 1937, recovery from the Depression seemed real: Employment was up, and even the stock market had recovered some of its losses. But in August the fragile prosperity collapsed. Unemployment shot back up nearly to the peak levels of 1934, industrial production fell, and Wall Street plummeted. Roosevelt had probably helped cause the recession by assuming that the prosperity of 1936 was permanent. A believer in balanced budgets, he had cut federal spending and reduced outlays for relief. Now, facing an embarrassing economic slump and charges that the New Deal had failed, he gave in to those of his advisers who were followers of British economist John Maynard Keynes.

Keynes argued that to get out of a depression, the government must spend massively on goods and services. This would spur demand and revive production. By increasing appropriations for the WPA and other agencies, Roosevelt's administration consciously incurred a deficit for the first time in order to stimulate the economy. It was not a well-planned effort, however. The economy responded slowly, never fully recovering until wartime expenditures, beginning in 1940, eliminated unemployment and ended the Depression.

The Third New Deal

Despite increasing hostility, Congress passed a number of important bills in 1937 and 1938 that completed the New Deal reform legislation. The Bankhead-Jones Farm Tenancy Act of 1937 created the Farm Security Administration (FSA) to aid tenant farmers, sharecroppers, and owners who had lost their farms. The FSA, which provided loans to grain collectives, also set up camps for migratory workers. But the FSA never had enough money to make a real difference.

Congress passed a new Agricultural Adjustment Act in 1938 that tried to solve the problem of farm surpluses by controlling production. Under the new act, the federal treasury made direct payments to farmers. It introduced a soil conservation program and tried to market surplus crops. But only the outbreak of World War II would end the problem of farm surplus—temporarily.

A shortage of urban housing continued to be a problem. Reformers who had worked in the first experiment with federal housing during World War I convinced FDR that federal low-cost housing should be part of New Deal reform. The National Housing Act of 1937 provided federal funds for slum clearance projects and the construction of low-cost housing. By 1939, however, only 117,000 units had been built—mostly bleak and boxlike structures that soon became a problem rather than a solution.

New Deal housing legislation had a greater impact on middle-class housing policies and patterns. During the first 100 days of the New Deal, Congress created the Home Owners Loan Corporation (HOLC) at Roosevelt's urging, which over the next two years made more than $3 billion in low-interest loans and helped over a million people save their homes from foreclosure. The HOLC also had a strong impact on housing policy by introducing the first long-term fixed-rate mortgages. (Formerly, mortgages ran no longer than five years and were subject to frequent renegotiation.) The HOLC also introduced a uniform system of real estate appraisal that tended to undervalue urban property, especially in old, crowded, and ethnically mixed neighborhoods. The system gave the highest ratings to suburban developments in which the HOLC determined there had been no "infiltration of Jews"—the beginning of the practice later called "redlining" that made it nearly impossible for certain prospective homeowners to obtain a mortgage.

The Federal Housing Administration (FHA), created in 1934 by the National Housing Act, expanded and extended many HOLC policies. The FHA insured mortgages, many of them for 25 or 30 years, reduced the minimum down payment from 30 percent to under 10 percent, and allowed over 11 million families to buy homes between 1934 and 1972. It also tended to favor purchasing new suburban homes rather than repairing older urban residences.

An equally important reform measure was the Fair Labor Standards Act, passed in June 1938. Roosevelt's bill proposed for all industries engaged in interstate commerce a minimum wage of 25 cents an hour and a maximum work week of 44 hours. Despite congressional watering down, when the act went into effect, 750,000 workers immediately got raises, and by 1940 some 12 million had them. The law also barred child labor in interstate commerce, making it the first permanent federal law to prohibit youngsters under 16 from working. And the law made no distinction between men and women, thus diminishing the need for special legislation for women.

The New Deal had many weaknesses, but it did dramatically increase government support for the needy. In 1913, local, state, and federal government spent $21 million on public assistance. By 1932, that had risen to $218 million; by 1939, it was $4.9 billion.

THE OTHER SIDE OF THE 1930s

The Great Depression and the New Deal so dominate the history of the 1930s that it is easy to conclude that there were only breadlines and relief agencies. But there is another side of the decade. A communications revolution changed the lives of middle-class Americans. The sale of radios and attendance at movies increased during the 1930s, and literature flourished. Americans were fascinated by technology, especially automobiles. Many people traveled and looked ahead to a brighter future of streamlined appliances and gadgets.

Taking to the Road

"People give up everything in the world but their car," a banker in Muncie, Indiana, remarked during the Depression, and that seems to have been true all over the country. Although automobile production dropped off after 1929 and did not recover until the end of the 1930s, the number of motor vehicles registered, which declined from 26.7 million in 1930 to just over 24 million in 1933, increased to over 32 million by 1940. Even the "Okies" fled the dust bowl of the Southwest in cars—secondhand, run-down ones, to be sure.

The American middle class traveled at an increasing rate after the low point of 1932 and 1933. In 1938, the tourist industry was the third largest in the United States, behind only steel and automobile production.

The Electric Home

If the 1920s was the age of the bathroom, the 1930s was the era of the modern kitchen. In 1930, the number of electric refrigerators produced exceeded the number of iceboxes for the first time, and refrigerator production peaked at 2.3 million in 1937. At first, the refrigerator looked like an icebox with a motor on top. In 1935, however, the refrigerator, like most other appliances, became streamlined. The Sears Coldspot, which quickly influenced the look of all other models, was designed by Raymond Loewy, one of a group of industrial designers who emphasized sweeping horizontal lines and rounded corners.

Replacing an icebox with an electrical refrigerator, as many middle-class families did in the 1930s, altered more than the appearance of the kitchen. Unlike the constant tending demanded by the icebox, the refrigerator required only an occasional defrosting.

Streamlining became the symbol of modern civilization in the 1930s. At the end of the decade, in 1939, the World's Fair in New York glorified the streamlined, planned, technologized future. This reverence for progress contrasted with the economic despair in the 1930s, but people adapted to it selectively. For example, the electric washing machine and electric iron revolutionized washday—although Monday continued to be washday and Tuesday ironing day.

Ironically, despite these new conveniences, a great many middle-class families maintained their standard of living during the 1930s only because the women in the family learned to stretch and save and make do, and most wives spent as much time on housework as before. Some also took jobs outside the home to maintain their level of consumption. The number of married women who worked increased substantially during the decade.

The Age of Leisure

During the Depression, many middle-class people found themselves with time on their hands. The 1920s had been a time of spectator sports watched by huge crowds. Those sports continued during the Depression decade, although attendance suffered. Cheap forms of entertainment like softball and miniature golf also became popular. But leisure in the 1930s actually grew into something on which professionals published some 450 new books.

Many popular games of the period had elaborate rules. Contract bridge swept the country. Monopoly was the most popular game of all, as Americans became fascinated by a game of building real estate and utility monopolies and bankrupting their opponents.

Literary Reflections of the 1930s

Though much of the literature of the 1930s reflected the decade's troubled currents, reading continued to be a popular and cheap entertainment. John Steinbeck described the plight of Mexican migrant workers in *Tortilla Flat* (1935) and in his 1939 novel *The Grapes of Wrath* followed the deteriorating fortunes of an Okie family. His novels expressed his belief that there was in American life a "crime . . . that goes beyond denunciation"—the crime being the toleration of suffering and injustice.

Other writers also questioned the American dream. John Dos Passos's trilogy *U.S.A.* (1930–1936) conveyed a deep pessimism about American capitalism that many intellectuals shared. Less political were the novels of Thomas Wolfe and William Faulkner, who more sympathetically portrayed Americans caught up in the web of local life and facing modern complexities. Faulkner's fictional Yoknapatawpha County, brought to life in *The Sound and the Fury, As I Lay Dying, Sanctuary,* and *Light in August* (1929–1932), documented the South's racial problems, poverty, and stubborn pride. But a far more optimistic and far less complex book about the South became one of the decade's best-sellers—Margaret Mitchell's Civil War novel *Gone with the Wind* (1936). Its success showed that most Americans read to escape, not to explore their problems.

Radio's Finest Hour

In Chicago's working-class neighborhoods in 1930 there was one radio for every two or three households but often families and friends gathered to listen to the radio. Radio purchases increased steadily during the decade. The radio became a focal point of the living room. Families gathered around it at night to laugh at Jack Benny, and during the day there were soap operas: "Between thick slices of advertising," wrote James Thurber, "spread twelve minutes of dialogue, add predicament, villainy, and female suffering in equal measure, throw in a dash of nobility, sprinkle with tears, season with organ music, cover with a rich announcer sauce and serve five times a week."

Radio allowed many people to feel connected to distant places and to believe they knew the performers personally. And for proof of radio's power, there was Orson Welles's Halloween 1938 broadcast of "The War of the Worlds," so realistic that thousands actually believed that Martians had just landed in New Jersey. It was one of history's greatest episodes of mass hysteria.

The Movies

Just as some historians have used fiction to help define the cultural history of a decade, others in the twentieth century have turned to film to describe the "spirit of an age." On an elementary level, the movies help us appreciate changing styles in dress, furniture, and automobiles. We can even get some sense of how a particular time defined a beautiful woman or a handsome man, and we can learn about ethnic and racial stereotypes and assumptions about gender and class.

The decade of the 1930s is sometimes called the "golden age of the movies." Careful selection among the 500 or so feature films Hollywood produced each year during the decade—ranging from gangster and cowboy movies to Marx brothers comedies, from historical romances to Busby Berkeley musical extravaganzas—could support a number of interpretations about the special myths and assumptions of the era. But one historian has argued that especially after 1934, "Not only did the movies amuse and entertain the nation through its most severe economic and social disorder, holding it together by their capacity to create unifying myths and dreams, but movie culture in the 1930s became a dominant culture for many Americans, providing new values and social ideas to replace shattered old traditions."

It Happened One Night (1934) and *Drums Along the Mohawk* (1939), two films out of thousands, illustrate some of the myths the movies created and sustained. Frank Capra, one of Hollywood's masters at entertaining without disturbing, directed *It Happened One Night,* a comedy-romance. A rich girl played by Claudette Colbert dives from her father's yacht off the coast of Florida and takes a bus for New York. She meets a newspaper reporter played by Clark Gable. They have a series of madcap adventures and fall in love. But mix-ups and misunderstandings make it appear that she will marry her old boyfriend. In the end, however, they are reunited and marry in an elaborate outdoor ceremony. Afterward, they presumably live happily ever after. The movie is funny and entertaining and presents a variation on the poor-boy-marries-rich-girl theme. Like so many movies of the time, this one suggests that life is fulfilled for a woman only if she can find the right man to marry.

Claudette Colbert also stars in *Drums Along the Mohawk,* this time with Henry Fonda. Based on a 1936 novel by Walter Edmonds, *Drums* is a sentimental story about a man who builds a house in the wilderness, marries a pretty girl, fights off the Indians, and works with the simple country folk to create a satisfying life in the very year the American colonies rebel against Great Britain. *Drums* was one of a number of films based on historical themes that Hollywood released just before World War II. *The Howards of Virginia* (1940), *Northwest Passage* (1939), and most popular of all, *Gone with the Wind* (1939) were others in the same genre. Historical themes had been popular before, but with the world on the brink of war, the story of men and women in the wilderness struggling for family and country against the Indians (stereotyped as savages) proved comforting as well as entertaining.

Can a historian use movies to describe the values and myths of a particular time, or are the complexities and exaggerations too great? Are the most popular or most critically acclaimed films more useful than others in getting at the "spirit of an age"? What films popular today tell us most about our time and culture? Is there too much sex and violence in movies today? Should the government control the language, themes, and values depicted in movies? Are movies as important today as they were in the 1930s in defining and influencing the country's myths and values?

A scene from *It Happened One Night*, 1934. (The Museum of Modern Art Film Stills Archive)

A scene from *Drums Along the Mohawk*, 1939. (The Museum of Modern Art Film Stills Archive)

The Silver Screen

The 1930s were the golden decade of the movies. Between 60 and 90 million Americans went to the movies every week. The medium was not entirely Depression-proof, but even in the depth of the Depression, movie money was almost as important as food money for many families.

Urban people could go to an elaborate movie palace and live in a fantasy world far removed from the reality of Depression America. In small towns across the country, for a quarter (a dime under age 12) people could see at least four movies during the week. There was a Sunday-Monday feature film (except in communities where the churches forbade Sunday movies), a different feature of somewhat lesser prominence on Tuesday-Wednesday, and another on Thursday-Friday. On Saturday there was a cowboy or detective movie. Sometimes a double feature played, and always there were short subjects, a cartoon, and a newsreel. The Saturday serial would leave the heroine or hero in such a dire predicament that patrons just had to come back the next week.

The animated cartoons of Walt Disney, one of the true geniuses of the movie industry, were so popular that Mickey Mouse was more famous and familiar than most human celebrities. In May 1933, halfway into Roosevelt's first 100 days, Disney released *The Three Little Pigs,* whose theme song "Who's Afraid of the Big Bad Wolf?" became a national hit overnight. One critic suggested that the moral of the Disney film was that the little pig survived because he was conservative, diligent, and hard-working; others felt that it was the pig who used modern tools and planned ahead who won out.

✦✦✦✦✦

CONCLUSION

The Ambivalence of the Great Depression

The New Deal, despite its great variety of legislation, did not end the Depression, nor did it solve the problem of unemployment. For many Americans looking back on the decade of the 1930s, the most vivid memory was the shame and guilt of being unemployed, the despair and fear that came from losing a business or being evicted from a home or an apartment. Parents who lived through the decade urged their children to find a secure job, get married, and settle down. "Every time I've encountered the Depression it has been used as a barrier and a club," one daughter of Depression parents remembered; "older people use it to explain to me that I can't understand anything: I didn't live through the Depression."

New Deal legislation did not solve the country's problems, but it did strengthen the federal government, especially the executive branch. Federal agencies like the Federal Deposit Insurance Corporation and programs like Social Security influenced the daily lives of most Americans, and rural electrification, the WPA, and the CCC changed the lives of millions. The New Deal also established the principle of federal responsibility for the health of the economy, initiated the concept of the welfare state, and dramatically increased government spending to help the poor. Federally subsidized housing, minimum-wage laws, and a policy for paying farmers to limit production, all aspects of these principles, had far-reaching implications.

TIMELINE

1929	1930	1932	1933	1934
Stock market crashes; Agricultural Marketing Act	Depression worsens; Hawley-Smoot Tariff	Reconstruction Finance Corporation established; Federal Home Loan Bank Act; Glass-Steagall Banking Act; Federal Emergency Relief Act; Bonus march on Washington; Franklin D. Roosevelt elected president	Emergency Banking Relief Act; Home Owners Loan Corporation; Twenty-first Amendment repeals Eighteenth Amendment, ending prohibition; Agricultural Adjustment Act; National Industrial Recovery Act; Civilian Conservation Corps; Tennessee Valley Authority established; Public Works Administration established	Unemployment peaks; Federal Housing Administration established; Indian Reorganization Act

1935	1936	1937	1938	1939
Second New Deal begins; Works Progress Administration established; Social Security Act; Rural Electrification Act; National Labor Relations Act; Public Utility Holding Company Act; Committee for Industrial Organization (CIO) formed	United Auto Workers hold sit-down strikes against General Motors; Roosevelt reelected president; Economy begins to rebound	Attempt to expand the Supreme Court; Economic collapse; Farm Security Administration established; National Housing Act	Fair Labor Standards Act; Agricultural Adjustment Act	John Steinbeck, *The Grapes of Wrath*; Margaret Mitchell, *Gone with the Wind*

The New Deal was as important for what it did not do as for what it did. It was not socialistic and did not redistribute income. It promoted social justice and social reform, but it provided little for people at the bottom of American society. In the long run, it probably strengthened corporate capitalism.

With his colorful personality and dramatic response to the nation's crisis, FDR dominated his times in a way few presidents have done. Yet for some who lived through the era, neither Roosevelt nor breadlines but a new streamlined refrigerator or a favorite movie symbolized the Depression decade.

Recommended Reading

General Accounts

Anthony J. Badger, *The New Deal: The Depression Years* (1989); Paul Conkin, *The New Deal* (1967); William E. Leuchtenburg, *Franklin D. Roosevelt and the New Deal* (1963); Robert S. McElvaine, *The Great Depression* (1984).

The Depression

Richard White, *The Roots of Dependency: Subsistence, Environment and Social Change Among the Choctaws, Pawnees, and Navajos* (1983); Studs Terkel, *Hard Times* (1970); Charles J. Shindo, *Dust Bowl Migrants in the American Imagination* (1997).

Roosevelt and the New Deal

Alan Brinkley, *Voices of Protest: Huey Long, Father Coughlin and the Great Depression* (1982) and *The End of Reform: New Deal Liberalism in Recession and War* (1995); James MacGregor Burns, *Roosevelt: The Lion and the Fox* (1956); Dan T. Carter, *Scottsboro* (1969); Lizabeth Cohen, *Making a New Deal: Industrial Workers in Chicago, 1919–1939* (1990); Nelson Lichtenstein, "The Most Dangerous Man in Detroit:" Walter Reuther and the Fate of American Labor* (1995); Blanche Wiesen Cook, *Eleanor Roosevelt* (1992); Steve Fraser and Gary Gertstle, eds., *The Rise and Fall of the New Deal Order* (1989); Abraham Hoffman, *Unwanted: Mexican Americans and the Great Depression* (1974); Joseph Lash, *Eleanor and Franklin* (1971); Richard Lowitt, *The New Deal and the West* (1984); Roy Lubove, *The Struggle for Social Security* (1968); Richard Pells, *Radical Visions and American Dreams* (1973); Kenneth R. Philip, *John Collier's Crusade for Indian Reform* (1977); Jordan A. Schwartz, *The New Dealers: Power Politics in the Age of Roosevelt* (1993); Harvard Sitkoff, *A New Deal for Blacks* (1978); Susan Ware, *Beyond Suffrage: Women in the New Deal* (1981).

The Other Side of the Thirties

Andrew Bergman, *We're in the Money* (1972); Richard Schickel, *The Disney Version* (1968); Terry A. Cooney, *Balancing Acts: American Thought and Culture in the 1930s* (1995); David Gelernter, *1939: The Lost World of the Fair* (1995); Sigfried Giedion, *Mechanization Takes Command* (1948); Marjorie Rosen, *Popcorn Venus: Women, Movies and the American Dream* (1971); Warren Sussman, ed., *Culture and Commitment* (1968).

Fiction

James Farrell describes growing up in Depression Chicago in *Studs Lonigan* (1932–1935); John Steinbeck shows Okies trying to escape the dust bowl in his novel, *The Grapes of Wrath* (1939); Richard Wright details the trials of a young black man in *Native Son* (1940).

CHAPTER 25

World War II

N Scott Momaday, a Kiowa Indian born at Lawton, Oklahoma, in 1934, grew up on reservations. He was only 11 when World War II ended, yet the war changed his life. Shortly after the United States entered the war, Momaday's parents moved to New Mexico, where his father got a job with an oil company and his mother worked in the civilian personnel office at an Army Air Force base. Like many couples, they had struggled through the hard times of the Depression. The war meant jobs.

Momaday's best friend was Billy Don Johnson. Together they played war, digging trenches and dragging themselves through imaginary minefields. They hurled grenades and fired endless rounds from their imaginary machine guns, pausing only to drink Kool-Aid from their canteens. At school, they were taught how to hate the enemy and be proud of America. They recited the Pledge of Allegiance to the flag and sang "God Bless America," "The Star-Spangled Banner," and "Remember Pearl Harbor." Like most Americans, they believed that World War II was a good war fought against evil empires. The United States was always right, the enemy always wrong. It was an attitude that would influence Momaday and his generation for the rest of their lives.

Momaday's only difficulty was that his Native American face was often mistaken for that of an Asian. Almost every day on the playground, someone would yell, "Hi ya, Jap," and a fight was on. Billy Don always came to his friend's defense, but it was disconcerting to be taken for the enemy. His father read old Kiowa tales to Momaday, who was proud to be an Indian but prouder still to be an American. On Saturday, he and his friends would cheer at the movies as they watched a Japanese Zero or a German ME-109 go down.

Near the end of the war, Momaday's family moved again, as so many families did, so that his father might get a better job. This time they lived right next door to an Air Force base, and Momaday fell in love with the B-17 "Flying Fortress," the bomber that military strategists thought would win the war in the Pacific and in Europe.

Looking back, Momaday reflected on the importance of the war in his growing up. "I see now that one experiences easily the ordinary things of life," he decided, "the things which cast familiar shadows upon the sheer, transparent panels of time, and he perceives his experience in the only way he can, according to his age." Though Momaday's life during the war differed from the lives of boys old enough to join the armed forces, the war was no less real for him.

The Momadays fared better than most Native Americans. Although they had been made U.S. citizens by an act of Congress in 1924, the Momadays, like all Native Americans living in Arizona and New Mexico, were denied the right to vote by state law. Jobs, even in wartime, were hard to find. Native American servicemen returning from the war discovered that as "Indians" they still faced blatant discrimination in many states. Still, Momaday thought of himself not so much as an Indian but as an American, and that too was a product of his generation. But as he grew to maturity, he became a successful writer and spokesman for his people. In 1969, he won the Pulitzer Prize for his novel *House Made of Dawn*. In his writing, he stresses the Indian's close identification with the land. Writing about his grandmother, he says: "The immense landscape of the continental interior lay like memory in her blood."

✦✦✦✦✦✦

No American cities were bombed and the country was never invaded, but still World War II influenced almost every aspect of American life. The war ended the Depression. Industrial jobs were plentiful, and even though prejudice and discrimination did not disappear, blacks, Hispanics, women, and other minorities had new opportunities. Like World War I, this second global war expanded cooperation between government and industry and increased the influence of government in all areas of American life. The war also ended the last remnants of American isolationism. The United States emerged from the war in 1945 as the most powerful and most prosperous nation in the world.

This chapter traces the gradual involvement of the United States in the international events during the 1930s that finally led to participation in the most devastating war the world had seen. It traces the diplomatic and military struggles of the war and the search for a secure peace. It also explores the war's impact on ordinary people and on American attitudes about the world, on patriotism and the American way of life. The war brought prosperity to some, death to others. It left Americans the world's richest people and the United States its most powerful nation.

THE TWISTING ROAD TO WAR

Looking back on the events between 1933 and 1941 that eventually led America into World War II, it is easy to criticize decisions made or actions not taken, or else to see everything as inevitable. But historical events are never inevitable, and leaders who must make decisions never have the advantage of hindsight. They must deal with situations as they find them, and they never have all the facts.

Foreign Policy in the 1930s

In March 1933, Roosevelt faced not only overwhelming domestic difficulties but also an international crisis. The worldwide depression had caused near financial disaster in Europe.

Roosevelt had no master plan in foreign policy, just as he had none in the domestic sphere. In the first days of his administration, he gave conflicting signals about the international situation. First it seemed that FDR would cooperate in some kind of international economic agreement on tariffs and currency, which was to be negotiated in London. But then he refused to go along with any such agreement. In 1933, it seemed to Roosevelt more important to solve the domestic economic crisis than to achieve international economic cooperation. His actions signaled a decision to go it alone in foreign policy.

Roosevelt did, however, alter some of the foreign policy decisions of previous administrations. For example, he recognized the Soviet government. In reversing the 1920s nonrecognition policy (which rested largely on anti-Communist sentiments), Roosevelt hoped to gain a market for surplus American grain—a trade bonanza that never materialized.

The administration also reversed earlier interventionist policies in Latin America. The United States continued to support dictators, especially in Central America, because they promised to promote stability and preserve U. S. economic interests. But Roosevelt, extending the Good Neighbor policy Hoover had initiated, completed the removal of American military forces from Haiti and Nicaragua in 1934. In a series of pan-American conferences, he joined in pledging that no country in the hemisphere would intervene in the "internal or external affairs" of any other.

The new policy's first test came in Cuba, where a revolution threatened American investments of more than a billion dollars. But the United States did not send troops. Instead, Roosevelt dispatched envoys to work out a conciliatory agreement. A short time later, when a coup led by Fulgencio Batista overthrew the revolutionary government, the United States not only recognized the Batista government but also offered a large loan and agreed to abrogate the Platt Amendment (which made Cuba a virtual protectorate of the United States) in return for continued rights to the Guantanamo naval base.

The Trade Agreements Act of 1934 empowered the president to lower tariff rates by as much as 50 percent and took the tariff away from the pressure of special-interest groups in Congress. Secretary of State Cordell Hull negotiated a series of pacts that improved trade. By 1935, half of American cotton exports and a large proportion of other products were going to Latin America. So the Good Neighbor policy was also good business for the United States. But increased trade did not solve the economic problems for either the United States or Latin America.

Another test for Latin American policy came in 1938 when Mexico nationalized the property of American oil companies. Instead of intervening, as many businessmen urged, the State Department patiently worked out an agreement that included some compensation for the companies. Washington might have acted differently had not the threat of war in Europe in 1938 created a sense that all the Western Hemisphere nations should cooperate. At a pan-American conference held that year, the United States and most Latin American countries agreed to resist all foreign intervention in the hemisphere.

Neutrality in Europe

On January 30, 1933, about two months before Roosevelt's inauguration, Nazi leader Adolf Hitler became German chancellor. Within a few months, he assumed dictatorial powers. Hitler intended to conquer Europe. As the first step, in 1934 he announced German rearmament, violating the Versailles Treaty. That same year, Italy's Fascist dictator Benito Mussolini (who had come to power a decade earlier) threatened to invade the East African country of Ethiopia. These ominous rumblings frightened Americans at the very time they were reexamining the history of American entry into the Great War and vowing that it would never happen again.

Senator Gerald P. Nye of North Dakota launched an investigation of the connection between corporate profits and American participation in World War I. His committee's public hearings revealed that many American businessmen had close relationships with the War Department. Though no conspiracy was proved, it was easy to conclude that the United States had been tricked into going to war by the people who profited heavily from it.

On many campuses, students demonstrated against war. Students protested Reserve Officer Training Corps programs and, like many adults, joined peace societies that pledged never to support a foreign war.

Ethiopia and Spain

In May 1935, Italy invaded Ethiopia after rejecting the League of Nations' offer to mediate disputes between the two countries. The remote Ethiopian war frightened Congress into passing the Neutrality Act, which authorized the president to prohibit all arms shipments to nations at war and to advise all United States citizens not to travel on belligerents' ships except at their own risk. Congress was determined to prevent America from being sucked into another world war.

Though he would have preferred a more flexible bill, Roosevelt used the authority of the Neutrality Act of 1935 to impose an arms embargo. The League of Nations condemned Italy as the aggressor. But neither Britain nor the United States wanted to stop oil shipments to Italy or join the fight. The embargo had little impact on Italy but was disastrous for the poor African nation. Having conquered Ethiopia, Mussolini made an alliance with Germany, the Rome-Berlin Axis, in 1936.

"We shun political commitments which might entangle us in foreign war," Roosevelt announced in 1936. But isolation became more difficult when General Francisco Franco, supported by the Catholic Church, large landowners, and reactionary politicians, revolted against the republican government of Spain. Germany and Italy aided Franco, sending planes and other weapons, while the Soviet Union supplied the Spanish republican Loyalists.

The Spanish Civil War polarized the United States. Most Catholics and many anti-Communists sided with Franco. But many American radicals, even those who said they opposed all war, found the republican cause worth fighting for. Over 3,000 Americans joined the Abraham Lincoln Brigade, and hundreds died fighting Fascism. "If this were a Spanish matter, I'd let it alone," wrote Sam Levenger, an Ohio State student. "But the rebellion would not last a week if it weren't for the Germans and the Italians." Levenger was killed in Spain in 1937 at the age of 20.

The U. S. government took neutrality seriously. The Neutrality Act, extended in 1936, did not apply to civil wars. However, when an American businessman tried to send 400 used airplane engines to the Loyalists, Roosevelt asked Congress to extend the arms embargo to Spain. While the United States, Britain, and France carefully stayed neutral, Franco consolidated his dictatorship with German and Italian help. Meanwhile, Congress in 1937 passed another Neutrality Act, this time forbidding American citizens to travel on belligerents' ships. The embargo on arms was tightened, and belligerents could buy even nonmilitary items only on a cash-and-carry basis.

So the United States tried to avoid repeating the mistakes that had led it into World War I. Unfortunately, World War II, which moved closer each day, would be a different kind of war, and the lessons of the first war would be of little use.

War in Europe

Roosevelt had no careful strategy to deal with the rising tide of troubles in Europe in the late 1930s. He was no isolationist, but he wanted to keep the United States out of any European conflict. When he publicly said "I hate war," he meant it. Unlike his distant cousin Theodore Roosevelt, he did not view war as a test of manhood. In foreign policy, as in domestic affairs, he responded to events, but he moved reluctantly toward greater American involvement.

In March 1938, Hitler annexed Austria and in September he occupied the Sudetenland, a part of Czechoslovakia. Within six months, Hitler seized the rest of that country. Little protest came from the United States. Most Americans sympathized with the victims of Hitler's aggression, and eventually some were horrified by rumors of the murder of hundreds of thousands of Jews. But because newspapers avoided intensive coverage of these well-documented but unpleasant stories, many Americans did not learn of the Holocaust until near the end of the war.

At first, almost everyone hoped that Europeans could work out compromises. But that notion was destroyed on August 23, 1939, by the news of a Nazi-Soviet pact. Many Americans had secretly hoped that Nazi Germany and Soviet Russia would destroy each other. Now these deadly enemies had signed a nonaggression pact. A week later, Hitler's army attacked Poland, marking the onset of World War II. Britain and France came to Poland's defense. "This nation will remain a neutral nation," Roosevelt said, "but I cannot ask that every American remain neutral in thought as well."

Roosevelt asked for repeal of the embargo section of the Neutrality Act and for approval of cash-and-carry arms sales to France and Britain. And he took some risks. In August 1939, physicist Albert Einstein, a Jewish refugee from Nazi Germany, warned him that German scientists were working on an atomic bomb. The president feared the consequences of Hitler being the first to possess such a weapon, and authorized secret exploratory work. The top-secret project—known only to a few advisers and key members of Congress—was officially launched in 1941. Ultimately it would change the course of human history.

There was a lull in the war after Germany and the Soviet Union crushed Poland in September 1939. A number of Americans, including the American ambassador to Great Britain, Joseph Kennedy, who feared Communist Russia more than Fascist Germany, urged the United States to take the lead in negotiating a peace settlement that would recognize the German and Russian occupation of Poland. The British and French were not interested, and neither was Roosevelt. Great Britain sent several divisions to aid the French against the expected German attack, but for months nothing happened.

The "phony war" dramatically ended on April 9, 1940, when Germany attacked Norway and Denmark. At the beginning of May, the German *Blitzkrieg* ("lightning war") swept into the Low Countries. A week later, mechanized

German forces stormed into France, sweeping around fortifications known as the Maginot line. France surrendered in June as the British army fled across the English Channel.

How should the United States respond to this desperate situation? Some concerned citizens organized the Committee to Defend America by Aiding the Allies, but others, including Charles Lindbergh, supported a group called America First. They argued that the United States should forget England and concentrate on defending America. Roosevelt steered a cautious course. He sent Britain 50 overage American destroyers. In return, the United States received the right to establish naval and air bases from Newfoundland to Bermuda and British Guiana. British Prime Minister Winston Churchill asked for much more.

But Roosevelt hesitated and emphasized U. S. preparedness. In July 1940, he authorized $4 billion for more American warships. In September, Congress passed the Selective Service Act, providing for America's first peacetime draft. Over a million men were to serve for one year, but only in the Western Hemisphere.

The Election of 1940

Part of Roosevelt's reluctance to aid Great Britain more energetically came from his genuine desire to keep the United States out of the war, but it also reflected the presidential campaign of 1940. Roosevelt broke tradition by seeking a third term. The increasing support he was drawing from the liberal wing of the Democratic party led him to select liberal Henry Wallace as his running mate.

The Republicans nominated energetic Wendell Willkie of Indiana. Despite his big-business ties, Willkie approved of most New Deal legislation and supported aid to Great Britain. Willkie was the most exciting Republican candidate since Theodore Roosevelt. Yet amid the international crisis, the voters stayed with FDR—27 million to 22 million, in 38 of the 48 states.

Lend-Lease

After the election, Roosevelt invented a "lend-lease" scheme for sending aid to Britain without demanding payment. He compared this to lending a garden hose to a neighbor whose house was on fire. Republican Senator Robert Taft thought it was more like lending chewing gum: "Once it had been used you did not want it back." Others were even more critical.

The Lend-Lease Act, which Congress passed in March 1941, destroyed the fiction of neutrality. By then, U-boats were sinking a half-million tons of Atlantic shipping each month. In June, Roosevelt proclaimed a national emergency. Then, on June 22, Germany attacked Russia.

When Roosevelt extended lend-lease aid to Russia in November 1941, many Americans were shocked. But most quickly shifted from viewing the Soviet Union as an enemy to treating it like a friend.

By the autumn of 1941, the United States was virtually at war with Germany in the Atlantic. On September 11, Roosevelt issued a "shoot on sight" order for all American ships operating in the Atlantic, and on October 30, a German submarine sank an American destroyer. The war in the Atlantic was undeclared, and many Americans opposed it. But it was not Germany that dragged the United States into World War II.

The Path to Pearl Harbor

Japan, controlled by ambitious military leaders, was the aggressor in the Far East as Hitler's Germany was in Europe. Intent on becoming a major world power yet desperate for natural resources, especially oil, Japan was willing to risk war to get them. It invaded Manchuria in 1931 and launched an all-out assault on China in 1937. But Japanese leaders wanted to put off attacking the Philippines. For its part, the United States feared a two-front war and was willing to delay a confrontation with Japan until it had dealt with the German threat. Thus between 1938 and 1941, the United States and Japan engaged in diplomatic shadow boxing.

America exerted economic pressure on Japan in July 1939, giving the required six months' notice for cancellation of the 1911 commercial agreement between the two countries. In September 1940, the administration forbade shipping aircraft fuel and scrap metal to Japan. Other items were added to the embargo until by the spring of 1941 only oil could be shipped to Japan; the administration hoped that the threat of cutting off that important resource would force negotiations and avert a crisis. Japan opened negotiations with the United States, but there was little to discuss. Japan would not withdraw from China and from 1940 to 1941 occupied French Indochina. In July 1941, Roosevelt froze all Japanese assets in the United States, effectively embargoing trade with Japan.

Roosevelt had an advantage in negotiating with Japan, for Americans had broken the Japanese secret diplomatic code. But Japanese intentions were hard to decipher from the intercepted messages. American leaders knew that Japan planned to attack, but they didn't know where. In September 1941, the Japanese decided to strike sometime after November unless the United States offered real concessions.

On the morning of December 7, 1941, Japanese airplanes launched from aircraft carriers attacked the United States fleet at Pearl Harbor, in Hawaii. The surprise attack destroyed or disabled 19 ships (including five battleships) and 150 planes and killed 2,335 soldiers and sailors and 68 civilians. On the same day, Japan invaded the Philippines, Guam, Midway, and British Hong Kong and Malaya. The next day, Congress declared war on Japan.

December 7, 1941, was a day that "would live in infamy," Franklin Roosevelt told Congress and the nation as he asked for the declaration of war. It was also a day that would have far-reaching implications for American foreign policy and for American attitudes toward the world. The surprise attack united the country—even isolationists and "America Firsters"—as nothing else could have.

After the shock and anger subsided, Americans searched for a villain. The myth still persists that the villain was Roosevelt, who supposedly knew of the Japanese attack but failed to warn the military so that the American people might unite behind the war against Germany. But Roosevelt did not know. There was no warning that the attack was coming against Pearl Harbor, and the American ability to read Japanese coded messages was no help because the fleet kept radio silence.

An exploding American destroyer at Pearl Harbor, December 7, 1941. The attack on Pearl Harbor united the country and came to symbolize Japanese treachery and American lack of preparedness. Photographs such as this were published throughout the war to inspire Americans to work harder. (National Archives)

The Americans underestimated the Japanese, partly because of racial prejudice. They ignored many warning signals because they simply did not believe the Japanese capable of attacking a target as far away as Hawaii. Roosevelt and most experts expected the Japanese to attack the Philippines or Thailand. Many people blundered, but there was no conspiracy.

Even more important in the long run was the Japanese attack's effect on a generation of military and political leaders. Pearl Harbor became the symbol of unpreparedness. For a generation that had been stunned by an unscrupulous enemy attack, the lesson was to be ready to stop an aggressor before it struck. That lesson would influence American policy in Korea, Vietnam, and beyond.

THE HOME FRONT

Too often wars are described in terms of leaders, grand strategy, and elaborate campaigns. But wars affect all people—the soldiers who fight and the women and children and men who stay home. World War II especially had an impact on all aspects of society—the economy, entertainment, even attitudes toward women and blacks. For many people, the war represented opportunity and the end of the Depression. On others, it left lasting scars.

Mobilizing for War

Converting American industry to war production was a complex task. Shortly after Pearl Harbor, Roosevelt created the War Production Board (WPB) and appointed a high executive at Sears, Roebuck to mobilize resources for an all-out war effort. The WPB offered businesses "cost-plus" contracts, guaranteeing a generous profit. Often the government also financed new plants and equipment. Secretary of War Henry Stimson explained: "If you . . . go to war . . . in a capitalist country, you have to let business make money out of the process or business won't work."

The Roosevelt administration leaned over backward to gain the cooperation of businessmen, many of them alienated by New Deal policies. The president appointed many business executives to key positions and abandoned antitrust actions in any industry that was remotely war-related.

The policy worked. Industrial production and net corporate profits nearly doubled during the war. Large commercial farmers also profited. The war years accelerated the mechanization of the farm and dramatically increased the use of fertilizer, but between 1940 and 1945 the farm population declined by 17 percent.

Many government agencies besides the War Production Board helped run the war effort efficiently. The Office of Price Administration (OPA) set prices to control inflation and rationed products—and because it affected so many lives so disagreeably, many Americans regarded it as oppressive. The National War Labor Board (NWLB) had authority to set wages and hours and to monitor working conditions, and it could seize plants whose owners refused to cooperate.

Union membership grew rapidly, aided by government policy. In return for a "no-strike pledge," the NWLB allowed agreements that required workers to retain their union membership through the life of a contract. Responding to labor leaders' protests, the NWLB finally allowed a 15 percent cost-of-living increase on some contracts, but that did not apply to overtime pay, which helped drive up wages in some industries during the war by about 70 percent. Not content with wages, John L. Lewis broke the no-strike pledge by calling a nationwide coal strike in 1943. When Roosevelt ordered a government seizure of the mines, Lewis called off the strike. But his bold protest did help raise miners' wages.

Besides imposing wage and price controls and rationing, the government fought inflation by selling war bonds and increasing taxes. The Revenue Act of 1942 raised tax rates, broadened the tax base, boosted corporate taxes to 40 percent, and set the excess-profits tax at 90 percent. In addition, the government initiated payroll deductions, making the income tax a reality for most Americans for the first time.

Despite some unfairness and much confusion, the American economy turned out the equipment and supplies that eventually won the war. American industries built 300,000 airplanes, 88,140 tanks, and 3,000 merchant ships. In 1944 alone, American factories produced 800,000 tons of synthetic rubber to replace natural rubber, cut off by the Japanese. By the war's end, the American economy was turning out an astonishing 50 percent of all the world's goods.

Although the national debt grew from about $143 billion in 1943 to $260 billion in 1945, taxation paid for about 40 percent of the war's cost. At the same time, full employment and the increase in two-income families, together with forced savings, helped amass capital for postwar expansion. In a limited way, the tax policy also tended to redistribute wealth, which the New Deal had failed to do. The top 5 percent income bracket, which controlled 23 percent of the disposable income in 1939, accounted for only 17 percent in 1945.

The war stimulated the growth of the federal bureaucracy and accelerated the trend, begun during World War I and extended in the 1920s and 1930s, toward a central governmental role in the economy. The war also increased the cooperation between industry and government, creating what would later be called a military-industrial complex. But for most Americans, despite their anger at the OPA and the income tax, the war meant the end of the Depression.

A World War II poster depicting the many nations united in the fight against the Axis powers. In reality there were often disagreements. Notice to the right the American sailor is marching next to Chinese and Soviet soldiers. Within a few years after victory they would be enemies. (Courtesy The American Legion)

Patriotic Fervor

The war, so horrible elsewhere, was remote in the United States—except for the thousands of families that received the official telegram telling of a loved one killed in action. The government tried to keep the conflict alive in Americans' minds, and the country united behind the war effort. The Office of War Information, staffed by writers and advertising executives, controlled the news that the public received about the war, presenting things in the best possible light. The government also sold war bonds, not only to help pay for the war and reduce inflation but also to sell the war to the American people. As during World War I, celebrities appeared at bond rallies. Schoolchildren purchased war stamps and pasted them in an album until they had accumulated stamps worth $18.75, enough to buy a $25 bond (redeemable ten years later). Their bonds, they were told, would purchase bullets or an airplane part to kill "Japs" and Germans. Working men and women purchased bonds through payroll deduction plans and looked forward to spending the money on consumer goods after the war. In the end, the government sold over $135 billion in war bonds. While the bond drives did help control inflation, they were most important in making millions of Americans feel that they were contributing to the war effort.

Those too old or too young to join the armed forces served as air raid wardens or civilian defense and Red Cross volunteers. They raised victory gardens, contributed to scrap drives, and did without. "Hoarders are the same as spies," one ad announced.

Japanese-American children on their way to a "relocation center." For many Japanese-Americans, but especially for the children, the nightmare of the relocation camp experience would stay with them all their lives. (Library of Congress)

Internment of Japanese-Americans

Cooperating with the war effort fostered pride and a feeling of community—but also hate for the enemy. The Nazis, especially Hitler and his Gestapo, were synonymous with evil before 1941. Later, most Americans ceased making distinctions between Germans and Nazis, although the anti-German hysteria that had swept the country during World War I never returned.

The Japanese were easier to hate. The attack on Pearl Harbor created a special animosity toward them, but depicting them as warlike and subhuman owed something to old fears of the so-called yellow peril. Two weeks after Pearl Harbor, *Time* magazine told Americans how to distinguish the friendly Chinese from "the Japs." "Chinese . . . have an easy gait. The Chinese expression is likely to be more kindly, placid, open; the Japanese more positive, dogmatic, arrogant."

Racial stereotypes played a role in the treatment of Japanese-Americans during the war. They were the only group confined in concentration camps, in the greatest mass abridgment of civil liberties in American history.

At the time of Pearl Harbor, about 127,000 Japanese-Americans lived in the United States, most on the West Coast. About 80,000 were *nisei* (Japanese born in the United States and holding American citizenship) and *sansei* (the sons and daughters of *nisei*); the rest were *issei* (aliens born in Japan who were ineligible for U.S. citizenship). They had long suffered from prejudice—barred, for example, from intermarriage with other groups and excluded from many clubs, restaurants, and recreation facilities. Many worked as tenant farmers, fishermen, or small businessmen, or were land-owning farmers, but some belonged to a small professional class of lawyers, teachers, and doctors.

Although many retained cultural ties to Japan and spoke Japanese, these people posed no more threat to the country than did the much larger groups of Italian-Americans and German-Americans. But their physical characteristics made them stand out. After Pearl Harbor, an anti-Japanese panic seized the West Coast. Rumors suggested that Japanese fishermen were preparing to mine harbors, blow up tunnels, and poison water supplies.

West Coast politicians and citizens urged the War Department to remove the Japanese. The president capitulated and issued Executive Order 9066, authorizing the evacuation in February 1942. "The continued pressure of a largely unassimilated, tightly knit racial group, bound to an enemy nation by strong ties of race, culture, custom and religion, constituted a menace which had to be dealt with," General John De Witt argued, justifying the removal on military grounds. But racial fear and hatred, not military necessity, stood behind the order.

"The Japs live like rats, breed like rats, and act like rats. We don't want them," the governor of Idaho announced. So it was in remote, often arid, sections of the West that eventually the government built the primitive "relocation centers." "When I first entered our room, I became sick to my stomach," a Japanese-American woman remembered.

The government evacuated about 110,000 Japanese, who lost almost all their property. Farmers left their crops to be harvested by their American neighbors. Store owners sold out for a small percentage of what their goods were worth. Japanese-Americans lost all their personal possessions, and something more—their pride and respect.

The evacuation appears unjustified in retrospect. In Hawaii, with its much larger Japanese-American population, authorities attempted no evacuation, and no sabotage and little disloyalty occurred. Late in the war, the government allowed Japanese-American men to volunteer for military service, and many served bravely in the European theater. The 442nd Infantry Combat Team, made up entirely of *nisei,* became the most decorated unit in all the military service—another indication of the loyalty and patriotism of the Japanese-Americans. In 1988, Congress belatedly apologized and voted limited compensation for Japanese-Americans relocated during World War II.

African- and Hispanic-Americans at War

Black Americans profited little from the wartime revival of prosperity and the expansion of jobs early in the war. Those who joined the military were usually assigned to menial jobs, always in segregated units with whites as the high-ranking officers. The myth persisted that black soldiers had failed to perform well in World War I.

Some black leaders found it especially ironic that as the country prepared to fight Hitler and his racist policies, the United States kept its own brand of racism. A black labor leader, A. Philip Randolph, decided to act. Randolph had worked with the first wave of African-Americans migrating from the South to the northern cities during and just after World War I. Afterwards he organized and led the Brotherhood of Sleeping Car Porters, and in 1937 finally won grudging recognition of the union from the Pullman Company.

Even before the United States entered the war, black families like this one moved north to look for work and a better life. This massive migration would change the racial mix in northern cities. (Library of Congress)

Admired by black leaders of all political persuasions, Randolph convinced many of them in 1941 to join him in a march on Washington to demand equal rights. The thought of as many as 100,000 African-Americans marching in protest in the nation's capital alarmed Roosevelt. At first, he sent his assistants and his wife Eleanor, who was greatly admired in the black community, to dissuade Randolph. Finally, he talked to Randolph in person on June 18, 1941, and they struck a bargain. Roosevelt refused to desegregate the armed forces, but in return for Randolph's calling off the march, the president issued Executive Order 8802, which stated that it was government policy that "there shall be no discrimination in the employment of workers in defense industries or government because of race, creed, color or national origin." To enforce the order, he established the Fair Employment Practices Commission (FEPC).

By threatening militant action, the black leaders wrested a major concession from the president. But the executive order did not end prejudice, and the FEPC (which its chairman described as the "most hated agency in Washington") had limited success in erasing the color line. Many black soldiers were angered and humiliated throughout the war by being made to sit in the back of buses and being barred from hotels and restaurants. A former black soldier recalled being refused service in a restaurant in Salina, Kansas, while the same restaurant served German prisoners from a camp nearby. "We continued to stare," he recalled. "This was really happening . . . . The people of Salina would serve these enemy soldiers and turn away black American G.I.'s."

Jobs in war industries helped many African-Americans improve their economic conditions. Continuing the migration that had begun during World War I, about 750,000 southern blacks moved to northern and western cities. Some became skilled workers and a few became professionals. The new arrivals increased pressure on overcrowded housing and other facilities, accentuating tension among all hard-pressed groups. In Detroit, a major race riot broke out in the summer of 1943 after Polish-Americans protested a public housing development that promised to bring blacks into their neighborhood. A series of incidents led to fights between black and white young people and then to looting in the black community. Before federal and state troops restored order, 25 blacks and 9 whites had been killed and more than $2 million worth of property was destroyed. Groups of whites roamed the city attacking blacks, overturning cars, setting fires, and sometimes killing wantonly. Other riots broke out in Mobile, Los Angeles, New York, and Beaumont, Texas. In all these cities, and in many others where the tension did not lead to open violence, the legacy of hate lasted long after the war.

Mexican-Americans, like most minority groups, benefited from wartime job opportunities, but they, too, faced prejudice. In California and in many parts of the Southwest, Mexicans could not use public swimming pools and certain restaurants. Usually they were limited to menial jobs and were constantly harassed by the police. In Los Angeles, anti-Mexican prejudice got violent. Most of the anger focused on Mexican gang members wearing zoot suits—long, loose coats with padded shoulders, ballooned pants, and a wide-brimmed hat.

Zoot-suiters especially angered soldiers and sailors in Los Angeles. After many provocative incidents, the violence peaked on June 7, 1943, when gangs of servicemen attacked all the young zoot-suiters they could find or anyone who looked Mexican. The servicemen, joined by others, beat up the Mexicans, stripped off their offensive clothes, and cut the long, duck-tailed hair that was part of the look. The police usually looked the other way or arrested the victims. The local press and the chamber of commerce hotly denied that race was a factor, but *Time* magazine was probably closer to the truth when it called the riots the "ugliest brand of mob action since the coolie race riots of the 1870s."

SOCIAL IMPACT OF THE WAR

Modern wars have been incredibly destructive of lives and property, but they have had social consequences as well. World War II altered patterns of work, leisure, education, and family life; caused a massive migration of people; created jobs; and changed lifestyles. It is difficult to overemphasize the war's social impact.

Wartime Opportunities

More than 15 million American civilians moved during the war. Like the Momadays, many left home seeking better jobs. For Native Americans, wartime opportunities caused a migration into the cities—as it did for countless other Americans who left farms and small towns for urban defense jobs. California alone gained more than two million people during the war. But Americans also moved from the rural South into northern cities, and a smaller number moved from the North to the South. Two hundred thousand came to the Detroit area, nearly a half-million to Los Angeles, and about 100,000 to Mobile, Alabama. They put pressure on the schools, housing, and other services. In Los Angeles, Mrs. Colin Kelley, the widow of a war hero, could find no place to live until a newspaper publicized her plight.

Nowhere was the change more dramatic than in the West, which the wartime boom transformed more dramatically than any development since the nineteenth-century economic revolution created by the railroads and mining. The federal government spent over $70 billion in California (one-tenth of the total for the entire country) on army bases, shipyards, supply depots, and testing sites. Private industry built so many facilities that the region became the center of a growing military-industrial complex. This spectacular growth created housing shortages and overwhelmed schools, hospitals and municipal services. Crime, prostitution, and racial tension all rose.

For the first time in years, many families had money to spend, but they had nothing to spend it on. The last new car rolled off the assembly line in February 1942. There were no washing machines, refrigerators, or radios in the stores, little gasoline and few tires. Even when people had time off, they tended to stay home, go to the movies or listen to the radio.

The war required major adjustments in American family life. With several million men in the service or working at faraway defense jobs, the number of households headed by a woman increased dramatically. The number of marriages also rose sharply. Early in the war, a young man could be deferred if he had a dependent, including a wife. Later, many servicemen got married, often to women they barely knew, because they wanted a little excitement and perhaps someone to come home to. Reversing a decline that extended back to the colonial period, the birthrate also began to rise in 1940, as young couples started families as fast as they could. Since birthrates had been especially low during the Depression, the shift marked a significant change. Some children—"good-bye babies"—were conceived just before the husband joined the military or went overseas. Illegitimacy and divorce rates also went up sharply. Yet most wartime marriages survived, and many of the women left behind looked ahead to a normal life after the war.

Women Workers for Victory

Thousands of women took jobs in heavy industry that once would have been considered unladylike. They built tanks, airplanes, and ships, but they still earned less than men. At first, women were rarely taken on because, as the war in Europe pulled American industry out of its long slump, unemployed men snapped up the newly available positions.

But by 1943, with many men drafted and male unemployment virtually nonexistent, the government was quick to suggest that it was women's patriotic duty to join the assembly line. A popular song was "Rosie the Riveter," who helped her marine boyfriend by "working overtime on the riveting machine."

At the end of the war, the labor force included 19.5 million women, but three-fourths of them had been working before the conflict, and some of the new ones might have sought work in normal times. The new women war workers tended to be older, and they were more often married than single. Some worked for patriotic reasons. "Every time I test a batch of rubber, I know it's going to help bring my three sons home quicker," said a woman worker in a rubber plant. But others worked for the money or to have something useful to do. Yet in 1944, women's weekly wages averaged $31.21, compared with $54.65 for men, reflecting women's menial tasks and low seniority as well as outright discrimination. Married women with young children found it difficult to obtain jobs. There were few day-care facilities, and women were often told that they should be home with their children. Women workers often had to endure overt sexual harassment. Still, most persisted, and they tried to look feminine despite work clothes.

Black women faced the most difficult situation. Often, when they applied for work, they were told something like "We have not yet installed separate toilet facilities." Not until 1944 did the telephone company in New York City hire a black operator. Still, some black women moved during the war from domestic jobs to higher-paying factory work.

Many women war workers quickly left their jobs after the war ended. Some left by choice, but dismissals ran twice as high for women as for men. Some women who learned what an extra paycheck meant for the family's standard of living would have preferred to keep working. But most women, and even more men, agreed at the war's end that women did not deserve an "equal chance with men" for jobs.

Entertaining the People

According to one survey, Americans listened to the radio an average of four and a half hours a day during the war. The major networks increased their news programs from less than 4 percent to nearly 30 percent of broadcasting time. Americans heard Edward R. Murrow broadcasting from London during the German air blitz with air raid sirens in the background. Often static made listening difficult, but the live broadcasts had an authenticity never before possible. Commentators became celebrities on whom millions depended for war news.

The war intruded on almost all programming. Ads reminded listeners of the fighting. Lucky Strikes, whose package color changed from green to white because there was a shortage of green pigment, made "Lucky Strike Green Has Gone to War" almost as famous as "Remember Pearl Harbor." Serials, the standard fare of daytime radio, adopted wartime themes. Popular music, which occupied a large share of radio programming, mirrored the war. There was "Goodbye, Mama (I'm Off to Yokohama)," but more numerous were songs of romance, love, separation, and hope for a better time after the war. The danceable tunes of Glenn Miller and Tommy Dorsey became just as much a part of wartime memories as ration books and far-off battlefields.

For many Americans, the motion picture became the most important leisure activity. Movie attendance averaged about 100 million viewers a week. There might not be gasoline for Sunday drives, but the whole family could go to the movies. Even those in the military could watch American movies on board ship or at a remote outpost. "Pinups" of Hollywood stars decorated barracks, tanks, and planes wherever American troops went.

The war engulfed Hollywood. Newsreels offering a visual synopsis of war news, always with an upbeat message and a touch of human interest, preceded most movies. Their theme was that the Americans were winning, even if early on there was little evidence of it. Many feature films also had a wartime theme, picturing the Pacific war complete with grinning Japanese villains (usually played by Chinese or Korean actors). In the beginning, the Japanese won, but in the end they always got "what they deserved." Movies set in Europe differed somewhat from those depicting the Pacific war. British and Americans heroes behind enemy lines outwitted Nazis at every turn, sabotaged installations, and escaped in a captured plane.

A number of Hollywood actors went into the service, and some even became heroes. Most, like Ronald Reagan, were employed to produce, narrate, or act in government films. The Office of War Information produced short subjects and documentaries, some of them distinguished, like John Huston's *Battle of San Pietro*, a realistic depiction of war on the Italian front. More typical were propaganda films aimed at American soldiers. *Letter from Bataan* (1942) portrayed a wounded GI who wrote home asking his brother-in-law to save his razor blades because "it takes twelve thousand razor blades to make a one-thousand-pound bomb." The film ended by announcing that the soldier had died in the hospital.

The GIs' War

GI, short for *government issue,* became the affectionate designation for the ordinary soldier in World War II. The GIs came from every background and ethnic group. Some served reluctantly, some eagerly. A few became genuine heroes, and all were turned into heroes by the press and the public, who seemed to believe that one American could easily defeat at least 20 Japanese or Germans. Ernie Pyle, a war correspondent who chronicled the authentic story of the ordinary GI, wrote of soldiers "just toiling from day to day in a world full of insecurity, discomfort, homesickness, and a dulled sense of danger."

In the midst of battle, the war was no fun, but only one soldier in eight ever saw combat, and even for many of them the war was a great adventure (just as World War I had been). "When World War II broke out I was delighted," Mario Puzo, author of *The Godfather,* remembered. "My country called."

Mexican-Americans were drafted and volunteered in great numbers. A third of a million served in all branches of the military, a larger percentage than for many other ethnic groups. Although they encountered prejudice, they probably found less in the armed forces than at home, and many returned to civilian life with new ambitions and self-esteem.

Many Native Americans also served, often recruited for special service in the Marine Signal Corps. One group of Navajo completely befuddled the Japanese with a code based on their native language. But the Navajo code talkers and all other Indians who chose to return to reservations after the war were ineligible for benefits like veterans' loans and hospitalization. (They lived on federal land, and that, by law, canceled the advantages that other veterans enjoyed.)

For African-Americans, who served throughout the war in segregated units and faced prejudice everywhere, the military experience also had much to teach. Fewer blacks were sent overseas (about 79,000 of 504,000 blacks in the service in 1943), and fewer were in combat outfits, so the percentage of black soldiers killed and wounded was low. Many illiterate blacks, especially from the South, learned to read and write. Blacks who went overseas began to realize that not everyone viewed them as inferior. Most realized the paradox of fighting for freedom when they themselves had little freedom; they hoped things would improve after the war.

Because the war lasted longer than World War I, its impact was greater. In all, over 16 million men and women served in the military. About 322,000 were killed, and more than 800,000 were wounded. The 12,000 listed as missing just disappeared. The war claimed many more lives than World War I and was the nation's costliest after the Civil War. But penicillin, blood plasma, sulfa drugs, and rapid battlefield evacuation made it twice as likely for the wounded in World War II to survive as in World War I. Penicillin also minimized the threat of venereal disease, but all men who served still saw an anti-VD film.

Women in Uniform

Women have served in all American wars as nurses and cooks and in other support capacities, and during World War II many continued in these roles. A few nurses landed in France just days after the Normandy invasion. Nurses with the Army and the Marines in the Pacific dug their own foxholes and treated men under fire. Sixty-six nurses spent the entire war in the Philippines as prisoners of the Japanese. Most nurses, however, were far behind the lines.

Although nobody objected to women nurses, not until April 1943 did women physicians win the right to join the Army and Navy Medical Corps. Despite some objections, Congress authorized full military participation (except combat duty) for women because they would free men for combat. World War II thus became the first U.S. war in which women received regular military status. About 350,000 women joined up, most in the Women's Army Corps (WACS) and the women's branch of the Navy (WAVES).

Many recruiting posters suggested that the services needed women "for the precision work at which women are so adept" or to attend to the wounded "as only women can do." Still, men and women were not treated equally. Women were explicitly kept out of combat situations and were often underused by male officers who found it difficult to view women in nontraditional roles. Army nurses with officer rank were forbidden to date enlisted men.

Men were informed about contraceptives and encouraged to use them, but information about birth control was explicitly prohibited for women. Rumors charged many servicewomen with promiscuity, spread apparently by men uncomfortable with women's invasion of the male military domain. Pregnancy brought instant dismissal; yet the pregnancy rate for both married and unmarried women remained low.

Thus, despite difficulties, women played important roles during the war, and when they left the service they had the same rights as male veterans. The women in the service did not permanently alter the military or the public's perception of women's proper role, but they did change a few minds, and many of these women had their lives altered and their horizons broadened.

A WAR OF DIPLOMATS AND GENERALS

Pearl Harbor thrust the country into war with Japan. On December 11, 1941, Hitler declared war on the United States. The reason why has never been fully explained. He was not required by his treaty with Japan to go to war with the United States, and without his action the United States might have concentrated on fighting Japan. Hitler forced the United States into war against the Axis powers in both Europe and Asia.

War Aims

What did the United States hope to accomplish? Roosevelt and other American leaders never really decided. In a speech before Congress in January 1941, Roosevelt had mentioned the four freedoms: freedom of speech and expression, freedom of worship, freedom from want, and freedom from fear. For many Americans, this was what they were fighting for. Roosevelt spoke vaguely of extending democracy and establishing a peacekeeping organization, but in direct contrast to Woodrow Wilson he never spelled out in any detail the political purposes for fighting. The only American policy was to end the war as quickly as possible and to solve the political problems it created when the time came.

Roosevelt and his advisers decided on a holding action in the Pacific while concentrating efforts against Hitler in Europe. But the United States was not fighting alone. It joined the Soviet Union and Great Britain in a difficult, but ultimately effective, anti-Nazi alliance. Churchill and Roosevelt got along well, although they often disagreed on strategy. Roosevelt's relationship with Stalin was much more strained, but often he agreed with the Soviet leader about the way to fight the war. Stalin, who had destroyed hundreds of thousands of potential or actual opponents, distrusted both the British and the Americans, but he needed them, just as they depended on him. Without the tremendous Russian sacrifices in 1941 and 1942, Germany would have won the war before the vast American military and industrial might could be mobilized.

Year of Disaster, 1942

The first half of 1942 was disastrous for the Allies. The Japanese captured the resource-rich Dutch East Indies, swept into Burma, took Wake and Guam, and invaded Alaska's Aleutian Islands. They pushed American forces in the Philippines onto the Bataan peninsula and finally onto the tiny island of Corregidor, where General Jonathan Wainwright surrendered more than 11,000 men to the Japanese. American reporters tried to play down the disasters, concentrating on tales of American heroism against overwhelming odds.

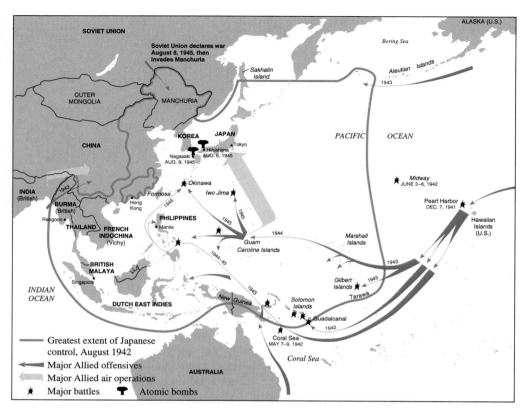

WORLD WAR II: PACIFIC THEATER   After the surprise attack on Pearl Harbor, the Japanese extended their control in the Pacific from Burma to the Aleutian Islands and almost to Australia. But after American naval and air victories at Coral Sea and Midway in 1942, the Japanese were increasingly on the defensive.

In Europe, the Germans pushed deep into Russia, threatening to take all the industrial centers, the valuable oil fields, and even Moscow. In North Africa, General Erwin Rommel's mechanized Afrika Korps neared the Suez Canal. U-boats sank British and American ships faster than they could be replaced. For a few dark months in 1942, it seemed that the Axis would win before the United States got ready.

The Allies could not agree on a military strategy in Europe. Churchill advocated tightening the ring around Germany, using bombing raids to weaken the enemy and encouraging resistance among the occupied countries but avoiding any direct assault on the continent until success was assured, thus preventing casualties on the scale of Britain's vast losses during World War I. Stalin demanded a second front, an invasion of Europe in 1942 to relieve the pressure on the Red Army, which faced 200 German divisions along a 2,000-mile front. Roosevelt agreed to an offensive in 1942. But the invasion in 1942 was not in France but North Africa. The decision was probably right from a military point of view, but it taught Russia to distrust Britain and the United States.

Landing in North Africa in November 1942, American and British troops tried to link up with a beleaguered British army fighting westward from Egypt. The

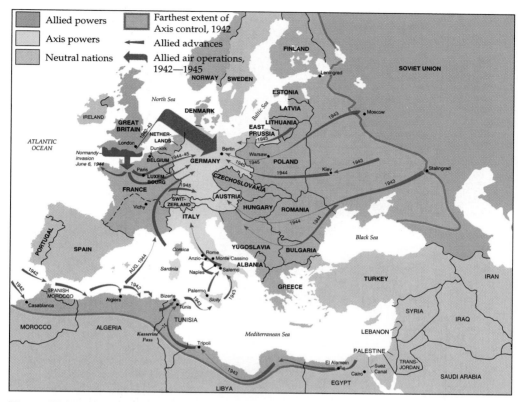

Allied powers	Farthest extent of Axis control, 1942	
Axis powers	Allied advances	
Neutral nations	Allied air operations, 1942—1945	

WORLD WAR II: EUROPEAN AND NORTH AFRICAN THEATERS The German war machine swept across Europe and North Africa and almost captured Cairo and Moscow, but after major defeats at Stalingrad and El Alamein in 1943, the Axis powers were in retreat. Many lives were lost on both sides before the Allied victory in 1945.

American army, enthusiastic but inexperienced, met little resistance until, at Kasserine Pass in Tunisia, the Germans counterattacked and destroyed a large American force, inflicting 5,000 casualties. Roosevelt, who launched the invasion in part to give the American people a victory to relieve dreary news from the Far East, learned that victories often came with long casualty lists.

Conquering French North Africa drew Roosevelt into unpleasant political compromises. To gain a cease-fire, the United States recognized a provisional government under Admiral Jean Darlan, a former Nazi collaborator. Did this mean that the United States would negotiate with Mussolini? Or with Hitler? The Darlan deal reinforced Soviet distrust of the Americans and angered many Americans.

Roosevelt never made a deal with Hitler, but he did aid Fascist Spain in return for safe passage of American shipping into the Mediterranean. But the United States did not aid only right-wing dictators like Franco. It also supplied arms to the left-wing resistance in France, to the Communist guerrilla Tito in Yugoslavia, and to Ho Chi Minh, the anti-French resistance leader in Indochina. Roosevelt also authorized large-scale, lend-lease aid to the Soviet Union. Although liberals criticized his support of dictators, Roosevelt was willing to do almost anything to win the war.

Only at the end of the war did the world learn of the horrors of the Nazi concentration camps and the gas chambers. (UPI/Corbis-Bettmann)

Even on the issue of the plight of the Jews in Nazi-occupied Europe, Roosevelt's solution was to win the war as quickly as possible. By November 1942, confirmed information reached the United States that the Nazis were systematically exterminating Jews. Yet the administration did nothing for more than a year, and even then it did scandalously little. Only 21,000 refugees were allowed to enter the United States over a period of three and a half years, just 10 percent of those who could have been admitted under immigration quotas. The War Department refused to bomb the Auschwitz gas chambers, and officials turned down many rescue schemes. Widespread anti-Semitism in the United States in the 1940s and fears of massive Jewish immigration help explain the administration's failure. The failure of the media, Christian leaders, and even American Jews to bring effective pressure on the government does not excuse the president for his shameful indifference to the systematic murder of millions of people. Roosevelt could not have prevented the Holocaust, but vigorous action by him could have saved many thousands of lives. Roosevelt was not always right, nor even consistent. People who assumed he had a master strategy or a fixed ideological position misunderstood him.

A Strategy for Ending the War

The commanding general of the Allied armies in the North African campaign emerged as a genuine leader. Born in Texas, Dwight D. Eisenhower spent his boyhood in Abilene, Kansas. His small-town background made it easy for the media to make him an American hero. Eisenhower, however, had not come to hero status easily. In World War I, he trained soldiers in Texas. He was only a lieutenant colonel when World War II erupted. But George Marshall, who became the Army's top general in September 1939, had discovered Eisenhower's talents even before the war began. He was quickly promoted to general and achieved a reputation as an expert planner and organizer. Gregarious and outgoing, "Ike" had a broad smile that made most people like him instantly. He was not a brilliant field commander and made many mistakes in the African campaign, but he could get diverse people working together, which was crucial where British and American units had to cooperate.

The American army moved slowly across North Africa, linked up with the British, invaded Sicily in July 1943, and finally stormed ashore in Italy in September. The Italian campaign proved long and bitter. After the overthrow of Mussolini and Italy's surrender in September 1943, the Germans occupied the country and bogged down the American army. The Allies did not reach Rome until June 1944, and they never controlled all of Italy.

Despite the decision to make the war in Europe the first priority, American ships and planes halted the Japanese advance in the spring of 1942. In the Battle of Coral Sea in May 1942, American carrier-based planes inflicted heavy damage on the Japanese fleet and probably prevented the invasion of Australia. It was the first naval battle in history in which surface ships did not fire on each other; airplanes did all the damage. In World War II, aircraft carriers were more important than battleships. A month later, at the Battle of Midway, American planes sank four Japanese carriers and destroyed nearly 300 planes. This first major Japanese defeat restored some balance of power in the Pacific and ended the threat to Hawaii.

In 1943, the American sea and land forces leapfrogged from island to island, retaking territory and building bases to attack the Philippines and eventually Japan. Progress often had terrible costs. In November 1943, about 5,000 Marines landed on the coral beaches of the tiny island of Tarawa. Despite heavy naval bombardment and the support of hundreds of planes, they met heavy resistance. The four-day battle killed more than 1,000 Americans and wounded over 3,000. One general thought it was all wasted effort—that the island should have been bypassed. Others disagreed. No one asked the Marines who hit the beaches. Less than half of the first wave survived.

The Invasion of Europe

Operation Overlord, the code name for the largest amphibious invasion in history, the invasion Stalin had wanted in 1942, began only on June 6, 1944. It was, according to Churchill, "the most difficult and complicated operation that has ever taken place." The initial assault along a 60-mile stretch of the Normandy coast was conducted with 175,000 men supported by 600 warships and 11,000 planes. Within a month, over a million troops and more than 170,000 vehicles had landed.

Eisenhower coordinated and planned the operation. During the first hours of the invasion, there seemed to be too many supplies. It cost 2,245 killed and 1,670 wounded to secure the beachhead. "It was much lighter than anybody expected," one observer remarked. "But if you saw faces instead of numbers on the casualty list, it wasn't light at all."

More than 1.5 million tons of bombs fell on Europe. Evidence gathered after the war suggests that this bombardment disrupted German war production less than Allied strategists expected. Often a plant or a rail center would be back in operation days or hours after an attack, and the bombing of the cities may have strengthened the German people's resolve to fight to the bitter end. Nor did the destruction of German cities come cheaply. Fighters and antiaircraft guns shot down 22 of 60 B-17s on June 23, 1943.

The most destructive bombing raid of the war, against Dresden on the night of February 13–14, 1945, had no strategic purpose. It was launched by the British and Americans to help demonstrate to Stalin that they were aiding the Russian offensive. Dresden, a city of 630,000, was a communications center. Three waves of planes dropped 650,000 incendiary bombs, causing a firestorm that swept over eight square miles, destroying everything in its path, and killing an estimated 60,000 civilians.

With eccentric General George Patton leading the charge and staid General Omar Bradley in command, the American army broke out of the Normandy beachhead in July 1944 and swept across France. American productive capacity and the ability to supply a mobile and motorized army eventually brought victory. But not all American equipment was superior. The American fighter plane, the P-40, could not compete early in the war with the German ME-109. The United States was far behind Germany in the development of rockets, but that was not as important as the American inability, until the end of the war, to develop a tank that could compete in armament or firepower with the German tanks. The American army partly made up for the deficiency of its tanks by having superior artillery. Perhaps even more important, most American soldiers had grown up tinkering with cars and radios. Children of the machine age, they managed to keep tanks, trucks, and guns functioning under difficult circumstances, which gave the American army superior mobility.

By late 1944, the American and British armies had driven across France, while the Russians had pushed far into eastern Europe. The war seemed nearly over. However, just before Christmas in 1944, the Germans launched a massive counterattack on the western front against thinly dispersed and inexperienced American troops. The Germans drove 50 miles inside the American lines before they were checked. During this so-called Battle of the Bulge, Eisenhower was so desperate for additional troops that he offered to pardon any military prisoners in Europe who would go into battle. Most declined. Eisenhower also promised any black soldiers in the service and supply outfits an opportunity to become infantrymen in the white units, though usually with a lower rank. However, his chief of staff pointed out that this was the "most dangerous thing I have seen in regard to race relations." Eisenhower recanted, not wishing to start a social revolution.

The Politics of Victory

As American and British armies assaulted Germany in the winter and spring of 1945, the political and diplomatic aspects of the war began to overshadow military concerns. Relations between the Soviet Union and the other Allies had been badly strained during the war; with victory in sight, tension grew. Although the American press idealized Stalin and the Russian people, a number of high-level American diplomats and presidential advisers distrusted the Russians and anticipated a postwar confrontation. They urged Roosevelt to make military decisions with the postwar political situation in mind.

The main issue in the spring of 1945 was who would capture Berlin. The British wanted to beat the Russians to the capital city. Eisenhower, however, fearing that the Germans might hold out indefinitely in the Alps, ordered the armies south rather than toward Berlin. He also wanted to avoid unnecessary American casualties, and he planned to meet the Russian army at an easily marked spot to avoid any unfortunate incidents. British and American forces could probably not have arrived in Berlin before the Russians, but Eisenhower's decision generated controversy after the war. Russian and American troops met on April 25, 1945, at the Elbe River. On May 2, the Russians took Berlin. Hitler had just committed suicide. The long war in Europe finally ended on May 8, 1945.

Meanwhile, throughout 1944, the United States had tightened the noose on Japan. Long-range B-29 bombers began sustained strikes on the Japanese mainland in June 1944, and by November they were firebombing Tokyo. In a series of naval and air engagements, especially at the Battle of Leyte Gulf, American planes destroyed most of the remaining Japanese navy. By the end of 1944, an American victory in the Pacific was all but assured. American forces recaptured the Philippines early the next year. Yet it might take years to conquer the Japanese home islands.

While the military campaigns reached a critical stage, Roosevelt ran for a fourth term. He dropped Vice President Henry Wallace from the ticket because some thought him too radical and impetuous. To replace him, the Democratic convention selected a relatively unknown senator from Missouri. Harry S Truman's only fame had come from leading a Senate investigation of war contracts.

The Republicans nominated Thomas Dewey, the colorless and moderate governor of New York, who had a difficult time criticizing Roosevelt without appearing unpatriotic. Roosevelt seemed haggard and ill during much of the campaign, but he won easily. He would need all his strength to deal with the difficult problems ahead.

The Big Three at Yalta

Roosevelt, Churchill, and Stalin met at the Soviet resort city of Yalta in February 1945 to discuss the peace settlements. Most of the Yalta agreements were secret, and during the subsequent Cold War they would become controversial. Roosevelt wanted Soviet help in ending the Pacific war, to avoid the slaughter of American men in an invasion of Japan. In return for a promise to enter the war within three months after the war in Europe was over, the Soviet Union was granted the Kurile Islands, the southern half of Sakhalin Island, and railroads and port facilities in

Korea, Manchuria, and Mongolia. That later seemed like a heavy price to pay, but realistically the Soviet Union controlled most of this territory and could not have been dislodged without war.

When the provisions of the secret treaties were revealed much later, many people would accuse Roosevelt of trusting Stalin too much. But Roosevelt wanted to retain a working relationship with Moscow to preserve the peace, and he hoped to get Soviet agreement to cooperate with the new peace-preserving United Nations.

The European section of the Yalta agreement proved even more controversial. It was decided to partition Germany and to divide Berlin. The Polish agreements were even more difficult to swallow. The Polish government-in-exile in London was militantly anti-Communist and looked forward to returning home after the war. Stalin demanded that eastern Poland be given to the Soviet Union. Churchill and Roosevelt finally agreed to the Russian demands with the proviso that Poland be compensated with German territory on its western border. Stalin agreed to include some London Poles in the pro-Soviet Polish government and to "free and unfettered elections as soon as possible."

The Polish settlement would prove divisive after the war, for it quickly became clear that what the British and Americans wanted in eastern Europe contrasted with what the Soviet Union intended. Yet at the time it seemed imperative that Russia enter the war in the Pacific, and the reality was that in 1945 the Soviet army occupied most of eastern Europe.

The most potentially valuable accomplishment at Yalta was Stalin's agreement to join Roosevelt and Churchill in calling a conference in San Francisco in April 1945 to draft a United Nations charter. The charter gave primary responsibility for keeping global peace to the Security Council, composed of five permanent members (the United States, the Soviet Union, Great Britain, France, and China) and six other nations elected for two-year terms.

The Atomic Age Begins

Two months after Yalta, on April 12, 1945, Roosevelt died suddenly. Hated and loved to the end, he was replaced by Harry Truman, who was more difficult to hate and harder to love. In the beginning, Truman seemed tentative and unsure. Yet it fell to him to make some of history's most difficult decisions.

The Manhattan Project, organized in 1941, was one of the best-kept secrets of the war. A distinguished group of scientists, headquartered at Los Alamos, New Mexico, had orders to build an atomic bomb before Germany did. But by the time the bomb was successfully tested in the New Mexico desert on July 16, 1945, the war in Europe had ended.

The scientists working on the bomb assumed they were perfecting a military weapon. Yet when they first saw its ghastly power, remembered J. Robert Oppenheimer, a leading scientist on the project, "some wept, a few cheered. Most stood silently." Some opposed using the bomb. They realized its revolutionary power and worried about the future reputation of the United States if it unleashed this new force. But a presidential committee made up of scientists, military leaders, and politicians recommended that it be dropped on a military target in Japan as soon as possible.

"The final decision of where and when to use the atomic bomb was up to me," Truman later remembered. "Let there be no doubt about it. I regarded the bomb as a military weapon and never had any doubt that it should be used." But the decision had military and political ramifications. Even though Japan had lost most of its empire by the summer of 1945, it still had several million troops and thousands of kamikaze planes, whose pilots gave their lives by crashing, heavily laden with bombs, into an American ship. There was little defense against them.

Even with the Russian promise to enter the war, it appeared that an amphibious landing on the Japanese mainland would be necessary. The month-long battle for Iwo Jima, 750 miles from Tokyo, had killed over 4,000 Americans and wounded 15,000, and the battle for Okinawa was even more costly. Invading the Japanese mainland would presumably be far worse. The bomb, many thought, could end the war without an invasion. Some people involved in the decision wanted to avenge Pearl Harbor, and still others felt they needed to justify spending over $2 billion on the project in the first place. To some historians, the timing of the first bomb indicates that the decision was intended to impress the Russians and ensure that they had little to do with the peace settlement in the Far East.

Historians debate whether the use of the atomic bomb on Japanese cities was necessary to end the war, but for the hundreds of thousands of American troops waiting to invade Japan, there was no question about the rightness of the decision. They believed that it saved their lives. On August 6, 1945, two days before the Soviet Union had promised to enter the war against Japan, a B29 bomber, the "Enola Gay," dropped a single atomic bomb over Hiroshima. It killed or severely wounded 140,000 civilians and destroyed four square miles of the city. One of the men on the plane thought that they had missed the target: "I didn't see any sign of the city." The Soviet Union entered the war on August 8. When Japan refused to surrender, a second bomb destroyed Nagasaki on August 9. The Japanese surrendered five days later. The war was over, but the problems of the atomic age and the postwar world were only beginning.

✦✦✦✦✦✦

CONCLUSION

Peace, Prosperity, and International Responsibilities

The United States emerged from World War II with an enhanced reputation as the world's most powerful industrial and military nation. The demands of the war had finally ended the Great Depression and brought prosperity to most Americans. The war had also increased the power of the federal government. The payroll deduction of federal income taxes, begun during the war, symbolized the growth of a federal bureaucracy that affected the lives of all Americans. The war had also ended American isolationism and made the United States into the dominant international power. Of all the nations that fought in the war, the United States had suffered the least. No bombs were dropped on American factories, and no cities were destroyed. Although more than 300,000 Americans lost their lives, even this carnage seemed minimal when compared with the more than 20 million Russian soldiers and civilians who died or the 6 million Jews and millions of others systematically exterminated by Hitler.

TIMELINE

1931–1932	1933	1934	1935	1936
Japan seizes Manchuria	Hitler becomes German chancellor; United States recognizes the Soviet Union; Roosevelt extends Good Neighbor policy	Germany begins rearmament	Italy invades Ethiopia; First Neutrality Act	Spanish civil war begins; Second Neutrality Act; Roosevelt reelected

1937	1938	1939	1940	1941
Third Neutrality Act	Hitler annexes Austria, occupies Sudetenland; German persecution of Jews intensifies	Nazi-Soviet Pact German invasion of Poland; World War II begins	Roosevelt elected for a third term; Selective Service Act	FDR's "Four Freedoms" speech; Proposed black march on Washington; Executive order outlaws discrimination in defense industries; Lend-Lease Act; Germany attacks Russia; Japanese assets in United States frozen; Japanese attack Pearl Harbor; United States declares war on Japan; Germany declares war on United States

1942	1943	1944	1945
Internment of Japanese-Americans; Second Allied front in Africa launched	Invasion of Sicily; Italian campaign; Italy surrenders; United Mine Workers strike; Race riots in Detroit and other cities	Normandy invasion (Operation Overlord); Congress passes GI Bill; Roosevelt elected for a fourth term	Yalta Conference; Roosevelt dies; Harry Truman becomes president; Germany surrenders; Successful test of atomic bomb; Hiroshima and Nagasaki bombed; Japan surrenders

Americans greeted the end of the war with joy and relief. They looked forward to the peace and prosperity for which they had fought. Yet within two years, the peace would be jeopardized by the Cold War, and the United States would be rearming its former enemies, Japan and Germany, to oppose its former friend, the Soviet Union. The irony of that situation reduced the joy of the hard-won peace and made the American people more suspicious of their government and its foreign policy.

Recommended Reading

General Accounts

A. Russell Buchanan, *The United States and World War II* (2 vols., 1964); Gerhard Weinberg, *A World at Arms: A Global History of World War II* (1994).

Diplomatic and Military

Gar Alperovitz, *Atomic Diplomacy* (1965); Richard M. Dalfiume, *Desegregation of the U.S. Armed Forces* (1975); John Dower, *War Without Mercy* (1986); Paul Fussell, *Wartime* (1989); Waldo Heinrichs, *Threshold of War* (1988); Akira Iriye, *The Origins of the Second World War in Asia and the Pacific* (1988); Gordon W. Prange, *At Dawn We Slept* (1981); Martin J. Sherwin, *A World Destroyed* (1975); Gaddis Smith, *Diplomacy During the Second World War* (1965); Russell F. Weigley, *Eisenhower's Lieutenants: The Campaigns in France and Germany* (1981); James Tobin, *Ernie Pyle's War* (1997); Stephen E. Ambrose, *D-Day* (1994) and *Citizen Soldiers* (1997).

The War at Home

Alison Bernstein, *American Indians and World War II* (1991); Roger Daniels, *Prisoners Without Trial: Japanese Americans in World War II* (1993); John Morton Blum, *V Was for Victory* (1976); D'Ann Campbell, *Women at War with America* (1984); Doris Kearns Goodwin, *No Ordinary Time: Franklin and Eleanor Roosevelt, The Home Front in World War II* (1994); Susan M. Hartman, *The Homefront and Beyond: Women in the 1940s* (1982); Nicholas Lemann, *The Promised Land: The Great Black Migration and How It Changed America* (1991); Ruth Milkman, *Gender at Work* (1987); Gerald D. Nash, *The American West Transformed: The Impact of the Second World War* (1985); Richard Polenberg, *War and Society* (1972); William Tuttle, *"Daddy's Gone to War"* (1993); Allan M. Winkler, *The Politics of Propaganda: The Office of War Information, 1942–1945* (1978); David S. Wyman, *The Abandonment of the Jews* (1984); Neil A. Wynn, *The Afro-American and the Second World War* (1976).

Fiction

In the *Dollmaker* (1954), Harriette Arnow tells the story of a young woman from Kentucky who finds herself in wartime Detroit; two powerful novels that tell the story of the battlefield experience are Norman Mailer, *The Naked and the Dead* (1948), and Irwin Shaw, *The Young Lions* (1948).

CHAPTER 26

Postwar Growth and Social Change

Ray Kroc, an ambitious salesman, headed toward San Bernardino, California, on a business trip in 1954. For more than a decade he had been selling "multimixers"—stainless steel machines that could make six milkshakes at once—to restaurants and soda shops around the United States. On this trip, he was particularly interested in checking out a hamburger stand run by Richard and Maurice McDonald, who had bought eight of his "contraptions" and could therefore make 48 shakes at the same time.

Always eager to increase sales, Kroc wanted to see the McDonalds' operation for himself. The 52-year-old son of Slavic parents had sold everything from real estate to paper cups before peddling the multimixers, but had enjoyed no stunning success. Yet he was still on the alert for the key to the fortune that was part of the American dream. As he watched the lines of people at the San Bernardino McDonald's, the answer seemed at hand.

The McDonald brothers sold only standard hamburgers and french fries, but they had developed a system that was fast, efficient, and clean. It drew on the heavy automobile traffic of Route 66. And it was profitable indeed. Sensing the possibilities, Kroc proposed that the two owners open other establishments as well. When they balked, he negotiated a 99-year contract that allowed him to sell the fast-food idea and the name—and their golden arches design—wherever he could.

On April 15, 1955, Kroc opened his first McDonald's in Des Plaines, a suburb of Chicago. Three months later, he sold his first franchise in Fresno, California. Others soon followed. Kroc scouted out new locations, almost always on highway "strips," persuaded people to put up the capital, and provided them with specifications guaranteed to ensure future success. For his efforts, he received a percentage of the gross take.

From the start, Kroc insisted on standardization. Every McDonald's was the same—from the two functional arches supporting the glass enclosure that housed the kitchen and take-out window to the single arch near the road bearing a sign indicating how many 15-cent hamburgers had already been sold. All menus and prices were exactly the same, and Kroc demanded that everything from hamburger size to cooking time be constant. He insisted, too, that the establishments be clean. No pinball games or cigarette machines were permitted; the premium was on a good, inexpensive hamburger, quickly served, at a nice place.

McDonald's, of course, was an enormous success. In 1962, total sales exceeded $76 million. In 1964, before the company had been in operation ten years, it had sold over 400 million hamburgers and 120 million pounds of french fries. By the end of the next year, there were 710 McDonald's stands in 44 states. In 1974, only 20 years after Kroc's vision of the hamburger's future, McDonald's did $2 billion worth of business. When Kroc died in 1984, a total of 45 billion burgers had been sold at 7,500 outlets in 32 countries. Ronald McDonald, the clown who came to represent the company, became known to children around the globe after his Washington, D.C., debut in November 1963. When McDonald's began to advertise, it became the country's first restaurant to buy TV time. Musical slogans like "You deserve a break today" and "We do it all for you" became better known than some popular songs.

❮❮❮❮❮❮

The success of McDonald's provides an example of the development of new trends in the United States in the post-World War II years. Kroc capitalized on the changes of the automobile age. He understood that a restaurant had a better chance of succeeding if it was located along the highway than in a city. His drive-in design, catering to a new and ever-growing clientele, soon became common.

He understood, too, that the franchise notion provided the key to rapid growth. Not prepared to open up thousands of stands himself, he sold the idea to entrepreneurs who stood to make sizable profits as long as they remained a part of the larger whole. In numerous other product areas as well as the hamburger business, franchises helped create a nationwide web of firms.

Finally, Kroc sensed the importance of standardization and uniformity. He understood the mood of the time, the quiet conformity of Americans searching for success. The very monotony of McDonald's image was part of its appeal. Customers always knew what they would get at the golden arches. If the atmosphere was "bland," that, too, was deliberate. As Kroc said, "Our theme is kind of synonymous with Sunday school, the Girl Scouts and the YMCA. McDonald's is clean and wholesome." It was a symbol of the age.

This chapter describes the structural changes in American society in the 25 years following World War II. Even as the nation became involved in the Cold War with the Soviet Union (a story we will take up in Chapter 27), Americans were preoccupied with the shifts in social and economic patterns that were taking place. This chapter examines how economic growth, spurred by technological advances, transformed the patterns of work and daily life in the United States and provided the context for the development of the liberal state described in Chapter 28. Self-interest triumphed over idealism as most people gained a level of material comfort previously unknown. Working-class Americans shared in the gains, as the union movement pressed its claims more successfully than it had ever done in the past, and workers entered into a new equilibrium with the world of management. Life for most Americans was more comfortable than it had ever been before. For many, this period promised to deliver the American dream.

But even as the nation prospered, it experienced serious social and economic divisions. This chapter also shows the enormous gaps that existed between rich and poor, even in the best of times. It shows the continuing presence of what one critic eloquently called "the other America" and documents the considerable income disparity and persistent prejudice that most minority groups encountered in their effort to share in the postwar prosperity. Their frustrations led to the reform movements described in Chapter 29 and highlighted the limits of the postwar American dream.

ECONOMIC BOOM

Despite Cold War anxieties, most Americans were optimistic after 1945. As servicemen came home, their very presence changed family patterns. A baby boom brought unprecedented population growth. The simultaneous and unexpected economic boom had an even greater impact. Large corporations increasingly dominated the business world, but unions grew as well, and most workers improved their lives. Technology appeared triumphant, with new products flooding the market and finding their way into most American homes. Prosperity convinced the growing middle class that all was well.

The Thriving Peacetime Economy

The return of prosperity during World War II continued in the postwar years, relieving fears of another depression. The next several decades saw one of the longest sustained economic expansions the country had ever known. The United States solidified its position as the richest nation in the world.

The statistical evidence was impressive. The gross national product (GNP) jumped from just over $200 billion in 1945 to almost $300 billion in 1950, and it surpassed $500 billion by 1960. It reached $685 billion in 1965, and by 1970 it soared to $970 billion. Per capita personal income rose from $1,223 in 1945 to $3,945 in 1970. Almost 60 percent of all families in the country were now part of the middle class, a dramatic change from the class structure in the nineteenth and early twentieth centuries.

Personal resources fueled economic growth. During World War II, with factories concentrating on military needs, American consumers could not spend all they earned, so at war's end they were ready to spend savings of $140 billion. Equally important, between 1946 and 1960 real purchasing power rose by 22 percent, which meant that families now had far more discretionary income—money to satisfy wants as well as needs—than before. At the end of the Great Depression, fewer than one-quarter of all households had any discretionary income; in 1960, three of every five did.

The United States, which produced half the world's goods, was providing new products that average Americans, unlike their parents, could afford. Higher real wages allowed people of all classes to buy consumer goods. That consumer power, unlike the underconsumption of the 1920s and 1930s, spurred the economy.

The automobile industry, which expanded dramatically after the war, played a key part in the boom. Two million cars were made in 1946; eight million were built in 1955, and more than nine million were built in 1965. Customers now chose from a wide variety of engines, colors, and options. Grills and tail fins distinguished each year's models. A fancy car could signal solid middle-class achievement. Younger people, especially from the working class, valued speed more.

Both the automobile culture and national prosperity got massive boosts from the interstate highway system launched by the Eisenhower administration in 1956. The Interstate Highway Act poured $26 billion—the largest public works expenditure in American history—into the construction of over 40,000 miles of federal highways, linking all parts of the United States. Eisenhower was right when he

McDonald's provided a model for other franchisers in the 1950s and the years that followed. The golden arches, shown here in an early version, were virtually the same wherever they appeared. Initially found along highways around the country, they were later built within cities and towns as well. (Courtesy McDonald's Corporation)

proudly said that "more than any single action by the government since the end of the war, this one would change the face of America." But there were costs. Money was not invested in mass transit. Highways spawned pollution, triggered urban flight, and helped increase national dependence on a constant flow of cheap oil.

A housing boom also fed economic growth. In 1940, 43 percent of all American families owned their own homes; by 1970, 63 percent did. Much of the stimulus came from the GI Bill of 1944. In addition to giving returning servicemen priority for many jobs and providing educational benefits, it offered low-interest home mortgages. Millions of former servicemen from all social classes eagerly purchased their share of the American dream.

The government's increasingly active economic role both stimulated and sustained the expansion. Businesses were allowed to buy almost 80 percent of the factories built by the government during the war for much less than they cost. Even more important was the dramatic rise in defense spending as the Cold War escalated. In 1947, Congress created the Department of Defense with an initial budget of $13 billion. With the onset of the Korean War, the defense budget rose to about $47 billion by 1953. Approximately half the total federal budget went to the armed forces, stimulating the aircraft and electronic industries. The close business-government ties of World War II grew stronger.

Most citizens welcomed these huge expenditures, not only because they supported a strong stand against communism (see Chapter 27), but also because they understood the economic impact of military spending. As a columnist noted in 1950, "Cold war is an automatic pump primer. Turn a spigot, and the public clamors for more arms spending."

Postwar American growth avoided some of the major problems that often bedevil periods of economic expansion—inflation and the enrichment of a few at the expense of the many. During the late 1940s inflation was indeed a problem, running at an annual average of 7 percent, but in the 1950s and 1960s it slowed to a gentle 2 to 3 percent annually. And though the concentration of income remained the same—the bottom half of the population still earned less than the top tenth—middle-class ranks grew.

A major economic transformation had occurred in the United States. Peaceful, prosperous, and productive, the nation had become what a prominent economist called "the affluent society." A veteran from Missouri later recalled: "I was a twenty-one-year-old lieutenant with a high school education, and my only prewar experience was as a stock boy in a grocery store. But on V-J day, I knew it was only a matter of time before I was rich—or well-off, anyway."

The Corporate Impact on American Life

After 1945, the major corporations tightened their hold on the American economy. Government policy in World War II had produced tremendous industrial concentration. Antitrust actions were suspended in the interest of wartime production, while government contracts spurred expansion of the big corporations at the expense of smaller firms.

Industrial concentration continued after the war, making oligopoly—domination of a given industry by a few firms—a feature of American capitalism. At the same time, the booming economy encouraged the development of conglomerates—firms with holdings in a variety of industries to protect themselves against instability in one particular area. It also led to the further development of finance capitalism to help put the deals together.

Expansion took other forms as well. Even as the major corporations expanded, so did franchise operations like Ray Kroc's pioneering McDonald's and emulators like Kentucky Fried Chicken and Burger King.

While expanding at home, large corporations also moved increasingly into foreign markets, as they had in the 1890s. At the same time, they began to build plants overseas, where labor costs were cheaper. A General Electric plant in Massachusetts might have to pay a worker $3.40 an hour, but for the same job a plant in Singapore paid only 30 cents an hour. In the decade after 1957, General Electric built 61 plants abroad. So did many other corporations. Corporate planning, meanwhile, developed rapidly, as firms sought managers who could assess information, weigh marketing trends, and make rational decisions to maximize profit.

Changing Work Patterns

As corporations changed, so did the world of work. Reversing a 150-year trend, in the years after World War II the United States became less of a goods producer and more of a service provider. Between 1947 and 1957, the number of factory workers fell by 4 percent, while clerical workers increased by 23 percent and salaried middle-class employees rose by 61 percent. By 1956, a majority of American workers held white-collar jobs, and that percentage rose in the years that followed. People lived comfortably, enjoying an abundance of leisure time. Experts predicted a four-day work week.

Yet white-collar employees paid a price. Work in the huge corporations became ever more impersonal and bureaucratic. Just as product standardization became increasingly important, individual acceptance of company norms became necessary. Social critic C. Wright Mills observed that "when white-collar people get jobs, they sell not only their time and energy but their personalities as well."

But not all Americans held white-collar jobs. Many were still workers on assembly lines. They, too, dreamed of owning a suburban home and several cars and providing more for their children than they had enjoyed while growing up. Their lives were now more comfortable than ever before, as the union movement brought substantial gains (see the next section). These were the more fortunate members of the working class.

Millions of others, perhaps 40 percent of the work force, held less appealing and poorer-paying positions as taxi drivers or farm laborers or dime-store sales clerks. Casual employment had involved manual labor in the past; now it consisted of service work, and much of this was done by minorities, teenagers, and women gradually returning to the labor force.

The Union Movement at High Tide

The union movement had come of age during the New Deal (see Chapter 24), and the end of World War II found it even stronger. There were more union members—14.5 million—than ever before. Having taken a wartime no-strike pledge and given the war effort their full support, they now looked forward to better pay and a greater voice in workplace management.

The immediate postwar period was difficult. Cancellations of defense orders laid off war workers and prompted fears of a depression. Even workers who held their jobs lost the overtime pay of the war years. As workers scrapped no-strike pledges, job actions soared. In 1946 alone, 4.6 million workers went out on strike— more than ever before in the history of the United States. These disruptions annoyed middle-class Americans in general and outraged conservative Republicans, who felt that unionization had gone too far.

In the late 1940s, a new equilibrium emerged. Big business at last accepted the basic rights of industrial workers, and unions in turn acknowledged the prerogatives of management and accepted the principle of fair profit. Corporations in the same industry agreed to cooperate rather than compete with one another over labor costs. This meant that once a leading firm reached agreement with the union, the other firms in that sector would adopt similar terms, and the costs of the new contract would be met by a general increase in prices.

At the same time, companies made material concessions to workers, for example protecting them against inflation. In 1948, General Motors offered the United Automobile Workers a contract that included a cost-of-living adjustment (COLA) and a 2 percent "annual improvement factor" wage increase intended to share GM's productivity gains with workers. By the end of the 1950s COLAs were built into most union contracts.

The union movement made peace with itself, too. The rivalry of trade and industrial unions, so bitter in the 1930s and with a history running back to the late-nineteenth century (see Chapter 18), largely ended in 1955 with the merger of the

AFL and CIO. The new organization represented more than 90 percent of the country's now larger cohort of 17.5 million union members.

Union gains, like middle-class affluence, came at a price. With higher, more predictable incomes, workers were more willing to limit strikes and surrender the last vestiges of workplace autonomy. Co-opted by the materialistic benefits big business provided, workers fell increasingly under the control of middle-level managers and watched anxiously as companies automated at home or expanded abroad, where labor was cheaper. But the agreements they had reached often precluded any response.

The union movement stalled in the 1960s. Stagnation began to afflict the heavy industries whose workers dominated the union movement. The unionized percentage of the nonfarm work force remained stable in the decade and a half following World War II but then began to fall. Unions tried to expand their base by reaching out to new groups—less skilled minority workers and white-collar, service-oriented employees—but these groups proved difficult to organize.

Agricultural Workers in Trouble

The agricultural world changed even more than the industrial world in the postwar United States. On the eve of World War II, agriculture had supported one of every five Americans. Now, in one generation, mechanization and consolidation forced that figure down to one in twenty.

New technology revolutionized farming. Improved planting and harvesting machines and better fertilizers and pesticides brought massive gains in productivity. Increasing profitability led to agricultural consolidation. In the 25 years after 1945, average farm size almost doubled. Farms specialized more in cash crops like corn or soybeans, which could be used to feed animals. Demanding large-scale investment, farming became a big business—"agribusiness," it was called.

More and more small farmers left the land. Some were midwestern whites, who generally found jobs in local offices and factories. In the South, however, the upheaval was more disruptive. Many of the uprooted agricultural workers were African-Americans, and they helped accelerate the huge migration that had been going north since World War I. Overall, from 1910 and 1970 more than 6.5 million African-Americans left the South; of these, 5 million went north after 1940. Most of them gravitated to cities, where they faced difficulties described later in this chapter.

DEMOGRAPHIC AND TECHNOLOGICAL TRENDS

The postwar economic boom intertwined with a series of demographic changes. The population grew dramatically and continued moving west. At the same time, millions of white Americans left the cities for the suburbs, which began to grow exponentially in the postwar years. New patterns, revolving around television and other gadgets pouring from modern technology's cornucopia, came to characterize the consumer culture of suburban life.

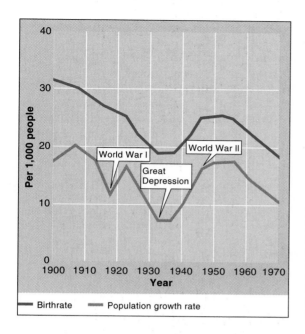

BIRTH AND POPULATION RATES, 1900–1970 Both birth and population rates increased dramatically after the difficult years of the Great Depression. Note the baby boom that began at the end of World War II and continued for the next several decades. Sources: U.S. Bureau of the Census and *Statistical Abstract of the United States*.

Population Shifts

In post-World War II America, a growing population testified to prosperity's return. The birthrate soared in the postwar years as millions of Americans started families. The "baby boom" peaked in 1957, with a rate of more than 25 births per 1,000. In that year, 4.3 million babies were born, one every seven seconds. While the population growth of 19 million in the 1940s was double that of the decade before, the latter increase paled against the increase in the 1950s, which totaled 29 million.

The death rate was also declining. Miracle drugs made a difference. Federal sponsorship of medical research during World War II had spurred the development of penicillin and streptomycin, now widely available in the United States. They helped cure strep throat and other bacterial infections, intestinal ailments, and more serious illnesses such as tuberculosis. A polio vaccine introduced a decade after the war virtually eliminated that dreaded disease. Life expectancy rose: Midway through the 1950s, the average life expectancy was 70 years for whites and 64 for blacks; in 1920 it was 55 for whites and 45 for blacks.

The baby boom shaped family patterns and material needs. Many women substituted housework for paid wartime work. Demand grew for diaper services and baby foods. Entering school, the baby boom generation strained the educational system. Since school construction had slowed during the Depression and had virtually halted during the Second World War, classrooms were needed. Teachers, too, were in short supply.

As Americans became more populous, they also became more mobile. For many generations, working-class Americans had been the most likely to move; now geographic mobility spread to the middle class. Each year in the 1950s, over a million farmers left their farms. Other Americans picked up stakes and headed on as well. Some moved to look for better jobs. Others simply wandered awhile after returning home from the war and then settled down.

The war had produced increasing movement, most of it westward. Although the scarcity of water in the West required massive water projects to support population growth, war workers and their families streamed to western cities. After the war, this migration pattern persisted. The Sun Belt—the region stretching along the southern tier of the United States from Florida to California—attracted new arrivals. Cities there expanded phenomenally. In the 1950s, Los Angeles pulled ahead of Philadelphia as the third-largest city in the United States. One-fifth of all the growth in the period took place in California. By 1963, California passed New York as the nation's most populous state.

Fueling the West's growth was the booming Cold War defense industry. Once the Korean War sparked increased military expenditures, California's economic growth outpaced that of the country as a whole. Aircraft production in the state accounted for more than 40 percent of the total increase in manufacturing employment there between 1949 and 1953. By 1962, the Pacific Coast as a whole held almost half of all Defense Department research and development contracts.

The West also benefited from the boom in the service economy. Many western workers in postwar America belonged to the service sector. The percentage of workers in such jobs was higher in virtually all western states than in eastern counterparts. Denver became a major regional center of the federal bureaucracy, with more people on the federal payroll in 1975 than any other city except Washington, D.C.

The New Suburbs

As the population shifted westward after World War II, another form of movement was taking place. Millions of white Americans fled the inner city to suburban fringes. Fourteen of the nation's largest cities lost population in the 1950s. As central cities became places where poor nonwhites clustered, new urban and racial problems emerged.

For people of means, cities were places to work but leave at five o'clock. In Manhattan south of City Hall, the noontime population of 1.5 million dropped to 2,000 overnight. "It was becoming a part-time city," wrote an observer, "tidally swamped with bustling humanity every weekday morning when the cars and commuter trains arrived, and abandoned again at nightfall when the wave sucked back—left pretty much to thieves, policemen, and rats." By the end of the 1950s, a third of all Americans resided in suburbs; in 1970 nearly 38 percent did.

Often rapidly constructed and overpriced, suburban tract houses provided the appearance of comfort and space and the chance to have at least one part of the American dream, a place of one's own. They seemed protected from the growing troubles of the cities, insulated from the difficulties of the world outside.

The pioneer of postwar suburbanization was William J. Levitt, a builder who had recognized the advantages of mass production during World War II, when his firm constructed housing for war workers. Aware that the GI Bill made mortgage money readily available, he saw the possibilities of suburban development. But to cash in, Levitt had to use new construction methods.

Step-by-step mass production, with units completed in assembly-line fashion, was the key to William Levitt's approach to housing. But the suburban developments he and others created were marked by street after street of houses that all looked the same. (Lambert/Archive Photos)

Mass production was the key. "The reason we have it so good in this country," he said, "is that we can produce lots of things at low prices through mass production." Houses were among them. Working on a careful schedule, Levitt's team brought precut and preassembled materials to each site, put them together, and moved on. As on an assembly line, tasks were broken down into individual steps. Groups of workers performed a single job on each tract.

Levitt proved that his system worked. Construction costs at Levittown, New York, a new community of 17,000 homes built in the late 1940s, were only $10 per square foot, compared with the $12 to $15 common elsewhere. The next Levittown appeared in Bucks County, Pennsylvania, several years after the first, and another went up in Willingboro, New Jersey, at the end of the 1950s. Levitt's success provided a model for other developers.

Government-insured mortgages, especially for veterans, fueled the housing boom. So did fairly low postwar interest rates. With many American families vividly remembering the Depression and saving significant parts of their paychecks, the nation had a pool of savings large enough to keep mortgage interest rates in the affordable 5 percent range.

Suburbanization transformed the American landscape in the 1950s. Huge tracts of former fields, pastures, and forests were now divided into standardized squares, each with a house, a two-car garage, and a manicured lawn. It was cheaper to cut trees down than to work around them.

As suburbs flourished, businesses followed their customers out of the cities. At the end of World War II, there were eight shopping centers, but the number multiplied rapidly in the 1950s. Shopping centers catered to suburbanites and transformed consumer patterns. If they wished, suburb dwellers could avoid the city entirely. Downtown department stores declined, further eroding urban health.

The Environmental Impact

Suburbanization had environmental consequences. Rapid development often took place without extensive planning and encroached on some of the nation's most attractive rural areas. Before long, every American city was ringed by an ugly highway sporting garish neon signs. Billboards filled whatever space was not yet developed.

Despite occasional protests against the spreading ugliness, there was little real consciousness of environmental issues in the early post-World War II years. The term *environment* itself was hardly used prior to the war. Americans had been concerned with conservation earlier in the century, focusing on efficient use and development of water and forests. Later they turned their attention to preservation.

The very prosperity that created dismal highway strips was leading more and more Americans to appreciate natural environments as treasured parts of their rising standard of living. The shorter workweek provided more free time, and many Americans now had the means for longer vacations. They began to explore mountains and rivers and ocean shores—and began to consider how to protect them. In 1958, Congress established the National Outdoor Recreation Review Commission, a first step toward consideration of environmental issues that became far more common in the next decade. In 1964, Congress went further, passing a National Wilderness Preservation Act, followed by a Wild and Scenic Rivers Act and a National Trails Act in 1968. Americans also began to recognize the need for open space in their communities to compensate for urban overdevelopment.

Technology Supreme

A technological revolution transformed postwar America. Some developments— the use of atomic energy, for example—flowed directly from wartime research. Federal support for scientific activity increased dramatically as the pattern of wartime collaboration continued. The government established the National Institutes of Health in 1948 to coordinate medical research and the National Science Foundation in 1950 to fund basic scientific research. The Cold War brought constantly increasing government research and development ("R & D") funding through the Atomic Energy Commission (1946) and the Department of Defense (1947). Money went to large research universities, which grew enormously. Basic and applied research developed not only nuclear weapons, jet planes, and satellites, but also the consumer goods that were often the spinoffs of military projects. Big business had its own R & D activities, often huge.

Computers both reflected and assisted technological development. Large calculators had been developed during the war, and in the immediate postwar years came machines with internal instructions and memories. In 1946, scientists at the University of Pennsylvania built the Electronic Numerical Integrator and Calculator, called ENIAC. It had 18,000 electronic tubes and required tremendous amounts of electricity and special cooling procedures, but it worked. In a widely publicized test, a reporter pushed the button, and in less than half a second it multiplied 97,367 by itself 5,000 times.

A key breakthrough in making computers faster and more reliable was the development of the transistor by three scientists at Bell Laboratories in 1948.

Computers were now on the way to transforming twentieth-century American society as radically as industrialization had revolutionized the nineteenth century. Computers were essential for space exploration. Airlines, hotels, and other businesses computerized their reservation systems. Business accounting and inventory control began to depend on computers. Computer programmers and operators were in increasing demand.

One ominous technological trend was automation. Mechanization was not new, but now it became far more widespread, threatening both skilled and unskilled workers. In 1952, the Ford Motor Company began using automatic drilling machines in an engine plant and found that 41 workers could do a job that 117 had done before. The implications of falling purchasing power as machines replaced workers were serious for an economy dependent on consumer demand.

The Consumer Culture

Americans fell in love with appliances and gadgets. By the end of the 1950s, most families had at least one automobile, as well as the staple appliances they had begun to purchase before—refrigerator, washing machine, television, and vacuum cleaner. Dozens of less essential items caught on, from electric can openers to aerosol sprays.

The greatest gadget of all was the TV. Developed in the 1930s, it became a major influence on American life after World War II. There were fewer than 17,000 sets in 1946, but by 1949 Americans were buying them at a rate of 250,000 a month. By 1960, three quarters of all families owned at least one set. Youngsters grew up with "Howdy Doody" and their parents followed "I Love Lucy." In 1955, the average family tuned in four to five hours each day.

Consumption, increasingly a pillar of the American economy, required a vast expansion of consumer credit. Installment plans facilitated buying a new car. For smaller purchases, the credit card became essential. Diner's Club, the first of the consumer credit cards, appeared in 1950, and by the end of the decade came the American Express card and the BankAmericard. By the end of the 1960s, about 50 million credit cards of all kinds were being used in the United States. Consumer credit—total private indebtedness—increased astronomically. It went from $8.4 billion in 1946 to nearly $45 billion in 1958, and reached $113.2 billion in 1968.

For consumers momentarily unsure about new purchases, a revitalized advertising industry was ready to convince them to go ahead. Advertising had come of age in the 1920s, as businesses persuaded customers that buying new products brought status and satisfaction. It faltered when the economy collapsed in the 1930s but began to revive during the war. With the postwar boom, admen were hawking wares more persuasively than ever before.

Motivational research discovered new ways of persuading people to buy. Unlike radio, which could only talk about new wonders, television could show them. Ads bombarded TV viewers with everything they needed to know about the luxuries indispensible to the good life. "The Price Is Right" went to the heart of the matter: Contestants won goods by guessing their correct retail price.

Having lived through poverty in the 1930s and sacrifices during the war, most Americans now regarded abundance and leisure as their due. A small minority of cultural critics, however, scolded them. The 1950s, one wrote, were a time of "self-satisfaction and gross materialism . . . . The loudest sound in the land has been the oink and grunt of private hoggishness . . . . It has been the age of the slob."

CONSENSUS AND CONFORMITY

As the economy expanded, an increasing sense of sameness pervaded American society. Some believed this was the great age of conformity, when members of all social groups learned to emulate those around them rather than strike out on their own. Third- and fourth-generation ethnic Americans became much more alike. As immigration slowed to a trickle after 1924, old-country ties weakened, assimilation speeded up, and inter-ethnic marriage sky-rocketed. Television gave young and old a shared, visually seductive experience. Escaping the homogenizing tendencies was difficult.

Conformity in School and Religious Life

The willingness to conform to group norms affected students at all levels. Elementary school children watched the same television shows and coveted the same toys. High school students—at an age when group norms are an obsession—dressed alike and took their vocabulary from TV programs and advertising jingles. College students seemed most concerned with security. They joined fraternities and sororities that engaged in panty raids and other pranks, but they usually took little interest in world affairs.

Postwar Americans discovered a shared religious sense and returned to their churches in record numbers. By the end of the 1950s, fully 95 percent of all Americans identified with some religious denomination. Church membership doubled between 1945 and 1970.

Part of this upsurge of church attendance grew out of anxieties about "godless Communism" and the threat of nuclear annihilation (see Chapter 27). Evangelist Billy Graham was in the forefront of the anti-Communist campaign in the 1950s and 1960s. He preached to millions at his revivals, and was a master of the mass media. "Hour of Decision," his radio ministry in the 1950s, tried to convert sinners and so save the nation. "When you make your decision for Jesus Christ," Graham said, "it is America making her decision through you."

The religious resurgence had other roots as well. Ecumenical activities—worldwide efforts on the part of different Christian churches—became more common following a first World Council of Churches meeting in 1948. These helped draw attention to the place of religion in modern life. In the early 1960s Pope John XXIII convened the Vatican Ecumenical Council to make the Catholic Church's traditions and practices more accessible, for example substituting modern languages for Latin in the liturgy. Judaism, likewise, went through important shifts in the postwar years. Second- and third-generation Jews became increasingly affluent, and between 1945 and 1965 a third of all American Jews left cities for the suburbs. There they built new synagogues, most of which adhered to the easier-to-follow patterns of Reform or Conservative, rather than Orthodox, Judaism. In part, this shift reflected an effort by Jews to seek greater acceptance in mainstream American society.

The religious revival resulted to some degree, as well, from the power of suggestion that led Americans to do what others did. As a billboard slogan put it, "The family that prays together stays together." The renewal of interest in religion also offered an acceptable means of escape from the anxieties of a middle-class executive's life. In the 1950s, the Full Gospel Businessmen's Fellowship not only provided religious camaraderie but also enjoyed access to the White House.

President Dwight Eisenhower reflected the national mood when he observed that "our government makes no sense unless it is founded in a deeply felt religious faith—and I don't care what it is." In 1954, Congress added the words "under God" to the pledge to the flag, and the next year voted to require the phrase "In God We Trust" on all U.S. currency. Yet the revival sometimes seemed to rest on a shallow base of religious knowledge. In one public opinion poll, 80 percent of the respondents avowed that the Bible was God's revealed word, but only 35 percent could name the four Gospels. Over half were unable to name even one.

Back to the Kitchen

World War II had interrupted traditional patterns of behavior for both men and women. As servicemen went overseas, women went to work. After 1945, there was a period of adjustment as the men returned and many working women were told that they were no longer needed in their jobs. In the 1950s, traditional gender roles were reaffirmed and women faced tremendous pressure to conform to accepted prewar patterns, even though, paradoxically, more women entered the work force than ever before.

Men and women had different postwar expectations. Most men planned to go to school and then find jobs to support a family. Viewing themselves as the primary breadwinners, they wanted their jobs back after the war. For women, the situation was more complex. While they wanted to resume disrupted patterns of family life, many had enjoyed working in the plants and were reluctant to retreat to the home, although the government and employers persistently told them to do so.

In 1947, *Life* magazine ran a long photo essay called "The American Woman's Dilemma." Women, it observed, were caught in a conflict between the traditional expectation to stay home and a new desire to have a paid job. Understandably, the sense of dilemma was strongest among white, well-educated, middle-class women; black and lower-class white women usually had to continue working outside the home whether they liked it or not.

By the 1950s, middle-class doubts had largely receded. The baby boom increased average family size and made the decision to remain home easier. The flight to the suburbs gave women more to do, and they settled into the routines of redecorating their homes and gardens and transporting children to and from activities and schools.

In 1956, when *Life* produced a special issue on women, the message had changed strikingly from that of nine years before. Profiling Marjorie Sutton, the magazine spoke of the "Busy Wife's Achievements" as "Home Manager, Mother, Hostess, and Useful Civic Worker." Married at the age of 16, Marjorie was now involved with the PTA, Campfire Girls, and charity causes. She cooked and sewed for her family, which included four children, supported her husband by entertaining 1,500 guests a year, and worked out on the trampoline "to keep her size 12 figure."

Marjorie Sutton typified the widespread social emphasis on marriage and home. Many women went to college to find husbands—and dropped out if they succeeded. Almost two-thirds of the women in college, but less than half the men, left before completing a degree. Women were expected to marry young, have children early, and support their husbands' careers. An article in *Esquire* magazine in 1954 called working wives a "menace." Adlai Stevenson, Democratic presidential candidate in 1952 and 1956, defined the female role in politics, telling a group of women that "the assignment for you, as wives and mothers, you can do in the living room with a baby in your lap or in the kitchen with a can opener in your hand." As in much of the nineteenth century, a woman was "to influence man and boy" in her "humble role of housewife" and mother.

Pediatrician Benjamin Spock agreed. In 1946 he published the first edition of *Baby and Child Care,* the book most responsible for the child-rearing patterns of the postwar generation. He advised mothers to stay at home if they wanted to raise stable and secure youngsters. Working outside the home might jeopardize their children's mental and emotional health.

Popular culture highlighted the stereotype of the woman concerned only about marriage and family. Author Betty Friedan described these patterns in her explosive 1963 critique, *The Feminine Mystique.* Through an exhaustive examination of women's magazines and other publications, she provided a profile of women in the 1950s and early 1960s. They "could desire no greater destiny than to glory in their own femininity . . . . All they had to do was to devote their lives from earliest girlhood to finding a husband and bearing children." Their role was clear. "It was unquestioned gospel," she wrote, "that women could identify with *nothing* beyond the home—not politics, not art, not science, not events large or small, war or peace, in the United States or the world, unless it could be approached through female experience as a wife or mother or translated into domestic detail."

Movies reinforced conventional images. Doris Day, charming and wholesome, was a favorite heroine. In film after film, she showed how an attractive woman who played her cards right could land her man.

The family was all-important in this scenario. Fewer than 10 percent of all Americans felt that an unmarried person could be happy. A healthy family strengthened the nation in its Cold War struggle. In the pattern endlessly reiterated by popular television programs, the family was meant to provide all satisfaction and contentment. The single-story ranch house that became so popular in this period reflected the focus on the family as the source of recreation and fun.

Sexuality was a troublesome if compelling postwar concern. In 1948, Alfred C. Kinsey published *Sexual Behavior in the Human Male.* Kinsey was an Indiana University zoologist who had been asked to teach a course on marriage problems but found little published material about human sexual activity. Collecting his own, he compiled case histories of 5,300 white males.

Kinsey shocked the country. Among males who went to college, he concluded, 67 percent had engaged in sexual intercourse before marriage, as had 84 percent of those who went to high school but not beyond. Thirty-seven percent of the total male population had experienced some kind of overt homosexual activity. Five years later, Kinsey published *Sexual Behavior in the Human Female,* detailing many of the same patterns. Although critics denounced Kinsey for his methodology and his results, both of his books sold widely, for they opened the door to a subject that had previously been considered taboo.

Interest in sexuality was reflected in the fascination with sex goddesses like Marilyn Monroe. With her blonde hair, breathy voice, and raw sexuality, she personified the forbidden side of the good life and became one of Hollywood's most popular stars. The images of such film goddesses corresponded to male fantasies of women, displayed in *Playboy* magazine, which first appeared in 1953 and soon achieved a huge readership. These men's wives were expected to manage their suburban homes and to be cheerful and willing objects of their husbands' desire.

Despite reaffirming the old ideology that a woman's place was in the home, the 1950s were years of unnoticed but important change. Because the supply of single women workers was diminished by the low birthrate of the Depression years and by increased schooling and early marriage, older married women continued the pattern begun during the war and entered the labor force in larger numbers than before. In 1940, only 15 percent of American wives had jobs. By 1950, 21 percent were employed, and ten years later, the figure had risen to 30 percent. Moreover, married women now accounted for more than half of all working women, a dramatic reversal of pre-World War II patterns. Although the media hailed those women who primarily tended to their families, some magazine articles, in fact, did stress the achievements of women outside the home.

Although many working women were poor, divorced, or widowed, many others worked to acquire the desirable new products that were badges of middle-class status. They stepped into the new jobs created by economic expansion, clustering in office, sales, and service positions, occupations already defined as female. They and their employers considered their work subordinate to their primary role as wives and mothers. The conviction that a woman's main role was homemaking justified low wages and the denial of promotions. Comparatively few women entered professions where they would have challenged traditional notions of a woman's place. As *Life* magazine pointed out in 1956, "Household skills take her into the garment trades; neat and personable, she becomes office worker and sales lady; patient and dexterous, she does well on competitive, detailed factory work; compassionate, she becomes teacher and nurse."

African-American women worked as always but often lost the jobs they had held during the war. As the percentage of women in the Detroit automobile industry, for example, dropped from 25 to 7.5 in the immediate postwar period, black women who had held some of the jobs were the first to go. Bernice McCannon, an African-American employee at a Virginia military base, observed, "I have always done domestic work for families. When war came, I made the same move many domestics did. I took a higher paying job in a government cafeteria as a junior baker. If domestic work offers a good living, I see no reason why most of us will not return to our old jobs. We will have no alternative." These jobs, however, did not pay well at all. In the 1950s, the employment picture improved somewhat. African-American women succeeded both in moving into white-collar positions and in increasing their income. By 1960, more than a third of all black women held clerical, sales, service, or professional jobs. The income gap between white women and black women holding similar jobs dropped from about 50 percent in 1940 to about 30 percent in 1960.

Clothing

Clothing can be an important source of information about the past. The clothes people wear often announce their age, sex, and class, and frequently transmit some sense of their origin, occupation, and even their politics. The vocabulary of dress includes more than garments alone: Hairstyles, jewelry, and makeup all contribute to the way people choose to present themselves. Clothing can signal strong emotions; a torn, unbuttoned shirt, for example, can indicate that a person who seldom dresses that way is really upset. Bright colors can demonstrate a daring sense and a willingness to make a strong statement. By examining clothing styles in a number of different decades, we can begin to understand something of the changing patterns of people's lives.

In the 1920s, flappers and other women often dressed like children, with loose dresses usually in pastel colors ending just below the knee. Large trimmings, like huge artificial flowers, accentuated the effect. A "boyish" figure was considered most attractive. The clothes conveyed a feeling of playfulness and a willingness to embrace the freedom of the young.

A couple of decades later, during World War II, styles changed dramatically. In the 1940s, young teenage girls frequently wore bobby socks, rolled down to their ankles. Working women wore overalls, but with their own adornments to maintain their femininity. Rosie the Riveter, drawn by noted artist Norman Rockwell, wore her overalls proudly as she sat with a riveting gun in her lap and an attractive scarf around her hair.

Harlem women in the 1920s. (Schomburg Collection, New York Public Library)

Then came the 1960s and an entirely new look. Casual clothing became a kind of uniform. The counterculture was a movement of the young, and clothing took on an increasingly youthful look. Skirts rose above the knee and then climbed to midthigh. Women began to wear pants and trouser suits. Men and women both favored jeans and informal shirts and let their hair grow longer. Men broke away from the gray flannel suits of the preceding decade and indulged themselves in bright colors in what has been called the "peacock revolution."

Look carefully at the pictures on these pages. They show fashions from different periods and can tell us a good deal about how these people defined themselves. Examine first the photo of the three black women from the 1920s. What kinds of adornments do you notice? What impression do these women convey?

In the picture of two drill press operators during World War II, the women are dressed to handle the heavy machinery. How have the women accommodated themselves to their work, while still maintaining their individuality?

Finally, examine the photograph of the man and woman at an outdoor music festival in the 1960s. What does their clothing remind you of? Where might it come from? What impression are these people trying to create by their dress?

World War II women at work. (Oregon Historical Society, Portland)

Countercultural dress in the 1960s. (Ken Heyman)

Some of the patterns of the 1950s persisted in the next decade. By the middle of the 1960s, however, the roots of what became a powerful women's movement were visible. Women challenged stereotypical patterns of behavior and patterns of dress. They demanded and seized greater control over their own lives, in a story we will take up in much greater detail in Chapter 29.

Cultural Rebels

Not all Americans fit the 1950s stereotypes. As young people struggled to meet the standards and expectations of their peers, they often contemplated Holden Caulfield, the central character in J. D. Salinger's novel *The Catcher in the Rye* (1951). Holden, a boarding school misfit, rebelled against the "phonies" around him who threatened his individuality and independence, and his ill-fated effort to preserve integrity in the face of pressures to conform struck a resonant chord.

Writers of the so-called "beat generation" espoused unconventional values. Stressing spontaneity and spirituality, they proclaimed intuition superior to reason and Eastern mysticism more satisfying than Western faith. The "beats" deliberately outraged respectability by sneering at materialism, flaunting unconventional sex lives, and smoking marijuana. Dispensing with punctuation and paragraphing, Jack Kerouac used a single 250-foot roll of paper to type his best-selling novel *On the Road* (1957), a saga of freewheeling trips across the country that glorified the beat life-style. Allen Ginsberg became equally notorious for his poem "Howl." Written during a wild weekend in 1955 while Ginsberg was under the influence of drugs, "Howl" assailed modern, mechanized culture and all its effects. Ginsberg became a celebrity when the poem appeared in print in 1956, particularly after it survived a court test on obscenity charges. Ginsberg, Kerouac, and the other beats would be models for countercultural rebellion in the 1960s, described in Chapter 29.

The popularity of Salinger, Kerouac, and Ginsberg owed much to a revolution in book publishing and to the democratization of education that accompanied the program of GI educational benefits. More Americans than ever before acquired a taste for literature, which they could satisfy with the huge numbers of inexpensive books made available by the "paperback revolution." The paperback, introduced in 1939, dominated the book market after World War II. By 1965, readers could choose among some 25,000 titles sold in bookstores, supermarkets, drugstores, and airplane terminals. They purchased nearly seven million copies per week.

The signs of cultural rebellion also appeared in popular music. Parents recoiled as their children flocked to hear Elvis Presley belt out rock-and-roll songs. Presley's sexy voice, gyrating hips, and other techniques borrowed from black singers made him the undisputed "king of rock-and-roll." A multimedia blitz of movies, television, and radio helped make his songs smash singles, and his black leather jacket and ducktail haircut became a virtual uniform for rebellious male teenagers.

American painters, shucking off European influences that had shaped American artists for two centuries, also became a part of the cultural rebellion. Led by Jackson Pollock and the "New York school," some artists discarded the easel, laid gigantic canvases on the floor, and then used trowels, putty knives, and sticks to apply paint, glass shards, sand, and other materials in wild explosions of color. Known as abstract expressionists, these painters regarded the unconscious as the source of their artistic creations. "I am not aware of what is taking place [as I paint]," Pollock explained; "it is only after that I see what I have done." Like much of the literature of rebellion, abstract expressionism reflected the artist's alienation from a world becoming filled with nuclear threats, computerization, and materialism.

THE OTHER AMERICA

Not all Americans shared postwar middle-class affluence. Poverty persisted in inner cities and rural areas. African-Americans, uprooted from rural ways and crowded into urban slums, were among the dispossessed. But other minorities and disadvantaged whites suffered similar dislocations, unknown to the middle class.

Poverty Amid Affluence

Economic growth favored the upper and middle classes. Although the "trickle-down" theory argued that economic expansion benefited all classes, little wealth actually reached people at the bottom. In 1960, according to the Federal Bureau of Labor Statistics, a yearly subsistence-level income for a family of four was $3,000 and for a family of six, $4,000. The Bureau reported that 40 million people (almost a quarter of the population) lived below those levels, with nearly the same number only marginally above the line. Two million migrant workers labored long hours for a subsistence wage. According to the 1960 census, 27 percent of the residential units in the United States were substandard, and even acceptable dwellings were often hopelessly overcrowded in some slums.

Michael Harrington, socialist author and critic, shocked the country with his 1962 book *The Other America*. The poor, Harrington showed, were everywhere. He described New York City's "economic underworld," where "Puerto Ricans and Negroes, alcoholics, drifters, and disturbed people" haunted employment agencies for temporary positions as "dishwashers and day workers, the fly-by-night jobs." In rural America, Appalachian mountain folk, Mississippi tenant farmers, and migrant farm workers everywhere suffered in the same relentless cycle of poverty.

Hard Times for African-Americans

African-Americans were among the postwar nation's least prosperous citizens. They had always known poverty. Now, however, most of them were concentrated in cities, driven from rural life by mechanization and the collapse of tenant farming. Millions of blacks moved to southern cities where they found better jobs, better schooling, and freedom from landlords. Some reached middle-class status; many more did not. They remained poor, with even less of a support system than they had before.

The millions of African-Americans who headed for northern cities after 1940 usually wound up in slums, where the growth of facilities and social services lagged behind population growth. At one point in the 1950s, Chicago's black population rose by more than 2,200 people each week.

The black ghetto that had begun to develop earlier in the twentieth century became a permanent fixture in the post-World War II years. African-Americans attempting to move elsewhere often found the way blocked, sometimes violently. In 1951, a black couple purchasing a home in Cicero, Illinois, was driven away when an angry white crowd broke the house's windows, defaced the walls, and shouted vile insults. Even passage in 1968 of the Fair Housing Act barring racial discrimination in housing failed to end such residential segregation.

Black novelist James Baldwin eloquently described slum conditions and their corrosive effect on African-Americans in his 1961 book *Nobody Knows My Name:*

> They work in the white man's world all day and come home in the evening to this fetid block. They struggle to instill in their children some private sense of honor or dignity, which will help the child to survive. This means, of course, that they must struggle, stolidly, incessantly, to keep this sense live in themselves, in spite of the insults, the indifference, and the cruelty they are certain to encounter in their working day. They patiently browbeat the landlord into fixing the heat, the plaster, the plumbing; this demands prodigious patience, nor is patience usually enough . . . . Such frustration, so long endured, is driving many strong and admirable men and women whose only crime is color to the very gates of paranoia.

Employment was the problem. Men had more difficulty finding work than women. Unemployment often had a chain effect of idleness, frustration, public drunkenness, and brawls. Inability to get steady work challenged black masculinity, which could devastate African-American family life. Despite all obstacles, the black family managed to hold together until the 1960s, with 70 percent of all units including both husband and wife. But by 1983, 50 percent of all black children under 18 lived in households headed by women, many suffering from seemingly inescapable poverty.

Still, the larger black community remained intact. Chicago's South Side neighborhood was a vibrant place, replacing New York's Harlem as black America's cultural capital in the 1950s. Here and elsewhere, the black church played an important role in sustaining African-American life. Blacks moving into the cities retained churchgoing habits and commitment to religious institutions from their rural days. Older, established churches assisted newcomers in the transition to urban America, while new religious groups began to form, creating a sense of community for recent arrivals. The churches offered more than just religious sustenance. Many provided day-care facilities, ran Scout troops, and sponsored other social services. These activities gave them a crucial place in the civil rights movement that began to flourish in these years (see Chapter 29).

The growth of the black urban population fostered businesses catering to the African-American community. Black newspapers now provided a more regional, rather than a national, focus, but magazines such as *Jet,* a pocket-size weekly with a large countrywide circulation, filled the void. Black-owned or -operated banks and other financial institutions proliferated.

Yet most African-Americans remained second-class citizens. Escape from the slums was difficult for many, impossible for most. Persistent poverty was a dismal fact of life, even as the rest of the United States enjoyed prosperous times.

Minorities on the Fringe

Other groups had similar difficulties in the postwar United States. Latino immigrants from Cuba, Puerto Rico, Mexico, and Central America, often unskilled and illiterate, followed other less fortunate Americans to the cities. In the face of persistent discrimination, these groups maintained strong group identities in their *barrios,* even in the midst of pervasive poverty. The ties fostered in these communities provided a strong base on which a growing political consciousness could rest as it emerged in the next decade (see Chapter 29).

Chicanos, as many Mexican-Americans called themselves, were the most numerous of the newcomers and faced special difficulties. During World War II, faced with a labor shortage, American farmers had sought Mexican *braceros* (helping hands) to harvest their crops. A U.S.-Mexican program to encourage the seasonal immigration of farm workers continued after the war. Between 1948 and 1964, some 4.5 million Mexicans were brought to the United States for temporary work. *Braceros* were expected to return to Mexico at the end of their contract, but often they stayed. Millions more entered the country illegally.

Conditions were harsh for *braceros* in the best of times, but in periods of economic difficulty, troubles worsened. During a serious recession from 1953 to 1954, the federal government mounted a massive attempt to round up and deport illegal Mexican immigrants. Some 1.1 million were expelled. As immigration officials searched out illegal workers, all Chicanos found themselves vulnerable. They bitterly protested the violations of their rights, to little effect.

Reliance on poor Mexican farm laborers continued despite the deportations. A coalition of southern Democrats and conservative Republicans, mostly representing farm states, wanted to continue to take advantage of cheap labor. Two years after the massive deportations of 1954, a record 445,000 *braceros* crossed the border.

A steady stream of immigrants had been coming to New York from Puerto Rico since the 1920s. As the island's sugarcane economy became more mechanized, nearly 40 percent of the inhabitants left their homeland. By the end of the 1960s, New York City had more Puerto Ricans than San Juan, the island's capital. El Barrio, in East Harlem, became the center of Puerto Rican immigrant life. Author Guillermo Cotto-Thorner described the place in his autobiographical novel *Trópico en Manhattan* through the words of Antonio, an older resident.

> This . . . is our neighborhood, El Barrio . . . . It's said that we Latins run things here. And that's how we see ourselves. While the American take most of the money that circulates around here, we consider this part of the city to be ours . . . . The stores, barbershops, restaurants, butcher shops, churches, funeral parlors, greasy spoons, pool halls, everything is all Latino. Every now and then you see a business run by a Jew or an Irishman or an Italian, but you'll also see that even these people know a little Spanish.

Puerto Ricans, like many other immigrants, hoped to earn money in America and then return home. Some did; others stayed. Like countless Latinos, most failed to enjoy the promise of the American dream.

Native Americans likewise remained outsiders. They faced the consequences of the same technological developments affecting other Americans, but often had greater difficulty coping with the changes they faced, given their long history of persistent discrimination. As power lines reached their reservations, Indians purchased

TIMELINE

1946	1947	1948	1950s	1950
4.6 million workers on strike; ENIAC computer built; Benjamin Spock, *Baby and Child Care*	Defense budget of $13 billion	GM offers UAW cost-of-living adjustment; Transistor developed at Bell Laboratories; Kinsey report on male sexuality	Each year a million farmers leave farms	Diner's Card inaugurated
1951	**1953**	**1954**	**1955**	**1956**
J.D. Salinger, *The Catcher in the Rye*	Defense budget of $47 billion; Operation Wetback begins	Congress adds "under God" to pledge to flag	First McDonald's opens in Illinois; Merger of AFL and CIO; Congress adds "In God We Trust" to currency	Interstate Highway Act; Majority of U.S. workers hold white-collar jobs; Allen Ginsberg, "Howl"
1957	**1960**	**1962**	**1963**	**1970**
Baby boom peaks; Jack Kerouac, *On the Road*	Three-quarters of all Americans own a TV set	Michael Harrington, *The Other America*	California passes New York as most populous state; Betty Friedan, *The Feminine Mystique*	38 percent of all Americans live in suburbs

televisions, refrigerators, washing machines, and automobiles. As they joined the consumer culture, reservation life lost its cohesiveness. Indians who gravitated to the cities often had difficulty adjusting to urban life and faced white hostility, much as did Latinos and blacks. They too began to protest in a movement that gained strength in succeeding years (see Chapter 29).

←←←←←

CONCLUSION

Qualms amid Affluence

In general, the United States during the decade and a half after World War II was stable and secure. Structural adjustments caused occasional moments of friction but were seldom visible in prosperous times. Recessions occurred periodically, but the economy righted itself after short downturns. For the most part, business boomed. The standard of living for many of the nation's citizens reached new heights, especially compared with standards in other parts of the world. Millions of middle-class Americans joined the ranks of suburban property owners, enjoying the benefits of shopping centers and fast-food establishments and other material manifestations of what they considered the good life. Workers found themselves savoring the materialistic advantages of the era.

Some Americans did not share in the prosperity, but they were not visible in the affluent suburbs. Many African-Americans and members of other minority groups were seriously disadvantaged, yet most still believed they could share in the American dream and remained confident that deeply rooted patterns of discrimination could be changed. Even when they began to mobilize, their protest was peaceful at first.

Beneath the calm surface, though, there were signs of discontent. The seeds for the protest movements of the 1960s had already been sown. Disquieting signs were likewise evident on other fronts. The divorce rate increased, as a third of all marriages in the 1950s broke apart. Americans more than doubled their use of tranquilizers between 1958 and 1959, in an effort to cope with problems in their lives. Some Americans began to criticize the materialism that seemed to undermine American efforts in the Cold War. Such criticisms in turn legitimized challenges by other groups, in the continuing struggle to make the realities of American life match the nation's ideals.

Criticisms and anxieties notwithstanding, the United States—for most whites and some people of color—continued to develop according to Ray Kroc's dreams as he first envisioned McDonald's establishments across the land. Healthy and comfortable, upper- and middle-class Americans expected prosperity and growth to continue in the years ahead.

Recommended Reading

Domestic Issues

Joshua Feeman, Nelson Lichtenstein, and Stephen Brier, et al, *Who Built America? Working People & the Nation's Economy, Politics, Culture, and Society* (1992); Peter Blake, *God's Own Junkyard: The Planned Deterioration of America's Landscape* (1964); David Brody, *Workers in Industrial America* (1980); Paul A. Carter, *Another Part of the fifties* (1983); James R. Green, *The World of the Worker* (1980); David Halberstam, *The Fifties* (1993); Samuel P. Hays, *Beauty, Health, and Permanence: Environmental Politics in the United States, 1955–1985* (1987); Daniel Horowitz, ed., *American Social Classes in the 1950s: Selections from Vance Packard's* The Status Seekers (1995); Kenneth T. Jackson, *Crabgrass Frontier: The Suburbanization of the United States* (1985); Alison Lurie, *The Language of Clothes* (1981); Zane L. Miller, *The Urbanization of Modern America* (1973); C. Wright Mills, *White Collar: The American Middle Classes* (1951); Richard Polenberg, *One Nation Divisible: Class, Race, and Ethnicity in the United States Since 1938* (1980); David Riesman, *The Lonely Crowd: A Study of the Changing American Character* (1950); Juliet B. Schor, *The Overworked American: The Unexpected Decline of Leisure* (1991); Richard White, *"It's Your Misfortune and None of My Own": A History of the American West* (1991); Robert H. Zieger, *American Workers, American Unions*, 2d ed. (1994) and *The CIO, 1935–1955* (1995).

Religious Developments

David Chidester, *Patterns of Power: Religion and Politics in American Culture* (1988); Erling Jorstad, *Holding Fast/Pressing On: Religion in America in the 1980s* (1990); R. Laurence Moore, *Selling God: American Religion in the Marketplace of Culture* (1994); Peter W. Williams, *Popular Religion in America: Symbolic Change and the Modernization Process in Historical Perspective* (1980); Garry Wills, *Under God: Religion and American Politics* (1990).

Women's Role in the 1950s

Beth L. Bailey, *From Front Porch to Back Seat: Courtship in Twentieth-Century America* (1988); William H. Chafe, *The American Woman: Her Changing Social, Economic, and political Roles, 1920–1970* (1972); Stephanie Coontz, *The Way We Never Were: American Families and the Nostalgia Trap* (1992); John D'Emilio and Estelle B. Freedman, *Intimate Matters: A History of Sexuality in America* (1988); Sara Evans, *Born for Liberty: A History of Women in America* (1989); Betty Friedan, *The Feminine Mystique* (1963); Susan M. Hartmann, *The Home Front and Beyond: American Women in the 1940s* (1982); Daniel Horowitz, *Betty Friedan and the Making of* The Feminine Mystique: *The American Left, the Cold War and Modern Feminism* (1998); Eugenia Kaledin, *Mothers and More: American Women in the 1950s* (1984); Elaine Tyler May, *Homeward Bound: American Families in the Cold War Era* (1988); Joanne Meyerowitz, ed., *Not June Cleaver: Women and Gender in Postwar America, 1945–1960* (1994).

African-Americans

James Baldwin, *Nobody Knows My Name* (1961); Claude Brown, *Manchild in the Promised Land* (1965); John Hope Franklin and Alfred A. Moss, Jr., *From Slavery to Freedom: A History of African Americans,* 7th ed. (1994); Jacqueline Jones, *Labor of Love, Labor of Sorrow: Black Women, Work, and the Family from Slavery to the Present* (1985).

Chicanos

Rodolfo Acuña, *Occupied America: A History of Chicanos,* 3d ed. (1988); George J. Sánchez, *Becoming Mexican American: Ethnicity, Culture and identity in Chicano Los Angeles, 1900–1945* (1993); Peter Skerry, *Mexican Americans: The Ambivalent Minority* (1993); Ronald Takaki, *A Different Mirror: A History of Multicultural America* (1993).

Native Americans

David Hurst Thomas, Jay Miller, Richard White, Peter Nabokov, Philip J. Deloria, *The Native Americans: An Illustrated History* (1993); Frederick E. Hoxie, ed., *Indians in American History* (1988); Peter Iverson, *"We Are Still Here:" American Indians in the twentieth Century* (1998); Alvin M. Josephy, Jr., *Now That the Buffalo's Gone* (1982); James S. Olson and Raymond Wilson, *Native Americans in the Twentieth Century* (1984).

Fiction

Jack Kerouac, *On the Road* (1957); J. D. Salinger, *The Catcher in the Rye* (1951); Sloan Wilson, *The Man in the Gray Flannel Suit* (1955).

CHAPTER 27

Chills and Fever During the Cold War

In November 1950, Val Lorwin learned of the charges against him. A State Department employee on leave of absence after 16 years of government service, he was in Paris working on a book. Now he had to return home to face an accusation that, as a Communist party member, he was a loyalty and security risk. It seemed to him a tasteless joke. Yet communism was no laughing matter in the United States. Suspicions of the Soviet Union had escalated after 1945, and a wave of paranoia swept the nation.

Lorwin had an unblemished record of government service. In 1935 he had begun working in a series of New Deal agencies. Before being drafted during World War II, he served on the War Production Board. While in the Army, he was assigned to the Office of Strategic Services, an early intelligence agency, and had frequently received security clearances in the United States and abroad.

Lorwin did have a left-wing past. In the 1930s, his social life had revolved around various Socialist party causes, particularly unionizing southern tenant farmers and aiding the unemployed. But that work had been open and legal, and Lorwin had always been aggressively anti-Communist.

Suddenly Lorwin, like others at that time, faced a nightmare. An unnamed accuser had identified him as a Communist. The burden of proof was entirely on him, and the chance of clearing his name was slim. He could undergo a hearing, or resign.

Lorwin requested a hearing, which was held late in 1950. Still struck by the absurdity of the situation, he refuted all accusations but made little effort to cite his own positive achievements. After the hearing, he learned that the government no longer doubted his loyalty but still considered him a security risk—likewise grounds for dismissal from his job. Appealing the ruling, Lorwin still was not told who had accused him.

At the appeal hearing, Lorwin produced 97 sworn witnesses who testified to his good character and meritorious service. The accuser, it came out, had once lived with Lorwin and his wife in Washington, D.C., and claimed that in 1935 Lorwin had revealed that he was holding a Communist party meeting in his home, even showing him a red party card. But Lorwin proved that in 1935 the *Socialist* party card was red, while the *Communist* party card was black. In March 1952, Lorwin was finally cleared for both loyalty and security.

Lorwin's troubles were not yet over. His name appeared on one of the lists produced by Senator Joseph McCarthy of Wisconsin, the most aggressive anti-Communist of the era. In 1953, Lorwin was indicted for making false statements to the State Department Loyalty Security Board. Again the charges proved specious. Finally, in May 1954, admitting that its special prosecutor had lied to the grand jury and had no legitimate case, the Justice

Department asked for dismissal of the indictment. Cleared at last, Lorwin went on to become a distinguished labor historian.

Lorwin was more fortunate than some victims of the anti-Communist crusade. People rallied around him and gave him valuable support. Despite considerable emotional cost, he survived the witch-hunt of the early 1950s, but his case still reflected vividly the ugly domestic consequences of the breakdown in relations between the Soviet Union and the United States.

The Cold War, which unfolded soon after the end of World War II and lasted for nearly 50 years, powerfully affected all aspects of American life. Rejecting for good the isolationist impulse that had governed foreign policy in the 1920s and 1930s, the United States began to play a major role in the world in the postwar years. Doubts about intervention in other lands faded as the nation acknowledged its dominant international position and resolved to do whatever was necessary to maintain it. The same sense of mission that had infused the United States in the Spanish-American War, World War I, and World War II now committed most Americans to the struggle against communism at home and abroad.

This chapter explores that continuing sense of mission and its consequences. It shows how basic beliefs about American destiny drove the United States forward in this latest struggle against forces that stood in its way. It examines the roots of the Cold War both in the idealistic aim to keep the world safe for democracy and in the pursuit of economic self-interest that had long fueled American capitalism. It records how the determination to prevent the spread of communism led American policy makers to consider vast parts of the world as pivotal to American security and to act accordingly, particularly in Korea and Vietnam. It examines the impact on economic development, particularly in the West, where the mighty defense industry flourished. And it considers the tragic consequences of the effort to promote ideological unity within the United States, where excesses threatened the principles of democracy itself.

ORIGINS OF THE COLD WAR

The two strongest powers after World War II—the United States and the Soviet Union—differed profoundly over the shape of the postwar world. European colonial empires were crumbling in Asia, Africa, and the Middle East. The United States was intent on spreading political freedom and free trade around the world to maintain its economic hegemony. The Soviet Union demanded politically sympathetic neighbors on its borders to preserve its security. Suppressed during World War II, these differences now surfaced in a Soviet-American confrontation.

The American Stance

The United States emerged from World War II as the most powerful nation in history, and it sought to use that might to achieve a world order that could sustain American aims. American policy makers, following in Woodrow Wilson's footsteps, hoped to spread the values—liberty, equality, and democracy—underpinning the American dream. They also hoped to forestall another depression. This meant promoting worldwide recovery from wartime devastation, supporting economic enterprise abroad, and opening markets for the industrial and agricultural products that poured out of the American economy, operating at full capacity as a result of the war. In 1947, the United States was the largest source of goods for world markets, with exports totaling $14 billion. To sustain economic growth, American officials reasoned, global trade barriers imposed by the Soviet Union and other nations had to fall. Americans assumed that their prosperity would benefit the rest of the world, even when other nations disagreed.

Soviet Aims

Historically, Russian governments had been strongly centralized autocracies. That authoritarian tradition—as much as Communist ideology, with its stress on class struggle and the inevitable triumph of a proletarian state—shaped Soviet goals after World War II.

During the war, the Russians had played down talk of world revolution, which they knew their allies found threatening, and had mobilized domestic support with nationalistic appeals. As the struggle drew to a close, the Soviets said little about world conquest and emphasized socialism within the nation itself.

Rebuilding was the first priority. Devastated by the war, Soviet agriculture and industry lay in shambles. But revival required internal security. At the same time, the Russians felt vulnerable along their western border, from which Napoleon in the nineteenth century and the Germans twice in the twentieth century had penetrated deep into Russia. Haunted by fears of a quick German recovery, the Soviets demanded defensible borders and subservient neighbors.

Early Cold War Leadership

Both the United States and the Soviet Union had strong leadership in the early years of the Cold War. On the American side, presidents Harry Truman and Dwight Eisenhower accepted the centralization of authority that Franklin Roosevelt had begun, as the executive branch became increasingly powerful in guiding foreign policy. In the Soviet Union, first Joseph Stalin, then Nikita Khrushchev provided equally forceful direction.

America's first postwar president, Harry S Truman, was an unpretentious man who took a straightforward approach to public affairs. But he was ill-prepared for the office he assumed in the final months of World War II. During Truman's three months as vice-president, Franklin Roosevelt had never confided in him, and Truman had been told nothing of the complexity of postwar issues. "I'm not big enough for this job," he groaned to a former Senate colleague.

Yet Truman matured quickly. Impulsive and aggressive, he made a virtue out of rapid response. At his first press conference, reporters could not keep up with his quick replies. A sign on his desk read "The Buck Stops Here," underscoring his determination to make speedy decisions—even though associates sometimes wondered whether he understood all the implications. His rapid-fire decisions had important consequences for the Cold War.

War hero Dwight Eisenhower, who was elected president in 1952 (the first Republican in 20 years), stood in stark contrast to Truman. His easy manner and warm smile made him widely popular. Sometimes he made convoluted comments at press conferences. Yet beneath his casual approach lay real shrewdness. "Don't worry," he once reassured officials briefing him for a press conference. "If that question comes up, I'll just confuse them."

Although his ambitions for high office may have grown during World War II, Eisenhower had not taken the typical route to the presidency. After the war he served successively as army chief of staff, president of Columbia University, and head of the North Atlantic Treaty Organization (NATO), but he made no bid for the presidency before 1952. Despite his apolitical background, he had a knack for getting people to compromise and cooperate. Whereas Truman loved political infighting and wanted to take charge, Eisenhower saw things differently. "You do not *lead* by hitting people over the head. Any damn fool can do that," he said, "but it's usually called 'assault,' not leadership." Even so, Ike knew exactly where he wanted to go and worked behind the scenes to get there.

Both presidents subscribed to traditional American attitudes about self-determination and the superiority of American political institutions and values. Viewing collaboration with the Soviet Union as a wartime necessity, Truman grew increasingly hostile to Soviet moves as the war neared its end. Like Truman, Eisenhower saw communism as a monolithic force struggling for world supremacy and believed that the men in the Kremlin were orchestrating subversion around the globe. Truman would have agreed with his denunciation of the Soviet system as "a tyranny that has brought thousands, millions of people into slave camps and is attempting to make all mankind its chattel." Yet Eisenhower was more willing than Truman to practice accommodation when it served his ends.

The Soviet leader at the war's end, Joseph Stalin, possessed almost absolute power. He had presided over monstrous purges against his opponents in the 1930s. Now he was determined to rebuild Soviet society, if possible with Western assistance, and to keep eastern Europe within the Soviet sphere of influence.

Stalin's death in March 1953 left a power vacuum that was eventually filled by Nikita Khrushchev, who by 1958 held the offices of both premier and party secretary. A crude man, Khrushchev once used his shoe to pound a table at the United Nations while the British prime minister was speaking. During Khrushchev's regime the Cold War continued, but there were now brief periods when Soviet-American relations became less hostile.

Disillusionment with the USSR

American support for the Soviet Union faded quickly after the war. In September 1945, a national poll revealed that 54 percent of the American public trusted the Russians to cooperate with the United States in the postwar years. Two months later, the figure had dropped to 44 percent, and by February 1946, to 35 percent.

As Americans soured on Russia, they began to equate the Nazi and Soviet systems. Just as they had in the 1930s, authors, journalists, and public officials pointed—sometimes legitimately—to similarities between the two regimes. Both states, critics contended, maintained total control over communications and could eliminate political opposition whenever they chose. Both used terror and concentration camps to silence dissidents. After the U.S. publication in 1949 of British writer George Orwell's frightening novel *1984*, an editorial in *Life* magazine noted that Orwell's ominous fictional figure "Big Brother" was but a "mating" of Hitler and Stalin. Truman spoke for many Americans when he said in 1950 that "there isn't any difference between the totalitarian Russian government and the Hitler government . . . . They are all alike. They are . . . police state governments."

A lingering sense that the nation had not been quick enough to resist totalitarian aggression in the 1930s heightened American fears. Had the United States stopped the Germans, Italians, or Japanese, it might have prevented the long, devastating war. The free world had not responded quickly enough before; postwar Americans were determined not to repeat that mistake.

The Troublesome Polish Question

The first East-West clash came, even before the war ended, over Poland. Soviet demands for a friendly Polish government collided with American hopes for a democratic one. The Yalta Conference of February 1945 had attempted to settle the question (see Chapter 25), with a loosely worded and imprecise agreement. When Truman assumed office, the Polish situation remained unresolved.

Truman assumed an unbending stance toward the Soviet Union over Poland. Meeting Soviet Foreign Minister Vyacheslav Molotov in April 1945, he insisted that the Russians were breaking the Yalta agreements and demanded a new democratic government for Poland. As Truman recalled in his memoirs, Molotov protested that "I have never been talked to like that in my life." "Carry out your agreements," Truman retorted bluntly, "and you won't get talked to like that."

Truman and Stalin met face-to-face for the first (and last) time at the Potsdam Conference, the final wartime Big Three meeting. There, outside devastated Berlin, the two leaders sized each other up as they considered the Soviet-Polish boundary, the fate of Germany, and the American desire to obtain Japan's unconditional surrender. It was Truman's first exposure to international diplomacy at the highest level, and it left him confident of his abilities. When he learned during the meeting of the first successful atomic bomb test in New Mexico, he became even more determined to get his way.

Economic Pressure on the USSR

One major source of controversy in the last stages of World War II was the question of U.S. aid to its allies. Responding to congressional pressure to limit foreign assistance as hostilities ended, Truman acted impulsively. Six days after Germany's surrender on V-E Day in May 1945, he issued an executive order cutting off lend-lease supplies to the Allies. Though the policy hurt all nations receiving aid, it hurt the Soviet Union most of all.

The United States intended to use economic pressure in other ways as well. The USSR desperately needed financial assistance to rebuild after the war and, in January 1945, had requested a $6 billion loan. Roosevelt hedged, hoping to win concessions in return. In August 1945 the Soviets renewed their application, this time for only $1 billion. Truman dragged his heels, hoping to use the loan as a lever to gain access to new markets in areas traditionally dominated by the Soviet Union. Unwilling to promote American trade in such areas, Stalin refused the offer of a loan with such conditions and launched his own five-year plan instead.

Declaring the Cold War

As Soviet-American disagreements increased, both sides stepped up their rhetorical attacks. In 1946, Stalin spoke out first, publicly asserting that capitalism and communism were on a collision course, that a series of cataclysmic disturbances would tear the capitalist world apart, and that the Soviet system would triumph. Stalin's speech, said Supreme Court Justice William O. Douglas, was "the declaration of World War III."

Long suspicious of the Soviet Union, former British prime minister Winston Churchill gave a Western response. Speaking in Fulton, Missouri, in 1946, with Truman listening on the platform, Churchill warned that a vigilant association of English-speaking peoples must contain Soviet designs. "From Stettin in the Baltic to Trieste in the Adriatic," he declared, "an iron curtain has descended across the Continent."

CONTAINING THE SOVIET UNION

"Containment" formed the basis of postwar American policy. Both Democrats and Republicans were determined to check Soviet expansion. In an increasingly contentious world, the American government formulated rigid anti-Soviet policies and the Soviet Union responded in an equally uncompromising way.

Containment Defined

George F. Kennan, the chargé d'affaires at the American embassy in the Soviet Union and an expert on Soviet matters, was primarily responsible for defining the new policy. After Stalin's ominous speech in February 1946, Kennan sent an 8,000-word telegram to the State Department. In it he argued that Soviet hostility stemmed from "the Kremlin's neurotic view of world affairs," which in turn came from "the traditional and instinctive Russian sense of insecurity." Soviet fanaticism would not soften, regardless of how accommodating American policy became. Therefore, it had to be opposed at every turn.

Kennan's "Long Telegram" struck a resonant chord in Washington. It made his diplomatic reputation and brought him into an influential State Department position. Soon he published an extended analysis in *Foreign Affairs* under the pseudonym "Mr. X." "The whole Soviet governmental machine, including the mechanism of diplomacy," he wrote, "moves inexorably along the prescribed path, like a persistent toy automobile wound up and headed in a given direction, stopping only when it meets with some unanswerable force." Many Americans agreed with Kennan that Soviet pressure must "be contained by the adroit and vigilant application of counterforce at a series of constantly shifting geographical and political points."

The concept of containment provided the philosophical justification for the hard-line stance that Americans, both in and out of government, adopted. Containment created the framework for military and economic assistance around to globe.

The First Step: The Truman Doctrine

In February 1947, the British ambassador to the United States informed the State Department that his exhausted country could no longer give the Greek and Turkish governments economic and military aid. The Soviet Union was demanding that Turkey agree to joint control of the Dardanelles, the strait separating the Black Sea and the Mediterranean. Meanwhile Communist-led forces were winning a civil war against a right-wing monarchy in Greece. Would the United States fill the void and help the two pro-Western governments resist Communist pressure? The State Department was willing to act in the eastern Mediterranean, which the United States had never before considered vital to national security, but it knew that a conservative, economy-minded Congress would likely object. A key Republican, Senator Arthur Vandenberg of Michigan, warned the top policy makers that they would have to begin "scaring hell out of the country" if they wanted to embark on a bold new containment policy.

Truman took Vandenberg's advice to heart. On March 12, 1947, he told Congress, in a statement that became known as the Truman Doctrine, "I believe that it must be the policy of the United States to support free peoples who are resisting subjugation by armed minorities or by outside pressures." Unless the United States acted, the free world might not survive. To avert that calamity, he urged Congress to appropriate $400 million for military and economic aid to Turkey and Greece. Not everyone agreed with Truman's overblown description of the situation, but Congress passed his foreign aid bill. The Truman Doctrine represented the first major application of containment policy.

In assuming that Americans could police the globe, the Truman Doctrine was taking a major step in the advent of the Cold War. Truman's address, observed financier Bernard Baruch, "was tantamount to a declaration of an ideological or religious war." Journalist Walter Lippmann was more critical. He termed the new containment policy a "strategic monstrosity" that could embroil the United States in disputes around the world. In the succeeding two decades, Lippmann proved correct.

The Marshall Plan, NATO, and NSC-68

The next step for American policy makers involved sending extensive economic aid for the postwar recovery of western Europe, which was economically and politically unstable. To forestall Communist movements there, decisive American action was needed. "The patient is sinking while the doctors deliberate," declared the new secretary of state, George Marshall. Another motive for action was to bolster the European economy to provide markets for American goods.

Marshall revealed the administration's willingness to assist European recovery in a speech in June 1947. He asked all troubled European nations to draw up an aid program that the United States could support, a program "directed not against any

country or doctrine but against hunger, poverty, desperation, and chaos."
Communist states were welcome to participate if they ceased being secretive about
their economic affairs, a condition that Marshall knew they were not likely to
accept. The proposed program would assist the ravaged nations, provide the
United States with needed markets, and advance the nation's ideological aims.
American aid, Marshall pointed out, would permit the "emergence of political
and social conditions in which free institutions can exist." The Marshall Plan and
the Truman Doctrine, Truman noted, were "two halves of the same walnut."

American officials agreed to provide $17 billion over a period of four years to
16 cooperating nations. Some members of Congress objected that the Marshall Plan
would spread U.S. resources too thin; on the left, former vice president Henry A.
Wallace, who had broken with the administration, blasted the "Martial Plan" as
another step toward war. But in early 1948, Congress committed the nation to funding European recovery, and the containment policy moved forward another step.

Closely related to the Marshall Plan was a concerted Western effort to integrate
a rebuilt Germany into a reviving Europe. Roosevelt, Churchill, and Stalin had
agreed at Yalta to divide Germany into four occupation zones (Soviet, American,
British, and French) and to force Germany to pay reparations. A year after the war
ended, however, the balance of power in Europe had shifted. With the Soviets
threatening to dominate eastern Europe, the West moved to fill the vacuum in central Europe. In late 1946, the Americans and British merged their zones economically and began assigning administrative duties to Germans. By mid-1947, despite
French worries, the process of rebuilding West German industry was under way.

In mid-1948 a crisis erupted when the Soviets attempted to force the Western
powers out of Berlin. The former German capital, deep in the Soviet occupation
zone, was itself divided into four occupation zones. When the Soviets refused to
allow their former allies land access to West Berlin, the U.S. Air Force and the
Royal Air Force responded by airlifting more than two million tons of supplies to
the beleaguered West Berliners. The airlift broke the Soviet blockade.

The next major link in the containment strategy was the creation of a military
alliance in Europe, complementing the Marshall Plan. After the Soviets tightened
their control of Hungary and Czechoslovakia, the United States in 1949 took the
lead in establishing the North Atlantic Treaty Organization (NATO). This alliance
of 12 nations, including the United States, vowed that an attack against one would
be an attack against all, to be met with appropriate armed force. The U.S. Senate
ratified the pact, which was the United States' first military alliance since the
American Revolution. Congress also voted military aid for the NATO allies. The
Cold War had softened long-standing American reluctance to become closely
involved in European affairs.

Two dramatic events in 1949—the Communist victory in the Chinese civil war
and the Russian detonation of an atomic device—jolted the United States into
sharpening its strategy. Responding to Truman's request for a full-fledged review
of U.S. policies, the National Security Council (an agency established in 1947 to
advise the president) produced the document called NSC-68. It shaped U.S. policy
for the next 20 years.

NSC-68 built on the cataclysmic Cold War rhetoric of the Truman Doctrine. It
assumed that East-West conflict was unavoidable and that negotiation with
Soviets—who could never be trusted to bargain in good faith—was useless.

An American and British airlift in 1948 brought badly needed supplies to West Berliners isolated behind a Soviet blockade of the city. By refusing to allow the Western powers to reach the city, located within the Soviet zone, the Russians hoped to drive them from Berlin, but the airlift broke the blockade. (Corbis-Bettmann)

Instead, it called for a massive increase in defense spending, from the $13 billion set for 1950 to as much as $50 billion per year. These huge costs, the document argued, were the price the United States must pay for the free world's survival.

Containment in the 1950s

When the Republicans took over the White House in 1953, containment, the keystone of American policy throughout the Truman years, came under attack by high officials of the Eisenhower administration. To them, containment seemed too cautious a response to the threat of communism.

Leading the charge was John Foster Dulles, secretary of state for most of Eisenhower's two terms. A devout Presbyterian who hated atheistic communism, Dulles sought to move beyond containment and mount a holy crusade to promote democracy and liberate Soviet-dominated countries.

Eisenhower, more conciliatory and realistic than Dulles, recognized the impossibility of changing the governments of Russia's satellites. He also understood the need for caution. In mid-1953, as East Germans mounted anti-Soviet demonstrations, the United States kept its distance. In 1956, when Hungarian "freedom fighters" rose up against Soviet domination, the United States again stood back as Soviet tanks smashed the rebels. Because Western action could have precipitated a

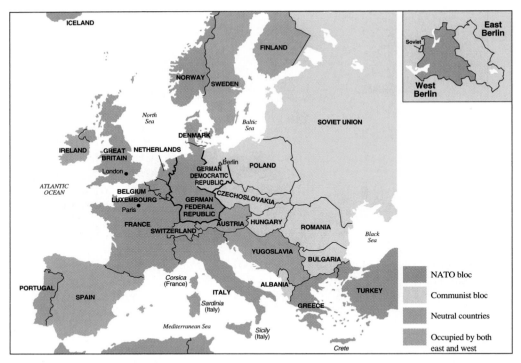

COLD WAR EUROPE IN 1950   This map shows the rigid demarcation between East and West during the Cold War. Although there were a number of neutral countries in Europe, the other nations found themselves in a standoff, as each side tried to contain the possible advances of the other. The small insert map in the upper-right-had corner shows the division of Berlin itself after World War II.

more general conflict, Eisenhower refused to translate rhetoric into action. Throughout the 1950s the policy of containment, largely as it had been defined earlier, remained in effect.

In the 1950s, however, the government depended increasingly on the Central Intelligence Agency (CIA). Established along with the National Security Council in 1947, the CIA conducted espionage abroad and analyzed the information it gathered. Some of its work was open; much was secret. Eisenhower appointed John Foster Dulles's brother Allen to head the agency. With presidential approval the CIA rearranged its priorities, so that by 1957 it was spending 80 percent of its budget on covert activities. Eisenhower used clandestine CIA actions to undermine unfriendly foreign governments, to subsidize sympathetic newspapers abroad, and to assist pro-American figures around the world.

CONTAINMENT IN ASIA, THE MIDDLE EAST, AND LATIN AMERICA

The containment policy in Europe represented an unprecedented American effort to promote continental stability. Soon the United States departed even further from its traditions by extending its commitments in a policy of *global* containment. As European colonial empires began disintegrating, Americans recognized that communism exerted a tremendous appeal in newly emerging nations. Even greater efforts were required to advance American aims.

The Shock of the Chinese Revolution

America's commitment to global containment became stronger with the Communist victory in the Chinese civil war in 1949. An ally during World War II, China had struggled against the Japanese while simultaneously fighting a domestic conflict rooted deeply in the Chinese past—in widespread poverty, disease, oppression by the landlord class, and national humiliation at the hands of foreign powers. Mao Zedong (Mao Tse-tung),* founder of the Chinese Communist Party, wished to reshape China in a distinctive Marxist mold. Opposing the Communists were the Nationalists, led by Jiang Jieshi (Chiang Kai-shek). By the early 1940s, Jiang's regime was exhausted, hopelessly inefficient, and corrupt. Mao's movement, meanwhile, grew stronger during World War II as it opposed the Japanese invaders and won the loyalty of the peasantry. Losing the civil war in 1949, Jiang fled to the island of Taiwan. There he nursed the improbable belief that his was still the rightful government of all China and that he would one day return to the mainland.

The United States failed to understand what had happened in China or to appreciate the immense popular support that Mao generated. As the Communist army moved toward victory, the *New York Times* dismissed it as a "nauseous force." Secretary of State Dean Acheson considered granting diplomatic recognition to the new regime but backed off after the Communists seized American property, harassed American citizens, and openly allied China with the USSR. Acheson and other American leaders mistakenly considered Mao a mere Soviet puppet.

Chinese-American tension increased during the Korean War and again in 1954, when Mao's government began shelling Nationalist positions on the tiny offshore islands of Quemoy and Matsu. But Eisenhower was unwilling to respond forcefully. Cautiously, he committed America only to defending the Nationalists on Taiwan.

Stalemate in the Korean War

The Korean War, on the other hand, highlighted growing U.S. intervention in Asia. Concern about China and determination to contain Communism led the United States into a bloody foreign struggle. But the sometimes fuzzy American objectives remained largely unrealized after three years of war.

The conflict in Korea stemmed from tensions lingering after World War II. Korea, long under Japanese control, hoped for independence after Japan's defeat. But the Allies temporarily divided Korea along the 38th parallel when the rapid end to the Pacific struggle allowed Soviet troops to accept the Japanese surrender in the north while American forces did the same in the south. Initially intended as a matter of military convenience, the Soviet-American line hardened after 1945, just

---

*Chinese names are rendered in their modern *pinyin* spelling. At first occurrence, the older but perhaps more familiar spelling (usually Wade-Giles) is given in parentheses.

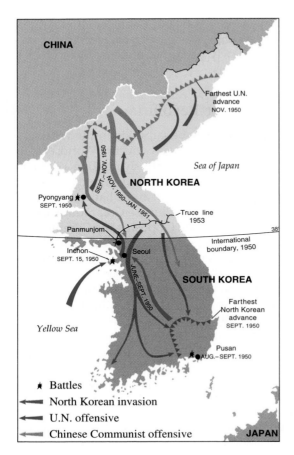

THE KOREAN WAR This map shows the ebb and flow of the Korean War. North Korea crossed the 38th parallel first, then the UN offensive drove the North Koreans close to the Chinese border, and finally the Chinese Communists entered the war and drove the UN forces back below the 38th parallel. The armistice signed at Panmunjom in 1953 provided a dividing line very close to the prewar line.

as a similar division became rigid in Germany. In time, the Soviets set up one Korean government in the north and the Americans another government in the south. Each Korean government hoped to reunify the country on its own terms.

North Korea moved first. The North Korean leader, Kim Il Sung, visited Moscow in early 1950 and spoke to Stalin about instability in the south. Although the Russians may have acquiesced in Kim's ideas, North Korea took the initiative in planning and timing. On June 25, 1950, it invaded South Korea. Following Soviet-built tanks, North Korean troops steadily advanced.

The United States had earlier seemed reluctant to defend South Korea but, taken by surprise, Truman responded vigorously to the invasion. "If this is allowed to go unchallenged," he declared, "it would mean a third world war, just as similar incidents had brought on the second world war." Truman directed General Douglas MacArthur, who headed the American occupation of Japan, to supply South Korea. Because Moscow was boycotting the UN to protest China's exclusion from it, the United States was able to get the Security Council to brand North Korea an aggressor and obtained another resolution calling on members of the organization to assist the South in repelling aggression and restoring peace.

On Truman's orders, American forces went into battle south of the 38th parallel: first naval and air units, then American ground forces. They, as well as other allied forces, fought together on behalf of the United Nations. Following a daring amphibious invasion in September that pushed the North Koreans back to the former dividing line, the UN forces crossed the 38th parallel and sought to reunify Korea under an American-backed government. Chinese warnings that this movement threatened their security were ignored. After briefly appearing in battle in October, the Chinese mounted a full-fledged counterattack in November 1950, which drove the UN forces below the dividing line.

In the stalemate that followed, the brilliant but arrogant MacArthur clashed openly with Truman, his commander-in-chief. MacArthur demanded retaliatory air strikes against China; Truman, trying to conduct a limited war, refused. MacArthur's public statements, issued from the field, finally went too far. In April 1951, he argued that the American approach to Korea was wrong—that "there is no substitute for victory." Truman had no choice but to relieve him for insubordination. An outraged public, remembering the stunning American victories of World War II, largely supported MacArthur and reviled Truman.

The Korean War dragged on into Eisenhower's presidency. Campaigning in 1952, Ike had promised to go to Korea, and go he did three weeks after he was elected. When truce talks bogged down again in May 1953, the new administration privately threatened China with atomic weapons and a massive military campaign. This threat brought about renewed negotiations. Finally, on July 27, 1953, an armistice was signed. The Republican administration had succeeded where the preceding Democratic administration had failed. After three long years, the unpopular war was over.

The Korean War carried a heavy price: 54,000 American dead and many more wounded. These figures paled beside as many as two million Koreans dead and countless others maimed.

The war significantly changed American attitudes and institutions. For the first time, American forces fought in racially integrated units. As commander-in-chief, President Truman had ordered the integration of the armed forces in 1948, over the opposition of many generals, and blacks became part of all military units. Their successful performance in Korea led to acceptance of military integration.

The Korean War years also saw military expenditures soar from $13 billion in 1950 to about $47 billion three years later as defense spending followed the guidelines of NSC-68. Whereas the military absorbed less than a third of the federal budget in 1950, a decade later it took one-half. More than a million military men were stationed around the world. At home, an increasingly powerful military establishment became closely tied to corporate and scientific communities, creating a military-industrial complex that employed 3.5 million Americans by 1960.

The Korean War had important political effects as well. It led the United States to sign a peace treaty with Japan in September 1951 and to rely on that nation to maintain the balance of power in the Pacific. At the same time, the struggle poisoned America's relations with the People's Republic of China and ensured a diplomatic standoff that lasted more than 20 years.

Turbulence in the Middle East

Cold War attitudes influenced American responses to dramatic events in the postwar Middle East, a part of the world that had tremendous strategic importance as

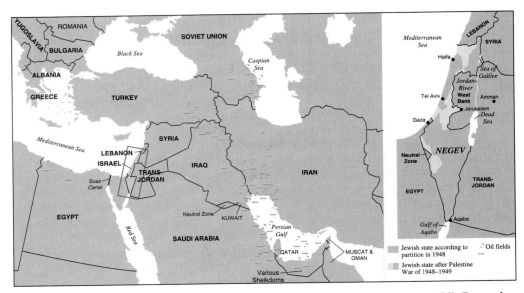

THE MIDDLE EAST IN 1949   This map shows the extensive oil resources that made the Middle East such an important region, and the shifting boundaries of Israel as a result of the war following its independence in 1948. Notice how its size increased after its victory in the first of a series of Middle Eastern conflicts.

the supplier of oil for the industrialized nations. During World War II, the major Allied powers (including the Soviet Union) had occupied Iran, agreeing that they would withdraw six months after the war's end. As of early 1946, both Great Britain and the United States had withdrawn, but the Soviet Union, which bordered on Iran, continued its occupation. Stalin claimed that earlier security agreements had not been honored and demanded oil concessions. Only a threat of vigorous American action forced the Soviets out.

The Eisenhower administration maintained its interest in Iran. In 1953, the CIA helped the Iranian army overthrow the government of Mohammed Mossadegh, which had nationalized formerly British oil wells, and placed the shah of Iran securely on the Peacock Throne. After the coup, British and American companies regained control of the wells, and thereafter the United States government provided military assistance to the shah.

A far more serious situation emerged in Palestine, which since the end of World War I had been under British rule. With British control set to end in 1948, the United Nations attempted to partition Palestine into an Arab state and a Jewish state. Truman officially recognized the new state of Israel 15 minutes after it was proclaimed. But American recognition could not end bitter animosities between Arabs, who felt they had been robbed of their territory, and Jews, who felt that they had finally regained a homeland after the horrors of the Holocaust. As Americans looked on, Arab forces from Egypt, Trans-Jordan, Syria, Lebanon, and Iraq invaded Israel, but the Israelis won the war and added territory to what the UN had given them.

The United States cultivated close ties with Israel but could not afford to alienate oil-rich Arab states or allow them to fall into the Soviet orbit. In Egypt, Arab nationalist Gamal Abdel Nasser, who seized power in 1952, planned a great dam on the Nile River to produce electricity—and proclaimed his country neutral in the Cold War. Dulles offered American financial support for the Aswan Dam project, but when Nasser also began discussions with the Soviet Union, the secretary of state furiously withdrew the American offer. Left without funds for the dam, Nasser nationalized the British-controlled Suez Canal in July 1956. He thereupon closed the canal to Israeli ships. All of Europe feared that Nasser would disrupt the flow of oil from the Middle East.

In October and November 1956, Israeli, British, and French troops invaded Egypt. Eisenhower, who had not been consulted, was irate. Realizing that the attack might push Nasser into Moscow's arms, the United States sponsored a UN resolution condemning the attack and cut off oil from Britain and France. These actions persuaded them, and the Israelis, to withdraw.

In 1958, the United States intervened in the Middle East to block perceived Soviet expansionism. Eisenhower landed 14,000 soldiers in Lebanon to prop up a right-wing government challenged from within.

The Middle East remained a battleground. In 1967, Israeli forces defeated an Arab coalition in the Six Day War and seized the West Bank and Jerusalem, the Golan Heights, and the Sinai Peninsula. Egypt struck again in 1973 in the Yom Kippur War, but Israel again prevailed. In both cases, the United States used its influence to halt the fighting in order to maintain regional stability and uninterrupted supplies of oil.

Restricting Revolt in Latin America

The Cold War also affected relations in Latin America, the United States' traditional sphere of influence, and provided fresh reasons for American intervention. In 1954, Dulles sniffed Communist activity in Guatemala, and Eisenhower ordered CIA support for a coup to oust the elected government of Colonel Jacobo Arbenz Guzmán. The property of the United Fruit Company that Arbenz had seized was restored, but at the cost of aborting needed reform. Interference in Guatemala fed anti-American feeling throughout Latin America.

In 1959, when Fidel Castro overthrew the dictatorship of Fulgencio Batista in Cuba, the shortsightedness of American policy became even clearer. Nationalism and the thrust for social reform were powerful forces in Latin America and other parts of the globe formerly dominated by imperialism, nations that now called themselves "the Third World." When Castro confiscated American property in Cuba, the Eisenhower administration cut off exports and severed diplomatic ties. Castro turned to Russia for support.

ATOMIC WEAPONS AND THE COLD WAR

Throughout the Cold War period, nuclear weapons were a crucial factor in world affairs. Atomic bombs were destructive enough, but when the United States and the Soviet Union both developed hydrogen bombs, an age of overkill began.

Sharing the Secret of the Bomb

The United States, with British aid, had built the atomic bomb in secrecy. Soviet spies, however, discovered that the Americans were at work on the bomb. By 1943, a program to create a Soviet atomic bomb was under way.

The question of sharing the atomic secret was considered in the immediate postwar years. Secretary of War Henry L. Stimson favored cooperating with the Soviet Union. Recognizing the futility of trying to cajole the Soviets while "having this weapon ostentatiously on our hip," he suggested that "their suspicions and their distrust of our purposes and motives will increase." Only mutual accommodation, he thought, could bring international cooperation.

But the United States never followed Stimson's advice. Truman, increasingly worried about the Soviet presence in eastern Europe, vowed to retain America's technological advantage. He resisted a more flexible approach until a "foolproof method of control" over atomic weapons could be devised. Most Americans agreed.

For a time the administration sought a means of international arms control. The United States proposed an international agency to provide atomic energy control. This plan failed when negotiations collapsed, and the United States moved toward its own internal mechanism of control. The Atomic Energy Act of 1946 established the Atomic Energy Commission to supervise all atomic energy development in the United States. It also opened the way to a nuclear arms race once the USSR developed its own bomb.

Nuclear Proliferation

As the atomic bomb found its way into popular culture, Americans at first showed more excitement than fear. In Los Angeles the "Atombomb Dancers" wiggled at the Burbank Burlesque Theater. Even so, anxiety lurked beneath the exuberance, though it did not surface while the United States held a nuclear monopoly. Then, in September 1949, reporters called to the White House were told: "We have evidence that within recent weeks an atomic explosion occurred in the U.S.S.R." Over the Labor Day weekend, a U.S. Air Force weather reconnaissance plane on a routine mission had picked up air samples showing higher than normal radiation counts. Scientists soon concluded that the Soviets had conducted a nuclear test.

The American public was stunned. Suddenly the security of being the world's only atomic power had vanished. Harold C. Urey, a Nobel Prize-winning scientist, summed up the feelings of many Americans: "There is only one thing worse than one nation having the atomic bomb—that's two nations having it."

In early 1950, Truman authorized the development of a new hydrogen superbomb, potentially far more devastating than the atomic bomb. Edward Teller, a physicist on the Manhattan Project, had theorized that nuclear fusion might release energy in even greater amounts than nuclear fission, which had powered the atomic bomb. Now he had the chance to prove it.

By 1953, both the United States and the Soviet Union had unlocked the secret of the hydrogen bomb. Rumors circulated that the first test of a hydrogen device in the Pacific Ocean had blasted a hole in the ocean floor 175 feet deep and a mile wide. Later, after the 1954 BRAVO test, Lewis Strauss, Atomic Energy

Commission chairman, admitted that "an H-bomb can be made . . . large enough to take out a city." Then, in 1957, shortly after the news that the Soviets had successfully tested their first intercontinental ballistic missile (ICBM), Americans learned that the Soviets had fired the first satellite, *Sputnik,* into outer space—with a rocket that could also deliver a hydrogen bomb on the United States. The apparent inferiority of American rocketry and the vulnerability of the country to attack shocked the nation.

But there was another dimension to the nuclear dilemma. The world learned about fallout when the BRAVO blast showered Japanese fishermen 85 miles away with radioactive dust. They became ill with radiation sickness, and several months later, one died. The Japanese, who had been the first to feel the effects of atomic weapons, were outraged and alarmed. Everywhere people began to realize the terrible consequences of the new weapons.

Authors in both the scientific and the popular press focused attention on radioactive fallout. Radiation, physicist Ralph Lapp observed, "cannot be felt and possesses all the terror of the unknown." Nevil Shute's 1957 bestseller *On the Beach,* and the film that followed, described a war that released so much radioactive waste that all life in the Northern Hemisphere perished, while the Southern Hemisphere waited for the residue to bring the same deadly end. In 1959, when *Consumer Reports* warned of the contamination of milk with strontium-90 from nuclear fallout, public alarm grew.

The discovery of fallout provoked a bomb shelter craze. Companies advertised prefabricated shelters to panicky customers. A firm in Miami reported many inquiries about shelters costing between $1,795 and $3,895, depending on capacity, and planned 900 franchises. By the end of 1960, some one million family shelters had been installed.

The Nuclear West

The nuclear arms race sparked an enormous increase in defense spending and created a huge nuclear industry, particularly in the West. Contractors liked the region because of its anti-union attitudes; labor stability, they said, would facilitate meeting government deadlines.

Several key facilities of the Manhattan Project had been located in the West. The plant at Hanford, Washington, was one of the important producers of fissionable material, and the bomb had been assembled at Los Alamos, New Mexico. Such activities continued after the war: Hanford produced plutonium; a facility outside Denver made plutonium triggers for thermonuclear bombs; and the Los Alamos laboratory remained a major research center. In 1951, the Nevada Test Site opened 65 miles north of Las Vegas. The local chamber of commerce published schedules of test shots, which people liked to watch.

Defense spending brought prosperity to these and other communities. Naval commands maintained headquarters in Seattle, San Francisco, San Diego, and Honolulu. Radar sites to track incoming missiles stretched all the way to Alaska. The Boeing Company, located in Seattle, stimulated tremendous development in that city as it produced the B-47s and B-52s that were the Air Force's main delivery vehicles for nuclear bombs.

"Massive Retaliation"

As Americans faced the implications of nuclear weaponry, government policy came to depend increasingly on an atomic shield. Truman authorized the development of a nuclear arsenal but also stressed conventional forms of defense. President Eisenhower, however, decided to rely on atomic weapons rather than combat forces as the key to American defense. Dulles developed a policy of threatening "massive retaliation:" the United States, he announced, was willing and ready to use nuclear weapons against Communist aggression "at places of our own choosing." The policy allowed troop cutbacks and promised to be cost-effective by giving "more bang for the buck."

Massive retaliation provided for an all-or-nothing response, leaving no middle course, no alternative between nuclear war and surrender. Critics called Dulles's foreign policy "brinksmanship" and wondered what would happen if the line was crossed in the new nuclear age. Eisenhower himself was horrified when he saw reports of what nuclear weapons could do, and with characteristic caution he did his best to ensure that the rhetoric of massive retaliation did not lead to war.

Atomic Protest

As the arms race spiraled, critics demanded that it end. In 1956, Democratic presidential candidate Adlai Stevenson called for a halt to nuclear tests that were "poisoning the atmosphere." Eisenhower did not respond, but Dulles minimized the hazards by claiming that "from a health standpoint, there is greater danger from wearing a wrist watch with a luminous dial."

Unimpressed, in 1957, anti-nuclear activists organized SANE, the National Committee for a Sane Nuclear Policy. One of its most effective advertisements featured the internationally known pediatrician Dr. Spock pondering a little girl with a frown on his face. "Dr. Spock is worried," the caption read, and the text went on to quote Spock's fears about the effects of fallout on children. Several years later, women who had worked with SANE took the protest movement a step further. Concerned about radiation in the milk they served their children, they called on women all over the country to suspend normal activities for a day and strike for peace. An estimated 50,000 women marched in 60 communities around the nation.

Pressure from many groups produced a political breakthrough and sustained it for a time. The superpowers began a voluntary test moratorium in the fall of 1958, which lasted until the Soviet Union broke it in September 1961. The United States resumed tests the following March.

THE COLD WAR AT HOME

The Cold War deeply affected domestic fears and led to the creation of an internal loyalty program that seriously violated civil liberties. As Americans began to suspect infiltration at home, some determined that they needed to root out any traces of communism inside the United States.

Truman's Loyalty Program

As the Truman administration mobilized support for containment, its rhetoric became increasingly shrill. An alarmed Attorney General J. Howard McGrath spoke of "many Communists in America," each bearing "the germ of death for society." When administration officials uncovered an internal threat to security, Truman appointed a Temporary Commission on Employee Loyalty—partly because he feared disloyalty and partly to undercut Republican charges that the Democrats were "soft on communism."

In 1947, having received the report of his temporary commission, Truman established a new Federal Employee Loyalty Program by executive order. As he articulated his containment policy, the president ordered the FBI to check its files for evidence of subversive activity and to bring suspects before a new Civil Service Commission Loyalty Review Board. Initially, the program contained safeguards and assumed that a challenged employee was innocent until proved guilty. But as the Loyalty Review Board assumed more power, it ignored individual rights. Employees under suspicion had little chance to fight back. Val Lorwin was one of many victims. Although the Truman loyalty program found grounds to dismiss only a few hundred government employees, it investigated several million, breeding unwarranted fears of subversion and legitimating investigatory tactics that were later used irresponsibly to harm many innocent people.

The Congressional Loyalty Program

While Truman's loyalty probe investigated government employees, Congress launched its own program. The Smith Act of 1940 had made it a crime to advocate or teach the forcible overthrow of the U.S. government. In 1949, Eugene Dennis and ten other Communist leaders were found guilty under its terms. In 1951, the Supreme Court upheld the Smith Act, clearing the way for the prosecution of nearly 100 other Communists.

The McCarran Internal Security Act of 1950 further circumscribed Communist activity by declaring it illegal to conspire to act in a way that would "substantially contribute" to establishing a totalitarian dictatorship in America. Members of Communist organizations had to register with the attorney general and could not obtain passports or work in national defense jobs. Passing the measure over Truman's veto, Congress provided further legal backing for the anti-communist crusade. The American Communist party, which even in the Depression had never been large, declined still further. Membership, numbering about 80,000 in 1947, fell to 55,000 in 1950 and 25,000 in 1954.

The investigations of the House Committee on Un-American Activities (HUAC) contributed to that decline. Intent on rooting out subversives, HUAC probed the motion picture industry in 1947. Protesting its scare tactics, some people whom the committee summoned refused to testify under oath and were scapegoated. The so-called Hollywood Ten, a group of film writers, went to federal prison for contempt of court. Hollywood then knuckled under and blacklisted anyone with even a marginally questionable past. No one on these lists could find jobs at the studios anymore.

Congress made a greater splash with the Hiss-Chambers case. Whittaker Chambers, a former Communist who had broken with the party in 1938 and had become a successful *Time* magazine editor, charged that Alger Hiss had been a Communist in the 1930s. Hiss was a distinguished New Dealer who had served in the Agriculture Department before becoming assistant secretary of state. Now out of the government, he was president of the Carnegie Endowment for International Peace. He denied Chambers's charge, and the matter might have died there had not freshman congressman Richard Nixon taken up the case. Nixon finally extracted Hiss's admission that he had once known Chambers. When Hiss sued Chambers for libel, Chambers changed his story and charged that Hiss was a Soviet spy.

Hiss was indicted for perjury—for lying under oath about his former relationship with Chambers. The case made front-page news. Chambers appeared unstable and changed his story several times. Yet Hiss, too, seemed contradictory in his testimony and never adequately explained how copies of stolen State Department documents had been typed on a typewriter he had once owned. The first trial ended in a hung jury; the second trial, in January 1950, sent Hiss to prison for almost four years. While Hiss maintained his innocence until his death, recently disclosed evidence seems to underscore his guilt.

Dean Acheson was Hiss's friend, and the secretary of state announced that, whatever happened, "I do not intend to turn my back on Alger Hiss." Decent though this affirmation was, it caused Acheson political trouble. Truman, too, was broadly attacked because of his comments about the case. The dramatic Hiss affair helped to discredit the Democrats and to justify the even worse witch hunt that followed.

The Second Red Scare

The key anti-Communist warrior in the 1950s was Joseph R. McCarthy. He had not distinguished himself since being elected to the Senate from Wisconsin in 1946; now, facing reelection in a state Harry Truman had carried in 1948, McCarthy needed an issue. Speaking before a women's club in Wheeling, West Virginia, in February 1950, not long after Hiss's conviction, McCarthy brandished what he said was a list of 205 known Communists in the State Department. Pressed for details, he first said that he would give his list only to the president and then reduced the number to 57.

McCarthy drew mixed early reactions. A subcommittee of the Senate Foreign Relations Committee, after looking into his charges, found them "a fraud and a hoax." Working-class ethnic groups liked his attacks on established elites, and conservative midwestern Republicans admired him for lambasting liberals. As his public support grew, other Republican senators realized his partisan value and egged him on.

He selected assorted targets. In the elections of 1950, he attacked Millard Tydings, the Democrat from Maryland who chaired the subcommittee that had dismissed McCarthy's first accusations. A doctored photograph, supposedly showing Tydings with deposed American Communist leader Earl Browder, helped bring

Senator Joseph McCarthy's spurious charges inflamed anticommunist sentiment in the 1950s. Here he uses a chart of Communist Party organization in the United States to suggest that the nation was at risk until subversives were rooted out. (Corbis-Bettmann)

about Tyding's defeat. McCarthy blasted Acheson as the "Red Dean of the State Department" and slandered George C. Marshall as "a man steeped in falsehood."

A veteran demagogue, McCarthy liked to play tough for press coverage. He did not mind appearing disheveled, unshaven, and half sober. He used obscenity and vulgarity freely. His tactics worked because the public feared the Communist threat. The arrest in 1950 of Julius and Ethel Rosenberg fueled hysteria. The Rosenbergs, a seemingly ordinary American couple with two small children, were charged with stealing and transmitting atomic secrets to the Russians. To many Americans, only treachery from within could explain how the backward Russians had built an atomic bomb. When the Rosenbergs were convicted and, in 1953, executed, pleas that they were victims of hysteria availed for nothing. While some continued to argue their innocence, documents released at the end of the Cold War affirmed Julius's guilt, though left Ethel's involvement in question.

McCarthy's power grew when the Republicans captured the Senate in 1952. He became chairman of the Government Operations Committee and head of its Permanent Investigations Subcommittee. He now had a stronger base and two dedicated assistants, Roy Cohn and G. David Schine. Eisenhower, who disliked McCarthy, grew uneasy but, recognizing his popularity, was reluctant to challenge him.

Finally, McCarthy, Cohn, and Schine pushed too hard. In 1953 the Army drafted Schine, refusing him preferential treatment. Angered, McCarthy began to investigate Army security and even top-level military leaders. When the Army charged that McCarthy was going too far, the Senate investigated the complaint. In April

1954 the Army-McCarthy hearings began. For 36 days a fascinated nationwide television audience witnessed the power of TV to shape public opinion. Americans saw McCarthy's savage tactics and judged him irresponsible and destructive, particularly in contrast to the quiet eloquence of the Army's lawyer, Boston attorney Joseph Welch. McCarthy's ruthless methods discredited him, and the Senate finally summoned the courage to condemn him. Conservatives then turned against him because by attacking Eisenhower and the Army, he was no longer venting his venom on liberals and Democrats. Although McCarthy remained in the Senate, his influence disappeared. Three years later, at the age of 48, he died a broken man.

The Casualties of Fear

The anti-Communist crusade kindled pervasive suspicion in American society. In the late 1940s and early 1950s, dissent no longer seemed safe. Civil servants, government workers, academics, and actors all came under attack and found that the right of due process often evaporated amid the Cold War red scare. Seasoned China experts lost their diplomatic jobs, and social justice legislation faltered.

The paranoia affected American life in countless ways. New York subway workers were fired for refusing to answer questions about their political beliefs. Arizona and New Mexico Navajos, facing starvation in the bitter winter of 1947–1948, were denied government relief because their communal way of life seemed "communistic." Black actor Paul Robeson, who, along with the aged W.E.B. Du Bois, criticized American foreign policy, was accused of Communist leanings and found few opportunities to perform. Eventually both Robeson and Du Bois (who actually joined the Communist party) lost their passports. Hispanic laborers faced deportation for belonging to left-wing unions. In 1949, the Congress of Industrial Organizations (CIO) expelled 11 unions with a total membership of more than a million members for alleged Communist domination. Many individual victims of the witch hunts were less lucky than Val Lorwin. They were the unfortunate victims as the United States became consumed by the passions of the Cold War.

CONTINUING CONFRONTATIONS WITH COMMUNISTS

The Cold War continued into the 1960s and 1970s. Presidents John F. Kennedy and Lyndon B. Johnson were both aggressive cold warriors who subscribed to their predecessors' policies. Their anti-Communist commitments kept the nation locked in the same bitter conflict that had dominated foreign policy in the 1950s and led to continuing global confrontations.

John F. Kennedy and the Bay of Pigs Fiasco

Kennedy, who won the presidency in 1960, wanted to take charge of the White House. At 43, he was the youngest man ever elected president, and he was impatient to "get the country moving again." He also intended to stand up to the Russians. The United States, he proclaimed in his inaugural address, would "pay any price, bear any burden, meet any hardship, support any friend, oppose any foe, to assure the survival and success of liberty."

Kennedy first clashed with communism in the spring of 1961. Fidel Castro's radical regime in Cuba not only leaned toward the Soviet Union but also provided a model for anti-American uprisings elsewhere in Latin America. Just before Kennedy took office, the United States broke diplomatic relations with Cuba. Meanwhile the CIA had begun training anti-Castro exiles to storm the Cuban coast and provoke the uprising that American planners assumed would follow. Told of the plan, Kennedy approved it.

The invasion, which struck a place called the Bay of Pigs on April 17, 1961, was an unmitigated disaster. Cuban forces stopped the invaders on the beach, and there was no popular uprising. The United States stood exposed of clumsily and unsuccessfully trying to overthrow a sovereign government and of breaking promises not to interfere in the internal affairs of hemispheric neighbors.

Chastened, Kennedy nevertheless remained determined to deal sternly with the perceived Communist threat. Having met a hostile Nikita Khrushchev at Vienna in June 1961, where tense discussions focused on Soviet demands for a permanent settlement of West Berlin's status that would close the city as an escape hatch from East Germany, Kennedy reacted aggressively. He asked Congress for $3 billion more in defense spending, for more men in the armed services, and for funds for a civil defense fallout shelter program, explicitly warning of the threat of nuclear war. The crisis eased only when the USSR erected a wall to seal off West Berlin permanently from East Germany.

The Cuban Missile Face-off

In 1962 a new crisis arose. Understandably fearful of the American threat after the Bay of Pigs invasion, Castro sought and secured Soviet assistance. American aerial photographs taken in October 1962 revealed that the USSR had begun to place what Kennedy considered offensive missiles on Cuban soil, although Cuba insisted they were defensive. The missiles did not change the strategic balance significantly; the Soviets could still wreak immense damage on American targets from more distant bases. But with Russian weapons installed just 90 miles from American shores, appearance was more important than reality. Kennedy was this time determined to win a confrontation with the Soviet Union over Cuba.

Kennedy went on nationwide TV to tell the American people about the missiles and to demand their removal. He declared that the United States would not shrink from the risk of nuclear war and announced a naval "quarantine"—not a blockade, which would have been an act of war—around Cuba to prevent Soviet ships from bringing in additional missiles.

As Soviet ships steamed toward the island and the nations stood "eyeball to eyeball" at the brink, the world held its breath. After several days, the tension broke, but only because Khrushchev called the Soviet ships back. Khrushchev then sent Kennedy a long letter pledging to remove the missiles if the United States lifted the quarantine and promised to stay out of Cuba altogether. A second letter demanded that America remove its missiles from Turkey as well. The United States agreed to the first letter, ignored the second, and said nothing about its intention, already voiced, of removing its own missiles from Turkey. With that, the crisis ended.

The Cuban missile crisis was the most terrifying confrontation of the Cold War. Yet the president emerged from it as a hero who had stood firm, and his party benefited a few weeks later in the congressional elections. As the relief began to fade, however, critics charged that what Kennedy saw as his finest hour was in fact an unnecessary crisis. One consequence of the crisis was the installation of a Soviet-American hot line to avoid similar episodes in the future. Another consequence was the USSR's determination to increase its nuclear arsenal so that it would never again be exposed as inferior to the United States.

Confrontation and Containment under Johnson

Upon Kennedy's assassination in 1963, Vice President Lyndon Johnson assumed the presidency. An extraordinarily effective legislative leader (see Chapter 28), he had considerably less experience in foreign affairs. Yet he shared many of Kennedy's assumptions, including the conviction, born of World War II, that aggressors had to be stopped before they committed more aggression. Like Kennedy, he also believed in the domino theory: If one country in a region fell, the others would follow. He was determined to preserve American power and contain the Communist menace. He assumed he could treat foreign adversaries just as he treated political opponents at home.

In 1965, believing that "Castro-type elements" might win a civil war in the Dominican Republic, he dispatched over 20,000 American troops to that Caribbean nation. In fact, the so-called Communist group was led by a former president, Juan Bosch, who had been overthrown by a military junta. The rueful Bosch complained that "this was a democratic revolution smashed by the leading democracy of the world." Johnson's credibility suffered badly from the episode.

THE QUAGMIRE OF VIETNAM

The commitment to stopping the spread of communism led to massive U.S. involvement in Vietnam. That struggle tore the United States apart, wrought enormous damage in Southeast Asia, and finally forced a reexamination of America's Cold War policies.

Roots of the Conflict

Indochina, including Vietnam, had been a French colony since the mid-nineteenth century. During World War II, Japan occupied it but allowed French collaborators to administer internal affairs. An independence movement, led by the Communist organizer and revolutionary Ho Chi Minh, sought to expel the Japanese. In 1945, the Allies faced the question of how to deal with Ho's nationalistic movement.

Franklin Roosevelt, like Woodrow Wilson, believed in self-determination and wanted to end colonialism. But France was determined to regain its colony, and by the time of his death, Roosevelt had backed down. Meanwhile Ho had proclaimed the Democratic Republic of Vietnam in 1945. Although the new government enjoyed widespread internal support, the United States refused to recognize it. The head of the American Office of Strategic Services mission predicted that if France sought to reassert control, the Vietnamese would fight to the death.

Indeed, a long, bitter struggle broke out between the French and Ho's forces, which became entangled with the larger Cold War. President Truman was less concerned about ending colonialism than with checking Soviet power. He needed France to balance the Soviets in Europe, and that meant cooperating with France in Vietnam.

Although Ho did not have close ties to the Soviets and was committed to his independent nationalist crusade, Truman and his advisers were fixated on the notion of monolithic communism. They wrongly assumed that Ho took orders from Moscow. Hence, in 1950 the United States recognized the French puppet government in Vietnam, and by 1954 Washington was paying over three-quarters of the cost of France's Indochina War.

After Eisenhower took office, France's position in Southeast Asia deteriorated. Dulles was eager to assist the French; the chairman of the Joint Chiefs of Staff even contemplated using nuclear weapons. But Eisenhower refused to intervene directly. After the French fortress of Dien Bien Phu fell to Ho's forces, an international conference in Geneva divided Vietnam along the 17th parallel. Elections were promised in 1956 that would unify the country and determine its political fate.

The Start of U.S. Involvement in Vietnam

The elections were never held, and two Vietnamese states emerged. Ho Chi Minh held power in the north, while in the south a fierce anti-Communist, Ngo Dinh Diem, formed a separate government. Intent on securing stability in Southeast Asia, the United States supported Diem and refused to sign the Geneva agreement. In the next few years, American aid increased and U.S. military advisers began assisting the South Vietnamese. The United States had taken the first steps toward direct involvement in a ruinous war halfway around the world that would later escalate out of control.

John Kennedy's commitment to Cold War victory led him to expand the U.S. role in Vietnam, the country he once called the "cornerstone of the free world in Southeast Asia." But American bolstering of Diem's regime had already ignited resistance by Communist-led guerrillas, called the Viet Cong. Viewing them as one more Communist threat, Kennedy stepped up American assistance to Diem's regime. During the Kennedy administration, the number of advisers rose from 675 to more than 16,000.

Despite American backing, however, Diem was losing support in his country. Buddhist priests burned themselves alive in the capital, Saigon, to protest the corruption and arbitrariness of the Diem regime. After receiving assurances that the United States would not object to a coup, South Vietnamese military leaders killed Diem and seized the government. Kennedy understood the importance of having a South Vietnamese government with popular support, but he was reluctant to withdraw and let the Vietnamese solve their own problems.

Lyndon Johnson shared the same reservations. After an early briefing he said that he felt like a catfish that had "grabbed a big juicy worm with a right sharp hook in the middle of it." But soon after becoming president, Johnson made a fundamental decision that guided policy for the next four years. With North Vietnamese aid, the Viet Cong and its political arm, the National Liberation Front, slowly gained ground. "I am not going to be the President who saw Southeast Asia go the way of China," Johnson vowed. He posed as a man of peace in the 1964 election campaign, promising that "We are not going to send American boys nine or ten thousand miles away from home to do what Asian boys ought to be doing for themselves." But secretly he was planning to escalate the American role.

Escalation

In August 1964, Johnson cleverly obtained congressional authorization for war by announcing that North Vietnamese torpedo boats had made unprovoked attacks on American destroyers in the international waters of the Gulf of Tonkin. Congress handed Johnson what he sought: a resolution which, he said, was "like grandma's nightshirt—it covered everything." The Tonkin Gulf Resolution gave him authority to "take all necessary measures to repel any armed attack against the forces of the United States and to prevent further aggression." Only later did it become clear that the incident resulted from American vessels violating North Vietnamese territorial waters by assisting South Vietnamese commando raids.

Military escalation began in earnest in February 1965. Retaliating for a guerrilla attack on an American base, Johnson ordered North Vietnam bombed to cut off the Viet Cong's supplies. Johnson personally authorized every raid, boasting that the Air Force "can't even bomb an outhouse without my approval." Saturation bombing, using both fragmentation bombs and napalm (which seared off human flesh), brought enormous destruction to both North and South Vietnam. A few months later he sent American ground forces into action, a crucial turning point in Americanizing the war. Only 25,000 Americans were in Vietnam at the beginning of 1965; there were 184,000 by the end of the year, 385,000 in 1966, 485,000 in 1967, and 543,000 in 1968. American forces had become direct participants in a struggle to prop up a faraway dictatorial regime.

Protesting the War

As escalation began, 82 percent of the public told pollsters that American forces should stay in Vietnam until the Communist elements withdrew. Then students began to question basic Cold War assumptions about battling communism around the globe. The first antiwar teach-in took place in March 1965, and as such campus gatherings became more frequent, they tended to turn into antiwar rallies. Draft resistance also grew, legitimated by boxing champion Muhammad Ali who declared, "I ain't got no quarrel with them Viet Cong." Soon activists were attacking the draft, ROTC programs, and firms that produced the destructive tools of war (see Chapter 29 for a full discussion of student activism).

The antiwar movement expanded. Women Strike for Peace, the most forceful women's antiwar organization, marched under such placards as "Stop! Don't drench the jungles of Asia with the blood of our sons." "Hey, hey, LBJ, How many

In this picture, General Loan, the chief of the South Vietnamese National Police, looks at a Viet Cong prisoner, lifts his gun, and calmly blows out the captive's brains. This prizewinning photograph captured the horror of the war for many Americans. (AP/Wide World Photos)

kids did you kill today?" chanted students. In 1967, some 300,000 people marched in New York, while 100,000 tried to close down the Pentagon.

Working-class and middle-class Americans began to sour on the war in early 1968, when North Vietnamese forces launched massive attacks throughout South Vietnam, including an assault on the U.S. embassy in Saigon. This so-called Tet offensive—it came while South Vietnamese were celebrating the lunar new year, or Tet—was a psychological victory for the Communists although militarily they were beaten back. American audiences now saw on television horrific images of the war (including the photograph on this page) and began to wonder about their nation's purposes and actions—indeed, about whether the war could be won at all.

When Richard Nixon assumed office in 1969, he understood the need to heal the rifts that the war had torn through American society. Wanting to extricate the United States while avoiding defeat, he devised a strategy called Vietnamization. Under it, American forces were withdrawn and replaced by South Vietnamese ones, while American air attacks on the North were stepped up. Between 1968 and 1972, American troop strength in South Vietnam fell from 543,000 to 39,000, winning Nixon political support at home. Yet as the transition occurred, South Vietnamese forces steadily lost ground. Realizing that Communist forces relied on supplies channeled through Cambodia, Nixon in 1970 sent American and South Vietnamese forces into that neutral country to clear out enemy bases there.

Antiwar demonstrations did not stop; indeed, they multiplied in 1969 and 1970. So did revulsion against the war. In November 1969, as a massive protest took place in Washington, D.C., stories surfaced about a horrifying massacre of civilians in Vietnam the year before. The small South Vietnamese village of My Lai allegedly had been harboring 250 Viet Cong guerrillas. American troops sent to clear the guerrillas out of My Lai lost control when they found only civilians in the village. "We huddled them up," confessed one GI,

> We made them squat down . . . I poured about four clips into the group . . . . The mothers was hugging their children . . . Well, we kept right on firing. They was waving their arms and begging . . . . I still dream about it. About the women and children in my sleep. Some days . . . some nights, I can't even sleep.

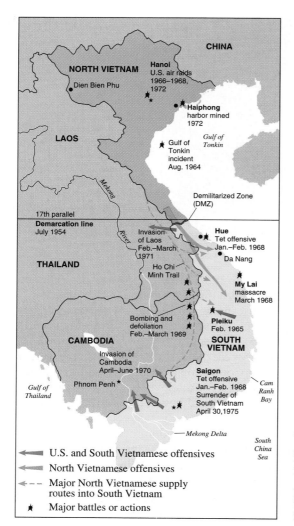

THE VIETNAM WAR This map shows the major campaigns of the Vietnam War. The North Vietnamese Tet offensive of early 1968 turned the tide against U.S. participation in the war and led to peace talks. The American invasion of Cambodia in 1970 provoked serious opposition.

Nixon's 1970 invasion of Cambodia brought renewed campus demonstrations, two with tragic consequences. At Kent State University in Ohio, the antiwar response was fierce. After students burned down the ROTC building, the governor of Ohio ordered the National Guard to the campus, and without provocation the soldiers fired on a gathering crowd. Two demonstrators, who were more than 250 feet away, were killed; so were two bystanders, almost 400 feet from the troops. Somewhat less media attention focused on a similar incident at a black institution, Jackson State College in Mississippi, where two black students were killed and two wounded, also by automatic weapons fired from National Guardsmen.

In 1971, the Vietnam War made major headlines once more when the *New York Times* began publishing a secret Defense Department account of American involvement. The so-called Pentagon Papers, leaked by defense analyst Daniel Ellsberg, gave Americans a firsthand look at the fabrications and faulty assumptions that

When Ohio National Guardsmen fired on a crowd of antiwar demonstrators and killed four students, even prowar Americans were shocked. This photograph shows the grief and outrage of others who survived the savage shooting of innocent bystanders. (Valley Daily News, Tarantum, Pennsylvania)

had guided the steady expansion of the struggle. Even though the study stopped with the Johnson years, the Nixon administration was furious and tried, unsuccessfully, to block publication.

Peace and Its Consequences

Vietnam remained a political football during the election of 1972. Just days before the vote, Nixon's chief foreign policy adviser, Henry Kissinger, announced that "peace is at hand." But Kissinger could not come to terms with the North Vietnamese until after the election, and while talks were still going on Nixon unleashed the war's most intensive bombing campaign, hitting hard at the North Vietnamese capital of Hanoi and mining the country's principal harbors.

Although American forces were withdrawn after the peace settlement was signed in January 1973, the war went on. In 1975, when the North Vietnamese forces were about to win and South Vietnamese units were disintegrating, Nixon's successor in the White House, Gerald Ford, called for another $1 billion in aid to stave off defeat. But Congress refused, leaving South Vietnam's crumbling government to its fate.

The long conflict had enormous consequences. Disillusionment with the war undermined assumptions about America's role in world affairs. In the longest war in its history, the United States lost almost 58,000 men, with far more wounded or maimed. Blacks and Chicanos suffered more than whites, since they were disproportionately represented in combat units. Financially, the cost was high: More than $150 billion was poured into an unsuccessful war. Domestic reform slowed, then stopped. Cynicism about government increased. American society was deeply divided. Only time would heal the wounds.

TIMELINE

1945	1946	1947	1948	1949
Yalta Conference; Roosevelt dies; Harry Truman becomes president; Potsdam Conference	American plan for control of atomic energy fails; Atomic Energy Act; Iran crisis; Churchill's "Iron Curtain" speech	Truman Doctrine; Federal Employee Loyalty Program; House Un-American Activities Committee (HUAC) investigates the movie industry	Marshall Plan launched; Berlin airlift; Israel created by United Nations; Hiss-Chambers case; Truman elected president	Soviet Union tests atomic bomb; North Atlantic Treaty Organization (NATO) established; George Orwell, *1984*; Mao Zedong's forces win Chinese civil war; Jiang Jieshi flees to Taiwan

1954	1956	1957	1958	1959
Fall of Dien Bien Phu ends French control of Indochina; Geneva Conference; Guatemalan government overthrown with CIA help; Mao's forces shell Quemoy and Matsu; Army-McCarthy hearings	Suez incident; Hungarian "freedom fighters" suppressed; Eisenhower reelected	Russians launch *Sputnik* satellite	U.S. troops sent to support Lebanese government	Castro deposes Batista in Cuba

1965	1967–1968	1968	1969	1970
Vietnam conflict escalates; Marines sent to Dominican Republic	Antiwar demonstrations	Tet offensive in Vietnam; Richard Nixon elected president; My Lai incident	Nixon Doctrine announced; Moratorium against the Vietnam War; SALT talks begin	U.S. invasion of Cambodia; Shootings at Kent State and Jackson State universities

Post-Vietnam Détente

If the Republicans' Vietnam policy was a questionable success, accomplishments were impressive in other areas. Nixon, the consummate Red-baiter of the past, dealt imaginatively and successfully with the major Communist powers, reversing the direction of a major part of American policy since World War II.

1950	1950–1953	1951	1952	1953
Truman authorizes development of the hydrogen bomb; Alger Hiss convicted; Joseph McCarthy's Wheeling (W. Va.) speech on subversion; NSC-68 McCarran Internal Security Act	Korean War	Japanese-American treaty; *Dennis* v. *United States*	Dwight D. Eisenhower elected president; McCarthy heads Senate Permanent Investigations Subcommittee	Stalin dies; Khrushchev consolidates power; East Germans stage anti-Soviet demonstrations; Shah of Iran returns to power in CIA-supported coup

1960	1961	1962	1963	1964
John F. Kennedy elected president	Bay of Pigs invasion fails; Khrushchev and Kennedy meet in Berlin; Berlin Wall constructed	Cuban missile crisis	Buddhist demonstrations in Vietnam; President Diem assassinated in Vietnam; Kennedy assassinated; Lyndon B. Johnson becomes president	Gulf of Tonkin resolution; Johnson reelected

1971	1972	1973	1975
New York Times publishes Pentagon Papers	Nixon visits People's Republic of China and Soviet Union; Nixon reelected; SALT I treaty on nuclear arms	Vietnam cease-fire agreement	South Vietnam falls to the Communists; End of the Vietnam War

Opening formal relations with the People's Republic of China was his most dramatic initiative. Ever since 1949 the United States had refused to recognize the Communist government on the mainland, insisting that Jiang Jieshi's rump regime on Taiwan alone was legitimate. In 1971, with an eye on upcoming elections, Nixon began softening his rigidity toward China and then announced that he would visit the People's Republic in 1972. Acknowledging what most nations already

Nixon shifted the course of Chinese-American relations by his dramatic visit to the People's Republic. He met Chinese officials for the first time, visited the Great Wall and other sites, and then reported back enthusiastically to the American people. (Sygma)

knew—that communism was not monolithic—he suspected that Chinese-American friendship could serve as leverage on the Soviet Union. Having long ago established his anti-Communist credentials, he realized, he could open a dialogue with Beijing without political harm. Finally, undertaking so dramatic a trip could boost his image.

Seeking to play one Communist state against another, Nixon also traveled to the Soviet Union in 1972 and likewise got a warm welcome. At a cordial summit meeting, the president and the Soviet leader, Leonid Brezhnev, signed the first Strategic Arms Limitation Treaty (SALT I). Besides making this agreement to limit missile stockpiles, the two nations also promised to cooperate in space and to ease long-standing trade restrictions. Business applauded the new approach, and most Americans approved of détente—a diplomatic term meaning a relaxation of tension.

When Gerald Ford assumed office in 1974 after Nixon's resignation, he followed Nixon's policies, even if he ceased calling them détente. He continued the strategic arms limitation talks that provided hope for eventual nuclear disarmament, which culminated in the signing of the even more comprehensive SALT II agreement—signed but never ratified during Jimmy Carter's administration (1977–1981).

←←←←←←

CONCLUSION

The Cold War In Perspective

The Cold War had a powerful impact on American society in the post-World War II decades. The Soviet-American standoff dominated international relations for nearly 50 years.

Historians have long differed over which side caused the Cold War. In the early postwar years, policy makers and commentators justified the American stance as a bold and courageous effort to meet the Communist threat. Later, particularly during the 1960s when the war in Vietnam was eroding confidence in American foreign policy, historians began to argue that American actions were misguided, insensitive to Soviet needs, and at least partially responsible for escalating friction. As with most historical questions, there are no easy answers, but both sides must be weighed.

The Cold War grew out of the two great world powers' competition for international influence. After World War II, the U.S. goal was to exercise economic and political leadership in the world and thus encourage capitalist economies and democratic political institutions throughout Europe and in nations emerging from colonialism. But these goals put the United States on a collision course with nations, such as the Soviet Union, that had a different vision of what the postwar world should be like, as well as with anticolonial movements around the globe. Perceiving threats from the Soviet Union, China, and other Communist countries, the United States clung to its deep-rooted sense of mission and embarked on an increasingly aggressive policy of containment, culminating in the ill-fated war in Vietnam. Here, as elsewhere, policy makers followed the advice of George Kennan as they sought to preserve and extend America's influence. The Cold War, with its profound effects at home and abroad, was the unfortunate result.

Recommended Reading

Background and Development of the Cold War

Stephen E. Ambrose, *Rise to Globalism: American Foreign Policy Since 1938*, 3rd ed. (1983); John Lewis Gaddis, *The Long Peace: Inquiries into the History of the Cold War* (1987) and *The United States and the Origins of the Cold War, 1941–1947* (1972); Michael J. Hogan, *The Marshall Plan: America, Britain, and the Reconstruction of Western Europe* (1987) and *A Cross of Iron: Harry S. Truman and the Origins of the National Security State, 1945–1954* (1998); Walter LaFeber, *America, Russia, and the Cold War, 1945–1990*, 7th ed. (1993); Melvyn P. Leffler, *A Preponderance of Power: National Security, the Truman Administration, and the Cold War* (1992); Ralph B. Levering, *The Cold War: A Post-Cold War History* (1994); Thomas J. McCormick, *America's Half Century: United States Foreign Policy in the Cold War* (1992); Thomas G. Patterson, *Meeting the Communist Threat: Truman to Reagan* (1988); Ronald A. Powaski, *The Cold War: The United States and the Soviet Union, 1917–1991* (1997); Daniel Yergin, *Shattered Peace: The Origins of the Cold War and the National Security State* (1977).

Foreign Policy in the Eisenhower Years

H. W. Brands, Jr., *Cold Warriors: Eisenhower's Generation and American Foreign Policy* (1988); Robert A. Divine, *Eisenhower and the Cold War* (1981) and *The Sputnik Challenge: Eisenhower's Response to the Soviet Satellite* (1993); Townsend Hoopes, *The Devil and John Foster Dulles* (1973).

The Korean War

Joseph C. Goulden, *Korea: The Untold Story of the War* (1982); Burton I. Kaufman, *The Korean War: Challenges in Crisis, Credibility, and Command* (1986).

The Nuclear Threat

Paul Boyer, *By the Bomb's Early Light: American Thought and Culture at the Dawn of the Atomic Age* (1985); McGeorge Bundy, *Danger and Survival: Choices About the Bomb in the First Fifty*

Years (1988); Gregg Herken, *Counsels of War* (1985); Richard G. Hewlett and Francis Duncan, *Atomic Shield: Volume II: A History of the United States Atomic Energy Commission, 1947–1952* (1972); Richard G. Hewlett and Jack M. Holl, *Atoms for Peace and War: Eisenhower and the Atomic Energy Commission, 1953–1961* (1989); John Newhouse, *War and Peace in the Nuclear Age* (1989); Spencer R. Weart, *Nuclear Fear: A History of Images* (1988); Allan M. Winkler, *Life Under a Cloud: American Anxiety About the Atom* (1993).

The Anti-Communist Crusade

Robert Griffith, *The Politics of Fear: Joseph R. McCarthy and the Senate* (1970); David M. Oshinsky, *A Conspiracy So Immense: The World of Joe McCarthy* (1983); Ronald Radash and Joyce Milton, *The Rosenberg File: A Search for Truth* (1984); Thomas C. Reeves, *The Life and Times of Joe McCarthy: A Biography* (1982); Richard H. Rovere, *Senator Joe McCarthy* (1960); Ellen W. Schrecker, *No Ivory Tower: McCarthyism and the Universities* (1986), *The Age of McCarthyism: A Brief History with Documents* (1994), and *Many Are the Crimes: McCarthyism in America* (1998); Allen Weinstein, *Perjury: The Hiss-Chambers Case* (1978).

The War in Vietnam

Christian G. Appy, *Working-Class War: American Combat Soldiers and Vietnam* (1993); Frances FitzGerald, *Fire in the Lake: The Vietnamese and the Americans in Vietnam* (1972); David Halberstam, *The Best and the Brightest* (1972); Le Ly Hayslip, *When Heaven and Earth Changed Places* (1989); George C. Herring, *America's Longest War: The United States and Vietnam, 1950–1975* (1979) and *LBJ and Vietnam: A Different Kind of War* (1994); Stanley Karnow, *Vietnam: A History: The First Complete Account of Vietnam at War* (1983); Jeffrey P. Kimball, *Nixon's Vietnam War* (1998); Ron Kovic, *Born on the Fourth of July* (1976); Guenter Lewy, *America in Vietnam* (1978); Robert S. McNamara, *In Retrospect* (1995); Al Santoli, *Everything We Had: An Oral History of the Vietnam War by Thirty-three American Soldiers Who Fought It* (1981).

CHAPTER 28

High Water and Ebb Tide of the Liberal State

Paul Cowan was an idealist in the 1960s. Like many students who came of age in these years, he believed in the possibility of social change and plunged into the struggle for liberal reform. He shared the hopes and dreams of other members of his generation who felt that their government could make a difference in people's lives.

Cowan's commitment developed slowly. He was a child of the 1950s, when most Americans were caught up in the consumer culture and paid little attention to the problems of less fortunate people. His grandfather had sold used cement bags in Chicago, but his father had become an executive at CBS television, and Cowan grew up comfortably. He graduated from the Choate School (where John Kennedy had gone) in 1958, and then from Harvard University (where Kennedy had also been a student) in 1963.

When he entered college, Cowan was interested in politically conscious writers like John Dos Passos, John Steinbeck, and James Agee, and folk singers like Pete Seeger and Woody Guthrie. They offered him entrance, he later recalled, into a "nation that seemed to be filled with energy and decency," one that lurked "beneath the dull, conformist facade of the Eisenhower years." While at Harvard, he was excited by antinuclear campaigns in New England and civil rights demonstrations in the South.

After college, he made good on his commitment to civil rights by going to Mississippi to work in the Freedom Summer project of 1964. He was inspired by the example of John Kennedy, the liberal president whose administration promised "a new kind of politics" that could make the nation, and the world, a better place. During that summer, he wrote, "it was possible to believe that by changing ourselves we could change, and redeem, our America."

The Peace Corps came next. Paul and his wife Rachel were convinced that this organization, the idea of the young president, "really was a unique government agency, permanently protected by the lingering magic of John F. Kennedy's name." They were sent to the South American city of Guayaquil, Ecuador. Their task was to serve as mediators between administrators of the city hall and residents of the slums. They wanted to try to raise the standard of living by encouraging local governments to provide basic services such as garbage disposal and clean water.

But the work proved more frustrating than they had imagined. They bristled at restrictions imposed by the Peace Corps bureaucracy. They despaired at the inadequate resources local government officials had to accomplish their aims. They wondered if they were just new imperialists, trying to impose their values on others who had priorities of their own. "From the day we moved into the barrio," Cowan later recalled, "the question we were most frequently asked by the people we were supposed to be organizing was whether we would leave them our clothes when we returned to the States."

Cowan came home disillusioned. "I saw that even the liberals I had wanted to emulate, men who seemed to be devoting their lives to fighting injustice, were unable to accept people from alien cultures on any terms but their own." He called his account of his own odyssey The Making of an Un-American.

✦✦✦✦✦

Paul Cowan's passage through the 1960s mirrored the passage of American society as a whole. Millions of Americans shared his views as the period began. Mostly comfortable and confident, they supported the liberal agenda advanced by the Democratic party of John Kennedy and Lyndon Johnson. They endorsed the idea that the government had responsibility for the welfare of all its citizens and accepted the need for a more active governmental role to help those who were unable to help themselves. That commitment lay behind the legislative achievements of the "Great Society," the last wave of twentieth-century reform that built upon the gains of the Progressive era and the New Deal years before.

Then political reaction set in, as the nation was torn apart by the ravages of the Vietnam War. Liberal assumptions eroded as conservatives argued that an activist approach was responsible for the chaos consuming the country. Republicans who assumed power at the end of the 1960s accepted the basic outlines of the welfare state but rejected many of the liberal initiatives of Democratic administrations as expensive failures. Under Richard Nixon and Gerald Ford, Republicans capitalized on disillusionment with federal policy and crafted a new consensus that kept them in the White House for most of the next decade and a half. The presidency of Democrat Jimmy Carter failed to reverse the conservative shift. Liberals despaired as they watched the destruction of their dreams.

This chapter describes the climax of twentieth-century liberalism and its subsequent decline. It focuses on the effort of the government, begun in Franklin Roosevelt's New Deal, to help those left behind by the advances of industrial capitalism. It examines first the initiatives in the 1940s and 1950s and early 1960s to provide necessary assistance to the less fortunate members of American society, then the efforts in the late 1960s and 1970s to limit such aid. In pondering the possibilities of reform, this chapter outlines the various attempts to devise an effective political response to the major structural changes in the post-World War II economy outlined in Chapter 26. It explores the debates that took place and the shifts that occurred as the political system struggled to cope with the problems of wholesale economic transformation and to maintain the promise of American life.

THE ORIGINS OF THE WELFARE STATE

The modern American welfare state originated in the New Deal. Roosevelt's efforts to combat the Great Depression and protect Americans from problems stemming from industrial capitalism (see Chapter 24) provided the basis for subsequent reform. Harry Truman's Fair Deal built on Roosevelt's New Deal, though Truman often found himself curbed by a conservative Congress. His Republican successor, Dwight Eisenhower, tried to scale down spending but made no effort to roll back the most important initiatives of the welfare state. Actions taken in the post-World War II years provided the groundwork for the major reforms of the 1960s.

Truman's Approach

Like FDR, Harry Truman believed that the federal government had the responsibility for ensuring the social welfare of all Americans. He shared his predecessor's commitment to assisting less comfortable inhabitants of the country in a systematic, rational way. Truman wanted his administration to embrace and act upon a series of carefully defined social and economic goals. Immediate problems of reconversion had to be resolved first, to be sure: demands for the return of servicemen, fears of inflation, and labor unrest. But even as he worked (not always successfully) to handle these issues, Truman outlined his vision of the welfare state.

Truman took the same feisty approach to public policy that characterized his conduct of foreign affairs (see Chapter 27). He stated his position clearly and simply, often in black and white terms, and seldom hesitated to let others know exactly where he stood. He attacked his political enemies vigorously and often took his case to the American people. He was, in many ways, an old-style Democratic machine politician who hoped to use his authority to benefit his political base of middle-class and working-class Americans.

Less than a week after the end of World War II, Truman called on Congress to pass a 21-point program that would produce postwar stability and security. He wanted housing assistance, a higher minimum wage, more unemployment compensation, and a national commitment to maintain full employment. During the next ten weeks, Truman sent blueprints of further proposals to Congress, including health insurance and atomic energy legislation. But this liberal program soon ran into fierce opposition.

The debate surrounding the Employment Act of 1946 hinted at the fate of Truman's proposals. This measure was a deliberate effort to apply the theory of English economist John Maynard Keynes to preserve economic equilibrium and prevent depression. Keynes had argued a decade earlier that massive spending was necessary to overcome a depression (see Chapter 24). The money spent during World War II caused the economy to respond precisely as Keynes had predicted. Now economists wanted to institutionalize his ideas to forestall problems. The initial bill, which enjoyed the strong support of labor, would have committed the government to maintaining full employment by monitoring the economy and taking remedial action in case of decline. These actions included tax cuts and spending programs to stimulate the economy and reduce unemployment.

While liberals and labor leaders hailed the measure, business groups condemned it. They claimed that government intervention would move the United States closer to socialism. Responding to the business community, Congress cut the proposal to bits. As finally passed, the act created a Council of Economic Advisers to make recommendations to the president, who was to report annually to Congress and the nation on the state of the economy. But it stopped short of committing the government to using fiscal tools to maintain full employment when economic indicators turned downward.

Truman's Struggle with a Conservative Congress

As the midterm elections of 1946 approached, Truman and his supporters knew they were vulnerable. Many Democrats still pined for FDR. Truman appeared to be a petty bungler, the butt of countless jokes. His support dropped from 87 percent of those polled after he assumed the presidency to 32 percent in November 1946. Gleeful Republicans asked the voters, "Had enough?"

They had. Republicans won majorities in both houses of Congress for the first time since the 1928 elections, and a majority of the governorships as well. Truman now faced an unsympathetic 80th Congress in which Republicans and conservative Democrats planned to reverse the liberal policies of the Roosevelt years. Hoping to reestablish congressional authority and cut the power of the executive branch, they insisted on less government intervention in business and private life. They demanded tax cuts and a curtailment of the privileged position they felt labor had come to enjoy.

When the new Congress met, it slashed spending and taxes. In 1947, Congress twice passed tax-cut measures. Both times Truman vetoed them, but in 1948, another election year, Congress overrode the veto.

Congress also struck at Democratic labor policies. Angry at the gains won by labor in the 1930s and 1940s, Republicans wanted to curtail unions' right to call disruptive strikes such as those after the war. Early in Truman's presidency, Congress had passed a bill requiring prior notice for strikes, as well as a cooling-off period if a strike occurred. Truman vetoed it. But in 1947, commanding more votes, the Republicans passed the Taft-Hartley Act, which intended to limit the power of unions by restricting the weapons they could deploy. Revising the Wagner Act of 1935, the legislation spelled out unfair labor practices (such as preventing nonunion workers from working if they wished) and outlawed the closed shop, in which an employee had to join a union before getting a job. The law likewise allowed states to prohibit the union shop, which forced workers to join the union after they had been hired. It also gave the president the right to call for an 80-day cooling-off period in strikes affecting national security and required union officials to sign non-Communist oaths.

Union leaders and members were furious. They argued vigorously that the measure eliminated many of their hard-won rights and set labor-management relations back to pre-New Deal days. Vetoing the measure, Truman went on nationwide radio to seek public approval. This regained him some of the labor support he had earlier lost when he tried to force strikers back to work. But Congress passed Taft-Hartley over his veto.

The Fair Deal and Its Fate

In 1948, Truman wanted a chance to consolidate a liberal program and to win the presidency in his own right. He knew that some Democrats wanted to replace him with Dwight Eisenhower or Supreme Court Justice William O. Douglas or anyone else. That effort failed, but Truman was left with what most people thought was a worthless nomination. Not only was his own popularity waning, but the Democratic party seemed to be falling apart.

In one of the nation's most extraordinary political upsets, Harry Truman beat Thomas E. Dewey in 1948. Here an exuberant Truman holds a newspaper headline printed while he slept, before the vote turned his way. (Corbis-Bettmann)

The civil rights issue, aimed at securing the vote for African Americans, split the Democrats. Truman hoped to straddle it, at least until after the election, to avoid alienating the South. When liberals defeated a moderate platform proposal and pressed for a stronger stand on black civil rights, angry delegates from Mississippi and Alabama stormed out of the convention. They later formed the States' Rights, or Dixiecrat, party, which nominated Governor J. Strom Thurmond of South Carolina for the presidency and affirmed support for segregation.

Meanwhile, Henry A. Wallace, for seven years secretary of agriculture, then FDR's vice president, and after that secretary of commerce, mounted his own challenge. Truman had fired Wallace from his cabinet for supporting a more temperate approach to the Soviet Union. Now Wallace became the presidential candidate of the Progressive party. Initially, he attracted widespread liberal interest because of his moderate position on Soviet-American affairs, his promotion of desegregation, and his promise to nationalize the railroads and major industries. But as Communists and "fellow travelers" surfaced in his organization, other support dropped off.

Once again the GOP nominated New York Governor Dewey, its unsuccessful candidate in 1944. Dewey was stiff and egocentric. Still, the polls uniformly indicated a Republicans victory. Dewey saw little value in brawling with his opponent and campaigned (said one commentator) "with the humorless calculation of a Certified Public Accountant in pursuit of the Holy Grail."

Truman, the underdog, ran a two-fisted campaign. He appealed to ordinary Americans as an unpretentious man in an uphill fight. He addressed Americans in familiar language. He called the Republicans a "bunch of old mossbacks" out to destroy the New Deal. He attacked the "do nothing" 80th Congress. Speaking without a prepared text in his choppy, aggressive style, he warmed to crowds, and they warmed to him. "Give 'em hell, Harry," they yelled. He did.

The pollsters were wrong. On election day, despite the early headline "Dewey Defeats Truman" in the *Chicago Daily Tribune,* the incumbent president scored one of the most unexpected political upsets in American history, winning 303–189 in the Electoral College. Democrats also swept both houses of Congress.

Truman won primarily because he was able to revive the major elements of the Democratic coalition that FDR had constructed more than a decade before. Despite the rocky days of 1946, Truman managed to keep labor, farm, and black votes. Labor's support made a big difference. Working men and women had been buoyed by his veto, even though unsuccessful, of the Taft-Hartley Act. Union leaders, less happy with Truman, backed him because they were afraid of being tarnished with the Communist label if they supported Wallace.

With the election behind him, Truman pursued his liberal program. In his 1949 State of the Union message, he declared, "Every segment of our population and every individual has a right to expect from our Government a fair deal." The Fair Deal became the name for his domestic program, which included the measures he had proposed over and over since 1945.

Parts of the Fair Deal passed; others did not. Lawmakers raised the minimum wage and expanded Social Security. A housing program brought modest gains but did not really meet housing needs. A farm program, aimed at providing income support to farmers if prices fell, never made it through Congress. Although he desegregated the military, other parts of his civil rights program failed to win congressional support (see Chapter 29). The American Medical Association successfully opposed national health insurance, and Congress rejected federal aid to education.

The mixed record was not entirely Truman's fault. Conservative legislators generally sabotaged his efforts. But critics charged correctly that Truman was often unpragmatic and shrill. He sometimes seemed to provoke the confrontations that became a hallmark of his presidency. Seeking bipartisan support for checking the perceived Soviet threat (see Chapter 27), he allowed his domestic program to suffer. As defense expenditures mounted, correspondingly less money was available for projects at home.

Still, Truman had kept the liberal vision alive. The Fair Deal had ratified many of the New Deal's initiatives and had led Americans to take programs like Social Security for granted. Truman had not come close to achieving everything he wanted, but the nation had taken another step toward endorsing liberal goals.

The Election of Eisenhower

Acceptance of the liberal state continued in the 1950s, even as the Republicans took control. By 1952, Truman's popularity had plummeted to only 23 percent of the American people, and all indicators pointed to a political shift. The Democrats nominated Adlai Stevenson, Illinois's able, articulate, and moderately liberal governor. The Republicans turned to Dwight Eisenhower, the World War II hero.

Stevenson approached political issues in intellectual terms. "Let's talk sense to the American people," he said. While liberals loved his approach, Stevenson himself anticipated the outcome.

The Republicans focused on communism, corruption, and Korea as major issues. They called the Democrats "soft on communism." They criticized assorted scandals involving Truman's cronies and friends. The president himself was blameless, but some of the people near him were not. The Republicans also promised to end the unpopular Korean War.

Ike proved to be a great campaigner. Though this was his first effort to win political office, he had a natural talent for taking his case to the American people. He spoke in simple, reassuring terms. He struck a grandfatherly pose, unified his party, and won with 55 percent of the vote and 41 states. He took office with a Republican Congress, and had little difficulty gaining a second term four years later.

"Modern Republicanism"

Eisenhower believed firmly in limiting the presidential role. He was uncomfortable with the growth of the executive office over the past 20 years. Like the Congressional Republicans with whom Truman had tangled, he wanted to restore the balance between the branches of government and to reduce the authority of the national government. He recognized, however, that it was impossible to scale back federal power to the levels of the 1920s, and he wanted to preserve social gains that even Republicans now accepted. Eisenhower sometimes called his approach "dynamic conservatism" or "modern Republicanism," something that was "conservative when it comes to money, liberal when it comes to human beings." Liberals quipped that this meant endorsing social projects but failing to authorize the funds.

The president and his chief aides wanted desperately to preserve the value of the dollar, to pare down levels of funding, cut taxes, and to balance the budget after years of deficit spending. To do that, the president appointed George Humphrey, a fiscal conservative, as secretary of the treasury. In times of economic stagnation, Humphrey and other Republicans were willing to risk unemployment to control inflation. Charles E. Wilson, the secretary of defense and former GM president, epitomized the administration's pro-business stance: "What is good for our country is good for General Motors," he declared, "and vice versa."

Eisenhower fulfilled his promise to reduce government's economic role. After Republicans received financial support from oil companies during the campaign, the new Congress, with a presidential strong endorsement, transferred control of about $40 billion worth of federal oil lands to the states. Eisenhower said privately about the Tennessee Valley Authority: "I'd like to see us sell the whole thing, but I suppose we can't go that far." He opposed a TVA proposal for expansion to provide power to the Atomic Energy Commission and authorized a private group to build a plant for that purpose. Later, when charges of scandal arose, the administration canceled the agreement, but the basic preference for private development remained.

Eisenhower's indirect approach and low-key public image made him popular throughout the 1950s. His intent gaze and wide smile gave Americans a sense of confidence that the country was in good hands. Here Ike greets a delegation of Republican National Committee women during the 1952 presidential campaign. (UPI/Corbis-Bettmann)

Committed to supporting business interests, the administration sometimes saw its program backfire. As a result of its reluctance to stimulate the economy too much, the annual rate of economic growth declined from 4.3 percent between 1947 and 1952 to 2.5 percent between 1953 and 1960. The country also suffered three recessions in Eisenhower's eight years, during which tax revenues fell and deficits increased. Liberal economists argued that Keynesian tools were available to avoid such troubles but were not being used.

Eisenhower's understated approach led to a legislative stalemate, particularly when the Democrats regained control of Congress in 1954. Opponents spoke of the Eisenhower doll—you wound it up, and it did nothing for eight years.

Yet Eisenhower understood just what he was doing and had a better grasp of public policy than his critics realized. He worked quietly to create the consensus that he believed was necessary to make legislative progress and from behind the scenes often pushed his favorite programs. His was what later scholars called a "hidden hand" presidency.

Even more important was his role in ratifying the welfare state. By 1960, the government had become a major factor in ordinary people's lives. It had grown enormously, employing close to 2.5 million people throughout the 1950s. Federal expenditures, which had stood at $3.1 billion in 1929, rose to $75 billion in 1953 and passed $150 million in the 1960s. The White House now took the lead in initiating legislation and steering bills through Congress. Individuals had come to expect old-age pensions, unemployment payments, and a minimum wage. By accepting the fundamental features of the national state the Democrats had created, Eisenhower ensured its survival. Now the debate about social policy broadened, as issues such as educational assistance, federal health care, and increased welfare benefits became part of the political agenda of the 1960s.

For all the jokes about him, Eisenhower remained popular. He accomplished most of the things he had wanted to do. He was one of the few presidents to leave office as highly regarded by the people as when he entered it. He was the kind of leader Americans wanted in prosperous times.

THE HIGH WATER MARK OF LIBERALISM

The commitment to a welfare state grew stronger in the 1960s. The Democrats who won office in these years wanted to broaden the role of government even further. Dismayed at the problems of poverty, unemployment, and racism, John F. Kennedy and Lyndon B. Johnson sought to manage the economy more effectively, eradicate poverty, and protect the civil rights of all Americans. Midway through the decade they came close to achieving their goals.

The Election of 1960

In the 1960 campaign, Kennedy argued that the government in general, and the president in particular, had to play an even more active role than they had in the Eisenhower years. He charged that the country had become lazy as it reveled in the prosperity of the 1950s. There were, he said, problems that needed to be addressed.

Kennedy squared off against Richard Nixon, the Republican nominee, in the first televised presidential debates. Seventy million Americans saw the two men in the first contest. The debates made a major difference in the campaign. From now on, television would play a major role in politics and reshape its character.

Kennedy overcame seemingly insuperable odds to become the first Catholic in the White House. Yet his victory was razor-thin. The electoral margin of 303 to 219 concealed the close popular tally, in which he triumphed by fewer than 120,000 of 68 million votes cast. If a few thousand people had voted differently in Illinois and Texas, the election would have gone to Nixon. While Kennedy had Democratic majorities in Congress, many members of his party came from the South and were unsympathetic to liberal causes.

Kennedy had a charismatic presence. He was able to voice his aims in eloquent yet understandable language. During the campaign, he pointed to "uncharted areas of science and space, unsolved problems of peace and war, unconquered pockets of ignorance and prejudice, unanswered questions of poverty and surplus" that Americans must confront, for "the New Frontier is here whether we seek it or not." He made the same point even more movingly in his inaugural address: "The torch has been passed to a new generation of Americans—born in this century, tempered by war, disciplined by a hard and bitter peace, proud of our ancient heritage." Many, like Paul Cowan whom we met at the start of the chapter, were inspired by Kennedy's concluding call to action: "And so, my fellow

Americans: Ask not what your country can do for you—ask what you can do for your country."

For Kennedy, strong leadership was all-important. The president, he believed, "must serve as a catalyst, an energizer." Viewing himself as "tough-minded," he was determined to provide firm direction and play a leading role in creating the national agenda, just as Franklin Roosevelt had done.

Kennedy had talented assistants. On his staff were 15 Rhodes scholars and several famous authors. The secretary of state was Dean Rusk, a former member of the State Department who had then served as president of the Rockefeller Foundation. The secretary of defense was Robert S. McNamara, the highly successful president of the Ford Motor Company, who had used computer analysis to turn the company around.

Further contributing to Kennedy's attractive image were his glamorous wife Jacqueline and the glittering dinners the couple hosted for Nobel Prize winners, musicians, and artists. Energy, exuberance, and excitement filled the air. It seemed like King Arthur's Camelot, popularized in a Broadway musical in 1960.

The New Frontier

Kennedy was committed to extending the welfare state by expanding the economy and enlarging social welfare programs. Regarding civil rights, Kennedy espoused liberal goals and social justice although his policies were limited (see Chapter 29). On the economic front, he tried to end the lingering recession by working with the business community while controlling inflation.

These two goals conflicted when, in the spring of 1962, the large steel companies decided on a major price increase after steel unions had accepted a modest wage package. The angry president termed the price increases unjustifiable and on television charged that the firms pursued "private power and profit" rather than the public interest. In the end, the large companies capitulated, but they disliked Kennedy's heavy-handed approach and decided that this Democratic administration, like all the others, was anti-business. Six weeks after the steel crisis, the stock market took its biggest drop since the Great Crash of 1929. Kennedy got the blame.

It now seemed doubly urgent to end the recession. Earlier a proponent of a balanced budget, Kennedy began to listen to liberal advisers who proposed a Keynesian approach. Budget deficits had promoted prosperity during World War II and might work in the same way in peacetime. By the summer of 1962, the president was convinced. In early 1963, he called for a $13.5 billion cut in corporate taxes over the next three years. That cut would cause a large deficit, but it would also provide capital to stimulate the economy and ultimately increase tax revenues.

Opposition mounted. Conservatives refused to accept the basic premise that deficits would stimulate economic growth. Some liberals claimed that it would be better to stimulate the economy by spending for social programs. Why not, economist John Kenneth Galbraith wondered, have "a few more dollars to spend if the air is too dirty to breathe, the water is too polluted to drink, the commuters are losing out in the struggle to get in and out of cities, the streets are filthy, and the schools are so bad that the young, perhaps wisely, stay away?" In Congress, where Democrats had thin majorities but still had to contend with conservative

Southerners within the party, opponents pigeonholed the proposal in committee, and there it remained.

On other issues on the liberal agenda, Kennedy met similar resistance. He proposed an increased minimum wage, federal aid for education, medical care for the elderly, housing subsidies, and urban renewal, but the results were meager. For example, his call for federal aid to education foundered amid debates about bureaucratic control and the funding of segregated and parochial schools. His only initiative that passed was a scaled-down minimum-wage hike.

Kennedy was more successful in securing funds for space exploration. As first Alan Shepard and then John Glenn flew in space, Kennedy proposed that the United States commit itself to landing a man on the moon and returning him to earth before the end of the decade. Congress assented, caught up in the glamour of the proposal and worried about Soviet achievements in space.

Kennedy also established the Peace Corps, which sent men and women to assist developing countries. Paul Cowan was one of thousands of volunteers who hoped that they could share their liberal dreams.

If Kennedy's successes were modest, he had at least made commitments that could be broadened later. He had reaffirmed the importance of executive leadership in seeking a broader welfare state. And he had committed himself to using modern economics to maintain fiscal stability. The nation was poised to achieve liberal goals.

Change of Command

Facing reelection in 1964, Kennedy wanted not only to win the presidency for a second term but also to increase liberal Democratic strength in Congress. In November 1963, he went to Texas, hoping to unite the state's Democratic party for the upcoming election. Dallas, one of the stops on the trip, was reputed to be hostile to the administration. Now, on November 22, Kennedy had a chance to see the city for himself. Arriving at the airport, Henry González, a congressman accompanying the president in Texas, remarked jokingly, "Well, I'm taking my risks. I haven't got my steel vest yet." As the party entered the city in an open car, the president encountered friendly crowds. Suddenly shots rang out, and Kennedy slumped forward as bullets ripped through his head and throat, and died a short time later. Lee Harvey Oswald, the accused assassin, was himself killed a few days later by a minor underworld figure as he was being moved within the jail.

Americans were stunned. For days people stayed at home and watched endless television replays of the assassination and its aftermath. These images were indelibly imprinted on people's minds. United around the event, members of an entire generation remembered where they had been when Kennedy was shot, just as an earlier generation recalled Pearl Harbor.

Vice President Lyndon Johnson became president. Less polished, Johnson was a more effective political leader than Kennedy and brought his own special skills and vision to the presidency.

Johnson was a man of elemental force. Always manipulative, he reminded people (so a White House aide said) of a riverboat gambler. Though he desperately wanted to be loved, he was, as former secretary of state Dean Acheson once told

John Kennedy seemed comfortable and relaxed as he rode in a motorcade through the streets of Dallas. This picture was taken just moments before bullets ended the Camelot dream. (Corbis-Bettmann)

him, "not a very likable man." A streak of vulgarity contributed to his earthy appeal but offended some of his associates. Asked once why he had not responded more sympathetically to a suggestion from Richard Nixon, he said to his friends in Congress, "Boys, I may not know much, but I know the difference between chicken shit and chicken salad."

Those qualities notwithstanding, he was successful in the passion of his life—politics. Schooled in Congress and influenced by FDR, Johnson was the most able legislator of the postwar years. As Senate majority leader, he became famous for his ability to get things done. Ceaseless in his search for information, tireless in his attention to detail, he knew the strengths and weaknesses of everyone he faced. The "Johnson treatment" became famous: As described by two knowledgeable columnists, LBJ would zero in, "his face a scant millimeter from his target, his eyes widening and narrowing, his eyebrows rising and falling." He usually got his way.

Johnson ran the Senate with tight control and established a credible record for himself and his party during the Eisenhower years. He was the Democrat most responsible for keeping liberal goals alive in a conservative time, as he tried to broaden his own appeal in a quest for the presidency. Unsuccessful in his bid for the White House in 1960, he took the second spot under JFK and helped Kennedy win the election. But then he went into eclipse. Useless, stiffled, and uncomfortable with the Kennedy crowd, he agreed with John Nance Garner, FDR's first vice president, that the office "wasn't worth a pitcher of warm spit."

Despite his own ambivalence about Kennedy, Johnson sensed the profound shock that gripped the United States after the assassination and was determined to utilize Kennedy's memory to achieve legislative success. Even more than Kennedy, he was willing to wield presidential power aggressively and to exploit the media to shape public opinion in pursuit of his vision of a society in which the comforts of life would be more widely shared and poverty would be eliminated once and for all.

The Great Society in Action

Johnson began to develop the support he needed the day he took office. In his first public address, delivered to Congress and televised nationwide, he embraced Kennedy's liberal program. "All I have," he began in a measured tone, "I would have given gladly not to be standing here today." "Let us continue" was his theme.

Johnson resolved to secure what Kennedy had been unable to extract from Congress. Bills to reduce taxes and ensure civil rights were his most pressing priorities, but he was interested, too, in aiding public education, providing medical care for the aged, and eliminating poverty. By the spring of 1964, he had begun to use the phrase "Great Society" to describe his expansive vision of reform.

Successful even before the election of 1964, his landslide victory over conservative Republican challenger Barry Goldwater of Arizona validated his approach. LBJ received 61 percent of the popular vote and an electoral tally of 486 to 52 and gained Democratic congressional majorities of 68–32 in the Senate and 295–140 in the House. Goldwater's candidacy reflected a growing conservatism within the Republican party—which drove moderate Republicans to vote Democratic and gave Johnson a far more impressive mandate than Kennedy had ever enjoyed.

Johnson knew how to get laws passed. He appointed task forces (which included legislators) to study problems and suggest solutions, worked with them to draft bills, and maintained close contact with congressional leaders through a sophisticated liaison staff. Not since the FDR years had there been such a coordinated effort.

Civil rights reform was LBJ's first legislative priority and an integral part of the Great Society program (see Chapter 29), but other measures were equally important. Accepting the Keynesian theory that managed deficits could promote prosperity, Johnson pressed for a tax cut to stimulate the economy. To gain conservative support, he agreed to hold down spending. Once, he applied such pressure that the author of an amendment ended up voting against his own proposal. Soon the tax bill passed.

With the tax cut in hand, the president pressed for the anti-poverty program that Kennedy had begun to plan. Such an effort was bold and unprecedented. In the Progressive era, at the turn of the century, some legislation had attempted to alleviate conditions associated with poverty. During the New Deal, FDR had proposed assisting the one-third of the nation that could not help itself. Now Johnson took a step that no president had taken before: In his 1964 State of the Union message, he declared "unconditional war on poverty in America."

The center of this utopian effort to eradicate poverty was the Economic Opportunity Act of 1964. It created an Office of Economic Opportunity (OEO) to provide education and training through programs such as the Job Corps for unskilled young people. VISTA (Volunteers in Service to America), patterned after the Peace Corps, offered assistance to America's poor, while Head Start tried to give disadvantaged children a chance to succeed in school. Assorted community action programs gave the poor a voice in improving their lot.

Aware of escalating medical-care costs, Johnson also proposed a medical assistance plan, which Truman and Kennedy had vainly sought. Johnson succeeded. To head off conservative attacks, the administration tied the Medicare measure to the Social Security system and limited the program to the elderly; Medicaid was for those on welfare and certain others who could not afford private insurance. The Medicare-Medicaid program was the most important extension of federally directed social benefits since the Social Security Act of 1935. By 1976 the two programs were paying for the medical costs of 20 percent of the American people.

Johnson was similarly successful in his effort to provide aid for elementary and secondary schools. Johnson, a Protestant, could deal with the ticklish religious question (which had stymied Kennedy) without charges of favoritism. His legislation allocated education money to the states based on the number of children from low-income families, which could then be used to assist deprived children in public as well as private schools.

LBJ's expansive vision saw federal government assuring everyone a share in the promise of American life. Under his prodding, Congress created the Department of Housing and Urban Development, gave rent supplements to the poor, and provided legal assistance for those who could not afford it. The scope of funding for higher education was expanded, and artists and scholars were subsidized through the National Endowments for the Arts and Humanities—the first such government aid programs since the New Deal's WPA.

Johnson's administration also provided much-needed immigration reform. The Immigration Act of 1965 replaced the restrictive immigration policy, in place since 1924, limiting immigration severely and favoring northern Europeans. Now the ceiling on immigration was raised much higher and the door opened to immigrants from Asia and Latin America, while exempting from the quotas family members of U.S. citizens and political refugees. This new and growing stream of immigration—largely from Asia and Latin America—created a population more diverse than it had been since the early decades of the twentieth century. The consequences of this new diversity were far-ranging and affected many areas of American life, from politics to street signs and classrooms.

The Great Society also reflected the stirring of the environmental movement. In 1962, naturalist Rachel Carson had alerted the public to the dangers of pesticide poisoning and environmental pollution (see Chapter 29). Though the chemical industry fought Carson, a special presidential advisory committee supported her. Johnson recognized the need to go further, dealing with caustic fumes in the air, lethal sludge in rivers and streams, and the steady disappearance of wildlife. The National Wilderness Preservation Act of 1964 set aside 9.1 million acres of wilderness. Lady Bird Johnson, the president's wife, led a beautification campaign to eliminate billboards and junkyards, and Congress passed other measures to combat air and water pollution.

A Sympathetic Supreme Court

With the addition of four new liberal justices appointed by Kennedy and Johnson, the Supreme Court promoted the liberal agenda. Under the leadership of Chief Justice Earl Warren, the Court followed the lead it had taken in the 1954 landmark civil rights case *Brown* v. *Board of Education* (see Chapter 29). Several other decisions outlawed Jim Crow practices in public establishments.

The Court also supported civil liberties. Where earlier judicial decisions had affirmed restrictions on members of the Communist party and radical groups, now the Court began to defend the rights of individuals with radical political views. Similarly, the Court sought to protect accused suspects from police harassment. In *Gideon* v. *Wainwright* (1963), the justices decided that poor defendants in serious cases had the right to free legal counsel. In *Escobedo* v. *Illinois* (1964), they ruled that a suspect had to be given access to an attorney during questioning. In *Miranda* v. *Arizona* (1966), they ordered that people in custody had to be warned that statements extracted by the police could be used against them and that they could remain silent.

Other decisions broke new ground. *Baker* v. *Carr* (1962) opened the way to reapportionment of state legislative bodies, according to the standard, defined a year later by Justice William O. Douglas as "one person, one vote." This crucial ruling helped break the political control of lightly populated rural districts in many state assemblies and similarly made the U.S. House of Representatives much more responsive to urban and suburban issues. And the Court outraged conservatives by ruling against prayer in the public schools and holding that obscenity laws could no longer restrict allegedly pornographic material if it had "redeeming social value."

The Great Society Under Attack

Supported by healthy economic growth, the Great Society worked for a few years as Johnson had hoped. After the tax cut's passage, the gross national product (GNP) rose steadily—7.1 percent in 1964, 8.1 percent in 1965, and 9.5 percent in 1966—while the budget deficit shrank, unemployment fell, and inflation remained under control. Medical programs provided basic security for the old and the poor. Schools were built and teachers' salaries increased.

Yet Johnson's Great Society dream proved illusory. Some programs promised too much, and the administration's rhetorical oversell led to disillusionment when problems failed to disappear. Other programs, planned in haste, simply did not work. Never were the massive sums allocated to these programs that, some argued, were necessary to make them successful.

Factionalism also plagued the Great Society. Johnson had reconstituted the old Democratic coalition in his triumph in 1964. But diverse interests within the coalition soon clashed. Conservative white southerners and blue-collar white northerners felt threatened by the government's support of civil rights. Urban bosses, long the backbone of the Democratic party, objected to grass-roots participation of the urban poor, which threatened their own control.

From across the political spectrum came criticisms of the Great Society, for much of which there had never been widespread enthusiasm. Conservatives attacked the centralization of authority and the government's increased role in defining the national welfare; they also questioned whether the poor, lacking a broad vision of national needs, should be involved in shaping reform programs. Even middle-class Americans, generally supportive of liberal goals, sometimes grumbled that the government neglected them in favor of the underprivileged. Meanwhile the radical left attacked the Great Society as a warmed-over New Deal whose real intent was to indoctrinate the working-class poor with middle-class values, while making no real effort to redistribute income.

The Vietnam War dealt the Great Society a fatal blow. LBJ wanted both to fight the war and to pursue his domestic reform programs. But pursuing these goals simultaneously produced serious inflation. The economy was already booming as a result of the tax cut and the spending for reform. As military expenditures increased, productivity lagged. When Johnson refused to raise taxes, trying to hide the costs of the war, inflation spiraled out of control. Congress finally got into the act and slashed Great Society programs. As hard economic choices became increasingly necessary, many decided the country could no longer afford social reform on the scale Johnson had proposed.

THE DECLINE OF LIBERALISM

After eight years of Democratic rule, many Americans became frustrated with liberalism. They questioned the liberal agenda and the government's ability to solve social problems. The war in Vietnam had polarized the country and fragmented the Democratic party. Capitalizing on the alienation, Republicans determined to scale down the commitment to social change. Like Eisenhower, they accepted some social programs as necessary for the well-being of modern America, but they resolved to cut spending and the federal bureaucracy. And they were determined to pay more attention to white, middle-class Americans, who disliked the mounting social disorder they saw as one of the consequences of rapid change and resented the government's perceived favoritism toward the poor and dispossessed.

The Election of 1968

Richard Nixon had pursued his dream of the White House ever since his days as Eisenhower's vice president. He had failed in his first bid in 1960, and two years later losing a race for governor of California seemed to kill his political career. But after the Goldwater disaster he made a comeback. By 1968 he had a good shot at the presidency again.

In the election, Nixon faced Vice President Hubert H. Humphrey. The war in Vietnam had fractured the Democratic party and made Johnson so unpopular that he chose not to run for reelection. The turbulent Democratic convention in Chicago, where police ran amok on nationwide TV, clubbing demonstrators, reporters, and bystanders alike, worked in Nixon's favor. But he faced a serious threat from Governor George C. Wallace of Alabama, the third-party candidate adept at

Policemen attacked demonstrators and bystanders alike at the turbulent Democratic convention of 1968. The senseless violence, pictured in graphic detail on national television, undermined the Democratic party and helped Nixon win the election. (UPI/Corbis-Bettmann)

exploiting social and racial tensions. Appealing to northern working-class voters as well as southern whites, Wallace baited "left-wing theoreticians, briefcase-totin' bureaucrats, ivory-tower guideline writers, bearded anarchists, smart-aleck editorial writers and pointy-headed professors."

Nixon addressed the same constituency, calling it the "silent majority." Capitalizing on the dismay these Americans felt over campus disruptions and inner-city riots and appealing to latent racism, he promised law and order. The Great Society was a costly mistake. Nixon left the shrill criticism to his running-mate, Governor Spiro Agnew of Maryland, who sounded like the Nixon of old.

Nixon received 43 percent of the popular vote, not quite 1 percent more than Humphrey, with Wallace capturing the rest. But it was enough to give the Republicans a majority in the electoral college and Nixon the presidency at last. Sixty-two percent of all white voters (but only 12 percent of black voters) had cast their votes for either Nixon or Wallace, suggesting the covert racial appeal had worked. But the Democrats won Congress.

A complex, remote man, Nixon was careful to conceal his private self that, said one of his aides, had "a mean side." Awkward and humorless, he was most comfortable alone or with a few wealthy friends.

"In the modern presidency," Nixon believed, "concern for image must rank with concern for substance." Publicly he posed as the defender of American morality, but in private he was frequently coarse and profane. Earlier in his career he had been labeled "Tricky Dick" for his apparent willingness to do anything to advance his career. He spent years creating the "new Nixon" image, but to many he still appeared always calculating his next step.

Philosophically, Nixon disagreed with the liberal faith in federal planning and wanted to decentralize social policy. But he agreed with his liberal predecessors that the presidency ought to be the engine of the political system. Faced with a Congress dominated by Democrats who allocated money for programs he opposed, he simply impounded—refused to spend—the funds. Later commentators would see the Nixon years as the height of the "imperial presidency."

Nixon's cabinet appointees were white, male Republicans. For the most part, however, the president relied on other White House staff members to make policy. In domestic affairs, one of his most important advisers was Daniel Patrick Moynihan, a Harvard professor of government (and a Democrat). In foreign affairs, the talented and ambitious Henry A. Kissinger, another Harvard government professor, was his chief adviser and later secretary of state.

Another tier of White House officials—none with policy-making experience but all intensely loyal to him—insulated Nixon from the outside world and carried out his commands. Advertising executive H. R. Haldeman became chief of staff, and lawyer John Ehrlichman soon rose to chief domestic adviser. John Mitchell, a tough attorney from Nixon's law office, became his fast friend, attorney general, and daily confidante.

The Republican Agenda

Accepting the basic contours of the welfare state, Nixon sought to scale it back. His goal was "to reverse the flow of power and resources" away from the federal government and back toward state and local governments.

Despite initial reservations, Nixon proved willing to use economic tools to maintain stability. When he assumed office the economy was faltering, beset by inflation that largely resulted from the Vietnam War. Nixon responded by reducing government spending and pressing the Federal Reserve Board to raise interest rates. Although parts of the conservative plan worked, a mild recession struck in the 1969–1970 period, and inflation continued to rise. Realizing the political dangers, Nixon shifted course, imposing wage and price controls to stop inflation and using monetary and fiscal policies to stimulate the economy. After his reelection in 1972, however, he lifted the controls and inflation resumed.

A number of factors besides the Vietnam War contributed to the troubling price spiral. Eager to court the farm vote, the administration made a large wheat sale to the Soviet Union in 1972—a major miscalculation, because with insufficient wheat left for the American market, grain prices soared. Between 1971 and 1974, farm prices rose 66 percent. The most critical factor in disrupting the economy, though, was an Arab oil embargo. Although the Organization of Petroleum Exporting Countries (OPEC) had slowly raised oil prices in the early 1970s, the 1973 Arab-Israeli war led Saudi Arabia to end oil shipments to Israel's ally, the United States. Other OPEC nations quadrupled their prices. Dependent on imports for one-third of their energy needs, Americans faced shortages and skyrocketing prices. When the embargo ended in 1974, prices remained high.

The oil crisis affected all aspects of American economic life. A loaf of bread that had cost 28 cents in the early 1970s jumped to 89 cents, and automobiles cost 72 percent more in 1978 than they had in 1973. Accustomed to filling up their gas tanks for only a few dollars, Americans were shocked at paying 65 cents a gallon. In 1974, inflation reached 11 percent. Then, as higher energy prices drove consumers to cut back on purchases, the nation entered a recession. Unemployment climbed to 9 percent, the highest level since the 1930s.

As economic growth and stability eluded him, Nixon tried to overhaul the rapidly expanding and expensive welfare programs. Critics claimed that welfare was inefficient and that benefits discouraged people from seeking work. Nixon recognized the conservative tide growing in the Sun Belt, where many voters wanted cutbacks in what they viewed as excessive government programs. But he also wanted to create a new Republican coalition by winning over traditionally Democratic blue-collar workers with reassurances that the Republicans would not dismantle the parts of the welfare state on which they relied.

Urged by Moynihan, Nixon endorsed an expensive but feasible new program that would have guaranteed a minimum yearly stipend of $1,600 to a family of four, with food stamps providing about $800 more. To crack down on "welfare cheaters" and encourage welfare recipients to work, all participants would have to register for job training and accept employment when found. But the plan was attacked by liberals as too little and by conservatives as too much. It died in the Senate.

As he struggled with the economy and the "welfare mess," Nixon irritated liberals with his pursuit of "law and order." Political protest, rising crime rates, increased drug use, and permissive attitudes toward sex all created a growing backlash among the working class and many middle-class Americans (see Chapter 29). Nixon decided to use government power to silence disruption and strengthen his conservative constituency.

Part of the administration's campaign involved denouncing disruptive elements. Nixon lashed out at demonstrators—"bums," he called student activists. But he generally relied on his vice president as the hatchet man. And Agnew had a sure eye for the jugular: Opponents (students in particular) were "ideological eunuchs" and an "effete corps of impudent snobs."

Nixon also attacked liberalism by lambasting the communications industry. Well aware of the power of radio and television and able to use it effectively, Nixon believed the media represented the "Eastern establishment," which he assumed hated him. He challenged the television networks, Agnew spearheading the attack.

The third and strongest part of Nixon's plan was Attorney General John Mitchell's effort to demonstrate administration support for the values of citizens upset by domestic upheavals. Mitchell sought enhanced powers for a war against crime, sometimes at the expense of constitutional liberties. This included reshaping the Supreme Court, which Republican leaders accused of being excessively concerned for lawbreakers. During his first term, Nixon had the opportunity to fill four Court vacancies, and he nominated men who shared his views. His first choice—the moderate Warren E. Burger as chief justice to replace the retiring liberal Earl Warren—was confirmed quickly. His next nominations, however, reflected Nixon's aggressively conservative approach. Appealing to white southerners, he selected two judges with racial biases so strong or limitations so great that the Senate refused to confirm them. Nixon then appointed Harry Blackmun, Lewis F. Powell, Jr., and William Rehnquist, all able and qualified—and all inclined to tilt the Court in a more conservative direction.

Not surprisingly, the Court gradually shifted to the right. It narrowed defendants' rights and slowed the liberalizing of pornography laws. It supported Nixon's assault on the media by ruling that journalists did not have the right to refuse to answer questions for a grand jury, even if they had promised their sources confidentiality. On other questions, however, the Court did not always act as the president had hoped. In the controversial 1973 *Roe* v. *Wade* decision, the Court legalized abortion, stating that women's rights included the right to control their own bodies. This decision was one that feminists, a group hardly supported by the president, had ardently sought.

The Watergate Affair

A solidly Democratic Congress blocked the administration's legislative initiatives. Nixon sought to end the stalemate by winning a second term and sweeping Republican majorities into both houses of Congress. But in his attempt for a decisive victory at the polls, he committed excesses that brought about his downfall.

Nixon's reelection campaign was even better organized than four years earlier. His fiercely loyal aides were prepared to do anything to win. Special counsel Charles W. Colson described himself as a "flag-waving, kick-'em-in-the-nuts, anti-press, anti-liberal Nixon fanatic" and had already busied himself with drawing up an "enemies list" of prominent anti-administration figures. White House counsel John Dean defined his job as finding a way to "use the available federal machinery to screw our political enemies." Commands were carried out by such men as E. Howard Hunt, a former CIA agent and specialist in "dirty tricks," and G. Gordon Liddy, a onetime member of the FBI who prided himself on a willingness to do anything without flinching.

The Committee to Re-elect the President (CREEP) was led by John Mitchell, who had resigned as attorney general. Its massive fund-raising drive tried to collect maximum money before contributions had to be reported under a new campaign-finance law. That money could be used for any purpose, including dirty tricks to disrupt the opposition's campaign. Other funds financed an intelligence branch within CREEP, headed by Liddy and including Hunt.

Early in 1972, Liddy proposed an elaborate scheme to wiretap the phones of various Democrats and disrupt their convention. Twice Mitchell refused to go along with what he saw as too risky and expensive an idea. Finally he approved a less ambitious plan to tap phones at the Democratic National Committee's headquarters in the Watergate apartment complex in Washington, D.C. Mitchell, formerly the nation's top law enforcement official, had authorized breaking the law.

The wiretapping attempt took place on the evening of June 16, 1972, and ended with the arrest of those involved. They carried with them money and documents that could be traced to CREEP. Top officials of the Nixon reelection team had to decide quickly what to do.

Reelection remained the most pressing priority, so Nixon's aides played down the matter and used federal resources to stifle an investigation. The president authorized the CIA to call off the FBI—which had quickly begun establishing the burglars' link to CREEP—on the grounds that national security was at stake. Though not privy to planning the break-in, the president was now party to the cover-up. In the succeeding months, he authorized payment of hush money.

DOONESBURY — by Garry Trudeau

Although Nixon steadfastly denied his complicity in the Watergate affair, his tape recordings of White House conversations told a different story. In this classic "Doonesbury" cartoon from September 17, 1973, Garry Trudeau notes Nixon's efforts to head off the investigation. (Universal Press Syndicate)

Members of the administration, including Mitchell, perjured themselves to shield the top officials who were involved.

Nixon trounced Democrat George McGovern in the election of 1972, receiving 61 percent of the popular vote. In a clear sign of the collapse of the Democratic coalition, 70 percent of southern voters cast their ballots for Nixon. The president, however, failed to gain the congressional majorities he desired.

When the Watergate burglars were brought to trial after the election, they pleaded guilty and were sentenced to jail, but the case refused to die. Judge John Sirica was not satisfied that justice had yet been done. Meanwhile, two zealous reporters, Bob Woodward and Carl Bernstein of the *Washington Post*, were following a trail of leads on their own. Slowly they recognized who else was involved.

The unraveling continued. The Senate Select Committee on Presidential Campaign Activities undertook an investigation, and one of the convicted burglars testified to White House involvement. Newspaper stories and Senate hearings brought out more. Eventually Nixon decided that Haldeman and Ehrlichman, his two closest aides, must be sacrificed to save his own neck.

In May 1973, the Senate committee began televised public hearings, watched by millions of Americans. Dean, to save himself, testified that Nixon knew about the cover-up, and other staffers revealed a host of illegal activities at the White House: money paid to the burglars; State Department documents forged to smear a previous administration; wiretaps used to stop top-level leaks. The most electrifying disclosure was that the president had installed a secret taping system that recorded all conversations in his office. Tapes could verify or disprove the growing rumors that Nixon had been party to the cover-up.

To show his honesty, Nixon appointed Harvard law professor Archibald Cox as a special prosecutor. But when Cox tried to gain access to the tapes, Nixon first resisted and finally fired him. Nixon's popularity plummeted, and even the appointment of another special prosecutor, Leon Jaworski, did not help. More and more Americans now believed that the president had played at least some part in the cover-up. Congress began considering impeachment.

The first steps, in accordance with constitutional mandate, began in the House of Representatives. The House Judiciary Committee, made up of 21 Democrats and 17 Republicans, began to debate the impeachment case in late July 1974. By sizable tallies, it voted to impeach the president on the grounds of obstruction of justice, abuse of power, and refusal to obey a congressional subpoena to turn over his tapes. A full House of Representatives vote still had to occur, and the Senate would have to conduct a trial and convict the president before removal could take place. But Nixon saw the handwriting on the wall.

After a brief delay, on August 5 Nixon obeyed a Supreme Court ruling and released the tapes. Besides a suspicious 18 1/2-minute gap, they contained the "smoking gun"—clear evidence of his complicity in the cover-up. Four days later, on August 9, 1974, the extraordinary episode came to an end, as Nixon became the first American president ever to resign.

The Watergate affair seemed disturbing evidence that the balance of power had disappeared. As the scandal wound down, many questioned the centralization of power in the American political system and cited the "imperial presidency" as the cause of recent abuses. Others simply lost faith in the presidency. On the heels of Lyndon Johnson's lying to the American people about Vietnam, the Watergate affair contributed to the cumulative disillusionment with politics in Washington and to the steady decrease in political participation. Barely half of those eligible to vote bothered to go to the polls in the presidential elections of 1976, 1980, and 1984. Even fewer cast ballots in nonpresidential contests.

Gerald Ford: Caretaker President

When Nixon resigned in disgrace, he was succeeded by Gerald Ford. An unpretentious middle-American Republican who believed in traditional virtues, Ford became vice president in 1973 when Spiro Agnew resigned for accepting bribes. The new president acknowledged that "I am a Ford, not a Lincoln."

More important were his views about public policy. Throughout his tenure in Congress, Ford voted according to the Republican convictions he shared with his Michigan constituents. Over the years he had opposed federal aid to education, the poverty program, and mass transit. He had voted for civil rights measures only when the weaker substitutes he favored had gone down to defeat. Like his predecessor, he was determined to stop the liberal advances promoted by the Democrats in the 1960s.

He faced a daunting task. After Watergate, Washington was in turmoil. Americans wondered whether any politician could be trusted. The new president had to use his authority to restore national confidence at a time when the misuse of presidential power itself had precipitated the crisis.

Ford worked quickly to restore trust in the government. He emphasized conciliation and compromise, and he promised to cooperate both with Congress and with American citizens. The nation responded gratefully. But the new feeling did not last long. Ford weakened his base of support by pardoning Nixon barely a month after his resignation. His decidedly conservative bent often threw him into confrontation with a Democratic Congress. Economic problems proved most pressing in 1974, as inflation, fueled by oil price increases, rose to 11 percent a year, unemployment stood at 5.3 percent, and GNP declined. Home construction slackened and interest rates rose while stock prices fell. Nixon, preoccupied with the Watergate crisis, had been unable to curb rising inflation and unemployment. Not since Franklin Roosevelt took office in the depths of the Great Depression had a new president faced economic difficulties so severe.

Like Hoover 45 years before, Ford hoped to restore confidence and persuade the public that conditions would improve with patience and goodwill. But his campaign to cajole Americans to "Whip Inflation Now" voluntarily failed dismally. At last convinced of the need for strong governmental action, the administration introduced a tight-money policy to halt inflation. The result was the worst recession since the Depression, with unemployment peaking at 12 percent in 1975. In response, Congress pushed for an anti-recession spending program. Recognizing political reality, Ford endorsed a multibillion-dollar tax cut coupled with higher unemployment benefits. The economy made a modest recovery, although inflation and unemployment remained high. Federal deficits soared.

Ford's dilemma was that his belief in limited presidential involvement set him against liberals who argued for strong executive leadership to make the welfare state work. When he failed to take the initiative, Congress intervened, and the two branches of government clashed. Ford vetoed numerous bills, including those creating a consumer protection agency and expanding programs in education, housing, and health. Congress overrode a higher percentage of vetoes than at any time since the presidency of Franklin Pierce more than a century before.

The Carter Interlude

In the election of 1976, the nation's bicentennial year, Ford faced Jimmy Carter, former governor of Georgia. Appealing to voters distrustful of political leadership, Carter portrayed himself as an outsider. He made a virtue of not being from Washington and of not being a lawyer. Carter's quest for the Democratic nomination benefited from reforms that increased the significance of primary elections in selecting a presidential candidate and decreased the influence of party professionals. Assisted by public relations experts, he effectively used the media, especially television, to bypass party machines and establish a direct electronic relationship with voters.

Most elements of the old Democratic coalition came together once again, as the Democrats benefited from the fallout of the Watergate affair. Carter won a 50 to 48 percent majority of the popular vote and a 297 to 240 tally in the Electoral College. He did well with working people, African-Americans, and Catholics. He won most of the South, heartening to the Democrats after Nixon's gains there. Racial voting differences continued, however, as Carter attracted less than half of all white voters but an overwhelming majority of black voters.

Carter stood in stark contrast to recent occupants of the White House. He was a peanut farmer who shared the rural South's values. He was also a graduate of the Naval Academy, trained as a manager and an engineer. A modest man, he was uncomfortable with the pomp and incessant political activity in Washington. He hoped to diminish the presidency's imperial trappings.

Initially, voters saw Carter as a reform Democrat committed to his party's liberal goals. When he had accepted the Democratic nomination, he had called for an end to race and sex discrimination. He had challenged the "political and economic

TIMELINE

1946	1947	1948	1949	1952
Employment Act	Taft-Hartley Act	"Dixiecrat" party formed; Truman defeats Dewey	Truman launches Fair Deal	Dwight D. Eisenhower elected president

1956	1960	1962	1963	1964
Eisenhower reelected	John F. Kennedy elected president	JFK confronts steel companies	Kennedy assassinated; Lyndon B. Johnson becomes president	Economic Opportunity Act initiates War on Poverty; Johnson reelected president

1965	1968	1972	1973	1974
Department of Housing and Urban Development established; Elementary and Secondary Education Act	Robert F. Kennedy assassinated; Police and protesters clash at Democratic national convention; Richard Nixon elected president	Nixon reelected	Watergate hearings in Congress; Spiro Agnew resigns as vice president	OPEC price increases; Inflation hits 11 percent; Unemployment reaches 7.1 percent; Nixon resigns; Gerald Ford becomes president; Ford pardons Nixon

1975	1976	1977
Unemployment reaches 12 percent	Jimmy Carter elected president	Carter energy program

elite" in America and sought a new approach to providing for the poor, the old, and the weak.

But Carter was hardly the old-line liberal for whom some Democrats had hoped. Though he called himself a populist, his political philosophy and priorities were never clear. Critics charged that he had no legislative strategy. Rather, they said with some truth that he responded to problems haphazardly and failed to provide firm direction. His stance as an outsider, touted during the campaign, led him to ignore traditional political channels after he assumed power. He became mired in detail, losing sight of larger issues. Like Herbert Hoover, he was a technocrat when liberals wanted a visionary to lead the country out of hard times.

Carter gave liberals some hope at first as he accepted deficit spending. When the Federal Reserve increased the money supply to help meet mounting deficits, which reached peacetime records in these years, inflation rose to about 10 percent a year. Seeking to reduce inflation in 1979, Carter slowed down the economy by cutting spending, and he dented the deficit slightly. Contraction of the money supply led to greater unemployment and many small-business failures. Budget cuts fell largely on social programs and distanced Carter from reform-minded Democrats who had supported him three years before. Yet even that effort to arrest growing deficits was not enough. When the budget released in early 1980 still showed high spending levels, the financial community reacted strongly. Bond prices fell, and interest rates rose dramatically.

Similarly, Carter disappointed liberals by failing to construct an effective energy policy. OPEC had been boosting oil prices rapidly since 1973. Americans began to resent their dependence on foreign oil—over 40 percent was being imported by the end of the decade—and clamored for energy self-sufficiency. Carter responded in April 1977 with a comprehensive energy program, which he called the "moral equivalent of war." (Critics dubbed it MEOW.) Never an effective leader in working with the legislative branch, Carter watched his proposals bog down in Congress for 26 months. Eventually, the program committed the nation to move from oil dependence to reliance on coal, possibly even on sun and wind, and established a new synthetic-fuel corporation. Nuclear power, another alternative, seemed less attractive as costs rose and the frightening Three Mile Island accident occurred.

Carter further upset liberals by beginning deregulation—the removal of governmental controls in economic life. Arguing that restrictions established over the past century hampered competition and increased consumer costs, he supported decontrol of oil and natural gas prices to spur production. He also deregulated the railroad, trucking, and airline industries.

Liberals were disappointed as the 1970s ended. Their hopes for a stronger commitment to a welfare state had been dashed and conservatives had the upper hand. Despite a tenuous Democratic hold on the presidency, liberalism was in decline.

✦✦✦✦✦✦

CONCLUSION

Political Readjustment

The course of public policy shifted significantly in the post-World War II years. In the late 1940s and 1950s, American leaders took the first steps toward consolidating the welfare state that Franklin Roosevelt had begun to create in the decade before. In the 1960s, liberal Democrats went even further, as they pressed for large-scale government intervention to meet the social and economic problems that accompanied the modern industrial age. They were inspired by John Kennedy's rhetoric and saw the triumph of their approach in Lyndon Johnson's Great Society, as the nation strengthened its commitment to a capitalist welfare state. When the Democratic party became impaled on the Vietnam War and lost the presidency, the Republicans began dismantling the Great Society programs. While accepting some provisions of the modern welfare state, they objected to the aggressive liberal effort to make the government the major player in the political game and took exception to many of the programs aimed at the poor.

Most Americans, like Paul Cowan, whom we met at the start of this chapter, embraced the message of John Kennedy and the New Frontier in the 1960s and endorsed the liberal approach. But over time, they began to question the tenets of liberalism as the economy faltered, as hard economic choices had to be made, and as the country became mired in Vietnam. Republicans challenging Democratic priorities gained the upper hand and disillusioned liberals like Cowan wondered if their approach could ever succeed.

Recommended Reading

General Works

Terry Anderson, *The Movement and the Sixties: Protest in America from Greensboro to Wounded Knee* (1995); Edward D. Berkowitz and Kim McQuaid, *Creating the Welfare State: The Political Economy of 20th-Century Reform* (1992); Mary C. Brennan, *Tuning Right in the Sixties: The Conservative Capture of the GOP* (1995); Paul Cowan, *The Making of an Un-American: A Dialogue with Experience* (1970); David Farber, *The Age of Great Dreams: America in the 1960s* (1994); Todd Gitlin, *The Sixties: Years of Hope, Days of Rage* (1987); Jim F. Heath, *Decade of Disillusionment: The Kennedy-Johnson Years* (1975); Godfrey Hodgson, *America in Our Time* (1976); Allen J. Matusow, *The Unraveling of America: A History of Liberalism in the 1960s* (1984).

Harry S Truman

Barton J. Bernstein and Allen J. Matusow, eds., *The Truman Administration: A Documentary History* (1966); Robert J. Donovan, *Conflict and Crisis: The Presidency of Harry S Truman, 1945–1948* (1977) and *Tumultuous Years: The Presidency of Harry S Truman, 1949–1953* (1982); Robert H. Ferrell, *Harry S. Truman and the Modern American Presidency* (1983); Alonzo L. Hamby, *Man of the People: A Life of Harry S. Truman* (1995); David McCullough, *Truman* (1992); Harry S. Truman, *Memoirs,* 2 vols. (1955, 1956).

Dwight D. Eisenhower

Charles C. Alexander, *Holding the Line: The Eisenhower Era, 1952–1961* (1975); Craig Allen, *Eisenhower and the Mass Media: Peace, Prosperity, and Prime-Time TV* (1993); Stephen E. Ambrose, *Eisenhower: The President* (1984); Günter Bischof and Stephen E. Ambrose, eds., *Eisenhower: A Centenary Assessment* (1995); Dwight D. Eisenhower, *Mandate for Change, 1953–1956* (1963) and *Waging Peace* (1965); Fred I. Greenstein, *The Hidden-Hand Presidency: Eisenhower as Leader* (1982); Herbert S. Parmet, *Eisenhower and the American Crusades* (1972).

John F. Kennedy and the New Frontier

Henry Fairlie, *The Kennedy Promise* (1972); James N. Giglio, *The Presidency of John F. Kennedy* (1991); Nigel Hamilton, *JFK: Reckless Youth* (1992); Seymour M Hersh, *The Dark Side of Camelot* (1997); Herbert S. Parmet, *Jack: The Struggles of John F. Kennedy* (1980) and *JFK: The Presidency of John F. Kennedy* (1983); Richard Reeves, *President Kennedy: Profile of Power* (1993); Thomas C. Reeves, *A Question of Character: A Life of John F. Kennedy* (1991); Arthur M. Schlesinger, Jr., *A Thousand Days: John F. Kennedy in the White House* (1965); Theodore C. Sorensen, *Kennedy* (1965).

Lyndon B. Johnson and the Great Society

Michael R. Bechloss (ed.), *Taking Charge: The Johnson White House Tapes, 1963–1964* (1997); Robert A. Caro, *The Years of Lyndon Johnson: The Path to Power* (1983) and *The Years of Lyndon Johnson: Means of Ascent* (1990); Robert Dallek, *Lone Star Rising: Lyndon Johnson and His Times, 1908–1960* (1990) and *Flawed Giant: Lyndon Johnson and His Times, 1961–1973* (1998); Robert A. Divine, ed., *Exploring the Johnson Years* (1981) and *The Johnson Years, Volume Two: Vietnam, the Environment, and Science* (1984) and *The Johnson Years: LBJ at Home and Abroad* (1994) Lyndon

Johnson, *The Vantage Point: Perspectives of the Presidency* (1971); Doris Kearns, *Lyndon Johnson and the American Dream* (1976); James T. Patterson, *America's Struggle Against Poverty* (1976).

Richard Nixon and Watergate

Stephen Ambrose, *Nixon: The Education of a Politician, 1913–1962* (1987); Rowland Evans, Jr., and Robert D. Novak, *Nixon in the White House* (1972); Stanley I. Kutler, *The Wars of Watergate: The Last Crisis of Richard Nixon* (1990); Stanley I. Kutler (ed.), *Abuse of Power: The New Nixon Tapes* (1997); J. Anthony Lukas, *Nightmare: The Underside of the Nixon Years* (1976); Richard Nixon, *RN: The Memoirs of Richard Nixon* (1978); Jonathon Schell, *The Time of Illusion: An Historical and Reflective Account of the Nixon Era* (1975); Garry Wills, *Nixon Agonistes: The Crisis of the Self-made Man* (1969); Bob Woodward and Carl Bernstein, *All the President's Men* (1974) and *The Final Days* (1976).

Gerald Ford

John Robert Greene, *The Limits of Power: The Nixon and Ford Administrations* (1992); John Hersey, *The President* (1975); Richard Reeves, *A Ford, Not a Lincoln* (1975).

Jimmy Carter

Jimmy Carter, *Keeping Faith: Memories of a President* (1982); Kenneth A. Morris, *Jimmy Carter: American Moralist* (1996); Gaddis Smith, *Morality, Reason, and Power: American Diplomacy in the Carter Years* (1985); Jules Witcover, *Marathon: The Pursuit of the Presidency, 1972–1976* (1977).

CHAPTER 29

The Struggle for Social Reform

Ann Clarke—as she chooses to call herself now—always wanted to go to college. But girls from Italian families rarely did when she was growing up. Her mother, a widowed Sicilian immigrant, asked her brother for advice: "Should Antonina go to college?" "What's the point?" he replied. "She's just going to get married."

Life had not been easy for Antonina Rose Rumore. As a child in the 1920s, her Italian-speaking grandmother cared for her while her mother supported the family, first in the sweat-shops, then as a seamstress. Even as she dreamed, Ann accommodated her culture's demands for dutiful daughters. Responsive to family needs, Ann finished the high school com-mercial course in three years. She struggled with ethnic prejudice as a legal secretary on Wall Street but still believed in the American dream and the Puritan work ethic. She was proud of her ability to bring money home to her family.

When World War II began, Ann wanted to join the WACS. "Better you should be a prostitute," her mother said. Ann went off to California instead, where she worked at resorts. When she left California, she vowed to return to that land of freedom and opportunity.

After the war, Ann married Gerard Clarke, a college man with an English background. Her children would grow up accepted with Anglo-Saxon names. Over the next 15 years, Ann devoted herself to her family. She was a mother above all, and that took all her time. But she still waited for her own chance. "I had this hunger to learn, this curiosity," she later recalled. By the early 1960s, her three children were all in school. Promising her husband to have dinner on the table every night at six, she enrolled at Pasadena City College. It was not easy. Family still came first. A simple problem was finding time to study. When doing dishes or cleaning house, she memorized lists of facts and dates for school. Holiday time was difficult. Ann occasionally felt compelled to give everything up "to make Christmas." Forgetting about a whole semester's work two weeks before finals one year, she sewed nightgowns instead of writing her art history paper.

Her conflict over her studies was intensified by her position as one of the first older women to go back to college. "Sometimes I felt like I wanted to hide in the woodwork," she admitted. Often her teachers were younger than she was. It took four years to complete the two-year program. But she was not yet done. She wanted a bachelor's degree. Back she went, this time to California State College at Los Angeles.

As the years passed and the credits piled up, Ann became an honors student. Her chil-dren, now in college themselves, were proud and supportive; dinners became arguments over Faulkner and foreign policy. Even so, Ann still felt caught between her world at home and out-side. Since she was at the top of her class, graduation should have been a special occasion.

But she was only embarrassed when a letter from the school invited her parents to attend the final ceremonies. Ann could not bring herself to go.

With a college degree in hand, Ann returned to school for a teaching credential. Receiving her certificate at age 50, she faced the irony of social change. Once denied opportunities, Italians had assimilated into American society. Now she was just another Anglo in Los Angeles, caught in a changing immigration wave; now the city sought Latinos and other minorities to teach in the schools. Jobs in education were scarce, and she was close to "retirement age," so she became a substitute in Mexican-American areas for the next ten years, specializing in bilingual education.

Meanwhile, Ann was troubled by the Vietnam War. "For every boy that died, one of us should lie down," she told fellow workers. She was not an activist, rather one of the millions of quieter Americans who ultimately helped bring about change. The social adjustments caused by the war affected her. Her son grew long hair and a beard and attended protest rallies. She worried that he would antagonize the ladies in Pasadena. Her daughter came home from college in boots and a leather miniskirt designed to shock. Ann accepted her children's changes as relatively superficial, confident in their fundamental values. She trusted them, even as she worried about them.

←←←←←

Ann Clarke's experience paralleled that of millions of women in the post-World War II years. Caught up in traditional patterns of family life, these women began to recognize their need for something more. Like blacks, Latinos, Native Americans, and members of other groups, American women struggled to transform the conditions of their lives and the rights they enjoyed within American society. In the process, they changed the nation itself.

This chapter describes the reform impulse that accompanied the effort to define the government's responsibility for economic and social stability described in Chapter 28. Like earlier reform efforts, particularly those during the Progressive era and the New Deal, this modern struggle sought to fulfill the promise of the American past and to provide liberty and equality in racial, gender, and social relations. The third reform cycle of the twentieth century, however, drew more from the militancy of those on the mudsills of society than from the pleas of middle-class activists. It reflected the attempt of often marginalized Americans to make the nation live up to its professed values. This chapter highlights the voices of such "outsiders" as it describes their efforts to square the ideals of American life with the realities many Americans faced. The chapter records the continuing frustrations of integrating diverse groups into American society while acknowledging their integrity and identity. And it notes the still-present tension accompanying the sharp debate over power and its distribution in the United States.

THE BLACK STRUGGLE FOR EQUALITY

African-Americans' quest for equality was central to the postwar struggle for civil rights by all minority groups in the United States. Stemming from an effort dating back to the Civil War and Reconstruction, the black movement gained momentum by the mid-twentieth century. African-Americans continued to press for reform through peaceful protest and political pressure. But change came slowly. Despite some major victories in the 1950s, rigid segregation remained the rule in the South. In the North, urban ghettos grew with the continuing influx of southern blacks. Crowded public housing, poor schools, and limited economic opportunities bred serious discontent.

Mid-Twentieth Century Roots

Having stepped up their demands for change in the 1930s and 1940s, African-Americans made significant gains during World War II (see Chapter 25). Black servicemen returning from the war vowed to reject second-class citizenship and helped mobilize a grass-roots movement to counter discrimination. In the postwar years, African struggles for independence inspired African-American leaders who now saw the quest for black equality in a broader context. As Adam Clayton Powell, a Harlem preacher (and later congressman), warned, the black man "walks conscious of the fact that he is no longer alone—no longer a minority."

The racial question was dramatized in 1947 when Jackie Robinson broke the color line and began playing major league baseball with the Brooklyn Dodgers. Sometimes teammates were hostile, sometimes runners slid into him with spikes high, but Robinson kept his frustrations to himself. A splendid first season helped ease the way, and after Robinson's trailblazing effort, other blacks, formerly confined to the old Negro leagues, started to move into the major leagues. Next came professional football and basketball.

The nation's racial problems became entangled with Cold War politics. As leader of the "free world," America sought support in Africa and Asia, but discrimination at home was an obvious embarrassment.

Somewhat reluctantly, Truman supported the civil rights movement. He believed in political, not social, equality, but he responded to the growing strength of the African-American vote. In 1946, he appointed a Committee on Civil Rights to investigate lynching and other brutalities against blacks and recommend remedies. The committee's report, released in October 1947, showed that black Americans remained second-class citizens in every area of American life. The first report set a civil rights agenda for the next two decades.

Though Truman hedged at first, in February 1948, he sent a ten-point civil rights program to Congress—the first presidential civil rights plan since Reconstruction. When the southern wing of the Democratic party bolted later that year (see Chapter 28), he moved forward even more aggressively. First he issued an executive order barring discrimination in the federal establishment. Then he ordered equality of treatment in the military services. Manpower needs in the Korean War broke down the last restrictions, particularly when the army found that integrated units performed well.

Elsewhere the administration pushed reforms as well. The Justice Department, not previously supportive of civil rights litigation from the National Association for the Advancement of Colored People (NAACP), now filed briefs challenging discrimination in housing, education, and interstate transportation. These actions helped build the pressure for change that influenced the Supreme Court. Congress, however, took little action.

Federal officials and local law enforcement authorities frequently had to assist African-American children attending integrated schools in the sometimes turbulent aftermath of the *Brown* v. *Board of Education* decision of 1954. (Printed by permission of the Norman Rockwell Family Trust Copyright ©1964 The Norman Rockwell Family Trust)

Integrating the Schools

As the civil rights struggle gained momentum during the 1950s, the judicial system played a crucial role. The NAACP was determined to overturn the 1896 Supreme Court decision *Plessy* v. *Ferguson,* in which the Court had approved of segregation if the facilities used by each race were "separate but equal." The decree had been used for generations to sanction rigid segregation, primarily in the South, though the separate facilities were seldom, if ever, equal.

In 1951, Oliver Brown sued the school board of Topeka, Kansas, to allow his 8-year-old daughter to attend a school for white children that she passed while walking to the bus that carried her to a black school farther away. The case reached the Supreme Court, which added other school segregation cases to this one.

On May 17, 1954, the Supreme Court released its bombshell ruling in *Brown* v. *Board of Education.* For more than a decade, Supreme Court decisions had gradually expanded black civil rights. Now the Court unanimously decreed that "separate facilities are inherently unequal" and concluded that the "separate but equal" doctrine had no place in public education. A year later, the Court declared that local school boards, acting with the guidance of lower courts, should move "with all deliberate speed" to desegregate facilities.

President Eisenhower privately disagreed with the *Brown* ruling, but he knew that it was his constitutional duty to see that the law was carried out. Even while urging sympathy for the South in its period of transition, he acted immediately to desegregate the Washington, D.C., schools as a model for the rest of the country. He also ordered desegregation in navy yards and veterans' hospitals.

The South resisted. In district after district, vicious scenes occurred. The crucial confrontation came in Little Rock, Arkansas, in 1957. A desegregation plan, beginning with the token admission of a few black students to Central High School, was ready. Governor Orval Faubus declared on television that it would not be possible to maintain order if integration took place. National Guardsmen, posted by the governor, turned away nine black students as they tried to enter the school. After three weeks, a federal court ordered the troops to leave. When the black children entered the building, the white students, spurred on by their elders, belligerently opposed them. In the face of mobs, the black children left the school.

With the lines drawn, attention focused on the moderate man in the White House, who faced a situation in which Little Rock whites were clearly defying the law. As a military officer, Ike knew that such resistance could not be tolerated, and he finally took the one action he had earlier called unthinkable. For the first time since the end of Reconstruction, an American president called out federal troops to protect the rights of black citizens. Eisenhower ordered paratroopers to Little Rock and placed National Guardsmen under federal command. The black children entered the school and attended classes with the military protecting their rights.

Black Gains on Other Fronts

The 1930s and World War II had seen the first modern black demonstrations and boycotts protesting job discrimination and segregation. Now, taking direct action, they were ready for an even more dramatic confrontation that would significantly advance the civil rights movement. The crucial event occurred in Montgomery, Alabama.

In December 1955, Rosa Parks, a 42-year-old black seamstress who was also secretary of the Alabama NAACP, sat down in the whites-only front section of a bus. Tired from a hard day's work, she refused orders to move to the back. The bus driver called the police at the next stop, and Parks was arrested and ordered to stand trial for violating the segregation laws. Her stance marked a new phase in the civil rights struggle. Like Rosa Parks, ordinary black men and women would challenge the racial status quo and force both white and black leaders to respond.

In Montgomery, black civil rights officials seized the issue. Fifty black leaders decided to organize a massive boycott of the bus system.

Martin Luther King, Jr., the 27-year-old minister of the Baptist church where the meeting was held, soon emerged as the preeminent spokesman of the protest. King was an impressive figure and an inspiring speaker. "There comes a time when people get tired . . . of being kicked about by the brutal feet of oppression," he declared.

Although King, like others, was arrested on a trumped-up speeding charge and jailed, grass-roots support arose. In Montgomery, 50,000 African Americans walked or formed car pools to avoid the transit system. Their actions cut gross revenue on city buses by 65 percent. Almost a year later, the Supreme Court ruled that bus segregation, like school segregation, violated the Constitution, and the boycott ended. But the mood it fostered continued, and for many blacks peaceful protest became a way of life.

Meanwhile, a concerted effort developed to guarantee black voting rights. Notwithstanding the Fifteenth Amendment (see Chapter 16), many states had

Baptist minister Martin Luther King, Jr., emerged as the black spokesman in the Montgomery, Alabama, bus boycott and soon became the most eloquent African-American leader of the entire civil rights movement. Drawing on his religious background, he was able to mobilize blacks and whites alike in the struggle for equal rights. (Bob Henriques/Magnum Photos)

disfranchised blacks for decades with a poll tax, a literacy test, or an examination of constitutional understanding.

Largely because of the legislative genius of Senate majority leader Lyndon Johnson, the first civil rights bill since Reconstruction moved toward passage. With his eye on the presidency, Johnson wanted to establish his credentials as a man who could look beyond narrow southern interests. Paring the bill down to provisions he felt would pass, Johnson pushed the measure through.

The Civil Rights Act of 1957 created a Civil Rights Commission and empowered the Justice Department to go to court in cases where blacks were denied the right to vote. Though a compromise measure, it was the first successful effort to protect civil rights in 82 years. A few years later, Congress passed the Civil Rights Act of 1960, which set stiffer penalties for people who interfered with the right to vote. But, like its predecessor, it stopped short of authorizing federal registrars to register blacks to vote and so was generally ineffective.

The civil rights movement made important strides during the Eisenhower years. Presidential leadership had little to do with it; rather, Supreme Court rulings and blacks' own efforts had brought the most significant changes, and grass-roots civil rights activity would continue in the 1960s.

Confrontation Continues

A spectrum of organizations—some old, some new—carried the fight forward. The NAACP, founded in 1910, remained committed to overturning the legal bases

In violation of southern law, black college students refused to leave a lunch counter, launching a new campaign in the struggle. Here the students wait patiently for service, or forcible eviction, as a way of dramatizing their determination to end segregation. (Bruce Roberts/Photo Researchers)

for segregation. The Congress of Racial Equality (CORE), an interracial group established in 1942, promoted change through peaceful confrontation. In 1957, after their victory in Montgomery, Martin Luther King, Jr., and others formed the Southern Christian Leadership Conference (SCLC), an organization of southern black clergy. Far more militant was the Student Nonviolent Coordinating Committee (SNCC, pronounced "snick"), which began to operate in 1960 and recruited young Americans who had not been involved in the civil rights struggle.

Confrontations continued in the 1960s. On January 31, 1960, four black college students from the Agricultural and Technical College in Greensboro, North Carolina, sat down at a segregated Woolworth's lunch counter and deliberately violated segregation laws by refusing to leave. Though they often met brutal treatment, the sit-ins captured media attention, and soon involved thousands of African-Americans.

The next year, 1961, the freedom rides began, aimed at testing southern transportation facilities, recently desegregated by a Supreme Court decision. Organized initially by CORE and aided by SNCC, the program sent groups of blacks and whites on buses heading south and stopping at terminals along the way. The riders, peaceful themselves, meant to publicize their cause and generate political support. They anticipated violent confrontations—and got them. Outside Anniston, Alabama, a white mob attacked and firebombed the bus. In Birmingham the police gave the Ku Klux Klan 15 minutes alone to beat the Freedom Riders. The FBI knew about the plan, but did nothing to stop it.

In North and South alike, consciousness grew of the need to combat racial discrimination. The civil rights movement became the most powerful moral campaign since the abolitionist crusade before the Civil War. Often working together closely, blacks and whites vowed to eliminate racial barriers.

Anne Moody, who grew up in a small town in Mississippi, personified the black awakening. As a child, she had seen friends and acquaintances killed for transgressing the limits set for blacks. Overcoming enormous hardships, she became the first member of her family to go to college, and at her all-black school joined the civil rights movement. Slowly, she noted, "I could feel myself beginning to change. For the first time I began to think something would be done about whites killing, beating, and misusing Negroes. I knew I was going to be a part of whatever happened." Participating in sit-ins where she was thrashed and jailed, she remained deeply involved in the movement.

Meanwhile Mimi Feingold, a white student at Swarthmore College, was picketing a Chester, Pennsylvania, Woolworths and helping to unionize Swarthmore's black dining hall workers. In 1961, after her sophomore year, she headed south to join CORE's freedom rides. There she, too, found herself in the midst of often-violent confrontations and went to jail as an act of conscience. In Jackson, Mississippi, she spent a month behind bars.

In 1962, the civil rights movement accelerated. James Meredith, a black air force veteran and student at Jackson State College, applied to the all-white University of Mississippi. He was rejected on racial grounds. Suing for admission, he won his case in the U.S. Supreme Court. Then Governor Ross Barnett, an adamant racist, announced defiantly that Meredith would not be admitted, whatever the Court decision. A major riot followed; tear gas covered the university grounds, and two men were killed and hundreds were hurt.

In April 1963 there was an even more violent confrontation in Birmingham, Alabama, a city 40 percent black and rigidly segregated. Local black leaders encouraged Martin Luther King, Jr., to launch another attack on southern segregation. "We believed that while a campaign in Birmingham would surely be the toughest fight of our civil rights careers," King later explained, "it could, if successful, break the back of segregation all over the nation."

Though the demonstrations were nonviolent, the responses were not. Over a five-week period, city officials arrested 2,200 blacks, some of them schoolchildren, for parading without licenses. Police Commissioner Eugene "Bull" Connor used high-pressure fire hoses, electric cattle prods, and police dogs to force the protesters back. As the media recorded the events, Americans watching television and reading newspapers were horrified. The images of violence created mass sympathy for black Americans' civil rights struggle.

Kennedy's Response

John F. Kennedy claimed to be sickened by the pictures from Birmingham but insisted that he could do nothing, even though he had sought and won black support in 1960. The narrowness of his electoral victory made him reluctant to press white southerners on civil rights when he needed their votes on other issues. Kennedy initially failed to propose any civil rights legislation. Nor did he fulfill a campaign promise to use his presidential power to end housing discrimination "with the stroke of a pen," despite being mailed numerous bottles of ink. Not until

November 1962, after the midterm elections, did he take a modest action—an executive order ending segregation in federally financed housing.

Events finally forced the president to act more boldly. In the confrontation at the University of Mississippi, Kennedy, like Eisenhower at Little Rock, had to send federal troops to restore control and enforce the Supreme Court's order that Meredith be allowed to attend. The administration also forced the desegregation of the University of Alabama and helped arrange a compromise providing for desegregation of Birmingham's municipal facilities. And when white bombings aimed at black leaders in Birmingham caused thousands of blacks to abandon nonviolence and rampage through the streets, Kennedy readied federal troops to intervene.

He also spoke out more forcefully than before. On national television, he called the quest for equal rights a "moral issue." Just hours after Kennedy spoke, assassins killed Medgar Evers, a black NAACP official, in Jackson, Mississippi.

Kennedy finally sent Congress a new and stronger civil rights bill, outlawing segregation in public places, banning discrimination in federally funded programs, and promoting school integration. Polls showed 63 percent public support.

To lobby for passage of this measure, civil rights leaders, pressed from below by black activists, arranged a massive march on Washington in August 1963. More than 200,000 people and numerous celebrities gathered, and popular folk singers led the crowd in "Blowin' in the Wind" and "We Shall Overcome." But the high point was the address by Martin Luther King, Jr. With all the power of a southern preacher, he implored his audience to share his faith in decency and equality.

"I have a dream," King cried, "that one day this nation will rise up and live out the true meaning of its creed: 'We hold these truths to be self-evident, that all men are created equal.' I have a dream that one day on the red hills of Georgia, the sons of former slaves and the sons of former slave-owners will be able to sit together at the table of brotherhood." It was a fervent appeal, and one to which the crowd responded. Each time King used the refrain "I have a dream," thousands of blacks and whites roared together. King concluded by quoting from an old hymn: "Free at last! Free at last! Thank God almighty, we are free at last!"

Not all were moved. Anne Moody, who had come up from her activist work in Mississippi to attend the event, sat on the grass by the Lincoln Memorial. "Martin Luther King went on and on talking about his dream," she said. "I sat there thinking that . . . we never had time to sleep, much less dream." Nor was Congress prompted to do much. Despite Democratic majorities, strong white southern resistance to civil rights remained, and when he was assassinated in November 1963, Kennedy's bill was still bottled up in committee.

Legislative Success in the Johnson Years

Lyndon Johnson was more successful than Kennedy in advancing the cause of civil rights. "No memorial oration or eulogy could more eloquently honor President Kennedy's memory," he told Congress in his first address after becoming president, "than the earliest possible passage of the civil rights bill." He pushed the bill through Congress, heading off a Senate filibuster by persuading his old colleague, Republican minority leader Everett Dirksen of Illinois, to work for cloture—a two-thirds vote to cut off debate. In June 1964, the Senate for the first time imposed cloture to advance a civil rights measure, and passage soon followed. "No army can withstand the strength of an idea whose time has come," said Dirksen.

The Civil Rights Act of 1964 outlawed racial discrimination in all public accommodations and authorized the Justice Department to act with greater authority in school and voting matters. In addition, an equal opportunity provision prohibited discriminatory hiring on grounds of race, gender, religion, or national origin in firms with more than 25 employees.

Despite the law being one of the great achievements of the 1960s, Johnson realized that it was only a starting point because widespread discrimination still existed in American society. African-Americans still found it difficult to vote in large areas of the South. Freedom Summer, sponsored by SNCC and other civil rights groups in 1964, sent black and white students to Mississippi to work for black rights. Early in the summer, two whites, Michael Schwerner and Andrew Goodman, and one black, James Chaney, were murdered. By the end of the summer, 80 workers had been beaten, 1,000 had been arrested, and 37 churches had been bombed. Early in 1965 there was another confrontation in the national headlines when Alabama police clubbed and tear-gassed demonstrators trying to march from Selma to Montgomery, the state capital. Sending the National Guard to protect another march to Montgomery, Johnson asked Congress for a voting bill to close loopholes in earlier civil rights laws.

The Voting Rights Act of 1965, perhaps the most important law of the decade, authorized the U.S. attorney general to appoint federal examiners to register voters where local officials were obstructing the registration of blacks. In the year after passage of the act, 400,000 blacks registered to vote in the Deep South; by 1968, the number reached a million.

Black Power Challenges Liberal Reform

As the struggle for civil rights moved north, divisions within the movement emerged. Initially, the civil rights campaign had been integrated and nonviolent. Martin Luther King, Jr., had become its acknowledged leader. But now black-white tensions flared within organizations, and younger black leaders began to challenge King's nonviolent approach. They were tired of beatings, jailings, church bombings, and the slow pace of change that was dependent on white liberal support and government action. Anne Moody, the stalwart activist in Mississippi, voiced the doubts so many blacks harbored about the possibility of real change. Discouraged after months of struggle, she boarded a bus taking civil rights workers north to testify about abuses. As "We Shall Overcome" reverberated around her, she was overwhelmed by the suffering she had so often seen. All she could think was, "I wonder. I really wonder."

One episode that raised many blacks' suspicion of white liberals occurred at the Democratic national convention of 1964. In Mississippi's Freedom Summer campaign, SNCC had founded the Freedom Democratic party as an alternative to the all-white regular state delegation. Testifying before the credentials committee, black activist Fannie Lou Hamer reported that she had been beaten, jailed, and denied the right to vote. Yet the committee's final compromise—pressed by President Johnson, who worried about losing southern support in the upcoming election—was to seat the white delegation while offering the protest organization two at-large seats. That hardly satisfied those who had risked their lives and families to try to vote in Mississippi. Said civil rights leader James Forman: "[The convention] was a powerful lesson . . . . No longer was there any hope . . . that the federal government would change the situation in the Deep South." SNCC, once a religious and integrated organization, began to turn into an all-black cadre dedicated to mobilizing poor blacks for militant action. "Liberation" replaced civil rights as a goal.

Increasingly, angry blacks argued that the nation must no longer withhold the rights pledged in its founding credo. Black author James Baldwin wrote in one of his eloquent essays that unless change came soon, the worst could be expected: "If we do not now dare everything, the fulfillment of that prophecy, recreated from the Bible in song by a slave, is upon us: God gave Noah the rainbow sign, No more water, the fire next time!"

Even more responsible for channeling black frustration into a new set of goals and tactics was Malcolm X. Born Malcolm Little and reared in northern ghettos, he had been a petty criminal. In prison, he became a convert to the Nation of Islam and a disciple of black leader Elijah Muhammad. He began to preach that the white man was responsible for the black man's condition and that blacks had to help themselves.

Malcolm was impatient with the moderate civil rights movement. He grew tired of hearing "all of this non-violent, begging-the-white-man kind of dying . . . all of this sitting-in, sliding-in, wading-in, eating-in, diving-in, and all the rest." Espousing black separatism and black nationalism for most of his public career, he argued for black control of black communities, preached an international perspective embracing African peoples in diaspora, and appealed to blacks to fight racism "by any means necessary."

Malcolm X became the most dynamic spokesman for poor northern blacks since Marcus Garvey in the 1920s. Though he was assassinated by black antagonists in 1965, his African-centered, uncompromising perspective helped shape the struggle against racism.

One man influenced by Malcolm's message was Stokely Carmichael. Born in Trinidad, he came to the United States at the age of 11 and grew up with an interest in politics and black protest. While at Howard University, he picketed and demonstrated and was beaten and jailed. Frustrated with civil disobedience as he became active in SNCC, he urged field-workers to arm for self-defense. It was time for blacks to cease depending on whites, he argued, and to make SNCC a black organization. His election as its head reflected SNCC's growing radicalism.

The split in the black movement was dramatized in June 1966 during a march in Mississippi, when Carmichael's followers challenged those of Martin Luther King, Jr., the advocate of nonviolence and interracial cooperation. Carmichael, just out of jail after arrest for his protest activities, shouted to the crowd: "This is the twenty-seventh time I have been arrested—and I ain't going to jail no more! The only way we gonna stop them white men from whippin' us is to take over. We been saying freedom for six years and we ain't got nothing. What we gonna start saying now is Black Power!" Carmichael had the audience with him as he repeated, and the crowd shouted back, "We . . . want . . . Black . . . Power!"

Black Power was a call for a broad-based campaign to build independent institutions in the African-American community. It drew on growing demands for an end to abuse of black women and fostered a powerful sense of black pride. Its most enduring legacy was political and cultural mobilization at the grass-roots level, even if it only partially realized its goals.

Black Power led to demands for more drastic action. Huey Newton's Black Panthers, radical activists who organized first in Oakland, California, militantly vowed to eradicate not only racial discrimination but capitalism as well. H. Rap Brown, who succeeded Carmichael as head of SNCC, became famous for saying that "violence is as American as cherry pie."

Black Power calls for sweeping social change and the ghetto riots that began erupting in the summer of 1964 showed that racial injustice was an American, not just a southern, problem. In 1965, in the Watts neighborhood of Los Angeles, a massive uprising lasted five days and left 34 dead, more than 1,000 injured, and hundreds of buildings burned to the ground. Other cities saw similar riots in 1966 and 1967. When Martin Luther King, Jr., fell to a white assassin's bullet in April 1968, angry blacks went on rampages in cities throughout the country.

"Southern Strategy" and Showdown on Civil Rights

Richard Nixon, elected president in 1968, was less sympathetic to the civil rights cause than his immediate predecessors. He had won only 12 percent of the black vote and concluded that trying to woo the black vote would endanger his white southern support.

From the start, the Nixon administration sought to scale back federal commitments to civil rights. It moved to reduce appropriations for fair-housing enforcement and tried to block an extension of the Voting Rights Act of 1965. When southern politicians sought to get federal school desegregation guidelines suspended, the Justice Department supported them, and Nixon publicly criticized a unanimous Supreme Court rebuff of the effort.

Nixon also faced the growing controversy over busing as a means of desegregation, a highly-charged issue in the 1970s. Transporting students from one area to another to attend school was nothing new. In the South, busing had long been used to maintain segregated schools. Yet when busing was used to break down racial barriers, it inflamed passions.

The issue came to a head in North Carolina's Charlotte-Mecklenburg school system. A desegregation plan involving voluntary transfer was in effect, but many blacks still attended largely segregated schools. In 1971, the Supreme Court ruled that district courts had broad authority to order the desegregation of school systems—by busing, if necessary.

Nixon opposed busing, and now he went on television to denounce it. Although Congress did not grant his request for a moratorium, southerners knew where he stood. So did northerners, for the issue became a national one. Many of the nation's largest northern cities had school segregation as rigid as in the South, largely because of residential patterns. Mississippi Senator John C. Stennis hoped to stir up the North by subjecting it to the same busing standards as the South. Court decisions subsequently ordered many northern cities to desegregate their schools.

Northern resistance to integration was fiercest in Boston, but the situation there was typical. In 1973, more than half of the African-American students were in schools that were 90 percent black. In June 1974, a federal judge ordered busing to begin. The effort went smoothly enough for many younger students, but whites boycotted South Boston High and stoned buses bringing in black students, injuring some children. White working-class South Bostonians felt that they were being asked to carry the burden of middle-class liberals' racial views. Often white families either enrolled their children in private schools or fled the city.

The Republicans slowed down the school desegregation movement. Nixon openly catered to his conservative constituents. His successor, Gerald Ford, never came out squarely against civil rights, but his lukewarm approach to desegregation demonstrated a further weakening of the federal commitment.

The situation was less inflamed at the college level, but the same pattern held. Blacks made significant progress until the Republican administrations in the late 1960s and 1970s slowed the movement for civil rights. Integration at the postsecondary level came easier as federal affirmative-action guidelines brought more blacks into colleges and universities. In 1950, only 83,000 black students were enrolled in institutions of higher education, in 1960, about one million. Black enrollment in colleges peaked at 9.3 percent of the college population in 1976, before falling back slightly.

Some whites protested "reverse discrimination." Allan Bakke, who was white, was twice rejected by the medical school at the University of California, Davis. He sued on the grounds that a racial quota reserving 16 of 100 places for minority-group applicants was discriminatory, violating the Civil Rights Act of 1964. In 1978, the Supreme Court ordered Bakke's admission. Its complex ruling allowed "consideration" of race in admissions policies but not quotas.

Jimmy Carter, president when the *Bakke* decision was handed down, was more supportive of civil rights than his Republican predecessors. He brought a large number of qualified blacks, some of them highly visible, into his administration. But Carter's lack of support for increased social programs for the poor hurt the majority of black citizens and strained their loyalty to the Democratic party.

The civil rights movement underscored the democratic values on which the nation was based, but the gap between rhetoric and reality remained. Most black families remained poor. African-American income was substantially below white income. After early optimism in the years when the movement made its greatest strides, blacks and sympathetic whites were troubled by the direction of public policy. Given a wavering national commitment to reform in the 1970s, only pressures from reform groups kept the faltering civil rights movement alive.

PRESSURE FROM THE WOMEN'S MOVEMENT

The black struggle in the 1960s and 1970s was accompanied by a women's movement that grew out of the agitation for civil rights but soon developed a life of its own. This struggle, like those of Latinos and Native Americans, employed the confrontational approach and the vocabulary of the civil rights movement to create pressure for change. Using proven strategies, it sometimes proceeded even faster than the black effort.

Attacking the Feminine Mystique

Many white women joined the civil rights movement only to find themselves second-class citizens. Men, black and white, held the top positions and gave women menial jobs when not actually involved in demonstrations or voter drives. Many women also felt sexually exploited. Stokely Carmichael underscored their point: "The only position for women in SNCC is prone."

Although the civil rights movement helped spark the women's movement, broad social changes provided the preconditions. During the 1950s and 1960s, increasing numbers of married women entered the labor force (see Chapter 26). Equally important, many more young women were attending college. By 1970, women earned 41 percent of all B.A. degrees awarded, in comparison with only 25 percent in 1950. These educated young women had high hopes for themselves, even if they still earned substantially less than men.

Just as in the civil rights movement, reform legislation played a part in ending sexual discrimination. Title 7 of the 1964 civil rights bill, as originally drafted, prohibited discrimination on the grounds of race. Conservatives opposed to black civil rights introduced an amendment also banning discrimination on the basis of gender, hoping to guarantee the entire bill's failure. But both the amendment and the full measure were approved, giving women a legal tool for attacking discrimination. They discovered, however, that the Equal Employment Opportunities Commission regarded women's complaints as far less important than those of blacks.

In 1966, a group of 28 professional women, including author Betty Friedan, established the National Organization for Women (NOW) "to take action to bring American women into full participation in the mainstream of American society now." By full participation the founders meant not only fair pay and equal opportunity but also a more egalitarian form of marriage. NOW also attacked the "false image of women . . . in the media." By 1967, some 1,000 women had joined the organization, and four years later, its membership reached 15,000.

NOW was a pressure group, dedicated to reforming American society by promoting equal opportunity for women. But radical feminists, who had come up through the civil rights movement, found NOW's agenda an inadequate answer to gender discrimination. "Women's liberation does not mean equality with men," said one, because "equality in an unjust society is meaningless." Through consciousness-raising, these feminists wanted to educate millions of discontented but unpoliticized women about their oppression—to demonstrate, in their phrase, that the personal was political.

The radicals caught mass-media attention at the Miss America pageant in September 1968. On the Atlantic City boardwalk, a hundred women nominated a sheep as their candidate for Miss America and filled a "freedom trash can" with "instruments of torture": bras, girdles, hair curlers, high heels, and copies of *Playboy* and *Cosmopolitan* magazines. In the pageant hall, they unfurled banners reading "Women's Liberation."

Feminism at High Tide

Real changes were under way. A 1970 survey of first-year college students showed that men interested in such fields as business, medicine, engineering,

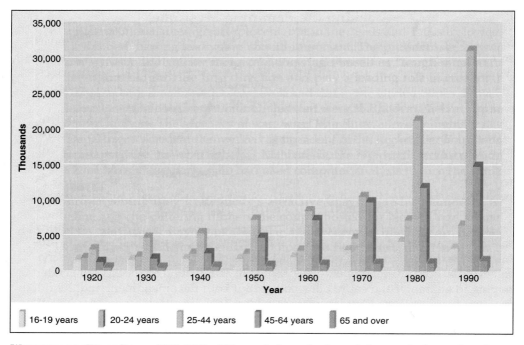

WOMEN IN THE WORK FORCE, 1920–1990 This graph shows the dramatic increase in the number of women in the work force in the 1970s and 1980s. Note particularly the rise in the number of working women 25 to 44 years old. Source: U.S. Bureau of the Census.

and law outnumbered women eight to one; by 1975, the ratio dropped to three to one. The proportion of women beginning law school quadrupled between 1969 and 1973. Women gained access to the military academies and entered senior officer ranks, although they were still kept out of combat command positions. According to the Census Bureau, 45 percent of mothers with preschool children held jobs outside the home in 1980—four times more than 30 years before. To be sure, many employers systematically excluded women from certain positions, and women usually held "female" jobs in the clerical, sales, and service sectors, but the progress was still unmistakable.

Legal changes brought women more benefits and opportunities. For example, Title 9 of the Education Amendments of 1972 broadened the Civil Rights Act of 1964 by barring gender bias in federally assisted educational activities and programs—which included sports teams, greatly boosting the visibility of women's sports.

A flurry of publications spread the principles of the women's movement. In 1972, journalist Gloria Steinem and several other women founded a new magazine, *Ms.*, which succeeded beyond their wildest dreams. By 1973, there were almost 200,000 subscribers. *Our Bodies, Ourselves,* a handbook published by a women's health collective, encouraged women to understand and control their bodies; it sold 850,000 copies between 1971 and 1976.

These new books and magazines differed radically from older women's magazines like *Ladies' Home Journal,* which focused on domestic interests and needs.

Women marched to mobilize support for ratification of the Equal Rights Amendment, but the campaign failed as opponents aroused public fears and blocked support in a number of key states. A decade after passage, the ERA was dead. (J. T. Alan/Sygma)

Ms. dealt with abortion, employment, discrimination, and other feminist issues such as the Equal Rights Amendment.

Women both in and out of NOW worked for congressional passage, then ratification, of the Equal Rights Amendment (ERA) to the Constitution. Passed by Congress in 1972, with ratification seemingly assured, it stated simply, "Equality of rights under the law shall not be denied or abridged by the United States or by any State on account of sex."

More radical feminists insisted that legal changes were not enough. Traditional gender and family roles would have to be discarded to end social exploitation. Socialist feminists claimed that it was not enough to strike out at male domination, for capitalist society itself was responsible for women's plight. Only through revolution could women be free.

Black women frequently viewed the women's movement ambivalently. Some became feminists; others insisted that race, more than gender, was the source of their oppression, and were suspicious of the middle-class orientation of many white feminists. Members of NOW and similar organizations, they claimed, "suffered little more than boredom, gentle repression, and dishpan hands."

Not all women were feminists. Many felt the women's movement was contemptuous of women who stayed at home to perform traditional tasks. Marabel Morgan was one who still insisted that the woman had a place at home by her husband's side. Phyllis Schlafly headed a nationwide campaign to block ratification of the ERA. "It won't do anything to help women," she said, "and it will take away from women the rights they already have, such as the right of a wife to be supported by her husband, the right of a woman to be exempted from military combat, and the right, if you wanted it, to go to a single-sex college." The ERA, she predicted, would lead to the establishment of coed bathrooms, the elimination of alimony, and the legalization of homosexual marriage.

Schlafly and her allies had their way. Within a few years after passage of the ERA, 35 states had agreed to the measure, but then the momentum disappeared. Even with an extension in the deadline granted in 1979, the amendment could not win support of the necessary 38 states. By mid-1982, the ERA was dead.

Despite the counterattacks, the women's movement flourished in the 1960s and 1970s. In the tenth anniversary issue of *Ms.* magazine, in 1982, founding editor Gloria Steinem noted the differences a decade had made. "Now, we have words like 'sexual harassment' and 'battered women,'" she wrote. "Ten years ago, it was just called 'life.'"

LATINO MOBILIZATION

Latinos, like women, profited from the example of blacks in the struggle for equality. They became more vocal and confrontational as their numbers increased dramatically in the postwar years. In 1970, some 9 million residents of the United States declared they were of Spanish origin; in 1980, the figure was 14.6 million. But median household income remained less than three-fourths that of Anglos and inferior education and political weakness reinforced social and cultural separation. Latinos comprised Puerto Ricans in the Northeast, Cubans in Florida, Chicanos in California, and Tejanos in Texas. Chicanos took the lead, though all developed a heightened sense of solidarity and group pride as they began to assert their rights.

Early Efforts for Equality

The roots of the Latino struggle dated back to the World War II years. Chicanos established the American GI Forum because a Texas funeral home refused to bury a Mexican-American casualty of World War II. When the group's protest led to a burial in Arlington National Cemetery, the possibilities of concerted action became clear. In the waning months of the war, a court case challenged Mexican-American segregation in the schools. In Orange County, California, Gonzalo Méndez, a U.S. citizen, sued to permit his children to attend the school reserved for Anglo-Americans rather than an inferior Mexican one. The federal courts backed him, opening the way for integration elsewhere. Meanwhile, Mexican-Americans returning from the military, where they had often been racially invisible, chafed at the discrimination they still met at home.

New organizations arose to struggle for equal rights. The Community Service Organization mobilized Chicanos against discrimination; the Asociación Nacional México-Americana took a more militant approach; the League of United Latin American Citizens continued efforts to promote educational reform.

Advances, however, came slowly. In the late 1940s, many Chicanos sought official classification as Caucasian, hoping that the change would lead to better treatment. But even when the designation changed, their status did not. They still faced discrimination and police brutality, particularly in the cities with the largest Chicano populations. Los Angeles, with its large number of Chicanos, saw incidents such as the 1951 "Bloody Christmas" case in which officers took seven Mexican-Americans from jail cells and beat them severely.

César Chávez organized the United Farm Workers to give migrant Mexican workers representation in their struggle for better wages and working conditions. Here he works with laborers in his tireless campaign for their support. (Bob Fitch/Black Star)

Protests continued, yet in the 1950s Chicano activism was fragmented. Some Mexican-Americans considered their situation hopeless. While new and aggressive challenges appeared, fully effective mobilization had to wait for another day.

César Chávez and the Politics of Confrontation

In the 1960s and 1970s, Mexican-Americans became more active politically. In 1960, Chicanos supported Kennedy, helping him win Texas, and started seeing the benefits of such support. Chicanos began to get elected to Congress.

Direct action was more immediately effective than political action. César Chávez, founder of the United Farm Workers, provided an example of its potential by organizing one of the most exploited and ignored groups of laboring people in the country, the western migrant farm workers. Chávez, himself of a farm worker family, concentrated on migrant Mexican field hands, who worked long hours for meager pay. By 1965, his organization had recruited 1,700 people and was beginning to attract volunteer help.

Chávez first took on the grape growers of California. His union struck for better pay, working conditions, and recognition. Chávez skillfully appealed to middle-class consumers nationwide to support his struggle by boycotting grapes. Some employers came to terms, but others held out or rigged the results of union elections. When California governor Edmund G. Brown, Sr., launched an investigation of such tactics, he became the first major political figure to support the long-powerless Chicano field hands. In a new election, Chávez's United Farm

Workers won. Later they won in boycotts of lettuce and other products harvested by exploited labor. In 1975, his long struggle on behalf of farm workers culminated with the enactment in California of a measure requiring growers to bargain collectively with the elected representatives of the workers. Farm workers had never been covered by the National Labor Relations Board. Now they had achieved the legal basis for representation that could help bring higher wages and improved working conditions. And Chávez had become a national figure.

Meanwhile, Mexican-Americans pressed for reform in other areas. In the West and Southwest, Mexican-American studies programs flourished. They offered degrees, built library collections, and gave Chicanos access to their own past. The campuses also provided a network linking students together and mobilizing them for political action. Such protests spread to the secondary-school level, where educational conditions were often deplorable. Walkouts in a number of western states brought about the hiring of more Latino teachers and better facilities.

Militant new Chicano organizations emerged. In East Los Angeles, Young Citizens for Community Action began as a neighborhood service club but adopted a paramilitary stance, trying to protect local residents. Its members became identified as the Brown Berets and formed chapters throughout the Midwest and Southwest.

Other Latinos followed a more political path. In Texas, José Angel Gutiérrez formed a citizens organization which developed into the La Raza Unida political party and successfully promoted Mexican-American candidates for political offices. This organization gained strength in the West and Southwest throughout the 1970s. In New Mexico, the charismatic preacher Reis López Tijerina, or "El Tigre," took up the land-grant cause and argued that the United States government had fraudulently deprived Chicanos of village lands. His organization, La Alianza Federal de Mercedes (the Federal Alliance of Land Grants), marched on the New Mexico state capitol and occupied national forests. Arrested, he stood trial and eventually served time in prison, where he became a symbol of political repression.

Latinos made a particular point of protesting the Vietnam War. Because the draft drew most heavily from the poorer segments of society, the Latino casualty rate was far higher than that of the population at large. In 1969, the Brown Berets organized the National Chicano Moratorium Committee and demonstrated against what they argued was a racial war. Some of the rallies ended in confrontations with the police. News reporter Rubén Salazar, active in exposing questionable police activity, was killed in one such episode in 1970, and his death brought renewed charges of police brutality.

Aware of the growing numbers and growing demands of Latinos, the Nixon administration tried to win them over. Cuban-American refugees, strongly opposed to communism, shifted toward the Republican party, which they saw as more vigorously anti-Castro than the Democratic party. Nixon courted Chicanos by dangling political positions, government jobs, and promises of better programs for Mexican-Americans. The effort paid off; Nixon received 31 percent of the Hispanic vote in 1972. But then the president moved to cut back the poverty program, begun under Johnson, that assisted many Hispanics.

Despite occasional gains, all Latinos faced continuing problems. Discrimination persisted in housing, education, and employment. Activists had laid the groundwork for a campaign for equal rights, but the struggle had just begun.

NATIVE AMERICAN PROTEST

Like Latinos, Native Americans continued to suffer second-class status as the 1960s began. But, partly inspired by the confrontational tactics of other groups, they mounted more aggressive efforts to claim their rights and to improve living and working conditions. Their soaring numbers—the census put them at 550,000 in 1960 and 1,480,000 in 1980—gave them greater visibility and political clout.

Origins of the Struggle

Native Americans began the struggle for equality well before the 1960s. They achieved an important victory just after the end of World War II when Congress established the Indian Claims Commission. The commission had a mandate to review tribal charges of ancestral lands being illegally seized and federal treaties violated. Hundreds of tribal suits against the government in federal courts were now possible. Many of them would lead to large cash settlements—a form of reparation for past injustices—and sometimes the return of long-lost lands.

In the 1950s, federal Indian policy shifted course. Hoping to limit the role of the national government, the Eisenhower administration turned away from the New Deal policy of government support for tribal autonomy. In the Indian Reorganization Act of 1934, the government had stepped in to restore lands to tribal ownership and end their loss or sale to outsiders. In 1953, instead of trying to encourage Native American self-government, the administration adopted a new "termination" policy. The government proposed settling all outstanding claims and eliminating reservations as legitimate political entities. To encourage their assimilation into mainstream society, the government offered small subsidies to families willing to leave the reservations and relocate in the cities.

The new policy victimized the Native Americans. With their lands no longer federally protected and their members deprived of treaty rights, many tribes became unwitting victims of people who wanted to seize their land. Though promising more freedom, the new policy caused great disruption as the government terminated a number of tribes.

An unintended consequence of the policy was increased Indian activism. The National Congress of American Indians mobilized opposition to the federal program. A Seminole petition to the president in 1954 summed up a general view:

> We do not say that we are superior or inferior to the White Man and we do not say that the White Man is superior or inferior to us. We do say that we are not White Men but Indians, do not wish to become White Men but wish to remain Indians, and have an outlook on all things different from the outlook of the White Man.

Not only did the termination policy foster a sense of Indian identity, but it also sparked an awareness among whites of the Indians' right to maintain their heritage. In 1958, the Eisenhower administration changed the policy of termination so that it required a tribe's consent. Implementation of the policy effectively ceased.

Tribal Voices

In the 1960s, Native Americans began to assert themselves even more. In 1961 several hundred Indians asked the Kennedy administration for the right to help make decisions about programs and budgets for the tribes, and college-educated Indians formed a National Indian Youth Council aimed at reestablishing Indian national pride. Over the next several decades, the council helped change the attitudes of tribal leaders, who were called Uncle Tomahawks for their willingness to submit to white demands.

Native Americans learned from the examples of protest in Third World nationalist movements and, even more important, in the civil rights revolution. They came to understand the place of interest-group politics in a diverse society, and in the Vietnam War they recognized a pattern of killing people of color.

Indians successfully promoted their own values and designs. Native American fashions became more common, museums and galleries displayed Indian art, and Indian jewelry found a new market. The larger culture came to appreciate important work by Native Americans. In 1968, N. Scott Momaday won the Pulitzer Prize for his book *House Made of Dawn*. Vine Deloria, Jr.'s *Custer Died for Your Sins* (1969) had even wider readership. Popular films sympathetically portrayed Indian history. Indian studies programs developed at universities. Organizations like the American Indian Historical Society protested traditional textbook treatment of Indians.

Confrontational Tactics

At the same time, Native Americans became more confrontational. Like other groups, they worked through the courts but also challenged authority more aggressively when necessary.

Led by a new generation of leaders, Native Americans tried to protect their remaining tribal lands. Intrusion had to cease. "Everything is tied to our homeland," D'Arcy McNickle, a Flathead anthropologist, told other Indians in 1961.

The protest spirit was apparent on the Seneca Nation's Allegany reservation in New York State. Although a 1794 treaty had established the Seneca right to the land, since 1928 the federal government wanted to build a flood control dam there. In 1956, after hearings to which the Indians were not invited and about which they were not informed, Congress appropriated funds for the project, and the dam was eventually built. Belated reparations of $15 million did not compensate for the loss of sacred sites, hunting and fishing grounds, and homes.

The Seneca did somewhat better in the 1970s. When New York State tried to build a superhighway through part of the same reservation, the Indians blocked it in court, and eventually negotiated an exchange: state lands, plus a cash settlement, in return for an easement through the reservation. That decision encouraged tribal efforts elsewhere to resist similar incursions.

Native American leaders found that lawsuits charging violations of treaty rights could give them powerful leverage. In 1967, in the first of many decisions upholding the Indian side, the U.S. Court of Claims ruled that in 1823 the government had forced the Seminole in Florida to cede their land for an unreasonably low

The American Indian Movement's armed occupation of Wounded Knee, South Dakota, site of a late-nineteenth-century massacre of the Sioux, resulted in bloodshed that dramatized unfair government treatment of Native Americans. (AP/Wide World Photos)

price; 144 years later, the government was directed to pay additional funds. In the 1970s, a number of tribes fought back when corporations, responding to the international oil shortage, tried to extend western coal strip-mining operations on a vast scale, infringing on Indian water rights. In a landmark 1973 case, a federal court ruled that the government must carry out its obligation as trustee to protect Indian property. The courts also upheld various Indian nations' rights to fish without state regulatory intrusion, as guaranteed by nineteenth-century treaties.

Urban Indian activism became highly visible in 1968, when George Mitchell and Dennis Banks, Chippewa living in Minneapolis, founded the American Indian Movement (AIM). It secured Office of Economic Opportunity funds for Indian-controlled organizations and established patrols to protect drunken Indians from police harassment. Chapters formed in other cities.

There were several well-publicized instances of Native American militancy. In 1969, a landing party of 78 Indians seized Alcatraz Island in San Francisco Bay. By converting the island and its defunct federal prison into a cultural and educational center, the protesters hoped (in the words of author Vine Deloria, Jr.) "to see what we could do toward developing answers to modern social problems . . . . It just seems to a lot of Indians that this continent was a lot better off when we were running it." In 1971 federal officials removed the Indians. Then, in 1972, other militants occupied the Bureau of Indian Affairs in Washington for six days. Finally, in

1973, AIM took over the South Dakota village of Wounded Knee, the site of the 1890 Sioux massacre, to dramatize the desperate impoverishment, alcoholism, and hopelessness of the people on the surrounding reservation and to draw attention to the 371 treaties AIM leaders claimed the government had broken. Federal officials encircled the area and, when AIM tried to bring in supplies, killed one Indian and wounded another. The confrontation ended with a government agreement to reexamine the treaty rights of the Indians, although little of substance was subsequently done.

Gaining education and legal skills became important for Native American peoples. The number of Indians in college increased from a few hundred in the early 1960s to tens of thousands by 1980. Because roughly half the Indian population lived on reservations, many tribal communities founded their own colleges. Indians studied law and acted as advocates for their own people in the court cases they were filing. In 1968, funding from the Office of Economic Opportunity helped the University of New Mexico Law School start a Native American scholarship program. Since 1971, that program has graduated 35 to 40 Indian lawyers each year. They have worked for tribes directly and have successfully argued for tribal jurisdiction in conflicts between whites and Indians on the reservations.

Government Response

Indian protest brought results. The outcry against termination in the 1960s led the Kennedy and Johnson administrations to steer a middle course, neither endorsing nor disavowing the policy. Instead they tried to bolster reservation economies and raise standards of living by persuading private industries to locate on reservations and by promoting the leasing of reservation lands to energy and development corporations. In the 1970s, the Navajo, Northern Cheyenne, Crow, and other tribes tried to cancel or renegotiate such leases, fearing "termination by corporation."

In the mid-1960s, the Native American cry for self-determination brought Indian involvement in the Great Society's poverty program. Two agencies, the Area Redevelopment Administration (later the Economic Development Administration) and the Office of Economic Opportunity, responded to pressure by letting Indians devise programs and budgets and to administer programs themselves. Indians were similarly involved with Great Society housing, health, and education initiatives.

Finally, in 1975, Congress passed Indian Self-determination and Education Assistance Acts. Five years earlier, Nixon had declared that self-determination had replaced termination as American policy. The self-determination act was a largely rhetorical statement, and the education act involved subcontracting federal services to tribal groups. Though both laws were limited, they nonetheless reflected the government's decision to respond to Indian pressure and created a framework to guide federal policy in the decades ahead.

SOCIAL AND CULTURAL PROTEST

As blacks, Latinos, and Native Americans agitated, white middle-class American society experienced an unprecedented upheaval. Young people in particular rejected the stable patterns of affluent life their parents had forged. Some embraced radical political activity; many more adopted new standards of sexual behavior, music, and dress. In time their actions spawned still other protests as Americans tried to make the political and social world more responsive.

Student Activism

Post-World War II demographic patterns help explain youthful activism and the "generation gap." Members of the baby boom generation came of age in the 1960s. Between 1950 and 1964, the number of students in college more than doubled. By the end of the 1960s, college enrollment stood more than four times above the 1940s level. In college, some students joined the struggle for civil rights. Hopeful at first, they gradually became discouraged by the gap between Kennedy's New Frontier rhetoric and the government's actual commitment.

Out of that disillusionment arose the radical spirit of the New Left. Civil rights activists were among those who in 1960 organized Students for a Democratic Society (SDS). In 1962, SDS issued a manifesto, the Port Huron Statement, written largely by Tom Hayden of the University of Michigan. "We are people of this generation, bred in at least modest comfort, housed now in universities, looking uncomfortably at the world we inherit," it began. It went on to deplore the vast social and economic distances separating people from each other and to condemn the isolation and estrangement of modern life. The document called for a better system, a "democracy of individual participation."

The first blow of the growing student rebellion came at the University of California in Berkeley. There, civil rights activists became involved in a confrontation soon known as the free speech movement. It began in September 1964 when the university refused to allow students to distribute protest material outside the main campus gate. When police arrested one of the leaders, students surrounded the police car and kept it from moving all night.

The university brought charges against the student leaders, and when the regents refused to drop the charges, students occupied the administration building. Mario Savio, one of the arrested, denounced the university as an impersonal machine: "It becomes odious, so we must put our bodies against the gears, against the wheels . . . and make the machine stop until we're free." Folk singer Joan Baez sang "We Shall Overcome," the marching song of the civil rights movement. Then, as in the South, police stormed in and arrested the students in the building. A student strike, with faculty aid, mobilized wider support for the right to free speech.

The free speech movement at Berkeley was basically a plea for traditional liberal reform. Students sought only the reaffirmation of the long-standing right to express themselves, and they aimed their attacks at the university, not at society. Later, in other institutions, the attack broadened. Students sought greater involvement in university affairs, argued for curricular reform, and demanded admission of more minority students. Their success in gaining their demands changed the shape of American higher education.

The mounting protest against the escalation of the Vietnam War fueled and refocused the youth movement. Confrontation became the new tactic of radical students, and protest became a way of life. Between January 1 and June 15, 1968,

Popular Music

One way to recover the past is through music. Popular songs not only provide insight into attitudes and beliefs but also quickly convey the mood and feelings of an era. As the United States confronted the challenges of the counterculture and the crosscurrents of political and social reform, new kinds of music reflected the changes taking place.

Folk music took off at the start of the period. Bob Dylan, a disheveled and gravelly-voiced singer from Minnesota, wrote a number of remarkable protest songs like "Blowin' in the Wind" that were soon sung by other artists like Peter, Paul and Mary as well. His song "The Times They Are A-Changin'" (included here) captured the inexorable force of the student protest movement.

But the 1960s were marked by far more than folk music alone. In early 1964, an English group from Liverpool called the Beatles released "I Want to Hold Your Hand" in the United States and took the country by storm. With *Sergeant Pepper's Lonely Hearts Club Band* a few years later, the Beatles branched out in new musical directions and reflected the influence of the counterculture with songs like "Lucy in the Sky with Diamonds" (which some people said referred to the hallucinogenic drug LSD). Another English group, the Rolling Stones, played a blues-based rock music that proclaimed a commitment to drugs, sex, and a decadent life of social upheaval.

Meanwhile, on the pop scene, Motown Records in Detroit popularized a new kind of black rhythm and blues. By 1960, the gospel-pop-soul fusion was gaining followers. Stevie Wonder, the Temptations, and the Supremes were among the groups who became enormously popular. The Supremes, led by Diana Ross, epitomized the Motown sound with such hits as "Where Did Our Love Go."

What songs come to your mind when you think of the 1960s? How is the music different from that of the 1950s? What do the lyrics tell you about the period?

Look at the lyrics for "The Times They Are A-Changin'" reprinted here. What do they tell you about the social upheaval of the 1960s? What, if anything, does the song imply can be done about the changes in the air?

The Beatles. (Archive Photos)

The Supremes. (Brown Brothers)

The Times They Are A-Changin'

Come gather 'round people
wherever you roam
And admit that the waters
Around you have grown
And accept it that soon
You'll be drenched to the bone.
If your time to you
Is worth savin'
Then you better start swimmin'
Or you'll sink like a stone
For the times they are a-changin'.

Come writers and critics
Who prophesize with your pen
And keep your eyes wide
The chance won't come again
And don't speak too soon
For the wheel's still in spin
And there's no tellin' who
That it's namin'
For the loser now
Will be later to win
For the times they are a-changin'.

Come senators, congressmen
Please heed the call
Don't stand in the doorway
Don't block up the hall
For he that gets hurt
Will be he who has stalled
There's a battle outside
And it is ragin'.
It'll soon shake your windows
And rattle your walls
For the times they are a-changin'.

Come mothers and fathers
Throughout the land
And don't criticize
What you can't understand
Your sons and your daughters
Are beyond your command
Your old road is
Rapidly agin'.
Please get out of the new one
If you can't lend your hand
for the times they are a-changin'.

The line it is drawn
The curse it is cast
The slow one now
Will later be fast
As the present now
Will later be past
The order is
Rapidly fadin'.
And the first one now
Will later be last
For the times they are a-changin'.

Bob Dylan. (AP/Wide World Photos)

hundreds of thousands of students staged 221 major demonstrations at more than 100 educational institutions.

One of the most dramatic uprisings, intertwining the antiwar and civil rights protests, came in April 1968 at Columbia University. A strong SDS chapter urged the university to break ties with military research projects. The Students' Afro-American Society tried to stop the building of a new gymnasium, which it claimed encroached on the Harlem community. Whites occupied one building, blacks another. Finally, the university president called in the police. Hundreds of students were arrested; many were hurt. A student sympathy strike followed, and Columbia closed for the summer several weeks early.

The next year, in October 1969, the Weathermen, a militant fringe group of SDS, attempted to show that the revolution had arrived by making a frontal attack on Chicago. Weathermen rampaged through the streets with clubs and pipes, chains and rocks, smashing whatever was in reach. "The status quo meant to us war, poverty, inequality, ignorance, famine and disease in most of the world," a Weatherman reflected. "To accept it was to condone and help perpetuate it. We felt like miners trapped in a terrible poisonous shaft with no light to guide us out. We resolved to destroy the tunnel even if we risked destroying ourselves in the process." Few other Americans were convinced by such logic.

The New Left was, briefly, a powerful force. Although activists never composed a majority, radicals attracted students and other sympathizers to their cause until the movement fragmented. But while it was healthy, the movement focused opposition to the Vietnam War and challenged inequities in American society in a more pointed way than ever before.

The Counterculture

"There was a general feeling that the platitudes of Americanism were horseshit," observed Joseph Heller, the irreverent author of the 1961 novel *Catch-22* . In the 1960s, many Americans, particularly young people, lost faith in the sanctity of the American system. Their protests exposed the emptiness of some old patterns, and many Americans—some politically active, some not—found new ways to assert individuality and independence. The young led the way, often inspired by the beats of the 1950s as they sought new means of self-gratification and self-expression.

Surface appearances were most visible and, to older Americans, most troubling. The "hippies" of the 1960s carried themselves in different ways. Men grew long hair and beards; men and women both donned simple garments. Stressing spontaneity above all else, some rejected traditional marital customs and gravitated to communal living groups. Their example, shocking to some, soon found its way into the culture at large.

A revolution in sexual norms occurred. A generation of young women came of age with access to "the pill"—an oral contraceptive that was effortless to use and freed sexual experimentation from the threat of pregnancy. Americans of all social classes became more open to exploring, and enjoying, their sexuality. Scholarly findings supported natural inclinations. In 1966, William H. Masters and Virginia E. Johnson published *Human Sexual Response,* based on intensive laboratory observation of couples engaged in sexual activities and destroying the myth of the sexually passive woman.

Nora Ephron, author and editor, summed up the sexual changes in the 1960s as she reflected on her own experiences. Initially she had "a hangover from the whole Fifties virgin thing," she recalled. "The first man I went to bed with, I was in love with and wanted to marry. The second one I was in love with, but I didn't have to marry him. With the third one, I thought I might fall in love."

The arts reflected the sexual revolution. Federal courts ruled that books like D. H. Lawrence's *Lady Chatterley's Lover*, earlier considered obscene, could not be banned. Nudity became more common on stage and screen.

Paintings reflected both the mood of dissent and the urge to innovate apparent in the larger society. "Op" artists painted geometric figures in vibrant colors, starkly different from the flowing work of the abstract expressionists. "Pop" artists such as Andy Warhol, Roy Lichtenstein, and Jasper Johns made ironic comments on American materialism and taste with their representations of soup cans, comic strips, or Marilyn Monroe.

Hallucinogenic drugs also became a part of the counterculture. Timothy Leary, a Harvard researcher experimenting with LSD, was fired for violating a pledge not to use undergraduates as subjects. Thereafter he dressed in long robes and preached "Tune in, turn on, drop out." Novelist Ken Kesey used the profits from his first book, *One Flew Over the Cuckoo's Nest*, to establish a commune of "Merry Pranksters" in California. In 1964, the group headed east in a converted school bus painted in psychedelic Day-Glo colors, wired for sound, and stocked with enough orange juice and "acid" (LSD) to sustain the Pranksters across the continent.

Drug use was no longer confined to urban subcultures. Soldiers brought experience with drugs back from Vietnam. Young professionals began trying cocaine, and a "tab" of LSD became part of the coming-of-age ritual for many middle-class college students. Marijuana became phenomenally popular in the 1960s.

Music was intimately connected with these cultural changes. The rock and roll of the 1950s and the gentle strains of folk music gave way to a new kind of rock that swept the country—and the world. Festivals at Woodstock and Altamont drew hundreds of thousands of young people.

But there was a disturbing underside to the counterculture, most visible in the Haight-Ashbury section of San Francisco, where runaway "flower children" mingled with "burned-out" drug users and radical activists. "Adolescents drifted from city to torn city, sloughing off both the past and the future as snakes shed their skins, children who were never taught and would never now learn the games that had held the society together," wrote essayist Joan Didion in 1967. For all the spontaneity and exuberance, the counterculture's darker side could not be ignored.

Gay and Lesbian Rights

Closely tied to the revolution in sexual norms was a fast-growing and increasingly militant gay liberation movement. There had always been people who openly accepted being "gay," but American society as a whole was unsympathetic, and many homosexuals kept their preferences private. The spirit of the times encouraged gays to "come out of the closet." In response to a police raid in 1969 on the Stonewall Inn, a homosexual bar in Greenwich Village in New York, a night-long riot helped spark a new consciousness and a movement for gay rights. Throughout the 1970s, homosexuals gained partial relief from some of the most blatant forms of discrimination against them. In 1973, the American Psychiatric Association ruled that homosexuality should no longer be classified as a mental illness, and that decision was overwhelmingly supported in a vote by the membership the next year. In 1975, the U.S. Civil Service Commission lifted its ban on the employment of homosexuals.

In this new climate, many gay men who had hidden or suppressed their sexuality revealed their secret. Homosexual women, too, became more open and a lesbian movement developed, sometimes involving feminists. But many Americans and some churches remained unsympathetic—sometimes vehemently so—to those who challenged traditional sexual norms.

Environmental and Consumer Agitation

Although many of the 1960s movements were defined by race, gender, and sexual preference, one cut across all boundaries. Beginning in the early 1960s, Americans concerned with the environment revived and broadened issues dating back to the Progressive era and attracted increasing attention. In the mid-1960s, a Gallup poll revealed that only 17 percent of the public included pollution among the three major problems of the day. By 1970, that figure had risen to 53 percent.

The modern environmental movement stemmed in part from post-World War II yearnings for a better "quality of life." Clear air, unpolluted waters, and unspoiled wilderness became, for many, indispensable to a decent existence (see Chapter 26). And threats to natural surroundings began to worry the public, particularly after naturalist Rachel Carson published her brilliant book *Silent Spring* in 1962. She took aim at chemical pesticides, especially DDT, which had increased crop yields with disastrous side effects. Earth Day in 1970 celebrated the world's natural resources and warned of continuing threats.

Public concern focused on a variety of targets. Americans were troubled in 1969 to learn how thermal pollution from nuclear power plants was killing fish in both eastern and western rivers. An article in *Sports Illustrated* aroused fishermen, sailors, and other previously unconcerned recreational enthusiasts. A massive oil spill off the coast of southern California turned white beaches black and wiped out much of the marine life in the immediate area. In 1978, the public became alarmed about the lethal effects of toxic chemicals dumped in the Love Canal neighborhood of Niagara Falls, New York. A few years later, attention focused on dioxin, one of the poisons in the Love Canal, which now surfaced in other areas in more concentrated form. Thousands of times more potent than cyanide, it was one of the most deadly substances ever made.

Equally frightening was the potential environmental damage from a nuclear accident. That possibility became more real as a result of a mishap at one of the reactors at Three Mile Island near Harrisburg, Pennsylvania, in 1979. A faulty pressure relief valve led to a loss of coolant. Initially, plant operators refused to believe indicators showing a serious malfunction. Part of the nuclear core became uncovered, part began to disintegrate, and the surrounding steam and water became highly radioactive. There was danger of an explosion releasing radioactivity into the atmosphere, and thousands of area residents fled. The scenario for nuclear disaster depicted in a current film, *The China Syndrome,* suddenly seemed frighteningly real. The worst never occurred, but the plant remained shut down and filled with radioactive debris, a monument to a form of energy once hailed as the wave of the future.

The threat of a nuclear catastrophe underscored the arguments of grass-roots environmental activists who campaigned aggressively against licensing new nuclear plants. While they did not always succeed, they mobilized opinion sufficiently that no new plants were authorized after 1978.

Western environmentalists were particularly worried about excessive use of water. The American West, wrote a critic, was "the greatest hydraulic society ever built in history." Massive irrigation systems had boosted the nation's use of water from 40 billion gallons a day in 1900 to 393 billion gallons a day by 1975, though the population had only tripled. Americans used three times as much water per capita as the world's average, and far more than other industrialized societies.

One serious source of concern was the Ogallala aquifer in the Great Plains. The drawing of enormous amounts of water in the 1950s and 1960s to make arid areas productive for farming had, by the mid-1970s, dramatically depleted the water stored in the aquifer. Conservation measures might delay, but not prevent, the day of reckoning.

The situation was similar in California. Naturally dry, the state's prosperity rested on massive irrigation projects. In the late 1970s, the state had 1,251 major reservoirs. Virtually every large river had at least one dam. Almost as much water was pumped from the ground, with little natural replenishment and even less regulation. Pointing to the destruction of the nation's rivers and streams and the severe lowering of the water table in many areas, environmentalists argued that something needed to be done before it was too late. Slowly, they attracted a following.

Environmental agitation produced legislative results in the 1960s and 1970s. Lyndon Johnson, whose vision of the Great Society included an "environment that is pleasing to the senses and healthy to live in," won basic legislation to halt the depletion of the country's natural resources (see Chapter 28). In the next few years, environmentalists went further, pressuring legislative and administrative bodies to regulate polluters. Under Nixon, Congress passed the Clean Air Act, the Water Quality Improvement Act, and the Resource Recovery Act and mandated a new Environmental Protection Agency (EPA) to spearhead the effort to control abuses. Initially, these measures aimed at controlling the toxic by-products of the modern industrial order. In subsequent years, environmentalists broadened the effort to include occupational health and social-justice issues.

One such effort developed into an extraordinarily bitter economic and ecological debate. The Endangered Species Act of 1973 prohibited the federal government from supporting any projects that might jeopardize species threatened with extinction. It ran into direct conflict with commercial imperatives in the Pacific Northwest. Loggers in the Olympic Peninsula had long exploited the land by clearcutting (cutting down all trees in a region). Environmentalists claimed that the forests they cut provided the last refuge for the spotted owl. Scientists and members of the U.S. Forest Service pushed to set aside timberland so that the owl could survive. Loggers protested that this action jeopardized their livelihood. As the issue wound its way through the courts, logging fell off drastically.

The Sagebrush Rebellion mounted another protest against regulation in the late 1970s and early 1980s. Critics argued that large federal landholdings in the

TIMELINE

1947 Jackie Robinson breaks the color line in major league baseball	**1950** Asociación Nacional México-Americana formed	**1954** *Brown* v. *Board of Education*	**1955** Montgomery, Alabama, bus boycott begins	**1957** Little Rock, Arkansas, school integration crisis; Civil Rights Act
1960 Civil Rights Act; Birth control pill becomes available; Sit-ins begin; Students for a Democratic Society (SDS) founded	**1961** Freedom rides; Joseph Heller, *Catch-22;* Ken Kesey, *One Flew Over the Cuckoo's Nest*	**1962** James Meredith crisis at the University of Mississippi; SDS's Port Huron Statement; Rachel Carson, *Silent Spring*	**1963** Birmingham demonstration; Civil rights march on Washington; Betty Friedan, *The Feminine Mystique*	**1964** Civil Rights Act; Free speech movement, Berkeley
1965 Martin Luther King, Jr., leads march from Selma to Montgomery; Voting Rights Act; United Farm Workers grape strike; Malcolm X assassinated; Riot in Watts section of Los Angeles; Ralph Nader, *Unsafe at Any Speed*	**1966** Stokely Carmichael becomes head of SNCC and calls for "Black Power"; Black Panthers founded; NOW founded; Masters and Johnson, *Human Sexual Response*	**1967** Urban riots in 22 cities	**1968** Martin Luther King, Jr., assassinated; Student demonstrations at Columbia University and elsewhere; Chicano student walkouts; American Indian Movement (AIM) founded	**1969** Woodstock and Altamont rock festivals; Weathermen's "Days of Rage" in Chicago; Native Americans seize Alcatraz; La Raza Unida founded
1971–1975 School busing controversies in North and South	**1972** *Ms.* magazine founded; Congress passes Equal Rights Amendment	**1973** AIM occupies Wounded Knee, South Dakota	**1975** Farmworkers' grape boycott; Indian Self-determination and Education Assistance Acts	**1978** *Bakke* v. *Regents of the University of California*
1979 Accident at Three Mile Island nuclear power plant	**1982** Ratification of ERA fails			

West put that region at a disadvantage in economic competition with the East. They demanded that the national government cede the lands to states, which could sell or lease them for local gain. Conservative state legislatures in the Rocky Mountain states supported the scheme, and ranchers applauded. In the end, it went nowhere, though the agitation did persuade federal authorities to endorse a less restrictive policy on grazing.

The consumer movement was related to the environmental movement. As they had during the Progressive era, Americans worried about unscrupulous sellers. In the 1970s, a stronger consumer movement developed, aimed at protecting the public and making business more responsible to consumers.

Ralph Nader led the movement. His book *Unsafe at Any Speed: The Designed-in Dangers of the American Automobile* (1965) argued that many cars were coffins on wheels. His efforts paved the way for the National Traffic and Motor Vehicle Safety Act of 1966, which set minimum safety standards for vehicles on public highways, provided for inspection to ensure compliance, and created a National Motor Vehicle Safety Advisory Council.

Nader's efforts attracted scores of volunteers, called "Nader's Raiders." They turned out critiques and reports and, more important, inspired consumer activists at all levels of government—city, state, and national. Consumer protection offices began to monitor a flood of complaints as ordinary citizens became more vocal in defending their rights.

✦✦✦✦✦

CONCLUSION

Extending the American Dream

The 1960s and 1970s were turbulent years. Yet this third major reform era of the twentieth century accomplished a good deal for the groups fighting to expand the meaning of equality. African-Americans now enjoyed greater access to the rights and privileges enjoyed by mainstream American society, despite the backlash the movement brought. Women like Ann Clarke, introduced at the start of the chapter, returned to school in ever-increasing numbers and found jobs and sometimes independence after years of being told that their place was at home. Native Americans and Latinos mobilized, too, and could see the stirrings of change. Environmentalists created a new awareness of the global dangers the nation and the world faced. Slowly reformers succeeded in pressuring the government to help the nation fulfill its promise and ensure the realization of the ideals of American life.

But the course of change was ragged. The reform effort reached its high-water mark during Lyndon Johnson's Great Society and in the years immediately following, then faltered with the rise of conservatism and disillusionment with liberalism, as we saw in Chapter 28. Some movements were circumscribed by the changing political climate; others simply ran out of steam. Still, the various efforts left a legacy of ferment which could help spark further change in future years.

Recommended Reading

The Civil Rights Movement

James Baldwin, *The Fire Next Time* (1962); Taylor Branch, *Parting the Waters: America in the King Years, 1954–1963* (1988) and *Pillar of Fire: America in the King Years, 1963–1965* (1998); Clayborne Carson, *In Struggle: SNCC and the Black Awakening of the 1960s* (1981); William H. Chafe, *Civilities and Civil Rights: Greensboro, North Carolina, and the Black Struggle for Freedom* (1980); Eric Foner, *The Story of American Freedom* (1998); John Hope Franklin and Alfred A. Moss, Jr., *From Slavery to Freedom: A History of African Americans,* 7th ed. (1994); David J. Garrow, *Bearing the Cross: Martin Luther King, Jr., and the Southern Christian Leadership Conference* (1986); Joanne Grant, *Ella Baker: Freedom Bound* (1998); Richard Kluger, *Simple Justice: The History of* Brown *v.* Board of Education *and Black America's Struggle for Equality* (1975); John Lewis with Michael D'Orso, *Walking with the Wind: A Memoir of the Movement* (1998); Malcolm X (with Alex Haley), *The Autobiography of Malcolm X* (1966); August Meier and Elliott Rudwick, *CORE: A Study in the Civil Rights Movement, 1942–1968* (1973); Anne Moody, *Coming of Age in Mississippi* (1968); Harvard Sitkoff, *The Struggle for Black Equality, 1954–1992,* revised ed. (1993); Ronald Takaki, *A Different Mirror: A History of Multicultural America* (1993).

The Women's Movement

William H. Chafe, *The American Woman: Her Changing Social, Political, and Economic Roles, 1920–1970* (1972); Sara Evans, *Personal Politics: The Roots of Women's Liberation in the Civil Rights Movements and the New Left* (1979); Peter Gabriel Filene, *Him/Her/Self: Sex Roles in Modern America,* second ed. (1986); Shulamith Firestone, *The Dialectic of Sex: The Case for Feminist Revolution* (1970); Jacqueline Jones, *Labor of Love, Labor of Sorrow: Black Women, Work, and the Family from Slavery to the Present* (1985); Alice Kessler-Harris, *Out to Work: A History of Wage-earning Women in the United States* (1982); Blanche Linden-Ward, *Changing the Future: American Women in the 1960s* (1993); Sheila M. Rothman, *Woman's Proper Place: A History of Changing Ideals and Practices, 1870 to the Present* (1978); Gloria Steinem, *Outrageous Acts and Everyday Rebellions,* second ed. (1995); Winifred D. Wandersee, *On the Move: American Women in the 1970s* (1988).

The Movement for Latino Rights

Rodolfo Acuña, *Occupied America: A History of Chicanos,* third ed. (1988); Mario T. García, *Memories of Chicano History: The Life and Narrative of Bert Corona* (1994) and *Mexican Americans: Leadership, Ideology, and Identity, 1930–1960* (1989); Ed Ludwig and James Santibañez, eds., *The Chicanos: Mexican American Voices* (1971); Beatrice Rodriguez Owsley, *The Hispanic-American Entrepreneur: An Oral History of the American Dream* (1992); Peter Skerry, *Mexican Americans: The Ambivalent Minority* (1993).

The Native American Struggle

Dee Brown, *Bury My Heart at Wounded Knee: An Indian History of the American West* (1971); Stephen Cornell, *The Return of the Native: American Indian Political Resurgence* (1988); Vine Deloria, Jr., *Custer Died for Your Sins: An Indian Manifesto* (1969); Frederick E. Hoxie, ed., *Indians in American History* (1988); Peter Iverson, *"We Are Still Here": American Indians in the Twentieth Century* (1998); Alvin M. Josephy, Jr., *Now That the Buffalo's Gone* (1982); James S. Olson and Raymond Wilson, *Native Americans in the Twentieth Century* (1984); David Hurst Thomas, Jay Miller, Richard White, Peter Nabokov, Philip J. Deloria, *The Native Americans: An Illustrated History* (1993).

Social and Cultural Protest

Terry Anderson, *The Movement and the Sixties: Protest in America from Greensboro to Wounded Knee* (1995); Beth L. Bailey, *From Front Porch to Back Seat: Courtship in Twentieth-Century America* (1988); David Burner, *Making Peace with the Sixties* (1996); David Chalmers, *And the Crooked Places Made Straight: The Struggle for Social Change in the 1960s* (1991); John D'Emilio and Estelle B. Freedman, *Intimate Matters: A History of Sexuality in America* (1988); Joan Didion, *Slouching Towards Bethlehem* (1968); Barbara Epstein, *Political Protest and Cultural Revolution: Nonviolent Direct Action in the 1970s and 1980s* (1991); David Farber, *The Age of Great Dreams: America in the 1960s* (1994); Todd Gitlin, *The Sixties: Years of Hope, Days of Rage* (1987); Neil A. Hamilton, *The ABC-CLIO Companion to the 1960s Counterculture in America* (1997); Charles A. Reich, *The Greening of America* (1978); W. J. Rorabaugh, *Berkeley at War: The 1960s* (1989); Theodore Roszak, *The Making of a Counter Culture* (1969); Milton Viorst, *Fire in the Streets: America in the 1960s* (1979); Jules Witcover, *The Year the Dream Died: Revisiting 1968 in America* (1998); Tom Wolfe, *The Electric Kool-Aid Acid Test* (1968).

The Environmental Movement

Rachel Carson, *Silent Spring* (1962); William Dietrich, *The Final Forest: The Battle for the Last Great Trees of the Pacific Northwest* (1992); Robert Gottlieb, *Forcing the Spring: The Transformation of the American Environmental Movement* (1993); Samuel P. Hays, *Beauty, Health, and Permanence: Environmental Politics in the United States, 1955–1985* (1987); Patricia Nelson Limerick, *The Legacy of Conquest: The Unbroken Past of the American West* (1987); John Opie, *The Law of the Land: Two Hundred Years of American Farmland Policy* (1987); Marc Reisner, *Cadillac Desert: The American West and Its Disappearing Water*, revised and updated ed. (1993); Kirkpatrick Sale, *The Green Revolution: The American Environmental Movement, 1962–1992* (1993); Richard White, *"It's Your Misfortune and None of My Own:" A History of the American West* (1991); Charles F. Wilkinson, *Crossing the Next Meridian: Land, Water, and the Future of the West* (1992); Donald Worster, *Rivers of Empire: Water, Aridity and the Growth of the American West* (1985).

Fiction

Sara Davidson, *Loose Change* (1977).

CHAPTER 30

The Revival of Conservatism

Craig Miller lived comfortably in the early 1990s. A sheet-metal worker for TWA, he earned $15.65 an hour. He, his wife, and their four children rented a pleasant house in suburban Overland Park, Kansas. They were saving money to buy their own home.

In the summer of 1992, Miller lost his job. The airline industry was financially troubled, and TWA began to lay off blue-collar workers. Miller looked without success for a comparable position with another company. Manufacturing jobs were drying up as American firms moved operations abroad, where labor costs were cheaper. Other positions were lost to advances in technology, which rendered old production methods obsolete.

Miller had no alternative but to piece together a living. He found work at McDonald's, taking orders for Quarter Pounders and Big Macs. He drove a school bus every morning and afternoon. He also started a small business, changing furnace filters. With the income from his various jobs and his wife's part-time position at Toys "R" Us, the family took in $18,000 a year, less than half of what Miller made as a sheet-metal worker.

The decline in their standard of living was hard to accept. Miller and his wife had worked hard and prospered modestly, but suddenly any security they had known had vanished. Before the layoff, they had moved comfortably in a middle-class world of backyard barbecues and church picnics. Now they struggled to make ends meet. They could have qualified for food stamps to supplement their income but refused to apply. Those were only for the really poor, they believed. "We're middle-class people," Miller said. "It's just that we have a lower-class income."

Gone was the pride Miller had once felt in his work. He had enjoyed fixing dents in the fuselages of jets. When other children boasted about what their parents did, his son Peter said, "My daddy can fix planes so they can fly high in the sky." That was the same feeling Miller had about his own father, also a blue-collar laborer, who had worked hard in a factory all his life, bought a two-story house for his family, and earned enough to provide summer vacations out West. Now all Miller could do was to take out his old tools, stroke them with his hands, and put them away again.

Miller still worked hard, only now he spent his time in nearly skill-less jobs. At McDonald's, he forced himself to be polite to rude teenage customers. "I still have some pride, you know," he said. "But what am I going to do? I think the needs of my children are a little more important than my ego."

But those needs were hard to meet. In mid-1994, the family fell $3,000 behind in medical bills. Miller bought one newspaper a week, to get the food coupons. If a child left a light burning, Miller's wife asked, "Have you got stock in the electric company? Well, neither do I." The dream of their own home disappeared.

After two years of struggle, neither Miller nor his wife expected conditions to improve for members of the working class. "For people like us," she said, "I'm afraid the good times are gone for good."

The Miller family's struggle unfolded against the backdrop of a conservative era marked by extravagance and a widening gap between rich and poor. Middle-class incomes, like the Millers', shrank, and it became increasingly difficult for many Americans to make ends meet. In this situation, members of minority groups had the most trouble finding jobs, just as they had in past decades. Then a deep recession in the early 1990s eroded the security of the middle and upper-middle classes as well. The national debt continued to climb and the stock market tumbled as investors, for a while at least, questioned the stability of the economy.

Within that economic framework, the nation struggled with questions about the government's responsibility for those who could not help themselves. The relentless shift toward a service economy left millions of people like the Millers either jobless or in positions far less attractive than the ones they had held before. Yet even as the nation's underclass and homeless population grew, the welfare system came under renewed attack from conservatives who argued that the government was trying to do too much. As discontent mounted, they managed to cut back on payments to millions of Americans who had relied on federal assistance in the past.

At the same time, cataclysmic events shook Communist governments in the USSR and Eastern Europe, ending nearly a half century of Cold War and requiring the United States to redefine its international role. A substantial debate ensued with conservative Republicans often arguing against an activist, and potentially expensive, American role abroad.

This chapter describes the enormous changes that occurred in the 1980s and 1990s. It highlights the economic and technological shifts that reshaped the daily lives of millions and the social, political, and diplomatic adjustments that affected the entire nation.

THE CONSERVATIVE TRANSFORMATION

In the 1980s, the Republican party again dominated national politics. The Republican ascendancy, begun in the Nixon era, was now largely complete. The liberal agenda that had governed national affairs ever since the New Deal gave way to a new Republican coalition determined to scale back the welfare state and prevent what it perceived as the erosion of the nation's moral values. Firmly in control of the presidency, sometimes in control of the Senate, and eventually holding both houses, the Republican party set the new national agenda.

The New Politics

Conservatism won new respect in the 1980s. It attracted new adherents upset at the upheavals of the 1960s, while new advertising and fundraising techniques capitalized on growing disaffection with liberal solutions to social problems. The conservative movement became almost unstoppable.

Conservatives seized on Thomas Jefferson's maxim "That government is best which governs least." They argued that the United States in the 1980s had entered an era of limits, with international competition making resources scarcer. The dramatic economic growth of the 1960s and 1970s, they believed, left a legacy of rising inflation, falling productivity, enormous waste, and out-of-control entitlements. The liberal solution of "throwing money at social problems" no longer worked. Conservatives intended to downsize government, reduce taxes, and roll back regulations in order to restore focus on individual initiative and private enterprise.

The conservative philosophy had tremendous appeal. It promised profitability to those who worked hard and showed initiative. It attracted middle-class Americans, thinking themselves forgotten in the commitment to assist minorities and the poor. And it offered hope for the revival of basic values that many citizens worried had been eaten away by rising divorce rates, legalized abortion, homosexuality, and media preoccupations with violence and sex.

The new conservative coalition covered a broad spectrum. Some embraced the economic doctrines of the University of Chicago's Milton Friedman, who advocated freeing market forces and sharply restricting governmental activism in the economy. Others applauded the social and political conservatism of North Carolina Senator Jesse Helms, a tireless foe of anything he deemed pornographic and a fervent campaigner for a limited federal role. Still others flocked to the Republican fold because of their conviction that civil rights activists and "bleeding heart liberals" practiced "reverse racism" with affirmative action, job quotas, and busing.

The conservative coalition also drew deeply from religious fundamentalists who advocated a literal interpretation of Scriptures. Millions—devout Catholics, orthodox Jews, evangelical Protestants—demanded stricter morality. They were offended by sexual permissiveness and gay rights and believed that the increased number of women working outside the home eroded family life. They were bothered by rising crime and drug use. Marijuana, they said, was not simply a youthful fad but an institution for a broad segment of society. In short, fundamentalists objected to what they viewed as the liberalizing tendencies of American life and sought to refashion society by reaffirming biblical morality and the centrality of religion in life.

Many activists belonged to the Moral Majority, a pressure group founded by Baptist preacher Jerry Falwell and other televangelists. They appealed to audiences who knew them only on the airwaves, focusing their followers on specific political ends. They also used their fundraising ability to support sympathetic political candidates. Moral Majority money began to fund politicians who demanded reinstituting school prayer, ending legalized abortion, and defeating the Equal Rights Amendment. Later a group calling itself the Christian Coalition became even more powerful in supporting—and electing—conservative candidates.

Conservatives from all camps capitalized on changing political techniques more successfully than their liberal opponents. They understood the importance of television in getting instant access to the American public. Politicians became increasingly adept at using "sound bites." By the 1990s, they were exploiting e-mail, fax, and the Internet to mobilize their followers. And they raised huge amounts of money, often through computerized direct-mail appeals.

Moreover, conservatives outdid liberals in using negative political advertising. Mudslinging has always been an American political tradition, but now carefully crafted television ads concentrated not so much on conveying a positive image of a candidate's platform but on destroying an opponent's character. That effort was visible in both presidential and congressional campaigns.

Conservatives led the way in refining their appeal to voters. Polls, sometimes taken daily, showed which part of a candidate's image needed polishing or where an opponent was vulnerable. "Spin doctors" put the best possible gloss on what politicians said. Small wonder that Americans became increasingly cynical about politics and avoided voting booths in record numbers.

Conservatives understood as well the need to provide an intellectual grounding for their positions. Conservative scholars worked in think tanks and other research organizations such as the Hoover Institution at Stanford University or the American Enterprise Institute in Washington, D.C., that gave conservatism a solid institutional base. Their books, articles, and reports helped elect Ronald Reagan and other conservative politicians.

Conservative Leadership

More than any other Republican, Ronald Reagan was responsible for the success of the conservative cause. An actor turned politician, during the Depression he had been a radio broadcaster in his native Midwest before launching a movie career. His success affected his political inclinations, and he changed his affiliation from Democrat to Republican. His visibility and ability to articulate corporate values as a TV spokesman for General Electric attracted the attention of conservatives who recognized his political potential and helped elect him governor of California in 1966. He failed in his first presidential bid in 1976 but gathered strength for the next four years. By 1980, he had the firm support of the growing right, which applauded his promise to reduce the size of the federal government but bolster military might.

Running against incumbent Jimmy Carter in 1980, Reagan scored a landslide victory—a popular vote of 51 to 41 percent and 489 to 49 in the Electoral College. He also helped the Republicans win the Senate for the first time since 1955. In 1984, he was reelected by an even larger margin, swamping Democrat Walter Mondale and losing only Mondale's home state of Minnesota and the District of Columbia. The Democrats, however, netted two additional seats in the Senate and held the House of Representatives.

Reagan had a pleasing manner and a special skill as a media communicator. Relying on his acting experience, he used television as Franklin D. Roosevelt had used radio. He was a gifted storyteller who loved using anecdotes or one-liners to make his point.

Reagan enjoyed enormous popularity. People called him the "Teflon" president, for even serious criticisms failed to stick and disagreements over policy never diminished his poll standings. When he left the White House, 68 percent of the American public approved of his performance.

But Reagan had a number of liabilities that surfaced over time. As the oldest president the nation had ever had, his attention often drifted. In press conferences,

Ronald Reagan drew on his experience in the movies to project an appealing, if old-fashioned, image. Though he was the nation's oldest president, he gave the appearance of vitality. Here he is pictured with his wife Nancy, who was one of his most influential advisers. (Michael Evans/The White House)

he was often unsure about what was being asked. He delegated much authority, which left him unclear about policy decisions. Worst of all, there were persistent charges of "sleaze" in his administration, with a number of aides and cabinet officers accused of influence-peddling.

In 1988, Republican George Bush, who served eight years as Reagan's vice president, ran for the presidency. Though a New Englander, he had prospered in the Texas oil industry, then served in Congress, as ambassador to China, and as head of the CIA. Sneered at by the press as a preppy wimp, he became a pit bull in a mudslinging campaign against Democrat Michael Dukakis, the governor of Massachusetts. Bush won, 54 to 46 percent in popular votes and with a 40-state, 426 to 112 Electoral College majority. But with Democrats controlling both houses of Congress, he did not have the kind of mandate Reagan had enjoyed eight years earlier.

Bush quickly put his imprint on the presidency. Despite his upper-crust background, he was an unpretentious man who made a point of trying to appear down-to-earth. More than a year and a half into his term, he was still on his political honeymoon, with a personal approval rating of 67 percent. Support grew even stronger as he presided over the Persian Gulf War in 1991. But then, as the economy faltered and the results of the war seemed suspect, approval levels began to drop.

Though the Democrats won the presidency in 1992, the Republicans won control of both houses of Congress in the midterm elections of 1994. Legislative leaders were now responsible for promoting the Republican cause. Robert Dole of Kansas became Senate majority leader. Newt Gingrich, a brash, aggressive Georgia congressman, became Speaker of the House and the most visible advocate of the conservative Republican agenda.

Republican Policies at Home

Republicans in the 1980s aimed to reverse the stagnation of the Carter years and to provide new opportunities for business to prosper. To that end Reagan proposed and implemented an economic recovery program that rested on the theory of supply-side economics. According to this much-criticized theory, reduction of taxes would encourage business expansion, which in turn would wipe out deficits. Even Bush, during his run for the Republican nomination in 1980, called Reagan's program "voodoo economics." Still, Republicans endorsed "Reaganomics" with its promise of a revitalized economy.

One early initiative involved tax reductions. A 5 percent cut in the tax rate was enacted to go into effect on October 1, 1981, followed by 10 percent cuts in 1982 and 1983. Although all taxpayers received some tax relief, the rich gained far more. Poverty-level Americans did not benefit at all. Tax cuts and enormous defense expenditures increased the budget deficit. From $74 billion in 1980, it jumped to $290 billion in 1992. Such massive deficits drove the gross federal debt—the total national indebtedness—upward from $909 billion in 1980 to $4.4 trillion in 1992. When Reagan assumed office, the per capita national debt was $4,035; ten years later, in 1990, it was about $12,400.

Faced with the need to raise more money and rectify an increasingly skewed tax code, in 1986 Congress passed and Reagan signed the most sweeping tax reform since the federal income tax began in 1913. It lowered rates, consolidated brackets, and closed loopholes to expand the tax base. Though it ended up neither increasing nor decreasing the government's tax take, the measure was an important step toward treating low-income Americans more equitably. Still, most of the benefits went to the richest 5 percent of Americans.

At the same time, Reagan embarked on a major program of deregulation. In a campaign more comprehensive than Carter's, he focused on agencies of the 1970s such as the Environmental Protection Agency, the Consumer Product Safety Commission, and the Occupational Safety and Health Administration. The Republican administration argued that regulations pertaining to the consumer, the workplace, and the environment were inefficient, paternalistic, and excessively expensive. They impeded growth and needed to be eliminated.

Meanwhile, Reagan challenged the New Deal consensus that the federal government should monitor the economy and assist the least fortunate. Reagan charged that government intruded too deeply into American life. It was time to eliminate "waste, fraud, and abuse."

Reagan needed to make cuts in social programs, both because of sizable tax cuts and because of enormous military expenditures. Committed to a massive arms buildup, over a five-year period the administration sought an unprecedented military budget of $1.5 trillion.

The huge cuts in social programs reversed the approach of liberals over the past 50 years. Republicans in the 1970s had begun to question the social policy goals of Johnson's Great Society (see Chapter 28). In the 1980s, they attacked those liberal aims head-on. They eliminated public service jobs and reduced other aid to the cities, where the poor congregated. They cut back unemployment compensation and required Medicare patients to pay more. They lowered welfare benefits and food stamp allocations. They slashed the Legal Services Corporation, which provided legal services for the poor. They replaced grants for college students with loans. Spending on human resources fell by $101 billion between 1980 and 1982. The process continued even after Reagan left office. Between 1981 and 1992, federal spending (adjusted for inflation) fell 82 percent for subsidized housing, 63 percent for job training and employment services, and 40 percent for community services. Middle-class Americans, benefiting from the tax cuts, were not hurt. But for millions of the poorest citizens there was real suffering.

Distrustful of centralized government, Reagan wanted to give more power to state and local governments and to reduce federal involvement in people's lives. His "New Federalism" attempted to shift responsibilities from the federal to the state level. Replacing federal funding with grants that states could spend as they saw fit, he hoped to fortify local initiative. Critics charged, with some justification, that the proposal merely moved programs from one place to another. When a recession began in 1990, the policy helped push some states and municipalities close to bankruptcy.

Reagan took a conservative approach to social issues as well. The support he gave to school prayer and to anti-abortionists, however, was largely symbolic.

George Bush followed directly in his predecessor's footsteps. Having forsworn objections to "voodoo economics" as soon as he received the vice-presidential nomination, Bush faithfully backed Reagan's general economic policy even after he became president. Running for president in 1988, he promised "no new taxes." Though he backed down from that pledge to join a bipartisan effort to bring the budget deficit under control, he renounced his own agreement to modest tax increases when he went back on the campaign trail in 1992.

Bush, like Reagan, wanted deep cuts in social programs. He vetoed measure after measure to assist those suffering in a recession that sent unemployment rates up to 8 percent and left one of every four urban children living in poverty.

Bush was more outspoken than Reagan in supporting conservative social goals. At the start of the 1980s, conservatives had questioned Bush's commitment to their agenda, and Bush had been pro-choice. As president, however, he firmly opposed abortion, and his Supreme Court appointments, like Reagan's, were meant to help roll back or overturn *Roe* v. *Wade.*

The Republican philosophy under Reagan and Bush dramatically reversed the nation's domestic agenda. Liberalism in the 1960s had reached a high-water mark in a time of steady growth, when hard choices about where to spend money had been less necessary. As limits appeared, decisions about social programs became more difficult, and millions of Americans came to believe that most of the Great Society programs had not only failed to conquer poverty but also created lifelong welfare dependency. Conservatism offered a more attractive answer, particularly to those Americans in the middle and upper classes.

But the transformation was accompanied by a number of serious problems that emerged in the early 1990s. Bush faced a crisis in the long-mismanaged savings and loan industry. Republican deregulation had allowed the owners of savings and loan institutions to operate without previous restrictions. Many, paying themselves lavish salaries, made unwise high-risk investments that eventually produced tremendous losses. To protect depositors who had lost assets, Congress approved a $166 billion rescue plan (that soon reached more than $250 billion) committing taxpayers to bail out the industry.

Republican policy also widened the gap between rich and poor. Tax breaks for the wealthy, deregulation initiatives, permissiveness toward mergers, and an enormous growth in the salaries of top business executives all contributed to the disparity. So did more lenient antitrust enforcement and a general sympathy for speculative finance.

The results were clear. "The 1980s," analyst Kevin Phillips observed, "were the triumph of upper America—an ostentatious celebration of wealth, the political ascendancy of the rich and a glorification of capitalism, free markets and finance." The share of national wealth of the richest 1 percent of the nation rose from about 18 percent in 1976 to 36 percent in 1989.

Meanwhile, less fortunate Americans suffered more than they had since the Great Depression. Liberal financial expert Felix Rohatyn decried the "huge transfer of wealth from lower-skilled, middle-class American workers to owners of capital assets and a new technological aristocracy." Millions of people, ranging from foreclosed farmers to laid-off industrial workers, were struggling to make ends meet.

Liberal Interlude

In 1992, the Democratic Party mounted an aggressive challenge to Republican rule. Fending off allegations of marital infidelity, youthful marijuana use, and draft evasion, Governor Bill Clinton of Arkansas won the nomination. Forty-six years old, he had reached maturity in the 1960s and stood in stark contrast to George Bush, a World War II veteran. An independent third candidate was H. Ross Perot, a quirky Texan who had made billions in computers.

On election day, Clinton won 43 percent of the popular vote to 38 percent for Bush and 19 percent for Perot. The electoral vote margin was even larger: 357 for Clinton and 168 for Bush. The Democrats retained control of both houses of Congress, with more women and minority members than ever before.

The president-elect quickly demonstrated his intention of shifting the nation's course. His cabinet nominations included four women, four African-Americans, and two Latinos. He held a televised "economic summit" to explore national options and demonstrated mastery of policy details. In his inaugural address, Clinton announced that "a new season of American renewal has begun."

Clinton soon found his hands full. Although the economy finally began to improve, the public gave the president little credit for the upturn. He gained Senate ratification of the North American Free Trade Agreement (NAFTA)—for free trade between Canada, Mexico, and the United States—in November 1993 after a bitter battle. He secured passage of a crime bill banning manufacture, sale, or possession of 19 different assault weapons (though not of a much larger number of semiautomatic guns).

But Clinton failed in his major legislative initiative: health care reform. Costs were escalating, yet the lack of universal medical care left 35 million Americans without insurance. Clinton's complicated proposal provoked intense opposition from all over the political spectrum. In the end he was unable to persuade Congress either to accept his approach or adopt a workable alternative.

Conservative Resurgence

Voters demonstrated their dissatisfaction in the midterm elections of 1994. Republicans swept control of both the Senate and the House for the first time in over 40 years. In the House, they made the largest gains since 1946, winning over 50 races against Democratic incumbents. Some of the most senior members lost their seats. At the state level, Republicans picked up 12 governorships and took control in seven of the eight largest states.

The election marked the end of the commitment to the welfare state. The 104th Congress moved aggressively to make good on its promises—outlined during the campaign in the Republicans' "Contract with America"—to scale back the federal government, eliminate troublesome regulations, reduce taxes, and balance the budget. Gingrich, as the new Speaker, pushed through changes in the House rules that gave him far greater power in appointing committee members and moving legislation along. Under his leadership, Congress launched a frontal attack on the budget, proposing massive cuts in virtually all social services. It demanded elimination of three Cabinet departments and insisted on gutting the National Endowment for the Humanities, the National Endowment for the Arts, and the Public Broadcasting System. When, at the end of 1995 the president and the speaker refused to compromise on a budget, the government shut down and 800,000 federal employees found themselves temporarily "furloughed."

While the House passed most of the "Contract with America" proposals, only a few became law. The Senate balked at some; the president vetoed others. As the election of 1996 approached, Gingrich found himself out of favor as millions of Americans began to realize that they would suffer from the cuts more aggressive Republicans wanted.

A Second Term for Clinton

As Clinton sought a second term in 1996, the Republicans nominated Senate Minority Leader Robert Dole. The 73-year-old Dole ran a lackluster campaign. Stung by Democratic congressional defeats two years before, Clinton reshaped his image and announced that the "era of big government is over." He co-opted Republican issues, pledging to balance the budget himself and enraging liberal supporters by signing a welfare reform bill that slashed benefits and removed millions of people from the rolls. At the same time, he posed as the protector of Medicare and other programs that were threatened by proposed Republican cuts.

Clinton's strategy worked. On election day, he won a resounding victory: 49 percent of the popular vote to 41 percent for Dole and 8 percent for Perot, who ran again. In the electoral tally, Clinton received 379 votes to 159 for Dole. Yet the Republicans still controlled Congress. Around the country, voters seemed willing to support Clinton, but not to give him a blanket mandate. In California, voters rejected affirmative action by approving Proposition 209, prohibiting preferential treatment based on gender or race.

Partisan Politics and Impeachment

Democrats made small gains in the midterm elections of 1998. They worried about their prospects as election day approached, for Clinton had been accused by an independent prosecutor, appointed by the Justice Department, of having engaged

Bill Clinton's relationship with Monica Lewinsky affected both the country and his own family. Here he heads off for vacation with wife Hillary and daughter Chelsea after acknowledging the relationship to the nation. (Brad Markel/Liaison Agency, Inc.)

in an improper sexual relationship with Monica Lewinsky, a White House intern. While Clinton denied the relationship at first, the lengthy report presented to Congress left little doubt that such a connection existed, and Clinton finally admitted to the relationship in a nationally televised address.

As Congress began to consider impeachment, Americans outside of Washington felt differently. Disturbed at what Clinton had done in his personal life, they nonetheless approved overwhelmingly of the job he was doing as president, and his approval ratings were higher than any of his predecessors in the recent past.

Those sentiments were reflected in the 1998 electoral vote. Republicans, who had hoped to score sizable gains in both house of Congress, maintained their 55–45 margin in the Senate, but lost 5 seats in the house of Representatives, ending up with a 223–211 margin that made it even more difficult to pursue their own agenda.

Despite that clear signal from the voters, House Republicans continued their efforts to remove the President. Just weeks after the election, a majority impeached him on counts of perjury and obstruction of justice. Then, at the start of 1999, the case moved to the Senate for a trial, where Clinton fought to retain his office, just as Andrew Johnson had done 131 years before. In the Senate, presided over by the chief justice of the Supreme Court, a two-thirds majority vote was necessary to find the president guilty and remove him from the White House. After weeks of testimony, despite a universal condemnation of Clinton's personal behavior, the Senate voted for acquittal. Democrats, who were joined by a number of Republicans, stood by the president and, with that coalition, neither charge managed to muster even a simple majority. The count of perjury was decided by a 45–55 vote, while the count of obstruction of justice failed on a 50–50 vote. At long last, the nightmare was over, and the country could again deal with more substantive issues.

AN END TO SOCIAL REFORM

The Republican attack on the welfare state included an effort to limit commitments to social reform. Enough had been done, conservatives argued. It was time to end federal "intrusion."

Slowdown in the Struggle for Civil Rights

Republican policies slowed the civil rights movement. Reagan opposed busing to achieve racial balance, and his attorney general worked to dismantle affirmative action programs. Initially reluctant to support extension of the enormously successful Voting Rights Act of 1965, Reagan relented only under severe bipartisan criticism. He directed the Internal Revenue Service to allow tax exemptions for private schools that discriminated against blacks, only to see that move overturned by the Supreme Court in 1983. He also launched an assault on the Civil Rights Commission and hampered it by appointing members who did not support its main goals.

The courts similarly weakened commitments to equal rights. As a result of Reagan's and Bush's judicial appointments, federal courts stopped pushing for school integration. In 1995, for example, the Supreme Court let stand a lower court ruling prohibiting colleges from giving special scholarships to African-Americans or other minorities.

That decision was part of a larger backlash against the policy of affirmative action. Energized by their political victories in 1994, conservatives launched a powerful attack on preferential treatments for minorities. Arguing that affirmative action had never been meant as a permanent policy, they pushed ballot initiatives and pressured public agencies to halt the practice.

Despite significant African-American progress in gaining important electoral offices, black-white relations remained tense. African-American historian John Hope Franklin, looking back in 1995 at the eight decades of his life, said, "Just about the time you sit down or sit back and say, 'Oh, yes, we're really moving,' you get slapped back down."

Obstacles to Women's Rights

Women had a similar experience in the 1980s and 1990s. They, too, made significant electoral gains. In 1981, President Reagan named Sandra Day O'Connor as the first woman Supreme Court justice, and in 1984 Democrat Geraldine Ferraro became the first major-party female vice-presidential nominee.

Yet women still faced serious problems, compounded by conservative social policies. Access to new positions did not change their concentration in lower-paying jobs. In 1985, most working women were still secretaries, cashiers, bookkeepers, registered nurses, and waitresses. Even when women moved into positions traditionally held by men, their progress often stopped at the lower and middle levels. Interruptions of work—to bear children or assume family responsibilities—impeded advancement. A "glass ceiling" seemed to prevent them from moving up, though by the late 1990s the ceiling began to crack.

Wage differentials between women and men continued. In 1985, full-time working women still earned only 63.6 cents for every dollar earned by men. Their concentration in traditional women's jobs made further improvement difficult. Comparable-worth arguments that women should receive equal pay for different jobs of similar value met conservative resistance.

Conservatives also waged a dedicated campaign against the right to legal abortion. Despite the 1973 Supreme Court decision legalizing abortion, the issue remained very much alive. The number of abortions increased dramatically in the decade after the decision. "Pro-life" forces mobilized. Opponents lobbied to cut off federal funds that allowed the poor to obtain abortions; they insisted that abortions should be performed in hospitals and not in less expensive clinics; and they worked to reverse the original decision itself.

Though the Supreme Court reiterated its decision in 1983, the pro-life movement was not deterred. In 1989, a solidifying conservative Court majority ruled that while a woman's right to abortion remained intact, state legislatures could impose limitations. A major legislative debate over the issue began, and numerous states began to mandate restrictions.

In 1992 the Supreme Court reaffirmed what it termed the essence of the right to abortion, while permitting further state restrictions. It declared that a 24-hour waiting period for women seeking abortions was acceptable and required teenage girls to secure the permission of a parent (or a judge) before ending a pregnancy. The ruling clearly gave states greater latitude in the overall restrictive effort and made an abortion harder to obtain, particularly for poor women and young women.

In response to a conservative backlash, the women's movement became more inclusive and more sensitive to race. Black women now found more common ground with white feminists. While black women in the early 1990s still earned less, on a weekly basis, than white men and white women, that situation began to improve. The dramatic confrontation between Supreme Court nominee Clarence Thomas and lawyer Anita Hill during confirmation hearings in 1991 dramatized both racial questions and the issue of sexual harassment. In the aftermath, Americans everywhere became more aware of inappropriate behavior that could no longer be tolerated.

The Limited Commitment to Latino Rights

Latinos likewise faced continuing problems in the 1980s and 1990s as commitments to reform eroded. Spanish-speaking students often found it difficult to finish school. In 1987, fully 40 percent of all Latino high school students did not graduate, and only 31 percent of Latino seniors were enrolled in college-preparatory courses.

College itself was another problem. Of those Latinos who went to college, 56 percent attended community colleges. Graduation often proved difficult; fewer than 7 percent completed a course of study. Forced to take courses with little connection to their background and less relevance to their lives, many students became frustrated and dropped out.

Like other groups, Latinos slowly extended their political gains. Henry Cisneros became mayor of San Antonio and Federico Peña was elected mayor of

Denver. In New Mexico, Governor Toney Anaya called himself the nation's highest elected Hispanic. The number of Latinos holding elective offices nationwide increased 3.5 percent between 1986 and 1987, and the number of Latina women in such offices increased 20 percent in that time. The first Latinos were appointed to President Clinton's cabinet beginning in 1988.

Latino workers, however, continued to have a hard time in the employment market. As the nation's overall unemployment rate dropped in the mid-1990s, the rate for the 12 million Latino workers barely budged—and worsened in relation to the rate for African-Americans. Many found themselves suffering from outdated skills and weak educational backgrounds.

Continuing Problems for Native Americans

Native Americans likewise experienced the waning commitment to reform, and their gains came as a result of their own efforts. Some tribal communities developed business skills, although traditional Indian attitudes hardly fostered the capitalist perspective. "The Crow believe in sharing wealth, and whites believe in accumulating wealth," explained Dale Old Horn, an MIT graduate and department head at Little Big Horn College in Crow Agency, Montana.

Some Indian groups did adapt to the capitalist ethos. The Choctaw in Mississippi were among the most successful. Before they began a drive toward self-sufficiency in 1979, their unemployment rate was 50 percent. By the middle of the 1980s, Choctaws owned all or part of three businesses on the reservation, employed 1,000 people, generated $30 million in work annually, and cut unemployment in half. The Pequot in Connecticut built a highly lucrative casino, as did many other tribes.

Indians still remained, as the 1990 census showed, the nation's poorest group. As Ben Nighthorse Campbell, Republican Senator from Colorado, noted in 1995, average Indian household income fell by 5 percent in the 1980s, while it rose for all other ethnic and racial groups. Average annual income for Native Americans on reservations was less than $5,000. There was still much to be done.

Pressures on the Environmental Movement

Environmentalists, too, were discouraged by the direction of public policy in the 1980s and 1990s. Activists now found that they faced fierce opposition. Reagan systematically restrained the EPA. The Department of the Interior opened forest lands, wilderness areas, and coastal waters to economic development, with no concern for preserving the environment. Bush initially proved more sympathetic to environmental causes, but as the economy faltered he drew back. In 1992, at a United Nations-sponsored Earth Summit that attracted 100 heads of government worldwide, Bush alone refused to sign a biological diversity treaty.

Clinton seemed to promise a new approach. Vice President Al Gore and Secretary of the Interior Bruce Babbitt were staunch environmentalists. The administration tried to take the middle ground in the spotted owl controversy. But Clinton, too, discovered that the issues could not easily be resolved in a conservative age.

THE POSTINDUSTRIAL ECONOMY

Republicans sought to reorganize the government against the backdrop of an economy growing ever more turbulent in the 1980s and 1990s. As patterns of employment changed in an increasingly mechanized workplace, millions of workers struggled to survive the shocks. Under Republican supply-side economics, the business cycle began to follow a boom-recession-boom pattern. When Reagan took office in 1980, the economy was reeling with declining productivity, galloping inflation, oil shortages, and high unemployment. Reagan's policies brought improvement in the early 1980s, particularly for middle- and upper-income people. But even renewed growth and higher employment rates could not help those less well off, as foreign competition contributed to continuing trouble in balancing budgets. The recession gripping the country from 1990 to 1992 underscored the need for renewed productivity, full employment, and equitable distribution of wealth.

The Changing Nature of Work

Automation and other technological advances had a powerful impact on the American workplace and caused a shift in the occupational structure of the working class. Once-lucrative jobs disappeared. Workers sat for hours before their screens, worried about radiation from the monitor or muscular fatigue at the keyboard.

Even as the nature of work changed, people seemed to be working more. In past decades leisure time had seemed to expand; there had been talk of a four-day workweek in the late 1950s. In the last 20 years, however, the amount of time Americans worked has steadily risen. In the mid-1990s, American employees toiled 320 hours more each year than their counterparts in Germany or France. Meanwhile they experienced more stress as they juggled the conflicts between employment and family life. Problems were particularly severe for women, still trying to cope with the pressures of maintaining the home while working outside of it.

The Shift to a Service Economy

The scarcity of good jobs stemmed in part from the restructuring of the economy that occurred in the 1980s. In a trend underway for more than half a century, the United States continued its shift from an industrial base, where most workers produced tangible things, to a service base, where most provided expertise or service to others in the work force. By the mid-1980s, three-fourths of the 113 million employees in the country worked in the service sector, as fast-food workers, clerks, teachers, lawyers, doctors, and bureaucrats.

That shift, in turn, had its roots in the decline of the country's industrial sector. The United States had been the world's industrial leader since the late nineteenth century. By the 1970s, however, the United States began to lose that position. After 1973, productivity slowed in virtually all American industries, a pattern that continued in the 1980s and 1990s. Economic growth in the early 1970s averaged 2.3 percent annually, compared to an average of 3.2 percent in the 1950s. In the early 1980s, during the worst recession since the 1930s, growth virtually ceased.

The causes of this decline in productivity were complex. The most important factor was a widespread and systematic failure on the part of the United States to invest sufficiently in its basic productive capacity. During the Reagan years, capital investment in real plants and equipment within the United States gave way to speculation, mergers, and spending abroad. Gross private domestic investment in national industries rose modestly during the boom years, though most companies became caught up in an acquisition mania that consumed even more resources. At the end of the 1980s, domestic investment was down—5.7 percent in 1990 and 9.5 percent in 1991. The energy crisis and rising oil prices (see Chapter 28) also contributed to the industrial decline. Finally, the war in Vietnam diverted federal funds from research and development.

While American industry became less productive, other industrial nations moved forward. German and Japanese industries, rebuilt after World War II with U.S. aid and aggressively modernized thereafter, reached new heights of efficiency. As a result, the United States began to lose its share of the world market for industrial goods. In 1946, the country had provided 60 percent of the world's iron and steel. In 1978, it provided a mere 16 percent. Foreign steel and automobile manufacturers captured huge market segments from American competitors. The auto industry, a mainstay of economic growth for much of the twentieth century, suffered plant shutdowns and massive layoffs. In 1991, its worst year ever, Ford lost a staggering $2.3 billion.

Workers in Transition

In the 1980s and 1990s, American labor struggled to hold on to the gains realized by the post-World War II generation of blue-collar workers. The largest problems involved adjusting to the nation's changing economic needs. The shift to a service economy was personally devastating for many workers, like Craig Miller, met at the start of the chapter. When new jobs were created in the cities, minority residents often lacked the skills to get them—or the transportation to get to them.

Meanwhile, the trade union movement faltered as the economy moved from an industrial to a service base. Union membership stood just over 25 percent in 1980 and barely over 16 percent a decade later. Between 1983 and 1993, union membership dropped further despite a substantial rise in the number of jobs.

Union membership declined for several reasons. One was the shift from blue-collar to white-collar work. The increase in the workforce of women and young people—both historically difficult to organize—was a second factor. A third was employers' growing willingness to use the Taft-Hartley Act of 1947 to restrict the tactics labor leaders could use.

Union vulnerability was visible early in Reagan's first term, when the Professional Air Traffic Controllers Organization (PATCO) went on strike. Charging that the strike violated the law, the president fired the strikers, decertified the union, and ordered the training of new controllers at a cost of $1.3 billion. The message was clear: Government employees must not challenge the public interest.

Antiunion sentiments reverberated throughout the nongovernment sector as well, as a 1983 strike by Arizona miners demonstrated. Confronted by falling prices and company losses, the management of Phelps Dodge, one of the world's largest copper producers, decided to end the cost-of-living allowance that enabled workers, many of them Mexican-Americans, to earn $12 an hour. When negotiations failed, workers struck, only to find that the company, working with antiunion experts at the University of Pennsylvania's Wharton School of Business, had hired permanent replacement workers. As the company president later acknowledged, "I had decided to break the union."

Strikers who kept their jobs found that their unions could not get favorable contracts. For example, in 1984 the United Auto Workers (UAW) ended a strike at General Motors by trading a pledge that GM would guarantee up to 70 percent of the production workers' lifetime jobs for a smaller wage increase than the union sought and a modification of the cost-of-living allowance that had been a part of UAW contracts since 1948. Company threats to move jobs overseas often made unions capitulate.

Continuing a trend that began in the early twentieth century, the number of farms and farmers declined steadily. The 6.7 million farms of 1933 shrank to 2.4 million in 1983. By 1989, farmers made up only 1.9 percent of the U.S. population. Farming income, meanwhile, became more concentrated. In 1983, the top 12 percent collected 90 percent of all farm income.

The extraordinary productivity of the most successful American farmers derived in part from the use of chemical fertilizers, irrigation, pesticides, and scientific management. Government price support programs helped too. Yet that very productivity caused unexpected setbacks. In the 1970s, food shortages abroad made the United States the "breadbasket of the world." Farmers increased their output to meet multibillion-bushel grain export orders and profited handsomely from high prices. To increase production, farmers often borrowed heavily at high interest rates. When a worldwide economic slump began in 1980, overseas demand for American farm products declined sharply and farm prices dropped. Thousands of farmers, caught in the cycle of overproduction, heavy indebtedness, and falling prices, watched helplessly as banks and federal agencies foreclosed on their mortgages and drove them out of business.

The Roller Coaster Economy

The economy shifted several times during the 1980s and 1990s. The Reagan years began with a recession that lasted for several years. An economic boom between 1983 and 1990 gave way to a punishing recession as the new decade began. It appeared that the United States had embarked on another boom-and-bust cycle.

The recession of 1980 to 1982 began during the Carter administration, when the Federal Reserve Board tried to deal with mounting deficits by increasing the money supply. To cool down the resulting inflation, Carter cut programs—but he succeeded only in bringing on a recession with substantial unemployment. During Reagan's first year, the job situation deteriorated further, and by the end of 1982, the unemployment rate had climbed to 10.8 percent (and over 20 percent among African-Americans). Nearly a third of the nation's industrial capacity lay idle, and 12 million Americans were out of work.

Inflation, accompanied by heavy unemployment, continued to be a problem. The inflation rate, which reached 12.4 percent a year under Carter in 1980, fell after Reagan assumed office, to 8.9 percent in his first year and about 5 percent during the remainder of his first term. But even the lower rate eroded the purchasing power of people already in difficulty.

The recession of 1980 to 1982 afflicted every region of the country. Business failures proliferated in every city and state, as large and small businesses closed their doors and fired employees. In 1982, business bankruptcies rose 50 percent from the previous year. In one week in June 1982, a total of 548 businesses failed, close to the 1932 weekly record of 612.

Economic conditions improved in late 1983 and early 1984, particularly for Americans in the middle and upper income ranges. The federal tax cut Reagan pushed through encouraged consumer spending, and huge defense expenditures had a stimulating effect. The Republican effort to reduce restrictions and cut waste sparked business confidence. The stock market climbed as it reflected the optimistic buying spree. Inflation remained low, about 3 to 4 percent annually from 1982 to 1988. Interest rates likewise fell from 16.5 percent in 1982 to 10.5 percent in the same period and remained thereafter under 11 percent. The unemployment rate at the end of the 1980s fell to below 6 percent nationally (though many of the new jobs created paid less than $13,000 per year). Between the start of the recovery and 1988, real GNP grew at an annual rate of 4.2 percent.

But the upswing masked problems. Millions of Americans remained poor. For many families, a middle-class living standard required two full-time income earners, and many took on heavy debt, at very high rates of interest for mortgages and credit cards. Under such circumstances, some young families struggled to remain in the middle class. Workers like Craig Miller, introduced at the beginning of the chapter, had to accept lower standards of living when they lost jobs. Single mothers were hit hardest of all.

The huge and growing budget deficits reflected the fundamental economic instability. Those deficits provoked doubts that resulted in the stock market crash of 1987. Six weeks of falling prices culminated with a 22.6 percent drop on Black Monday (October 19, 1987), almost double the plunge of Black Tuesday in 1929. The deficits, negative trade balances, and exposures of Wall Street fraud all combined to puncture the bubble. Later the market revived, but problems remained.

In the early 1990s the country experienced another recession. Deficits became enormous under the weight of extravagant military spending, the uncontrolled growth of entitlements—programs such as Medicare and Medicaid, which provided benefits for millions of Americans on the basis of need—and the tax cut. As bond traders in the 1980s speculated recklessly and pocketed huge profits, the basic productive structure of the country continued to decline. The huge increase in the national debt eroded business confidence, and this time the effects were felt not simply in the stock market but in the economy as a whole.

American firms suffered a serious decline as corporate profits fell from $327 billion in 1989 to $315.5 billion in 1991. To cope with declining profits and decreased consumer demand, companies scaled back dramatically. For example, General Motors closed 21 plants in late 1991, laid off 9,000 white-collar employees the next year, and planned to eliminate more than 70,000 jobs over the next several years. The unemployment rate rose once again. In mid-1991, it reached 7 percent, the highest level in nearly five years.

Around the nation, state governments found it impossible to balance their budgets without massive spending cuts. Reagan's efforts to move programs from the federal to the state level worked as long as funding lasted, but as national support dropped and state tax revenues declined, states found themselves in budget gridlocks, forced to slash spending for social services and education.

After several false starts, recovery began in mid-1992. Unemployment dropped from 7.4 percent that year to 5.6 percent in mid-1995. The productivity index maintained a steady rise. And a concerted effort reduced the federal deficit and led to the announcement of a surplus in 1998. One reflection of renewed prosperity was the soaring stock market, as the Dow Jones, average passed 10,000 for the first time in 1999.

DEMOGRAPHIC AND REGIONAL CHANGE

As the American people dealt with the swings of the economy, demographic patterns changed significantly. The nation's population increased from 228 million to approximately 250 million between 1980 and 1990—a rise of 9.6 percent (as opposed to 11.5 percent in the 1970s) that was one of the lowest rates of growth in American history. At the same time, the complexion of the country changed. In 1992 the country's non-white population—blacks, Latinos, Asians, and Native Americans—stood at an all-time high of 25 percent, the result of increased immigration and of minority birthrates significantly above the white rate. The population shifted as well. Suburban growth continued, leaving ever larger minority populations in the cities. In the West a pattern of urban and regional development underway since World War II continued and provided a model for the rest of the country.

Urban and Suburban Shifts

American cities increasingly became concentrations of minorities. White families continued to leave for the suburbs, which by 1990 contained almost half the population, more than ever before. In 15 of the nation's 28 largest central cities, minorities made up at least half the population.

The cities also grew steadily poorer. In Houston, for example, although increasing numbers of blacks, Hispanics, and Asians lived in the suburbs, most of the poorest minority families concentrated in the city itself. As had been the case since World War II, commuters from the suburbs took the better-paying jobs, while people living in the cities held lower-paying positions.

Western Development

At the same time, the population was moving west. In 1900, the Mountain and Pacific states contained about 5 percent of the nation's population. By 1990 that figure stood at 21 percent. The population of the nation as a whole rose by less than 10 percent in the 1980s, but the population of the West increased by 22 percent.

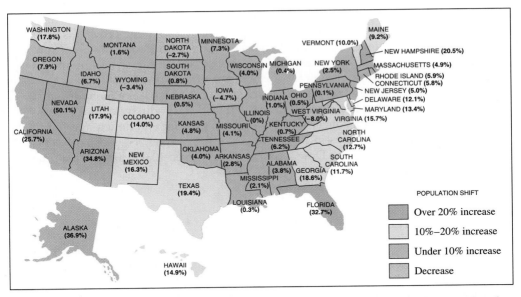

POPULATION SHIFTS, 1980–1990   This map shows the population shifts between 1980 and 1990. Note the substantial increases in western regions of the country and the much smaller increases along the Atlantic seaboard.

That population was becoming much more urbanized. In the 50 years following 1940, the six largest metropolitan areas in the West grew by 380 percent; the six largest in the East expanded by only 64 percent. By 1990, 80 percent of all westerners lived in metropolitan areas, compared to 76 percent of the people in the rest of the United States.

With its urban development, the West became a pacesetter for the rest of the country. If the New England village had been a representative symbol of the 18th century and the midwestern town a similar symbol of the 19th century, now in the late twentieth century the western metropolis had special symbolic importance. Western cities were unbounded, open-ended, sprawling in all directions. They seemed capable of expanding indefinitely. Horizontal, low-slung homes made western neighborhoods look very different from those in the Northeast. Tourism became a dynamic industry, with the West in the forefront. The motel, a western invention, made automobile travel easier. Western cities were among the most popular tourist destinations, drawing visitors from all over the world.

California was the nation's fastest-growing state, its population increasing in the 1980s by nearly 26 percent. Responding to a question about California's impact on the rest of the country, writer Wallace Stegner replied, "We *are* the national culture, at its most energetic end." Los Angeles became the most dynamic example of American vitality and creativity. The motion picture industry exerted a worldwide impact. The city became a capital of consumption.

The New Pilgrims

The second great wave of immigrants in the twentieth century brought about another demographic shift. The number of immigrants has risen dramatically in the past 30 years. In the 1970s the number averaged 450,000 a year, far higher than in the decade before. In the 1980s, it averaged 730,000. In 1990, more people arrived than in any single year in this century. Altogether, a fifth of the population growth in the 1980s stemmed from immigration.

The influx was spurred by the Immigration Act of 1965 (see Chapter 28). Part of the Great Society program, this act authorized the acceptance of immigrants impartially from all parts of the world. The result in the 1980s and 1990s, as in the 1970s, was far greater numbers of Asians and Latin Americans. In this latter decade, 37 percent of the new arrivals came from Asia, and 47 percent came from Mexico, the Caribbean, and Latin America. Always a nation of immigrants, the United States was once again receiving new, and very different, ethnic infusions.

As has long been true, the desire for jobs fostered immigration. But foreign crises also fueled the influx. After 1975, the United States accepted more than a half million Vietnamese refugees. In 1980, the nation admitted 125,000 Cuban and Haitian refugees.

Millions more arrived illegally. As the populations of Latin American nations soared and as economic conditions deteriorated, more and more people looked to the United States for relief. In the mid-1970s, it was estimated that there might be 12 million foreigners in the nation illegally.

Several legislative measures sought to rationalize the immigration process. In 1986, Congress passed the Immigration Reform and Control Act, aimed at curbing illegal immigration while offering amnesty to aliens who had lived in the United States since 1982. As the mid-1988 deadline approached, 50,000 per week applied to stay. The Immigration Act of 1990 revised the level and preference system for admitting immigrants and refined naturalization procedures. Raising immigration quotas by 40 percent per year, the act cut back on restrictions based on ideology or sexual orientation that had denied entry in the past. It also set aside a substantial number of visas for large investors and provided for swift deportation of aliens who committed crimes.

The more than ten million immigrants who arrived between 1976 and 1990 belonged to two very different economic classes. In the 1970s and early 1980s, about 25 percent were professionals, and more than 40 percent were white-collar employees. Many brought skills, funds, and family support networks that could assist in business ventures in America. At the same time, the United States absorbed a large group of less skilled workers. In this decade and a half, about 46 percent of all employed immigrants were laborers, service sector workers, and semiskilled employees. The flow of this group increased in the 1980s and 1990s.

This new wave of immigration changed the complexion of the United States, as it had in decades past. Once again, as before 1924, the nation was a refuge for people from very different parts of the world.

These groups left a new imprint on the United States. As African-Americans and Latinos became major figures in the urban equation, the number of Asians in

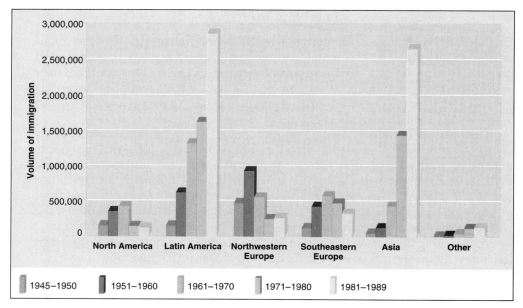

IMMIGRATION: VOLUME AND SOURCES, 1945–1989   This map shows the shifting patterns of American immigration in the postwar years. In particular, note the large increase in Asian and Latin American immigration in the past several decades.

the country doubled in the 1980s, and they made up nearly half of all immigrants by the end of the decade. They often brought skills and professional expertise, although Southeast Asian refugees were frequently less well off when they arrived. The Asian immigrants, following a pattern established decades before, sought better and better opportunities for their children, and in California they became the largest group of entering students at a number of college campuses.

Sometimes the media highlighted the successes of Asian immigrants, particularly in contrast to the problems encountered by other groups. In 1986, *U.S. News & World Report* noted Asian-American advances in a cover story, while *Newsweek* ran a lead article on "Asian Americans: A 'Model Minority.'" Asian-Americans were proud of the exposure but pointed out that many members of the working class still struggled for a foothold, especially in the Chinatowns of San Francisco, Los Angeles, and New York. Chinese immigrant women, in particular, often had little choice but to work as seamstresses, just as women from other nationalities had earlier in the century.

Professionals often had a hard time. Frequently, training in their country of birth had little bearing in the United States. One Vietnamese physician who resettled in Oklahoma noted, "When I come here, I am told that I must be a beginner again and serve like an apprentice for two years. I have no choice, so I will do it, but I have been wronged to be asked to do this."

In the 1970s and 1980s, America's efforts to help immigrants coincided with still-intact social assistance programs of the liberal welfare state. Affirmative action programs aided both legal and illegal arrivals. Bilingual classrooms became more common, and multiculturalism, stressing the different values that made up a larger American identity, became a dominant theme in many schools.

Yet those efforts brought increasing resistance from Americans already here, particularly as the structure of the economy changed and good jobs became more scarce. That opposition, which echoed anti-immigrant feeling of the past, included strenuous efforts to restrict illegal immigration and a move to lower annual quotas for new arrivals. Resistance came to a head in California in 1994, where a referendum issue, Proposition 187, was passed, requiring teachers and clinic doctors to deny assistance to illegal aliens and to report them to police. It provided a model for other states to follow, and caught the attention of national legislators as the Republicans took control.

Growing Up

In the mid-1970s, the birthrate began to rise slowly after a decade and a half of decline. The baby boom, which had created a population explosion in the years after World War II, peaked in 1960 with a rate of 24 births per 1,000 people. In 1981, the rate stood at 16, then rose to nearly 17 in 1990, as demographers viewed the new increase in births as part of a long-term trend.

But children less frequently had traditional homes. The Labor Department estimated that by the late 1970s only 7 percent of the nation's families matched the stereotypical pattern of the breadwinner father, the homemaker mother, and two children. Divorce shattered the mold. In 1980, the courts granted nearly 1.2 million divorces, the highest total in the nation's history. In 1990, the figure of 1.175 million was almost as high. For each 1,000 marriages there were 480 divorces, compared to 258 per 1,000 in 1960. The social stigma once attached to divorce disappeared; Reagan was the first divorced person to be elected president. "Nonfamily households" became increasingly common. Between 1980 and 1990, such households, led by either a man or a woman, increased from 26 to 29 percent of the total, while the percentage of full-family households declined. For African-Americans, the proportion of families headed by women was three times as great as for whites.

During hard times, new children could pose problems. An extra mouth could make a difference to a family on the fringe. New children also required women of all classes to consider the relationship between family and career. Women entering the work force faced the daunting problem of juggling work and home schedules and finding adequate child care facilities.

The rising death rate among the young was disturbing. In 1982 it was reported that the death rate for most Americans had dropped significantly over a 30-year period, and it continued to drop throughout the decade, but the rate for those between 15 and 24 rose steadily after 1976. Automobile accidents, murders, and suicides accounted for three out of four deaths for this group.

AIDS (acquired immune deficiency syndrome), surfacing in 1981, complicated the process of growing up. The sexual revolution of the 1960s had brought a major change in sexual patterns, particularly for the young, but sexual experimentation now involved facing a deadly threat. AIDS became the leading cause of death in Americans between the ages of 25 and 44. The growing number of deaths—more than 250,000 by 1995—suggested that the disease would reach epic proportions.

Growing Old

As concern with the problems of the young increased, awareness of the plight of the old also grew. Between 1900 and 1980, when the population of the country tripled, the number of people over 65 rose eightfold and continued to rise in the next decade. In the 1980s, the number of Americans over 75 grew by more than 27 percent. Underlying the rapid increase was the steady advance in medical care, which in the twentieth century had increased life expectancy from 47 to 74 years. Americans became aware of the "aging revolution," which promised to become the most lasting of all twentieth-century social changes.

The elderly raised new issues in a nation suffering periodic recession. Many wanted to continue working and opposed mandatory retirement rules that drove them from their jobs. Legislation in 1978 that raised the mandatory retirement age from 65 to 70 helped older workers but cut employment opportunities for younger workers seeking jobs, a pattern that became even more problematical in the 1990s.

Generational resentment over jobs was compounded by the knotty problems faced by the Social Security system established a half century before. As more and more Americans retired, the system could not generate sufficient revenue to make the payments due without assistance from the general governmental fund. In the early 1980s, it appeared that the entire system might collapse. A government solution involving higher taxes for those still employed and a later age for qualifying for benefits rescued the fund. But many Americans in the 1990s wondered whether Social Security would survive.

As Americans lived longer, they suffered increasingly from Alzheimer's disease, an affliction that gradually destroyed a patient's memory and brought on infantile behavior. No treatment was available to reverse the ailment, and no family felt secure. In 1995, the family of former President Ronald Reagan disclosed that he was stricken by the disease.

American families faced difficult decisions about caring for older parents. In the past, the elderly often came into their children's homes, but attitudes and family patterns had changed. As women entered the paid workforce, they were less able to give elderly parents home-care. Retirement villages and nursing homes provided two alternatives, but the decision to institutionalize a parent was often excruciating.

Growing Poor

Meanwhile, despite the increase in wealth enjoyed by already-rich Americans, many people were growing poorer. According to the 1990 census, nearly 32 million people now found themselves below the poverty line, defined as an income of $13,000 for a family of four. That number included one out of every three *working* Americans. As always, minorities fared worse than whites. The net worth of a typical white household was 12 times greater than the net worth of a typical black household and 8 times greater than the net worth of a typical Latino household. Minorities and women continued to lose ground faster than the rest of the population.

Just as the United States rediscovered its poor in the 1960s, so it rediscovered its homeless in the 1980s and 1990s. Even as unemployment dropped in the 1980s, the number of homeless quadrupled during that time. Numbers were hard to ascertain, but one estimate in 1990 calculated that six or seven million people had been home-less at some point in the past five years. A more careful study in 1994 scaled that figure down to 500,000, still a huge number for the richest nation on earth.

People became homeless for a variety of reasons. Some started life in seriously disturbed or dysfunctional families. Others fell prey to alcohol and drugs. Still others had health or learning problems that eroded possibilities for a stable life. For millions of working Americans, homelessness was just an unaffordable illness away. Though many Americans initially regarded the homeless as "bag ladies, winos, and junkies," they gradually came to realize that the underclass category included others as well.

The growing disparity in wealth and the neglect of the urban poor and resur-gent racism, noted earlier in this chapter, became horrifyingly visible in the terrible rioting that engulfed Los Angeles in the spring of 1992. The year before, Americans had watched videotape of a savage beating of black motorist Rodney King by white police officers, the most dramatic of a long string of incidents involving police brutality. When a California jury, which contained no African-Americans, acquitted the policemen, many people throughout the country became convinced that people of color could not get equal justice. In Los Angeles, arson and looting swept uncontrollably through many neighborhoods. Irresponsible as such behav-ior might be, there was also a sense of the social contract having been broken by politicians and the rich. Several days later, after the riot had run its course, 51 people (most of them black and Hispanic) lay dead, 2,000 were injured; and $1 bil-lion in damage had been done to the city. It was the worst riot in decades, more deadly than the Watts uprising 27 years before.

THE UNITED STATES IN A CHANGED WORLD

In the 1980s and 1990s, the United States emerged triumphant in the Cold War that had dominated international politics since the end of World War II. In one of the most momentous turns in modern world history, communism collapsed in Eastern Europe and in the Soviet Union, and the various republics in the Soviet orbit moved toward capitalism and democracy. Other regions—the Middle East and Africa—experienced equally breathtaking change.

This international tumult forced the United States to reexamine its own assumptions about its role in the world. What kind of leadership would the United States exert as the one remaining superpower on the globe? What kind of assistance would it extend to developing nations once the competition with the Soviet Union that had fueled foreign aid was over? These questions, asked in dif-ferent forms over the course of past centuries, helped shape foreign policy in transitional times.

Triumph in the Cold War

The Cold War was very much alive when Reagan assumed power in 1981. The new president asserted U.S. interests far more aggressively than had President Carter. Like most of his compatriots, Reagan believed in large defense budgets and

a militant approach toward the Soviet Union. He wanted to cripple the USSR economically by forcing it to spend more than it could afford on defense.

Viewing the Soviet Union as an "evil empire" in his first term, Reagan promoted a bigger atomic arsenal by arguing that a nuclear war could be fought and
won. The administration dropped efforts to obtain Senate ratification of SALT II,
the arms reduction plan negotiated under Carter, although it observed the pact's
restrictions. Then Reagan proposed the enormously expensive and bitterly criticized Strategic Defense Initiative, popularly known as "Star Wars" after a 1977
movie, to intercept Soviet missiles in outer space.

In his second term, Reagan softened his belligerence. Mikhail Gorbachev, the
new Soviet leader, watching his own economy collapse under the pressure of the
superheated arms race, realized the need for accommodation with the West. He
therefore proposed a policy of *perestroika* (restructuring the economy) and *glasnost*
(political openness to encourage personal initiative). His overtures opened the
way to better relations with the United States.

Conscious of his place in history, Reagan met with Gorbachev, and the two
developed a close working relationship. Summit meetings led to an Intermediate-
Range Nuclear Forces Treaty in 1987 that provided for withdrawal and destruction
of 2,500 Soviet and American nuclear missiles in Europe.

Bush maintained Reagan's comfortable relationship with Gorbachev. At several summit meetings in 1989 and 1990, the two leaders signed agreements reducing the number of long-range nuclear weapons, ending manufacture of chemical
weapons, and easing trade restrictions. The Strategic Arms Reduction Treaty
(START) signed in 1991 dramatically cut stockpiles of long-range weapons.

Hailed around the world for helping end the Cold War, Gorbachev encountered trouble at home. In mid-1991, he faced an old-guard Communist coup, led by
those who opposed *glasnost* and *perestroika* and wanted to slow the process of
change. He survived, but he could not resist those who wanted to go even further
to establish democracy and capitalism. The forces he had unleashed finally
destroyed the Soviet system and tore the USSR apart.

Boris Yeltsin, president of Russia, the strongest and largest of the Soviet
republics, emerged as the dominant leader, but even he could not stop disintegration. Independence movements in the tiny Baltic republics began the dismantling
of the Soviet Union, and other republics likewise went their own way. The once-
powerful superpower was now a collection of separate states.

Early in 1992, Bush and Yeltsin proclaimed a new era of "friendship and partnership" and formally declared an end to the Cold War. After half a century of confrontation, the United States had won. Yeltsin abandoned the quest for nuclear
parity—maintaining an arsenal equal to that of the United States—and agreed to
cut back Russian conventional forces. The United States then extended aid to the
former Soviet republics, which needed help in reorganizing their economies as
free enterprise systems. Relations became strained in 1994, when Russia moved
aggressively to subdue a rebellion in the republic of Chechnya. The brutality of
Yeltsin's response led to questions about both his democratic values and his ability to govern, yet the West continued to support him for lack of a better alternative.

Communist regimes in Eastern Europe had already collapsed. The most dramatic episodes unfolded in Germany in November 1989. Prodded by Gorbachev,
East Germany's Communist boss announced unexpectedly that citizens could

The destruction of the Berlin Wall in November 1989 was a symbolic blow to the entire Cold War structure that had grown up in Europe in the postwar years. The fall of the Wall touched off joyous celebrations. (AP/Wide World Photos)

leave. Within hours, thousands gathered on both sides of the 28-mile Berlin Wall— the symbol of the Cold War division of Berlin. As border guards stepped aside, East Germans flooded into West Berlin amid dancing, shouting, and fireworks. Within days, sledgehammer-wielding Germans were pulverizing the wall. By October 1990, less than a year after the end had began, the two Germanys were reunited.

The fall of the Berlin Wall reverberated all over Eastern Europe. Everywhere it brought the pell-mell overthrow of Communist regimes. In Poland, the Solidarity movement triumphed in its ten-year struggle against Soviet domination and found itself in power. The nation, however, faced enormous economic problems, and Americans had to decide just how much help they could afford to give. In Czechoslovakia, two decades after Soviet tanks had rolled into Prague to suppress liberalization, the forces of freedom were victorious. Dissident playwright Václav Havel was elected president. But not even economic assistance could keep the federation intact, and separate Czech and Slovak republics emerged. New post-Communist regimes emerged in Bulgaria, Hungary, Romania, and Albania, but they were also politically and economically troubled.

Yugoslavia, held together by a Communist dictatorship since 1945, proved to be the extreme case of ethnic hostility resurging amid collapsing central authority. In 1991 Yugoslavia splintered into its ethnic components. In Bosnia, the large Serbian minority resisted Muslim and Croatian attempts to secede from Serbian-dominated Yugoslavia. The result was a civil war, a brutal siege of the city of Sarajevo, and an even more ruthless "ethnic cleansing" campaign. The United States stayed out of the conflict, but the United Nations failed to bring about peace.

Only in mid-1995 did a NATO bombing campaign force the Bosnian Serbs into negotiations, and a peace conference held in Dayton, Ohio, led to the commitment of American troops, along with soldiers from other countries. Even that effort failed to end all hostilities.

STEPS TOWARD PEACE IN THE MIDDLE EAST

The United States was equally involved with events in the Middle East. Here again the nation sought to preserve stability as the Cold War drew to an end. The most dramatic crisis occurred in 1990 when Saddam Hussein, the dictator of Iraq, invaded and annexed his oil-rich neighbor Kuwait. Saddam seemed intent on unifying Arab nations, threatening Israel, and dominating the Middle Eastern oil on which the West, including the United States, relied.

President Bush reacted vigorously. Working through the United Nations, as Truman had done in Korea, the United States persuaded the Security Council to vote unanimously to condemn the attack and impose an embargo on Iraq. After Saddam refused to relinquish Kuwait, in mid-January 1991 a 28-nation coalition struck at Iraq with an American-led multinational army of nearly half a million troops. In Operation Desert Storm, the coalition forces' sophisticated missiles, aircraft, and tanks swiftly overwhelmed the Iraqis. Americans were initially jubilant. Then the euphoria soured as Saddam used his remaining military power against minorities in Iraq. Bush's unwillingness to become bogged down in an Iraqi civil war and his eagerness to return U.S. troops home left the conflict unfinished. A year after his defeat, Saddam was as strongly entrenched as ever.

Meanwhile, the United States was involved in a larger, and ultimately more important, effort to bring peace to the Middle East. In the early 1990s, Secretary of State James Baker finally secured agreement from the major parties in the region to speak to one another face-to-face. A victory in the Israeli parliamentary elections in mid-1992 for Yitzhak Rabin, a soldier who recognized the need for peace and was ready to compromise, offered further hope for the talks.

During his first year in office, President Clinton played the part of peacemaker, just as Jimmy Carter had done 15 years before. On September 13, 1993, in a dramatic White House ceremony, Palestine Liberation Organization leader Yasir Arafat and Israeli prime minister Rabin signed an agreement that promised the Palestinians a step-by-step progression toward self-rule. A subsequent treaty between Jordan and Israel brought peace on still another border. While extremists tried to destroy the peace process by continued violence, the effort to heal old animosities continued.

Turbulence in Latin America

The United States intervened frequently in Latin America, as it had in the past, hoping to impose stability. Viewing Central America as a Cold War battlefield, President Reagan opposed left-wing guerrillas in El Salvador struggling against a repressive right-wing regime. Efforts to destroy the radicals failed, despite the expenditure of about $1 million a day. When in 1989 a far-right faction won

Salvadoran elections and polarized the country, U.S. officials despaired of finding a solution.

Nicaragua became an even bloodier battleground. In 1979, revolutionaries calling themselves Sandinistas (after César Sandino, who in the 1920s had fought against U.S. occupation) overthrew the repressive Somoza family dictatorship. President Carter, who at first recognized and aided the Sandinistas, cut off support when they curbed civil liberties and allegedly helped the rebels in El Salvador. Reagan took a far tougher stand. Circumventing congressional opposition, in November 1981 he authorized the CIA to arm and train counterrevolutionaries known as *contras*.

The *contras* began to attack from bases outside the country, and Nicaragua descended into civil war. When things went badly for the *contras*, the CIA secretly mined Nicaraguan harbors, violating international law. Learning about this, Congress cut off military aid to the *contras*. Peaceful elections in early 1990 finally drove out the Sandinistas and brought the fighting to an end. But the Nicaraguan morass had already caused a major political scandal in Washington.

In 1987, Congress learned that the National Security Council had launched an effort to free American hostages in the Middle East by selling arms to Iran and then using the funds to aid the *contras*, in direct violation of both the law and congressional will. Oliver North, the National Security Council official responsible for the policy, was brought to trial on charges of lying to congressional committees and destroying crucial documents. Convicted in 1989, North received a light sentence with no prison time from a judge who recognized that he had been not acting entirely on his own. Reagan's possible involvement never became quite clear.

Reagan found it easier to maintain stability on the tiny Caribbean island of Grenada. The president ordered marines there in October 1983, after a coup installed a government sympathetic to Castro's Cuba. Concerned about the construction of a large airfield there, 2,000 marines invaded the island, rescued a number of American medical students, and claimed triumph. Though the United Nations condemned it, Americans cheered the administration's "rescue mission."

Bush took credit for a similar incursion in Panama. Despite memories of past imperialism, the United States invaded Panama, it said, to protect the Canal, defend American citizens, and stop drug trafficking. Panamanian military leader Manuel Noriega, notorious for his involvement in drugs, was captured and brought to the United States, convicted of drug-trafficking, and given a long prison sentence.

Stabilization efforts enjoyed more success in the mid-1990s, in the aftermath of the Cold War. El Salvador and Nicaragua seemed to emerge from the turbulence of the preceding decade. In Haiti, after seeking for several years to restore deposed president Jean Bertrand Aristide to power, Clinton threatened an invasion. A last-minute visit by an American delegation including Jimmy Carter forced Haiti's military dictatorship to relinquish power.

Upheaval in Africa

The United States likewise found itself drawn into turbulent African affairs. In South Africa, the United States supported the long and ultimately successful

TIMELINE

1980	1980–1982	1981	1981–1983	1982
Ronald Reagan elected president	Recession	Reagan breaks air controllers' strike; AIDS (acquired immune deficiency syndrome) discovered	Tax cuts; deficit spending increases	U.S. invasion of Lebanon
1989	**1990**	**1990–1992**	**1991**	**1991–1999**
Federal bailout of savings and loan industry; Fall of the Berlin Wall	National debt reaches $3.1 trillion; Immigration Act of 1990; Sandinistas driven from power in Nicaragua; Nelson Mandela freed in South Africa; U.S. population reaches 250 million	Recession	Persian Gulf War; Failed coup in Soviet Union; Disintegration of the Soviet Union; Strategic Arms Reduction Treaty (START) signed	Ethnic turbulence in fragmented former Yugoslavia
1999				
Bill Clinton acquitted by the Senate; Stock market soars as Dow Jones average passes 10,000				

struggle against apartheid—the policy of the white minority (only 15 percent of the population) to segregate and deny human rights to the black majority. While the United States had long expressed its dislike of this extreme system of segregation, in past years it had refused to go further. Then the ferment within the United States, sparked by the civil rights movement and opposition to dictatorships in Central America, generated domestic pressure for a stronger stand. In 1986, over Reagan's objections, Congress imposed sanctions. The pressure damaged the South African economy and persuaded more than half of the 300 American firms doing business there to leave.

The final blow to apartheid was dealt by Nelson Mandela, South Africa's leading black activist who had become the symbol of resistance during 27 years in prison. In 1990, Prime Minister Frederik W. De Klerk succumbed to American and international pressure by freeing Mandela and pledging to end apartheid gradually. De Klerk's

1983	1984	1986	1987	1988
Reagan proposes Strategic Defense Initiative ("Star Wars")	Reagan reelected	Tax reform measure passed; Immigration Reform and Control Act	Iran-*contra* affair becomes public; Stock market crashes; Intermediate Range Nuclear Forces Treaty signed	George Bush elected president

1992	1993	1994	1996	1998
Bill Clinton elected president; Czechoslovakia splits into separate Czech and Slovak Republics; Riots erupt in Los Angeles	North American Free Trade Agreement (NAFTA) ratified; Palestine Liberation Organization and Israel sign peace treaty	Nelson Mandela elected president of South Africa	Bill Clinton reelected	Budget Surplus announced; Bill Clinton impeached by the House of Representatives

white government and Mandela's African National Congress negotiated a transition to multiracial democracy. In 1994 peaceful elections were held, in which blacks voted for the first time. After years of struggle, the African National Congress assumed power and dismantled apartheid. Mandela became president of a nation that began building itself anew. American aid provided crucial support.

Elsewhere in Africa, U.S. policy makers had greater difficulty in maintaining post-Cold War stability. Somalia, an impoverished East African nation, suffered from a devastating famine, compounded by struggles between warlords that led to an almost total disintegration of order. In 1992, Bush sent U.S. troops to assist a United Nations effort to stop the starvation and stabilize the country. But six months after Clinton became president, a firefight with one Somali faction resulted in several dozen American casualties. The shooting prompted the American public, still haunted by memories of Vietnam, to demand withdrawal. Reluctant to back down as he groped to define a policy, Clinton first increased the number of U.S. troops, then in 1993 recalled the soldiers without having restored order.

The United States was similarly baffled by a crisis in the tiny Central African country of Rwanda. There a fragile balance of power between two hostile ethnic groups—the Tutsis and the Hutus—broke down. Hard-line Hutus attacked Tutsi rebels and embarked on an appalling genocidal campaign in which hundreds of thousands of innocent Tutsis and moderate Hutus perished. As the world followed the carnage on television, the United States, like many European nations, debated intervention on humanitarian grounds but in the end did nothing. Eventually the killing stopped, although ethnic friction remained.

The post-Cold War world remained an unsettled and uncertain place. While the United States was committed to nourishing democracy and protecting its economic interests, Americans remained wary of foreign intervention, even to prevent genocide or massive violations of human rights. They continued to be haunted by the ghost of Vietnam. Yet powerful political, military, and economic interests still required attention, just as they had for the past 50 years, and the United States remained deeply involved in the effort to promote international stability. Despite hopes that money formerly allocated for defense could be used for domestic needs, the military budget remained huge. Even with the Cold War over, global responsibilities remained.

❧❧❧❧❧❧

CONCLUSION

The Recent Past in Perspective

In the 1980s and 1990s, the United States witnessed the resurgence of conservatism. The assault on the welfare state, dubbed the "Reagan Revolution," created a less regulated economy, whatever the implications for less fortunate Americans. The policies of Ronald Reagan and George Bush continued the trend begun by Richard Nixon in the 1970s. They reshaped the political agenda and reversed the liberal approach that had held sway since the New Deal of Franklin Roosevelt in the 1930s. Bill Clinton's brief effort to revive the liberal welfare state failed to reverse the conservative momentum. In foreign affairs, Republican administrations likewise shifted course. Reagan first assumed a steel-ribbed posture toward the Soviet Union, then moved toward détente, and watched as his successor declared victory in the Cold War. When Democrats were in charge, they followed much the same approach. Yet leaders of both parties still faced resistance to an active role abroad, particularly in time of economic distress at home.

To be sure, there were limits to the transformation. Such fundamental programs as Social Security and Medicare remained securely in place, accepted by all but the most implacable splinter groups. Even the most conservative presidents of the past half century could not return to an imagined era of unbridled individualism and puny federal government. On the international front, despite the end of the Cold War, the nation's defense budget remained far higher than many Americans wished, and the nuclear arsenal continued to pose a threat to the human race.

Nor was the transformation beneficial to everyone. Periods of deep recession wrought havoc on the lives of blue-collar and white-collar workers alike. Working-class Americans like Craig Miller, introduced at the start of the chapter, were caught in the spiral of downward mobility that made them question the ability of the nation's economy to reward hard work. Liberals and conservatives both worried about the mounting national debt and the capacity of the economy to compete with Japan, South Korea, Germany, and other countries. Countless Americans fretted about the growing gaps between rich and poor. They fought with one another over what rules should govern a woman's right to an abortion. For the first time in American history, many children could not hope to do better than their parents had done. Reluctantly they tried to prepare themselves to accept a scaled-down vision of the future.

In the 1980s and 1990s, the United States sought a new stability, at home and abroad. In the process, the nation struggled to adhere to its historic values in a complex and changing world. Despite shifts in policy during the Republican resurgence, those basic values still governed, as the American people continued their centuries-old effort to live up to the promise of the American dream.

Recommended Reading

Historians have not yet had a chance to deal in detail with the developments of the immediate past, so full descriptions must be found in other sources, such as newspaper and magazine accounts. But a number of useful treatments about selected topics provide good starting points in various areas.

General and Statistical Works

Stephanie Coontz, *The Way We Really Are: Coming to Terms with America's Changing Families* (1997); U.S. Bureau of the Census, *Statistical Abstract of the United States: 1994 & 1998*; U.S. Bureau of the Census, *U.S. Census of Population, 1990*; Alan Wolfe, *One Nation, After All: What Middle-Class Americans Really Think About: God, Country, Family, Racism, Welfare, Immigration, Homosexuality, Work, the Right, the Left, and Each Other* (1998).

Religious Developments

David Chidester, *Patterns of Power: Religion and Politics in American Culture* (1988); Yvonne Yazbeck Haddad and Jane Idleman Smith, *Muslim Communities in North America* (1994); Erling Jorstad, *Holding Fast/Pressing On: Religion in America in the 1980s* (1990); R. Laurence Moore, *Selling God: American Religion in the Marketplace of Culture* (1994); Garry Wills, *Under God: Religion and American Politics* (1990).

The Reagan Presidency

Paul Boyer, ed., *Reagan as President: Contemporary Views of the Man, His Politics, and His Policies* (1990); Lou Cannon, *President Reagan: A Role of a Lifetime* (1991); Ronnie Dugger, *On Reagan: The Man and His Presidency* (1983); Fred I. Greenstein, ed., *The Reagan Presidency: An Early Assessment* (1983); Godfrey Hodgson, *The World Turned Right Side Up: A History of the Conservative Ascendency in America* (1997); Haynes Johnson, *Sleepwalking Through History: America Through the Reagan Years* (1991); William E. Pemberton, *Exit with Honor: The Life and Presidency of Ronald Reagan* (1998); Garry Wills, *Reagan's America: Innocents at Home* (1985).

The Bush Presidency

Colin Campbell, S.J. and Bert A. Rockman, eds., *The Bush Presidency: First Appraisals* (1991); Herbert S. Parmet, *George Bush: The Life of a Lone Star Yankee* (1997).

The Decline of Social Reform

Rodolfo Acuña, *Occupied America: A History of Chicanos,* third ed. (1988); Stephen Cornell, *The Return of the Native: American Indian Political Resurgence* (1988); Susan Faludi, *Backlash: The Undeclared War Against American Women* (1991); John Hope Franklin and Alfred A. Moss, Jr., *From Slavery to Freedom: A History of African Americans,* seventh ed. (1994); David G. Gutiérrez, *Walls and Mirrors: Mexican Americans, Mexican Immigrants, and the Politics of Identity* (1995); Jacqueline Jones, *Labor of Love, Labor of Sorrow: Black Women, Work, and the Family from Slavery to the Present* (1985); Peter Skerry, *Mexican Americans: The Ambivalent Minority* (1993); Studs Terkel, *Race: How Blacks and Whites Think and Feel About the American Obsession* (1992); Stephan Thernstrom and Abigail Thernstrom, *America in Black and White: One Nation, Indivisible* (1997); David Hurst Thomas, Jay Miller, Richard White, Peter Nabokov, Philip J. Deloria, *The Native Americans: An Illustrated History* (1993).

The Economy

William Bamberger and Cathy N. Davidson, *Closing: The Life and Death of an American Factory* (1998); Kathryn Marie Dudley, *The End of the Line: Lost Jobs, New Lives in Postindustrial America* (1994); Christopher Jencks, *The Homeless* (1994); Jacqueline Jones, *The Dispossessed: America's Underclasses from the Civil War to the Present* (1992) and *American Work: Four Centuries of Black and White Labor* (1998); Katherine S. Newman, *Falling from Grace: The Experience of Downward Mobility in the American Middle Class* (1988); Kevin P. Phillips, *The Politics of Rich and Poor: Wealth and the American Electorate in the Reagan Aftermath* (1990); Juliet B. Schor, *The Overworked American: The Unexpected Decline of Leisure* (1991); John C. Teaford, *Cities of the Heartland: The Rise and Fall of the Industrial Midwest* (1993).

Unionization

Richard B. Freeman and James L. Medoff, *What Do Unions Do?* (1984); Arthur B. Shostak, *Robust Unionism: Innovations in the Labor Movement* (1991).

The West

Carl Abbott, *The Metropolitan Frontier: Cities in the Modern American West* (1993); John M. Findlay, *Magic Lands: Western Cityscapes and American Culture After 1940* (1992); Timothy Egan, *Lasso the Wind: Away to the New West* (1998); William G. Robbins, *Colony and Empire: The Capitalist Transformation of the American West* (1994); Richard White, *"It's Your Misfortune and None of My Own": A New History of the American West* (1991).

Immigration

Roger Daniels, *Coming to America: A History of Immigration and Ethnicity in American Life* (1990); David M. Reimers, *Still the Golden Door: The Third World Comes to America* (1985); Paul James Rutledge, *The Vietnamese Experience in America* (1992); Al Santoli, *New Americans: An Oral History: Immigrants and Refugees in the U.S. Today* (1988); Ronald Takaki, *A Different Mirror: A History of Multicultural America* (1993) and *A Larger Memory: A History of Our Diversity, With Voices* (1998); Reed Ueda, *Postwar Immigrant America: A Social History* (1994).

Foreign Affairs

Paul Kennedy, *The Rise and Fall of the Great Powers: Economic Change and Military Conflict from 1500 to 2000* (1987); Walter LaFeber, *America, Russia, and the Cold War, 1945–1992,* seventh ed. (1993) and *Inevitable Revolutions: The United States in Central America* (1983); Robert Scheer,

With Enough Shovels: Reagan, Bush & Nuclear War (1982); Ronald Steel, *Temptations of a Superpower* (1995); Strobe Talbott, *The Russians and Reagan* (1984).

Fiction

Sherman Alexie, *The Lone Ranger and Tonto Fistfight in Heaven* (1993); Tim O'Brien, *The Nuclear Age* (1985); Anne Tyler, *Dinner at the Homesick Restaurant* (1982); Tom Wolfe, *The Bonfire of the Vanities* (1987).

Appendix

❖❖❖❖❖

The Declaration of Independence In Congress, July 4, 1776

THE UNANIMOUS DECLARATION OF THE THIRTEEN UNITED STATES OF AMERICA

When, in the course of human events, it becomes necessary for one people to dissolve the political bonds which have connected them with another, and to assume, among the powers of the earth, the separate and equal station to which the laws of nature and of nature's God entitle them, a decent respect to the opinions of mankind requires that they should declare the causes which impel them to the separation.

We hold these truths to be self-evident: That all men are created equal; that they are endowed by their Creator with certain unalienable rights; that among these are life, liberty, and the pursuit of happiness; that, to secure these rights, governments are instituted among men, deriving their just powers from the consent of the governed; that whenever any form of government becomes destructive of these ends, it is the right of the people to alter or to abolish it, and to institute new government, laying its foundation on such principles, and organizing its powers in such form, as to them shall seem most likely to effect their safety and happiness. Prudence, indeed, will dictate that governments long established should not be changed for light and transient causes; and accordingly all experience hath shown that mankind are more disposed to suffer, while evils are sufferable, than to right themselves by abolishing the forms to which they are accustomed. But when a long train of abuses and usurpations, pursuing invariably the same object, evinces a design to reduce them under absolute depotism, it is their right, it is their duty, to throw off such government, and to provide new guards for their future security. Such has been the patient sufferance of these colonies; and such is now the necessity which constrains them to alter their former systems of government. The history of the present King of Great Britain is a history of repeated injuries and usurpations, all having in direct object the establishment of an absolute tyranny over these states. To prove this, let facts be submitted to a candid world.

He has refused his assent to laws, the most wholesome and necessary for the public good.

He has forbidden his governors to pass laws of immediate and pressing importance, unless suspended in their operation till his assent should be obtained; and, when so suspended, he has utterly neglected to attend to them.

He has refused to pass other laws for the accommodation of large districts of people, unless those people would relinquish the right of representation in the legislature, a right inestimable to them, and formidable to tyrants only.

He has called together legislative bodies at places unusual, uncomfortable, and distant from the depository of their public records, for the sole purpose of fatiguing them into compliance with his measures.

He has dissolved representative houses repeatedly, for opposing, with manly firmness, his invasions on the rights of the people.

He has refused for a long time, after such dissolutions, to cause others to be elected; whereby the legislative powers, incapable of annihilation, have returned to the people at large for their exercise; the state remaining, in the mean time, exposed to all the dangers of invasions from without and convulsions within.

He has endeavored to prevent the population of these states; for that purpose obstructing the laws for naturalization of foreigners; refusing to pass others to encourage their migration hither, and raising the conditions of new appropriations of lands.

He has obstructed the administration of justice, by refusing his assent to laws for establishing judiciary powers.

He has made judges dependent on his will alone, for the tenure of their offices, and the amount and payment of their salaries.

He has erected a multitude of new offices, and sent hither swarms of officers to harass our people and eat out their substance.

He has kept among us, in times of peace, standing armies, without the consent of our legislatures.

He has affected to render the military independent of, and superior to, the civil power.

He has combined with others to subject us to a jurisdiction foreign to our constitution, and unacknowledged by our laws, giving his assent to their acts of pretended legislation:

For quartering large bodies of armed troops among us;

For protecting them, by a mock trial, from punishment for any murder which they should commit on the inhabitants of these states;

For cutting off our trade with all parts of the world;

For imposing taxes on us without our consent;

For depriving us, in many cases, of the benefits of trial by jury;

For transporting us beyond seas, to be tried for pretended offenses;

For abolishing the free system of English laws in a neighboring province, establishing therein an arbitrary government, and enlarging its boundaries, so as to render it at once an example and fit instrument for introducing the same absolute rule into these colonies;

For taking away our charters abolishing our most valuable laws, and altering fundamentally the forms of our governments;

For suspending our own legislatures, and declaring themselves invested with power to legislate for us in all cases whatsoever.

He has abdicated government here, by declaring us out of his protection and waging war against us.

He has plundered our seas, ravaged our coasts, burned our towns, and destroyed the lives of our people.

He is at this time transporting large armies of foreign mercenaries to complete the works of death, desolation, and tyranny already begun with circumstances of cruelty and perfidy scarcely paralleled in the most barbarous ages, and totally unworthy the head of a civilized nation.

He has constrained our fellow-citizens, taken captive on the high seas, to bear arms against their country, to become the executioners of their friends and brethren, or to fall themselves by their hands.

He has excited domestic insurrection among us, and has endeavored to bring on the inhabitants of our frontiers the merciless Indian savages, whose known rule of warfare is an undistinguished destruction of all ages, sexes, and conditions.

In every stage of these oppressions we have petitioned for redress in the most humble terms; our repeated petitions have been answered only by repeated injury. A prince, whose character is thus marked by every act which may define a tyrant, is unfit to be the ruler of a free people.

Nor have we been wanting in our attentions to our British brethren. We have warned them, from time to time, of attempts by their legislature to extend an unwarrantable jurisdiction over us. We have reminded them of the circumstances of our emigration and settlement here. We have appealed to their native justice and magnanimity; and we have conjured them, by the ties of our common kindred, to disavow these usurpations, which would inevitably interrupt our connections and correspondence. They, too, have been deaf to the voice of justice and of consanguinity. We must, therefore, acquiesce in the necessity which denounces our separation, and hold them, as we hold the rest of mankind, enemies in war, in peace friends.

We, therefore, the representatives of the United States of America, in General Congress assembled, appealing to the Supreme Judge of the world for the rectitude of our intentions, do, in the name and by the authority of the good people of these colonies, solemnly publish and declare, that these United Colonies are, and of right, ought to be, FREE AND INDEPENDENT STATES; that they are absolved from all allegiance to the British crown, and that all political connection between them and the state of Great Britain is, and ought to be, totally dissolved; and that, as free and independent states, they have full power to levy war, conclude peace, contract alliances, establish commerce, and do all other acts and things which independent states may of right do. And for the support of this declaration, with a firm reliance on the protection of Devine Providence, we mutually pledge to each other our lives, our fortunes, and our sacred honor.

JOHN HANCOCK

BUTTON GWENNETT	THS. NELSON, JR.	RICHD. STOCKTON
LYMAN HALL	FRANCIS LIGHTFOOT LEE	JNO. WITHERSPOON
GEO. WALTON	CARTER BRAXTON	FRAS. HOPKINSON
WM. HOOPER	ROBT. MORRIS	JOHN HART
JOSEPH HEWES	BENJAMIN RUSH	ABRA. CLARK
JOHN PENN	BENJA. FRANKLIN	JOSIAH BARTLETT
EDWARD RUTLEDGE	JOHN MORTON	WM. WHIPPLE
THOS. HEYWARD, JUNR.	GEO. CLYMER	SAML. ADAMS
THOMAS LYNCH, JUNR.	JAS. SMITH	JOHN ADAMS
ARTHUR MIDDLETON	GEO. TAYLOR	ROBT. TREAT PAINE
SAMUEL CHASE	JAMES WILSON	ELBRIDGE GERRY
WM. PACA	GEO. ROSS	STEP. HOPKINS
THOS. STONE	CAESAR RODNEY	WILLIAM ELLERY
CHARLES CARROLL OF CARROLLTON	GEO. READ	ROGER SHERMAN
GEORGE WYTHE	THO. MiKEAN	SAMiEL. HUNTINGTON
RICHARD HENRY LEE	WM. FLOYD	WM. WILLIAMS
TH. JEFFERSON	PHIL. LIVINGSTON	OLIVER WOLCOTT
BENJA. HARRISON	FRANS. LEWIS	MATHEW THORNTON
	LEWIS MORRIS	

The Constitution of the United States of America

PREAMBLE

We the People of the United States, in Order to form a more perfect Union, establish Justice, insure domestic Tranquility, provide for the common defence, promote the general Welfare, and secure the Blessings of Liberty to ourselves and our Posterity, do ordain and establish this Constitution for the United States of America.

ARTICLE I.

Section 1 All legislative Powers herein granted shall be vested in a Congress of the United States, which shall consist of a Senate and House of Representatives.

Section 2 The House of Representatives shall be composed of Members chosen every second Year by the People of the several States, and the Electors in each State shall have the Qualifications requisite for Electors of the most numerous Branch of the State Legislature.

No Person shall be a Representative who shall not have attained to the Age of twenty five Years, and been seven Years a Citizen of the United States, and who shall not, when elected, be an Inhabitant of that State in which he shall be chosen.

Representatives and direct Taxes shall be apportioned among the several States which may be included within this Union, according to their respective Numbers, *which shall be determined by adding to the whole Number of free Persons, including those bound to Service for a Term of Years, and excluding Indians not taxed, three fifths of all other Persons.* The actual Enumeration shall be made within three Years after the first Meeting of the Congress of the United States, and within every subsequent Term of ten Years, in such Manner as they shall by Law direct. The Number of Representatives shall not exceed one for every thirty Thousand, but each State shall have at Least one Representative; *and until such enumeration shall be made, the State of New Hampshire shall be entitled to chuse three, Massachusetts eight, Rhode-Island and Providence Plantations one, Connecticut five, New-York six, New Jersey four, Pennsylvania eight, Delaware one, Maryland six, Virginia ten, North Carolina five, South Carolina five, and Georgia three.*

When vacancies happen in the Representation from any State, the Executive Authority thereof shall issue Writs of Election to fill such Vacancies.

The House of Representatives shall chuse their Speaker and other Officers; and shall have the sole Power of Impeachment.

Section 3 The Senate of the United States shall be composed of two Senators from each State, chosen by the Legislature thereof, for six Years; and each Senator shall have one Vote.

Immediately after they shall be assembled in Consequence of the first Election, they shall be divided as equally as may be into three Classes. The Seats of the Senators of the first Class shall be vacated at the Expiration of the second Year, of the second Class at the Expiration of the fourth Year, and of the third Class at the Expiration of the sixth Year, so that one third may be chosen every second Year; and if Vacancies happen by Resignation, or otherwise, during the Recess of the Legislature of any State, the Executive thereof may make temporary Appointments until the next Meeting of the Legislature, which shall then fill such Vacancies.

No Person shall be a Senator who shall not have attained to the Age of thirty Years, and been nine Years a Citizen of the United States, and who shall not, when elected, be an Inhabitant of that State for which he shall be chosen.

The Vice President of the United States shall be President of the Senate, but shall have no Vote, unless they be equally divided.

The Senate shall choose their other Officers, and also a President *pro tempore*, in the Absence of the Vice President, or when he shall exercise the Office of President of the United States.

The Senate shall have the sole Power to try all Impeachments. When sitting for that Purpose, they shall be on Oath or Affirmation. When the President of the United States is tried the Chief Justice shall preside: And no Person shall be convicted without the Concurrence of two thirds of the Members present.

Judgment in Cases of Impeachment shall not extend further than to removal from Office, and disqualification to hold and enjoy any Office of honor, Trust or Profit under the United States: but the Party convicted shall nevertheless be liable and subject to Indictment, Trial, Judgment and Punishment, according to Law.

Section 4   The Times, Places and Manner of holding Elections for Senators and Representatives, shall be prescribed in each State by the Legislature thereof; but the Congress may at any time by Law make or alter such Regulations, except as to the Places of chusing Senators.

The Congress shall assemble at least once in every Year, and such Meeting *shall be on the first Monday in December, unless they shall by Law appoint a different Day.*

Section 5   Each House shall be the Judge of the Elections, Returns and Qualifications of its own Members, and a Majority of each shall constitute a Quorum to do Business; but a smaller Number may adjourn from day to day, and may be authorized to compel the Attendance of absent Members, in such Manner, and under such Penalties as each House may provide.

Each House may determine the Rules of its Proceedings, punish its Members for disorderly Behaviour, and, with the Concurrence of two thirds, expel a Member.

Each House shall keep a Journal of its Proceedings, and from time to time publish the same, excepting such Parts as may in their Judgment require Secrecy; and the Yeas and Nays of the Members of either House on any question shall, at the Desire of one fifth of those Present, be entered on the Journal.

Neither House, during the Session of Congress, shall, without the Consent of the other, adjourn for more than three days, nor to any other Place than that in which the two Houses shall be sitting.

Section 6   The Senators and Representatives shall receive a Compensation for their Services, to be ascertained by Law, and paid out of the Treasury of the United States. They shall in all Cases, except Treason, Felony and Breach of the Peace, be privileged from Arrest during their Attendance at the Session of their respective Houses, and in going to and returning from the same; and for any Speech or Debate in either House, they shall not be questioned in any other Place.

No Senator or Representative shall, during the Time for which he was elected, be appointed to any civil Office under the Authority of the United States, which shall have been created, or the Emoluments whereof shall have been encreased during such time; and no Person holding any Office under the United States, shall be a Member of either House during his Continuance in Office.

Section 7 All Bills for raising Revenue shall originate in the House of Representatives; but the Senate may propose or concur with Amendments as on other Bills.

Every Bill which shall have passed the House of Representatives and the Senate, shall, before it become a Law, be presented to the President of the United States; If he approve he shall sign it, but if not he shall return it, with his Objections to that House in which it shall have originated, who shall enter the Objections at large on their Journal, and proceed to reconsider it. If after such Reconsideration two thirds of that House shall agree to pass the Bill, it shall be sent, together with the Objections, to the other House, by which it shall likewise be reconsidered, and if approved by two thirds of that House, it shall become a Law. But in all such Cases the Votes of both Houses shall be determined by yeas and Nays, and the Names of the Persons voting for and against the Bill shall be entered on the Journal of each House respectively. If any Bill shall not be returned by the President within ten Days (Sundays excepted) after it shall have been presented to him, the Same shall be a Law, in like Manner as if he had signed it, unless the Congress by their Adjournment prevent its Return, in which Case it shall not be a Law.

Every Order, Resolution, or Vote to which the Concurrence of the Senate and House of Representatives may be necessary (except on a question of Adjournment) shall be presented to the President of the United States; and before the Same shall take Effect, shall be approved by him, or being disapproved by him, shall be repassed by two thirds of the Senate and House of Representatives, according to the Rules and Limitations prescribed in the Case of a Bill.

Section 8 The Congress shall have Power:

To lay and collect Taxes, Duties, Imposts and Excises, to pay the Debts and provide for the common Defence and general Welfare of the United States; but all Duties, Imposts and Excises shall be uniform throughout the United States;

To borrow Money on the credit of the United States;

To regulate Commerce with foreign Nations, and among the several States, and with the Indian Tribes;

To establish an uniform Rule of Naturalization, and uniform Laws on the subject of Bankruptcies throughout the United States;

To coin Money, regulate the Value thereof, and of foreign Coin, and fix the Standard of Weights and Measures;

To provide for the Punishment of counterfeiting the Securities and current Coin of the United States;

To establish Post Offices and post Roads;

To promote the Progress of Science and useful Arts, by securing for limited Times to Authors and Inventors the exclusive Right to their respective Writings and Discoveries;

To constitute Tribunals inferior to the supreme Court;

To define and punish Piracies and Felonies committed on the high Seas, and Offences against the Law of Nations;

To declare War, grant Letters of Marque and Reprisal, and make Rules concerning Captures on Land and Water;

To raise and support Armies, but no Appropriation of Money to that Use shall be for a longer Term than two Years;

To provide and maintain a Navy;

To make Rules for the Government and Regulation of the land and naval Forces;

To provide for calling forth the Militia to execute the Laws of the Union, suppress Insurrections and repel Invasions;

To provide for organizing, arming, and disciplining, the Militia, and for governing such Part of them as may be employed in the Service of the United States, reserving to the States respectively, the Appointment of the Officers, and the Authority of training the Militia according to the discipline prescribed by Congress;

To exercise exclusive Legislation in all Cases whatsoever, over such District (not exceeding ten Miles square) as may, by Cession of particular States, and the Acceptance of Congress, become the Seat of the Government of the United States, and to exercise like Authority over all Places purchased by the Consent of the Legislature of the State in which the Same shall be, for the Erection of Forts, Magazines, Arsenals, dock-Yards, and other needful Buildings;—And

To make all Laws which shall be necessary and proper for carrying into Execution the foregoing Powers, and all other Powers vested by this Constitution in the Government of the United States, or in any Department or Officer thereof.

Section 9   *The Migration or Importation of such Persons as any of the States now existing shall think proper to admit, shall not be prohibited by the Congress prior to the Year one thousand eight hundred and eight, but a Tax or duty may be imposed on such Importation, not exceeding ten dollars for each Person.*

The Privilege of the Writ of Habeas Corpus shall not be suspended, unless when in Cases of Rebellion or Invasion the public Safety may require it.

No Bill of Attainder or ex post facto Law shall be passed.

No Capitation, or other direct, Tax shall be laid, unless in Proportion to the Census or Enumeration herein before directed to be taken.

No Tax or Duty shall be laid on Articles exported from any State.

No Preference shall be given by any Regulation of Commerce or Revenue to the Ports of one State over those of another: nor shall Vessels bound to, or from, one State, be obliged to enter, clear, or pay Duties in another.

No Money shall be drawn from the Treasury, but in Consequence of Appropriations made by Law; and a regular Statement and Account of the Receipts and Expenditures of all public Money shall be published from time to time.

No Title of Nobility shall be granted by the United States: And no Person holding any Office of Profit or Trust under them, shall, without the Consent of the Congress, accept of any present, Emolument, Office, or Title, of any kind whatever, from any King, Prince, or foreign State.

Section 10   No State shall enter into any Treaty, Alliance, or Confederation; grant Letters of Marque and Reprisal; coin Money; emit Bills of Credit; make any Thing but gold and silver Coin a Tender in Payment of Debts; pass any Bill of Attainder, ex post facto Law, or Law impairing the Obligation of Contracts, or grant any Title of Nobility.

No State shall, without the Consent of the Congress, lay any Imposts or Duties on Imports or Exports, except what may be absolutely necessary for executing it's inspection Laws: and the net Produce of all Duties and Imposts, laid by any State on Imports or Exports, shall be for the Use of the Treasury of the United States; and all such Laws shall be subject to the Revision and Controul of the Congress.

No State shall, without the Consent of Congress, lay any Duty of Tonnage, keep Troops, or Ships of War in time of Peace, enter into any Agreement or Compact with another State, or with a foreign Power, or engage in War, unless actually invaded, or in such imminent Danger as will not admit of delay.

ARTICLE II.

Section 1   The executive Power shall be vested in a President of the United States of America. He shall hold his Office during the Term of four Years, and, together with the Vice President, chosen for the same Term, be elected, as follows

Each State shall appoint, in such Manner as the Legislature thereof may direct, a Number of Electors, equal to the whole Number of Senators and Representatives to which the State may be entitled in the Congress: but no Senator or Representative, or Person holding an Office of Trust or Profit under the United States, shall be appointed an Elector.

The Electors shall meet in their respective States, and vote by Ballot for two Persons, of whom one at least shall not be an Inhabitant of the same State with themselves. And they shall make a List of all the Persons voted for, and of the Number of Votes for each; which List they shall sign and certify, and transmit sealed to the Seat of Government of the United States, directed to the President of the Senate. The President of the Senate shall, in the Presence of the Senate and House of Representatives, open all the Certificates, and the Votes shall then be counted. The Person having the greatest Number of Votes shall be the President, if such Number be a Majority of the whole Number of Electors appointed; and if there be more than one who have such Majority, and have an equal Number of Votes, then the House of Representatives shall immediately chuse by Ballot one of them for President; and if no Person have a Majority, then from the five highest on the List the said House shall in like Manner chuse the President. But in chusing the President, the Votes shall be taken by States, the Representation from each State having one Vote; A quorum for this Purpose shall consist of a Member or Members from two thirds of the States, and a Majority of all the States shall be necessary to a Choice. In every Case, after the Choice of the President, the Person having the greatest Number of Votes of the Electors shall be the Vice President. But if there should remain two or more who have equal Votes, the Senate shall chuse from them by Ballot the Vice President.

The Congress may determine the Time of chusing the Electors, and the Day on which they shall give their Votes; which Day shall be the same throughout the United States.

No Person except a natural born Citizen, *or a Citizen of the United States, at the time of the Adoption of this Constitution,* shall be eligible to the Office of President; neither shall any Person be eligible to that Office who shall not have attained to the Age of thirty five Years, and been fourteen Years a Resident within the United States.

In Case of the Removal of the President from Office, or of his Death, Resignation, or Inability to discharge the Powers and Duties of the said Office, the Same shall devolve on the Vice President, and the Congress may by Law provide for the Case of Removal, Death, Resignation or Inability, both of the President and Vice President declaring what Officer shall then act as President, and such Officer shall act accordingly, until the Disability be removed, or a President shall be elected.

The President shall, at stated Times, receive for his Services, a Compensation, which shall neither be encreased nor diminished during the Period for which he shall have been elected, and he shall not receive within that Period any other Emolument from the United States, or any of them.

Before he enter on the Execution of his Office, he shall take the following Oath or Affirmation: "I do solemnly swear (or affirm) that I will faithfully execute the Office of President of the United States, and will to the best of my Ability, preserve, protect and defend the Constitution of the United States."

Section 2 The President shall be Commander in Chief of the Army and Navy of the United States, and of the Militia of the several States, when called into the actual Service of the United States; he may require the Opinion, in writing, of the principal Officer in each of the executive Departments, upon any Subject relating to the Duties of their respective Offices, and he shall have Power to grant Reprieves and Pardons for Offences against the United States, except in Cases of Impeachment.

He shall have Power, by and with the Advice and Consent of the Senate, to make Treaties, provided two thirds of the Senators present concur; and he shall nominate, and by and with the Advice and Consent of the Senate, shall appoint Ambassadors, other public Ministers and Consuls, Judges of the supreme Court, and all other Officers of the United States, whose Appointments are not herein otherwise provided for, and which shall be established by Law: but the Congress may by Law vest the Appointment of such inferior Officers, as they think proper, in the President alone, in the Courts of Law, or in the Heads of Departments.

The President shall have Power to fill up all Vacancies that may happen during the Recess of the Senate, by granting Commissions which shall expire at the End of their next Session.

Section 3 He shall from time to time give to the Congress Information of the State of the Union, and recommend to their Consideration such Measures as he shall judge necessary and expedient; he may, on extraordinary Occasions, convene both Houses, or either of them, and in Case of Disagreement between them, with Respect to the Time of Adjournment, he may adjourn them to such Time as he shall think proper; he shall receive Ambassadors and other public Ministers; he shall take Care that the Laws be faithfully executed, and shall Commission all the Officers of the United States.

Section 4 The President, Vice President and all civil Officers of the United States, shall be removed from Office on Impeachment for, and Conviction of, Treason, Bribery, or other high Crimes and Misdemeanors.

ARTICLE III.

Section 1 The judicial Power of the United States, shall be vested in one supreme Court, and in such inferior Courts as the Congress may from time to time ordain and establish. The Judges, both of the supreme and inferior Courts, shall hold their Offices during good Behaviour, and shall, at stated Times, receive for their Services, a Compensation which shall not be diminished during their Continuance in Office.

Section 2   The judicial Power shall extend to all Cases, in Law and Equity, arising under this Constitution, the Laws of the United States, and Treaties made, or which shall be made, under their Authority;—to all Cases affecting Ambassadors, other public Ministers and Consuls;— to all Cases of admiralty and maritime Jurisdiction;—to Controversies to which the United States shall be a Party;—to Controversies between two or more States;—*between a State and Citizens of another State;*—between Citizens of different States;—between Citizens of the same State claiming Lands under Grants of different States, and between a State, or the Citizens thereof, and foreign States, Citizens or Subjects.

In all Cases affecting Ambassadors, other public Ministers and Consuls, and those in which a State shall be Party, the supreme Court shall have original Jurisdiction. In all the other Cases before mentioned, the supreme Court shall have appellate Jurisdiction, both as to Law and Fact, with such Exceptions, and under such Regulations as the Congress shall make.

The Trial of all Crimes, except in Cases of Impeachment, shall be by Jury; and such Trial shall be held in the State where the said Crimes shall have been committed; but when not committed within any State, the Trial shall be at such Place or Places as the Congress may by Law have directed.

Section 3   Treason against the United States, shall consist only in levying War against them, or in adhering to their Enemies, giving them Aid and Comfort. No Person shall be convicted of Treason unless on the Testimony of two Witnesses to the same overt Act, or on Confession in open Court.

The Congress shall have Power to declare the Punishment of Treason, but no Attainder of Treason shall work Corruption of Blood, or Forfeiture except during the Life of the Person attainted.

ARTICLE IV

Section 1   Full Faith and Credit shall be given in each State to the public Acts, Records, and judicial Proceedings of every other State. And the Congress may by general Laws prescribe the Manner in which such Acts, Records and Proceedings shall be proved, and the Effect thereof.

Section 2   The Citizens of each State shall be entitled to all Privileges and Immunities of Citizens in the several States.

A Person charged in any State with Treason, Felony, or other Crime, who shall flee from Justice, and be found in another State, shall on Demand of the executive Authority of the State from which he fled, be delivered up, to be removed to the State having Jurisdiction of the Crime.

No Person held to Service or Labour in one State, under the Laws thereof, escaping into another, shall, in Consequence of any Law or Regulation therein, be discharged from such Service or Labour, but shall be delivered up on Claim of the Party to whom such Service or Labour may be due.

Section 3   New States may be admitted by the Congress into this Union; but no new State shall be formed or erected within the Jurisdiction of any other State; nor any State be formed by the Junction of two or more States, or Parts of States, without the Consent of the Legislatures of the States concerned as well as of the Congress.

The Congress shall have Power to dispose of and make all needful Rules and Regulations respecting the Territory or other Property belonging to the United States; and nothing in this Constitution shall be so construed as to Prejudice any Claims of the United States, or of any particular State.

Section 4   The United States shall guarantee to every State in this Union a Republican Form of Government, and shall protect each of them against Invasion; and on Application of the Legislature, or of the Executive (when the Legislature cannot be convened) against domestic Violence.

ARTICLE V

The Congress, whenever two thirds of both Houses shall deem it necessary, shall propose Amendments to this Constitution, or, on the Application of the Legislatures of two thirds of the several States, shall call a Convention for proposing Amendments, which, in either Case, shall be valid to all Intents and Purposes, as Part of this Constitution, when ratified by the Legislatures of three fourths of the several States, or by Conventions in three fourths thereof, as the one or the other Mode of Ratification may be proposed by the Congress; Provided *that no Amendment which may be made prior to the Year One thousand eight hundred and eight shall in any Manner affect the first and fourth Clauses in the Ninth Section of the first Article; and* that no State, without its Consent, shall be deprived of its equal Suffrage in the Senate.

ARTICLE VI

All Debts contracted and Engagements entered into, before the Adoption of this Constitution, shall be as valid against the United States under this Constitution, as under the Confederation.

This Constitution, and the Laws of the United States which shall be made in Pursuance thereof; and all Treaties made or which shall be made, under the Authority of the United States, shall be the supreme Law of the Land; and the Judges in every State shall be bound thereby, any Thing in the Constitution or Laws of any State to the Contrary notwithstanding.

The Senators and Representatives before mentioned, and the Members of the several State Legislatures, and all executive and judicial Officers, both of the United States and of the several States, shall be bound by Oath or Affirmation, to support this Constitution; but no religious Test shall ever be required as a Qualification to any Office or public Trust under the United States.

ARTICLE VII

The Ratification of the Conventions of nine States, shall be sufficient for the Establishment of this Constitution between the States so ratifying the Same.

Done in Convention by the Unanimous Consent of the States present the Seventeenth Day of September in the Year of our Lord one thousand seven hundred and Eighty seven and of the Independence of the United States of America the Twelfth. IN WITNESS whereof We have hereunto subscribed our Names,

GEORGE WASHINGTON,
President and Deputy from Virginia

North Carolina
WILLIAM BLOUNT
RICHARD DOBBS
SPRAIGHT
HU WILLIAMSON

Pennsylvania
BENJAMIN FRANKLIN
THOMAS MIFFLIN
ROVERT MORRIS
GEORGE CLYMER
THOMAS FITZSIMONS
JARED INGERSOLL
JAMES WILSON
GOUVERNEUR MORRIS

Delaware
GEORGE READ
GUNNING BEDFORD, JR.
JOHN DICKINSON
RICHARD BASSETT
JACOB BROOM

South Carolina
J. RUTLEDGE
CHARLES C. PINCKNEY
PIERCE BUTLER

Virginia
JOHN BLAIR
JAMES MADISON, JR.

New Jersey
WILLIAM LIVINGSTON
DAVID BREARLEY
WILLIAM PATERSON
JONATHAN DAYTON

Maryland
JAMES MCHENRY
DANIEL OF ST. THOMAS
JENIFER
DANIEL CARROLL

Massachusetts
NATHANIEL GORHAM
RUFUS KING

Connecticut
WILLIAM S. JOHNSON
ROGER SHERMAN

New York
ALEXANDER HAMILTON

New Hampshire
JOHN LANGDON
NICHOLAS GILMAN

Georgia
WILLIAM FEW
ABRAHAM BALDWIN

AMENDMENTS TO THE CONSTITUTION*

*The first ten amendments (the Bill of Rights) were adopted in 1791.

Amendment I

Congress shall make no law respecting an establishment of religion, or prohibiting the free exercise thereof; or abridging the freedom of speech, or of the press; or the right of the people peaceably to assemble, and to petition the Government for a redress of grievances.

Amendment II

A well regulated Militia, being necessary to the security of a free State, the right of the people to keep and bear Arms, shall not be infringed.

Amendment III

No Soldier shall, in time of peace be quartered in any house, without the consent of the Owner, nor in time of war, but in a manner to be prescribed by law.

Amendment IV

The right of the people to be secure in their persons, houses, papers, and effects, against unreasonable searches and seizures, shall not be violated, and no Warrants shall issue, but upon probable cause, supported by Oath or affirmation, and particularly describing the place to be searched, and the persons or things to be seized.

Amendment V

No person shall be held to answer for a capital, or otherwise infamous crime, unless on a presentment or indictment of a Grand Jury, except in cases arising in the land or naval forces, or in the Militia, when in actual service in time of War or public danger; nor shall any person be subject for the same offence to be twice put in jeopardy of life or limb; nor shall be compelled in any criminal case to be a witness against himself, nor be deprived of life, liberty, or property, without due process of law; nor shall private property be taken for public use, without just compensation.

Amendment VI

In all criminal prosecutions, the accused shall enjoy the right to a speedy and public trial, by an impartial jury of the State and district wherein the crime shall have been committed, which district shall have been previously ascertained by law, and to be informed of the nature and cause of the accusation; to be confronted with the witnesses against him; to have compulsory process for obtaining witnesses in his favor, and to have the Assistance of Counsel for his defence.

Amendment VII

In Suits at common law, where the value in controversy shall exceed twenty dollars, the right of trial by jury shall be preserved, and no fact tried by a jury, shall be otherwise re-examined in any Court of the United States, than according to the rules of the common law.

Amendment VIII

Excessive bail shall not be required, nor excessive fines imposed, nor cruel and unusual punishments inflicted.

Amendment IX

The enumeration in the Constitution, of certain rights, shall not be construed to deny or disparage others retained by the people.

Amendment X

The powers not delegated to the United States by the Constitution, nor prohibited by it to the States, are reserved to the States respectively, or to the people.

Amendment XI [Adopted 1798]

The Judicial power of the United States shall not be construed to extend to any suit in law or equity, commenced or prosecuted against one of the United States by Citizens of another State, or by Citizens or Subjects of any Foreign State.

Amendment XII [Adopted 1804]

The Electors shall meet in their respective states, and vote by ballot for President and Vice-President, one of whom, at least, shall not be an inhabitant of the same state with themselves; they shall name in their ballots the person voted for as President, and in distinct ballots the person voted for as Vice-President, and they shall make distinct lists of all persons voted for as President, and of all persons voted for as Vice-President, and of the number of votes for each, which list they shall sign and certify, and transmit sealed to the seat of the government of the United States, directed to the President of the Senate;—The President of the Senate shall, in the presence of the Senate and House of Representatives, open all the certificates and the votes shall then be counted;—The person having the greatest number of votes for President, shall be the President, if such number be a majority of the whole number of Electors appointed; and if no person have such majority, then from the persons having the highest numbers not exceeding three on the list of those voted for as President, the House of Representatives shall choose immediately, by ballot, the President. But in choosing the President, the votes shall be taken by states, the representation from each state having one vote; a quorum for this purpose shall consist of a member or members from two thirds of the states, and a majority of all the states shall be necessary to a choice. And if the House of Representatives shall not choose a President whenever the right of choice shall devolve upon them, before *the fourth day of March* next following, then the Vice-President shall act as President, as in the case of the death or other constitutional disability of the President.

The person having the greatest number of votes as Vice-President, shall be the Vice-President, if such number be a majority of the whole number of Electors appointed, and if no person have a majority, then from the two highest numbers on the list, the Senate shall choose the Vice-President; a quorum for the purpose shall consist of two thirds of the whole number of Senators, and a majority of the whole number shall be necessary to a choice. But no person constitutionally ineligible to the office of President shall be eligible to that of Vice-President of the United States.

Amendment XIII [Adopted 1865]

Section 1   Neither slavery nor involuntary servitude, except as a punishment for crime whereof the party shall have been duly convicted, shall exist within the United States, or any place subject to their jurisdiction.

Section 2   Congress shall have power to enforce this article by appropriate legislation.

Amendment XIV [Adopted 1868]

Section 1   All persons born or naturalized in the United States, and subject to the jurisdiction thereof, are citizens of the United States and of the State wherein they reside. No State shall make or enforce any law which shall abridge the privileges or immunities of citizens of the United States; nor shall any State deprive any person of life, liberty, or property, without due process of law; nor deny to any person within its jurisdiction the equal protection of the laws.

Section 2   Representatives shall be apportioned among the several States according to their respective numbers, counting the whole number of persons in each State, excluding Indians not taxed. But when the right to vote at any election for the choice of electors for President and Vice-President of the United States, Representatives in Congress, the Executive and Judicial officers of a State, or the members of the Legislature thereof, is denied to any of the male inhabitants of such State, being twenty-one years of age, and citizens of the United States, or in any way abridged, except for participation in rebellion, or other crime, the basis of representation therein shall be reduced in the proportion which the number of such male citizens shall bear to the whole number of male citizens twenty-one years of age in such State.

Section 3   No person shall be a Senator or Representative in Congress, or elector of President and Vice-President, or hold any office, civil or military, under the United States, or under any State, who, having previously taken an oath, as a member of Congress, or as an officer of the United States, or as a member of any State legislature, or as an executive or judicial officer of any State, to support the Constitution of the United States, shall have engaged in insurrection or rebellion against the same, or given aid or comfort to the enemies thereof. But Congress may by a vote of two thirds of each House, remove such disability.

Section 4   The validity of the public debt of the United States, authorized by law, including debts incurred for payment of pensions and bounties for services in suppressing insurrection or rebellion, shall not be questioned. But neither the

United States nor any State shall assume or pay any debt or obligation incurred in aid of insurrection or rebellion against the United States, or any claim for the loss or emancipation of any slave; but all such debts, obligations and claims shall be held illegal and void.

Section 5   The Congress shall have power to enforce, by appropriate legislation, the provisions of this article.

Amendment XV [Adopted 1870]
Section 1   The right of citizens of the United States to vote shall not be denied or abridged by the United States or by any State on account of race, color, or previous condition of servitude.

Section 2   The Congress shall have power to enforce this article by appropriate legislation.

Amendment XVI [Adopted 1913]
The Congress shall have power to lay and collect taxes on incomes, from whatever source derived, without apportionment among the several States, and without regard to any census or enumeration.

Amendment XVII [Adopted 1913]
The Senate of the United States shall be composed of two Senators from each State, elected by the people thereof, for six years; and each Senator shall have one vote. The electors in each State shall have the qualifications requisite for electors of the most numerous branch of the State legislatures.

When vacancies happen in the representation of any State in the Senate, the executive authority of such State shall issue writs of election to fill such vacancies: *Provided,* That the legislature of any State may empower the executive thereof to make temporary appointments until the people fill the vacancies by election as the legislature may direct.

This amendment shall not be so construed as to affect the election or term of any Senator chosen before it becomes valid as part of the Constitution.

Amendment XVIII [Adopted 1919; Repealed 1933]
Section 1   After one year from the ratification of this article the manufacture, sale, or transportation of intoxicating liquors within, the importation thereof into, or the exportation thereof from the United States and all territory subject to the jurisdiction thereof for beverage purposes is hereby prohibited.

Section 2   The Congress and the several States shall have concurrent power to enforce this article by appropriate legislation.

Section 3   This article shall be inoperative unless it shall have been ratified as an amendment to the Constitution by the legislatures of the several States, as provided in the Constitution, within seven years from the date of the submission hereof to the States by the Congress.

Amendment XIX [Adopted 1920]
Section 1   The right of citizens of the United States to vote shall not be denied or abridged by the United States or by any State on account of sex.

Section 2 Congress shall have power to enforce this article by appropriate legislation.

Amendment XX [Adopted 1933]
Section 1 The terms of the President and Vice-President shall end at noon on the 20th day of January, and the terms of Senators and Representatives at noon on the third day of January, of the years in which such terms would have ended if this article had not been ratified; and the terms of their successors shall then begin.

Section 2 The Congress shall assemble at least once in every year, and such meeting shall begin at noon on the third day of January, unless they shall by law appoint a different day.

Section 3 If, at the time fixed for the beginning of the term of the President, the President elect shall have died, the Vice-President elect shall become President. If a President shall not have been chosen before the time fixed for the beginning of his term, or if the President elect shall have failed to qualify, then the Vice-President elect shall act as President until a President shall have qualified; and the Congress may by law provide for the case wherein neither a President elect nor a Vice-President elect shall have qualified, declaring who shall then act as President, or the manner in which one who is to act shall be selected, and such person shall act accordingly until a President or Vice-President shall have qualified.

Section 4 The Congress may by law provide for the case of the death of any of the persons from whom the House of Representatives may choose a President whenever the right of choice shall have devolved upon them, and for the case of the death of any of the persons from whom the Senate may choose a Vice-President whenever the right of choice shall have devolved upon them.

Section 5 Sections 1 and 2 shall take effect on the 15th day of October following the ratification of this article.

Section 6 This article shall be inoperative unless it shall have been ratified as an amendment to the Constitution by the legislatures of three fourths of the several States within seven years from the date of its submission.

Amendment XXI [Adopted 1933]
Section 1 The eighteenth article of amendment to the Constitution of the United States is hereby repealed.

Section 2 The transportation or importation into any State, Territory, or possession of the United States for delivery or use therein of intoxicating liquors, in violation of the laws thereof, is hereby prohibited.

Section 3 This article shall be inoperative unless it shall have been ratified as an amendment to the Constitution by conventions in the several States, as provided in the Constitution, within seven years from the date of the submission hereof to the States by the Congress.

Amendment XXII [Adopted 1951]
Section 1 No person shall be elected to the office of the President more than twice, and no person who has held the office of President, or acted as President, for

more than two years of a term to which some other person was elected President shall be elected to the office of the President more than once. But this Article shall not apply to any person holding the office of President when this Article was proposed by the Congress, and shall not prevent any person who may be holding the office of President, or acting as President, during the term within which this Article becomes operative from holding the office of President or acting as President during the remainder of such term.

Section 2   This article shall be inoperative unless it shall have been ratified as an amendment to the Constitution by the legislatures of three fourths of the several States within seven years from the date of its submission to the States by the Congress.

Amendment XXIII [Adopted 1961]
Section 1   The District constituting the seat of Government of the United States shall appoint in such manner as the Congress may direct:

A number of electors of President and Vice-President equal to the whole number of Senators and Representatives in Congress to which the District would be entitled if it were a State, but in no event more than the least populous State; they shall be in addition to those appointed by the States, but they shall be considered, for the purposes of the election of President and Vice-President, to be electors appointed by a State; and they shall meet in the District and perform such duties as provided by the twelfth article of amendment.

Section 2   The Congress shall have power to enforce this article by appropriate legislation.

Amendment XXIV [Adopted 1964]
Section 1   The right of citizens of the United States to vote in any primary or other election for President or Vice-President, for electors for President or Vice-President, or for Senator or Representative in Congress, shall not be denied or abridged by the United States or any State by reason of failure to pay any poll tax or other tax.

Section 2   The Congress shall have power to enforce this article by appropriate legislation.

Amendment XXV [Adopted 1967]
Section 1   In case of the removal of the President from office or his death or resignation, the Vice-President shall become President.

Section 2   Whenever there is a vacancy in the office of the Vice-President, the President shall nominate a Vice-President who shall take the office upon confirmation by a majority vote of both houses of Congress.

Section 3   Whenever the President transmits to the President pro tempore of the Senate and the Speaker of the House of Representatives his written declaration that he is unable to discharge the powers and duties of his office, and until he transmits to them a written declaration to the contrary, such powers and duties shall be discharged by the Vice-President as Acting President.

Section 4 Whenever the Vice-President and a majority of either the principal officers of the executive departments, or of such other body as Congress may by law provide, transmit to the President pro tempore of the Senate and the Speaker of the House of Representatives their written declaration that the President is unable to discharge the powers and duties of his office, the Vice-President shall immediately assume the powers and duties of the office as Acting President.

Thereafter, when the President transmits to the President pro tempore of the Senate and the Speaker of the House of Representatives his written declaration that no inability exists, he shall resume the powers and duties of his office unless the Vice-President and a majority of either the principal officers of the executive department, or of such other body as Congress may by law provide, transmit within four days to the President pro tempore of the Senate and the Speaker of the House of Representatives their written declaration that the President is unable to discharge the powers and duties of his office. Thereupon Congress shall decide the issue, assembling within 48 hours for that purpose if not in session. If the Congress, within 21 days after receipt of the latter written declaration, or, if Congress is not in session, within 21 days after Congress is required to assemble, determines by two-thirds vote of both houses that the President is unable to discharge the powers and duties of his office, the Vice-President shall continue to discharge the same as Acting President; otherwise, the President shall resume the powers and duties of his office.

Amendment XXVI [Adopted 1971]
Section 1 The right of citizens of the United States, who are eighteen years of age or older, to vote shall not be denied or abridged by the United States or any state on account of age.

Section 2 The Congress shall have power to enforce this article by appropriate legislation.

Amendment XXVII [Adopted 1992]
No law, varying the compensation for the services of Senators and Representatives, shall take effect until an election of Representatives have intervened.

PRESIDENTIAL ELECTIONS

Year	Candidates	Parties	Popular Vote	Electoral Vote	Voter Participation
1789	GEORGE WASHINGTON		*	69	
	John Adams			34	
	Others			35	
1792	GEORGE WASHINGTON		*	132	
	John Adams			77	
	George Clinton			50	
	Others			5	
1796	JOHN ADAMS	Federalist	*	71	
	Thomas Jefferson	Democratic-Republican		68	
	Thomas Pinckney	Federalist		59	
	Aaron Burr	Dem.-Rep.		30	
	Others			48	

Year	Candidates	Parties	Popular Vote	Electoral Vote	Voter Participation
1800	THOMAS JEFFERSON	Dem.-Rep.	*	73	
	Aaron Burr	Dem.-Rep.		73	
	C. C. Pinckney	Federalist		64	
	John Jay	Federalist		1	
1804	THOMAS JEFFERSON	Dem.-Rep.	*	162	
	C. C. Pinckney	Federalist		14	
1808	JAMES MADISON	Dem.-Rep.	*	122	
	C. C. Pinckney	Federalist		47	
	George Clinton	Dem.-Rep.		6	
1812	JAMES MADISON	Dem.-Rep.	*	128	
	De Witt Clinton	Federalist		89	
1816	JAMES MONROE	Dem.-Rep.	*	183	
	Rufus King	Federalist		34	
1820	JAMES MONROE	Dem.-Rep.	*	231	
	John Quincy Adams	Dem.-Rep.		1	
1824	JOHN Q. ADAMS	Dem.-Rep.	108,740 (10.5%)	84	26.9%
	Andrew Jackson	Dem.-Rep.	153,544 (43.1%)	99	
	William H. Crawford	Dem.-Rep.	46,618 (13.1%)	41	
	Henry Clay	Dem.-Rep.	47,136 (13.2%)	37	
1828	ANDREW JACKSON	Democratic	647,286 (56.0%)	178	57.6%
	John Quincy Adams	National Republican	508,064 (44.0%)	83	
1832	ANDREW JACKSON	Democratic	687,502 (55.0%)	219	55.4%
	Henry Clay	National Republican	530,189 (42.4%)	49	
	John Floyd	Independent		11	
	William Wirt	Anti-Mason	33,108 (2.6%)	7	
1836	MARTIN VAN BUREN	Democratic	765,483 (50.9%)	170	57.8%
	W. H. Harrison	Whig		73	
	Hugh L. White	Whig	739,795 (49.1%)	26	
	Daniel Webster	Whig		14	
	W. P. Magnum	Independent		11	
1840	WILLIAM H. HARRISON	Whig	1,274,624 (53.1%)	234	80.2%
	Martin Van Buren	Democratic	1,127,781 (46.9%)	60	
	J. G. Birney	Liberty	7069	—	
1844	JAMES K. POLK	Democratic	1,338,464 (49.6%)	170	78.9%
	Henry Clay	Whig	1,300,097 (48.1%)	105	
	J. G. Birney	Liberty	62,300 (2.3%)	—	
1848	ZACHARY TAYLOR	Whig	1,360,967 (47.4%)	163	72.7%
	Lewis Cass	Democratic	1,222,342 (42.5%)	127	
	Martin Van Buren	Free-Soil	291,263 (10.1%)	—	
1852	FRANKLIN PIERCE	Democratic	1,601,117 (50.9%)	254	69.6%
	Winfield Scott	Whig	1,385,453 (44.1%)	42	
	John P. Hale	Free-Soil	155,825 (5.0%)	—	
1856	JAMES BUCHANAN	Democratic	1,832,955 (45.3%)	174	78.9%
	John C. Fremont	Republican	1,339,932 (33.1%)	114	
	Millard Fillmore	American	871,731 (21.6%)	8	
1860	ABRAHAM LINCOLN	Republican	1,865,593 (39.8%)	180	81.2%
	Stephen A. Douglas	Democratic	1,382,713 (29.5%)	12	
	John C. Breckinridge	Democratic	848,356 (18.1%)	72	
	John Bell	Union	592,906 (12.6%)	39	

Year	Candidates	Parties	Popular Vote	Electoral Vote	Voter Participation
1864	ABRAHAM LINCOLN	Republican	2,213,655 (55.0%)	212	73.8%
	George B. McClellan	Democratic	1,805,237 (45.0%)	21	
1868	ULYSSES S. GRANT	Republican	3,012,833 (52.7%)	214	78.1%
	Horatio Seymour	Democratic	2,703,249 (47.3%)	80	
1872	ULYSSES S. GRANT	Republican	3,597,132 (55.6%)	286	71.3%
	Horace Greeley	Democratic; Liberal Republican	2,834,125 (43.9%)	66	
1876	RUTHERFORD B. HAYES	Republican	4,036,298 (48.0%)	185	81.8%
	Samuel J. Tilden	Democratic	4,300,590 (51.0%)	184	
1880	JAMES A. GARFIELD	Republican	4,454,416 (48.5%)	214	79.4%
	Winfield S. Hancock	Democratic	4,444,952 (48.1%)	155	
1884	GROVER CLEVELAND	Democratic	4,874,986 (48.5%)	219	77.5%
	James G. Blaine	Republican	4,851,981 (48.2%)	182	
1888	BENJAMIN HARRISON	Republican	5,439,853 (47.9%)	233	79.3%
	Grover Cleveland	Democratic	5,540,309 (48.6%)	168	
1892	GROVER CLEVELAND	Democratic	5,556,918 (46.1%)	277	74.7%
	Benjamin Harrison	Republican	5,176,108 (43.0%)	145	
	James B. Weaver	People's	1,041,028 (8.5%)	22	
1896	WILLIAM McKINLEY	Republican	7,104,779 (51.1%)	271	79.3%
	William J. Bryan	democratic People's	6,502,925 (47.7%)	176	
1900	WILLIAM McKINLEY	Republican	7,207,923 (51.7%)	292	73.2%
	William J. Bryan	Dem.-Populist	6,358,133 (45.5%)	155	
1904	THEODORE ROOSEVELT	Republican	7,623,486 (57.9%)	336	65.2%
	Alton B. Parker	Democratic	5,077,911 (37.6%)	140	
	Eugene V. Debs	Socialist	402,283 (3.0%)	—	
1908	WILLIAM H. TAFT	Republican	7,678,908 (51.6%)	321	65.4%
	William J. Bryan	democratic	6,409,104 (43.1%)	162	
	Eugene V. Debs	Socialist	420,793 (2.8%)	—	
1912	WOODROW WILSON	Democratic	6,293,454 (41.9%)	435	58.8%
	Theodore Roosevelt	Progressive	4,119,538 (27.4%)	88	
	William H. Taft	Republican	3,484,980 (23.2%)	8	
	Eugene V. Debs	Socialist	900,672 (6.0%)	—	
1916	WOODROW WILSON	Democratic	9,129,606 (49.4%)	277	61.6%
	Charles E. Hughes	Republican	8,538,221 (46.2%)	254	
	A. L. Benson	Socialist	585,113 (3.2%)	—	
1920	WARREN G. HARDING	Republican	16,152,200 (60.4%)	404	49.2%
	James M. Cox	Democratic	9,147,353 (34.2%)	127	
	Eugene V. Debs	Socialist	919,799 (3.4%)	—	
1924	CALVIN COOLIDGE	Republican	15,725,016 (54.0%)	382	48.9%
	John W. Davis	Democratic	8,386,503 (28.8%)	136	
	Robert M. La Follette	Progressive	4,822,856 (16.6%)	13	
1928	HERBERT HOOVER	Republican	21,391,381 (58.2%)	444	56.9%
	Alfred E. Smith	Democratic	15,016,443 (40.9%)	87	
	Normal Thomas	Socialist	267,835 (0.7%)	—	
1932	FRANKLIN D. ROOSEVELT	Democratic	22,821,857 (57.4%)	472	56.9%
	Herbert Hoover	republican	15,761,841 (39.7%)	59	
	Norman Thomas	Socialist	881,951 (2.2%)	—	

Year	Candidates	Parties	Popular Vote	Electoral Vote	Voter Participation
1936	FRANKLIN D. ROOSEVELT	Democratic	27,751,597 (60.8%)	523	61.0%
	Alfred M. Landon	Republican	16,679,583 (36.5%)	8	
	William Lemke	Union	882,479 (1.9%)	—	
1940	FRANKLIN D. ROOSEVELT	Democratic	27,244,160 (54.8%)	449	62.5%
	Wendell L. Willkie	Republican	22,305,198 (44.8%)	82	
1944	FRANKLIN D. ROOSEVELT	Democrat	25,602,504 (53.5%)	432	55.9%
	Thomas E. Dewey	Republican	22,006,285 (46.0%)	99	
1948	HARRY S TRUMAN	Democratic	24,105,695 (49.5%)	303	53.0%
	Thomas E. Dewey	Republican	21,969,170 (45.1%)	189	
	J. Strom Thurmond	State-Rights Democratic	1,169,021 (2.4%)	39	
	Henry A. Wallace	Progressive	1,156,103 (2.4%)	—	
1952	DWIGHT D. EISENHOWER	Republican	33,936,252 (55.1%)	442	63.3%
	Adlai E. Stevenson	Democratic	27,314,992 (44.4%)	89	
1956	DWIGHT D. EISENHOWER	Republican	35,575,420 (57.6%)	457	60.5%
	Adlai E. Stevenson	Democratic	26,033,066 (42.1%)	73	
	Other	—	—	1	
1960	JOHN F. KENNEDY	Democratic	34,227,096 (49.9%)	303	62.8%
	Richard M. Nixon	Republican	34,108,546 (49.6%)	219	
	Other	—	—	15	
1964	LYNDON B. JOHNSON	Democratic	43,126,506 (61.1%)	486	61.7%
	Barry M. Goldwater	Republican	27,176,799 (38.5%)	52	
1968	RICHARD M. NIXON	Republican	31,770,237 (43.4.%)	301	60.6%
	Hurbert H. Humphrey	Democratic	31,270,633 (42.7%)	191	
	George Wallace	American Indep.	9,906,141 (13.5%)	46	
1972	RICHARD M. NIXON	Republican	47,169,911 (60.7%)	520	55.2%
	George S. McGovern	Democratic	29,170,383 (37.5%)	17	
	Other	—	—	1	
1976	JIMMY CARTER	Democratic	40,828,587 (50.0%)	297	53.5%
	Gerald R. Ford	Republican	39,147,613 (47.9%)	240	
	Other	—	1,575,459 92.1%)	—	
1980	RONALD REAGAN	Republican	43,901,812 (50.7%)	489	52.6%
	Jimmy Carter	Democratic	35,483,820 (41.0%)	49	
	John B. Anderson	Independent	5,719,722 (6.6%)	—	
	Ed Clark	Libertarian	921,188 (1.1%)	—	
1984	RONALD REAGAN	Republican	54,455,075 (59.0%)	525	53.3%
	Walter Mondale	Democratic	37,577,185 (41.0%)	13	
1988	GEORGE H. W. BUSH	Republican	48,886,000 (45.6%)	426	57.4%
	Michael S. Dukakis	Democratic	41,809,000 (45.6%)	112	
1992	William J. CLINTON	Democratic	43,728,375 (43%)	370	55.0%
	George H. W. Bush	Republican	38,167,416 (38%)	168	
	Ross Perot	—	19,237,247 (19%)	—	
1996	William J. CLINTON	Democratic	45,590,703 (50%)	379	48.8%
	Robert Dole	Republican	37,816,307 (41%)	159	
	Ross Perot	Independent	7,866,284 (9%)	—	

CREDITS

INDEX

AAA. *See* Agricultural Adjustment Act (AAA)
Abortion rights, 764, 817
  pro-choice movement and, 812
  pro-life movement and, 817
Abraham Lincoln Brigade, 660
Abstract expressionist painters, 704–705
Acheson, Dean, 721, 731, 755–756
Activism. *See also* Protests
  civil rights and, 775–784
  consumer, 803
  Counterculture and, 798–799
  environmental, 800–803
  gay and lesbian, 799–800
  of Latinos, 788–791
  of Native Americans, 791–794
  of Roosevelt, Theodore, 529
  student, 736, 795–798
  of women, 784–788
Adams, Brooks, 501
Adams, Henry, 434, 435, 496
  on civil service reform, 499
  on future, 514
Adamson Act, 581
Addams, Jane, 477, 502–503
  anti-liquor movement and, 550
  Niagara movement and, 566
  Progressive party and, 567
  segregation and, 565
  Women's International League for Peace and Freedom and, 596
  women's rights and, 506
  World War I and, 576
Advertising
  automobile and, 607
  Barton, Bruce, and, 618
  political, 808–809
  after World War II, 697
Affirmative action
  backlash against, 816
  in California, 814
  immigrants and, 826–827
  programs for, 784
Affluent society, 690. *See also* Prosperity
  middle class and, 692
AFL. *See* American Federation of Labor (AFL)
AFL-CIO, 692
Africa
  black migration to, 458
  Garvey and, 613
  South Africa and, 833–835
  after World War I, 596
African-Americans. *See also* Race and racism; Race riots; Reconstruction;

Slaves and slavery
  as agricultural workers, 692
  in armed forces, 723
  black codes and, 419–420
  Black Power movement and, 782–783
  Brown v. *Board of Education* and, 759
  in CIO, 645
  in city neighborhoods, 475
  congressional Reconstruction and, 430–431
  equality for, 773–784
  farmers' alliances and, 461
  Freedmen's Bureau and, 425–426
  Garvey and, 612–613
  in Great Depression, 645–646
  Harlem Renaissance and, 614
  integration in North and, 783–784
  job discrimination and, 480
  lifestyle after slavery, 424–430
  migration to cities by, 472
  migration to North by, 592–593, 600, 612
  NAACP and, 565–566
  in New South, 455–458
  Niagara movement and, 566
  postwar poverty of, 705–706
  Progressive party (1912) and, 568
  progressivism and, 565–566
  responses to discrimination against, 458–459
  Scottsboro Boys and, 645
  self-help institutions of, 428–430
  in southern workforce, 454–455
  Spanish-American War and, 525
  surnames of freedmen, 418–419
  tensions in, 816
  as unskilled labor, 491
  urban areas and, 823
  voting rights of, 508, 776–777
  women, 484, 671, 701, 787, 817
  World War I armed forces and, 586, 587, 589–590
  World War I labor force and, 592–593
  World War II and, 668–670, 674
African Methodist Episcopal Church, 428
African National Congress, 835
Afrika Korps, 676
Afro-American League, 458
Age and aging. *See* Elderly
Agee, James, 745
Agnew, Spiro, 761, 763, 766
Agribusiness, 692
Agricultural Adjustment Act (AAA) of 1933, 636–637

of 1938, 648
Agricultural Marketing Act (1929), 629
Agriculture
  cattle frontier and, 446–447
  in 1880s, 446 (map)
  modernization of, 442–449, 472
  productivity of, 821
  southern blacks and, 426–427
  after World War II, 692
Aguinaldo, Emilio, 517
AIDS (acquired immune deficiency syndrome), 827
AIM. *See* American Indian Movement (AIM)
Airlift, Berlin, 718, 719
Airline industry, 806
Airplanes
  Lindbergh and, 609
  in World War I, 577
  in World War II, 679, 680
Air pollution, 758
Alaska
  mining in, 567
  purchase of, 520
Albania, post-Communist regime in, 831
Alcatraz Island, Indian occupation of, 793
Alcohol. *See also* Prohibition
  Prohibition and, 623
  Women's Christian Temperance Union (WCTU) and, 500, 549
Algeciras Conference, 539
Alger, Horatio, 479
Ali, Muhammad, 736
Aliens. *See* Immigrants and immigration; Naturalization process
Alliances. *See also* Allies (World War I); Allies (World War II); Southern Farmers' Alliance; specific alliances
  military, 718
  Rome-Berlin Axis, 660
  in World War I, 576 (map)
Allies (World War I), 575, 576 (map), 577–578
  U.S. and, 587–590
Allies (World War II), 675, 676
  aid to, 715
  European invasion by, 679–680
  postwar world and, 681
  Yalta and, 681–682
Allston family, 416, 426
Altamont festival, 799
Altgeld, Richard, 489
Alzheimer's disease, 828
Amalgamated Clothing Workers, 644

The World

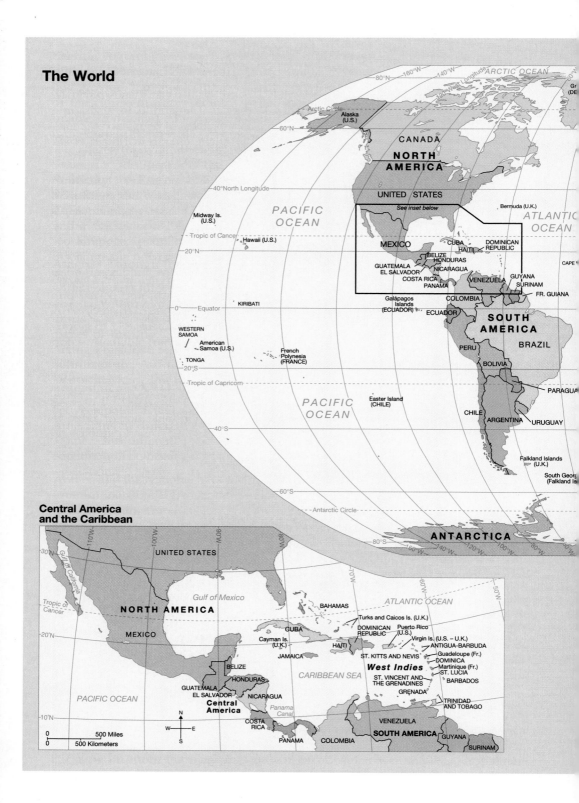

80°N · 160°W · 140°W · West Longitude · ARCTIC OCEAN

Gr
(DE

Arctic Circle

Alaska
(U.S.)

60°N

CANADA

**NORTH
AMERICA**

40°North Longitude

UNITED STATES

See inset below

Bermuda (U.K.)

ATLANTIC
OCEAN

PACIFIC
OCEAN

Midway Is.
(U.S.)

Tropic of Cancer · Hawaii (U.S.)

20°N

MEXICO

CUBA

HAITI

DOMINICAN
REPUBLIC

CAPE V

BELIZE
HONDURAS
GUATEMALA
EL SALVADOR · NICARAGUA
COSTA RICA
PANAMA

VENEZUELA

GUYANA
SURINAM

FR. GUIANA

Galápagos
Islands
(ECUADOR)

COLOMBIA

0° · Equator

KIRIBATI

ECUADOR

**SOUTH
AMERICA**

WESTERN
SAMOA

American
Samoa (U.S.)

French
Polynesia
(FRANCE)

PERU

BRAZIL

TONGA

20°S

BOLIVIA

Tropic of Capricorn

Easter Island
(CHILE)

PARAGUA

PACIFIC
OCEAN

CHILE

ARGENTINA · URUGUAY

40°S

Falkland Islands
(U.K.)

South Georg
(Falkland Is

60°S

Antarctic Circle

80°S · 160°W · 140°W · 120°W · 100 · 80°W · 60°W

ANTARCTICA

Central America
and the Caribbean

30°N

110°W

100°W

90°W

UNITED STATES

Gulf of
California

80°W

Tropic of
Cancer

Gulf of Mexico

NORTH AMERICA

BAHAMAS

ATLANTIC OCEAN

70°W

60°W

50°W

20°N

MEXICO

CUBA

Cayman Is.
(U.K.)

JAMAICA

HAITI

Turks and Caicos Is. (U.K.)

DOMINICAN
REPUBLIC

Puerto Rico
(U.S.)

Virgin Is. (U.S. – U.K.)
ANTIGUA-BARBUDA
Guadeloupe (Fr.)
DOMINICA
Martinique (Fr.)
ST. LUCIA

BELIZE

HONDURAS

GUATEMALA
EL SALVADOR · NICARAGUA

**Central
America**

CARIBBEAN SEA

ST. KITTS AND NEVIS

West Indies

ST. VINCENT AND
THE GRENADINES

GRENADA

BARBADOS

TRINIDAD
AND TOBAGO

PACIFIC OCEAN

10°N

N
W · E
S

COSTA
RICA

Panama
Canal

VENEZUELA

0 ____ 500 Miles
0 ____ 500 Kilometers

PANAMA

COLOMBIA

SOUTH AMERICA

GUYANA

SURINAM

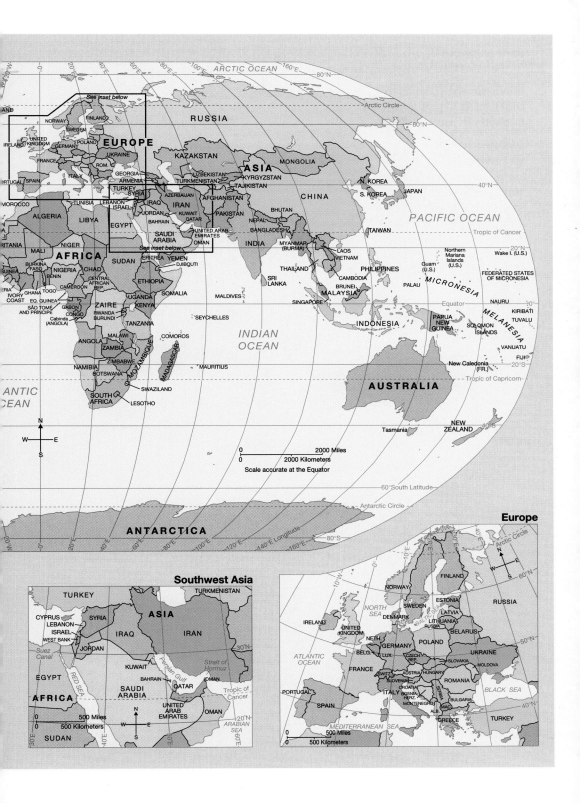

ARCTIC OCEAN

80°N

Arctic Circle

See inset below

RUSSIA

NORWAY
FINLAND

SWEDEN

60°N

UNITED
KINGDOM
POLAND

IRELAND
EUROPE

GERMANY

KAZAKSTAN

ASIA

MONGOLIA

FRANCE
UKRAINE

ROM.

ITALY

GEORGIA

UZBEKISTAN

KYRGYZSTAN

TAJIKISTAN

40°N

PORTUGAL
SPAIN

ARMENIA
TURKMENISTAN

N. KOREA

TURKEY

AZERBAIJAN

AFGHANISTAN

CHINA

S. KOREA
JAPAN

SYRIA

MOROCCO

TUNISIA

LEBANON
ISRAEL

IRAQ

IRAN

PACIFIC OCEAN

PAKISTAN

KUWAIT

ALGERIA

LIBYA

JORDAN

BAHRAIN
QATAR

NEPAL

BHUTAN

Tropic of Cancer

EGYPT

SAUDI
ARABIA

UNITED ARAB
EMIRATES
OMAN

INDIA

BANGLADESH

TAIWAN

20°N

MAURITANIA

MALI

NIGER

SUDAN

See inset below

ERITREA

YEMEN

MYANMAR
(BURMA)

LAOS
VIETNAM

Northern
Mariana
Islands
(U.S.)

Wake I. (U.S.)

NIGERIA
CHAD

DJIBOUTI

THAILAND

Guam
(U.S.)

FEDERATED STATES
OF MICRONESIA

BURKINA
FASO

CENTRAL
AFRICAN
REP.

ETHIOPIA

SRI
LANKA

CAMBODIA

MICRONESIA

BENIN

PHILIPPINES

PALAU

NIGERIA

GHANA
TOGO

CAMEROON

SOMALIA

BRUNEI

NAURU

IVORY
COAST

EQ. GUINEA

UGANDA
KENYA

MALDIVES

MALAYSIA

KIRIBATI

SÃO TOMÉ
AND PRINCIPE

GABON
CONGO

RWANDA
BURUNDI

SINGAPORE

Equator

MELANESIA

TUVALU

Cabinda
(ANGOLA)

AFRICA

ZAIRE

TANZANIA

INDONESIA

PAPUA
NEW
GUINEA

SOLOMON
ISLANDS

SEYCHELLES

VANUATU

ANGOLA

MALAWI

COMOROS

INDIAN
OCEAN

FIJI

ZAMBIA
ZIMBABWE

MAURITIUS

New Caledonia
(FR.)

20°S

NAMIBIA

MOZAMBIQUE

MADAGASCAR

Tropic of Capricorn

BOTSWANA

AUSTRALIA

ATLANTIC
OCEAN

SOUTH
AFRICA

SWAZILAND

LESOTHO

N

W   E

S

NEW
ZEALAND

Tasmania

2000 Miles
2000 Kilometers

Scale accurate at the Equator

60°South Latitude

Antarctic Circle

ANTARCTICA

80°S

Europe

See inset below

Southwest Asia

TURKEY

TURKMENISTAN

CYPRUS

SYRIA

ASIA

LEBANON
ISRAEL
WEST BANK

IRAQ

IRAN

JORDAN

30°N

Suez
Canal

KUWAIT

Strait of
Hormuz

EGYPT

BAHRAIN

AFRICA

RED SEA

SAUDI
ARABIA

QATAR

OMAN

Tropic of
Cancer

UNITED
ARAB
EMIRATES

OMAN

20°N

N

W   E

S

ARABIAN
SEA

500 Miles
500 Kilometers

SUDAN

Arctic Circle

N

W   E

S

60°N

FINLAND

NORWAY

ESTONIA

SWEDEN

RUSSIA

NORTH
SEA

DENMARK

LATVIA

IRELAND

LITHUANIA

UNITED
KINGDOM

RUSSIA

BELARUS

NETH.

GERMANY

POLAND

50°N

ATLANTIC
OCEAN

BELG.
LUX.

UKRAINE

FRANCE

CZECH
REP.

SLOVAKIA

MOLDOVA

SWITZ.

AUSTRIA
HUNGARY

ROMANIA

SLOVENIA

PORTUGAL

CROATIA

ITALY

BOSNIA
HERZ.

SERBIA

BLACK SEA

SPAIN

MONTENEGRO

BULGARIA

MAC.

ALB.

40°N

MEDITERRANEAN SEA

GREECE

TURKEY

500 Miles
500 Kilometers